The Life of W. B. Yeats

𝔹

BLACKWELL CRITICAL BIOGRAPHIES

General Editor: Claude Rawson

This acclaimed series offers informative and durable biographies of important authors, British, European and North American, which will include substantial critical discussion of their works. An underlying objective is to re-establish the notion that books are written by people who lived in particular times and places. This objective is pursued not by programmatic assertions or strenuous point-making, but through the practical persuasion of volumes which offer intelligent criticism within a well-researched biographical context.

Also in this series

Visit our website at http://www.blackwellpublishers.co.uk

The Life of
W. B. YEATS
A Critical Biography

Terence Brown

'But whoever had to create also had his prophetic dreams
and astral themes – and a faith in faith.'
Friedrich Nietzsche, *Thus Spake Zarathustra*

Copyright © Terence Brown 1999, 2001

The right of Terence Brown to be identified as author of this work has been
asserted in accordance with the Copyright, Designs and Patents Act 1988.

First published 1999
Reprinted 2000 (twice)

First published in paperback 2001

Blackwell Publishers Ltd
108 Cowley Road
Oxford OX4 1JF
UK

Blackwell Publishers Inc.
350 Main Street
Malden, Massachusetts 02148
USA

British Library Cataloguing in Publication Data

A CIP catalogue record for this book is available from the British Library.

Library of Congress Cataloging-in-Publication Data

The life of W. B. Yeats: a critical biography / Terence Brown.
p.   cm.
— (Blackwell critical biographies ; 12)
Includes bibliographical references and index.
ISBN 0–631–18298–5 (hbk: alk. paper); 0–631–22851–9 (pbk)
1. Yeats, W. B. (William Butler), 1865–1939.   2. Ireland—Intellectual
life—19th century.   3. Ireland—Intellectual life—20th century.
4. Poets, Irish—19th century Biography.
5. Poets, Irish—20th century Biography.   I. Title.   II. Series.
PR5906.B76   1999   821'.8—dc21   [B]   99–28388   CIP

Typeset in 10 on 11.5 pt Baskerville
by Kolam Information Services Pvt Ltd, Pondicherry, India

This book is printed on acid-free paper.

Contents

List of Illustrations   vii

Preface and Acknowledgements   viii

Abbreviations   xi

Prologue: Sindbad's Yellow Shore   1

1   Victorian Cities: London and Dublin   22

2   The English 1890s   47

3   *Poems* 1895   71

4   Conflicts and Crises   84

5   Patronage and Powers   105

6   An Irish Ireland   126

7   The Strong Enchanter   147

8   The Mid-life Mask   168

9   Darkened Rooms   187

10 The Lonely Height   208

11 All Changed   227

12 Occult Marriage   246

13 The Weasel's Tooth   267

14 Senator and Seer   286

15 Visionary Modernist   304

16 Home and Abroad   324

17   An Old Man's Frenzy   345

18   Stroke of Midnight   364

     Epilogue: Afterlife   377

     Works Cited   383

     Select Bibliography and Guide to Further Reading   392

     Index   399

Illustrations

The illustrations appear between pages 208 and 209

1   W. B. Yeats by John Sargent, 1908 (National Portrait Gallery)
2   John Butler Yeats, the poet's father (Rex Roberts)
3   Susan Yeats, the poet's mother (Rex Roberts)
4   John O'Leary, the old Fenian, 1894 (Rex Roberts)
5   Yeats by Charles Beresford (National Portrait Gallery)
6   Maud Gonne (National Library of Ireland)
7   Olivia Shakespear (Bodleian Library/*Literary Yearbook*, 1897)
8   Florence Farr (Department of English, University of Reading)
9   Lady Augusta Gregory, patron and friend (National Gallery of Ireland)
10   John Millington Synge (Hugh Lane Municipal Gallery of Modern Art, Dublin)
11   Iseult Gonne from a pastel by Maud Gonne (National Library of Ireland)
12a & b   W. B. and 'George' Yeats (née Georgie Hyde-Lees) (Rex Roberts)
13   W. B. and 'George' with their children, Anne and Michael, 1929 (Rex Roberts)
14   W. B. Yeats, *c.* 1935 (National Library of Ireland)

Preface and Acknowledgements

This book is very significantly concerned with contexts so a prefatory word on the contexts in which it came to be written may be in order. That I should attempt such a work was initially suggested to me by Professor Claude Rawson at a conference on Joyce and History at Yale University. That academic event was itself a notable indication of how things were changing in the academy in North America in the early 1990s, for the discussion of Joyce, as of so much else, had in the 1970s and 1980s taken a distinctly theoretical turn, in which historical context and biography had figured little. At Yale the clock seemed to be turning, not back to a version of literary history in which literature was situated most meaningfully against an historical 'background', but forward towards a view of things in which writer, work and context are imbricated with one another in ways which involve ideologies of class, ethnicity, nation and gender. This book, without overt reference to such theoretical issues, seeks to do its work in the context of a significantly reinvigorated historical criticism. It does so with a keen sense of how a biographical and historical criticism has obligations to a general readership.

Yeats certainly offers an appropriate object for such study. Not only is his life an extraordinary tale but much of his writing is a charged, dramatic encounter with the history of Ireland and a reflection of the country's conflict with Britain. Furthermore his works were themselves interventions in that history in ways that still affect how Irish men and women understand their world and how they are understood by others.

Yeats's historical imagination meant too that his writings could never be completely detached, even by the most determined New Critic or Deconstructionist, from the contexts in Ireland and Britain which gave them birth and in which they initially lived, for their field of allusion involved the extensive annotation that undeniably forced the aesthetic to consort with the contingent.

And it may be as well that it is the intensity of Yeats's engagement with the history of his times in Britain and Ireland and with modernity itself that accounts for the amount of major historical research and scholarship that his life and works have attracted even in the decades since the 1960s during which university

English has been engaged in protracted theory and culture wars. Without such labour, no work like this one, which offers itself as an interpretative synthesis, would have been possible.

Accordingly I must acknowledge my signal indebtedness to the following works and scholars: the basic chronology has been supplied by earlier biographers, Hone, Jeffares, Ellmann, and by the richly detailed chronologies provided in the first three volumes of the *Collected Letters* appearing under the general editorship of John Kelly; the appendices of these volumes, are furthermore, treasure-troves of information and data; William Murphy's *Prodigal Father: The Life of John Butler Yeats*, and his *Family Secrets: William Butler Yeats and His Relations*, were also highly informative. A. N. Jeffares', *A New Commentary on the Poems of W. B. Yeats* was an invaluable tool; Margaret Ward's *Maud Gonne: A Life* (1990) and May Lou Kohfeldt's *Lady Gregory: The Woman Behind the Irish Renaissance* (1985) were also useful; the Herculean labours of George Mills Harper and his team have allowed us to examine the collaboration between the poet and his wife in psychic experiment and literary creation; Anna MacBride White and A. Norman Jeffares have given us the fascinating *Gonne–Yeats Letters*; David Pierce's *Yeats's Worlds: Ireland, England and the Poetic Imagination* is full of intriguing detail and guided me to some contemporary accounts of Yeats the man; the *Yeats Annual*, (vols 1 and 2 edited by Richard Finneran, subsequently, 1985 to the present by Warwick Gould and his appointees) both intimidated and exhilarated by the depth of its scientific scholarship; it has been a major resource; Adrian Frazier's *Behind the Scenes: Yeats, Horniman, and the Struggle for the Irish Theatre* was a stimulating guide; and R. F. Foster's magisterial *W. B. Yeats: A Life* (1997) is exemplary in its learning and searching analysis of Yeats in his almost daily experience.

Conversations with friends, colleagues and students over the years also played their part: with Derry and Jeanne Jeffares, Ann Saddlemyer, Adrian Frazier (who supplied a useful reference to Yeats at art school), Peter Costello (who supplied material on Bedford Park), Helen Vendler, Antoinette Quinn, Nicholas Grene, Declan Kiberd, W. J. Mc Cormack (who gave me access to his unpublished essay on the Yeats family background), Derek Mahon, Gerald Dawe, Ian Campbell Ross, Robert Welch, the late Augustine Martin, the late F. S. L. Lyons. Joseph M. Hassett alerted me to an unpublished letter; John Devitt, Bruce Stewart, Patrick Gallagher, Nicholas Allen helped with some references. Thanks are due to Margaret Mills Harper for permission to quote from the typescript of a lecture; and to R. Dardis Clarke, 21 Pleasants Street, Dublin 8, for permission to quote from unpublished letters by Austin Clarke.

My agent Jonathan Williams was always helpful and encouraging.

I am also most grateful to the Provost of Trinity College, Dublin, Dr T. N. Mitchell, who made available a grant from the Provost's Academic Development Fund, which allowed me a year's leave-of-absence to work on this book. The Arts and Social Sciences Benefactions Fund, Trinity College, Dublin made a grant towards research costs, for which I am grateful.

My family put up with a lot and here I must express gratitude to my wife Suzanne, to my son Michael and my daughter Carolyn, all of whom have found their lives affected by the presence of a mighty ghost in the household, but kept their good humour.

It was the poet Brendan Kennelly who first helped me to grasp the essentially dramatic nature of Yeats's imagination, in a series of tutorials in Trinity College, Dublin in 1965. Since then we have discussed the poetry and drama on many occasions, through the years in which Irish history ran on in ways that made Yeats seem a constant, necessary presence. My debt to Brendan is great and is reflected in the dedication of this volume.

Terence Brown
Dublin, June, 1999

Abbreviations

The abbreviations below are used to make for ease-of-reference in the text. Note, however, that quotations from Yeats's poetry and drama are taken from individual volumes as they appeared in first or early editions. These works are identified in the text. Readers will sometimes note, especially in respect of the early verse, differences between versions of poems given here and the form in which they appear in the modern collected and selected editions. Yeats was an obsessive reviser of his own early work. This study, which sets Yeats's writings in the context of his life and experience, 'prefers' the early versions to those that resulted from later revision. Readers are directed to *The Poems*, ed. Daniel Albright (London: Dent, Everyman Library, 1992), *The Poems: Revised*, ed. Richard Finneran (London: Macmillan, 1983, 1984) and to *The Collected Plays of W. B. Yeats* (London: Macmillan, 1953) and *W. B. Yeats: Selected Plays*, ed. Richard Allen Cave (Harmondsworth: Penguin Books, 1997) for 'canonical' versions of the plays and poems considered in this book. Information on other works cited in the text is given in Works Cited listed at the end of the book. I have retained Yeats's unstable spelling, which is given in the first three volumes of the *Collected Letters* and in *Yeats's* Vision *Papers* and in the Gonne–Yeats letters.

AM	*W. B. Yeats: A Life*, vol. 1: *The Apprentice Mage* by R. F. Foster (Oxford: Oxford University Press, 1997)
Au	*Autobiographies* (London: Macmillan, 1955)
AVA	*A Vision* (1925); repr. *A Critical Edition of Yeats's* A Vision, eds. George Mills Harper and Walter Kelly Hood (London: Macmillan, 1978)
AVB	*A Vision* (London: Macmillan, 1937)
CH	*W. B. Yeats: The Critical Heritage*, ed. A. Norman Jeffares (London: Routledge and Kegan Paul, 1977)
CK	*The Countess Kathleen and Various Legends and Lyrics* (London: T. Fisher Unwin, 1892)
CL1	*The Collected Letters of W. B. Yeats*, vol. 1, *1865–1895* ed. John Kelly, associate ed. Eric Domville (Oxford: Clarendon Press, 1986)

CL2	*The Collected Letters of W. B. Yeats*, vol. 2, *1896–1900* eds Warwick Gould, John Kelly and Deirdre Toomey (Oxford: Clarendon Press, 1997)
CL3	*The Collected Letters of W. B. Yeats*, vol. 3, *1901–1904*, eds John Kelly and Ronald Schuchard (Oxford: Clarendon Press, 1994)
CT	*The Celtic Twilight* (London: Lawrence and Bullen, 1893)
CT2	*The Celtic Twilight*, with an introduction by Kathleen Raine (Gerrard's Cross: Colin Smythe, 1987)
E&I	*Essays and Introductions* (London: Macmillan, 1961)
EM	*Early Memories: Some Chapters of Autobiography by John Butler Yeats* (Dublin: Cuala Press, 1923)
Ex	*Explorations* (London: Macmillan, 1962)
GYL	*The Gonne–Yeats Letters, 1893–1938*, eds Anna MacBride White and A. N. Jeffares (London: Hutchinson, 1992)
Hone	*W. B. Yeats, 1865–1939*, by Joseph Hone (London: Macmillan, 1942)
ISW	*In the Seven Woods* (Dundrum: Dun Emer Press, 1903)
JS	*John Sherman and Dhoya*, Ganonagh; pseud. W. B. Yeats (London: T. Fisher Unwin, Pseudonym Library, 1891)
KOGCT	*The King of the Great Clock Tower, Commentaries and Poems by W. B. Yeats* (Dublin: Cuala Press, 1934)
L	*The Letters of W. B. Yeats*, ed. Allan Wade (London: Rupert Hart-Davis, 1954)
LTNI	*Letters to the New Island by William Butler Yeats*, ed. Horace Reynolds, (Cambridge, Mass.: Harvard University Press, 1934)
LTWBY 1 and 2	*Letters to W. B. Yeats* eds Richard Finneran, George Mills Harper and William M. Murphy (London and New York: Macmillan, and Columbia University Press, 1977)
Mem	*Memoirs, Autobiography – First Draft, Journal* ed. Denis Donoghue (London and Basingstoke: Macmillan, 1972)
Myth	*Mythologies* (London: Macmillan, 1959)
NL	National Library of Ireland
OTB	*On the Boiler* (Dublin: Cuala Press, 1939)
PASL	*Per Amica Silentia Lunae* (London: Macmillan, 1918)
PFEP	*A Packet for Ezra Pound* (Dublin: Cuala Press, 1929)
SR	*The Secret Rose* (London: Lawrence and Bullen, 1897)
TOL	*The Tables of the Law; & The Adoration of the Magi* (Stratford-upon-Avon: The Shakespeare Head Press, 1914)
TOV	*The Trembling of the Veil* (privately printed, Werner Laurie Ltd, 1922)
TWATR	*The Wind Among the Reeds* (London: Elkin Mathews, 1899)
UP1	*Uncollected Prose*, vol. 1, ed. John P. Frayne (London: Macmillan, 1970)
UP2	*Uncollected Prose*, vol. 2, eds John P. Frayne and Colton Johnson (London: Macmillan 1975)

VP	*The Variorum Edition of the Poems of W. B. Yeats*, eds Peter Allt and Russell K. Alspach, fourth printing (London: Macmillan, 1968)
VPs 1, 2, 3	*Yeats's* Vision *Papers*, gen. ed. George Mills Harper, assisted by Mary Jane Harper, eds S. L. Adams, B. J. Frieling and S. L. Sprayberry (London and Basingstoke: Macmillan, 1992)
VSR	*The Secret Rose, Stories by W. B. Yeats: A Variorum Edition*, eds Warwick Gould, Phillip L. Marcus and Michael J. Sidnell (London and Basingstoke: Macmillan, 1992)
W & B	*Wheels and Butterflies* (London: Macmillan, 1934)
WS	*The Winding Stair and Other Poems* (London: Macmillan, 1933)

For Brendan Kennelly

Prologue: Sindbad's Yellow Shore

County Sligo, observed a lecturer addressing the Belfast Natural History Society in the museum in that city in 1887, is 'classic Irish soil'. Its ancient history, 'if recorded by another Walter Scott, would lend a charm and an interest to it, equal to any in Europe' (O'Rourke 1889: xix). It would have perhaps gratified the speaker to learn that the year before he spoke, a young Dublin-born man then about to move with his family to London, but with strong Sligo associations, had published an article which served as a manifesto for a literature which would make Sligo, town and county, in subsequent years as famous in the literary firmament as Scott's Highlands. For in that article, published in the *Dublin University Review* in November 1886, W. B. Yeats had contributed a stirring memorial essay on the recently dead Irish poet and antiquary, Sir Samuel Ferguson, which opened with an expression of regret that Ireland was not Scotland either creatively or critically: 'In the literature of every country', Yeats boldly asserted, 'there are two classes, the creative and the critical. In Scotland all the poets have been Scotch in feeling, or, as we would call it, national, and the cultured and critical public read their books, and applauded, for the nation was homogeneous. Over here things have gone according to a very different fashion' (*UP1*: 88).

For the young Yeats in this polemical essay, the scandal of Ferguson's career was that, properly national as it had been, it had not been given its due by a professional class in his own country 'who, in Ireland, at least, appear at no time to have thought of the affairs of their country till they first feared for their emoluments' (*UP1*: 104) and where 'the shoddy society of "West Britonism"' (ibid.) egregiously ignored 'the greatest poet Ireland has produced, because the most central and most Celtic' (*UP1*: 103). In stark antithesis to that unworthy spectacle of mediocre opportunism, national apostasy and heterogeneity, Yeats summons into existence in his essay an improbable image (for the dead man had been knighted for his services not to poetry but to archaeology; the *Athenaeum* reckoned 'there was never a more loyal or orderly British citizen'; *UP1*: 89) of

Ferguson as a founding, progenitive figure in the new national literature which a dispersed but unified nation would shortly bring into mature existence:

> Whatever the future may bring forth in the way of a truly great and national literature – and now that the race is so large, and so widely spread, and so conscious of its unity, the years are ripe – will find its morning in these ... volumes of one who was made by the purifying flame of National sentiment the one man of his time who wrote heroic poetry – one who, among the somewhat sybaritic singers of his day, was like some aged sea-king sitting among the inland wheat and poppies – the savour of the sea about him. (*UPI*: 103–4)

It is not difficult in this passage, where Yeats celebrates a chosen precursor and announces a literary creed of buoyant nationalism, to discover the source of its imagery. It is in that 'classic Irish soil' of Sligo, identified by the Belfast lecturer, where land and sea are intimate in a county which faces the Atlantic on a wild western shore. For we know that, as a child-exile in London in the 1870s, the poet-to-be felt himself 'so full of love for the fields and roads of Sligo that I longed – a strange sentiment for a child – for earth from a road there that I might kiss it' (*Au*: 472). And as he remembered in adulthood the more than two full years he lived in Sligo as a child of seven and eight, and the holidays passed with relatives in the town and county, he reminisced how 'All my dreams were of ships; and one day a sea-captain who had come to dine with my grandfather put a hand on each side of my head and lifted me up to show me Africa' (*Au*: 15).

Ships, sailing, sailors and the lore of the sea mingling with mythology and history weave their spell on the imagination of the young child, whom Yeats recreates as his boyish self in *Reveries Over Childhood and Youth* (1916). In the channel a steamer designed by one his relatives could be heard 'wheezing ... like an asthmatic person' (*Au*: 16). When his younger brother Robert dies in infancy and Yeats comes to a 'realization of death', he and his sister draw ships with flags at half-mast: 'We must have heard or seen that the ships in the harbour had their flags at half-mast. Next day at breakfast I heard people telling how my mother and the servant had heard the banshee crying the night before he died' (*Au*: 27). Yeats remembers too how he 'was often at Sligo pier to sail my boat' and was imaginatively gratified that the family-owned SS *Liverpool* 'had been built to run the blockade during the war of the North and the South' (*Au*: 49) in the United States and had once nearly foundered. We hear of fishing, an anchored ship, a distant lighthouse, as constituents of the poet's ideal world: 'I have walked on Sindbad's yellow shore and never shall another's hit my fancy' (*Au*: 52). Indeed, much of the wonder of Sligo for the growing boy was not because the county was a site of Celtic legendry and Gaelic tradition (a much greater knowledge of that was to come later for Yeats), but because Sligo town as a thriving port was where he was touched with the romance of the mysterious and the exotic. A place and his imagination wove together a primal magic of their own:

> Indeed, so many stories did I hear from sailors along the wharf, or around the fo'castle fire of the little steamer that ran between Sligo and Rosses, or from boys

out fishing that the world seemed full of monsters and marvels. The foreign sailors wearing earrings did not tell me stories, but like the fishing boys I gazed at them in wonder and admiration. (*Au*: 52)

Childhood, however, was not all an idyll of sea and shore. 'I remember little of childhood but its pain' (*Au*: 11) asserts Yeats in *Reveries Over Childhood and Youth*, in a passage in which he seeks to exonerate his family of responsibility for what is represented as an unaccountable aspect of an innate temperament: 'I have grown happier with every year of life as though gradually conquering something in myself, for certainly my miseries were not made by others but were a part of my own mind' (*Au*: 11). An acquaintance with the facts of the poet's formative years suggests that either he was being disingenuous here, or he was sparing a still-living father, who was unquestionably implicated in a family tragedy, or that even in middle life he was incapable of confronting directly a childhood, youth and young manhood that had included its share of trauma and confusion. Perhaps all three were at work in a text that hides as much as it reveals.

John Butler Yeats, the poet's father, was born in County Down in the province of Ulster in 1839, the third child of the Reverend William Butler Yeats, Rector in the Church of Ireland parish of Tullylish. The two older children had not survived, so John was in effect the first-born in a family that was not to be enlarged for some years. The Church of Ireland (Anglican and established until 1869) was a family affair, for William's own father had been Rector in Drumcliffe parish in County Sligo. There legend had him an apparently agreeable soul, whose name as late as 1889 was 'still popular as that of a straightforward, high-principled man' (O'Rourke 1889: 27). The tale was told of Rector John that once, when he accompanied a local landlord's agent and bailiff in an attempt to enrol the children of the tenantry in the local Protestant school, he commended one who declared that no child of his would ever darken the school's doors 'for his spirit, and observed, that he was the honestest man they had come across that day' (O'Rourke 1889: 27). The local landlord, whose emissaries 'Parson John', as he was known, accompanied that day, was Sir Robert Gore-Booth of Lissadell, the local 'big house'; and however whimsically the clergyman may have represented himself in the exchanges he was engaged in with his companions, it cannot be set aside that they were at work in a context of peculiarly noxious power relations that made sectarian headcounts a feature of the larger Irish polity.

Yeats himself in *Reveries Over Childhood and Youth* confessed that he was 'delighted with all' that joined his life 'to those who had power in Ireland' and, although he qualifies this with the phrase 'or with those anywhere that were good servants and poor bargainers' (*Au*: 22), it is clear from his pondering their miniatures, as he represents himself as doing in the text (soldier, or lawyer, or Castle official), it is state service, rather than anything more menial, that he has in mind.

The Yeats family established itself in Ireland at the beginning of the period that set in place the structure of power which had one of its least attractive manifestations in the kind of early nineteenth-century Irish day when a land agent, a bailiff and a parson sought to persuade a Catholic tenantry to send their children to a Protestant school.

The earliest known Yeats is one Jervis Yeats. With a Yorkshire background, he was probably a demobbed soldier who set himself up in Ireland in the wake of the Williamite Settlement. He began civilian life in Ireland as a small trader and rose in the world as a wholesale linen-merchant and eventual freeman of the city. This success story was one of the many that could be recounted of those newcomers to Ireland who had grasped the opportunities laid open to individuals of Protestant profession after 'Aughrim's great disaster', when Gaelic and Catholic Ireland had been defeated on the battlefield of 1691 and its leaders cast into European exile. His commercial success soon made possible a fortunate family marriage. Jervis's grandson Benjamin Yeats married Mary Butler, linked by name to the Anglo-Norman family which since medieval times had been a great power in the land, led by the Dukes of Ormonde. The marriage certainly brought the Yeats family actual power in Ireland (Yeats based the constant aggrandisement of his not especially remarkable paternal ancestry on this assumed Butler connection) for it involved the acquisition of substantial lands. Mary Butler brought 560 acres of land and a pension from the War Office to marriage with Benjamin Yeats. It was fortunate that she was a woman of means for her husband's business failed. So her income allowed their son to attend Trinity College, Dublin, to prepare for his ordination as a priest of the Church of Ireland, when the family was released from the embarrassment of trade, about which their caste, obsessively alert to gradations of calling and breeding, was decidedly snobbish.

The Reverend John Butler Yeats married soundly. His wife was sister of a powerful official in Dublin Castle (from where following the Act of Union in 1800, the Westminster government ruled Ireland through its agents and representatives drawn mainly from the caste into which the Yeatses had managed to penetrate), and he became that Rector in Drumcliffe we have already seen about his complicated duties. His son, the first William Butler Yeats (the tenuous Butler connection had always meant a lot), followed his father to the university and into the Church. Unfortunately, the living he acceded to, following marriage to Jane Corbet of Sandymount, sister of the Governor of Penang, was not in the Sligo that his parents had apparently found congenial (and where some of his siblings settled) but in Tullylish, County Down, where he set himself up as a gentleman and prolific *paterfamilias*.

Although he had disliked the gentility of his childhood home (*AM*: 2), to J. B. Yeats his father, the County Down Rector, was a model in one crucial respect: 'My father was an Irish gentleman of the old school and not at all thrifty' (*EM*: 1), he declared in old age after a lifetime in which he had proved himself his father's son. For the ideal of the essentially leisured life his father had led was encompassed in John Butler Yeats's own understanding of that term 'a gentleman', while thrift was foreign to his nature.

In 1848 the Reverend William Butler Yeats, according to the poet's first biographer, had given clear evidence of his admirable hierarchy of values. When Macaulay's *History of England* was published, he 'threw the parish to his curate and went to bed until he had read all the volumes' (Hone 1946: 5). There were five of them published between 1849 and 1861, so we must imagine that the curate had his work cut out as his Rector dealt with the early volumes. Few of the inhabitants of the region in which he found himself could have spared the time for such literary indulgences. For Tullylish, during the Reverend Yeats's time there, was experiencing the swift, often brutal changes in Ulster rural society that were effected by a burgeoning industrial revolution. It was a centre of the linen business, that motor of a distinct Northern Irish identity in the period. The population of the district underwent a rapid increase during the Reverend Yeats's time in County Down. And the Presbyterianism of many of its inhabitants became fervently evangelical, as a religion of a new class in Ireland, the industrial proletariat, began to replace in the north of the country the more even-tempered version of Anglican evangelical orthodoxy favoured by the Reverend Yeats. As one historian has reported it, during his incumbency, 'the industrial capitalists in Tullylish overshadowed their landlord in power and wealth' (Cohen 1997: 127). We can be sure they overshadowed the local Rector.

This new Irish arena of capitalists and proletariat in a few short years was to be one of the epicentres of a millenialist and ecstatic religion of the dispossessed, the great revival of 1859, the Year of Grace. William Butler Yeats withdrew from his parish at the age of forty-seven, several years before this epoch-making event in Ulster (in an unpublished essay W. J. Mc Cormack has shown that the local Presbyterian minister in the Reverend Yeats's time was a notable orator and a leading figure in the revival). Nevertheless, one does not have to be unduly speculative to find in Yeats's reported dislike for Presbyterians (they were to the fore in revival enthusiasm), and in the fact that he 'could never come to an understanding with the aggressive North' (*Hone*: 5–6), not only evidence that 'his Evangelicism belonged to the cultivated classes', but that instead of being a hatred of human nature was 'an intense pity mixed with an affectionate and human delight'. (*Hone*: 6) Rather, it strikes one as perhaps the earliest occasion on which a Yeats encountered the challenge of a detested and feared modernity which was to affront the family for the next two generations. Indeed a convinced dislike for the North of Ireland is a leitmotif which connects the Yeatses – father, son and grandchild – in a way which makes it something more than just the expression of the conventional distaste members of an old and landed caste feel for new money. The North is detested not only for what it represents – puritanism, money-grubbing, bumptiousness – but almost as a personal and familial insult.

In J. B. Yeats's memoir of his youth, composed in New York, when, after a life of much sponsored leisure, some equanimity might have been expected, the city of Belfast is positively an obsession. It is as if it still pursued him to the end as the dystopia of his worst fears. 'Though I hate puritanism', he announces, 'I don't think I would like it to be entirely removed from the world, unless it be the Belfast variety, which like the east wind is good for neither man nor beast' (*EM*: 15). He also recalls how his father believed ' "nothing can exceed the vulgar assumption of a Belfast man" ' (ibid.: 15–16). J. B. Yeats damns too the religion of the city since 'it may be stated in a single sentence: "The man who sells his cow too cheap goes to hell" ' (ibid.: 48) and is sardonically dismissive of the 'will power which has made the dull people of Belfast such an edifying success' (ibid.: 81).

In fact Sligo town, which occupies so crucial a role in the Yeats family's perception of its history, in the early twentieth century was known to its inhabitants and to others as 'Little Belfast'. As a county that lies close to the Ulster counties of Donegal and Fermanagh, Sligo's links of kin and custom have always been across a provincial border with the north of the country, as well as with its southern hinterland in Connacht. In modern times railway communication was established with the town and county in 1862 when the Midland Great Western Railway provided services mediately or immediately with the three southern provinces of Ireland. The Sligo Leitrim and Northern Counties service began operating in 1882, carrying passengers to and from the North. The railways brought tourists to the county and to the town and added to the sense they both possessed of wider contacts in the great world than were common in much of provincial Ireland. For as a county with a small but busy port, even the peasant inhabitants of the Rosses (a sandy promontory with a village to the north of the town), as Yeats's friend Arthur Symons discovered in 1896, knew 'more of the coast of Spain, the River Plate, and the Barbadoes' than they knew 'of the other side of their own mountains, for seafaring men go far'. (Symons 1918: 328). What the coming of the railways did was to draw the town and county into a process of social and economic modernization that was at work in Ireland as a whole in the Post-famine era.

Emigration had for decades been a principal business of the port. For between the famine years of the 1840s and the 1880s Ireland exported a significant proportion of its population to North America, where the emigrants would constitute a major force in the Irish nationalism that during Yeats's lifetime would overturn the world from which he came. Concurrently the country also became a commercial, self-consciously progressive, modernizing province of Queen Victoria's rapidly increasing empire. Sligo was very much a part of this. In Yeats's boyhood the town boasted those characteristically Victorian institutions – an infirmary, a fever hospital, a workhouse and a district lunatic asylum. It also possessed banks, a military barracks (which in time made soccer the local game, rather than Gaelic football) and a variety of churches.

The county was of course markedly Catholic in religious profession. By 1881, even though emigration had reduced their numbers somewhat (as indeed it had Protestant numbers) since 1861, there were over 100,000 Catholics recorded in the Census and a mere 10,000 Protestants of one kind or another. Of these, 8,000 or so were members of the Church of Ireland in which the Yeats family had served for two generations. There were also Presbyterians, Methodists and Christian Brethren. The Masonic movement had been socially influential since the late eighteenth century. The main ecclesiastic presence in the county, however, was the Roman church, which in the post-Famine period was a prime agent of modernization. Under the energetic leadership of Ireland's first cardinal, Paul Cullen, the church had set in motion a sustained wave of church building as it sought to centralize local religious practice in socially dominant institutions. Public, civic space was being appropriated by an increasingly ultramontanist authority and the demonstration of this was to be found in the bricks and mortar of ostentatious social presence. Sligo Cathedral was consecrated on 25 July 1874 in the presence of Cardinal Cullen. An imposing, even triumphalist expression of ecclesiastic presence, it was designed to accommodate a congregation of 4,000.

The Catholic Church's drive to seize the social highground (a new college founded subsequently in Sligo to serve as a seminary, was built 'on a commanding position, above the presbytery, overlooking the town', Wood-Martin 1992: 133) had a cultural impact on town and county. As Lawrence Taylor has concluded of the process at work throughout the country, the church was creating a new social geography in Ireland. He speaks of a 'substantial restructuring of the geography – the rise of the street town, the building of roads – a redefinition of domesticity and the household'. He recognizes that landlords and their agents were also involved in this restructuring, but emphasizes that the church and its parish priest were

> a part of the interpretative community which was in the process of forming and defining itself which included teachers and doctors. Their civil religion took shape in townscape, but also within the changing domestic space, where Victorian parlours and the act of reading entailed a discipline of the body as significant in its own way as the penitential exercises self-inflicted in devotional occasions. (Taylor 1995: 243)

In Sligo town and county all this had direct effects. Schools were founded and flourished and illiteracy levels fell markedly.

This progressive incorporation of a small western Irish seaport into a recognizably Victorian world, in which the dominant church played its own distinctive part, was not achieved without stress. In *Reveries Over Childhood and Youth* the poet remembers how he was introduced to rhyme in a stable-boy book of Orange ballads. He continues: 'Later on I can remember being told, when there was a rumour of a Fenian rising, that rifles had been served out to the Orangemen; and presently, when I had begun to dream of my future life, I thought I would like to die fighting the Fenians' (*Au*: 14). The poet offers here an evocation of a colourful, archaic, pre-modern world, inhabited as an Irish childhood's dreamtime. One suspects that that is less than the whole story. Yeats first lived in Sligo in 1869, two years after the Fenian rising (his first visit had been for a family holiday in the summer of 1868), so what he is recalling cannot have been that event. Probably this is an adult recollection of the older generation's engrained attitude, bred of the fear that dangerous year had provoked among Irish loyalists.

And Sligo was not immune to the party spirit that made the greater Belfast a byword for sectarian strife in the nineteenth century as in the twentieth. O'Rourke, one of the county's nineteenth-century historians, admitted in 1889 that Sligo was 'a county in which sectarian and party feelings have run perhaps higher than any other county in Ireland' (O'Rourke 1889: xxiii). He cautioned 'there are some silly people who think if our English and Scotch settlers took themselves away tomorrow, bag and baggage, the county would be well rid of them. This is not the opinion of those whose opinion carries weight' (ibid.: 586). Three years earlier in 1886, the year of the failed Home Rule Bill, the sectarian outrages that broke out in Belfast, had their echo on the streets of Sligo town. The cathedral was damaged, as was the entrance to the Presbytery. It transpired that passions had been roused by three Catholic *agents provocateurs*, who were subsequently imprisoned, but the coals were there for the spark to ignite.

John Butler Yeats married the Sligo-born Susan Pollexfen in 1863. In so doing, he brought himself within the orbit of new local power in the county where his grandfather had served as a parish priest. For the Pollexfen family was making its mark in the town.

J. B. Yeats had first come within the magnetic force-field of the Pollexfen dynasty as a schoolboy in the rough and tumble world of an Isle of Man school, Atholl Academy, to which his father had despatched him. Possibly its avowed ethos reflected to some extent the evangelicalism of his churchmanship (the headmaster was a Scots Calvinist, renowned as a disciplinarian). It was a fateful encounter, certainly more profoundly influential in his life than anything he might have acquired in the brutally controlled classrooms of a Manx Dotheboys Hall. From the start, J. B. Yeats was mesmerized by George Pollexfen, a fellow pupil at the school, along with his brother Charles. George seemed a primitive – unresponsive, self-contained, a compelling impromptu storyteller after dark in the dormitory, a centre of unregenerate energy, at one with the place from which he derived. J. B. Yeats recalled him talking 'poetry though he did not know it' (*EM*: 18).

The Pollexfens were not native to Sligo. They were descendants of a notable Devonshire family. Had John Butler Yeats's dynastically inclined son William been as ready to appreciate fully his maternal ancestry as he was his paternal, he would have found in Pollexfen history much matter for a myth of family. The ancestral home was Kitley, Devon and the line had been distinguished in law and commerce since the seventeenth century. The family's relationship with Sligo began in 1813, when the fifteen-year-old Elizabeth Pollexfen accepted the marriage proposal of a Sligo merchant named William Middleton, whose business profited on the fruits of a career as a sea-captain and smuggler. The Sligo connection was strengthened when the young William Pollexfen, who had run away to sea when he was twelve years old, came to Sligo in the early 1830s. William Middleton had died during a recent cholera epidemic, so when William Pollexfen arrived 'almost by chance' (*AM*: 4) in the town, he stayed to help his widowed cousin, and in 1837 married her eldest daughter, another Elizabeth. With her brother, another William Middleton, as partner, he helped to build up a milling company and a shipping line. Business flourished mightily.

William Pollexfen plays a major role in Yeats's *Reveries Over Childhood and Youth*, where he appears, in the poet's terms, as a patriarch of Lear-like proportions. Yet there is an air of anachronism about the way in which the poet represents old Pollexfen and everything to do with the family business in Sligo. In all his writings on his maternal ancestry, Yeats makes them seem a dynasty of 'Half legendary men' ('Are You Content?'), fixed in some eighteenth-century version of mercantilism, invested in its Sligo dispensation with the romance and folklore of seafaring and adventurism. It would be difficult to realize from Yeats's celebration of an '*Old merchant skipper that leaped overboard / After a ragged hat in Biscay Bay*' or of a '*silent and fierce old man*' who taught him that ' "*Only the wasteful virtues earn the sun*" ' ('*Pardon, Old Fathers*') that the firm of Middleton and Pollexfen and the Sligo Steam Ship Navigation Company were among the principal forces at work in the modernization of their Sligo. A modern historian of the port of Sligo in fact argues that the partnership 'was to be synonymous with the commercial life and trade of Sligo for over a century' (McTernan 1992: 40) – though its fortunes did begin to wane in the 1880s after the death of William Middleton, who, it seems, possessed the more astute business brain. In the early years, the two men extended the tradition of Sligo's historic maritime trade which since the mid-fifteenth century had been with France and Spain. Their grain barges and a fleet of schooners traded even as far away as the Black Sea. The names of their craft gave no sense of their Irish provenance, with family names like *Susan, Jesse* and *Jane* vying with those such as *Effort, Commerce,* even *Teetotaller*.

When steam came, the firm went into steam, playing what part they could on the western Atlantic seaboard in the vibrant era of steamboat capitalism which, in the second half of the nineteenth century, was laying down a network of commercial links between northern British ports and cities – Belfast, Liverpool and Glasgow in particular. The family's steamers plied between Sligo and Liverpool and Sligo and Glasgow. When in 1856 they chartered the steamer *Lyra*, 'one of the fastest steamers around', it was greeted by cheering crowds as it berthed for the first time in Sligo. In 1857 the company took delivery of the purpose-built SS *Sligo*. Their business, so obviously a version of Victorian capitalist enterprise (as they went into steam, they advertised under the slogan 'Encourage Irish enterprise'), was established in the face of competition. The SS *Liverpool*, on which the poet travelled as a boy, was sabotaged on its maiden voyage. There were fights for limited berth-space in the port in which the police were required to keep the peace, and in 1890 the company faced a difficult industrial conflict when it refused to pay an extra gratuity to which the dock workers, upon whom they depended to load and unload their ships, felt entitled. Like any Victorian Gradgrind, the company called in scab labour from the surrounding countryside. A large force of police was deployed, and the workers were defeated within eight days. Foster reports that in contemporary local reputation William Middleton 'emerges as the voice of hard-headed and belligerent business interests' (*AM*: 10), while William Pollexfen 'was among those found guilty of bribing voters in 1860' (*AM*: 10).

The Middleton and Pollexfen partnership was not the only manifestation of local commercial ambition. In 1870 substantial deposits of sulphate of barium began to be exploited industrially. These had been located between Glencar ('Where the wandering water gushes / From the hills above Glen-Car'; 'The Stolen Child') and Glenade on the border with County Leitrim. Mining went on for five years and recommenced in 1888. Sir Henry Gore-Booth of Lissadell, the local squire, was part of the company which was exploiting this valuable resource. In 1885 it was reported that in a local river a salmon had been caught with a nose curved like a hawk's bill: a Celtic metamorphosis out of folklore or a hint of the 'filthy modern tide' that had already begun to flow, even in Yeats's childhood paradise?

When John Butler Yeats married a Pollexfen, he must have seemed a promising young man, a good catch for the daughter of a provincial Victorian entrepreneur and founding partner of an ambitiously successful business enterprise. The estate in Kildare (although heavily encumbered) and a house in Dublin, both of which had come into his hands on his father's death two months after his engagement to Susan Pollexfen, gave him an annual income of fairly comfortable proportions, certainly sufficient to support a family in decent middle-class comfort, while providing security as the young husband prepared himself for a remunerative career.

J. B. Yeats had enrolled in Trinity College, Dublin in 1857 where he found the atmosphere utilitarian and stultifying. But he was fortunate in his friends among whom pre-eminently were John Todhunter, who was to become moderately well known as a poet of the Celtic mode; Edward Dowden, who would hold his university's first Professorship of English Literature and a renowned critic and scholar; and his brother John, who was to finish a distinguished career as a churchman as bishop of Edinburgh. At college they formed a coterie dedicated to conversation and literary and metaphysical speculation. Only John, the future bishop, was religiously orthodox and the talk dwelt on Comptean positivism, Darwinism, J. S. Mill and the novels of George Eliot. In the way of gifted young men, they felt constrained by a Dublin they thought provincial and dull. They knew they deserved better. However, money was a problem. Todhunter came of solid Quaker stock but he made it his business to qualify with an MD, though he practised only briefly before turning to schoolmastering and a life of minor literary and dramatic success in London. The Dowdens were the sons of a Cork tradesman whose linen company eventually would supply some private means, but which could not support them as they made their way in the world. A profession was a sad necessity, undertaken, especially by Edward Dowden, with a deep sense of foreboding. Writing to J. B. Yeats in 1869 about the chair of English Literature he had accepted as a very young but promising man in 1867, and which he was to occupy for nearly half a century, he lamented the prospect of academic employment: 'I wish I could live in the deepest solitude with a few friends, and no acquaintances! But if I were to give up my Professorship I should be obliged to work for my bread, and go to London and become a hack for the magazines, which consummation I fully intend to avert' (Eglinton 1914: 45).

Edward's brother John was, not unexpectedly, ordained in the Church of Ireland, though not until he had experienced a typical crisis of Victorian doubt. Doubt defeated, he found himself appointed curate in a County Sligo parish and subsequently in the town itself, where his high, liturgically based churchmanship, in the fraught period of disestablishment, made his tenure there extremely painful. In 1870 he was appointed chaplain to the Lord Lieutenant of Ireland, before escaping to Scotland and eventually a bishopric, in which office he resisted even the holidays to which he was entitled (Mitchell 1914: 273).

That was one temptation J. B. Yeats had no trouble resisting. After graduating from Trinity, he read for the bar and seemed set fair for the career of landlord and barrister which his young bride must have reckoned to be part of the unspoken contract upon which she had entered on marriage. They had set up house together in Sandymount, a village-like district on the south side of Dublin which faces the bay. Here W. B. Yeats was born on 13 June 1865. Their semi-detached home was close to Sandymount Castle, then in the possession of J. B. Yeats's uncle, Robert Corbet. J. B. Yeats's own father had settled next door to the castle upon withdrawal from his parish in the North of Ireland and had made his residence there until his death in 1862. J. B. Yeats himself had lived there as a college student. There were aunts living in the Castle too. So there must have been something pleasantly familial and familiar about these early years of the Yeatses' marriage when the poet was an infant and John Buter Yeats was reading for the bar. The nearby castle with its castellations, grounds and pond may have given Susan a sense that she had married into a family that counted in the capital in a way in which her own father, who as local magnate moved into a substantial house ('Merville') outside Sligo in 1867, could never quite do in the rigidly stratified county world. Her husband was called to the bar in 1866.

Yet in the spring of 1867 J. B. Yeats – the coming man in Dublin, with influential friends, a young family (a daughter Susan, known as 'Lily' had been born in 1866) and the gifts as an orator that seemed to suit him for his chosen profession – to the chagrin of wife and the astonishment of his extended family announced that he intended to abandon the law for art. William Murphy, J. B. Yeats's warmly partisan biographer, has explained this professional *volte face* as the revolt of an essentially artistic spirit against the burdensome fatuity of courtroom advocacy, in which commitment to a cause is immaterial to due process. It can be read too as putting into practice J. B. Yeats's frequently professed creed that ' "a Gentleman . . . is such simply because he has not the doctrine of *getting on* and the habit of it. The contest is not against material things, but between those who want and those who don't want to get on, having other important things to attend to" ' (*Hone*: 24). The Pollexfens, who were obviously intent on getting on, he tended to patronize; rather too easily it must be said. To the more critical Gifford Lewis, in her study of the Yeats daughters and the printing and publishing press they established together, J. B. Yeats's decision was the act of a profoundly irresponsible man who could turn his charm on and off at will, but who sacrificed his family's security and chances for happiness on a whim and in answer to his own feckless sense of how an Irish gentleman should conduct himself. Yet such a severe view fails to reckon with the sheer exuberance of the man, his vital spirits and with the touch of artistic genius he undoubtedly possessed. His larger-than-life bohemianism strikingly contrasts both with the slightly frozen personality Susan Yeats had inherited from her Pollexfen forbears and with her unadventurous provincialism of mind.

J. B. Yeats enrolled as an art student in London and took a lease on a house, 23 Fitzroy Road, near Regent's Park. Since he no longer was in command of an income from any profession, he made vitiating demands on the heavily encumbered inheritance his father had left him (*AM*: 9). It became not the helpful cushion it had been at the start of their marriage, but a serious liability which he eventually sold out. When Uncle Robert fell into financial difficulty and committed suicide in 1870 it might have been read as a terrible warning to the Yeats household of what financial ruin could mean to a family. Furthermore, failure to make good John Butler Yeats's hopes of commercial success as an artist (he was almost incapable of completing such commissions as his friends in desperation arranged for him) meant that the family spent much of the 1870s apart and in a kind of peripatetic disorder which could have done little for any of the children's well-being. What one critic has described as the 'wretched saga of the period 1869 to 1877' when the poet passed through boyhood and entered on the challenges of youth, meant that 'in the first twelve years of [his] life he was never more than two years in the one place' (Toomey 1993: 6). A third child, Elizabeth, known as 'Lollie', had been born in London in 1868 and the following year J. B. Yeats left the three children in Sligo, after a summer holiday, where they were looked after by their grandparents in the latter half of the year. In 1870 a son, Robert, was born; he would die in Sligo (when the flags were at half-mast in the bay) in 1873, during a two-year period when Susan Yeats and the children lived apart from her husband with her family, so precarious had finances become in London. Jack Yeats, the Yeatses' last child to survive and the future painter, was born in 1871.

The family was back together in London in late 1874. The lease on their first London tenancy had run out, so it was at 14 Edith Villas, in what is now West Kensington, that the Yeatses tried to re-establish their domestic life together. Nothing much improved and tragedy struck. A daughter Jane, the couple's last child, died in infancy in June 1876 and the family parted again when J. B. Yeats returned alone to London after a summer holiday in Sligo. Yeats was called to London by his father that autumn, though his mother and siblings did not return until the new year. Part of this time was spent in Farnham Royal, near Slough, where J. B. Yeats hoped to improve his technique as a landscape painter. This was by no means the end of their comings and goings. In 1879 the family moved to the artist's colony in the new garden suburb of Bedford Park, where they spent two settled years. Then J. B. Yeats decided to return to Dublin since Edward Dowden had offered him his rooms in the university, until he, ever hopeful, had established himself back in Ireland. The first house they took proved too expensive, so J. B. Yeats transported his family across the city to the village of Howth on a small peninsula ten miles to the north on Dublin Bay. Jack was not with the family at this time, since he had been settled with his grandparents in Sligo. The Yeatses spent two-and-a-half years in Howth, occupying two houses in succession, before they moved back into the city where J. B. Yeats had taken a studio. A drab terrace house in Terenure was their last Dublin address before, in April 1887, they set off once more for London and an even more disagreeable residence in South Kensington. It was there that Susan Yeats was to suffer the first of the strokes which would eventually kill her. In the spring of 1888 the family settled again in Bedford Park, this time at 3 Blenheim Road, in a house which, however difficult it may have been for them to pay the rent, at least gave space for the painter father to have a studio and his son, the poet-to-be, a study.

W. B. Yeats records that his father's friends during their first period in Bedford Park were 'painters who had been influenced by the Pre-Raphaelite movement but had lost their confidence' (*Au*: 44). J. B. Yeats was himself an admirer of Dante Gabriel Rossetti, and he and his artist friends had, in his early London years, christened themselves 'The Brotherhood' in conscious emulation of the Pre-Raphaelite Brotherhood. Rossetti indeed favourably noticed one of J. B. Yeats's pictures in 1871 (Murphy 1979: 74). Perhaps the young aspirant artist imagined that such art as the Pre-Raphaelites had produced was the kind of work, with its powerful evocation of a life lived for art itself and in the service of a spiritualized eroticism, that a gentleman could produce and remain a gentleman; an art unsullied in its ethereal preoccupations by obvious commercialism. In idealizing Pre-Raphaelitism at the beginning of his career (as he matured, he tended more towards realistic, representational modes), J. B. Yeats was making a more serious error about the society in which he lived than when he had in rather cavalier fashion patronized the Pollexfen commitment to worldly success. For the artists who founded that short-lived movement, despite their apparent aesthetic-ism, had a concept of manhood that was foreign to J. B. Yeats's vision of the painter as gifted amateur who retains his status as a gentleman even as he creates. As Herbert Sussmann has shown, the Pre-Raphaelite's creed was informed by a 'secular cult of labour' (Sussmann 1995: 118), in which a complex attitude to entrepreneurship was encoded. Art, masculinity and work were being incorpor-ated in a progressive aesthetic. Sussmann notes particularly the way Hunt and Millais made their art dependent on the hard labour of accurate scientific observation. He also astutely identifies the Brotherhood, which had broken up in 1853 after five years of semi-collective labour, as the moment when profession-alization as a social force in Victorian England had had a decisive effect on artistic production. A merging of the 'artist as professional with the artist as gentleman' (ibid.: 155) generated severe contradictions. It was not possible to be a gentleman without work; but work set at risk, unless transcended in some way, the essential leisure that defined the life of a gentleman. J. B. Yeats himself in an uncharacteristically gloomy letter (probably written in 1873) to the wife who was to become the chief victim of these contradictions as they affected the Yeats household, reveals that he had some understanding of the bind he found himself in as a Victorian artistic hopeful:

> I know that years back I have night and day thought of nothing else except how to get a competency. Time can only tell whether I am on the right track. . . . I have hopes, expectations, but no certain knowledge. I am going on trying to get skill. . . . Possess skill and you possess money – and great skill means a great deal

of money. . . . I must grind on as everyone else has done and be patient. Of course it is very unpleasant, and very galling and very humiliating, but to me quite as certainly as to you, unless it is that *I know* that the event will be a success. Show me a better course and I will take it.   (Murphy 1979: 83)

Missing here is any sense of Victorian zest in the manly heroism of art (in Browning's 'Fra Lippo Lippi', for example, male artistic daring coexists with sexual potency; in Holman Hunt's 'The Scapegoat' it involves the artist risking his life in a dangerous desert for the sake of authenticity) which was part of the nexus of Victorian feeling about such work. All is Micawberism and querulous complaint at injured dignity. But for once J. B. Yeats appreciated that skill and money were intimately connected and a competency must be had.

Over the years it was a lesson he failed to apply. And family circumstances changed in Sligo, to add to his wife's constant concerns. Following the death of William Middleton in 1882, William Pollexfen found that his finances were not as secure as he had believed. He soon retired and moved from 'Merville' to a smaller house in Sligo. In as much as the Yeats family possessed a real home, it was 'Merville'. Its sale must have reinforced Susan Yeats's very understandable anxiety about her offsprings' economic future. There was no longer a securely rich grandfather at the height of his powers to come to the rescue if things became impossible. By the end of 1886, the Ashbourne Act of 1885 supplying the means, J. B. Yeats had set in motion the process whereby he rid himself of the estate in County Kildare. The nest-egg was gone.

What effect all this family commotion had on the poet is of course a matter for speculation. *Reveries Over Childhood and Youth* has a curious remoteness of tone, as if the inner life of the child it remembers cannot or must not be recreated. Yeats's companion of his youth, AE (the poet, visionary and co-operative worker, George William Russell) remarked, unfairly but in some irritation, that the book is a thing of 'pure externalities. . . . The boy in the book might have become a grocer as well as a poet' (Eglinton 1937: 111).

Many of those who met or knew Yeats as a man have left accounts of his unsettlingly cold nature, his distance from quotidian human warmth despite the passion of his poetry. One acquaintance was struck by 'a certain malicious vein in his nature' and thought his 'worst personal fault' was 'a lack of ordinary good nature' (Mikhail 1977: 33). Perhaps it was the younger Ulster writer St John Ervine who expressed this view of the mature Yeats's personality most critically when he wrote in 1920 of the poet in his mid-fifties:

He is a tall man, with dark hanging hair that is now turning grey, and he has a queer way of focussing when he looks at you. I do not know what is the defect of sight from which he suffers, but it makes his way of regarding you somewhat disturbing. He has a poetic appearance, entirely physical, and owing nothing to any eccentricity of dress; for, apart from his necktie, there is nothing odd about his clothes. It is not easy to talk to him in a familiar fashion, and I imagine he has difficulty in talking easily on common topics. I soon discovered that he is not comfortable with individuals: he needs an audience to which he can discourse in a pontifical manner. . . . I doubt very much whether he takes any intimate interest in any human being. (ibid.: 103)

Perhaps we can trace the source of what Yeats as public man seemed to many (in private he could certainly be expansive and sometimes Rabelaisian) – cold, aloof, curiously without evident affect – to the lack of warm maternal affection in the troubled currents of the Yeats household in his most impressionable years.

The Pollexfens, for all the grandfather's ambition and commercial determination to found a dynasty, were a family haunted by the malign spirit of mental instability. Gloom was the prevailing family climate, interrupted only by periods of what must be identified as the troughs of melancholia, the clinical depression of modern diagnosis. A florid hypochondriasis afflicted J. B. Yeats's brother-in-law George, while patriarch William inhabited a world of chronic irritation and settled, lowering silences, broken by violent fits of rage. Another Pollexfen, who had been an inventor, spent his days incarcerated in an asylum for the insane. Feelings were unexpressed; stoicism and constitutional pessimism often made daily life among them a chilling of the blood.

J. B. Yeats, after the brief infatuation that provoked courtship and the essentially unworkable marriage, had soon begun to feel that his wife was her father's daughter, a true Pollexfen. Certainly he gave her much to be cool about, but the problems posed for this loquacious and sociable man who found his wife an uncommunicative, apparently emotionless companion, must have been genuinely perturbing of his usually most genial spirits. He was to write later to his New York friend and patron, John Quinn, of how in their marriage Susan 'was not sympathetic. The feelings of people around her did not concern her. She was not aware of them. She was always in an island of her own.' He acknowledges in the same letter that this was a false impression, for beneath the surface she was all 'occupied with thoughts of other people and of how to help', but he also reflects 'there is a good deal of his mother in Willie' (Reid 1968: 425–6). The Welsh writer Ernest Rhys, remembering the family in London in the 1880s, recalled: 'it was the mother with her strange dark eyes who seemed nearest in mould to her unaccountable eldest son' (Mikhail 1977: 35).

If J. B. Yeats as an adult found a relationship with the undemonstrative Pollexfen in his unfortunate wife so difficult, how must his nervous, imaginative, neglected child, the future poet, have found his emotional development marred in a life of constant relocations and familial conflict? From that childhood may indeed derive the existential anxiety, the sense of incompletion which Yeats identified in *Reveries Over Childhood and Youth* as his defining mode of consciousness as an adult: 'all life weighed in the scales of my own life seems to me a preparation for something that never happens' (*Au*: 106).

It is from the evidence of Yeats's own silence about his mother that critics and biographers have sought to assess what their relationship was. In *Reveries Over Childhood and Youth* she is little more than a series of vaguely realized images. 'I always', the poet avers, 'see her sewing or knitting in spectacles and wearing some plain dress' (*Au*: 31), though his memory of 'what she was like in those days' had 'grown very dim, but I think her sense of personality, her desire for any life of her own, had disappeared in her care for us and in much anxiety about money' (ibid.). His final chastened estimate of her life, as strokes and emotional and mental deterioration made her a ghostlike figure in the Bedford Park house where she ended her days, is shocking in the way it composes a Victorian cameo of geriatric pathos and social irrelevancy. He recalls her when 'her mind had gone in a stroke of paralysis and she had found, liberated at last from financial worry, perfect happiness feeding the birds at a London window' (*Au*: 62). When Yeats first published these words, he was fifty. His mother's age when she died in 1900 had been fifty-nine.

Reveries Over Childhood and Youth does make perfectly plain, for all its Oedipal preoccupation with father and the 'old fathers' of the poet's ancestry, that Susan Yeats was a profoundly unhappy woman. She detested the London to which her husband had dragged her against her will; she found some contentment only in the years in which the family lived in Howth (a substitute for the Sligo of her childhood) when she could spend time among common people, the fisher-folk and their wives of that harbour village, with whom she seemed able to establish genuine rapport.

Susan Yeats, her poet-son tells us, had one crucial effect upon his developing sense of the world as a child. She kept alive his love of Sligo in the dismal London years: 'She would spend hours listening to stories or telling stories of the pilots and fishing-people of Rosses Point, or of her own Sligo girlhood, and it was always assumed between her and us that Sligo was more beautiful than other places' (*Au*: 31)'. From her he heard tales 'Homer might have told' (ibid.: 61) and, as Deirdre Toomey (to whose article 'Away' I am indebted) has argued, from her he derived, as well as a profound sense of place, a life-long respect for the folk imagination: 'Inasmuch as Yeats is an *Irish* poet and a poet of *Irish* place, landscape and legend, of the "cairn-heaped grassy hill/Where passionate Maeve is stony-still"...we can thank Susan Pollexfen...She gave value to folklore, legend, country wisdom, the irrational, traditional, "unthinking" "lunar" side of life – all that J. B. Yeats rejected' (Toomey 1993: 24–5)

As the one who opened a channel to the land of fairy and the lore of the countryside, Susan Yeats in London was striking a blow in her son's mind for an archaic, immemorial world. She was, by virtue of her solitude in an unhappy marriage and her instinctively unlettered response to experience ('She read no books', Yeats records, *Au*: 61), cut off in exile not only from her own immediate social world but from an Ireland which was swiftly abandoning the sacral, magical, mythic consciousness of its traditional life, for a modernized, Catholic-dominated, Victorian normality. She, the troubled, intense woman that she was, mute in her personal relations with inexpressible feeling in the Pollexfen way, was intimate in her memories of place and custom, with a primal Irish sense of things which modernity sought to efface. So when J. B. Yeats, in a frequently cited phrase, said of his marriage to Susan that 'We have ideas and no passions, but by marriage with a Pollexfen we have given a tongue to the sea cliffs' (*Au*: 23), he perhaps spoke more than he knew. For Susan Yeats, the silent, difficult, disappointed woman, who ended her days in cerebral disintegration, was the conduit through whom flowed to the poet-to-be the energy of a folk tradition that had its roots in pagan, pre-Christian Ireland. She introduced her sensitive, dreamy son, who like his mother must have taken refuge from the pain of daily life in a dysfunctional family in an otherworld of story-telling, to a way of comprehending reality remote from his father's rationalism and positivism. She introduced him to a tradition in story, narrative, myth, folk-custom and belief, which, the adult Yeats believed, 'binds the unlettered, so long as they are masters of themselves, to the beginning of time and to the foundation of the world' (*E&I*: 6).

Yeats was most a Pollexfen in his refusal or inability to confront in his writings in any direct way the pain of his childhood and the confused emotions which must have been stirred up by the parental conflict of his home and his mother's unhappiness, depression and eventual, pitiful fate. As a poet in the Romantic tradition, nurtured by reading Shelley and Blake, he is curiously chary of child-hood as a poetic subject; though it must also be noted that the image of motherhood is one that recurs in his poetry and prose. And it does so often at moments of intensifying feeling as if escaping from some subterranean source in the poet's psyche, released under pressure. Some of his early work does however allow us to reckon with the feelings which a troubled childhood provoked in him in a way in which the pages of *Reveries Over Childhood and Youth* do not, even as they suggest in their elisions and silences the existence of such feeling.

In 1887–8, when he was twenty-two, Yeats set his hand to a novel set in Sligo and London. *John Sherman*, which he published pseudonymously in 1891, in part as an attempt to help the family's customarily precarious finances, is a pallid enough performance. It recounts the tale of a young man who forsakes Sligo and the woman there who loves him, for a suburban London in which he hopes to make a financially advantageous marriage. What saves it from a sepia-tinted indeterminacy of focus is a rising wave of ambiguous sexual longing which makes of the young woman left behind a substitute mother figure. Indeed, when in a unsatisfyingly obvious ending Sherman returns to his first love who has patiently waited for him, their erotic entanglement is compact of passivity and a yearning for a breast more nurturing than that of a lover: 'She looked upon him whom she loved as full of a helplessness that needed protection, a reverberation of the feeling of the mother for the child at the breast' (*JS*: 170).

While Yeats was waiting to place his novel with a publisher in 1891, he confessed to Katherine Tynan, Irish poet and novelist and one of his earliest woman friends, that it contained 'more of myself... than in any thing I have done (*CL1*: 245–6); and when it was published, he told her how its powerful sense of place expressed something of his own memories of Sligo and the mother with whom they were associated: 'I remember when we were children how intense our devotion was to all things in Sligo & still see in my mother the old feeling' (ibid.: 275). So when Yeats supplies John Sherman with an intense nostalgia for Sligo in a London in which he increasingly feels alienated, he is not simply transferring feelings of his own to a literary creation, but seeking to give his mother's repressed and inarticulate sensibility a voice it would not otherwise have had, since following her stroke in 1887 and subsequent protracted ill-health, she sank into silence. A walk in London made Sherman

> remember an old day-dream of his. The source of the river that passed his garden at home was a certain wood-bordered and islanded lake, whither in childhood he had often gone blackberry-gathering. At the further end was a little islet called Inniscrewin. Its rocky centre, covered with many bushes, rose some forty feet above the lake. Often when life and its difficulties had seemed to him like the lessons of some elder boy given to a younger by mistake, it had seemed good to dream of going away to that islet and building a wooden hut there and burning a few years out, rowing to and fro, fishing, or lying on the island slopes by day, and listening at night to the ripple of the water and the quivering of the bushes – full always of unknown creatures – and going out at morning to see the island's edge marked by the feet of birds.   (*JS*: 122–3)

This passage, which is a prose version of one of Yeats's most famous early poems, 'The Lake Isle of Innisfree' (begun in 1888 and completed in 1890), is redolent of primal associations, fertility, mysterious presences and a longing for pre-conscious harmony with nature. In the novel, however, it is Sherman who must bear the burden of bringing such depth of feeling into the conscious world. For his mother is represented as 'a spare, delicate-featured woman, with somewhat thin lips tightly closed as with silent people, and eyes at once gentle and distrustful, tempering the hardness of the lips' (ibid.: 19). A very Pollexfen, indeed, as is the young woman, Mary Carton, who teaches school in Ballah (the fictional Sligo) in a regime of quiet but enforced discipline. It is as if mother and prospective bride are a composite character, the one silent but a focus for nostalgic feeling, the other a puritan, to be transformed by love for the increasingly dreamy, imaginatively passive, eponymous hero. It is a magic land where such miracles of synthesis can take place. John Sherman is back in Ballah/Sligo:

> Sherman began to mount the hill to the vicarage. He was happy. Because he was happy he began to run. Soon the steepness of the hill made him walk. He thought about his love for Mary Carton. Seen by the light of this love everything that had happened to him was plain now. He had found his centre of unity. His childhood had prepared him for this love. He had been solitary, fond of favourite corners of fields, fond of going about alone, unhuman like the birds and the leaves, his heart empty.   (ibid.: 152)

Childhood, sexuality, the primal unity with nature and the mother, are here compacted in heightened anticipation of the novel's iconographic display of religio-erotic emotion in its concluding image of a Madonna and child.

Yeats's fascination for folklore as a young man was also a transposition into literary activity of his feelings for the mother who had introduced him to the magic world of story and oral tradition. Through the 1880s and 1890s, in the first phase of his career as a man of letters in Victorian London, he sustained a commitment to the folk imagination as it is expressed in the lore and tradition of the Irish countryside. In 1888 he edited *Fairy and Folk Tales of the Irish Peasantry*, and in 1893 *The Celtic Twilight* offered a series of folk narratives in the poet's own artful versions. In this period, too, he published essays and articles which sought to register as proper to serious literary attention the imaginative world of the western Irish countryman and woman. In so doing, he was well aware that he was bringing into the light a world hitherto usually regarded as inhabiting only the darkness of superstition. As he admitted in 1890, 'When I tell people that the Irish peasantry still believe in fairies, I am often doubted. They think that I am merely trying to weave a forlorn piece of gilt thread into the dull grey worsted of this century' (Welch 1993: 60). Furthermore, he was aware that modernity was an antithetical force to the world he wished to make available to a sceptical reader-ship. Such doubting folk, he observed in 1892, 'think I am merely trying to bring back a little of the old dead beautiful world of romance into this century of great engines and spinning-jinnies. Surely the hum of wheels and clatter of printing presses, to let alone the lecturers with their black coats and tumblers of water, have driven away the goblin kingdom and made silent the feet of the little dancers' (ibid.: 77). In 1890 Yeats had asserted that this is 'quite wrong' since 'ghosts and goblins do still live and rule in the imaginations of innumerable Irish men and women, and not merely in remote places, but close even to big cities' (ibid.: 60).

It is noteworthy, however, that when in 1897 and 1898 Yeats conducted intensive folkloric fieldwork, from which came his most densely written, locally rooted series of reports on folk-customs and beliefs, he conducted his researches not near Sligo nor close to any large town, let alone city, but in the wild districts in south County Galway. There, under the guidance of his new friend and patron, Lady Gregory (who also made her unpublished work on the subject available to him), he found material that fed in rich detail one of his own, highly revelatory, youthful obsessions: the motif of the changeling.

Yeats's poem 'The Stolen Child' introduces us to this uncanny imagining. This poem first appeared in the *Irish Monthly* in December 1886 when the poet was twenty-one. In a work, which provoked Yeats himself to identify his early verses as 'a flight into fairyland, from the real world... the cry of the heart against necessity' (*CL1*: 54–5), the fairies call to a human child, inviting it to forsake domesticity and security for a more compelling reality: '*Come away, O human child! / To the waters and the wild*'. The implication of course is that when the human child heeds their call, the fairies will leave behind one of their own in its place, as the folklore belief has it. In Yeats's play *The Land of Heart's Desire* (his second venture as an adult in the dramatic medium), we see such a transaction from the point of view of a family. In the company of a local priest, they watch their daughter-in-law, a newly married bride, being lured away. In this play (which ran successfully for six weeks at the Avenue Theatre, London in 1894, though it was greeted with laughter on its opening night (the audience expected panto-mime, the theatre's customary fare), it is striking that it is the restlessness of the young married woman which alerts her family to the strange fate that awaits her. The priest predicts that she will settle down in time, as responsibility enforces dutifulness (the family complains that she is 'dull' and would 'never do a turn' unless ordered to do so). The appeal of fairy, however, is greater than the promise of a familial future in this poignantly fantastical play.

When Yeats came at the end of the 1890s to do the fieldwork which gave him an even more intimate knowledge of such Irish folklore as the changeling motif, the six articles he wrote subsequently on the subject (drawing on Lady Gregory's manuscript, which deals with County Clare as well as County Galway) reinforce the impression, present in an artful, highly poeticized fashion in this play – all trembling other-worldliness and glamorous mystique – that such beliefs have social and psychological significance. They seem to be ways of explaining and coping with the manifold shocks and sorrows of a rugged rural life of peasant poverty in an unrelenting environment. The accidents, drownings, mysterious illnesses, sudden deaths (particularly of children), in which the church and the local healer, a redoubtable woman, compete for social power, are given some kind of meaning for the people in the narratives of the supernatural world interacting with the natural. For all Yeats's own supernaturalism (by this time he had definitely renounced his father's Comptean positivism), Yeats seems aware of the sociological and psychological import of what he has been observing. He remarks, as if all too conscious of the wish-fulfilment element in their folk-beliefs: 'It is not wonderful [that is, it is understandable], when one remembers this nearness of the dead to the living, that the country people should sometimes go on half-hoping for years, that their dead might walk in at the door, as ruddy and warm as ever, and live with them again. They keep their hopes half-living with many stories, but I think only half-living.' (Welch 1993: 172). Yet when he confronts the changeling motif, a preoccupation, once again, of these writings, Yeats emphasizes the magical, even religious, significance of the occurrences he reports.

It is perfectly clear in these detailed accounts of personality changes, which are attributed to a changeling being left by the fairies, that such tales of the 'taken' and of those who are 'away' deal with the onset and the course of mental illnesses of one kind or another – depression, madness. In Ireland, to be 'away in the head' is slang for bizarre, even insane, behaviour. Yeats tells his stories, many of which 'are about women who are brought back by their husbands, but almost always against their will, because their will is under enchantment' (ibid.: 173), of unfortunates who sink into protracted silences, or who take to their beds, or to night wandering, or grow thin and emaciated, refusing food. All is to be accounted for by the belief in fairy interference. The woman, the child, the man, is 'away'. A changeling has come among the people.

At a crucial point in the series, his essay on changelings, starkly entitled 'Away', Yeats does acknowledge that even his country people, who like 'all premature people' see mystery in madness, sometimes associate it with 'the others' (their euphemistic term for the feared fairy folk). That is an association he seems at pains to avoid himself since he writes of how the country people believe that when you are 'away', 'lying in a faint on the ground, or in your bed or even going about your daily work', some dead person has been substituted for you. Of this he advises:

> This substitution of the dead for the living is indeed a pagan mystery, and not more hard to understand than the substitution of the body and blood of Christ for the wafer and the wine in the mass; and I have not yet lost the belief that some day, in some village lost among the hills or in some island among the western seas, in some place that remembers old ways and has not learned new ways, I will come to understand how this pagan mystery hides and reveals some half-forgotten memory of an ancient knowledge or of an ancient wisdom.   (Welch 1993: 317)

Yeats, as Deirdre Toomey tells us, drafted this essay in 1898, when, as she bluntly puts it, 'Susan Yeats had been "away" for a decade' (Toomey 1993: 20). She was to die, with the poet present, in January 1900 in her hated London, but to earn from her poet son no elegy or eulogy: unless we can read this passage with its melancholic dying fall, its evasive elevation of the pain of his own childhood and youth and of more recent tragic years into a sacramental dimension and with its evocation of a place of rural, islanded archaism, of the kind his mother had introduced him to in her own storytelling, as his fullest memorial to her. Perhaps it was all he could bring himself to say of a mother who had been 'taken' from her Sligo home.

1

Victorian Cities: London and Dublin

In 1888 Henry James recalled his first sight of England, twenty years earlier. He had arrived by ship and he remembered how 'the sense of approach was already intolerably strong at Liverpool' and how 'the perception of the English character of everything was as acute as a surprise' (James 1905: 2). Many Irish men and women have shared this experience of the foreignness of England on first disembarking at that same port. The young W. B. Yeats frequently made the journey to Liverpool on his grandfather's craft, though perhaps because he first set foot in the country as a very young child, we have no description of a sea voyage to the neighbouring island as Irish rite of passage, to set beside those of various other Irish writers. *Reveries Over Childhood and Youth*, by contrast, records the excitement of a return journey to Ireland through Liverpool. In fact the England in which Yeats was to spend much of his life plays surprisingly little part in his writings and is specifically referred to only three times in his poetry.

Yeats as a schoolboy in London seems to have been almost completely immune to the undoubted atmospherics of the world's largest metropolis. The city in which his family settled in 1877 for sufficient time for the future poet to attend a school, the Godolphin in Hammersmith, was unquestionably a challenge to the imagination. The paintings of Turner had opened English eyes to the beauty of an urban sunset. Whistler did for London's famous fogs what Turner had done for sunsets (J. B. Yeats disapproved of Whistler, but his son felt that his work reflected an aesthetic in which 'creation should be deliberate'; *Au*: 83). And it was in 1877 that Whistler's *Nocturne in Black and Gold; The Falling Rocket*, that distillation of an urban mood, inspired by a fireworks display on the Thames, led to Ruskin's denunciation of his talent and a famous libel trial. London as artistic subject was available and controversial. In the 1890s Yeats's friend Arthur Symons would evoke it as an art object in its own right: 'continually changing, a continual sequence of pictures, and there is no knowing what mean street corner may not suddenly take on a glory of its own' (Symons 1918: 164).

The young Irish schoolboy Willie Yeats, who spent over three formative years in London in the late 1870s and early 1880s does not seem to have been affected by such urban aestheticism. The pages in *Reveries Over Childhood and Youth* dedicated to this period of his life are marked by the settled distaste with which he had viewed most things English, as if he had in part been responding to the world though his mother's jaundiced eyes. For it is she who had taught him, on noticing how the English kiss at railway stations, 'to feel disgust at their lack of reserve'. Since she hated London and longed for Sligo, so her son for some days told himself 'that whatever' he 'most cared for had been taken away' (*Au*: 32). No identification with his surroundings, normal in childhood, filled this vacuum. Rather, a developing sense of his own distinctiveness as an Irish son of an artist overcame him and anti-Englishness began to coalesce, indeed, into a distinct sense of the individual and his world. Where another imaginative and sensitive child might have developed a romance of the city, Yeats began to respond to the glamour of a country whose name was danger. At school, he tells us: 'Anti-Irish feeling was running high, for the Land League had been founded and landlords had been shot, and I, who had no politics, was yet full of pride, for it is romantic to live in a dangerous country' (*Au*: 35).

One part of London did, however, offer some attractions: the garden suburb of Bedford Park where the family, as we saw, took a house in the spring of 1879. Yeats remembered that 'for years Bedford Park was a romantic excitement' (*Au*: 42) and how when they lived there he and his siblings 'could imagine people living happy lives as we thought people did long ago when the poor were picturesque and the master of a house could tell of strange adventures over the sea' (*Au*: 43); almost as he would have done in an ideal Sligo.

The London of the 1870s and 1880s in which Yeats spent part of his boyhood and young manhood was a city undergoing rapid transformation. Its ancient 'agglomerating habit' (Waller 1983: 24) had, since the the 1860s, become a kind of mania. Indeed the population in the greater London conurbation grew by 125 per cent in the period 1861 to 1911 when the population of England as a whole grew by 80 per cent. A huge public housing crisis developed and by the 1880s there was a widespread sense that London, a city increasingly of migrants and immigrants (from a depopulating countryside, from various parts of the Empire, including Ireland, and from repressive regimes in Europe), was becoming dangerously overinhabited. There was a reactive fear that the city was becoming overpopulated by undesirable elements. Voices were raised to express an apocalyptic premonition of imminent urban degeneration, there were social commentators who suggested the forced removal of unwanted people. One less drastic response was for capital to flow to the periphery of the city, where new middle-class housing estates sprang up to meet the demand for salubrious dwelling-houses with rail links to the city, secure from the threat posed to daily life by the immiserated urban poor. The era of the speculative builder had arrived with a vengeance.

Where Sligo had not been immune to the forces of Victorian change, in London the Yeats family was close to the heart of the monster. And its power was not only extending in tentacles of suburban blight – it was changing the social environment and the psychic landscape. For the nature of city life was altering, as one social historian reports: 'Between 1870 and 1900, there was a sterilisation of public space as activities moved into specialised and purpose-built locations: the music hall, sports ground and department store. Streets were not used in the same way as they had been in the past in British cities, or as they continued to be used in most European cities' (Olsen 1976: 67). The era had dawned when privacy would be a prime value in the world of Pooterism and the semi-detached villa on a suburban line. The city Dickens had celebrated, in which public and private intermingled in the thronged streets of a socially variegated capital, was rapidly disappearing. Class and location became instinctively associated in a universally comprehended mental map, with the working class East End as a version of the inferno.

Bedford Park was purpose-built in the era of the purpose-built; but, paradoxically, its purpose was to resist the spirit of the times. The district which G. K. Chesterton dubbed 'the fantastic suburb' and described as a 'queer artificial village' (Chesterton 1992: 139) had been deliberately envisaged as an artists' colony by its architect, Jonathan Carr. When the Yeatses moved in it was still very new and worthy of comment. In 1881, for example, *Harper's Monthly Magazine* featured it in a lengthy illustrated article which caught the atmosphere of the place, where in little more than three years, 350 houses had been constructed (many of them built by Norman Shaw in the 'Queen Anne' style; interior decor tended to be William Morris). *Harper's* commended its sanitary efficiency (which deteriorated swiftly), its elegant lack of fussy ostentation, its air of instant antiquity, its adjacency to the city by rail, its co-operative stores, club-house (built in 1879 and progressively open to men and women 'on a perfect equality') and a tavern named after Chaucer's Tabard Inn.

The journalist reckoned that the suburb met two needs. It offered a solution to the problem that 'the people who most desired beautiful homes were those of the younger generation whom the new culture had educated above the merg pursuiv of riches, at the same time awakening in them refined tastes which only through riches could obtain their satisfaction' ('Bedford Park' 1881: 482). In other words, affordable chic. And in as much as it functioned co-operatively, it did not mean that an exquisite environment and domestic regime had to be bought at the cost of destructive personal toil. The Yeats family should have thrived.

To a limited extent it did. The children enjoyed the garden and the adventure of living in so new a place. A governess was employed for the young ones, while Willie continued to attend the Godolphin. There was a cheerfully complete Devon family holiday in 1879, when Willie was fourteen. There, Jack's talents as an artist began to show themselves in a family of sketchers. Willie even started to excel in school, though he hated its bullying and English complacency. He exhibited great promise in scientific subjects. His father was gratified when in his son's last year at the school the 'reports were written in rose-water'. He recalled: '"Of exceptional ability" was a blessed phrase that once occurred, and I said to myself, "He will be a man of science; it is great to be a man ofscience"' (Murphy 1979: 122). J. B. Yeats remained true to Comptean positivism.

Perhaps the family's comparative happiness in these years, despite the chronic money worries, can be explained by the simple fact that they were occupying a house that they liked. For in the Anglo-Irish way, houses were a measure for the Yeatses not only of social standing but of how well life was being lived, a tribute paid to ideals of amplitude and traditional hierarchy. Their home at this time 'was the biggest and most elegant house the Yeatses ever lived in alone as a family' (Murphy 1995: 47) so perhaps there was an underlying familial satisfaction that, in a world of suburban mediocrity and privacy, the Yeatses were living with stylish creativity among talented people in the Bedford Park collective (as well as artists, there were professional men and retired military types), as befitted the family of the Irish gentleman John Butler Yeats believed himself to be. For although the house lacked grandeur of scale, it was very charming and airy, its formal rooms giving on a well-designed garden that extended the living space in the integrated fashion William Morris had originated when he had built his own house at Upton, near London, in 1859/60. (MacCarthy 1995: 165).

Certainly Yeats as poet was to take 'the house' as theme. He would discover in the metaphor of a country house in its landscape, dynastic and cultural lessons for a degraded present. His ideal was to become a complex blend of memories of the long avenues of the Big Houses in County Sligo, Lissadell pre-eminently, from which his essentially middle-class family had been excluded in his childhood years, of images drawn from the poetry of Jonson and Marvell, and his own social experience of country-house life as a guest, in Ireland and in England, when he was a mature man. Anything approaching an actual, secure personal hold on even an approximation of such a residential ideal was not to be his until after his marriage, in his fifty-second year.

Yeats's parents were never again really to enjoy a sense of being at ease in an appropriate house with their children around them. For in 1881 the family returned to Ireland and domestic uncertainty reasserted itself. Perhaps one may account for Yeats's preoccupation in his work with the ideal of the house as not only a consequence of a characteristic caste concern, but as a compensation for what had been so absent in his own immediate background. There was no Yeats house, for memory and legend to mythologize, until the poet purchased a Norman keep at Thoor Ballylee in County Galway in 1917 – only a series of addresses. And these (the Sandymount villa, a long, low cottage on the cliffs at Howth, a villa overlooking Howth harbour, the Bedford Park residences) symbolize the social precariousness of a family existing between the rooted, customary life of the country-house ideal, with, in Ireland, its estates and agreeably collective life of farm, stable-yard, horse-boxes, well-run kitchen and the modern anonymity of a suburban villa in such a place as Dublin's Rathgar, to which the Yeatses must at times have felt themselves ignominiously reduced. Yeats himself recalled in a letter written in 1922 'that Rathgar villa where we all lived when I went to school, a time of crowding & indignity' (*CL1*: 9). The offence still rankled after almost forty years.

The return to Ireland in 1881 meant a new school for Willie – the Erasmus Smith High School in Harcourt Street in central Dublin. It is from this period that we begin to have records of the poet-to-be as he was seen by people other than his immediate relatives and to gain an impression of the young person beginning to emerge from the family chrysalis. The scientific bent, already noted in London, blossomed, in the way of boyhood's obsessional hobbies, into a fascination for entomology. His capacities and curious incapacities began to reveal themselves too. His school-fellows sensed his reserve and observed his distracted air. He could not spell and had no talent for foreign languages. What may have been a mild form of dyslexia and a tone-deaf ear made it always difficult for Yeats to rectify these deficiencies in later life. He was also very short-sighted. However at school, as one acute fellow pupil recalled, he evinced strong ability in Euclid and algebra. Arcane geometric and mathematical interests would resurface in later life.

Yeats was in fact somewhat older than his fellows in the High School classroom and was already displaying in elaborate conversations the wide reading he had done and his commitment to the discussion of general issues of life and art. He spoke of T. H. Huxley and Herbert Spencer. He seemed to come and go as the fancy took him, as if attendance was a matter for himself alone. Shortly after he left the school in December 1883, he loaned one senior pupil A. P. Sinnett's *Esoteric Buddhism*, a book to which his Aunt Isabella Pollexfen had introduced him.

By his own admission, Yeats departed school with 'small Latin and less Greek'. It scarcely mattered, for his real education had been going on elsewhere. Daily he and his father left Howth for the train journey to Dublin, where J. B. had his studio just off St Stephen's Green in the centre of the city. They breakfasted together there and Yeats returned from the nearby school at midday for a light meal. Edward Dowden frequently joined them; he was now a distinguished professor at J. B. Yeats's old university and author of a popular study of Shakespeare which had made his academic name in 1875. There was much wide-ranging talk. Charles Johnston, another High School boy, who shared Yeats's burgeoning interest in theosophy and the occult – which dates from this period – recorded his impressions of that studio, where the poet experienced his intellectual awakening:

Many of the finer qualities of Willie Yeats' mind were formed in that studio on St Stephen's Green, in long talks on art and life, on man and God, with his sensitive, enthusiastic father. One remembers the long room, with its skylight, the walls of pale green, frames and canvasses massed along them; a sofa and a big armchair or two; the stout iron stove with its tube; and, filling the whole with his spirit, the artist stepping forward along a strip of carpet to touch his work with tentative brush, then stepping back again, always in movement, always meditating high themes, and now and then breaking into talk on the second part of 'Faust,' or the Hesperian apples, or the relation of villainy to genius. (Mikhail 1977: 9–10)

It was hardly surprising that Yeats preferred the studio to the High School, where the headmaster measured the worth of his pupils solely by examination prowess.

The Dowden who came visiting in those Dublin days was no longer the impecunious young man who had looked on a Trinity chair with trepidation. The Professor's stipend and fees for the diverse literary tasks he performed (as well as income deriving from the family business in Cork) had brought him a large house in the prosperous suburb of Rathmines. His mild bohemianism found occasional expression; he irritated the Board of his college by lecturing on risky literary topics. He was an advocate of Whitman, with whom he had corresponded. He was becoming too a pronounced Unionist. Although his marriage was less than happy, he must have seemed an object lesson to the young Yeats in how it was possible to shape a cultivated life in the Ireland in which his own future might lie. For a time Yeats seems to have hero-worshipped the elegant, ironical older man until, as is the way with such youthful enthusiasms, he began to suspect feet of clay. J. B. Yeats had always reckoned Dowden a traitor to his own poetic nature, one who had forsaken the cause of art for security (though he was not averse to borrowing money from his old friend, who never pressed for repayment). He told Dowden that all his poems had 'a furtive look' (Eglinton 1914: 187), as if Dowden were ashamed to confess himself a poet. W. B. Yeats, later, when his own personal identity as the distinctive kind of Irishman he became, was more secure, was to indict the professor and family friend as the chief representative of an intellectual Unionism which in Victorian Dublin had betrayed Irish possibility.

In the autumn of 1882, in Howth, Yeats caught sight of a red-headed girl driving in a dog-cart. He was smitten. She was in fact a distant cousin, so a meeting came easily enough with the Laura Armstrong for whom Yeats wrote some of his earliest verses. In 1889 he remembered her 'wild dash of half insane genius' (*CL1*: 155). Perhaps he was recalling her performance in *Vivienne and Time*, a play he had written for her. It was put on in a local judge's house in Howth, in the home of the family's landlord in fact.

Armstrong was engaged to be married when Yeats fell for her. She would scarcely have taken his poetic suit too seriously. The daughter of an army sergeant, she had set her cap higher than the son of an impoverished portrait painter. For in the stratified, genteel world of Protestant Dublin Yeats's status was unquestionably anomalous. Trinity College would have helped to clarify that uncertain marginality which made him a somewhat solitary figure as a Dublin schoolboy, even when putting on a play he had written in Judge Wright's imposing redbrick house overlooking the sea at Howth. At Trinity he could have mixed with the scions of Ireland's Protestant middle class (the Ascendancy proper preferred Oxbridge for their sons) and, by his gifts for debate and conversation, have made a name for himself in the Historical Society, where many an Irish lad of parts had caught the public eye and established the contacts which in later life could compensate for lack of family means. Yeats's paper qualifications, when he left school in December 1883, were too poor to allow matriculation. Instead, in May 1884, he enrolled in Dublin's Metropolitan School of Art, Kildare Street, in sight of his father's *alma mater* but different in tone and social composition for it was less conventional politically, with a touch of bohemian eccentricity among its students. There he met George Russell (AE), just the kind of person Trinity would scarcely have produced for him as a possible soul-mate. They shared a dislike of the School's teaching methods, which Yeats later characterized as 'destructive of enthusiasm' (*Report* 1906: 60).

Russell was a native of Lurgan, County Armagh. He was the son of an accountant who had settled in Dublin when George was eleven. When Yeats met him, he had been attending the art college in a desultory way since his arrival in Dublin. He had a fluent, facile style with the brush, but (much more significantly for Yeats) he painted the visions which rose up before him like emanations from some alternative reality. Russell was one of those people (William Blake, whose work Yeats was to edit in the 1890s, was another) who have what can only be described as the capacity for waking dreams. He truly 'saw' the mythological personages, the angelic or fairy folk, who appeared before him as in some mysterious tableau. For Yeats, who was beginning to revolt against his father's materialism and the realistic Rembrandt-inspired art he had turned to after his Pre-Raphaelite phase, Russell was like a messenger sent to set him on a true path. He was a godsend to a dreamy youth who was beginning to make poetry, not painting, his avocation.

Russell was not the only acquaintance outside the social circle of the family whom Yeats was developing at this crucial point of his development. There were others as involved in heterodox speculation as Russell who were ready to explore occult possibilities. Among them were Charles Johnston (son of a Unionist MP and fanatical Orangeman from the North of Ireland) and Charles Alexandre Weekes, another High School boy who sought occult illumination. Yeats also became a regular attender at the Contemporary Club, which met initially in the college rooms of a Trinity don, C. H. Oldham, and then took a more public address in Grafton Street, near the college but distinct from it. The Club for Yeats was an introduction to political, social and cultural debate superior to anything the college's Historical Society could have supplied, with its essentially undergraduate atmosphere. For under the Protestant Home-Ruler Oldham's liberal-minded regime, its meetings attracted some of the most energetic and persuasive of contemporary public speakers. The ethos was one of freedom of speech, with no holds barred. Yeats encountered a range of Irish opinion, the kind of thing the Unionist-dominated university would not have offered. And he was challenged to overcome innate shyness and personal insecurity when confronted by polemical opposition. He remembered it as a test of his 'self-possession' (*Au*: 94). His experience in the Club meant that Yeats put himself to the hard school of public debate, seeking out controversy where he could find it, as a means of honing his own rhetorical skills.

The principal orator at the Contemporary Club and Yeats's chief antagonist was John F. Taylor, in whom the young poet faced the force of histrionic authority in the service of a windy, essentially pious Catholic nationalism (James Joyce rescued Taylor from obscurity, only to immortalize him as a Victorian windbag in the 'Aeolus' chapter of *Ulysses*). In the figure of John O'Leary, another Club disputant, he met a man whom, he believed, exerted a more effective and profound (because moral) authority in the Ireland of his day.

John O'Leary (1830–1907) was a Fenian (the revolutionary Brotherhood that had risen in 1867 to assert Ireland's right to independence by force of arms), an associate of those who had provoked alarm in the Sligo of the poet's childhood. For the Yeats who was beginning to suspect Dowden of an artistic bad faith disguised in an ironical pose, and whose own father must at times have seemed a loquacious but ineffectual dilettante, O'Leary was a new mentor. And where Taylor was loudly contentious, O'Leary was courteous and noble in demeanor. He had been sentenced to twenty years' penal servitude in 1865 for treason-felony, which added romance and danger to his record for the impressionable youth inebriated by the headier passages of Shelley's romantic and revolutionary verses (Yeats had made *Prometheus Unbound* a 'sacred book'; *Au*: 87). O'Leary had been released from prison in England in 1871, on condition that he would not live in Ireland. His protracted Parisian exile invested his return to the country in 1885, when Yeats met him, with further glamour. Here was a man who had suffered and had kept the faith. That he was bookish and cultivated added to the appeal of a figure who began to occupy the role of a substitute father for the poet.

In *Reveries Over Childhood and Youth* O'Leary is represented as a foil for Dowden, the one's austere, classical dignity rebuking the other's suave, condescending provincialism. With O'Leary came his politics, the antithesis of Dowden's and apparently more hard-edged than J. B. Yeats's unfocused if good-hearted national feelings. He was anti-clerical, suspicious of Parnell and, as a landlord himself, his attitude to tenant rights was decidedly cool. O'Leary believed that ultimately 'a people who are not prepared to fight in the last resort rather than remain slaves will never be made free by any sort of Parliamentary legerdemain whatsoever' (Pierce 1995: 87). But he combined this with a conviction that a country must be worth fighting for. It must, accordingly, have a cultural life of its own and its citizens must be the epitome of the moral virtues. There was something Robespierre-like in O'Leary's sense of the revolutionary as just man, and his *obiter dicta*, brief and stoical, in a country of garrulous overstatement, impressed Yeats enormously: 'There are things a man must not do to save a nation' (*Au*: 96); 'I have but one religion, the old Persian: to bend the bow and tell the truth' (*P&I*: 2) (O'Leary was quoting a character in a Charles Kingsley novel). Yeats judged that O'Leary had 'the moral genius that moves all young people' (*Au*: 95) and deemed him 'the one indispensable man' (*Mem*: 52). Late in life he reflected in valedictory self-assessment that he was 'a nationalist of the school of John O'Leary' (*L*: 920–1), as if to remind himself that he had never abandoned the curious blend of public spirit with individual hauteur in the service of a revolutionary elitism, which O'Leary had preached verbally and represented in what Yeats had regarded as his dignified person ('O'Leary's noble head'; 'Beautiful Lofty Things').

O'Leary, so different in his austere single-mindedness, which Yeats subsequently was to find abstract and uncreative, shared with Yeats's father a pecuniary problem. Although he had embarked on a medical education, he had no actual profession. He depended on the rents from his property in County Tipperary, which dried up during a bitterly fought rent strike that lasted from 1889 to 1891. A man who counselled that it might be better to wait 100 years before Home Rule lest it be 'an altogether wrong sort' (Pierce 1995: 86), was directly affected by the more pragmatic revolutionary energies which had been released in a swiftly modernizing Ireland by the Land War of the 1880s. Agitation and consequent land reform were transferring power from the ascendant landowning Protestant caste, with its ecclesiastical, legal and professional penumbra (in which decent, even ample, livings could be achieved), to an emerging class of former tenant farmers who believed they had at last come into their national inheritance. They were flexing their political muscles in a demand for Home Rule, of a kind which O'Leary the landlord found distinctly threatening.

In June 1885 Yeats met a Miss Katherine Tynan to discuss with C. H. Oldham plans for the recently founded *Dublin University Review*, at her father's residence ('a pretty thatched . . . farmhouse'; *LTNI*: 85) in Clondalkin, then a village to the west of Dublin. Tynan's father was a prosperous Catholic farmer and entrepreneur, who had seen to it that his daughter, one of twelve children, had been provided with a genteel, convent education. His hopes for his daughter were well founded, for not only did she share her father's strong support of Parnell's crusade for legislative independence, she displayed distinct literary gifts. In 1885, through a fatherly subvention, she published a first volume of verse; it met with a gratifying critical reception. Seven years older than Yeats (though she claimed she was only four years his elder), she already had the self-confidence to conduct a regular 'evening' of literary conversation in her Clondalkin home. For Yeats, this was an introduction to the middle-class Irish Catholic world that hitherto would have been closed to him in Sligo and Dublin. Friendship developed. Tynan would stay with the Yeatses in Dublin and the poet corresponded frequently with her on his family's return to London in 1887. It is in these letters from the English capital that we find the young poet trying out ideas about poetry and, with Tynan (whom he feared, rather presumptuously, might wish to marry him) as confidante and sounding-board, dealing surprisingly frankly with the insecurities of late adolescence amid minor illnesses and frequent debilitating nervous crises.

Among the pressures provoking these distresses were a father's financial inadequacy and a growing awareness that, by finding employment himself, he could ameliorate the family's exiguous circumstances. To make matters worse, his father disapproved of his literary son seeking regular work. In a letter of 12 February 1888, this anxiety about work, and the conflict with his father, comes to a head. Yeats felt caught in a 'web of thoughts' (*CL1*: 48): 'To me the hope of regular work is a great thing for it would mean more peace of mind than I have had lately but Papa see all kinds of injury to me in it' (*CL1*: 48). Things did not improve. In June the family finances reached a crisis. Yeats was at work, with a July deadline, on a collection of Irish folk tales for the Camelot Classic series which he hoped would bring ready cash. Still his father disapproved, yet the poet bowed to practical literary industry. Over the next two months the word 'work' recurs in his letters in the context of the lists and prospectuses of a young man desperate to establish himself in a career or its literary equivalent. It all took its toll. As usual the motherly Tynan received the *cri de coeur*: 'I have had three months incessant work without a moment to read or think and am feeling like a burnt out taper' (*CL1*: 92). He had been reduced to a job of mere transcription to raise some ready cash.

Autumn was a rush of proofs and scrabbling for new commissions, with 'as much work' as he could manage, 'only badly paid' (*CL1*: 95). In mid-December he began to compose 'The Lake Isle of Innisfree', with its longing for 'peace . . . dropping slow' (*CL1*: 121). A year of literary drudgery reached its ironic conclusion when Oscar Wilde, then thirty-four years old, invited Yeats for Christmas dinner at the elegant home he shared with his wife in Tite Street. He thought the young man alone in London. The poet was impressed by the precious interior of the house beautiful, by Wilde's studied act of self-fashioning and by his commitment, in disdain of the market-place, to art as a form of moral vision. It was this latter aspect of his fellow Irishman's experiment in living that was to mean most to Yeats. He would remember how Wilde in his person and in his critical writings had espoused a doctrine which made the aesthetic a force for the spiritual transformation of human consciousness. After dinner Wilde read aloud to Yeats from the proofs of his iconoclastic treatise 'The Decay of Lying'.

Yeats's conflict with his father was not only about the conventional employment which J. B. Yeats believed was inimical to creative freedom. It was, even more seriously, a religious conflict. The mature Yeats recalled the religious crisis he had experienced as a youth in the following terms:

> I was unlike others of my generation in one thing only. I am very religious, and deprived by Huxley and Tyndall, whom I detested, of the simple-minded religion of my childhood, I had made a new religion, almost an infallible Church of poetic tradition, of a fardel of stories, and of personages, and of emotions, inseparable from their first expression, passed on from generation to generation by poets and painters with some help from philosophers and theologians. I wished for a world where I could discover this tradition perpetually, and not in pictures and in poems only, but in tiles around the chimney-piece and in the hangings that kept out the draught. (*Au*: 115–16)

This passage, despite Yeats's claim of generational uniqueness, seems to recall a quintessentially Victorian crisis of faith – the dogmas of orthodox Christianity melting in contact with Darwinian evolutionism and scientific humanism. Yet there was little in his immediate family background to suggest that he was so earnestly instructed in Christianity that he would have found its abandonment psychologically disturbing. For although he had been baptised and confirmed and had been taken to church by his mother, religion played little part in his upbringing, despite the clerical tradition of the Yeats family. In fact Yeats as a man and writer shows few signs that his developing imagination was much affected by religion as he could have experienced it in church service and school teaching as a child and youth. His religious feelings in childhood were expressed in private prayer and an overly scrupulous conscience. In as much as Christian liturgy and symbology surfaces in his poetry, it is the iconography of a more Catholic faith that fires his imagination (the true cross, the Madonna with Child, the image of the Holy Family), rather than anything redolent of the low-church, Biblically earnest piety of the nineteenth-century Church of Ireland. Losing orthodox Christian faith can scarcely have been traumatic.

What Yeats may mean in the passage cited above is that for him religion is related to his perennial sense that life must be comprehended systematically. For the poet refers there to his first attempt to construct a religious system of his own. And, as we shall see, religious speculation and system-building are inseparable in Yeats's mature intellectual processes, in a way which makes his spiritual nature not at all one that deals in piety, faith or good works, but in systematic knowledge, structured ritual and organized power. In this, of course, the no-nonsense scepticism of Huxley and Tyndall and his father's Comptean rationalism were just as much the enemies of what he sought to build as of the childhood Christianity he had shed.

So religious ambition meant that he was seriously at odds with his father. In the early months of his friendship with Russell, both paternal parents, in a nice irony, disapproved of the new relationship. Russell's father deprecated Yeats as an influence luring George away from orthodox faith; J. B. Yeats feared that Russell would encourage his son in the foolish irrationality, towards which he seemed attracted like a moth to a flame. Oddly enough, though, it was Dowden's account of Shelley's diabolism at Eton College, in his biography of the English poet, which prompted the friends to try raising spirits. The fundamental conflict between Yeats and his father, however, was about much more than a parent's concern at a son's youthful follies among dubious companions. A clash of outlooks and of ways of being in the world was in the making.

How intense this conflict became is clear in the disturbing incidents that the poet described in the first draft of an autobiographical account (it remained unpublished in his lifetime) of the years following the family's return to London in 1887. The poet remembers a quarrel over Ruskin which turned physical. Ruskin 'added to [the poet's] interest in psychical research and mysticism' (*Mem*: 19), enraged J. B. Yeats. One night he broke the glass of a picture with the back of his son's head as he put him out of the room. Another night he ended a similar argument in a challenge to fisticuffs.

'I was much among the Theosophists, having drifted there from the Dublin Hermetic Society' (*Mem*: 23), recalled Yeats of his early years in London as a young man. The Dublin society had been founded on 16 June 1885, with Yeats as the president of a small group of spiritual neophytes. George Russell, no joiner of groups, disapproved of their aims and kept himself apart. It was an early hint of the controversy Yeats would discover in the worlds of occultism and Theosophy where disagreements were endemic. It was also an introduction to the way in which leadership and conflict are inevitably joined in human affairs.

When Yeats wrote to John O'Leary in 1892 that 'the mystical life is the centre of all that I do & all that I think & all that I write. It holds to my work the same relation that the philosophy of Godwin held to the work of Shelley & I have all-ways considered my self a voice of what I beleive to be a greater renaisance – the revolt of the soul against the intellect – now beginning in the world', (*CL1*: 303), he was identifying what had been his principal preoccupation since he had left the High School: the occult. And the occult was to remain a controlling, energizing obsession throughout his life.

Yeats's fascination for and deep interest in the possibility of occult reality and powers which might be acquired through esoteric knowledge, had, by 1892, brought him into contact with some individuals whom his rationalist father must have found alarming in the extreme. They were individuals who fed on a diet of controversy in a world of claim and counter-claim to magical authority and of scandalous revelations of fraud and deception. The Dublin Hermetic Society itself had been founded in 1885 in emulation of a branch of the Theo-sophical Society in London (Kuch 1986: 14). One of the most extraordinary of the many extraordinary figures who made late Victorian London an emporium of exotic cults, creeds, social experiments and outright religious lunacies was the presiding genius of Theosophy.

Madame Helena Petrovna Blavatsky (1831–91) was a native of southern Russia. Following a life of colourful international gypsydom, marital confusions and (or so her followers were required to believe) religious initiation in the tenets of what came to be called Esoteric Buddhism, at the hands of occult masters in Tibet, she fetched up in London in 1887. She had founded the Theosophical Society in 1875 and had communicated her religious discoveries to the world in general through her treatise *Isis Unveiled* (1877). From 1879 to 1885 she had been in India where she established the headquarters of her movement. One of her main, if not unambiguously loyal, advocates in Europe was A. P. Sinnett, author of *Esoteric Buddhism* (1883).

Sinnett's book, together with his earlier more anecdotal text *The Occult World* (1881), was Yeats's introduction to a way of thinking about reality that retained the supernaturalism of Christian faith, but in a totally different doctrinal context. Sinnett's writings revealed that there were living in the world, in the secret land of Tibet or in inaccessible northern India, a group of spiritual masters, or Mahatmas, who shared their occult knowledge of the very nature of the universe with selected individuals with whom they could communicate at a distance. Madame Blavastsky was one such privileged messenger, who was empowered to inform all who would listen of the truths vouchsafed to her. High romance indeed for the young poet already entranced by Shelley's Neoplatonism, full of revolt against scientific positivism. In his early poetry, India, the India to which Sinnett's writings had introduced him, became indeed a version of the Sligo of his dreams, a secret place apart, where, as on an isle in a western lake, the modern world could be escaped in a transcendental eastern peace. As 'An Indian Song' (sub-sequently 'The Indian to His Love') had it: 'there we will moor our lonely ship/ And wander ever with woven hands'. Yet it is also a place, like the west of Ireland, where immemorial folk wisdom has its roots in deep antiquity, of great spiritual power, where the gods 'dwell on sacred Himalay – / On the far Golden Peak;

enormous shapes −/Who still were old when the great sea was young' ('Jealousy', subsequently retitled 'Anshuya and Vijaya').

Sinnett's books, moreover, offer a thoroughgoing system, albeit one that comes from oral sources. Yeats, who esteemed his mother's innocence of literature in her direct contact with the 'folk', must have been pleased to hear that the Mahatmas were the custodians of an unwritten tradition. It was a system too that claimed to take account of science, even that of Darwin. The opening sections of *Esoteric Buddhism* seek indeed to defend the new creed as a higher form of evolutionary theory, one that avoids the scientific reductionism of the Darwinian version. Sinnett attacked what he termed 'Dense materialism which cannot conceive of consciousness as anything but a function of flesh and blood' (cited in Oppenheim 1985: 161). And in letters in *The Occult World*, purportedly from a very Mahatma himself (one Koot Hoomi Lal Singh), Yeats heard a refreshing counter-voice to his father's philosophical complacency − 'Full always of Mill and humanitarianism' (Kuch 1986: 11). Here was secret doctrine, anti-materialistic and reserved for the privileged few:

> The mysteries never were, never can be, put within the reach of the general public.... The adept is the rare efflorescence of a generation of enquiries; and to become one, he must obey the inward impulse of his soul, irrespective of the prudential considerations of worldly science or sagacity. (Sinnett 1881: 101)

Sagacity, whether prudential or not, was something Yeats, in his lifelong quest for occult knowledge and power, never quite abandoned. His sensibility was always to be marked by extremes of enthusiasm, held in check by a canny circumspection, and his intelligence, in a curious dialectic, was simultaneously credulous and sceptical. Throughout his life he remained hungry for belief, but inveterately the investigator who seeks demonstrable proof of the supernaturalism he could not live without. When in 1886 the Dublin Hermetic Society, which he had sought as president to direct towards metaphysical rather than ethical concerns, became a branch of the Theosophical Society, Yeats disassociated himself. Theosophy as a body of esoteric doctrine appealed to him to be sure, but not the atmosphere of pious moral uplift and vaguely progressive self-improvement its initiates also encouraged (Chesterton similarly noted the Theosophists' irritating complacency as they 'waited for others to rise to the spiritual plane where they themselves already stood'; Chesterton 1992: 148–9). Nevertheless when an Indian missionary, Mohini Chatterjee, had arrived in Dublin in 1885 to instruct the members of what would become the new branch, Yeats had begun to waver. And Blavatsky worked her curious magic too.

Chatterjee, from whom, the poet later testified, he learnt more as a young man than from any book, was an Indian associate of Blavatsky. Yeats recalled him as a 'handsome young man with the typical face of Christ' (*Au*: 92) and as 'beautiful, as only an Eastern is beautiful' (cited in Sri 1994: 62). This orientally glamorous personage was helping HPB, as Blavatsky was known to her acolytes, to recover in London from the damning report on her activities in India, which the Society for Psychical Research had commissioned in 1884. That report had concluded that HPB's repertoire of mediumistic tricks – flowers mysteriously falling from ceilings, 'precipitated' letters which inexplicably arrived bearing messages from the Mahatmas, astral bells, music, moving bodies – was wholly fraudulent. Its conclusion managed to be both damning and oddly celebratory. It had determined of HPB that she was 'neither the mouth-piece of hidden seers, nor...a mere vulgar adventuress; we think she has achieved a title to a permanent remembrance as one of the most accomplished, ingenious, and interesting imposters of history' (cited in Washington 1993: 83).

It was the impact of Chatterjee and especially that of Blavatsky herself that for a time made Yeats a   member of a section of the Theosophical Society. From Chatterjee he had acquired that pose of world-weary longing for a reality where will is forsaken for dream, which invests such early poems as 'The Song of the Happy Shepherd' and 'Fergus and the Druid'. Blavatsky offered information about that reality. The poet, it seems, fell under the spell of her extraordinary, even mesmeric, personality. It was not that he disregarded the evidence of the Psychical Society's report (though he did reflect in 1889: 'the fraud theory in its most pronounced form I have never held for more than a few minutes as it is wholly unable to cover the facts'; *Mem*: 281). For as Peter Washington has observed of Theosophy's attractions: 'it appeals to passionate amateurs and spiritual auto-didacts' (Washington 1993: 53). Yeats as a young man was assuredly both and, essentially motherless, was vulnerable to the authority of a powerful woman (though he detected something masculine in her, the spirit of a female Dr Johnson) who unabashedly sought to dominate through the force of her legend and her bizarre, psychologically uninhibited personality. In 1889 Yeats dubbed her in an American newspaper 'the pythoness of the Movement'. Still in the coils of her strange hold on him, he tried in a flippant tone to assert his intellectual independence as he reports how HPB 'holds nightly levees at Lansdowne Road. She is certainly a woman of great learning and character. A London wit once described her as the low comedian of the world to come' (*LTNI*: 84). 'Great learning' was accompanied by ample girth. Her favourite dish was fried eggs floating in butter and on this diet she weighed in at over seventeen stones.

Madame Blavatsky's learning was not in fact as substantial as her person. It was almost completely second-hand, even plagiarized. An early critic of her book *Isis Unveiled* assessed that volume as a 'rehash of Neo-Platonist and Kabbalistic mysticism with Buddhist terminology' (cited in Oppenheim 1985: 165). A proven charlatan, she yet managed to influence individuals whose distaste for the materialism of much Victorian science made them ready to grasp at spiritual straws. Derivative as it was, her system of doctrines did, nevertheless, amount to a largely coherent account of reality which could command credence among the susceptible. They were doctrines which Yeats was to embrace and hold to with great tenacity. For, as Graham Hough has argued, they were, when stripped of much nonsense and a farrago of mystificatory mumbo-jumbo, the elements of what can be deemed a perennial occultist philosophy, which has found expression in a variety of religious traditions. Ignoring for the most part the complex cosmology of the Society itself, Yeats took from Theosophy the doctrines which can be made readily comprehensible in Hough's succinct summary:

> The idea of an age-old secret doctrine, passed on by oral tradition from generation to generation. He found a God seen only as the boundless, Absolute, impassible, unknowable, indescribable. He found a world consisting of emanations from this Absolute, and souls who were sparks or separated fragments of the same substance. Their object was to return to the One from which they came, but to accomplish this they have to make a long pilgrimage through many incarnations, live through many lives both in this world and beyond. (Hough 1984: 39)

The concept of each soul experiencing many lives meant much to Yeats. It appealed at the outset, one may surmise, to his own youthful crises of identity, as his early encounters in Dublin and London offered him a range of possible modes of life and challenged the shy, insecure youth to acts of social self-definition: in 1933 Yeats remembered how in his youth 'sometimes the barrier between [himself] and other people filled [him] with terror' and recalled how he had in 'an extreme degree the shyness... that keeps a man from speaking his own thought' (*LTNI*: xii). The doctrine of many lives allowed that the self was not an absolute but a site of possibility. The principle of *karma*, also annunciated in the Theosophical creed, implied too that a spiritual destiny would work itself out in many times and places, in many human guises. Perhaps Yeats's mature belief in the dramatic mask as a self-fashioned expression of a complex, polar human identity, has its source in the occult doctrine of the soul's reincarnation, which he espoused as a young man under the tutelage of the redoubtable HPB. For in both conceptions the self is denied singularity, is subject to change and reconstitution. In the one it experiences dramatic duality; in the other plurality.

In Theosophy Yeats also met with the idea that reality is antinomial, that, in Hough's words, there are 'two alternating phases in the self-unfolding of the one – active and passive, objective and subjective; called in *Isis Unveiled* "the days and nights of Brahma"' (Hough 1984: 40). Such a teaching must have touched a chord in the youthful poet whose verses were beginning to exhibit a fascination for a world imagined in terms of ubiquitous oppositions and polarities – between the domesticated and the wild, between the quotidian and the claims of fairyland, between sun and moon, between reality and romance.

There was more to Yeats's membership of the Theosophical Society in London than a desire for religious truth. Theosophy itself had emerged alongside the rich Victorian sub-culture of Spiritualism. That movement offered to those who put their faith in mediumship more than a metaphysical account of the universe. It promised direct experience of the supernatural, contact with the dead and with spirits. It was an era of table-rappings and spirit manifestations. Spiritualism had indeed almost achieved the status of a religion in its own right as belief in orthodox Christianity waned in a climate of middle-class speculation about such topics as mesmerism, phrenology, clairvoyance and faith healing. The young Yeats was avidly curious about all such matters. Madame Blavatsky, who had begun her strange career as a religious teacher in the increasingly competitive world of mediumship, had by the 1880s abandoned its practice and she discouraged her disciples from experimentalism in the spiritualist field. No doubt as a proven fraudster, she had good reason to direct acolytes to the doctrinal content of her teachings, rather than to her discredited 'powers'. She told Yeats that 'mediumship and insanity are the same thing' (*CL1*: 164).

Yeats was not to be curtailed. As if to give him his head, while keeping the reins in her own hands, HPB allowed the formation in 1888 of an esoteric section of the London lodge, in which Yeats sought to expand his knowledge of practical magic, whatever the personal risks. In January 1888 he had attended a seance in Dublin at which he had been forced to rely on the opening lines of *Paradise Lost* (he could remember no prayer) to protect himself from a terrifying experience. Then his 'whole body', already depleted by bouts of anxiety, depression and by chronic minor infections, 'moved like a suddenly unrolled watch-spring'. He was 'thrown backward on the wall'. 'For years afterwards', he confessed, 'I would not go to a séance or turn a table and would often ask myself what was that violent impulse that had run through my nerves. Was it a part of myself – something always to be a danger perhaps; or had it come from without, as it seemed?' (*Au*: 103–5)

The following month he heard from one of HPB's disciples of the even more terrible things which can happen at a seance. He reported to Tynan who had been present with him at the Dublin 'occurrences'. His tone in this letter is chastened; he is at pains to set her tender Catholic conscience at rest by assuring her that he has learnt his lesson: 'When she heard I had been to a spiritualistic sceance, she told me she had gone to many till Madame Blavatsky told her it was wrong. So you need not fear for spiritualistic influence coming to me from that quarter. She told me of horrible things she has seen or beleives she has seen at sceances. She has seen the medium thrown down by a spirit and half-stifled, the marks of fingers coming on his throat and finally his clothes set on fire' (*CL1*: 49). Yeats's curiosity conquered his caution, however, in other branches of occult experiment, even if his hold on mental health occasionally seemed tenuous. At the end of 1888 he wrote to Tynan of one of his 'collapses' and of how a 'single vigerous conversation, especially if any philosophic matter comes up, leaves me next day dry as a sucked orange' (*CL1*: 118).

Yeats was clearly living on a knife-edge in these difficult years of his young adulthood. But he pressed on, whatever the psychological and social risks, with attempts to disprove the Victorian materialism he found so threatening. In February 1890 he wrote to Tynan once more, whom he had earlier assured that mesmerism held no appeal, of recent experiments in mesmerism and clairvoyance he had made with colleagues and of their shattering implications: 'To prove the action of man's will, man's soul, outside his body would bring down the who[le] thing – crash – at least for those who beleived one but then who will beleive' (*CL1*: 212).

It was perhaps inevitable that the young Yeats should have been intrigued by the experimental aspect of the material he was studying (and his commitment to such study provoked his expulsion from the esoteric section of the Theosophical Society in 1890). His sister 'Lily' was gifted with 'second sight' in the Irish way. Uncle George Pollexfen's servant, Mary Battle, also had 'the gift'. The folklore of the Irish countryside too, with its hauntings, revenants and changelings, its Hallowe'en games to placate the walking spirits of the dead, was an integral part of everyday awareness, even in the middle-class world of Yeats's childhood. What seems like an innate Gothicism in the Ascendancy caste's preoccupation with dynasties, misalliance, ancestral houses – repeated motifs in their nine-teenth-century fictions – meant as well that spectral matters were never far from a social consciousness that anticipated, but feared it could not prevent, imminent ruin. The uncanny and the weird often broke through the surface of polite Irish convention, as spiritualist obsessions, and like the prevailing hypo-chondriasis, found ready soil as the political unconscious maybe sensed seismic, threatening shifts. In an Irish setting, the young Yeats, who on reading a work of astrology persuaded fellow esotericists to seek to summon the phantom of a flower from its ashes under a bell-glass, is certainly no singular figure. There is something characteristic, even traditional, about his Irish instinct for the spooky and the domestic supernatural (Foster 1989: 251–3).

There were, however, implications in the mid-Victorian occultism, which quickly became an obsession with Yeats, that were anything but traditional; for more was at stake than the scientific world-view which Yeats thought could come crashing down if his kind of experimentalism could gain a hearing. The role of woman was intimately bound up with the emergence of Spiritualism and of occultism as a kind of counter-culture in a society governed by ideals of empiri-cism, scientific validity and material, technological progress.

The great majority of the mediums who had made Spiritualism a fashionable craze and something of a religious cult in Britain since the 1840s were women. A historian comments of the period: 'the typical spiritualist experience involves a female medium and a male spirit or control' (Skultans 1983: 17). A census of hallucinations by the Society for Psychical Research in the years 1889–92 con-firmed this gender difference when it found that women were twice as prone as men to mediumistic experiences (ibid.). In one way this gender imbalance among the Spiritualists simply tended to consolidate conventional Victorian estimates of female character. For the irrationalism of the Spiritualist and occult movements, their opening up of zones of bizarre experience and belief beyond the purview of empirical philosophy, could readily be dismissed as forms of pathology, hysteria, at the further reaches of typical feminine psychology. Theoretically such an analysis might have seemed satisfactory to a certain kind of rationalist; in experience, however, more complex relations and exchanges between the sexes were being actualized and figured in the worlds of mediumship, magic and occult adeptship. For although the image of female medium and male spirit control might appear to replicate in the supernatural world the social relations of the actual one, the feminized spirituality vested in mediumship gave to women a symbolic power as desire, insecurity, religious doubt and sexual ambivalence circulated in the foggy late Victorian cultural atmosphere. Woman, as Alex Owen has argued in *The*

Darkened Room, became a site of divinatory, almost priestly energy, at the point in Victorian culture where medicine, law, and science vied with religion for authority over the human body (much was made of corporeal manifestations, even to the point of eroticism, in the Spiritualist repertoire).

As a version of female power, Spiritualism and its sister, the Victorian flowering of occult magic, became a handmaid of the vigorous contemporaneous crusade for female emancipation. Indeed, a religious fashion which may have had its roots in the 'frustrations experienced by uncounted mid-Victorian women barred from gainful and stimulating employment by social conventions, with horizons limited by the predictable routine that domestic responsibilities imposed' (Oppenheim 1985: 10), in time became one inspiration in an emancipatory movement that sought a social order in which such frustrations would be a thing of the past. For Spiritualism and occultism offered a mode of behaviour for women which signalled that they would no longer accept the prescribed roles that society had determined for them in suburban isolation from political and social power.

For Yeats, occultism was a way of defining himself as a man who had revolted against his father's materialism. It did not, by contrast, offer him any stable vision of masculinity as he sought to carve a role for himself as an adult in the insecure space between the Ireland he considered his home and the England in which he tried to make his way. Indeed in stepping into the the world of occultism, he was entering a psychological zone in which sexuality and gender, the role of woman, and correlatively, the role of man, were set in question in the eddying confusions of power relations and of gendered identity itself. It was not a world for a young man whose own sense of selfhood and of masculinity were inchoate. In a poignant, even distressing letter of 6 September 1888, written from Blenheim Road to Tynan, Yeats, on the day on which he received a first proof of his first volume of verse, *The Wanderings of Oisin and other poems* (1889), admits to the terrible self-consciousness that he fears has made him an inarticulate victim of his own nature. It is a letter which betrays the anxiety of the man who is not as yet assured of a self, who has tried to make that uncertainty the stuff of his art:

> Some thing I had to say. Dont know that I have said it. All seems confused incoherent inarticulate. Yet this I know I am no idle poetaster. My life has been in my poems. To make them I have broken my life in a mortar as it were. I have brayed in it youth and fellowship and worldly hopes. I have seen others enjoying while I stood alone with myself – commenting, commenting – a mere dead miror on which things reflect themselves. I have buried my youth and raised over it a cairn – of clouds.   (*CL1*: 93–4)

There is in this fraught confession a history of self-inspection, of repeated assessments of many selves which seem to be mere reflections of an external world. The self is incoherent. That was something the worlds of Spiritualism and occult experiment confirmed. For not only were the two movements loaded with ambiguous messages about sexual difference and power exchanges between the sexes, but their intimacy with altered states of consciousness, trances, visions, out-of-body experiences, astral-travel, mediumistic possession, challenged the very basis of individual personality. As Owen astutely observes, mediumship in particular (and her words hold good for the other phenomena encountered in occultism and magical experiment) 'helps to lay bare the paucity of any analysis based on the often unacknowledged notion of the unified subject. Mediumship, because it so often involved the disclosure of a multivalent and disruptive unconscious, revealed the inconsistency, heterogeneity, and precariousness of human identity' (Owen 1989: 226).

For the immature Yeats Theosophy and occultism performed one signal service. It offered social acquaintanceship with a range of spirited women for whom respectable domestic life in a Victorian marriage offered few attractions. Mrs Annie Besant, for example, the socialist activist and progressive advocate of women's rights, turned to the oriental creed in 1889. She had separated from her boring, authoritarian clergyman husband in 1873 to travel a well-publicized route that took her from secular atheism to Theosophy and prophetic leadership of a section of the movement after HPB's death in 1891. Yeats found her a 'very courteous & charming woman' (*CL1*: 184). She became one of his occult experimental coterie, whose dabblings in practical magic led to Yeats's expulsion from the esoteric section of the movement in October 1890.

Florence Farr, the actress, and sexually free spirit, who in 1894 produced and acted in Yeats's *The Land of Heart's Desire*, also shared Yeats's occult interests. They began their friendship in 1888 and by May 1889 he trusted her sufficiently to read a scene of an earlier play *The Countess Kathleen* to her for comment. A year later she appeared in one of the two main roles in Todhunter's pastoral romance, *A Sicilian Idyll*. This had its première in the Clubhouse on an early summer evening in Bedford Park, where the residents were much given to fancy-dress balls, amateur theatricals and masques (Fletcher 1987: 65–7). The play itself, with its Alma-Tadema classical poses in self-conscious expression of a titillating sexual modernity, was of a piece with such cultivated entertainments for relaxed, mildly bohemian, metropolitan suburbanites at leisure. Fashionably progressive attitudes were aired amid the wine-glasses, the flower-boxes and good taste of a slightly precious night out. Farr, in the person of Amaryllis, a classical prototype of the New Woman, got to denounce marriage (her own had ended after four years, though she still employed her former husband's name). The ambiance was one of vaguely realized Sapphism (the published version of the play has an epigraph from the poet of Lesbos).

Yeats was enraptured by Farr's beauty and the enchantment of her voice. For on stage she and her fellow actor Heron Allen sought to speak verse with 'a passionate austerity that made it akin for certain moments to the great poetry of the world.' (*Au*: 120–1). Farr possessed for the youthful Yeats 'three great gifts, a tranquil beauty like that of Demeter's image near the British Museum Reading-Room door, and an incomparable sense of rhythm and a beautiful voice, the seeming natural expression of the image' (*Au*: 121).

Yeats understood that the occult was a feminized spirituality. In the revised and enlarged edition of *The Celtic Twilight* (1902) he averred that 'women come more easily than men to that wisdom which ancient peoples, and all wild peoples even now, think the only wisdom' (*CT2*: 132–4). Furthermore he was entering on manhood in a era when the concept of masculinity was undergoing the sea-change which in the 1890s would allow the epicene heroes of Wilde's boulevard comedies to situate the androgynous dandy at the apex of a decadence that had its many layers of ambivalent and inverted sexuality. In 1873 Walter Pater had published *The Renaissance: Studies in Art and Poetry*, in which a series of impression-istic meditations in art history and literary criticism were an elaborately disguised paean to an equivocal aestheticized eroticism, at its most narcotic in his prose poem on the famously enigmatic smile of the *Mona Lisa*. It influenced a genera-tion for whom the idea of the beautiful in the 1880s and 1890s came charged with a bisexual voltage, when it was not in direct contact with socially repressed homoerotic energies.

For Yeats 'beauty' was quintessentially a female attribute. Although he had entered a milieu in 1880s' London where sexual difference had been made problematic in all sorts of ways (Farr wore her hair short in the deliberate fashion of New Womanhood), his own sexual nature was positively heterosexual. Hetero-sexual, but not uncomplicatedly so. For constitutional shyness and social inse-curity, together with a touch of Protestant Irish prudery (he was uncomfortable with friends' crude conversation), together with his sheer impecuniousness as a prospective suitor, meant that his sexual initiation was delayed until his thirty-first year. Some of the most anguished passages of the autobiographical draft which he began in 1915 recount with raw adult pain how the shock of sexual awakening in his teens inaugurated a lengthy period of unbearable sexual starvation and nervous tension. There he recalls how his struggle with his senses made him dread the subject of sex and 'the almost unendurable strain' of his chaste life. His confession in that text to the effects of masturbation on his overwrought sensi-bility is a reminder that he lived at a time when, for all the sexual *frisson* of its art and social experimentalism, self-relief was regarded as moral pollution. It was 'plain ruin' (*Mem*: 72) and filled him with self-loathing.

However difficult Yeats found the demands of the flesh, the object of his desire was the opposite sex. None of the friendships of his early youth seem to have involved the kind of homoerotic intimacy with another young man that had reached its Victorian apogee in Tennyson's regard for the short-lived Arthur Hallam and which had characterized the male-bonding atmosphere in which Pre-Raphaelitism had its inception. Yeats himself, in what he identified as an 'incredible timidity' (*Mem*: 33) found it easier to make intimate intellectual contact with women, since in a man he always found 'some competing thought' (*Au*: 153). For him, however, sexual desire was strikingly modulated by a sense of female beauty which art had stimulated, for all its urgent, bodily imperatives and frustrations. He was not necessarily unusual as a young man in the way he read the world in terms of literature and painting. Many literary-minded people instinctively do so. That, in as immediate and pressing a dimension of experience as the sexual, he so readily turned to iconographic representation as a means of coping with such a disturbed aspect of his life tells us, nevertheless, in a markedly distinctive way, something crucial about his sensibility. And it is something which offers a guide to the peculiar quality of his own artistic procedures, the governing principles of his *oeuvre*.

When Yeats remembered how Farr had seemed a very Demeter to his youthful eye, like a statue he saw frequently, he was recalling how, even as a young man, life and image were for him in complex relationship. A habit had established itself early whereby experience was interpreted in terms of its iconographic potentiality, its tendency to approximate to pre-existing forms, to enter relationship with its own dynamic capacity for taking on significance. An agenda had begun to be set, in which the poet's own life could be rescued from mere individual inconsequence and become the stuff of an exemplary, formal art. It could do so in an artistic transcendence as image among the many images which tradition and certain contemporary writers and artists had bequeathed to a world rapidly losing any significant form in the incoherence of urban modernity.

Images of women nevertheless had their direct effect on the young Yeats, as he confessed in 1915: 'women filled me with curiosity and my mind seemed never long to escape from the disturbance of my senses, I was a romantic, my head full of the mysterious women of Rossetti and those hesitating faces in the art of Burne-Jones which seemed always anxious for some Alastor at the end of a long journey' (*Mem*: 33). In the poetry he composed in the 1880s Yeats was willing to represent himself as just such a Shelleyan figure, in thrall to an ideal of female beauty that represented sexual desire as a quest romance. The intensity of sexual longing finds expression in an erotically inspired dedication. Its object is unambiguously female, though Yeats does derive from the art and poetry of Morris, Swinburne and Rossetti, if not its equivocal images of sexual difference, then its acknowledgement of the unsettling power vested in the beauty of woman. For as Nina Auerbach has shown, in *Woman and the Demon*, Victorian culture, for all its attempts to restrict woman to the domestic sphere, was granting her, in its poetry and art, symbolic power as enchantress, sybil or goddess. The courtly hero on his quest (the Arthurian cycle of tales was a constant source of imagery) may be a figure of noble ardour, but he is captive to a power – his own desire – that the woman in her beauty provokes. She becomes masterful, dangerous, sinister, even mortally threatening, since her power so unmans the hero. Elizabeth Cullingford astutely comments on this process: 'Woman' is granted immense textual and symbolical significance in order to disguise (or to maintain against increasingly vehement feminist demands) her lack of social significance' (Cullingford 1993: 34). Yet the permission so granted for woman to enter iconographic and textual space in art and literature – paradoxically – unleashes her power.

Yeats's 1880s' apprentice verse is populated by figures of woman as enchantress and as agent of occult power in a context of quest and death. George Bornstein (1995: 21) points out that: 'Female magicians' appear in all four of the verse-plays that Yeats published at this initial stage of his career. His masters as he set his hand to verse-making were the Keats of 'La Belle Dame Sans Merci' and the Shelley of 'Prometheus Unbound' and, especially, 'Alastor', as the images of Rossetti and Burne-Jones and the Pre-Raphaelite school gave flesh to literary imagining. In *Mosada* (published in 1886 and the most fully realized of these early dramatic experiments) a Moorish lady, who is to be condemned by the Inquisition as a witch and who dies at her own hand, summons

> a phantom fair
> And calm, robed all in raiment moony white.
> She was a great enchantress once of yore,
> Whose dwelling was a tree-wrapt island, lulled
> Far out upon the water world and ringed
> With wonderful white sands, where never yet
> Were furled the wings of ships. There in a dell,
> A lily-blanchèd place, she sat and sang,
> And in her singing wove around her head
> White lilies, and her song flew forth afar
> Along the sea; and many a man grew hushed
> In his own house or 'mong the merchants grey,
> Hearing the far-off singing guile, and groaned,
> And manned an argosy and sailing died.

Woman is the enchanting, magically powerful alternative to the worlds of domesticity and commerce, but she can be deadly in her mesmeric 'guile'.

Woman as beautiful temptress reaches its apotheosis in Yeats's 1880s' poetry in the figure of the fairy Niam in his first major poem, 'The Wanderings of Oisin', which he completed in its earliest version in November 1887 after almost two years of dedicated work. The poem was the title poem of the poet's first collection. It was heavily revised in later publications. The question as to where it should stand in any collected edition of Yeats's poems became one of the many editorial cruces which have marked the publishing history of this most self-revising of authors (he came to fear that when placed at the head of his work, the poem tended to distract from what followed). For from the first Yeats was conscious that a poem is more than an individual work, that it finds richer meaning and new kinds of life in the many contexts in which it appears, until it rests in the canonical finality of a posthumously established *Collected Poems*. This means that, from a very early stage in his career, Yeats had a clear and abiding sense of himself as a poet, for all his social insecurity and personal and sexual timidity. The fact that over the years he returned frequently in his writings to 'The Wanderings of Oisin' to comment on it, suggests that it was in this work that he felt he had come into possession of his own talent, had become sure of a poetic destiny. If so, he was assuredly right, for it was a truly impressive debut.

In 1931 Yeats offered what Harold Bloom has identified as 'the most illuminating of his many insights into his own poem' (Bloom 1970: 100). In an introduction to his play *The Resurrection* Yeats wrote:

> When I was a boy everybody talked about progress, and rebellion against my elders took the form of aversion to that myth. I took satisfaction in certain public disasters, and felt a sort of ecstasy at the contemplation of ruin, and then came upon the story

of Oisin in Tír na nOg and reshaped it into my *Wanderings of Oisin*. He rides across the sea with a spirit, he passes phantoms, a boy following a girl, a hound chasing a hare, emblematic of eternal pursuit, he comes to an island of choral dancing, leaves that after many years, passes the phantoms once again, comes to an island of endless battle for an object never achieved, leaves that after many years, passes the phantoms once again, comes to an island of sleep, leaves that and comes to Ireland, to S Patrick and old age. I did not pick these images because of any theory, but because I found them impressive, yet all the while abstractions haunted me. I remember rejecting, because it spoilt the simplicity, an elaborate metaphor of a breaking wave intended to prove that all life rose and fell as in my poem.   (*W&B*: 101–2)

Such a passage gives a critic leave to read the poem so summarized not only as autobiography, but as a poem of Victorian crisis, a revolt, couched as apocalypse, against the dominant myth of social progress.

Richard Ellmann took the autobiographical hint. He suggested that the three islands where Oisin spends 100 years apiece can be associated with the three phases of Yeats's early life: the isle of dancing and song with the Sligo of 'Sindbad's yellow shore'; the isle of battles with his unhappy years at school in London when he was locked in futile conflict with his English school-fellows; and the island of sleep with the idyllic days in Howth (Ellmann 1964: 18). He also recognized how such a pattern, which Yeats himself, in his late poem 'The Circus Animals' Desertion', saw as one of 'Vain gaiety, vain battle, vain repose', was that not only of youth, but of life as a whole. Other critics have sought not only to read 'The Wanderings of Oisin' as a social and human document, but as a work which gives insight into the poet's psyche. David Lynch makes much of the heavily charged eroticism of the work, with its crowded symbolic landscapes, which he finds all too open to a reading where the vain battle with a continually reviving monster in the second isle can be reckoned an oedipal conflict with the father which is repetitive, futile and issueless (Lynch 1979: 92–138). Another critic finds the 'dusky demon' of the same book 'orgasm incarnate' (cited in Archibald 1986: 87).

The most admiring account of the poem is Bloom's (though he addresses the poem in its revised form). He prefers it to some of Yeats's later and more widely regarded works. For Bloom 'The Wanderings of Oisin' is a late and notable entry in the tradition of romantic quest poems in which the epic action of a major narrative becomes the vehicle for a subjective spiritual history. In this, Yeats observes the emotional trajectory of his high romantic precursors (Blake and especially Shelley) but makes his poem, for all its commitment to the direct expression of transformative feeling in the person of the poet/Oisin, subject to the implacable, divisive forces of nature. The poem ends with Oisin, who has abandoned his fairy-bride for love of his old warrior companions, arguing with the St Patrick who has conquered pagan Ireland with a new faith. When Oisin touches the earth, the weight of the ages falls on him and he perishes. It is an ambiguous victory, which allows Oisin's poetic imagination only the consolation of nostalgia. He will 'go to the house of the Fenians, be they in flames or at feast'.

For Yeats, if not for Oisin/Yeats (and the poem is the one where the poet and his hero are the least distinct) however, the ambiguity was potentially more tragic than nostalgic, since in entering so Shelleyan a subjectivity, he was forced to embrace 'the quester's natural defeat as a victory... of a man divided against himself, natural against imaginative, neither capable of final victory over the other' (Bloom 102–3).

Such a formulation for all its force lacks, it is necessary to add, a sense of history. Bloom is so anxious to set the text in the ideal dimension of a literary tradition that history – which is represented by the querulous voice of St Patrick in the poem – is ignored. For Patrick speaks to Oisin not simply as the voice of the reality before which the timeless world of vision in the land of youth must wither, but as a force for the very progress that Yeats had rejected in the poem's defiance of his own social world. In fact in Victorian Ireland St Patrick was not simply a figure in an antique source text from which Yeats took the matter for a poem, nor indeed just a folkloric motif (the debate between Oisin and St Patrick was extant in contemporary Irish folklore) but a living presence in national self-understanding. The Catholicism which was transforming Yeats's Ireland in the post-Famine period regarded the coming of St Patrick to the country in the fifth century as a progressive event, which had resulted in its own increasingly hegemonic if benign power over the social order. The centre of that power was St Patrick's College, Maynooth, the national seminary founded in 1795. Yeats, by contrast, offers in this initiatory work a vision of apocalypse in which the concept of progress itself seems paltry and sacrilegious in face of a Celtic *Götterdämmerung* in which old age consumes the pride of life, and death is preferable to mere existence among 'a small and a feeble populace stooping with mattock and spade,/Or weeding or ploughing with faces a-shining with much-toil wet' in the land of St Patrick's 'bell-mounted churches'.

It is these historical implications of Yeats's text which also make Richard Ellmann's negative critique of the poem wide of the mark. Ellmann reckoned that among the work's weaknesses were inconsistencies in its symbology: 'a powerful contrast which Yeats draws in the poem between Oisin and Patrick, as representatives of pagan and Christian Ireland, seems irrelevant to the timeless portrait of life in the three islands' (Ellmann 1964: 19–20). In fact that contrast is of the essence since the pagan world of fairy is rendered in terms which make it seem non-teleological, non-purposive, ahistorical. It is repetitive, patterned as if obeying typological imperatives, cyclical. Yeats himself indeed, in his introduction to *The Resurrection*, as he thought of the image of life as a process of rising and falling, continued: 'How hard it was to refrain from pointing out that Oisin after old age, its illumination half accepted, half rejected, would pass in death over another sea to another island (*W&B*: 102). He would be free not only of the biological and human facts of life, but of the progressive history over which St Patrick and his followers assume they have authority.

Presumably he would be led onwards by the fairy Niam. For she is the poem's female presiding genius. And 'The Wanderings of Oisin' is a poem which, as Yeats told Tynan, contained nothing in 'clear outline', and things 'under disguise of symbolism' (*CL1*: 98), to which only he possessed the key, where a tapestry, a 'cloud and foam' of interrelating images of bird, tree, water, sea, glimmers with indeterminate implication, like shot-silk in changing light. It is a poem which sets the magic power of enchantment against history; secret lore, the hermetic, against what is conventionally known of life and destructive time.

Yeats as he worked on this poem sought to comprehend much he had experienced and felt in his life. His mother had suffered her first stroke in the late summer of 1887, so it was also a time of anxiety. Both personal life and the work of creation took their toll. That autumn in Sligo he finished the poem and brought the last part round to read to his Uncle George. He could hardly read so 'collapsed' he felt, his voice 'quite broken' (*CL1*: 98). Subsequently he endured a period of weeks when his voice deserted him and he suffered a series of minor nervous collapses. That part of the poem, he told Tynan a year after he had finished it, 'really was a kind of vision it beset me night and day' (*CL1*: 98). The poem as a whole has a dreamy visionary quality, and perhaps no moment seems more the stuff of dreams than that when Oisin first glimpses Niam:

> Her eyes were soft as dewdrops hanging
> Upon the grass-blades' bending tips,
> And like a sunset were her lips,
> A stormy sunset o'er doomed ships.
> Her hair was of a citron tincture,
> And gathered in a silver cincture;
> Down to her feet white vesture flowed,
> And with the woven crimson glowed
> Of many a figured creature strange,
> And birds that on the seven seas range.
> For brooch 'twas bound with bright sea-shell,
> And wavered like a summer rill,
> As her soft bosom rose and fell.

A Rossetti temptress, with Burne-Jones coloration and William Morris costuming. Yet a vibrant erotic longing energizes the verse with youthful desire, despite the obligatory gesture, in such conventional Victorian imagining of alluring womanhood, to the female as death-dealer. This is the poem of a young man anxious to meet his own amatory destiny. He had not long to wait.

2

The English 1890s

In 'The Wanderings of Oisin' the young Yeats had summoned the creative energy to make of his troubled feelings about the modern world an image of mesmeric beauty. In that shimmering, dream-like text, the fairy Niamh inhabits a fantastic territory of trees, birds, waters and seas, where local detail seems to hover continually between the dimensions of symbolism and myth. The materialism of the modern world with its belief in progress can be forgotten. Sexual frustration can find a symbolic release. When he completed the poem in its first version in the fraught autumn of 1887, Yeats could not have known that, a few weeks after its publication, a figure would step into his everyday world like an emissary from the symbolic and mythological zone of his own artifact.

On 30 January 1889 Yeats, at home in Blenheim Road, welcomed a new caller who arrived in a hansom-cab. Maud Gonne, whom John O'Leary's sister Ellen had introduced to the household, had read Yeats's new book (O'Leary had helped to find the subscribers which had made its publication possible) with its title poem, the first of what the poet hoped would be 'a sort of *Légende des Siècles* of Ireland . . . having something of every age' (*Mem*: 184). A fervent twenty-two-year-old nationalist, one of O'Leary's circle, Gonne approved, and was keen to meet the poet, or as she believed, to renew an acquaintance. Yeats famously remembers what he thought was their first encounter as an event of mythological import:

> I was twenty-three years old when the troubling of my life began . . . she drove up to our house in Bedford Park with an introduction from John O'Leary to my father. I had never thought to see in a living woman so great beauty. It belonged to famous pictures, to poetry, to some legendary past. A complexion like the blossom of apples, and yet the face and body had the beauty of lineaments which Blake calls the highest beauty because it changes least from youth to age, and a stature so great that she seemed of divine race. Her movements were worthy of her

form, and I understood at last why the poet of antiquity, where we would but speak
of face and form, sings, loving some lady, that she paces like a goddess.   (*Mem:* 40)

The poet dined that evening with this divinity and they met frequently over the
coming days during her brief visit to London. Yeats was transfixed. The fact that
Gonne managed to surround herself over the next few years, 'no matter how
rapid her journey and how brief her stay at either end of it, by cages full of birds,
canaries, finches of all kinds, dogs, a parrot, and once a full-grown hawk from
Donegal' (*Au:* 123) added to the phantasmagoric impression she created. She
might have stepped out of the elaborate picture in which she belonged, accompanied as she was by a retinue appropriate to some mythological personage.

From the very beginning of what was to prove a long and troubled relationship
Yeats saw Gonne through the veils of literature and art. Two days after he met
her, he informed John O'Leary in a letter that she was 'very Irish, a kind of
"Diana of the Crossways"' (*CL1:* 137). He had read Meredith's novel of that
name, with its romantic Irish heroine, who is represented by its author as a
modern incarnation of the huntress goddess And Yeats certainly was a victim of
another such incarnate deity, for he informed Ellen O'Leary two days later: 'Did
I tell you how much I admire Miss Gonne? . . . If she said the world was flat or the
moon an old caubeen tossed up into the sky I would be proud to be of her party'
(*CL1:* 140–1). By the spring he had worked up the courage to tell Tynan, who had
heard of Yeats's infatuation, about her. It is a fascinating letter which tells us a lot
about Yeats's complex feelings at this time and about the nature of his obsession
with Gonne. Early in this letter he blurts out in some embarrassment: 'Who told
you that I am "taken up with Miss Gonne"', to continue defensively: 'I think she
is, "very good looking" and that is all I think about her. What you say of her
fondness for sensation is probably true. I sympathise with her love of the national
idia rather than any secondary land movement but care not much for the kind of
red Indian feathers in which she has trapped out that idea . . .' (*CL1:* 154). He is
obviously anxious that Tynan might conceivably be jealous; he clumsily adverts
to the now safely married Laura Armstrong, but in terms which in fact reveal
how Gonne is entering his affections in the same complex way Laura had: as an
object of worship whom he could transform into myth and symbol.

For Yeats's relationship with Maud Gonne over the next decade was to be a
highly charged literary romance in which difficult experience was made amenable to the transfiguring power of poetry. To accept that Yeats simply fell in love
with her and that he endured the pains of an unrequited passion, a theme of his
own verses during this period, is to evade what was psychologically a more
problematic and ambiguous matter than any such high tale of spurned ardour.

Richard Ellmann's *Yeats: The Man and the Masks* identified Yeats's meeting with
Gonne and his instant infatuation, as the stimulus for the poet to confront the
implications of his own bifurcated nature, torn as it was between the dreaming
and retiring poet and the man who aspired to action and achievement in the
social sphere. It is a persuasive account which allows us to read such works as
Yeats's novel *John Sherman* (complete in draft form by October 1888; *CL1:* 104) as

a study of a divided soul. Young Sherman is Yeats as poet, the Reverend William Howard, a Sligo curate (who was in part based on John Dowden, with something of his successful brother Edward in him too), all purpose and career-conscious, is the kind of man Yeats knew he would have to become if he was to win the hand of any woman. So Yeats, in Ellmann's version of him, entered the lists of Irish nationalist politics in the 1890s as a kind of courtly lover, anxious to prove his worth before a scornful and very nationalistic mistress's eye. Since he found her unresponsive (he proposed marriage unsuccessfully in July 1891, after a period when his emotions had cooled and then revived), he developed a concept of personal transformation through the agency of failure: 'He must try to change Ireland or the world, or to win his mistress's favour, and fail, and in failure find apotheosis. Yeats makes a cult of frustration, and courts defeat like a lover' (Ellmann 1987: 85).

Modern biographical researches have made this account seem too close to the romanticism of Yeats's own re-creation of his experience in art. John Harwood, for example, has argued forcefully that Yeats from the first moment of his encounter with Gonne was 'engineering a life in which the natural man will forgo as many "heavenly mansions" as he can bear to pass by' (Harwood 1992: 16). So he offers a version of this strange relationship which correlates more fully with the sense of Yeats we have already established. For Harwood's Yeats is one for whom life and image are in a constant relationship, whereby art assimilates what it purports to represent. So Yeats is understood to have seen in Gonne what his imagination had already determined from poetry and art she should be – an image of womanhood, like the fairy Niamh, before which he would worship in frustrated, spiritual, unrequited 'love'. While recognizing that in their 'day-to-day encounters' their relationship partook of existential contingencies, Harwood nevertheless concludes:

> Yeats's composite heroine directed his response to Maud Gonne from the moment he set eyes on her. To call this 'idealisation' in the conventional sense is inadequate; the process is much more systematic, more directed. Maud Gonne did not overpower his imagination; his imagination overpowered 'Maud Gonne', and he then began, in life, to enter into a relationship 'with the image he had made'. (Harwood 1992: 18)

Deirdre Toomey, in her detailed study of this phase of Yeats's life (1993: 13–15) accepts Harwood's conjecture, but adds her own explanation of Yeats's vulnerability to such a strangely self-constructed kind of obsession. She reads his curiously concocted passion for Gonne as the dramatic consequence of the family stresses that had come to a crisis in the recent past, as his mother suffered her first strokes, his 'Oedipal' quarrel with his father intensified and he was assailed by anxieties and 'collapses'. The strain of first publication in full-volume form could be added to the list. Be these speculations as they may, a dynamic was set in motion in which life and art do not occupy separate compartments of consciousness but feed on one another in a compulsive fashion, with art as a kind of voracious predator of the stuff of experience, seeking imaginative mastery. This confirmed Yeats in the youthful habit which had begun in the mid-1880s whereby he made the image-making faculty a mode of perception and interpretation.

The problem of course was that such a radical approach to the difficulty of relating to the opposite sex, while also being a poet, did nothing to meet the demands of actual, intense sexual desire. Nor was the object of this imaginative stratagem merely a figure in a poem or picture. No living woman could have been expected to acquiesce with total comprehension in this psychological manoeuvre – least of all a vital and adventurous woman such as Gonne. Yeats was storing up trouble for himself and over the years he was to have a full share.

When Yeats met her Gonne was considerably more experienced in matters of the heart and certainly of the body than the dreamy poet who would immortalize her in his verses. To his family, on that January day when she entered their lives, she was less than godlike. Yeats's sisters noted somewhat sniffily the royal airs she gave herself and that she had arrived wearing slippers. Had they known more about Gonne's recent doings, one suspects that familial disfavour would have been absolute.

Gonne (b. 1866) was the English-born daughter of a British army officer. In 1869 he had been posted to Ireland where she spent her early years. Captain Gonne had been widowed in 1871, so his daughter's girlhood had been as peripatetic an affair as Yeats's boyhood – a matter of governesses in England and France, which prepared her for a role in society as the Colonel's daughter (father rose in the ranks). Posted back to Dublin, he had been happy to have a beautiful daughter to serve as his hostess in the social life of the garrison and Dublin Castle. His death in 1886 had left Gonne and her almost equally beautiful sister, Kathleen, financially secure (though this fact was kept from her for a time), independent and apparently marriageable. But Gonne was not inclined to dwindle into the wife of some respectable Victorian burgher. She hated the Dublin round of middle-class dinner-parties, at which doctors and lawyers complimented her on her looks. She expected more from life and pursued it with little regard for convention. For a time the theatre seemed a channel for her rebellious nature, but politics soon became her arena of action. In France she fell in love with a lawyer and journalist named Lucien Millevoye and in 1888 she became his mistress (bearing him a son in January 1890). Strenuously Boulangist, he recruited Gonne to the cause of Alsace-Lorraine. She had seen evictions in County Donegal and this experience, when combined with Boulangist anti-British feeling, made of her an Irish revolutionary. She attached herself to O'Leary's circle and set about a career of agitation, which her ample private means allowed her to undertake without the regard for personal security that inhibited so many of her less fortunate Victorian sisters.

O'Leary was not especially impressed. As Yeats himself reported, he 'saw but a beautiful woman seeking excitement' (*Mem*: 60–1). In fact Gonne was a firebrand, ready to countenance violence with few, if any, qualms. This certainly set her apart from O'Leary's gentlemanly, Roman concern with moral rather than physical force. On her first visit to Blenheim Road, to J. B. Yeats's considerable irritation, she had celebrated warfare. If Yeats *père* had feared for his son among the occultists, he now had new grounds for concern. For Gonne's activities were of a kind which interest policemen.

Yeats may have joined the secret Irish Republican Brotherhood, which traced its origins to the Fenian Brotherhood that had risen in futile rebellion in 1867, some time after 1885 (*AM*: 112). He certainly reckoned that his literary work contributed generally to the cause of Irish separatism for which the secret, sworn association stood. Gonne wanted immediate, not literary, results and threw herself into a campaign for tenant rights in Donegal, made a fiery speech in the Liberal cause in Barrow-in-Furness in the north of England and by the autumn of 1890 she was in poor health and under threat of arrest. That she had also, unknown to Yeats, conceived and given birth to a son by her French lover, made this a period of great intensity in her life, which reached one full tide of emotionalism when Yeats made that first proposal of marriage in August 1891.

They then spent a day on the cliffs at Howth, which had meant so much to Yeats and his mother and which had played a part too in Gonne's personal mythology. From this charged encounter came one of Yeats's most remarkable early lyrics, 'The White Birds' – a poem that imagines, even at the moment of ecstatic transport, a post-coital *tristesse* and a terminal weariness. It is as if the poet seeks to protect himself by the knowledge of mutability, which the poem also seeks to deny, from the pain of what cannot be:

> I would that we were, my beloved, white birds on the foam of the sea,
> We tire of the flame of the meteor, before it can pass by and flee;
> And the flame of the blue star of twilight, hung low on the rim of the sky,
> Has awakened in our hearts, my beloved, a sadness that never may die.
>
> (*CK*: 106).

Gonne was to know her own sadness almost immediately, for her son died in France from meningitis on 31 August.

In the draft of his autobiography, Yeats recalls how in the early 1890s he found Gonne's political single-mindeness and commitment deeply unsettling until he admits 'I came to hate her politics, my one visible rival' (*Mem*: 63). What helped to keep them in contact was her undoubted affection for Yeats, which she could not easily express (even had she wished to do so), given the complications of her personal life, and a shared interest in occultism and paranormal experience.

Early in their friendship, Yeats discovered that Gonne 'seemed to understand every subtlety of my own art and especially all my spiritual philosophy... We worked much with symbols, and she would pass at once into a semi-trance and see all very distinctly' (ibid.: 61). Yeats was impressed by her divinatory powers, though he sensed in her a divided nature until he dreamed himself of 'a thimble, and a shapeless white mass that puzzled me. The next day on passing a tobacconist's I saw that it was a lump of meerschaum not yet made into a pipe. She was complete; I was not' (ibid.: 63). The search for personal completion continued, with woman's magical powers as a guide.

For when he had been expelled from the Esoteric Section of the Theosophical Society in the autumn of 1890, Yeats had by no means abandoned his quest for a religious system which would 'complete' his sense of reality and explain to him his complex, multiple nature as a being in the world. Earlier in the year he had been initiated into a hermetic society which called itself the Order of the Golden Dawn. The Order would occupy a central role in his life for more than a decade and remain important to him until the 1920s. He persuaded Gonne to enter the Golden Dawn too in late 1891.

Gonne's private grief was intense in the autumn of 1891. By fateful accident it provoked a curious drama as, on the Irish national stage, a tragedy of historic proportions unfolded. For in 1890 Charles Stewart Parnell's adulterous affair with the wife of a fellow-member of the Irish political party he led, became public knowledge. The greatest national leader since Daniel O'Connell was forced to resign his post amid much acrimony. This event must have confirmed Gonne in her disdainful attitude to what she saw as the futility of constitutional politics. Perhaps it reminded her too of the dangers she was running in her own life, as she sought to achieve the status of an Irish Joan of Arc. For if a man of Parnell's stature and popularity could be destroyed by a sexual scandal, how much more as a woman was she open to destructive censure.

On 7 October 1891 Parnell died in England after a hectic period in which he had sought to appeal over the heads of his party to the Irish electorate. By chance the boat that brought his remains to Ireland for burial also carried Gonne to Dublin, still deeply grieving her lost child. In her ostentatious mourning, she seemed a figure of Mother Ireland, in a spectacular conjunction of private life with public disaster. She attended the interment at Glasnevin cemetery in Dublin, which Yeats did not, to report with others that a star had fallen from the heavens as the coffin had been laid to rest. Yeats composed a bad, opportunistic poem on the dead 'Chief', 'Mourn – And Then Onward!', which he sent to the nationalistic periodical *United Ireland*, which obliged by publishing it immediately.

Gonne's fascination with the occult, was deepened by her bereavement (she told Yeats that, sadly, a child she had adopted, had passed away). She wanted to renew contact with her dead son and was immensely relieved to learn from George Russell that the soul of a child could be reincarnated quite quickly in the family from which he had been taken by death. Yeats was doubtful but kept his council. Neither man suspected the reason for her concern.

Yeats's dedication to the quest for magical powers and occult lore, which brought him from the Theosophical Society to the Golden Dawn, had involved him in forms of experience which set in question the fixed nature of human and sexual identity. In this unstable psychological territory, feminism and spirituality had found common cause in opposition to materialist philosophy and repressive social structures. There was a more mundane sense in which occultism and magic represented a pressure point in late Victorian cultural life. For it was in debates about the authenticity of spiritualist, magical and occult practices that the idea of professional qualification took on a particularly keen edge. From the 1860s onwards, women in particular had been laying claim to social roles – in healing, personal therapy, psychological insight, the acquisition and control of knowledge – that increasingly were contested by the rising professional bodies of Victorian male institutionalism.

The 'woman question' in fact had been raised for late Victorian society not only because a vociferous minority had insisted that it be on the public agenda, but because demography had inescapably placed it there. The 1851 census of population had shown that there were half a million more women than men in Britain. By 1911 this figure had risen to one-and-a-half million. It was also significant that about 20 per cent of men never married. Marriage accordingly was a crucial element in a social order which left many women without employment or other means of support. Thus there was a 'surplus' of nubile young women in a society where a substantial number of men chose not to marry, which further unbalanced what demography had already destabilized. Yeats's friend Florence Farr observed in 1910 that there were at that date two-and-a-half million 'grown women in a dependent position without a husband or occupation in England and Wales alone' (Farr 1910: 17). How, the 'woman question' really asked, were unmarried women to survive? The answer that many of them in the middle class gave was that women should participate with their brothers in the increasing professionalization of work.

Moreover, this was the era of an enlarging middle class for which, as we saw, suburbia was a new home. Increasingly, entry to this class was by way of academic and professional qualifications, as professions such as those of medicine, university teaching, scientific research, sought to achieve secure status. 'The late nineteenth century', as one social historian has put it, 'saw a considerable competition for professional status as emerging occupations tried to join their more established colleagues. In order to do so they had to combine an ideology of service with the mastery of a differentiated body of knowledge' (Gourvish and O'Day 1988: 17). For women, nursing and schoolteaching, particularly at the primary level, offered a route to this kind of economic security. It was a route Yeats's own sister Elizabeth ('Lollie') embarked upon when she trained as a teacher at the Bedford Froebel College in the early 1890s. Others even chose the stage, which became an increasingly respectable option for a young woman as the professions became too crowded. And the rewards were good. As Farr, who had left a marriage for the stage, records, an average successful woman in the theatre in 1910 could bring in £500 a year, when the business income of 'an everyday sort of woman, working hard, is less than £100 a year' (Farr 1910: 26).

Other women were not content to settle for what were coming to be seen as women's professions (in 1901, 75 per cent of teachers listed in the census were women). They were determined to breach the walls of male status at the highest academic and professional levels. The women's colleges at Oxbridge had been founded with such serious intent and could not be made to seem anomalous, as Tennyson had sought to do with his mildly erotic vision of 'Sweet girl-graduates in their golden hair', in his poem 'The Princess' (1847). By 1889 the reformer

Maria Corey was pleased to welcome the fact that a few years had brought 'a vast and sweeping change ... of unprecedented rapidity, causing a reaction from this doctrine of idleness and dependence on essential ladyhood toward the opposite extreme, of work and independence as essential to honourable womanhood; work meaning paid work, and independence meaning life apart from home life, and free from the duties and continuing order of the home' (cited in Perkin, 1993: 168).

In a letter Yeats wrote to Tynan in April 1889, the poet opined of the process:

> What poor delusiveness is all this 'higher education of women'. Men have set up a great mill, called examinations, to destroy the imagination. Why should women go through it, circumstance does not drive *them* [Yeats's emphasis]. They come out with no repose no peacefulness – their minds no longer quiet gardens full of secluded paths and umbrage circled nooks, but loud as chaffering market places. (*CL1*: 161)

Yeats clearly sensed that he was at risk in this new world of professional opportunity based on examination success, even if he was insufficiently attentive to his younger sister's attempt to adapt to it. Circumstance was clearly involved in her decision to enrol at the local teacher training college. As a trainee teacher she was required to work for the first year as a kind of unpaid apprentice, as well as to undertake a course of formal study (and to pass examinations). However, as he grew a little older Yeats could not have been unaware that the women he chose to cultivate as friends tended to be unmarried, or separated and with access to private means, which allowed some of them to lead the kinds of reposeful, imaginatively rich and artistically productive lives that he thought appropriate to their sex. The revolutionary Gonne was also free of concerns about money. And in the Order of the Golden Dawn the poet found himself in a milieu where not only female spiritual power was accounted for, but where women comprised almost half the membership. One member was the wealthy Annie Horniman, who was to be so useful to Yeats's later theatrical exploits. The spiritually minded women of the Golden Dawn were women with independent wealth, a profession, or more usually a comfortable marriage. In the main they did not have to worry that the professionalization of Victorian society was making things difficult for their poorer sisters in the lower orders of society who had made spiritual mediumship and faith a paying concern. It was in fact the overwhelming middle-class complacency of the Order that offended Gonne. She left when credible opportunity presented itself (she repudiated the Order's ostensible links with anti-Catholic Freemasonry implicit in some shared symbolism).

Yeats's own position, as an aspirant poet and man of letters in the 1890s, was extremely insecure, even as he circulated among financially independent or securely placed women. Without academic qualifications, he might have been expected to show greater sympathy than he did for women like his sisters who, because of their gender and impecunious situation, found the new world of professionalization an arduous one. For he suffered analogous disadvantages, lacking as he did certified competence in any field or even a successful, influential father who could petition for some agreeable sinecure in the establishment's gift for an unusual son.

The problem of paid work had troubled the young Yeats in the exiguous circumstances of the Blenheim Road household. He must too have been alert enough to notice (though he never acknowledged the fact) that his sisters were the mainstay of the household's domestic regime. Their brother Jack had wisely left home. In 1894 he married a woman of some means, and was making his own way in the world as a periodical illustrator (sporting events were his forte). 'Lollie' taught and lectured in salaried employment between 1893 and 1902. 'Lily' acquired skill as a needlewoman and set to work as a seamstress at William Morris's design workshop, first at Kelmscott House which she liked, then in Hammersmith, under the gimlet eye of Morris's daughter May, which she hated (Florence Farr also did a short stint in Hammersmith). 'Lily's' health failed in 1895, after a brief spell as an unpaid governess, that expedient of Victorian female desperation, in the south of France. She caught typhoid fever in France and her health was uncertain for the rest of the decade.

London could be exciting for a young man prepared to take it on. It was after all the place where ambition could meet with worthy challenge. The journalist Frank Harris, vulgar and invincibly ambitious, remembered the excitement of his early career in London in the 1880s, how it 'made [him] drunk for years and in memory still the magic of those first years ennobles life' (cited in Waller 1983: 33). Harris's London was the site of opportunity and infinite variety. For Yeats however, even when his own place in English literature was assured, the city was remembered as an almost unbearable burden, where he had become oppressed by the ' "great weight of stone" ' and the ' "miles and miles of stone and brick" ' (*Au*: 154), which made the city an overwhelming metropolis. Yeats furthermore recalled how he lived as a young man in the city on a diet of bread and tea. Asceticism, he suggests was necessary to his professional advancement: 'More than thirty years have passed and I have seen no forcible young man of letters brave the metropolis without some like stimulant; and all after two or three, or twelve or fifteen years, according to obstinacy, have understood that we achieve, if we do achieve, in little sedentary stitches as though we were making lace' (*Au*: 154).

The impression this passage gives is of a man recalling how the literary life is one of unremitting, cumulative dedication to a modest craft, in which achievement is less than assured. In adopting such a tone, Yeats was retrospectively responding to the conditions of the literary market place as it had developed in Britain since the 1880s. For recent studies and researches have shown that the high period of the 'Man of Letters' in literary London had passed by the 1880s (though Yeats and his contemporaries could not have been fully aware of this) and, like so much else in the final decades of the century, was coming under the intense pressures of professionalization. By the 1890s the kinds of people identified by Stefan Collini as 'public moralists', writers, editors and journalists, who had enjoyed a heyday in mid-Victorian Britain, could still sustain a middle-class life without salaried employment (a comfortable ménage for a married man with a family was possible on *c.* £500 per annum; a single man could manage on £250), but it was becoming increasingly difficult to do so.

In an apparent paradox, it was increased literacy which put the role of the man of letters in question. As literacy rates among men and women in England and Wales rose, until in 1900 they stood at 97.2 and 96.8 per cent respectively, a huge market for cheap prints of all kinds was created. Newspapers, sensationalist novels, cheap magazines, works of self-improvement, encyclopaedias flooded the market. The old role of the man of letters as arbiter of taste, of political, social and cultural ideas, of public opinion, was superseded to a disturbing extent by that of the hack writer, who catered for a growing, often philistine readership. A historian of this process has observed: 'what had been created was a mass semi-literate, working-class, reading public, about whom the serious literary figures knew almost nothing and felt little commonality of interests and values, and yet who threatened to win the dominant position in political and economic life. This new public was to unsettle literary authors as much as any feature of modern life' (Heyck 1982: 199). Nor were the suburban middle classes a substitute audience for the old intellectual elites in Church, Government, the Law, who had once provided the readership for periodical publications in which substantially remunerated men of letters reflected on and informed influential opinion in the capital. For as mass publication intensified, publishers who sought to do something more serious than issue pot-boilers, penny-dreadfuls and titillating gossip, tried to adapt by safe specialization. They catered for a middle-class readership eager for undemanding reading material on specific topics. All this led to a fragmentation of the literary market place in which the number of outlets for serious literary and intellectual work that might appeal to a general audience fell markedly in the 1880s and 1890s. Yeats himself noted how in the 1890s 'the world was now a bundle of fragments' (cited in Alford 1994: 16). So while the 1890s was a period in which many books on poetry and drama were in fact published, it is also the decade in which the aspirant author had to fear grinding poverty and the indignity of Grub Street (memorably evoked in its modern form in Gissing's novel of 1891, *New Grub Street*).

There were some new, specialist periodicals where the young Yeats found hospitable editors, if not ample financial reward. But the periodicals which published his reviews, articles and poems in 1890s' London do suggest that literary culture in the decade was forced to situate itself not at the centre of British culture, but at its periphery, in the limited interstices of an increasingly philistine and homogenous social order. As educated society became more and more professionalized, conformist and suburban, intellectual life became fissiparous. Accordingly, the diverse interests represented by the periodicals in which Yeats achieved publication in the 1890s alert us to how fragmented literary culture had become by the last decade of the century. They also suggest how insecure the young poet's identity was in the complex urban environment in which he was seeking to make his way.

Yeats as a young man was strikingly impressionable. Madame Blavatsky had been the first to win his attention in the capital. Soon she was followed as the principal star in his firmament by William Morris. In 1886 Morris had offered support to the Irish cause (MacCarthy 1995: 540), in the year of the first Home Rule Bill. This must have drawn the young Yeats to him, as must the older man's revulsion from urban chaos and the vulgarity of mass production. In 1887 and the next year Yeats attended Morris's Coach House lectures in Kelmscott House and was invited with the select few to stay for supper and talk. Yeats found in Morris, 'Something childlike and joyous' which in 1915 still left him his 'chief of men' (*Mem*: 20). But he disliked the 'working-men revolutionists' (ibid.: 21) he met at Kelmscott House and the frequent attacks on religion which they mounted. He drifted away, from socialism and from Morris.

Had he stayed, he might have found himself personally involved in one of the two movements of the *fin de siècle* which offered a collective challenge to the suburban conformities of middle-class life in the last decade of the century. For socialism, with its pamphleteering, its Fabian Society (in which Yeats's fellow-Dubliner George Bernard Shaw cut his polemical teeth in the 1880s), its workers' organizations and strike committees (Yeats's colleague in occultism Annie Besant had helped to mount a famous strike among female match manufacturers in 1888) was laying the foundations for the modern Labour Party which in the twentieth century would replace the Liberal Party as the main party of opposition to traditional Tory rule in Britain.

The other movement which stirred minds to idealism in the 1890s was British imperialism. Between 1870 and 1914, on the eve of the Great War, the Empire added about five million square miles to its territory as, in the words of one of its principal ideologues, Britain 'conquered and peopled half the world in a fit of absence of mind' (J. R. Seeley, cited in Sigsworth 1988: 169). Many young men were fired by a vision of 'the white man's burden' (the phrase is Kipling's in a poem of that title, published in 1899), which involved him in pacifying and civilizing less fortunate peoples than the English, at sacrificial cost to himself. The cult of self-sacrifice in imperialist ideology, which was given more popular, cruder expression in jingoistic songs in the numerous music-halls of *fin de siècle* London, made the movement one which challenged the liberal belief in inevitable social progress that had characterized Victorian bourgeois sentiment. Imperialism by contrast offered a life of struggle, conflict, personal suffering in service of a noble crusade fought in the teeth of dangerous and cunning adversaries – the period was marked by the publication of novels which warned of the imminence of a French invasion of England. The movement found vigorous journalistic support in the early 1890s from W. E. Henley in the newly named *National Observer* (until 1890, the *Scots Observer*).

A gifted talent-spotter among the literary young, Henley recruited a team of coming men (the cartoonist Max Beerbohm satirically dubbed them 'Henley's Regatta') for his publication, among whom, surprisingly, we find W. B. Yeats. First in Henley's *Observer* and then in the *New Review*, which he also edited, Yeats found a paying outlet for his poems and stories, although, as he was later at pains to insist, he did not share the editor's beliefs. Yet he had found in Henley (a poet himself, who had in 1892 gone to the lengths of publishing a very popular anthology of patriotic poems for use in the education of the young for an imperial age) a man to whom he was drawn, on account of 'his aristocratic attitudes, his hatred of the crowd and of that logical realism which is but popular oratory, as it were frozen and solidified' (*Mem:* 39). He even allowed Henley, though it irritated him, to amend some of his own poems, so respectful was he forced to be of the man he named in retrospect 'my chief employer' (ibid.: 37).

In recollecting Henley as a splenetic aristocrat of the leading article, disdainful of the herd, Yeats made him a kind of rebarbative cousin of his other mentor, the Fenian O'Leary, as if to explain, perhaps even to himself, how he could have associated so paradoxically with two men whose politics were polar opposites. Apparent contradiction, however, was becoming a feature of the young Yeats's developing artistic personality – toying with socialism, joining an elite hermetic religious order, publishing poems and stories of Celtic mysticism in an imperialist organ. So it should not really disconcert us that the young man who found in Henley a man who 'alarmed' and 'impressed' (*Mem* 38) could also find in aestheticism an inspiration and a publishing opportunity.

The aesthetic movement of the 1890s, at its most self-conscious in coterie periodicals which were receptive to Yeats, such as *The Savoy* (edited by Yeats's friend Arthur Symons), *The Yellow Book* and *The Dome*, although very much the concern of a minority of exotic, even outrageous, individuals, at least shared with the imperial ideal a contempt for the mediocrity of conventional English bourgeois respectability. For all the epicene posturing, the homoerotic and lubricious fantasies indulged in the pages of those publications, which flew in the face of the kind of healthily male Christianity imperialism encouraged as the ethos of empire-building, the aesthetic movement's sense of the artist as superior being in a degraded society made it part of the general challenge of the 1890s to the long-established Victorian consensus. Walter Pater had enunciated the doctrine of aestheticism in 1873 when he had declared that 'All art constantly aspires to the condition of music' (Pater 1986: 86). For music in Pater's terms was the art in which matter was most subservient to the ideality of form, subject was secondary to style. Yeats, in revolt against the materialism of the age and its doctrine of social progress, was only one, if perhaps the most gifted, of an alienated minority in conflict with their elders, for whom such aestheticism – art as a supreme good – rather than socialism or imperialism, represented a credible alternative to the meaningless, vulgarizing rhythms of modernity.

Yeats is accordingly most fully representative as a late Victorian, not when he is attending to the mysteries of occult lore in the Order of the Golden Dawn, listening to William Morris's Coach House lectures, or even when he allows his work to appear in the pages of an organ of imperialist propaganda, but when, affecting the dress and manners of the poet as dandy and aesthete, he publishes in those periodicals which inevitably associated his name (to his friend AE's disapproval) with the risqué and risky artistic daring of Decadence. For in the idea of Decadence, which could incorporate any amount of ostentatiously extreme political, religious, sexual and aesthetic attitudinizing, the age found a concept and implied way of life so disturbing that it brought the decade to its strange crisis in the trial and conviction of Oscar Wilde for sodomy in 1895.

The sense that the 1890s was infected by a terminal malaise was widespread among concerned social commentators and moralists in church and politics. The *outré* antics of the small literary and artistic avant garde, at their most reprehensible in Aubrey Beardsley's notorious illustrations to Oscar Wilde's chillingly aestheticized, langorously lush, dramatic version of the gospel story of Salomé, could be read by an outraged bourgeoisie as a ghastly sign of the times. *Salomé* was refused a production licence in 1892. Also seriously in doubt were the increasingly frank literary celebrations of the homoerotic in the cult of Uranian love of beautiful boyhood and the suggestive implications of bisexuality in the figure of the dandy. The study of sexuality itself was suspect, for in 1897 the publication of Havelock Ellis's *Studies in the Psychology of Sex: Sexual Inversion* saw its hapless publisher in court. In the aftermath of Wilde's conviction and incarceration in Reading Gaol, this was an unsettling signal that society was fighting back.

It is now possible for us to see how much of the literary and artistic activity of the 1890s was analagous to the experimentalism and the elitist social attitudes of the Modernist avant garde of the second and third decades of the twentieth century. Decadence, we can now recognize, was a transitional phase in English cultural history, rather than the terminal condition many anxious or censorious contempories feared it to be. Yet as a period in which the artist and writer felt under social threat and responded with varying degrees of defiance of respectable mores, the 1890s was a period culturally significant in its own right. For Decadence made a life of literary bohemianism in an increasingly conformist mass-society, a beguiling if perilous possibility for the alienated young, for those disinclined or unable to follow their fellows into the tediums of secure professional life.

There was often something heroic about such bohemianism. Its peril was part of its appeal. For it certainly involved the kind of self-sacrifice which Pater had envisaged when he had conceived of 'success in life', in an image which blends machismo with exoticism in a frisson of charged sexuality, as the capacity to 'burn always with a hard, gem-like flame' (Pater 1986: 152). Yeats himself was to designate the friends of his youth – who in his version of their lives, ended in dissipation, Paterian burn-out, despair and madness – 'The Tragic Generation'. In a brief passage in his draft autobiography he catches the quintessence of the Decadence when he recalls a visit he and his friend Arthur Symons made to the flat of the publisher Leonard Smithers, proprietor of *The Savoy* and as Yeats himself avers, 'a most disreputable man' (*Mem*: 90).

Smithers and Beardsley had gone on ahead of us, and when we arrived Beardsley was lying on two chairs in the middle of the room and Smithers was sweating at his hurdy-gurdy piano. His piano was at ordinary times worked by electricity, but at the moment his electricity had been cut off or he had not paid the bill and could only make music by turning the handle. Beardsley was praising the beautiful tone, the incomparable touch – going at intervals into the lavatory to spit blood – and Smithers, flattered, sweated on. (*Mem*: 91)

A decadent mixture of the sordid, danger and style, which so often involved personal disaster, appealed in a direct way only to the few for whom bohemianism was an essential alternative to middle-class respectability. Symons was certainly one of them, for he had welcomed the decadence not only as a way of avoiding conventional life, but as an escape from the restrictions of a peculiarly stifling background. The Welsh-born son of a gloomy Wesleyan preacher, Symons had endured an even more geographically disrupted childhood than Yeats, in a sober and pious household which bred in him a desire for some more entrancing life. Literature, with Swinburne, Browning and Pater affecting a transition from religion to art, was his chosen form of salvation. Both London and the Paris where he met his ideal of the poetic life in the decayed, flagrantly drunken person of the symbolist poet Paul Verlaine, offered him the opportunity to practise a literary creed which demanded that he accept that 'for the respectable virtues poetry has but the slightest use' (cited in Sturgis 1995: 76). In 1890 Symons had taken up residence in Fountain Court in the Temple. The Inns of Court there were chambers for barristers, but they also offered to literary men a chance to roost close to the newspaper offices of Fleet Street and the theatres of the West End. The novelist George Moore and the poet John Gray had already established themselves therein. It was to this quiet oasis in central London that Yeats moved when, in October 1895, he left his father's house in Blenheim Road for good. A decisive break was necessary for he was about to embark on a first sexual affair. He needed clear water between himself and his family. He stayed for four months and nurtured a talent for bohemian individualism on a modest budget which was to mark his domestic arrangements as a Londoner for years to come.

It was well that such a mode of living could just about be sustained in the 1890s on the income to be derived from the life of letters. Yeats on his departure from Bedford Park, had hoped to live on ten shillings a week ('Let him try' said his sister 'Lily' (Hardwick 1996: 93). Certainly the blend of decadence and aestheticism associated with the bohemian figures of the age – Beardsley, Gray, Symons and Yeats himself – constituted one of the most vital of contemporary currents in late Victorian artistic life. Yet it remained more a matter of a coterie enthusiasm than a movement which could hope to compete with mass taste and the financial rewards it offered to those willing and able to satisfy it. Nor could it compete with the wider appeals of socialism and imperialism (with both of which it shared an instinct for self-sacrifice) as an inspiring alternative to bourgeois complacency. In fact as a tendency which can be identified in the work of a variety of artists and writers – for the farouche, the exotic (Chinoiserie and Japanaiserie enjoyed a vogue in the decorative arts of the period), the degraded and sexually outrageous, for the altogether other – rather than as a movement in its own right, Decadence and the aesthetic movement were vulnerable to the stronger currents which swept Britain towards the crises of the new century. A symbol of this might be read in the crude imperialist jingoism with which the poet Swinburne, a precursor of and presiding genius for Decadence, greeted the Boer War in 1899. For Swinburne the Boers were 'dogs agape, with jaws afoam' ('The Transvaal'), in a poetic tirade that singularly lacked the Decadents' appreciation of strange forms of life.

It is telling that neither *The Yellow Book* nor *The Savoy* achieved long-term financial viability (*The Savoy* in fact paid well and 'went out of business within a year'; Pittock 1993: 167) and that at the end of the decade *The Dome* could exist only because of the commitment of a patron. Only the Rhymers Club offered the London poets of the period a chance to develop some solidarity in what was becoming a depressingly difficult vocation in the era of mass markets and professional specialization.

In 1896 Arthur Symons bemoaned the lack of a London café life of the kind he had found so agreeable in Paris when he had met the French Symbolists and enjoyed the controversy and conversation of the Latin quarter. To this lack of 'easy meeting and talking' (Symons 1918: 198) he attributed the fact that 'there have been in England many great writers but few schools' (ibid.). In default, he observed, 'different taverns were at different times haunted by young writers; some of them came for the drink and some for the society; and one bold attempt was made to get together a *cénacle* in quite the French manner in the upper room of a famous old inn' (ibid.). This was the Rhymers Club, which from about May 1890 until 1894 met weekly, usually in an upstairs room in the Cheshire Cheese pub, off Fleet Street. There were occasional weeks when the meeting took place in a private house.

Yeats had been a prime mover in getting the Club going, along with the young London-born poet of Welsh background, Ernest Rhys (in his memoirs Yeats refers to Rhys as 'for a few years my closest friend'; *Mem*: 35). In 1892 Yeats reckoned that 'England [was] the land of literary Ishmaels' (*LTNI*: 143) and he had hoped, in founding the Club that it would help him to get to know literary London, and would allow him to overcome his jealousy of other poets. He told Rhys, 'we will all grow jealous of each other unless we know each other and so feel a share in each other's triumph' (*Au*: 164). This suggests that Yeats was certainly aware that literary London was a competitive field and that an amount of judicious co-operation would be useful.

Membership of the Club (men only) was by a fairly loosely defined system of election and the principal names associated with its meetings, apart from Yeats and Rhys, were Ernest Dowson, Lionel Johnson and John Davidson. Wilde made an occasional appearance. Other members and associates were such now almost forgotten minor poets as Victor Plarr, Richard Le Gallienne and Selwyn Image. Two members of note, besides Yeats and Wilde, were indisputably Irish: Yeats's father's old friend John Todhunter and T. W. Rolleston, the editor of the *Dublin University Review*, where Yeats had published *Mosada*. Others, chief among whom was Lionel Johnson, affected an Irish identity, to which ancestry and social formation barely entitled them.

Karl Beckson has observed of the Rhymers Club that 'not since the Pre-Raphaelite Brotherhood in the 1860s [*sic*] had artists united out of a sense of isolation from the dominant culture' (Beckson 1992: 75). Their sense of collective endeavour, which had them listening to and commenting on each others' works, after dinner and ale (for those who could afford it), at their regular meetings, bore fruit in the publication by the Bodley Head of two anthologies (in which Yeats's poems 'The Lake Isle of Innisfree', 'The Man who Dreamed of Faeryland', 'The Cap and Bells' and the poem which would later bear the title 'The Poet pleads with the Elemental Powers', as well as others, appeared). Members also engaged in literary journalism, in which they went in for the enthusiastic log-rolling of their various books which anonymous reviewing in the press made all too possible.

In early July 1891 Yeats wrote to Tynan to inform her that owing to the Rhymers Club (which began meeting in early 1890) he had achieved 'a certain amont of influence with reviewers' (*CL1*: 255) and that he would try to get a book of hers favourably noticed. He was ready to review it himself and in several places, for he was far from averse to the kind of puffing, or 'booming', of his friends, for which the Rhymers Club was the butt of criticism and satire. Yet in the flood of publications which a modern mass society was producing, such less-than-principled promotion, which Yeats undertook with panache and a good deal of organizational acuity, was necessary to get any notice for new literary works. For there were too many hopefuls seeking to exploit the market, as Yeats himself announced at a meeting of the Rhymers: 'I remember saying one night at the Cheshire Cheese, when more poets than usual had come, "None of us can say who will succeed, or even who has or has not talent. The only thing certain about us is that we are too many"' (*Au*: 171).

Yeats in October 1892 reported in an article how he had found an unreceptive audience among the Rhymers for the brand of Irish nationalism which he was developing in the early years of the decade: 'I well remember' he commented, 'the irritated silence that fell upon a noted gathering of the younger English imaginative writers once, when I tried to explain a philosophy of poetry in which I was profoundly interested, and to show the dependence, as I conceived it, of all great art and literature upon conviction and upon heroic life' (*UP1*: 248). For many of the Rhymers aesthetic commitment to art for art's sake combined with a desire simply to allow poetry to inhabit a world of urban impressionism. This undoubtedly made the kind of 'conviction' (Yeats's own word in this article), which nationalism involved, seem antithetical to their concerns. An aestheticized Celticism in poetry and the fine arts was acceptable, as one more variant of the exoticism that had fed a decadent taste for artistic novelty – 'any stirring of the senses, strange dyes, strange colours, and curious odours, or work of the artist's hands' (Pater 1986: 152). A philosophy, or worse, a programme of action was much less acceptable.

Celticism had, it is true, become a pervasive literary doctrine in London among young Irish men and women emigrés, for whom it offered a distinctive artistic identity if they wished to represent themselves as writers. This meant that there was considerable overlap between the fairly well-defined membership of the Rhymers Club and the looser associations of Irish residents in London who had constituted the Southwark Irish Literary Club (founded in 1883, its aims were 'the cultivation of Irish history, art, and literature, and the providing of a medium of social and intellectual intercourse for Irish people of both sexes'; Ryan 1894:

16). This Club prepared the way for what in 1892 became, less locally and under Yeats's influence, the Irish Literary Society of London.

The idea of the Celt had been given wide dissemination in a famous series of lectures which Matthew Arnold had published in 1866. Arnold had argued in *The Celtic Element in Literature*, drawing on the work of such French ethnographic thinkers as Henri Martin and Ernest Renan, that what characterized the Celt, in Martin's resonant phrase was a disinclination to 'bow to the despotism of fact' (Matthew Arnold 1866: 543). This for Arnold made the Celt Nature's dreamer, one close to the 'natural magic' of the earth whose characteristic art was the lyric and whose spirituality was ethereal, impractical and intimate with the supernatural. Such attributes clearly meant that the Celt had a great deal to give in symbiosis with the much duller Saxon, but unfitted him for self-government.

It is difficult to trace the lines of filiation which tie the Celticism of the 1880s and 1890s in literary London to Arnold's prescriptive account of the 1860s. Many Irish *littérateurs* and poetasters however seemed all too ready to supply the kind of literary fare for which Arnold's lectures were a recipe. This ready route to some minor literary notice was to be sniffily dismissed by James Joyce in the early twentieth century in the person of Little Chandler in 'A Little Cloud' (one of the short stories collected in *Dubliners*, 1914), who imagines his poetic success as a writer of the Celtic School, if he can escape provincial Dublin for London and change his name to something more obviously Irish.

Yeats himself exploited this version of Irishness, even though his ancestors on both sides of the family were indisputably Anglo-Irish and English. An early, colourful sighting we have of him among his compatriots in the Southwark Irish Literary Club, which he had begun attending in 1888, reveals him in ostentatiously Celtic mode. W. P. Ryan recalls how he lectured on Irish fairies in that year:

> In appearance he was tall, slight, and mystic of the mystical. His face was not so much dreamy as haunting: a little weird even – so that really if one were to meet him on an Irish mountain in the moonlight he would assuredly hasten away to the nearest fireside with a story of a new and genial ghost which had crossed his path. He spoke in a hushed, musical, eerie tone: a tone which had constant suggestions of the faery world, of somebody 'in em' (that is, in the councils of the fairies), as we say in Ireland. (Ryan 1894: 229)

It seemed to Ryan that Yeats spoke of the fairyfolk 'as one who took his information first hand' (ibid.). Others were ready to see in Yeats's mystical manner not intimations of direct access to the land of fairy, but the affectation of a poseur. In Max Beerbohm's famous cartoon of the young Yeats introducing George Moore to the Queen of the Fairies he is pilloried as a foppish dilettante of the spiritual life.

Beerbohm may have been astute enough in sending Yeats up as a professional Celt purveying mystery as a literary property. Indeed, the reputation this suggests he had acquired as the fey dreamer of the 1890s may be, as John P. Frayne has suggested (*UP1*: 24), why the imperialist and Unionist Henley made space for him in his publications. For Yeats as dreamy Celt merely confirmed Arnold's assessment of the Celt as one incapable of the organizational complexities of self-government. Better leave such practicalities to a benign imperial power and give the Celts themselves licence to dream. So while Yeats thought that the Celtic 'natural magic' that Arnold valued was a residue of an ancient world religion where Arnold thought it a racial characteristic, the Irish poet confirmed in his poetry and person an English estimate of the Celt as a mere dreamer, however much he may have deprecated the way that view of the Celt impacted on contemporary politics.

Yeats as a young man was certainly aware in opportunist fashion that a degree of Irishness was a distinct advantage to the literary hopeful in London. In 1889 he had written to a young woman who had sought his advice about the literary market-place. Lamenting that few periodicals actually paid, he observed: 'You will find it a good thing to make verses on Irish legends and places and so forth. It helps origonality and makes one's verses sincere, and gives one less numerous compeditors. Besides one should love best what is nearest and most interwoven with ones life' (*CL1*: 131). This blends economic realism and an eye for the main chance with youthful altruism in a way which perfectly captures what was involved in his own strategically conducted attempt to make his way in the literary world.

Despite such worldly perspicacity, there was, it should nevertheless be stressed, much more to Yeats's Celticism and his Irishness than the ersatz concoction of a literary *arriviste* in the English capital. Certainly Celticism and an Irish mystique, portentous and other-worldly, could be deployed in London when the need arose to clear a space in a crowded marketplace, but elsewhere, where market forces were more directly involved with nationalist politics, it was possible to employ a Celtic identity as one might a weapon.

Between 1888 and 1892 Yeats contributed, as a cis-Atlantic correspondent, a series of articles and reviews to two Irish American publications, the Boston *Pilot* and the *Providence Sunday Journal* (O'Leary put him in touch with the *Pilot*). In these, he presented himself for an émigré audience (some of whom may have been children of the Famine years, whose parents had escaped to North America by way of Sligo itself) as a Celt of an altogether more robust and politicized kind than the dreamy version allowed poetic expression in England. The political and literary Fenianism he had learnt from O'Leary, which he had begun to explore in 1887 in an article on the popular ballad poetry of Ireland (it was published in 1889 in London) is given frank, repeated expression in these articles. In November 1892, for example, Yeats informed his undoubtedly nationalistic readership, many of whom saw imperial England as the immediate cause of their own exile from Erin, 'Your Celt has written the greater bulk of his letters from the capital of the enemy' (*LTNI*: 152). This is of a piece with a writer who had announced in the same publication in February, 1890, with all the certitude of the youthful convert to nationalism: 'Whenever an Irish writer has strayed away from Irish themes and Irish feeling, in almost all cases he has done no more than make alms for oblivion' (*LTNI*: 103); and 'There is no great literature without nationality, no great nationality without literature' (*LTNI*: 103–4).

Observations of this kind tell us that, while the idea of the Celt in London may have involved a good deal of posturing and an exoticism which gave a distinctive accent to some of the decadent art of the period, elsewhere it had purchase on a considerable social and political force – the power of cultural nationalism. For as at the heart of the empire socialism and imperialism challenged the Victorian liberal consensus of benignly inevitable social progress, in the provinces of the Victorian world nationalism was developing a vision of cultural and social distinctiveness to be asserted in defiance of the increasingly uniform culture of modernity. In much of his work in the late 1880s and in the early 1890s, Yeats revealed himself as a fervent Irish cultural nationalist. In this commitment, the idea of the Celt had a complex social and political valency.

In Yeats's mature recollection of the years 1887–91 he remembered how he had felt his mind abstract, yet desirous of 'images because I had gone to the art schools instead of a university' (*Au*: 166). He recognized, however, that had he gone to a university and acquired 'all the classical foundations of English litera-ture and English culture' (*Au*: 166) he 'should have had to give up [his] Irish subject matter, or attempt to found a new tradition' (*Au*: 166). He blamed his youthful abstractness of mind on this predicament for, as he recalled, 'Lacking sufficient recognized precedent, I must needs find out some reason for all I did. I knew almost from the start that to overflow with reasons was to be not quite well-born; and when I could I hid them, as men hide a disagreeable ancestry; and that there was no help for it seeing that my country was not born at all' (*Au*: 166).

In these years, Yeats had a pervasive sense that his country lacked an adequate identity (such as it possessed was a vulgar, tawdry tapestry of sentimental symbols and a conviction of grievance) and that he must labour to supply it with one as he himself sought to determine his own role in the world and to fashion an independent selfhood. Much of his editorial activity, while undertaken with a canny eye on possible financial rewards, had as its inspiration the desire to construct a sense of a tradition from the very limited resources of Irish writing in English. After the disintegration of Gaelic Ireland (that had reached its climax in the Famine of the 1840s), these were all the country could boast as a living literature. It was as if his own consciousness of the inchoate, plastic nature of selfhood was projected onto the screen of his native land, where cloudy, frag-mentary images of nationality – some the remnants of a vanished civilization, some as yet not fully limned – awaited directorial decisions and editorial skills to bring to birth an inspirational country of the mind and of the imagination.

Minor English language poets of the nineteenth century were rescued from obscurity. In articles and essays, Thomas Davis, Mangan, Ferguson and Allingham were construed as precursors. Davis was exemplary, whatever his faults as a propagandist poet, as a writer who had wedded art to a national ideal of unity among Irish people in the terrible decade of the 1840s. From James Clarence Mangan, Yeats gained a sense of how misery, like the poet's and that of the country he wrote of, could be 'regal and terrible' in contrast to 'your drawing-room bards of fashionable pessimism' (*UPI*: 155). From Ferguson he had early intimations of the epic grandeur of the Celtic sagas of antiquity and a sense of the strangeness and poetic power of Irish place-names in English language verse. From William Allingham he sensed the power of place itself as a source of poetic energy, even for a 'non-national' poet: 'He has expressed that curious devotion of the people for the earth under their feet, a devotion that is not national, but local' (*UPI*: 260).

From early on Yeats had worked assiduously to make Irish writing in English available. In 1888 *Poems and Ballads of Young Ireland* was published in Dublin. He had helped with its production and was also a contributor. One of his best early poems, 'King Goll (Third Century)' (subsequently 'The Madness of King Goll') was included, associating that poem of isolated mystic intensity with the cultural and political echoes which the anthology's title summoned (Thomas Davis had been a leader of the Young Ireland movement in the 1840s). Later in the year came his own London-published anthology of Irish folk and fairy lore *Fairy and Folk Tales of the Irish Peasantry*. There Yeats included his own poem 'The Stolen Child', in a work which drew on a wide range of nineteenth-century English-language literary sources in its quest for the timeless, visionary realm of the Celt. He believed the 'innermost heart of the Celt' (Welch 1993: 5) was still discoverable in superstitions of the Irish country people about the fairy folk, upon which his writers had drawn. In 1889 Yeats selected for the Camelot series five stories by the Tyrone-born novelist William Carleton whose *Traits and Stories of the Irish Peasantry* (1830–3) was a mine-shaft into the subterranean world of late eighteenth-century peasant life in the author's native county. Yeats was already immersed in the nineteenth-century fiction from which he selected stories by Carleton and others which appeared in 1891 as *Representative Irish Tales*. In both these works, as Mary Helen Thuente has pointed out (Thuente 1979: 12), Yeats sought to discern in his chosen texts the essential characteristics of a peasantry that had been the butt of much English opprobrium and a good deal of Irish sentimentality. For Yeats, by contrast, the literary record could be made to exhibit the Irish peasant as a figure in whom passion, deep feeling and an extravagant, vital energy could be the basis of a national image and a literary inspiration. As he himself recalled in 1908 of this period of intense editorial sifting among the scattered literary remains of nineteenth-century Irish fiction in English: 'I do not speak carelessly of the Irish novelists, for when I was in London during the first years of my literary life, I read them continually, seeking in them an image of Ireland that I might not forget what I meant to be the foundations of my art, trying always to winnow as I read' (*Samhain*, November, 1908: 8)

In May 1893, during one of his visits to Dublin, Yeats gave a lecture in which he summarized many of the views about Ireland and literature which had been gestating in these early years of assiduous reading and editorial labour. The substance of his remarks was recorded in the *United Irishman* under the heading 'Nationality and Literature'. Here he affirms of the Irish: 'we are a young nation with unexhausted material lying within us in our still unexpressed national character, about us in our scenery, and in the clearly marked outlines of our national life, and behind us in our multitude of legends' (*UP1*: 273). So while Ireland may not have been fully born when Yeats began his literary life, the materials to create a literature, without which, he believed, there could be no true nationality, were to hand. Only the willing workers were needed, for in Ireland, he admonished his audience, there had been too much faith in inspiration and not enough 'labours at rhythm and cadence, at form and style.... We have shrunk from the labour that art demands...' (*UP1*: 274). For Yeats such inspirational dedication is to be found not only in a Flaubert, whom he mentions admiringly, but in the man he honours in the same lecture as his 'master', the English poet William Blake.

Yeats, along with his father's friend, the poet and painter Edwin Ellis, had begun editing the works of William Blake in 1889 and their co-edition was published in London in 1893. Yeats was convinced that Blake was a true Celt and was ready to believe that he was in fact blessed with the requisite Irish ancestry. In August 1889 he excitedly informed an Irish acquaintance: 'His grandfather was a Cornelious O'Neal who changed his name to Blake. Ireland makes much noise in his Mystic system & always holds a high ideal place' (*CL1*: 183). Yeats remained unshaken in this erroneous conviction. It allowed his work on Blake to take its place in the more general labour of these years as the poet sought in all this work to give Ireland an image of itself which could inform national identity. Blake was one more Irish arrow in the quiver of an ardent cultural nationalist: 'The very manner of Blake's writing has an Irish flavour, a lofty extravagance of invention and epithet, recalling the *Tain Bo Cuilane* [sic] and other old Irish epics' (*The Works of William Blake*, vol. 1: 3–4).

In Blake Yeats found too a confirmation of the innate spirituality of the Celt, for in the English poet's profound antipathy for materialism he had met a soulmate. He discovered in Blake's prophetic works, with their huge, epic canvases in which an essentially lyric, romantic artist communed with the spirits of ancient, Celtic Britain and with mythological figures conjured from the depths of mental life, an intimation of what an Irish literature could be like. It would not only take its sense of the other-world from the fairy lore of the countryside, its understanding of an essentially wild national character from the Irish peasantry, but its vision of racial mystique and primal splendour from the kind of mythopoeic imagination which had informed Blake's monumental broodings on antiquity and on the current state of the spiritual world.

In the early 1890s, when he was at work on Blake, Yeats had access to the mythic world of the Celtic sagas (to the world of Cuchulain, hero of the *Táin Bó Cúalnge*) through the English language versions Standish James O'Grady had published in 1878 and 1880 as *History of Ireland*. The grandiloquent, glamorous prose of these volumes had deeply affected the young AE with a vision of Ireland's heroic age. And when Yeats wrote of the Irish bards of the Celtic past his prose took on some of the coloration of O'Grady's heady rhetoric. He added his own Blakean sense of occult spirituality and mythopoeic drama:

> Instead of the well-made poems we might have had, there remains but a wild anarchy of legends – a vast pell-mell of monstrous shapes: huge demons driving

swine on the hill-tops; beautiful shadows whose hair has a peculiar life and moves responsive to their thought; and here and there some great hero like Cuchullin, some epic needing only deliberate craft to be scarce less than Homer. There behind the Ireland of today, lost in the ages, this chaos murmurs like a dark and stormy sea full of the sounds of lamentation. And through all these throbs one impulse – the persistence of Celtic passion. . . . the Celtic Irish seem of the fellowship of the sea: ever changing, ever the same.   (*UP1*: 165–6)

In his effort to construct a distinctive national literature Yeats did not only have to depend, as he set himself to the task, on a limited English-language literary inheritance, in which fairyland and the peasant cottage played their parts, and on a cycle of sagas realized into modern prose. There was also the folklore and story-telling of the countryside and a deposit of English-language ballad verse which since the eighteenth century had been broadcast in town and country through the medium of broadside prints. The folklore kept alive belief in an animistic world of spirits of place and of nature. Exchanges between natural and supernatural orders of being were assumed. Story-tellers still recounted wonder-tales and kept fresh the memory of Oisin and other heroes. In the ballads, the local politics of landlord and tenant, as well as the more legendary exploits of such as Napoleon Bonaparte and Daniel O'Connell, made historical consciousness a matter of exciting, swift-paced narrative in a timeless world.

Yeats was fortunate to begin his career at just the moment when knowledge about this hidden Ireland, of interest to ethnology since about the 1830s, was being expanded by the work of a very gifted linguist and folklorist. Douglas Hyde was the son of a bibulous Church of Ireland clergyman who had served as a Rector in County Roscommon. Hyde had acquired the Irish language in child-hood and youth from the country people in his locality, so possessed an intimacy with the folk tradition which Yeats's lack of linguistic ability made problematic for him. He and Hyde, who was a founding member of the Contemporary Club, had met in 1885 and since then they had frequently corresponded and talked together. In 1890 Hyde published *Beside the Fire*, a collection of Gaelic folk-tales in Irish with English translations, which sought authenticity of speech and content. Yeats praised it profusely. In 1893 Hyde's highly influential bilingual collection of poems from the Gaelic tradition, *The Love Songs of Connacht*, appeared. This made it possible for non-Irish-speaking Irish readers to believe that in Hyde's versions of the poems they were entering a fresh, rural Gaeldom, in which uncontaminated emotion ran deep and nature was unsullied by commerce or industrialism. To Yeats (who thought these poems, along with Allingham's, 'the blossom of all that is most winning in Irish character'; *CL1*: 444) it was a confirmation of his conviction that Ireland could be a site of renewal, where a new nation might be brought to birth.

For Yeats, all this involvement in things Irish and Celtic, this earnest attempt in the early 1890s to invent an Ireland since no adequate Ireland had yet come into existence, using such resources as could be mustered in the worlds of print and oral tradition, by no means meant that he neglected the occultism that had preoccupied him since he had left school. As he busied himself with literary work he was simultaneously engaged at a most serious level, in private, in a religious quest for arcane, obscure knowledge and for magical powers that made him, even among his fellow adepts, unusually dedicated to esotericism and fixed in his commitment to it.

It was in the Order of the Golden Dawn that this commitment found expression in a highly structured course of study (his Blake studies in poetic mythology were a cognate discipline). The young man who had missed out on a university education set himself to an idiosyncratic curriculum as he sought to rise in the several degrees, with their appropriate graduation ceremonies and rituals, that the Order had established for its initiates. Founded by William Wynn Westcott in 1888 with the co-operation of the charismatic MacGregor Mathers (Yeats thought him on first encounter 'a figure of romance'; *Au*: 183), the Order offered its members instruction in a series of Rosicrucian doctrines and in a symbolism owing something to Masonic traditions. It established itself in 1888 as the Isis-Urania Temple of the Hermetic Order of the Golden Dawn, the London branch of an Order that traced its origins to Germany. By 1896 it had a membership in London of 315 persons (Harper 1974: 12). Light was the Order's prime symbol, illumination its purpose. To that end, initiates were set to studying 'alchemical and astrological symbolism, the Hebrew alphabet, the ten Sephiroth and twenty-two Paths of the Cabbalistic Tree of Life, and the tarot trumps'. (*CL1*: 487). Mathers was the guiding, organizing spirit of the Order and it was he who set in place an elaborate hierarchy, with examinations preceding entry to the higher grades, where secrecy was required by oath at a theatrical ritual of advancement. This took place at the Second Order of the Temple's premises in Clipstone Street where a simulacrum of Father Rosenkreuz's legendary tomb had been set up in a vault, decorated with rich symbolism.

Yeats in flight from his father's scepticism and the materialism of the age, suspicious of abstraction and mere intellect, found the Order profoundly absorbing. The practice of ritual magic, with its hierarchical drama and invocation of powerful mind-altering symbolism, was exciting, compulsive and imaginatively enlarging. In January 1893 he passed through what was called the Portal, into the Second Order. At the same time he graduated from the lowest to the third grades of the Second Order, and moved from the state of being 'in the outer' to being 'in the inner'. To achieve this ascension the poet was required to undergo a series of ritual experiences which would have satisfied the most sacerdotal of natures. The poet was tied, hands, waist and feet, to a Cross of Suffering, and in a lengthy exchange of liturgical formalities with more senior adepts he was informed 'that the Mysteries of the Rose and of the Cross have existed from time immemorial, and that the Rites were practiced . . . in Egypt, Eleusis, Samothrace, Persia, Chaldea and India, and in far more ancient lands. The story of the introduction of these mysteries into Medieval Europe has thus been handed down to us' (Virginia Moore 1964: 150).

Released from the cross, Yeats was then told the story of the entirely fictitious Father Rosenkreuz who was reputedly the fifteenth-century conduit of this ancient wisdom to modern Europe. Further lengthy ritual and symbolic enactments, (the proceedings took place over two days), with the chief adept marvellously attired in the tomb as Father Rosy Cross, brought the (by now, we must assume), exhausted if imaginatively transported poet, to the knowledge that he had become a Rosicrucian. At the last he 'saw a golden Greek cross and red rose of forty-nine petals; and as instructed, made the LUX sign of light' (Virginia Moore, 1964: 155) and was sworn to eternal secrecy. His motto and name in the Order was *Demon Est Deus Inversus* (D.E.D.I.).

The Order for the impressionable Yeats, still a sexual virgin at twenty-seven when this initiation took place, and in thrall to the image of Maud Gonne, must, with its invocation of sacrifice and purity, of cleansing in preparation for occult illumination and service, have been a powerful reinforcement of a sense of a special destiny in love and life. There was a good deal of sublimated eroticism in the Order's theatricality (Frazier 1990: 158–9; Howe 1972: 75–90). It must also have fed the poet's imagination with a richly profuse symbolism, invested with the systematic order and religious authority for which his nature had craved. It was the Order, as well as his youthful enthusiasm for Shelley and his researches for the edition of Blake, that were making of Yeats a symbolist poet. As such, he would expect poetry to serve as a handmaiden to magic, to transform a desacralized modernity, and to make his native country (itself a repository of ancient magic) the heart of that supernatural rebirth, as the national culture awakened to spiritual life.

3

Poems 1895

Symbols played a special role in the instruction Yeats received in the Order of the Golden Dawn for the adept was required to put his or her mind to the regular contemplation of figures, images and diagrams derived and adapted from occult tradition and to use these as a means to spiritual transformation. Yeats, the devoted student of magic, in the 1890s believed that symbols in poetry should perform a similar religious service for humankind. They must be much more than merely a means of communication which the poet could exploit along with other linguistic resources. They were at the heart of the spiritual task he had set himself as a man and artist.

Yeats was encouraged in his belief that poetry could employ symbols in as radically religious a manner as he sensed he must, by his friendship with Symons. For Symons brought him news of and contact with poets in France who similarly believed that Symbolism represented more in poetry than merely a literary technique. For among them too the power of words was reckoned to possess magical properties and the symbol was its secret.

Symons had first visited Paris in late 1889, in company with Havelock Ellis, where artistic experimentalism and bohemia mixed a heady cocktail for a young man. He had met Verlaine and had become his devout disciple. During his stay in the city, which lasted until June 1890, Symons also encountered Mallarmé, Huysmans, Rodin, Redon and Toulouse-Lautrec and became convinced of the superiority of Parisian artistic life to anything London could offer. His admiration for Verlaine and his zest for café society enliven the essentially journalistic work of synthesis on modern French poetry and drama which he published in 1899 as *The Symbolist Movement in Literature*. The volume was dedicated to W. B. Yeats (who had helped him with it), as 'the chief representative of that movement in our country'. Yeats was in Paris in February 1894 when he had stayed with MacGregor Mathers and his wife (the sister of the French philosopher Henri Bergson) for the best part of the month. It was probably Symons who arranged for Yeats to meet Verlaine. Verlaine set up an interview with Mallarmé, but this came to nothing. Yeats's purpose in Paris was to see Gonne and to attend with her a performance of Villiers de l'Isle-Adam's Rosicrucian and symbolist play *Axël*. So he found it disappointing that Verlaine misinterpreted, as he thought, a work which had impressed him deeply. Verlaine cut a striking figure nevertheless. For Yeats he 'possessed the joyous serenity and untroubled perception of those who commune with spiritual ideas'. Yeats saw in Verlaine one who had sacrificed himself in the dangerous service of art as a vision of truth. Even the dissipation of his life had religious import: ' "He who sees Jehovah dies." The ideal world, when it opens its fountains, dissolves by its mysterious excitement in this man sanity, which is but the art of understanding the mechanical world, and in this man morality, which is but the art of living there with comfort' (*UP1*: 399).

It cannot be said that Yeats grasped all the subtleties of French Symbolist doctrine at this time. His poor grasp of French would have made that a difficult task. What can be said is that Yeats's conversations with Symons and his visit to Paris led him to believe his commitments to magic and the power of symbolic expression did not make him an isolated figure in contemporary letters. The information Symons supplied (and when they shared quarters in Fountain Court, Symons read translations to him of Baudelaire, Verlaine and Mallarmé) in John Kelly's words 'gave him confidence to pursue his own aesthetic more vigorously' (Kelly 1989: 160). As Denis Donoghue justly puts it: 'Conversation with Symons confirmed him in his feeling, that his early verses, 'however fragile they might eventually appear, were notations in the spirit of the age.... For the moment, then, it was enough. When Yeats spoke of symbols, he had French authority to associate them with the condition of trance, the ultimate liberation of mind from the pressure of will, a sense of timelessness, and the corresponding rhythms' (Donoghue 1986: 35).

Yeats in fact as he espoused Symbolism in the 1890s had ambitions for his poetry that distinguised his aesthetic from the French variety at its most pure in Mallarmé. He shared certainly the French Symbolist sense of poetry as an art form that could induce transcendental consciousness, but for Yeats, increasingly, that transformation was to have significance in the human world. His ambitions for poetry were actively religious rather than essentially quietist, as they were with Mallarmé, for whom the world was well lost in the delicate intricacies of poetic verbal magic. Indeed it would seem that his emphasis on the real religious significance of poetry led to disagreement between Yeats and Symons, who speaks, in his dedication to his book on the Symbolist movement of 'gradually finding [his] way' towards mysticism (Symons 1899: vi). One senses that in the word 'mysticism' here, Symons acknowledges how seriously Yeats took Symbolism as a vital religious practice.

So it was probably the clarification of Yeats's thoughts in discussion with Symons, with his visit to Paris as a confirmatory experience, which allowed him slowly to systematize his beliefs about the role of Symbolism in poetry in the 1890s, until he presented them in fully developed form in essays published in the early 1900s.

In September 1901 Yeats issued his frankest, most unambiguous published statement of his religious convictions and pondered their implications for his vocation as a poet. This essay indeed represented an attempt to bear witness to a religious world-view, forged in the difficult crucible of his youth and young manhood. He writes as if preparing for the next stage of life, the knowledge he has gained hitherto now fully a possession of emerging maturity. 'I believe', he affirms, as if issuing a manifesto:

(1) That the borders of our mind are ever shifting, and that many minds can flow into one another, as it were, and create or reveal a single mind, a single energy.
(2) That the borders of our memories are as shifting, and that our memories are a part of one great memory, the memory of Nature herself.
(3) That this great mind and great memory can be evoked by symbols. (*E & I*: 28)

Later in the essay Yeats reveals that by 'symbols' in this creed he means the special inheritance of occult learning – such things as solar symbols which 'often call up visions of gold and precious stones' (ibid.: 48). This leads him to ponder how such symbolism relates to the symbolism of poetry. He admits that he had toyed with a possible distinction between what he had called 'inherent symbols' and 'arbitrary symbols' (ibid.: 49), but is happier now in stating: 'I cannot now think symbols less than the greatest of all powers whether they are used consciously by the masters of magic, or half unconsciously by their successors, the poet, the musician and the artist' (ibid.: 49). The poet does not therefore deal in a merely arbitrary Symbolism, but, whether he fully knows it or not, in a system of occult iconography which can evoke the great mind and great memory. As Yeats had stated it in a *Savoy* essay of 1896, 'William Blake and his Illustrations to the *Divine Comedy*': 'A symbol is indeed the only possible expression of some invisible essence, a transparent lamp about a spiritual flame' (ibid.: 116). In other words, it is a magical formula, a potent image, an invocatory word, which is essentially related to the transcendent reality it evokes. There is nothing arbitrary about it. Signifier and signified are united by a sacred bond. We see through the glass of the lamp to be illuminated by the flame within.

In 1892 and 1895 Yeats published collections of his verse which bear the imprint of a conviction that 'poetry moves us because of its symbolism' (ibid.: 163) for they contain poems which tell us how far he was advancing along the road to Symbolist writing even before Symons had introduced him to the French poets and he had elaborated his own theory of the symbol. Ellmann indeed argues that his father by 'teaching his son that the only criterion in life as in art is the fullness or totality of one's personality' had prepared the way for Yeats: 'the external world's importance could therefore easily be reduced to the role of the stimulus upon the self. From here it was but a short distance to the theory that the external world could be used to represent states of mind' (Ellmann 1987: 56). And Shelley and Blake had shown him too how that could be achieved in

verse, while his occult and religious interests had led him to study Swedenborg
and Boehme who encouraged him to believe that what the imagination revealed
must be truth and that things above have their correspondences in things below.

The Countess Kathleen and Various Legends and Lyrics (1892) and *Poems* (1895) drew
on much of the work he had produced since he had set his hand to poetry and
allowed Yeats to undertake a good deal of selection, rewriting and reordering of
his work, so that the volume *Poems*, when it was published in 1895, could, as he
entered on the fourth decade of his life, represent his achievement to that date in
a highly formalized and structured fashion. As his friend and fellow Rhymer
Ernest Rhys noted, in a review of the volume, with *Poems* 'we have the total
accomplishment in poetry, so far, of Mr Yeats' (*CH*: 92). Consequently it was this
volume which established Yeats's reputation as one of the truly significant
English-language poets of the period. For it served notice that the major poets
of mid-Victorian Britain and even the now middle-aged Swinburne, who to
many had seemed the only possible successor to Tennyson for the Poet Laureateship (the office fell vacant on Tennyson's death in 1892 and was eventually filled
to almost universal scorn by Alfred Austin), might possibly have a credible
successor. *The Bookman* observed of the collection: 'there is not one commonplace
line. There is hardly a misused term. There is no exaggeration, no eccentricity. It
is the verse of a man born into the ranks of the poets, who sees poetry and
breathes it, and who happens to have the gift of words' (*CH*: 91).

The volume contained a rewritten version of 'The Wanderings of Oisin' (with
'Oisin' now spelt 'Usheen'), the texts of Yeats's plays *The Countess Cathleen* (with the
countess's name now spelt with a 'C', in a new version of the play), *The Land of
Heart's Desire* and a selection of Yeats's poems, some of these also somewhat
rewritten for this publication. Yeats took the opportunity to arrange his early
work in two sections; one he entitled 'Crossways', in reference to the many
'pathways tried' (*Poems*, preface), at the outset of his career. This section contains
poems which had originally been collected in *The Wanderings of Oisin and other poems*
in 1889, with the addition of two ballads (published in 1892). The other section
he named 'The Rose' to contain a selection of newer poems from the 1892
volume (which had also re-collected poems from the 1889 volume). These two
sections became the basis, with the poems in some cases substantially rewritten,
for the opening 'books' of various collected editions of Yeats's poems, though they
never actually appeared as individual volumes. The fairly complex way in which
Yeats was arranging and rearranging the contexts in which his poems appeared
in volume form in the 1890s, was the culmination of the first stage in what was to
prove a continuing obsession. For throughout his career, as we have already
noted, he was conscious to an unusual degree that he was not only issuing
individual poems and volumes, but constructing an *oeuvre* which after his death
would achieve an independent life of its own.

Yeats also cared deeply about how his works were given to the public in his
own lifetime. In the 1890s, fired with Symbolist faith and as an earnest devotee of
the Golden Dawn, one in possession of occult knowledge, it was especially
desirable that his poems appear in appropriate editions. Both *The Countess Kathleen*

and *Poems* were exquisitely designed physical objects which advertised their distinctiveness as works of high art and spiritual intention in the mannered Celticism and medievalism of their production. The 1892 volume included as a frontispiece a rather fey drawing of 'Cuchullin Fighting the Sea' by John Butler Yeats's friend J. T. Nettleship. Yeats, as he later reported, found it 'rather disappointing' (*CL1*: 306). *Poems* employed the artwork of the English artist Herbert Granville Fell, to suggest mystical spirituality. Its binding was a notable if precious artifact in the Celtic revival mode, a development of the Arts and Crafts movement set in motion by William Morris. Yeats, who had taken a good deal of trouble to get the right person to design his book in fact hated 'the expressionless angel' (*CL1*: 462) Fell had supplied for the cover.

It mattered a lot, for in this volume Yeats was engaging with spiritual powers for whom such a vacant icon could not have been any kind of adequate representation. Of 'The Rose' section of the book, he avers that their author had 'found... the only pathway whereon he can hope to see with his own eyes the Eternal Rose of Beauty and of Peace' (*Poems*: vi).

The poems in this section of the book include some of Yeats's most characteristic and achieved works in the magical, Symbolist mode. 'To the Rose upon the Rood of Time', 'The Rose of Peace', 'The Rose of Battle' evoke in hypnotic, languorous rhythms a reality of ideal beauty and peace which rebukes the sordid conditions of the mundane. The tones of passive fatigue, interrupted by phases of windy passion, in which the poet greets the '*Red Rose, proud Rose, sad Rose of all*' his days, are invested with a sense of terminal melancholy, as if beauty and peace are intimates of death and of an advanced necrophilia. Disturbingly 'A Dream of Death' has first to bury a beloved in a foreign land and surround her with the solitude of a kind of non-being and with the imagery of mourning, before the poem can honour her with an apt epitaph:

> *She was more beautiful than thy first love,*
> *This lady by the trees.*

The poems in 'The Rose', as in the volume more generally, are marked by a thematic preoccupation with polarities – between action and dream, time and eternal beauty, the material world and fairyland. The Rose of the poems is variously a beautiful but unattainable woman and some state of ecstatic transcendence. Yet, as Yeats himself later insisted, the Rose is seen 'as suffering with man and not as something pursued and seen from afar' (*VP*: 842). The poet's stance is one in which he is caught irresolutely between the poles of his experience, indulging his weary sorrow at mutability and longing for some transformative moment which will lift the world out of its decadence into a new dispensation. Yet the verse syntactically inhabits a continuous present tense (a key word in all Yeats's early verse is 'wandering'), slowing down the passage of time, in which memory and optative moods do not threaten the curious stasis of the tapestry-like effects of an ornately formal mode of being. Change is desired, but the poems appear to deny its possibility.

The tall thought-woven sails, that flap unfurled
Above the tide of hours, trouble the air,
And God's bell buoyed to be the water's care;
While hushed from fear, or loud with hope, a band
With blown, spray-dabbled hair gather at hand.

('The Rose of Battle')

Despite the action such a stanza describes, it seems to unfold in a dreamy slow-motion sequence of soft-focus imagery. The poem gestures towards a state of consciousness where defeat is eternal (the poem in the 1892 volume bore the title 'They went forth to the Battle but they always Fell'), where nothing can change. Yet there is also hovering over the poems in 'The Rose' a suggestion that there is a power in the universe which might lift the heavy burden of the everyday world, torpid and deathly, and render it overwhelmingly beautiful, harmonious and actively significant. Some revelation is at hand, if we can quieten ourselves to receive it and accept the gifts of 'the long dew-dropping hours of the night,/And the stars above' ('A Faery Song'). The Rose, one of the Golden Dawn's prime symbols, that so preoccupies the semi-entranced poet, may come to fill the mind of the reader too and allow him or her to share an awakening to a transcendent yet intimately compassionate beauty, in which male and female power intermingle. As Jeffares reports it: 'In the Rosicrucian symbolism a conjunction of rose (with four leaves) and cross forms a fifth element – a mystic marriage – the rose possessing feminine sexual elements, the cross masculine; the rose being the flower that blooms upon the sacrifice of the cross' (Jeffares 1984: 21).

These poems compose a telling paradox. At one level they are poems of acquiescence in a state of mere longing, loss and the decay of dreams. Their present tense is emotionally frozen time, in which action to realize dream is impossible. The diction is that of an uncertain soul ('drifting', 'waver', 'thought-woven', 'glimmer', 'mused', 'half-forgotten') adrift in a world in which death beckons to seductive repose or to the 'peace' which 'comes dropping slow' in 'The Lake Isle of Innisfree'. The rhythms, by contrast, although meditative and stately, do move the poems to moments of resonant closure. And they do so in stanzas which, for all the vagueness of theme, are often complex, masterfully wrought structures. As Helen Vendler has observed of Yeats's youthful style in general: 'At the other extreme from hovering sensitivity, undecidability, lack, and ambiguity stand full power and command'. (Vendler 1991: 16). She rightly attributes those moments in the early poetry which hint at such 'full, even coercive, rhetorical strength' with 'language used...with magical intent and confident will' (ibid.). For Yeats's poetic when he composed such poems as these in 'The Rose' allowed for a technique which was much more than merely the artistic strategy of a poet who wished to symbolize a state of being. It was a technique exactly suited to a poet who believed he was using symbols with real magical capacities.

In his essay 'The Symbolism of Poetry' (published in *The Dome* in 1900), Yeats advised of the purpose of rhythm in his early poetry. If we were 'to accept' he argues, 'that poetry moves us because of its symbolism' and to abandon the realism of the Victorian poetic in a 'return to the imagination' (*E&I* 163), then

> we would cast out of serious poetry those energetic rhythms, as of a man running, which are the invention of the will with its eyes always on something to be done or undone; and we would seek out those wavering, meditative, organic rhythms, which are the embodiment of the imagination, that neither desires nor hates, because it has done with time, and only wishes to gaze upon some reality, some beauty. (*E&I*: 163)

Yeats, in eschewing will here, probably has in mind the energetic, robust rhythms of the patriotic school for whom W. E. Henley was a mentor. Henley's popular poem 'Out of the night that covers me', with its violent assertion 'I am the master of my fate:/I am the captain of my soul', might be taken to be just the kind of wilfully powerful show of individual strength he wished to avoid as a poet. It did not mean that he was forswearing power of another kind – the occult mastery of symbolism. Such poems as he wished to write, which would 'give a body to something that moves beyond the senses' (*E&I*: 164) would exploit rhythm to induce a state of receptive reverie. For as he had made clear earlier in the essay:

> The purpose of rhythm, it has always seemed to me, is to prolong the moment of contemplation, the moment when we are both asleep and awake, which is the one moment of creation, by hushing us with an alluring monotony, while it holds us waking by variety, to keep us in that state of perhaps real trance, in which the mind liberated from the pressure of the will is unfolded in symbols. (ibid: 159)

The technique of these early poems accordingly is one in which incantatory rhythms lull the listener (and the poems seem composed for declarative recitation, which would raise them from mere textuality into communal existence, as a sacred book is the basis in its rubrics and verbiage of liturgical celebration) into a state of receptive reverie. In that reverie the mind can accommodate the bold assertiveness of some of the final lines of these deceptively authoritarian poems: 'He made the world to be a grassy road/Before her wandering feet' ('The Rose of the World'); 'And above the deep of heaven,/Flame on flame and wing on wing.' ('A Dream of a Blessed Spirit', subsequently 'The Countess Cathleen in Paradise'). Meditative rhythms allow, as they prepare for the grandeur and portentousness of sacred annunciation, the unfolding of the mind in symbols. So also do the repetitive structures of the syntax in many of the poems, executed with manifest exercise of will and control. As Vendler has commented: 'The incantatory power of reduplictive language (learned in part from Swinburne but not abused) served Yeats as an index of magical writing all his life. . . . Repetition, by spell-casting, is the guarantee of revolution; and so transformative or revolutionary spells must be repetitive first, and then . . . revolutionary' (Vendler 1991: 19):

And then you came with those red mournful lips,
And with you came the whole of the world's tears,
And all the sorrows of her labouring ships,
And all the burden of her myriad years.
And now the sparrows warring in the eaves,
The curd-pale moon, the white stars in the sky,
And the loud chaunting of the unquiet leaves,
Are shaken with earth's old and weary cry.

('The Sorrow of Love')

There are magical properties in the rhymes in such a poem. Yeats, as an atrocious speller is also one of the least etymologically engaged of the English-language poets. He seems to employ words, especially in his early work, as objects which he has been forced by near-dyslexia to investigate and with which he has become fascinated. Vendler, one of the few critics to have examined his early poetry in anything other than thematic terms (Frank Kinahan in his book *Yeats, Folklore and Occultism: Contexts of the Early Work and Thought*, (1988: 127) is particularly helpful on themes, especially on the conflict between 'worldly and other worldly realms') has astutely identified how Yeats often develops his rhymes by addition, as in 'The Sorrow of Love' where 'eaves' becomes 'leaves', and how he seems constantly alert to the odd ways in which words contain other words. 'Leaves' contains 'eaves'. The keyword of this poem in its revised form in the *Collected Poems*, upon which the two final stanzas turn, is 'arose', which of course makes Helen, more explicitly present in the amended work – 'a rose' in a sequence entitled 'The Rose'. The rhyme on 'lips' and 'ships' links the girl and her beauty which launched a thousand ships 'magically' as in Marlowe's lines, where face and ships are linked. For Helen, along with the Irish Deirdre, is a presiding presence in the sequence (alluded to directly in 'The Rose of the World').

The texts of Yeats's early poems are scrupulously fabricated artifacts. They are poems composed by a poet for whom language seems to have been a complex system of interrelating, essentially significant signs which could be shaped by diligent work and craft, and, possibly, according to complicated occult and numerological rules learnt in the secrecies of the Golden Dawn, into magical mandalas, mantra-like symbols, which would unlock the door to transcendental awareness. This too is a poet instructed, through his Blakean researches, in the Swedenborgian doctrine of 'correspondences'. In this theory, ' "Whatever originates in the ultimate parts of nature on account of its deriving its origin from heaven, involves something celestial in what is terrestrial or something spiritual in what is natural" ' (Virginia Moore 1964: 94, citing Swedenborg). All of which gives a special meaning to the line 'Words alone are certain good', in 'The Song of the Happy Shepherd', in 'Crossways', the poem which Yeats chose to stand at the head of his *Collected Poems*. For, in Vendler's own words, 'magical, non-rational, non-etymological connections between words are as important to Yeats as logical, semantic, or etymological relations' (Vendler 1991: 17).

Such a conception of art, language and poetry, which finds its fullest expression in *Poems* and in 'The Rose' in the elaborate, formal repetitions, magic naming of place and authoritative full- and half-rhyming, the intricate tapestry of assonance, of 'The Man Who Dreamed of Faeryland', assuredly made Yeats an antithetical figure, at odds with the spirit of the age in England and with much of the more accessible writing of the final years of the nineteenth century. Where others in the 1890s, ill-at-ease with the Victorian complacencies about progress and modern social advances in city life, settled for critical urban realism in fiction and art, or urban impressionism in painting, prose and verse, or found release in exquisite aestheticisms or in imperial romance, Yeats sought to make consciousness amenable to a religious dimension, magically invoked. For him a poem was part object, a construct of language which possessed precise magical attributes, part pattern of sounds that lulled auditors into an appropriate state of being. Most of all it was a symbol that held up the process of mere chronological time in a timeless world, where eternal movement rendered all things motionless, unfolded in a vision of reality. In an era of materialist desacralization and highly self-conscious modernity (Wilde make much ironical play with the word 'modern' in his dramas) he sought to 'discover' as he wrote in 1895 'immortal moods in mortal desires, an undecaying hope in our trivial ambitions, a divine love in sexual passion' (*E&I*: 195). For he believed the arts were about to 'take upon their shoulders the burdens that have fallen from the shoulders of priests, and to lead us back upon our journey by filling our thoughts with the essences of things, and not with things' (*E&I*: 193).

It was the precision and magical purport of Yeats's poetic in the 1890s which made his early verses more than a re-enactment at the century's end of the central tenets of English Romanticism, which otherwise they might seem. Shelley, Wordsworth and Coleridge had all believed in the power of the imagination to save humankind in a world emptied of significance by scientific accounts of its miracles. They relied on an often vague transcendental inspiration and on a faith in Nature as a benign force which can sustain, and in Wordsworth's case, even stimulate, humane feeling in despite of science's depredations. By contrast Yeats, who saw in mere nature a cold and alien otherness (in 'The Man who Dreamed of Faeryland' nature presents in images of ineluctable alteriety), could depend for his faith in transformative possibilities for consciousness on the complex doctrines and practices of magic. He could depend furthermore on a deposit of symbology which had been vested with the authority of occult tradition and, perhaps most tellingly, he believed this tradition possessed a local habitation and a name, for one of its names was Ireland. This gave it, he believed, a valency altogether more potent than Romantic Nature ever had, even when discovered in a territory like Wordsworth's Lake District. The Ireland which did not yet exist in literary terms was an Ireland, nevertheless, that in its spiritual resources was richer than anyone had yet imagined. It was where an ancient magical faith was still residual, awaiting a resurrection. The force and conviction with which Yeats held to this idea should not be underestimated, for it energized him throughout his thirties and early forties in a way which brought him into stressful and invigoratingly creative conflict with his native country of a kind that would not have occurred had he not believed the curious things about it that he did. And it was that conflictual experience which made him acutely aware of the recalcitrance of history. From this dialectic some of his finest poetry eventually sprang. Only a man of conviction would have tried to do the things which he did in the first phase of his maturity in the early twentieth century, only to discover the limitations of symbolism as a mode of art and the forces with which magic must contend on the level of the quotidian.

In his essay 'William Blake and his Illustrations to the *Divine Comedy*', Yeats, in reference to Blake's ideas on the relations between mind and symbol, alludes to 'not a few doctrines which, though they have not been difficult to many simple persons, ascetics wrapped in skins, women who had cast away all common knowledge, peasants dreaming by their sheepfolds upon the hills, are full of obscurity to the man of modern culture' (*E&I*: 116). Ireland of course provided Yeats, or so he liked to think, with such a dreamy peasantry and a country which, in the ethnography of the period and in Irish folklore, was deemed so essentially feminine as to allow her to be represented by Yeats as a repository of uncommon knowledge. Both Renan and Arnold had identified the Celtic spirit as female and given to heights of mystical transport. Ireland in the native folklore was variously the Hag of Beare, the poor old woman, Kathleen the daughter of Houlihan, the Shan van Vocht of revolutionary ballad, or *Róisín Dubh* (Little Black Rose) of a famous poem by Mangan, a version of an eighteenth-century Irish verse. There was even the occasional ascetic and seer in the land, like Yeats's own friend AE, whom in an essay of 1891 the poet evoked as a kind of holy fool who had forsaken the life of the artist, which he thought bad for him, for that of a vision of the 'great Celtic phantasmagoria'.

Poems as a volume inhabits an indisputably Irish world when it forsakes the orientalism of Mohinee Chaterjee's India. It is however an Ireland of the mind, a literary fabrication. It is a world of mythic titanism, in which Deirdre is the equal of a Helen of Troy, Cuchulain an epic hero from noble saga; it is a world too where occultism and elaborate symbology find appropriate setting in a stylized version of an Irish landscape – all cloud, seas, leaves aflutter, 'cold wet winds ever blowing' ('The Pity of Love') and twilight, 'the moth-hour of eve' (The Ballad of Father Gilligan'). The poetry enters secret zones of experience, straying deliberately on the feminized territory of the emotions ('Beloved, gaze in thine own heart,/The holy tree is growing there' ('The Two Trees')) and of occult knowledge, so that the poet can murmur 'a wizard song'. It is as if Ireland herself is the female spirit medium in whom the poet gains access to an occult power which releases his own Druidic genius:

> *Nor may I less be counted one*
> *With Davis, Mangan, Ferguson,*
> *Because, to him who ponders well,*
> *My rhymes more than their rhyming tell*

Of the dim wisdoms old and deep
That God gives unto man in sleep.
(*'To Ireland in the Coming Times'*)

He follows '*After the red-rose-bordered hem*' so that he might intone:

Ah, faeries, dancing under the moon,
A Druid land, a Druid tune!

Yeats also seeks to enter the folk-mind of the peasantry in *Poems*, through the medium of the ballad form. In 1893 he had published *The Celtic Twilight*, his account of the lore and legendry of the Irish countryside and of its villages, in which he had recounted tales told to him by the firesides of cottagers and of experiences of the other-world, of portents and mystical intimations he had himself undergone in the Irish West. He had recreated in prose an Ireland where 'To the wise peasant the green hills and woods round him are full of never fading mystery' (*CT*: 139). In *Poems* Ireland is similarly a liminal region between the world of wise peasants and never-fading mystery, in which supernatural events are recorded in the ostensibly down-to-earth narrative form of the traditional broadside, Anglo-Irish ballads. These had customarily borne news of political events, local tragedies and strange occurrences. Yeats makes them poems of a folk-world which takes the supernatural for granted in the rhythmic pace of their quatrains and demotic diction. The result is a poetry, in such pieces as 'The Ballad of Moll Magee', 'The Ballad of Father O'Hart' and 'The Ballad of Father Gilligan' of *faux-naif* simplicity, as the poet rather uncertainly seeks a tonal register that can suggest rustic authent-icity without condescension. Where, however, they do achieve real authority as poems is in their apparently unself-conscious, subtly modulated reverence for the aural implications of Irish place-names, with their Gaelic-language origins. So the well-loved priest Father O'Hart is buried, despite his wish to suppress traditional Irish keening of the dead, to a requiem of bird calls and magical nomenclature.

There was no human keening;
The birds from Knocknarea
And the world round Knocknashee
Came keening in that day.

The young birds and the old birds
Came flying, heavy and sad;
Keening in from Tiraragh,
Keening from Ballinafad;

Keening from Innismurray,
Nor stayed for bite or sup;
This way were all reproved
Who dig old customs up.

The cultural import of such poems in the 1890s, slight as they now may seem, is certainly worth nothing. In 1888 Henry James had observed that 'the capital of the human race happens to be British' and had reflected, accordingly, of London and the English language: 'It is the headquarters of that strangely elastic tongue' (James 1905: 12). In the 1890s the fortunes of the English language, celebrated in this imperial fashion by James, were clearly associated with the fortunes of the Empire. Its very elasticity meant that it could be exported to the ever-expanding territories under British control and influence. By contrast, Yeats's use of Irish place-names in *Poems* suggested that in certain corners of the Empire the imperial language was beholden to other tongues, could find itself transformed in contact with the accents and tones of a spoken English, which had for centuries been undergoing a sea-change in the waters of Irish. And instead of being a language which extended its influence as if inevitably and by divine right throughout an ever-widening empty or cleared space of geographic and political manifest destiny, English found itself halted and transformed, by the names and mythic sites of a small west of Ireland region (all the place names in 'The Ballad of Father O'Hart' are local, Knocknarea is the grave of Queen Maeve of the sagas). Its imperial elasticity was stretched to the limit in the hybrid condition of Hiberno-English naming, in poems that made such nomination part of a magical, symbolist, occult universe, a universe entered through the portals of the folk-mind, of the secret knowledge of ascetics and empowered women and of the poet as mage. Entered, one might say, through Yeats's Ireland and the poems it inspired.

It is easy to forget, so familiar have the properties of Yeats's early poems become in literary consciousness, how strangely they must have sounded to the ears of his first readers. For not only had they to respond to the unfamiliarity of the poems' points of reference, but the texture of the verse suggested an ear tuned not only to the various registers of English-language verse, but to translations from the Irish which carry something of the rhythmic pulse of Gaelic poetry (Meir 1974: 47–54).

The close-knit patterns of alliteration, assonance and consonance in perhaps the finest single poem in *Poems*, 'The Man who Dreamed of Faeryland', are by no means foreign to English poetics. Yet in the compression of their usage in this particular instance, they suggest a poetry that is paying its respects to the complex prosody of Irish-language verse, which Yeats knew in translation:

> As he went by the sands of Lisadill,
>   His mind ran all on money cares and fears,
>   And he had known at last some prudent years
> Before they heaped his grave under the hill;
> But while he passed before a plashy place,
>   A lug-worm with its grey and muddy mouth
>   Sang how somewhere to north or west or south
> There dwelt a gay, exulting, gentle race.

The very unfamiliarity of the properties and some of the tones of Yeats's early verse, as it imagined an Ireland of the mind into existence, gave it a particular force. The late Victorian world was opening its imagination to the artistic potential of mythology in new ways. Myth was increasingly to be seen not as an attribute of barbarism now superseded in a rational world by science, but as a means of interpreting reality and offering insight into human consciousness and the unconscious. The 1890s were a decade of perfect and imperfect Wagnerians. Wagner's musical dramas, based on Nordic mythology, had cult followings amongst the literary-minded. Arthur Symons was a devotee, as was George Moore. And Wagner's works could be read as mythological explorations of the great conflicts in human experience, which worked themselves out at the unconscious level. They could find expression in the heroes of Nordic myth. Freud too was soon to employ Greek mythology in a related fashion in his studies of father/son relations as an unconscious Oedipal conflict.

Yeats seems quickly to have realized the potential for Irish mythology in this climate, for its very strangeness meant that it seemed to operate not in a familiar world of known narratives, but in a primitive yet symbolist dimension which bore on the ramifications of the self and of the psyche in a more arresting way than in Wagner's works. So one does not have to press the biographical argument very far to see in Yeats's poem 'The Death of Cuhoollin' (later 'Cuchulain's Fight with the Sea') in *Poems*, with its dramatizing of the murder of a son by a father, a study of the powerful emotions at work in Yeats's relationship with his own father, and implicit in all generational struggle. As Denis Donoghue has eloquently stated, while admitting the problems of unfamiliarity involved in Yeats's recourse to Celtic symbols and legends as the matter of his early art,

> the legends which allowed Yeats's mind to move freely and suggestively along their margins allowed him also to find their analogies in his own life; they gave him a terminology which he was free to apply and, applying it, to move from legend into history, his own history but history nonetheless. In that sense, a mythology reflects not only its region, as Stevens said, but the experience of the mind that receives it. (Donoghue 1986: 46)

So Irish legend gave Yeats a way to be something more than the kind of symbolist who would have wished only to forsake history for eternal vision. Why he felt the need to be more than such a poet and what were the biographical sources and artistic consequences of that aspiration, will be a matter for subsequent chapters.

4

Conflicts and Crises

'It is one of the great troubles of life that we cannot have any unmixed emotions. There is always something in our enemy that we like, and something in our sweetheart that we dislike. It is this entanglement of moods which makes us old, and puckers our brows and deepens the furrows about our eyes' (*CT*: 108). Yeats was twenty-eight when these weary words were published. In his maturity he would make ageing one of his great poetic themes. That process had, it seemed, overtaken him prematurely, when as a young man, he struggled with the forces of his own entangled moods in the contested arena of his own nature. In this struggle for self-definition, Ireland offered not only a locus of symbolic, occult possibility but a theatre of life where dramatic action might make a forceful personality of a self which, he feared, emotional confusion had made old before its time.

For Yeats had believed for a period in the early 1890s that not only was Ireland a country which had not yet been born, but that the moment was particularly propitious for an intervention of the kind he could imagine himself as making. Following the death of Parnell in 1891, he had sensed that Ireland was ripe for an intellectual movement. This was a moment of insight that, he recalls, involved 'the sudden certainty that Ireland was to be like soft wax for years to come' (*Au*: 199). The exhaustion and disappointment in the political sphere, riven by quarrels about Parnell, could leave the field open to a nationally minded intellectual movement in which Yeats could play a leading role. The malleability of Irish public life gave real opportunity to one ready to mould the soft wax as he wished, while the paucity of the country's cultural resources made leadership in Ireland more readily accessible than it ever would have been in the English metropolis. In fact, in Yeats's critical writings of the early 1890s he gives the distinct impression that he envisages for himself in Ireland something of the role formerly occupied in England by opinion-forming men of letters. It was a softly waxen and culturally bereft Ireland that might supply the idealistic and impecunious young poet not only with a cause but with a social role and even a modest competence.

Yeats's 'sudden certainty' about the condition of Ireland, as Roy Foster has argued (Foster 1993: 260–80), in the 1890s was significantly in error. For the ranks of political nationalism which he thought in disarray, were by no means in so supine a state as Yeats imagined. And he was quickly to come into conflict with their representatives, in the first of the many public crises of his adult life that would in time make him more than a transcendental symbolist poet.

In the spring of 1892 Yeats entered a controversy (he himself had helped to engineer it) which had been running in the pages of a Dublin periodical. The subject of controversy was where was the true intellectual capital of Ireland, in Dublin or in London? In London when the Irish Literary Society had been established in early 1892, the *Daily Telegraph* had editorialized that it was 'eminently fitting that, if an Irish Literary Society is to be formed, its seat should be in London, not Dublin' (*CL1*: 297). Since English was the language of Ireland, 'the literary and oratorical and characteristic genius of the country' (ibid.) must of necessity gravitate towards the English capital. Yeats was having none of it and pressed the idea of Dublin as an Irish intellectual capital, since it was at least the capital of a country which appreciated books, even if the population did not read them. In this respect it was quite dissimilar to England, where, whatever the claims of London as an intellectual capital, people in general showed no respect for books whatsoever. What Ireland lacked was the infrastructure to support cultural life.

A National Literary Society in Dublin (founded June 1892) and a circulating library would help meet that need. Under the auspices of the London-based Irish Literary Society with input from the Irish 'branch' appropriate books would be selected for republication to be circulated by the library in Ireland. From the first the project was dogged by bickering about aims and policy. Thomas William Rolleston, former editor of the *Dublin University Review*, was appointed secretary of the London society. He had rather academic ideas about how the society should seek to spread its cultural gospel in Ireland through a series of lectures. Yeats wanted to reach a truly popular audience, so he had hurried over to Dublin in May of a busy year to help found the National Literary Society and to make sure that it did what he thought had to be done, which was to get the right books selected for publication and have them distributed as widely as possible. He thought that with O'Leary as ally he would get his own way. The poet's energetic commitment to the cause must also have been intended to impress Gonne, who had ideas of her own for a travelling theatre company for Ireland. Her role was to help with fund-raising in France. Yeats's *The Countess Cathleen* would be part of its repertoire.

There was a fatal flaw in the enterprise. For the particular Ireland Yeats was trying to manipulate to his agenda was less soft wax than all too brittle clay, which cracked as stresses intensified. Sir Charles Gavan Duffy had been appointed president of the Irish Literary Society in London and although his position was essentially an honorary one he became involved in the library and publishing project. Indeed Duffy quickly came to believe he was the leading spirit in the enterprise, for he was a man used to power and to getting his own way. In the

1840s he had been a leader of the Young Ireland movement and editor of *The Nation*, the most successful and popular of all nineteenth-century Irish nationalist publications. He had been tried and acquitted on a charge of treason-felony, so he had impeccable patriotic credentials. He had also spent much of his life in Australia, where he had served in the 1870s as prime minister of Victoria. He was unlikely therefore as an elderly, substantial man of achievement to have bowed to the opinions of a young poet who sought to wrest from him the authority he believed was his by right.

Yeats and Duffy disagreed about what the contents of an Irish library should be and, after a hectic period of politicking, plotting and lobbying, Yeats lost control of the venture. There were some terrible rows. They could not agree on the books to be published by the London publisher Fisher Unwin. Duffy thought that literature should serve the national cause in the basically cultural way the poets of Young Ireland and their anthology *The Spirit of the Nation* had done. He did not wish to foment extreme separatist opinion (*AM*: 122). He was also anxious to publish rather tired works by friends of his youth. Yeats, by contrast, had wanted the publications to bare sharp political teeth. In his own dealings with Unwin, he was convinced that he had been betrayed by Rolleston in alliance with Duffy and never forgot how foolish he had been in speaking frankly to all and sundry of his own plans. He had been blooded in the dangerous, slippery bull-ring of Irish cultural politics and would never be so innocently open again. He had learnt that his increasingly radical nationalism, the friendship of a Fenian like John O'Leary, and his own talent could not protect him from a skilled rhetorician like J. F. Taylor, whom he had first encountered in the Contemporary Club. Taylor had taken Duffy's part in the controversy.

In the event few enough books were published – to little success, so the scheme was stillborn. For Yeats, however, the experience of attempting co-operative work for Ireland was an unsettling introduction as an adult to the country for which he had felt nostalgia as a boy in London, but which he knew imperfectly. Some of what he discovered was certainly gratifying. He gave lectures on the library project in provincial towns where he was greeted respectfully. One woman finished a speech of welcome 'by telling her children never to forget that they had seen' the poet (*Au*: 201). A man compared Yeats to the Young Irelander Thomas Davis – praise indeed. Dublin however, in his recollection of this period, was anything but pliant to his will. It was a city where a rancorous, middle class established the tone of debate, where 'opinion crushes and rends, and all is hatred and bitterness: wheel biting upon wheel, a roar of steel or iron tackle, a mill of argument grinding all things down to mediocrity' (*Au*: 231).

Dublin had failed the test as an intellectual capital. It was a city in the grip of an almost Blakean principle of spiritual atrophy, ground down as if by a middle-class emanation of Urizen. Yeats felt himself caught in the machinery of Dublin's dark satanic mills in the city which he had hoped would allow him to fashion, more easily than in London, a social role as an influential man of letters.

In the two difficult years (1892–4) when Yeats was actively involved in the politics of the Irish literary societies, the poet had opportunity to renew his acquaintance with the social geography of his native city. In November 1892 he took rooms in Lonsdale House, on St Lawrence Road, Clontarf, a suburb on the north side of the city. John O'Leary also lodged there in the house of a female cousin. Yeats kept this accommodation until about the end of February 1893, an extended, if temporary experiment in living away from the family home or outside the circle of his relatives (the real break came, as we noted, in the autumn of 1895). Yeats's grandfather, the patriarch William Pollexfen had died on 12 November, 1892, bringing a Sligo era to an end for the family as a whole (*AM*: 125). In late September 1893 Yeats shared lodgings with his friend the poet Lionel Johnson, whom Yeats had introduced to the Irish cause, on the North Circular Road, near the Mater Misericordia Hospital. A medical student friend of Yeats billeted with them and worked in the hospital. Both addresses could have instructed Yeats in the complex social faultlines that ran through the city, which in the 1890s made it a provincial version of London with sectarian division as a complication of the class strata.

Like London, Dublin was becoming notably suburban, but given the preponderance of Protestants in the upper reaches of government, professional and civic life, that process was creating districts to the south of the city marked by a distinctly confessional atmosphere. The inner city was being abandoned to the Catholic poor in notorious and ghastly slums. Areas like Clontarf, which had traditionally been home as a village outside Dublin to prosperous Protestants, were beginning to offer respectable villas to Catholics anxious for social advancement. Clontarf as a district was close to the suburb of Drumcondra, which had been deliberately laid out by Catholic nationalist developers as an area in which the city's Catholic lower middle class could reside in decent comfort. Drumcondra was also the site of important Catholic institutions and buildings. The North Circular Road nearby contained lengthy terraces of houses which catered for the families of skilled Catholic artisans, minor functionaries of one kind and another, shopkeepers and tradespeople. The hospital at hand where Yeats's friend studied was part of an ecclesiastical attempt to break a Protestant hegemony in the city's medical services.

As Yeats tried to live on a bare minimum (on one occasion he lacked the funds to get back to London for a crucial meeting) it was clear that Dublin held no real future for him. He recalls in his autobiography how at this time he 'thought many a time of the pleasant Dublin houses that would never ask me to dine; and the still pleasanter houses with trout-streams near at hand, that would never ask me upon a visit' (*Au*: 233–4). For he had by his political commitments and associations with people such as Gonne and O'Leary placed himself beyond the pale of polite Protestant society and Catholic Dublin, the Dublin of nationalist politics and oppressive opinion, could offer no alternative for such as he in its suffocating suburbs.

Yeats's discomfiture at being out-manoeuvred by the elderly Duffy was not cushioned by any happier developments in his personal life. Gonne had come to Ireland from France in February 1893, to help with the libraries venture. However, she was friendly with Taylor (*AM*: 127), Yeats's enemy in the battle against

Duffy. They quarrelled. Then Gonne became seriously ill with congestion of the lungs and her physician, another of the partners in their joint cultural venture, with whom Yeats had also rowed, forbade Yeats to see her. A nasty-minded, half-insane woman whom Gonne had charitably befriended kept Yeats from her in her lodgings and when Gonne had returned to Paris she spread the rumour in Dublin that Yeats had made his beloved pregnant and that there had been an abortion. Yeats fled for a brief visit to Sligo where he could ponder for the first time what he would later call 'the daily spite' of an 'unmannerly town'. He felt himself 'burning in fires of a slanderous tongue', as a poem composed in June of that year had it.

He spent most of the summer in the family home in London as his mind began to refocus on the English metropolitan literary scene and he continued his deep commitment to the Order of the Golden Dawn. For while he would continue to review books on Irish themes and engage in literary polemics in Dublin periodicals, one senses that for the next few years he was chary of direct political involvement in any complicated Irish scheme. When he visited Ireland, more often than not it was to stay with his Uncle George Pollexfen in Sligo, with whom he shared membership of the Golden Dawn and occult convictions, and to talk with the second-sighted Mary Battle, who seemed to Yeats an avenue to the Celtic other-world. Yeats made Sligo his base between late October 1894 and May 1895. He had the satisfaction in November and December 1894 of staying briefly at the Gore-Booth house, Lissadell, which as a child he had glimpsed as the epitome of unattainable graciousness. During the visits he even considered proposing to the younger daughter of the house, but realized she could hardly take seriously as impecunious a suitor as he. For, as Yeats admits in his draft autobiography, he 'had not solved the difficulty of living' (*Mem*: 75). There is evidence that his uncle allowed him a small allowance of a pound a week at this time, which scarcely suggests he was in any position to marry (Pethica 1992: 89).

Yeats had felt moved to declare his love for Eva Gore-Booth since he recalled how his hero Blake had married his beloved Catherine when she had pitied him on account of his unrequited love of another. Yeats too had confessed his unhappiness in love and found Eva sympathetic. He would certainly have been even more distressed, as he spoke with Eva of his amatory sorrow, had he known that on 6 August, three months earlier, Gonne had been delivered of a second child by Millevoye, a girl whom Gonne named Iseult. On his first visit to Paris the previous February, when together they had attended the theatre to see *Axël* Yeats had noted a certain distance in her manner and demeanour. Gonne had been noticeably pregnant, but had disguised the fact from her Irish admirer.

The Irish controversies Yeats engaged in in early 1895 had a distinct intellectual edge to them, as if his recent experience had convinced him that an ideological battle had to be won among an elite, before a more popular movement could be trusted to impel the country in the directions he wished to see it go. For Yeats hoped that an inclusive cultural nationalism would prove a spiritual resource in which the divisions of Irish society between Catholic and Protestant, Nationalist and Unionist, Parnellite and anti-Parnellite, which he had begun to understand as he sought to work in Ireland, could be made nugatory in a rich harmony of independent, freedom-loving, national self-assurance. In a letter to the Ulster poet and nationalist Alice Milligan, he explained in September, 1894: 'My experience of Ireland, during the last three years, has changed my views very greatly, & now I feel that the work of an Irish man of letters must not be so much to awaken or quicken or preserve the national idea among the mass of the people but to convert the educated classes to it' (*CL1*: 399).

In a demoralized country, without a real literary culture, a genuine space for intellectual life had to be carved out. So Yeats steadily kept on with his various literary tasks. He was collecting and editing his poems and plays for *Poems* and working slowly on a verse drama, *The Shadowy Waters*, which he had embarked on soon after seeing Villiers' play. In March 1895 his anthology of Irish poetry appeared in London as *A Book of Irish Verse*. The poet's introduction to this volume of Irish verse in English bore the unmistakeable traces of his recent immersion in the murky waters of Irish cultural politics, for he was determined to set the record straight about the poetic deficiencies of the Young Irelanders, as he insisted on the essential individuality of a true poet: 'They were full of earnestness, but never understood that though a poet may govern his life by his enthusiasms, he must when he sits down at his desk, but use them as the potter his clay' (*A Book of Irish Verse*: xiv). Yet he had come to know what he was up against in sponsoring such an aesthetic: 'The Irishman of to-day, for the most part, loves so deeply those arts which build up a gallant personality, ready talking, effective speaking, rapid writing, that has no thought for the arts which consume the personality in solitude' (ibid.: xxi–xxii). He feared that if men of letters 'have not a passion for artistic perfection . . . the deluge of incoherence, vulgarity, and triviality will pass over our heads (ibid.: xxii). Most tellingly Yeats admits that he envisages his book being 'only a little for English readers, and not at all for Irish peasants, but almost wholly for the small beginning of that educated and national public, which is our greatest need and perhaps our vainest hope' (ibid.: xxvii).

This introduction, like his letter to Alice Milligan, is a valuable indication that Yeats in the mid-1890s was coming to appreciate his anomalous status in Irish life. He had been defeated in the libraries venture by a combination of old-style popular nationalism with its roots in the Young Ireland movement, and his own naiveté. There had even been a suggestion of sectarianism in some of the ammunition deployed against him, as if, as a Protestant, he could be tolerated with his vision of the Celtic pre-Christian Irishry, only so long as he did not become too influential. He had begun to understand the nature of the enemy against whose power he was bound to protest. The problem was that in defending artistic values he might seem to be allying himself with that educated elite in the country which also insisted on aesthetic standards in the arts, whose politics tended, more often than not, to be Unionist rather than Nationalist. His father's old friend Dowden, whose 'orderly, prosperous house where all was in good taste, where poetry was rightly valued [had] made Dublin tolerable' (*Au*: 85–6) for the poet in his youth, supplied Yeats with the opportunity to define the narrow ground upon which he wished to make his Irish stand. He would defend artistic

standards from the levelling vulgarity of the more popular and political nationalists, crusading for aesthetic rigour, but distinguish himself clearly from the
cultural values of Unionist Ireland, at their most obvious in the figure of Dowden.

Dowden, as an eminent Victorian professor of English whose literary hero was
Goethe, was fearful of contamination by what he thought was the provincialism
of the Irish literary revival Yeats wished to sponsor. He was concerned too, as a
vigorous defender of the Union, about the implicit political separatism of its
ethos. Yet his actual critique of Irish poetry was telling for he censured sentimental rhetoric and poor technique. In January 1895 Yeats used the occasion of
some reported deprecatory remarks by Dowden about Irish poetry in general, to
launch propaganda against him which went on sporadically for some months.
The substance of his attack was to admit that he shared Dowden's anxiety about
standards. He suggested in a letter to the Dublin *Daily Express*, that Dowden had
examined the Irish literary tradition insufficiently, and had therefore missed its
successes, or was failing in his duty to reckon with the new literature in sympathetic criticism.

Dowden was unimpressed (though he did admire Yeats's verses). Later in the
year his observations about the Irish revival (in press during this contretemps) in
his introduction to a selection of his essays were uncompromising: 'If the Irish
literary movement were to consist in flapping a green banner in the eyes of the
beholders, and upthrusting a pasteboard "sunburst" high in the air, he for one
should prefer to stand quietly apart from such a movement'. (Dowden 1895: 18).
The controversy included an argument about the canon of Irish literature, with
Yeats listing books he thought should be included in the national pantheon. He
dismissed his adversary as being 'upon the side of academic tradition in that
eternal war which it wages on the creative spirit' (*UP1*: 353).

What comes across from this very public engagement of literary fire (Dowden
was a distinctly prominent Dublin figure) is that while the professor possessed the
more wide-ranging knowledge, in dispute he lacked the younger Yeats's capacity
to go for the jugular. There is something blustering and unconvincing about
Dowden's professorial stooping to polemic. Yeats cut his man up without compunction. He was scathing about the vacant verses produced by the graduates
and undergraduates of Dowden's own university.

Yeats's brutal self-assurance in his dispute with Dowden (in the year in which
he published in October the well-received collection *Poems*) indicates a gathering
confidence. That confidence did not extend to his personal life. There all was
confusion and uncertainty. His quarrel with Gonne in 1893 and the defeat of his
plans for the circulating libraries had certainly been crisis points for Yeats in his
relationship with Ireland. By the beginning of 1895 he had recovered the public
confidence to wage an intellectual Irish campaign on his own, if narrowly
defined, terms. The impression of authority was deceptive, however, for in the
early months of 1895 he was in a state of disturbed transition, which would make
1895 a year of further crises.

In April 1894 Yeats had met Olivia Shakespear, a beautiful married English
woman, two years his elder, accomplished in languages and generally cultivated.

Her family background was strongly military, with traditions of service in India. In 1885 she had married a London solicitor, Henry Hope Shakespear, and although the couple produced one child, the marriage seems to have broken down sexually soon after their honeymoon and by 1894, as far as Olivia was concerned, was little more than a respectable shell. Hope was a worthy, dull sort of man, no real companion for the imaginative young woman who found marriage a more than difficult constraint on a warm, generous and amatory nature. A novelist, the books she published, without success, have as a recurrent theme the unhappiness of women in disagreeable marital relationships. She shared her military family pedigree with her cousin Lionel Johnson. By the time Yeats met Shakespear she had moved away not only from her father's world of staunch, if sometimes critical, imperial loyalty (he had left the British Army as a major-general), but from the decent tedium of life as a solicitor's wife. She enjoyed the company of writers and artists. So it was at the inaugural dinner of *The Yellow Book*, in a rather tatty hotel off Charing Cross Road in London, that she met Yeats. Yeats sat opposite the fascinated Shakespear who was able to arrange a subsequent meeting with the poet through her cousin's good offices, within a month. It seems that she had semi-consciously set her cap at the poet, who still believed himself in unrequited love with the beauty of the age. Certainly as their relationship developed, it was she who took charge, giving Yeats to know that she was available to him, delicately manoeuvring the inhibited poet into a position where he had to make some hard personal decisions.

In the final months of 1894 and the early months of 1895, when Yeats was staying with his uncle in Sligo, he corresponded with Shakespear, discussing her work as a novelist. She was later to claim that he had been writing her unconscious love letters at that time. She herself had begun work on a heady if unfocused romantic novel, *The False Laurel*, which was to appear in 1896. This work was an unconvincing study of a doomed relationship between a closet woman poet and her lover, a publicly honoured male bard. As a novel it is too underdeveloped to allow any precise biographical parallels to be drawn. Yet one of the heroine's observations rings with exact pertinence to the author's own situation when she met Yeats again in the summer of 1895 after his return from Sligo. Shakespear has her heroine declare: 'A man may love, and acknowledge it; a woman must not listen to her heart till she is sure her love is desired – God help her if she does!' (Shakespear 1896: 71) Shakespear must have felt her love indeed was desired for she told the surprised poet of her empty marriage and of her love for him. Yeats in retrospect recalls Shakespear as speaking 'of her pagan life' in a way which made him 'believe that she had had many lovers and loathed her life' (*Mem*: 85). He asked for a fortnight to ponder a response. When next they discussed the matter he learnt that her 'wickedness' was a figment of his sexual innocence and that he would be her first extra-marital lover. They each agreed to select a woman friend to act as a sponsor of their relationship as over the ensuing month they sought to make some arrangement, whereby their love might find bodily expression.

Shakespear was taking a huge risk in seeking to find sexual satisfaction with Yeats. As a married woman she might have found herself involved in a civil court action as the adulterous wife of an aggrieved husband, who could have sued for divorce and custody of their child. Furthermore the house she shared with Hope in Porchester Square, Bayswater, was spacious and comfortable. Yeats had little money, no home of his own and both the lovers could have been ruined financially by a scandalous divorce. They met surreptitiously for about eight months trying to work out what to do. He had moved in to the halfway-house which Symons' rooms in Fountain Court represented. After much cautious hesitancy on Yeats's part, the pair decided not to elope. Yeats then took rooms of his own in Woburn Buildings, near Euston Station. This would have made an illicit liaison possible, though in far from salubrious circumstances, for the kind of lodgings Yeats could afford were to be found only in rundown sections of the city. Suddenly Gonne, who had been less than communicative for some time, wrote to say that she had seen Yeats's ghost in a hotel room in Dublin, as if she sensed the act of betrayal Yeats was about to commit, though probably she was simply keen to keep him emotionally in touch with her as a supportive and valued friend. Shakespear and the sponsors tried to bring things further along. Shakespear asked her husband for a separation. He refused, but may have suggested that he would be complaisant if she sought sexual satisfaction outside their marriage. Yeats and Shakespear at last became lovers (not however until they had endured the embarrassment of buying a bed together, appropriately to furnish Yeats's sparse chamber). After an initial anxiety-induced episode of impotence they enjoyed, as Yeats put it, 'many days of happiness' together (*Mem*: 88).

Yet Gonne and all she stood for as an image to which he owed a courtly, chivalric and chaste devotion, cannot have been absent from the poet's mind, even though as a man he was discovering, after years of anguished sexual frustration, the satisfactions of the body with a woman whose 'great beauty' he later would characterize as possessed of its own iconographic power: 'Her face had a perfectly Greek regularity' (*Mem*: 72). For Yeats, sharing snatched hours with his married English lover in his London lodgings, was still mindful of the Irish destiny fate had surely prepared him for and remained anxious to discover what it might be. Gonne, whom he knew to be irrevocably committed to Irish nationalism, could not be expelled from his imagination, even as he enjoyed sexual relations with Shakespear. She had settled in those areas of his psyche which were wedded to the country she seemed to symbolize.

In the second half of the 1890s, Yeats's plans for his imaginary Ireland were those of one anxious to influence an elite in the country. They were, too, of an altogether more esoteric nature than the earlier library scheme, in which he had come to grief. In April 1895, while on a visit to the folklorist and Irish-language enthusiast Douglas Hyde in County Roscommon, Yeats had discovered the island of Castle Rock in Lough Key. It was just the place, he believed, where he could centre a Celtic Order of Mysteries in a Castle of the Heroes. This would infuse Irish reality, through symbolic rites and ritual enactments, with an ancient spirituality in which paganism and heterodox Christianity combined would help Ireland achieve a transcendent liberation from the crassly materialist world of England's commercial empire. MacGregor Mathers was the man to supply the symbology and rituals of such an order and Yeats visited Paris at the end of 1896, as his feelings for Shakespear were cooling, to discuss the Celtic Mysteries with him. He was also looking for material for a novel. For Gonne, whom he met again in Paris to involve her in his plans, the proposed order would have been attractive since it might have served as a political counterweight to the Orange and Masonic lodges which held sway in Unionist Ireland, particularly in the north of the country. It would have satisfied Yeats's taste for the occult, the dramatic and for hierarchical power vested in special individuals. He could have expressed his own sense of special destiny while impressing Gonne that he was engaged in nationally useful activity (for more immediate national purposes they founded 'a Paris branch of the Young Ireland Societies'; *AM*: 172). The two set about experiments in clairvoyance, in which she was efficient, to develop the symbolism of the order which was based on what they believed were the four talismans of the Tuatha de Danaan (the mythogical Celtic conquerors of Ireland): the sword, the stone, the spear and the cauldron (*CL2*: 665). They hoped to intermingle their visions, Yeats supplying a masculine, Gonne a feminine, energy. And Yeats was stimulated in this gendered view of Celtic possibility by his friendship with the Scottish writer William Sharp who was at this time his conduit to the Celtic 'wise woman' (Halloran 1998: 79–88) Fiona Macleod (in fact a literary invention of Sharp himself), who was the author of appropriately visionary Celtic texts. Yeats wrote to her from Paris in January 1897 of how he was seeking to 'go back, from the medieval magic ... to the old celtic gods' (*CL2*: 74) and of his hopes 'for the beginning of what might become celtic magic' (*CL2*: 75). Yeats later became aware of Sharp's literary fabrication. Yet for a few years at the end of the 1890s Yeats indulged a Pan-Celtic universalism (Scotland, Wales, Brittany had their roles to play in all of this), in which Ireland, as a place where Celtic energies could be tapped, might be the epicentre of a seismic shift in European consciousness. So could be restored 'the ancient religion of the world' (*E&I*: 176). Macleod seemed a hint of the revolution to come. When it failed to arrive by the century's end the poet's Pan-Celtic ardour cooled, as he turned to concentrate on the potential of an Irish dramatic movement. By then Macleod's true identity was known to him.

Yeats's hopes that Gonne would be an inspiring co-worker in a Celtic Order suggest that he was drifting away from Shakespear. By March 1897 Yeats's affair with her had come to an end (though Harwood in his study of Yeats and Shakespear has conjectured that Yeats's affections had been waning since the previous summer). Gonne was in London and Yeats had been to dine with her. Shakespear suspected that she was not the only one in Yeats's heart and broke off their relationship. We have no direct records of how this conclusion to an intense and difficult three years of entanglement with Yeats affected Shakespear and her attitude to what had transpired between them. Her novel *Rupert Armstrong* (1899) suggests that it had been both an inspiring and a painful experience. For Harwood has argued that the volume contains in one of its plot-lines 'an ideal version of her affair with Yeats', as well offering elsewhere in the text a projection of 'her feelings of grief and rejection' (Harwood 1989: 103) at the hands of her less than constant lover. It was a period in her life marked by sorrow. Her father had died at a great age in August 1896 and in 1897 Lionel Johnson, for whom she felt deep affection, was well-advanced on the last terrible phase of the alcoholism that would be a contributory factor to his early death in 1902 at the age of thirty-five.

By contrast, there is evidence that the ending of the affair was a matter of profound significance for the poet which went to the heart of how he understood life in its relationship with art. He undoubtedly felt guilty and knew that he had hurt Shakespear as his feelings for her had patently drained away. The poem he was to include in his next volume of verses, *The Wind Among the Reeds* (1899), under the title 'Aedh Laments the Loss of Love', put the matter with autobiographical frankness in a heavily draped, hermetic collection:

> Pale brows, still hands and dim hair,
> I had a beautiful friend
> And dreamed that the old despair
> Would end in love in the end:
> She looked in my heart one day
> And saw your image was there;
> She was gone weeping away.

The passage in Yeats's draft autobiography begun in 1915, where he addresses the pain of that parting, is less frank and curiously more revelatory for that, since it alerts us in its evasions to some of the ambiguities that his poem had hinted at in its enigmatic title (who is the principal victim of the loss of love it records, Aedh or his 'beautiful friend'?). Yeats wrote of his remembrances of his time with Shakespear:

> It will always be a grief to me that I could not give the love that was her beauty's right, but she was too near my soul, too salutary and wholesome to my inmost being. All our lives long, as da Vinci says, we long, thinking it is but the moon we long [for], for our destruction, and how, when we meet [it] in the shape of a most fair woman, can we do less than leave all others for her? Do we not seek our dissolution upon her lips.　(*Mem*: 88)

There is in this strange confession an underlying philosophy of life, with crucial implications for the way the poet had come to understand the possibilities open to the human self by the time he penned it. The passage suggests furthermore that the affair with Shakespear and his abandonment of her for an ideal image ('the shape of a most fair woman') had powerfully affected the development of Yeats's sense of self as an artist who must live in a very special way.

The passage quoted above indicates that Yeats was aware that he had possessed in his early thirties the quick of existential being, a selfhood that was offered in an erotic encounter with a living woman the possibility of life lived just for the sake of life. His 'soul', his 'inmost being' could have entered, however unsettling the social risks for him, his lover and her child, on a daily existence that would have sustained that living soul, that inmost person. He had to refuse it as too salutary, too wholesome. He might have become at ease in the world, as a nature at peace with itself. One suspects, certainly, that the social challenges of life with Shakespear may have begun to give him qualms as the excitement of sexual initiation wore off and he may have felt uneasy about the constraints that a more public relationship with a married woman and her child would undoubtedly have imposed. These understandable if not very honourable inhibitions, if he felt them, were subsumed for the poet in a view of things which made the acceptance of life lived as it came and went a betrayal not only of an ideal woman, but of what she iconographically represented: the dissolution of the self in some ecstatic union with the transcendent.

The life Shakespear offered the poet had to be sacrificed, I am suggesting, so that his experience could become an image among other images drawn from his occult studies, that find a place in his early poetry. His life was being arranged, he felt, almost as if by the hand of fate, or by higher powers whose energies he sought to invoke through magical ritual. His own selfhood with its conflicting energies, must therefore be made available for art – that art which was to play a role in his magical project for Ireland and for a de-spiritualized modernity. His life must be made the stuff of sacred books which could employ those images of himself as symbols in acts of magical conjuration that would bring consciousness to the point of spiritual transformation. His soul, or innermost being sustained in a loving relationship with a gentle and generous woman, was the price demanded by his occult aesthetic.

For Yeats believed that his own life was to be represented as a series of symbols (from the start he had interpreted the world through the images of art) in the spiritual sphere, where symbols are potent in a way mere life can never be. There the symbols of his life can function like the liturgical acts of a magical ritual. In intently composed sacred books they can bring about transformative visionary experiences in his readers' minds.

The cost of all this was extremely high for the man who, for all his spiritual ambition as a magician, had not only an innermost being, which required emotional nourishment of an ordinarily human kind, but bodily desires. In his draft autobiography he recalls the anguish to which the end of the affair with Shakespear was a prelude:

> It was a time of great personal strain and sorrow. Since my mistress had left me, no other women had come into my life, and for nearly seven years none did. Often ...it would have been a relief to have screamed aloud. When desire became an unendurable torture, I would masturbate, and that no matter how moderate I was, would make me ill. It never occurred to me to seek another love. I would repeat to myself again and again the last confession of Lancelot, and indeed it was my greatest pride, 'I have loved a queen beyond measure and exceeding long.' I was never before or since so miserable as in those years. (*Mem*: 125)

A book which Yeats worked intently to complete, as the consequences of his aesthetic took their emotional toll, suggests that the cost of vision could be even higher than starved sexual misery. It might be death itself, a final, apocalyptic, dissolution. In April 1897 Yeats published in volume form a series of stories which had been published individually in periodicals during the 1890s (the earliest had been published in 1892, the most recent in 1896). Entitled *The Secret Rose*, the book employs a chronological structure, as the stories take us historically from pagan to Christian Ireland through the seventeenth and eighteenth centuries, to conclude with a tale set in the strange, decadent climacteric of the *fin de siècle*. This final story 'Rosa Alchemica' was intended to initiate a kind of triptych of mystical tales, which was completed in the private publication together in the same year of two further prose works 'The Tables of the Law' and 'The Adoration of the Magi' (Yeats's publisher at first disliked the last two tales and demanded their removal from *The Secret Rose*, then changed his mind and issued them privately as a separate work).

As one reads the collection in sequence, a strong sense emerges of history as a series of eras which Yeats seeks to represent in appropriate styles. This perhaps accounts for the sense of stylistic uncertainty in sections of the book. There is an impression of an author straining to fulfil a literary and doctrinal plan, rather than responding to the immediate stylistic demands of his narratives. Yet the volume does provoke a strong sense of period following period, as if obeying the imperatives of an underlying pattern of disintegrative change. In each era, the stories cumulatively inform us, there are, moreover, those who seek to comprehend and be subsumed by the spiritual powers which account for an unending process of historical formation and dissolution. This is symbolized by the Rose, which is invoked by the poet in the introductory poem to the volume '*To the Secret Rose*', which makes of the book not merely an exploration of a literary historical theme, but an act of magical conjuration. The poet is one with the various figures in his volume, who throughout the ages have desired to escape the cycle of historical time for the timelessness of transcendental vision and spiritual transformation.

> *I, too, await*
> *The hour of thy great wind of love and hate.*
> *When shall the stars be blown about the sky,*
> *Like the sparks blown out of a smithy, and die?*
> *Surely thine hour has come, thy great wind blows,*
> *Far off, most secret, and inviolate Rose?*

Accordingly Yeats asserts, in a dedicatory note to his friend AE, that 'So far ... as this book is visionary it is Irish; for Ireland, which is still predominantly Celtic, has preserved with some less excellent things a gift of vision, which has died out among more hurried and more successful nations' (*SR*: vii). For the Irish countryside, where the stories are mainly set, is a magical territory of visionary possibility where the 'one subject' of the book – 'the war of spiritual with natural order' (*SR*: vii) – is waged as era succeeds era. It is that war indeed which accounts for that succession, in which solitary souls like magicians, quest heroes and the poet's surrogate, Red Hanrahan (a version of an eighteenth-century Gaelic poet, Eoghan Rua Ó Súilleabháin), aspire to eternal reality beyond the flux of time and the mortal veil.

In almost all the stories the truth is admitted that to seek such transcendence and transformation of the world will involve the loss, certainly, of the comforts of the common round, but probably the loss also of life itself. It was as if Yeats knew that the way in which he was willing to devote the stuff of his own experience to a magical ordering of its various elements in the symbolic dimension of artistic conjuration, was to risk a kind of emotional and psychological death, fatal to his 'innermost being'. The book begins with a grim intimation of this ghastly pre-occupation which reaches its apotheosis in the concluding mystical triptych in its complete form. In 'The Binding of the Hair', first published in *The Savoy* in January 1896, Yeats has the severed head of a poet serve as an emblem (the symbolism is too overt to be wholly successful) of ecstatic, visionary song, in praise of eternal beauty, as the weird fruit of the ultimate sacrifice. Even the lusty, philandering Hanrahan in the book finds fleshly love inadequate, in thrall as he is to the allure of a woman of the Shee (she is an Irish folkloric motif) to find himself, like a peasant version of Keats's pale and loitering knight in 'La Belle Dame Sans Merci', alone in a deathly desolation, 'shivering on the earthen floor' of a cave. It is at the moment of his death that earthly and spiritual love meet. He dies in the arms of an old hag, with the voice of his fairy bride (for they are one and the same) whispering in his ear: 'You will seek me no more upon the breast of women'.

The Secret Rose, especially in the full form in which the poet intended it first to appear, becomes an increasingly elaborate book as it proceeds. The sense of pattern and structure which is established early by chronology, in the last three tales becomes overwhelming. We enter a world where symbolic implication becomes so over-determined that it is a telling reminder of how a hierophantic, Pateresque style, a mesmeric incantatory, magisterial prose rhythm in the service of a religiose art, can crush the life out of a literary text which threatens to become no more than a book of occult rubrics, a *grimoire*. The emphasis on death as intimate with the moment of revelation, of personal and historical apocalypse as ever-present companion of 'immaterial ecstasy', alerts us, however, to Yeats's awareness of the stakes involved in the experiment in magic he was conducting with his own life and art as the constituent elements. The narrator in 'Rosa Alchemica', at the moment when vision is about to subsume him, renounces it, for he knows it will involve the loss of his personality, his very personhood. In 'The Tables of the Law', he realizes that that can be a spiritual death even more terrifying than physical dissolution, for he sees that 'the Order of the Alchemical Rose was not of this earth, and that it was still seeking over this earth for whatever souls it could gather within its glittering net' (*VSR*: 164)). He recognizes that to accept its hegemony would mean the loss of his very humanity and the end of communal existence. He fears: 'all I held dear, all that bound me to spiritual and social order would be burnt up, and my soul left naked and shivering among the winds that blow from beyond this world and from beyond the stars' (*VSR*: 164).

It is the conflict in *The Secret Rose* between commitment to vision and the feared death of the soul, that does give the book its literary impact. In 'The Tables of the Law', the narrator encounters one who admits 'I have lost my soul because I have looked out of the eyes of the angels.' Critics have read this central conflict in the text as the consequence of the doubts Yeats was beginning to feel about the kind of Faustian bargain he had struck with himself in making his life the material from which he would fashion an art in the service of magic (Watson 1991: xxxv). Certainly his mature poetry would dramatize the cost in frustration, deprivation and suffering which the decisions he took in the 1890s made likely. However the formality and authorial control of the book, its exquisite design which was executed to Yeats's satisfaction by Althea Gyles, an artist friend, its suggestion of an esoteric system of imagery and symbol hermetically sealed to all but occult initiates, gives the reader to believe that Yeats was prepared to risk all for the sake of vision. The work salutes an elite who might save the world and Yeats's text is their testament and prophetic book. Writing to John O'Leary in May 1897, Yeats described it as 'an honest attempt to wards that aristocratic esetoric Irish litera-ture, which has been my chief ambition' (*CL2*: 104). For his purposes in this work were less to dramatize a conflict within himself than to supply his nation with a volume that could inform the religious mind of an elite.

There are, however, signs in the work, as Pierce has argued (Pierce 1995: 52) that Yeats was troubled by the way in which his commitment to an elitist conception of a magical role for himself in Ireland could have difficult social consequences. He had already experienced the manner in which he could be marginalized as a Protestant, when he had suffered defeat at the hands of Duffy. As a poet/mage, adept of the Order of the Golden Dawn, at work on the Celtic Mysteries, he was even more vulnerable to a charge in Catholic Ireland that his brand of cultural nationalism was contaminated by an unacceptable paganism. Owen Aherne in 'The Tables of the Law' acknowledges that his moment of visionary sight from an angel's eyes has been bought at the cost of his own damnation. He accedes to the primacy of the Christian doctrine of sin and redemption, despite his moment of angelic vision. In 'The Adoration of the Magi', the narrator rejects a new annunciation of a sacred birth, and assures the reader, as he reflects on the Magi of the gospels who seem in quest of a new deity, about to come into the world: 'Whatever they were, I have turned into a pathway which will lead me from them, and from the Order of the Alchemical Rose' (*VSR* 171).

Ironically, the ending of the poet's affair with Shakespear, when the image of Gonne as the most beautiful woman in the world had once again begun to exercise the power over him that he had earlier determined it should, was to provide Yeats with an immediate Irish role. In that was to be combined leader-ship, significant popular esteem *and* an occult, spiritual idealism. For Gonne and he were to work together in the aftermath of the poet's affair with Shakespear in opposition to the Queen's Jubilee in Ireland and to participate in a nationwide effort to have the United Irish rebellion of 1798 inspiringly commemorated.

For Irish nationalists the 1890s were years of regrouping. The defeat and death of Parnell had seemed to set back the cause of Home Rule indefinitely (the second Home Rule Bill fell in 1893). Futhermore the obviously political energies which had sustained Parnell's long crusade for a form of independence now tended to find expression, not in the formerly effective obstructionist tactics of the Irish Parliamentary Party at Westminster, which was now bitterly split into pro- and anti-Parnell factions, but in pressure for land reform and control of local government which could be effected within the constitutional *status quo*. And 'Constructive Unionism' waited in the wings ready to seek to kill Home Rule with kindness, however much some people hoped land agitation would have constitutional implications. In the new century this would set in train the kind of land reform in Land Acts of 1903 and 1909 that should have eroded definitively the social base of separatist and republican ideology in the countryside. Revolutionary Fenianism in the 1890s, with its elitist vision of a radical vanguard leading the people to rebellion, seemed to many the fantastical fanaticism of the few, which only gained substance by means of its links with militant Irish nationalist factions in the United States. The huge crowds which turned out to greet Queen Victoria in Dublin in 1900 also suggested that Ireland was safely in the bosom of the Empire, whatever literary cultural nationalists with Fenian sympathies, like Yeats, or extreme revolutionary separatists, like Gonne cared to believe.

The impending Diamond Jubilee of the Queen of England three years earlier had been the catalyst which had re-energized Gonne's interest in direct action in Ireland. It had seemed outrageous to her that the Queen's long rule should be celebrated in Dublin. The revolutionary cabals of Dublin, London and the United States concurred, but could not agree about who should lead the protest movement, riven as they were by disputes and personality clashes. The centenary of the United Irish rebellion of 1798 had been identified as a date which could be exploited to fan the flames of rebellion in Ireland and in March 1897 John O'Leary chaired a well-attended meeting which set in motion the establishment in Ireland, Britain and the United States of Centenary Commemoration Committees. A primary aim of this movement was to erect a statue, at the head of Grafton Street in central Dublin, of the United Irish patriot and martyr Wolfe Tone. Gonne decided to go to America to help raise funds for this project, but found, so divided was the movement between its London and Dublin wings by the bitter and deadly disputes of the past, that she could not get the necessary authorization to speak officially for the cause. Yeats summoned the Londoners in the movement to a meeting in his rooms in Woburn Buildings where he had himself elevated by election to the post of chairman of the Executive Committee of the Centenary Association for Britain and France. He hoped thereby not only to provide Gonne with the chance she sought to fund-raise effectively, but to heal the divisions in the movement. For he also intended to persuade its members to establish a 'convention' which in time, as Irish political parties transferred their allegiance to it, could remove legislative authority from Britain to Ireland.

All this as the months went on, led Yeats, still profoundly shaken by the termination of his affair with Shakespear, into a good deal of dramatic posturing and stridently extreme rhetoric. His intentions, however, were rather those of the elitist magician who dreamed of restoring the Celtic Mysteries in Lough Key, to strengthen the leadership of the country, than the revolutionary agitator. He hoped what he was doing in the spiritual and political spheres would combine to allow Ireland a peaceful means of exit from a materialist empire that was assuredly destroying its soul. He could comfort himself, in these emotionally painful, even guilty, months, that he was pleasing Gonne by his commitment to action, but helping to ensure that action would not result in a bloody rebellion in which she would almost certainly perish.

The contradictions in his position quickly became apparent. With strategic intent, a Convention of the Centenary Committee in Dublin was to be held in the city on Jubilee Day itself, 22 June 1897. The socialist agitator James Connolly, also realizing the propaganda opportunity which the occasion offered, asked Gonne to speak at a Dublin meeting on the 21st. The meeting went ahead though not before a crowd of Trinity College students was prevented from protesting against the insult that was being paid to the English queen (*CL2*: 113). On the evening of the 22nd, after the Centenary Committe Convention, a street riot broke out as the police baton-charged a crowd outside the National Club in Rutland Square, causing many injuries. In the mêlée an old woman died.

In her account of the evening, Gonne states that she had to insist that she be allowed to leave the National Club, where Yeats and she had gone to view, on the windows of the Club premises there, a limelight show on national themes (*CL2*: 113). She wanted to join the action outside, though Yeats had locked the door of the Club to prevent her doing so. Yeats's version has him successful in restraint of his firebrand companion and immediately informing a Dublin newspaper that he had restrained her, to exonerate her from any charge of cowardice. Whatever the exact truth, Yeats found himself compromised when confronted by the call to arms. As if to indicate his chagrin, he had in fact lost his voice during the day's stresses. Gonne told him in a letter shortly afterwards in affectionate but firm terms that the '*outer* side of politics' (*GL*: 72) was not for him. She would not work with him where physical danger was involved.

Gonne's work over the next few months did not involve physical danger apart from the risks to her own health that she took as she followed a hectic schedule of speaking, organizing and travelling. Yeats accompanied her on a lecture tour in Scotland and the English Midlands before she sailed for America in October. Despite being accused of being a spy by one of the leaders of nationalist opinion there, she raised about $4,500 (*GL*: 79) for the cause. On her return she and Yeats spent time together in the west of Ireland communing with the Celtic spirits of the land. Famine was again threatening mass starvation, and the movement to commemorate the dead of 1798 became linked to the memory of the famine dead of the hungry forties. Gonne embarked on a policy of resistance and attempted to organize a relief scheme, but in highly politicized terms. She made Mayo, where the French had landed in 1798 and where hunger was gnawing intensely, the focus of her campaign. She felt that she could stir a crowd and become a figure in the popular imagination. In old age she recalled how the peasantry rallied to her in Mayo. She remembered 'the confused murmur of [a] great throng and the strange soft sound of thousands of bare feet beating on the hard earth' (MacBride 1994: 255), though a government agent reported at the time that her meetings were poorly attended (Balliett 1979: 25).

It was, though, a time for crowds. The prospect of the centenary of 1798 was releasing something in the Irish masses which had not found expression since the monster meetings called by Daniel O'Connell in the 1820s and 1840s. Now however, the crowds were gathering not to demand emancipation or repeal of the Union, but to honour the heroes of militant republican separatism. The statuary erected in many towns and villages at this time, though Yeats was to find it vulgar and unappealing, bore witness to the fact that the tradition of Irish armed rebellion still had an imaginative purchase on many Irish minds at a level beneath the apparent passivity of the population at large. The blend of this military symbolism with Catholic iconography of sacrifice and bloodshed, with processions that seemed at once ceremonial celebration and funeral cortège, gave to mass meetings the quasi-mystical appeal of some religious, even occult, gathering. In a culture where funerary traditions were potent ritual expressions of communal solidarity there was a sense that a people was at last defining sacred, cultural spaces for itself in the modernized cityscape.

The site in Dublin for the Tone monument was chosen to assert that Protestant Unionist Dublin did not have full authority over the city's imagination or memory. The dedication of the stone on which the monument was to stand (in the event the statue was not put in place and Tone is today commemorated nearby in the modern city) was the great event of the centenary year. As one historian has commented, reflecting on what had amounted to 'a unique experiment in mass education' (Owens 106), 'this was the most concentrated outpouring of commemorative statuary that Ireland had ever seen' (Owens 109). Yeats declared that 'Ireland was appealing to the past to escape the confusions of the present' (cited Owens 1994: 106). Gonne, though she confessed herself disappointed with the impact of the centenary in general, sensed how the past was reasserting itself among the great crowds which had gathered in many places, almost like some revenant from the racial memory: 'the preparations for it had been the really important part, for it had given an opportunity to bring the hope of complete independence and of the means of its attainment – Wolfe Tone's means – slumbering in the hearts of the whole Irish race, to the surface consciousness of the people' (MacBride 1994: 259).

Although the period following his break with Shakespear was one of deep unhappiness for Yeats, at least he had the satisfaction during work for the Centenary Commemoration of seeing how the idea of a life lived so that it might be the material of art, of living sculpture indeed, was certainly no idle dream for which he had already sacrificed too much. For Gonne at this time seemed to be making of herself an image possessed of magical powers that could sway the multitude and embody its unified mind. He remembered when her 'power over crowds was at its height' how

> Her beauty, backed by her great stature, could instantly affect an assembly, and not, as often with our stage beauties, because obvious and florid, for it was

incredibly distinguished, and if – as must be that it might seem that assembly's very self, fused, unified, and solitary – her face, like the face of some Greek statue, showed little thought, her whole body seemed a master-work of long labouring thought. (*Au*: 364)

The living statue shattered in December 1898. Yeats had been keeping a notebook of his dreams and visions since the previous summer. He and Gonne had both experimented with hashish, and Yeats also tried mescalin, in pursuit of altered states of consciousness. They were accustomed to the experience of out-of-body awareness and believed the spirit could act independently of the body. On the night of 6 December the nature of the poet's frequent dreams of Gonne changed dramatically: 'I woke in my hotel somewhere near Rutland Square with the fading vision of her face bending over mine and the knowledge that she had just kissed me' (*Mem*: 131). Apparently what made this so new was that it was the first time in his dream and visionary life that a kiss between them had been mutual (Toomey, 1992: 96). They met after breakfast, for Yeats punctiliously insisted that when they were in Dublin they should stay in separate hotels, and the poet told her what had occurred. That evening, after they had dined together, as Yeats records it, she announced ' "I will tell you now what happened. When I fell asleep last night I saw standing at my bedside a great spirit. He took me to a great throng of spirits, and you were among them. My hand was put into yours and I was told that we were married. After that I remember nothing." Then and there for the first time with the bodily mouth, she kissed me' (*Mem*: 132). The next day she confessed all the facts of her life, some of which Yeats had heard about through innuendo and dismissed as impossible. He heard of how as a girl she had made a pact with the devil if he would give her 'control over her own life' (ibid.). Within a fortnight her father had died. He heard moreover how she had been Millevoye's mistress and had borne him two children. He must have been especially shocked when she told him how Millevoye and she had made love in the vault under the memorial chapel where her first-born was buried, in the hope that his soul might be reincarnated in another child. He heard about the now four-year-old child of that encounter, the daughter she had named Iseult.

The outcome of this extraordinary moment was a 'spiritual marriage' begun in a shared vision. On 17 December, as Yeats recalled, they were sitting together when Gonne said:

'I hear a voice saying "You are about to receive the initiation of the spear." ' We became silent; a double vision unfolded itself, neither speaking till all was finished. She thought herself a great stone statue though which passed flame, and I felt myself becoming flame and mounting up through and looking out of the eyes of a great stone Minerva. Were the beings which stand behind human life trying to unite us, or had we brought it by our own dreams? She was now very emotional, and would kiss me very tenderly, but when I spoke of marriage on the eve of her leaving said, 'No, it seems to me impossible.' And then, with clenched hands, 'I have a horror and terror of physical love.' (*Mem*: 134)

Love on the astral plane in a spiritual marriage which Gonne offered did not lack intensity and erotic implication, however impossible these were at the sublunary level. Gonne made that clear when she wrote from Paris in graphically phallic terms at the end of the month about a vision of her Initiation of the Spear in which Lug, the Celtic god of the sun, appeared to purify her for service against the forces of darkness and the enemies of Eire: 'He touched me on the chest with the spear & I fell down on the ground & the fountain of fire played over me' (*GYL*: 99).

Yet what exactly had transpired between Gonne and Yeats when she had told him of their marriage and they had kissed for the first time? Was she merely tantalizing him or was her behaviour, as Harwood imagines, 'the expression of a temporary outpouring of emotion' (Harwood 1989: 89) from which she soon recovered? Or was it, as Deirdre Toomey argues, that Gonne was at last prepared to marry Yeats, but the poet recoiled from the prospect. Sensing hesitation and rejection on Yeats's part in the days following her 'confession' and moment of erotic vulnerability, Gonne, a sensitive woman, co-operated in the idea of a spiritual marriage which she and Yeats jointly developed from then on. Accordingly, and in order to save both their feelings, she pleaded sexual inhibition in a final renunciation, when Yeats did propose once more on 18 December. Foster reckons that, neither of them knowing what they wanted, 'in a sense they both backed off' (*AM* 203). Lady Gregory noted in her diary how ill Gonne looked on that painful day: 'Instead of beauty' she saw 'a death's head' (Gregory 1996: 197).

Harwood offers an important speculation on all this. For he believes mystical sexual union was all Yeats really desired of his 'fairy bride' at this time, since, in a period when he was still exceptionally insecure following the break with Shakespear, such an arrangement 'probably released him from the most self-destructive aspects of his obsession' (Harwood 1989: 90) with Gonne. Indeed he argues that Gonne's confession of her affair with Millevoye may have saved his life, since it woke him out of a morbid fascination for dissolution as the inevitable end of a doomed love: 'Yeats's later, ambivalent preoccupation with the doomed Rhymers perhaps reflects the sense that he came close to sharing their fate' (Harwood 1992: 25).

Certainly spiritual marriage, which Yeats probably preferred to the demands of conventional married life with Gonne and her daughter, saved something from this emotional muddle for the poet as poet. It obviated the immediate need for him to confront how profound a challenge to his aesthetic and his view of the world had been posed by Gonne's shocking revelations. Though he knew that challenge assuredly existed, for on 26 December, 1898 he confessed to Lady Gregory: 'I feal that the seas & the hills has been upheaved..... My whole imagination has shifted its foundation' (*CL2*: 329). And he perhaps realized then that the past reality of his relationship with Gonne over almost a decade was not something which in the future could easily be raised to the symbolist and magical levels of an art invested with occult power. He could however let residual aspirations to such an aesthetic find expression, after the crisis, in the zone of spiritual communion and the visions it might offer as poetic inspiration. Immediate marriage to Gonne would in all likelihood have meant a huge, perhaps disabling challenge to his sense of life and art.

The poet's emotional stratagem to meet this dilemma was only temporarily efficacious. For the Yeats who believed he had sacrificed living on the quotidian plane with Shakespear for the higher destiny of art and magic, in which an unrequited love for Gonne played a crucial part, had now discovered that he had comprehensively risked his peace of mind for almost ten years in seeking to make a transformed version of his life the material of a revelatory, powerful art. His response to Gonne as a living person began to torment him: 'Many a time since then' (he wrote, referring to the time when he first heard from Gonne of her complex past), 'as I lay awake at night, have I accused myself of acting, not as I thought from a high scruple, but from a dread of moral responsibility, and my thoughts have gone round and round, as do miserable thoughts, coming to no solution' (*Mem*: 133). For history – embodied in the undeniable, living reality of another's complex, flawed experience – had taken its revenge. Symbolism alone, even when possessed of magical powers, could not, it seemed, cope with the shocking challenges of actuality. A 'spiritual marriage' and a dream of collabora-tive work for an Order of Celtic Mysteries might help to susain his art (if it could not assuage his conscience), or so he perhaps hoped in the confusion of his emotional situation.

That was not to be. For as Roy Foster's detailed narrative in *W. B. Yeats: The Apprentice Mage* suggests, the developing moods of the spiritual marriage con-tracted in troubled fashion in 1898 paradoxically involved for Yeats over the following five years a deepening, though chaste love for Gonne, which replaced the besotted excitement of youthful infatuation. Yet this new stage in their relationship could neither attain to the satisfactions of marital love, nor prove adequate fully to renew his poetic. In the crisis of December 1898 and its aftermath of unconsummated love for an actual woman, the poet needed resources other than symbolism and spiritual escapism if he was to survive into full maturity as a man and artist. Although he would continue to defend the efficacy of symbolism for some years to come (in such essays as 'Magic' and 'The Symbolism of Poetry') it was upon the enabling powers of drama and mythology, which he had already begun to exploit as an artist in the 1890s, that his imaginative survival would increasingly come to depend in the new century.

5

Patronage and Powers

On 4 February 1909 Yeats recorded in a journal entry how he had received a very disturbing letter, telling of a serious illness that had struck Lady Gregory. He was distraught:

> She has been to me mother, friend, sister and brother. I cannot realize the world without her − she brought to my wavering thoughts steadfast nobility. All day the thought of losing her is like a conflagration in the rafters. Friendship is all the house I have. (*Mem*: 161−1)

Yeats had first met Lady Augusta Gregory of Coole Park, near Gort in County Galway, in London in 1894. Her husband Sir William Gregory had died in 1892 and she had inherited his estate in trust for her only son Robert. Augusta Gregory was the seventh daughter of Dudley Persse of Roxborough, also in County Galway. The Persses had been Irish notables since at least the seventeenth century and she accordingly numbered among her ancestors the soldiers, churchmen and government officials who had constituted the ruling elite in Ireland since 1690. Her marriage to Sir William in 1880 had brought her immediately in contact with contemporary grandees in the British polity, for her husband had recently retired as governor of Ceylon and he enjoyed access to and friendship with socially powerful members of the British establishment. During her married years she had frequently travelled with Sir William on excursions in Europe, in Egypt and in India and she had moved in a world of ambassadors, aristocrats and such gifted men of achievement as Heinrich Schliemann, the discoverer of the remains of Troy. In girlhood she had shared the Unionist political attitudes of her caste, but her nature was touched with an ethical intensity that in her teens had found expression in an evangelical conviction of personal salvation and individual calling to a life of good works. She had felt a kinship with the self-sacrificing heroine of George Eliot's novel *Middlemarch* when, as a young woman, she had contemplated her forthcoming marriage to the elderly and twice-widowed Sir

William. Her youthful religious intensity (and she never abandoned the practice of her Anglican faith), in adulthood was directed by a deep sense of duty, which made her often seem a formidable, even a chilling, presence. Yet her immediate family included enough black sheep to suggest that a strain of wildness ran in the blood. Augusta Gregory was susceptible to the charms of adventurers and poets. She had found brief adventure and poetry in the arms of Wilfrid Scawen Blunt, the promiscuous, anti-imperialist Englishman with whom she had a passionate affair in 1882 and 1883. They had found common cause in Egyptian nationalism.

Following the death of her husband, Lady Gregory took to wearing black, as if in perpetual mourning, but also one suspects as a signal that she did not intend to fall sexually from grace again (the poems she wrote of that experience mingle gratitude with guilt; she did in fact have at least one love affair during her long widowhood). Collecting a poet, whom she could manage and support and make a collaborator in some great work, was by contrast very much on the agenda. That such a poet would be Irish rather than English, was determined by the fact that Lady Gregory had come to understand that the Irish cause, like the Egyptian, was a just one, and that the fortunes of her own landowning caste were dependent on the goodwill of the majority population of Catholic tenants. For a governing principle of Lady Gregory's busy and dutiful life was that her son should eventually enjoy Coole Park as his seat, in the way his ancestors had done. In an era of anti-landlord agitation, which the Land War of the 1880s had inaugurated, and eventual revolution, this was to prove an enduringly difficult and ultimately fruitless task. Robert Gregory died in action in the Great War, and after Lady Gregory's death, the house at Coole fell into dereliction and eventually was demolished.

Yeats first saw Coole, not perhaps in its heyday, but when the evidence of the kind of life it had represented was all about. In the summer of 1896, Arthur Symons and he visited Ireland together to enjoy the West and to journey to the little known Aran Islands, off the west coast of County Galway. They put up for a time in the home of another Co. Galway landlord with literary tastes and ambition, Edward Martyn of Tillyra Castle. There Yeats had outraged his almost pathologically pious Catholic host by invoking lunar power in a room directly over the house's private chapel. Yeats had recently been troubled by the direction of his work and felt at an impasse. He had sought the clairvoyant advice of Olivia Shakespear who had supplied advice in sentences 'unintelligible to herself' (*Mem*: 100): 'He is too much under solar influence. He is to live near water and to avoid woods, which concentrate the solar power' (ibid.). On the ninth night of lunar evocations Yeats was granted a vision, which was to obsess him for years to come. What made it even more impressive a visitation was the fact that Symons had dreamed a similar dream on the same night (Yeats would soon afterwards learn moreover that the writer William Sharp/'Fiona Macleod' had published a story which included imagery of the kind Yeats had seen in his vision). As he fell asleep in Tillyra he saw 'a centaur and then a marvellous naked woman shooting an arrow at a star. She stood like a statue upon a stone pedestal, and the flesh tints of her body seemed to make all human flesh in contrast seem unhealthy' (ibid.). All was portents and premonitions, expectation of some new door about to open. The door of Coole Park was a portal Yeats was ready to cross.

Lady Gregory had called with an invitation for Yeats, whom she had first met in 1894. A long, wonderfully supportive relationship had begun when on about 10 August Yeats had driven over to Coole with Martyn. He had found a *home* for the first time. There were woods at Coole, against which he had been warned, but there was a lake and Yeats quickly convinced himself: 'I had evoked only the moon and water' (ibid.: 101). He could see that Coole could be important to him.

The house, although not by any means a great house on a European or English scale, was comfortable enough. It was furnished and decorated in a manner which reflected good taste, familial power and the accumulation of a stable inheritance. The drawing-room and breakfast-room boasted William Morris wallpaper (Gregory 1971: 58; 67). The library held an impressive collection of vellum-bound volumes. Family portraits mixed with a print of Pitt and a portrait of Burke; there was also a portrait of Gladstone (Pierce 1995: 235). Yeats was attracted by a vision of domestic order, for which he had no personal responsibility, of a kind he had never before known. Lady Gregory had found her Irish poet (at the outset she may have been a little in love with him) and in the soil of mutual need grew a relationship of deep obligation, creative collaboration and a degree of opportunistic exploitation, at least on Yeats's part. It has been astutely observed by John Kelly that Lady Gregory drew Yeats into her world by her assured ability to act as a surrogate mother (Kelly 1987: 194–8). In the summer of 1897, when their relationship flowered, the poet's health was at a dangerously low ebb. The aftermath of his affair with Shakespear had left him guilty and emotionally confused. The Jubilee had been a crisis of another sort. He spent two summer months at Coole enjoying Lady Gregory's devoted ministrations. It was the start of a habit which for more than fifteen years would see the poet spend part of every summer in his Galway 'home'. He had found what he knew he had always wanted, 'a life of order and of labour, where all outward things were the image of an inward life' (*Mem*: 101). As he confessed later of his early years at Coole: 'In the second, as during the first visit my nervous system was worn out. The toil of dressing in the morning exhausted me and Lady Gregory began to send me cups of soup when I was called' (ibid.: 125–6). In 1899 he spent from May to November settled at Coole.

Lady Gregory's solicitous motherliness was not restricted to the regime of healthy food and exercise which she imposed in Galway. It extended to London where she kept a flat for her frequent visits to the capital. Yeats had held on to his rooms in Woburn Buildings when Shakespear had gone sorrowing away. Lady Gregory tried to make them more comfortable, sending him new curtains along with gifts of wine, biscuits, bottled fruit, food-hampers – in time an armchair. Even Yeats, used to accepting hospitality where it was available, especially from older, attentive women, felt a little embarrassed. He wrote to his benefactor: 'I have a kind of feeling that I ought not to let you do all these little kind things for me, things I should do for myself' (cited in Saddlemyer and Smythe 1987: 200). Yet Augusta Gregory knew what she was doing and her relationship with the poet, thirteen years younger than herself, was by no means just a matter of maternal feeling, mixed with some sexual interest, finding an object beyond her only child (Lady Gregory came of a large family, so she may have felt maternally unfulfilled). She had plans for Yeats; and there were elements too in her relationship with him akin to that between a demanding father and his uncertain son. She was determined to get Yeats working in a more regular fashion and to set his life in the order it had so signally lacked throughout the 1890s. She wanted to . make sure he would fulfil his promise and, perhaps, to share in the acclaim that would follow success.

Yeats, as we have seen, had been highly impressionable as a young man to strong, surrogate father figures. O'Leary, Morris, even Henley had all occupied the role of substitute father-figure for a time in their various ways. He himself had recognized the deficiencies of J. B. Yeats as a father and the dangers of the enervating atmosphere of the household over which he so ineffectually reigned. He told a friend many years later how distressed he had been as a young man by his father's 'infirmity of will which . . . prevented him from finishing his pictures and ruined his career . . . I had to escape this family drifting, innocent and helpless, and the need for that drew me to dominating men like Henley and Morris and estranged me from his friends' (cited in Reid 1968: 493–4). Now he was drawn into the orbit of a dominating woman. Lady Gregory not only had the table set at regular hours, but made sure that the poet had clean nibs, paper and ink ready each day. She was displeased when his early visits did not prove creatively or professionally fruitful (Pethica 1992: 64).

There were real grounds for concern for Yeats in these years. His health could be established through a sound diet and settled habits, but both his social role and his ability to support himself were uncertain. Money was almost always a problem. Yeats had reached what was a decent income in 1896 when, thanks to handsome rates paid by *The Savoy* he had 'probably earned close to £200' (ibid.: 89). A publisher at the end of December 1896 had offered him £105 as an advance on royalties (his first) for an autobiographical novel. He had received the first half of this in twenty-five weekly instalments, but the work, although it grew to a document of 150,000, words caused Yeats great difficulty and was to be abandoned in 1902. The weekly subvention his Uncle George allowed him, for a time, in the mid-1890s was probably withdrawn on account of Yeats's nationalistic activities leading up to the Queen's Jubilee. Furthermore, as Toomey has pointed out, in the emotionally intense eighteen months after Gonne's confession Yeats dried up poetically. She explains the monetary consequences of this block: 'Poetry was better paid than prose at this time. Thus this eighteen-month hiatus represents a financial as well as an artistic disaster. Yeats could get on average £5 for a lyric poem, yet only £15 for a long article: in fact in the summer of 1899, the *North American Review* offered him a fee of £20 for a poem, which he was unable to supply, although this sum would have represented two months income' (Toomey 1992: 125). Lady Gregory's support of Yeats during this crisis and for some years to come extended to financial advances that carried him through lean periods. Over a span of five or six years she subsidized him to the tune of about £500, which made her subventions to Yeats a significant item in her personal budget (Pethica 1992: 65–6) and a real cushion for him.

Throughout the 1890s Yeats had felt himself a slave to literary journalism. It had kept the wolf from the door, but had eaten into the time he would have preferred to have given to his art. In 1897 he told Robert Bridges, 'one has to give something of one's self to the devil that one may live. I have given my criticism' (*CL2*: 111). Lady Gregory's support helped him to escape the treadmill of constant reviewing (in the 1890s he published about seventy-five reviews, as well as a good deal of other literary journalism). So it was while he was holidaying with his patron at a County Galway shooting lodge in July 1899 that he wrote to his sister 'Lily': 'I have made up my mind to review no more books because, though it brings in money more quickly [than his more creative work], it gets me into all kinds of difficulties & quarrels & wastes my time' (ibid.: 433). Although he did not obey this self-denying ordinance completely he felt freed to choose more circumspectly the literary proposals he would entertain (articles on Shakespeare's plays for a volume of his own essays, an introduction to his own selection of Spenser's poems, undertaken in 1901 and 1902 respectively). In May 1901 he felt sufficiently confident of his marketability as a man of letters (Lady Gregory's subventions allowed him to sustain that increasingly archaic role in the era of professionalism) to appoint A. P. Watt as his literary agent in respect of all publishing matters – though muddles about legal rights and copyright in Britain and in North America, following more than a decade in which he had handled his own literary career, must also have influenced this decision.

The patronage Yeats now enjoyed did more than release him from much prosaic drudgery. It also helped to resolve the problem of his social role as an unmarried man who lacked the resources to establish himself in a permanent home of his own. Lady Gregory noted in her diary that Yeats told her how the hard struggle he had endured in the past, had induced a 'bitter feeling of degradation' (Gregory 1996: 151). This had haunted him for a long time. Now, without any feeling of humiliation, he could retain his rooms in Woburn Buildings, where, amid the rackety seediness of the district, he was looked after adequately by a loyal housekeeper, Mrs Old. He had a bohemian perch in the middle of a city where his professional life as a writer lay. He could hold his weekly 'evenings' there on Monday nights, when literary and artistic guests would assemble for conversation and debate. For he knew that for several weeks each year he could find comfort and consideration for his needs in the Coole that increasingly became an Irish base. It was this regular rhythm in his life that would enable him to keep a foot in the camp of Irish cultural politics and annually to renew his imaginative links with the landscape and associations of the Irish countryside, while maintaining the London *pied-à-terre* that made him an exotic, sought-after figure in the English capital's literary and social scene. And all this on a limited budget, for the basic rent in Woburn Buildings was never more than £50 per annum (*CL2*: 727).

Guests at Yeats's 'evenings' (he was known in the district as 'the toff what lives in the buildings', Mikhail 1977: 47) would have found Yeats's rooms impressively appropriate to his poetic vocation, combining as they did the spartan with the carefully deliberate artistic statement. Without electric light, they were a shrine to art and magic. Yeats in fact kept his own small shrine in his apartments (*CL3*: 303). A copy of Morris's Kelmscott Press Chaucer on a blue lectern was tribute to one of Yeats's first mentors (it was the gift of admirers on Yeats's fortieth birthday in 1905), while the Blake engravings on the walls were a testament to a principal imaginative and spiritual source. There was a favourite Jack Yeats painting too, *Memory Harbour*, works by his father, highlighting what a remarkable family these Yeatses were. As the years passed the poet improved his London quarters (a gas stove was a great addition) and took over more of the house.

It was well that a degree of security had become a possibility for Yeats at this time and that Lady Gregory had made a regular pattern of life available to him. For as the nineteenth gave way to the twentieth century there was much both in his personal and public life to disturb his always shaky emotional and physical equilibrium. The home at Coole where he knew he could find the stability he had never known before, was of immense importance to him as crisis followed crisis over the next decade.

The turmoil of Yeats's emotional life in the years which brought his affair with Shakespear and the 'mystical marriage' with Gonne following her confession, creates the climate of feeling in the poet's collection of 1899, *The Wind Among the Reeds*. This volume contains poems which Yeats had written for Maud Gonne as far back as 1892 and 1893, together with poems written before, during and after his affair with Shakespear, but before Gonne's confession. It is preoccupied, in an oppressively moody atmosphere redolent of imminent disaster, with 'youth's bitter burden', the travail of love. Though a few poems do still inhabit the geography and tonal register of a recognizably Irish balladry (especially 'The Host of the Air' and 'The Fiddler of Dooney'), the territory this volume occupies is a landscape of the unconscious, appropriated for consciousness in a poetic which seems to demand of symbolism its ultimate revelatory powers.

Yeats himself, in a note published in 1908, stated that he 'had so meditated over the images' in this volume that they had become 'true symbols' and had seemed accordingly 'part of a mystic language, which seemed always as if it would bring some strange revelation' (*VP*: 800). In the poems all is suggestion, twilight intimations of transcendence, iconography deployed as if in some temple of occult wisdom:

> The dew-cold lilies ladies bore
> Through many a sacred corridor
> Where such gray clouds of incense rose
> That only the god's eyes did not close...
> ('Michael Robartes Remembers Forgotten Beauty')

Language seems to be employed at its most ritualistic, least denotively precise, as if to indicate that it attends to a moment when vague suggestion itself must give way to a quite new form of spiritual communication. In this shadowland of half-tints and curiously ill-defined imagery ('candle-like foam on the dim sand', 'Aedh Gives his Beloved Certain Rhymes'), a narrative of sorts is apparently played out as a psycho-pageant realized as formal, static tableaux (Yeats himself referred to the poems, 'curiously elaborate in style', he had composed for Shakespear; *Mem*: 86). In this the poet, represented by three imaginary personae – Aedh, Michael Robartes and Hanrahan (Robartes and Hanrahan already familiar as figures in *The Secret Rose* and the triptych with which that volume was to have concluded) – passively contemplates love in its mortal and immortal guises. He rouses himself to moods of momentary self-assertion, which are easily subsumed in a more general acquiescence and self-abasement, in despair before the powers of the universe. In one of the extensive, often less than explanatory notes which Yeats appended to the poems in the collection, the poet informed his readers that he had used personae in his book 'more as principles of the mind than as actual personages' (*TWATR*: 73). Yet these shadowy figures are apparently caught in a love triangle which bears loosely on the poet's own situation. This gives the volume such limited dramatic tension as it possesses.

The love triangle in *The Wind Among the Reeds* involves the poet in his several personae seeking respite from the overwhelming powers of the universe in a bodily relationship with a woman whose hair (and hair threads through the volume as a token of erotic entanglement) forms a protective tent in which, as lover, he seeks sanctuary. He is in thrall nevertheless to the image of a perfected woman, a lost love, ardour for whom involves death and dissolution. Harwood, who has studied this period of Yeats's life in detail and who relates it scrupulously to the poetry, wisely counsels against reading the work in a directly biographical way. He demonstrates how the book brings together 'a cluster of female attributes to form a composite icon which could be associated with either woman' (Harwood 1989: 73). Yet the volume does revolve around a mortal love, which had, it seems, offered impermanent fulfilments, sacrificed in pursuit of an ideal beauty:

> Though I am old with wandering
> Through hollow lands and hilly lands,
> I will find out where she has gone,
> And kiss her lips and take her hands;
> And walk among long dappled grass,
> And pluck till time and times are done,
> The silver apples of the moon,
> The golden apples of the sun.
> ('The Song of Wandering Aengus')

Harwood summarizes:

The poems in *The Wind Among the Reeds*, read in chronological order, form a relatively coherent narrative. The early, ambivalent longing for union with the immortals, presented through myth and folklore, is set in opposition to the attraction of the mortal beloved in the poems of 1895–6. But the seductive power of the immortals is then transferred to the poet's quasi-immortal 'lost love', for whom he surrenders the mortal beloved, and is left helpless and desolate in consequence. The chronology of this unfolding pattern fits exactly with that of the parallel events in Yeats's life. (Harwood 1989: 79)

Harwood rightly insists that Yeats may not have been fully conscious of how much this book revealed of his own situation. Concerned to protect his privacy the poet may nevertheless have directed attention in the notes to the complex occult significance of the text to prevent readers drawing any biographical conclusions. Be that as it may, as he waited in Paris in February 1899 for news about the book's imminent publication which had been delayed by technical problems, he certainly must have been all too aware that his volume bore only partly on the unhappy, complicated truth of the decade through which he had lived. For Gonne was also in the city and it was made definitively clear to him that no marriage with her was possible. He must accordingly have felt that the obfuscation of his forthcoming book's biographical origins was fortunate indeed, given what he then had come to know. Harwood is also right to highlight as he does the apocalyptic atmosphere which prevails in the volume, for it is the chiliastic note that gives to many of the poems an aura of universality, as if personal turmoil is an aspect of a wider calamity.

Yeats was not alone in nurturing apocalyptic imaginings as the century drew to its close. Apocalypsism was a fairly widely shared apprehension in his circle. He and the Mathers, husband and wife, had even shared a vision of Armageddon. In 1895 Yeats had written to Florence Farr to alert her to the possibility that the international political situation seemed a fulfilment of that and other millenarian prophecies; 'what a dusk of the nations it would be!' (*CL1*: 477). In June 1896 AE had written to him that he believed in Ireland there was 'a hurrying of forces and swift things going out' (Denson 1961: 17). AE had declared, 'I believe profoundly that a new Avatar is about to appear and in all spheres the forerunners go before him to prepare' (ibid.). In mid-1897 AE wrote to tell his friend that he sensed the whereabouts of the Avatar who 'lives in a little whitewashed cottage ... in Donegal or Sligo' (cited in Kuch 1986: 119). That summer Yeats and AE spent time looking for Russell's Avatar, a middle-aged man, with a grey golden beard and hair. In Sligo they talked of Yeats's Castle of the Heroes and shared a vision of the supernatural beings whom Russell regularly entertained in his mind's eye. In the months following Yeats was haunted by the possibility of some apocalyptic event.

Yeats's doom-laden yearnings in *The Wind Among the Reeds*, strike a note of real terror in an artfully arranged text. Harwood goes so far as to attribute the undeniable energies that give one of the poems in the volume – 'The Valley of the Black Pig' – its rhetorical sweep in celebration of destruction, to the state of Yeats's troubled emotions as a frustrated lover during the years when the poems in this volume were composed. Yeats was trapped by the inadequacies of his own nature and the excruciating consequences of the symbolist aesthetic he had espoused in compensation. He was trammelled in the paradox that he could gain occult power as man and poet only through the ultimate sacrifice of himself, which is no power at all:

Yeats's invocations of apocalypse are another manifestation of that self-division which locates power and energy outside, and effectively inaccessible to, the poet. More specifically, the longing for the end can be read as a manifestation of dissociated anger: the turmoil of the heavens is the poet's projected on a cosmic scale. Given Yeats's acknowledged misery and self-flagellation during the years 1897 to 1899, it is hardly surprising that the volume contains some heavily displaced expressions of frustrated rage.　(Harwood, *Shakespear and Yeats* 80)

The dilemma explored with more composure and fictional distance in *The Secret Rose*, in this view of things, has become monstrously personal because it threatens emotional and actual annihilation.

Certainly Yeats's self-obsession in the final years of the century and in the early years of the new one give good grounds for accepting that this volume of lyric poems is charged with biographical implication, however disguised that is by the elaboration of the symbolism and the implied presence of an occult system determining the order and contents of a *grimoire*. The fact too that the evidence for that self-obsession is the autobiographical novel (*The Speckled Bird*, posthumously published with variant versions) Yeats was working on before and after the publication of *The Wind Among the Reeds*, adds weight to the argument. For that inchoate, self-communing and uncertainly inward work is an unfinished autobiographical *roman à clef*. Set in Paris, the west of Ireland and London it seeks to explore the relationship between the central character's life and the way the world and love are represented to him in iconographic and symbolist terms. In the highly subjective prose of a novel that sought to explore the poet's own experience of transforming his life into art, Yeats could not achieve the measured authority of form and structure that is so much an aspect of the artful poetic sequence, with its repeated motifs of wind, roses, hair, lips, iconographic female presences, mortal lover and demon lover and its subtly modulated prosodic effects. Yet the emotional pressure that makes *The Speckled Bird* a heady, intensely felt if muddled performance, breaks through in the much more managed sequence as a combined fear and relish of terminal things, anguish and despair in face of 'evil in the crying of wind' ('Hanrahan Reproves the Curlew').

The overall impression created by *The Wind Among the Reeds*, Yeats's most structurally organized book of poems in the nineteenth century (although some contemporary critics complained of its recondite imagery, Arthur Symons insisted that it expressed 'the elemental desires of humanity'; *CH*: 113), is of a poet seeking to gain authority over his own overwrought emotions and the divisions in his nature. The self cannot be represented as singular and in control but in the various personae of the text, all of them, in their several ways, in thrall to the complex lure of the feminine. Yet such self-division and ambiguous longing is denied substantial dramatic impact since these figures are to be read as principles and not as dynamic energies in their own right (from this requirement derives, in part, the tableau-like quality of the work as a whole). As such, they must be held in significant place by a system of mystical doctrine which the detailed notes indicate is the framework maintaining the structure of the text. Self and experience may be incoherent and fissiparous to the point of breakdown, but system is imposed according to a detailed, if only partially revealed, set of doctrines, rituals and symbols, which holds the world momentarily in place, though apocalypse threatens. As Steven Putzel succinctly states: 'the notes become a dictionary that almost forces us to read the poems as part of a mystic code. As a result, we are encouraged to see the connections between the poems and Yeats's folkloric and occult research, as well as the connections between the poems themselves' (Putzel 1986: 169). It is as if such order as the work achieves is both established and guaranteed by the existence of a body of knowledge which has been codified and given a stamp of institutional authenticity. When as a child Yeats felt the need of a faith to replace orthodox Christianity he had made up his own, with the vulnerability that entailed. Now as an adult undergoing a profound crisis in his personal life, he could depend (in a way which would recur at further crisis points in his turbulent life) not only on a set of doctrines to maintain order among his emotions but on a living community with its institutional authority to calm his mind with a sense of acquired power. That community was of course the Order of the Golden Dawn.

Yeats had invested a lot in the Order of the Golden Dawn. It was imperative to him that it was in fact conducted with decorum, for upon it, he must have sensed, significantly depended the possibility of a creative exchange between his own life and his art after the crisis of 1898. It was appalling when events in 1900 and 1901 threatened to split the Order into quarrelling factions. The poet threw himself into the struggle to save it from itself with a determination and imperious energy that betrays how crucial a role it played in his imagination and sense of reality.

The trouble affected the second level of the Order into which Yeats had been received so ceremoniously in 1893. MacGregor Mathers had settled in Paris in 1892. However authoritative he must have seemed when Yeats was received, distance from London diminished his influence. To remind the London adepts of their obligations to him he had demanded that they submit to his authority in writing. He expelled one recalcitrant member, Annie Horniman, in 1896. Following a resignation, which may have been engineered by Mathers, Florence Farr, whom Yeats had so admired in Todhunter's play, took over as leader. She decided to abandon examinations as a means of procedure through the various levels of the Order and allowed factions to form as secret 'groups', dedicated to various kinds of magic and experiment. She herself was a devotee of Egyptian mysteries. Yeats maintained contact with Mathers, despite these unsettling developments, working with him, as we have seen, on the symbolism for his own projected Order of Celtic Mysteries. In 1899 their relationship cooled. In 1900 it froze.

Mathers sensed that power was slipping from his hands. By now the figure whom Yeats had so admired was lost in the maze of egomania, paranoia and an ostentatious eccentricity, which rendered him a deranged stray from a Bulwer-Lytton novel (he had declared himself in a fit of bravura, Celtic extravagance and self-delusion, 'the Comte de Glenstrae'). He announced that he alone was in touch with the Secret Spirits upon whose instructions the Order depended. The foundational documents that the London adepts revered, he denounced as fraudulent. A committee was formed in London, against Mathers' orders, to assess the matter. Yeats and Farr were members. Mathers was having none of it and despatched the subsequently notorious wizard Aleister Crowley to enforce discipline by force. Crowley surpassed even Mathers in his passion for self-advertisement and outrageous claims of diabolic power. He entered the headquarters of the Order in Hammersmith on 17 April 1900, to occupy it in the name of Mathers. Farr summoned the law and Crowley was expelled. Yeats had the locks changed, but Crowley tried again. He turned up on 19 April in preposterous garb that combined Scottish aristocratic pretension with *opera bouffe* absurdity. He was armed with a dirk and, reportedly, wearing the 'Mask of Osiris' (Harper, 1974: 24). This time it was Crowley who called a constable. He was advised to go quietly and fortunately he did, but not before threatening legal action (this never came to anything). On 21 April the committee decided to expel Mathers, who had unleashed so dangerous an emissary upon them. In the consequent reorganization, Yeats became Imperator of the First Order and Instructer in Mystical Philosophy to the Second.

Yeats's tribulations among the magicians were only beginning. And what had started as unsettling farce became an altogether more serious threat to the Order's survival (Howe 1972: 203–51). At Yeats's instigation, the wealthy and strong-willed Horniman had been reinstated and she and Farr became unyielding antagonists in a dispute that threatened the Order's very existence, or so Yeats imagined. The issue was that of the secret 'groups' which Farr had authorized. Horniman shared Yeats's view that they undermined the very basis of the Order (Yeats also feared that they might allow the Order to be contaminated by 'black magic' which he feared), and by February 1901 the conflict had reached a climax in a highly contentious argument about procedure, legality and executive authority. Yeats fought his corner on the issue through a series of open letters, but at a general meeting on 26 February, when things turned decisively against his party and his own integrity was impugned, Yeats joined his resignation to that of Horniman, which had been tendered following an earlier bitter meeting.

Before settling for defeat, his pride undoubtedly stung, and disturbed by the imminent disintegration of an institution in which he placed much faith, Yeats stepped back from the fray to compose a remarkable document. He issued a privately printed and circulated pamphlet entitled 'Is the Order of the R.R. & A.C. to remain a Magical Order?' (the initials stand for the Latin name of the second level of the Order, *Rosea Rubae et Aurea Crucis*). He wrote this in March 1901 and had it distributed among members in April of that year, which suggests how deliberately he set down his convictions as the turmoil of the previous months fell into shape in his mind. This work was a compelling, even rather unnerving, production. It revealed aspects of Yeats's personality which came into play when, in hand-to-hand conflict, he was acting from a full sense of his own formidable powers. And as George Harper concludes, the essay 'represents his most thoughtful philosophic observation about the nature of the universe and of man's relationship to everything outside himself' (Harper 1974: 70).

Much of Yeats's prose of the 1890s, for all its polemical intention, its tendent-
ious asperities in controversy with such as Dowden, was marked by hesitancies of
style and manner, uncertainties of tone, a period air. This document, by contrast,
forged in the heat of a fundamental challenge to his convictions demanded from
Yeats a prose of urgent directness and measured authority. In his pamphlet we
encounter depth of commitment and exorbitance of conviction, together with an
analytic, adroitly engaged political intelligence. Yeats has learnt from controversies how men and women function as individuals and in groups. He knows how
disruptive undisciplined egotism and social fragmentation invariably are in the
conduct of human affairs. When they erupt it can be impossible to 'avoid passing
from the quiescence of a clique to the activity of a caucus' (ibid.: 263). That telling
observation, a sharp apophthegm, has the ring of bitter experience. Yet the force
of the document is not only dependent on Yeats's acute social awareness,
manifested in the controlled, occasionally caustic and satiric engagement of the
writing with an intended readership, but on the assured manner with which the
poet deals with his metaphysical certitudes. A mind so often curiously sceptical,
when most engaged with belief, here utters itself in the accents of certitude.

His faith is in three things: in the existence of spiritual powers above and
beyond the material world and which exist independently of human consciousness; in the practice of ritual magic; and in the efficacy of a magical order,
properly constituted to evoke those powers as agents of spiritual illumination
able to raise humankind to the level of divinity.

'The central principle of all the Magic of power', Yeats avers, 'is that everything we formulate in the imagination, if we formulate it strongly enough, realizes
itself in the circumstances of life, acting either through our own souls, or through
the spirits of nature' (ibid.: 265). The implications of this are immense, for it
means that the spiritual validity of an Order such as the Golden Dawn does not
ultimately depend on the authenticity or otherwise of its founding documents, but
on the strength with which the imagination formulates its codes and maintains it
in structured existence. For Yeats, strength involves discipline. He reckons that
the Order is, in a key phrase, 'a discipline that is essentially symbolic and
evocative' (ibid.: 260). As such it must be structured so that its systematic
organization symbolizes what it purports to do – that is, to raise select beings,
by the practice of ritual magic, through the various degrees of awareness which
will eventually permit full illumination and a spiritual apotheosis. It cannot be a
Magical Order unless it observes hierarchical order, governed by degree and the
discipline which examinations and rites of initiation demand. 'Groups' pursuing
their own experimental interests threaten the symbolic integrity of the Order in
the way Protestant sectaries threaten the body of Christ which is the one true
church of traditional Catholicism. Yeats holds out a vision of what the Order can
effect, if it remains true to this calling, in a passage of ebullient faith:

> If we preserve the unity of the Order, if we make that unity efficient among us, the
> Order will become a single very powerful talisman, creating in us, and in the world
> about us, such moods and circumstances as may best serve the magical life, and best

awaken the magical wisdom. Its personality will be powerful, active, visible afar, in that all powerful world that casts downward for its shadows, dreams, and visions. The right pupils will be drawn to us from the corners of the world by dreams and visions and by strange accidents; and the Order itself will send out Adepts and teachers, as well as hidden influences that may shape the life of these islands nearer to the magical life. (ibid.: 267)

Yeats challenged his readers to a life of sacrifice (he was insistent on the ethical efficacy of the Christian symbolism of the cross in the Order's rituals) as he penned a portrait of the great Adept (his own vocation) and excoriated an age of trivial individualism: 'The great adept may indeed have to hide much of his deepest life, lest he tell it to the careless and the indifferent, but he will sorrow and not rejoice over this silence, for he will be always seeking ways of giving the purest substance of his soul to fill the emptiness of other souls' (ibid.). Those who would impede his mission do so in the name of a false idea of freedom. The tone is magisterial:

> I have preferred to talk of greater things than freedom. In our day every idler, every trifler, every bungler, cries out for his freedom; but the busy, and weighty minded, and skilful handed, meditate more upon the bonds that they gladly accept, than upon the freedom that has never meant more in their eyes than right to choose the bonds that have made them faithful servants of law. (ibid.: 267–8)

Both tone and content here betray a mind that did not shrink from embracing authoritarian, elitist notions of its own destiny. In an increasingly democratic age, Yeats countenanced ideas which allowed for hierarchy, order imposed by established authority, the leadership of the many by the elect. In the first decade of the twentieth century he would become embroiled in many public controversies and bitterly fought debates in the country of his birth. In these he would prove a doughty champion of artistic freedom and intellectual independence. However, his defence of these ostensibly libertarian values was rooted, not in a vision of the equal right of every man or woman to participate in a popular democracy, but in a conviction that religious freedoms were at stake, freedoms which permitted the artist and the magician to pursue true illumination and to exercise the power which was its concomitant. Only in the disciplined order of a true, magical community (at his most doctrinally severe, religion and art almost become one for Yeats) would such illumination and power be vouchsafed. An undisciplined, slackly egalitarian democracy would constantly show itself as destructive, Yeats believed, of the spiritual life such as he summoned the few to make their own. As he frankly admitted, in a postscript he wrote to this document in May 1901, 'individuality is not as important as our age has imagined' (ibid.: 270). The adept and the artist must be free to follow their calling as those in possession, through the disciplines they accept, of higher powers.

The mind revealed by this pamphlet and its postscript, when taken together with the essay 'Magic', published in the same year, reveals how spectacularly at odds Yeats was with the spirit of his own period. In a democratic, increasingly secular age he had suffused his being with magical concepts and symbols to the degree that his sensibility might be reckoned more that of a Renaissance, neo-Platonic image, than that of a modern man. There was one aspect of his thinking in the pamphlet, however, that bore on contemporary concerns. Though even there Renaissance belief in a hierarchical cosmology – in which things in the higher dimension are matched in the lower – played its part.

The pamphlet, intended for a very limited readership, is much more open about Yeats's developing beliefs at this time than the published essay. So where the essay is unremarkably absorbed by 'the power of many minds to become one' (*E&I*: 36), the pamphlet places a distinctive emphasis on the body as a primary metaphor of communal experience. Yeats queries whether or not the Order 'has been sufficiently embodied in London' to bear the burden of Mathers' expulsion. He insists: 'Because a Magical Order differs from a society for experiment and research in that it is an Actual Being, an organic life holding within itself the highest life of its members now and in past times, to weaken its Degrees is to loosen the structure, to dislimn, to disembody, to dematerialize an Actual Being' (Harper 1974: 261). This metaphoric use of the body as a living reality in which spiritual realities can be incarnate (embodied) is new in Yeats. As recently as 1898 he had in fact been ready, in an essay entitled 'The Autumn of the Flesh' to declare his age one in which the most significant poetry would be part of an 'arduous search for an almost disembodied ecstasy' (*E&I*: 194, retitled 'The Autumn of the Body'). Now in his anxiety for the Order as a living body, Yeats introduces to his pamphlet one of the major obsessions of his later poetry and drama: the body of society itself at risk from disease and social decline. For he feared that the 'Groups' were 'astral diseases sapping up, as it were, its vital fluids' (Harper 1974: 262). Such a metaphor, in the guise of a Renaissance imagining, was, it is true, merely giving expression to a fairly widespread late Victorian and Edwardian concern for social purity. It indicates, however, that Yeats was shifting his attention from the realms of the ethereal to the regeneration of things on the lower plane, to a magical order conceived of as a living body.

Not of course that the Order of the Golden Dawn was any body. It was a living communion, already raised above the common life of humanity, poised to experience further spiritual elevation. Yet in comparison with the impalpable world in which so many of the conflicts in Yeats's early writings had been realized as a kind of immaterial shadow-boxing or dehumanized symbolism, this corporeal metaphor has a ring of new-found interest in the human frame as the locus of real possibility and actual processes, of good and evil at war in living personalities. The site of drama in fact.

Yeats had been intrigued by the artistic challenge of drama since his boyhood. Even as a callow, infatuated youth he had realized instinctively that the composition of drama and a living theatre are intimately connected. He had written *Vivien and Time* for Laura Armstrong to perform in a Howth drawing-room. As a young man he had admired the beauty of the voice when Farr played in *A Sicilian Idyll*. He had also been shocked into an awareness of the impact of live theatre at two remarkable theatrical performances he had attended in the 1890s. Villiers de l'Isle-Adam's *Axël*, as we saw, had stimulated him to attempt a similar work of symbolist world-rejection. The resulting drama *The Shadowy Waters*, with its navigator hero in quest of a transcendent love, absorbed Yeats for years to come, as he pondered and experimented with a kind of theatre in which action is at a minimum and words and symbolist motifs combine like notes in music to induce a state of dreamlike beauty, for which the world is well-lost in 'the ecstasy and terror of transcendence' (Kelly 1989: 169). In the 1890s he was denied the opportunity to see this work on stage. It was only when he saw it performed in 1904 and in 1905 (with Farr taking a starring role) that he was enabled to recast it as something that would play in the theatre (there were some further changes for a 1906 performance).

The highlight of Yeats's second visit to Paris in December 1896, had been another epoch-making opening night. He was in the city, as we noted, primarily to further his plans for an Order of Celtic Mysteries. He was also looking for copy for his projected novel *The Speckled Bird*. He met Strindberg, took hashish with a group of mystics and met a young Irishman, John Millington Synge, for the first time, who, though Yeats could not have known it at the time, was to play a major part in his own life and in the history of Irish drama in the first decade of the fast-approaching new century. All this paled before the horrendous assault upon theatrical decorum which the anarchic Alfred Jarry set in motion on 12 December. The play was his *Ubu Roi*, a work which seemed not only to blaspheme against the pieties of past and present, but to announce the birth of a new, cruel age.

Yeats was horrified by what he saw. On stage a king carried a toilet brush as a mock sceptre. The players acted as gross, animalistic marionettes. Yeats understood, nevertheless, that Jarry's iconoclastic, subversively mocking work came from more primitive sources in human psychology, in myth and religious ritual than any of his own writings had yet done. What he had seen had saddened him, but he had also, one senses, been excited by a glimpse of a theatrical energy he had hitherto found unimaginable. The passage in *Autobiographies* in which he recalls an iconoclastic theatrical evening in the company of Arthur Symons, is regretful, but moves to a moment of overwhelming revelation – a dynamic Yeats could never resist, however terrible the revelation. He had witnessed the awesome birth of 'the Savage God' (*Au*: 349)

As an aspirant dramatist, Yeats must have been enormously impressed by the way these two live performances affected him. For both experiences indicated that theatre as an art form was capable of expressing philosophic and religious questions of great moment. Both plays in their strikingly different ways challenged the dominance of realism, with its elaborate sets in the contemporary bourgeois theatre, and gave Yeats the hope that he might also contribute innovative work as a man of the theatre. What he needed was a theatre of his own where he could experiment and adapt his own drama before live audiences. For he had seen in Paris the electrifying effects that daring drama could achieve and he was keen to try out and adapt his own works in performance. Where that might be possible remained an open question until the early years of the twentieth century; yet from Yeats's theatrical needs as an apprentice playwright grew a movement which in time was to give his native country a national theatre of international significance and renown.

The idea of an Irish theatre had appealed to Yeats at least since the production in London of his Irish play *The Land of Heart's Desire*. It was not until 1897, however, that this began to seem practical. That summer he, Lady Gregory and Edward Martyn, in drama an Ibsenite, mooted the possibility of an Irish Celtic Theatre, one wet afternoon while they were visiting in County Clare. Martyn was a particularly useful ally since he was wealthy and was ready to act as a patron as well as a participant in the project. Less than two years later (in the interim George Moore was recruited as an ally with professional experience of the theatre), their plans came to fruition when the first season of what was proposed to be an annual spring festival of Celtic and Irish plays was announced.

In their eventual prospectus for what became the Irish Literary Theatre (Foster gives the earliest version which was in Yeats's own hand; see *AM*: 184) the collaborators made clear that they saw their role as highly innovative:

> We hope to find in Ireland an uncorrupted and imaginative audience trained to listen by its passion for oratory, and believe that our desire to bring upon the stage the deeper thoughts and emotions of Ireland will ensure for us a tolerant welcome, and that freedom to experiment which is not found in theatres of England, and without which no new movement in art or literature can succeed. We will show that Ireland is not the home of buffoonery and of easy sentiment, as it has been represented, but the home of ancient idealism. We are confident of the support of all Irish people, who are weary of misrepresentation, in carrying out a work that is outside all the political questions that divide us. (Gregory 1914: 8–9)

These earnest words, undoubtedly a compromise between the Ibsenite Martyn who was footing the bills and Yeats (no Ibsenite) who dreamed of a poetic drama, highlight both the problems such an enterprise faced and the role the group wished their theatre to play. The reference to the English stage indicated that they felt they could make little headway with the kind of drama they envisaged in a country where a commercial theatre held sway (in the early Yeatsian version there had been, too, an implicit critique of Ibsenism). In Ireland they hoped that an audience could be found which was not slave to such vulgarity. However they knew that the demeaning image of the stage Irishman – a butt of English comedy since at least the eighteenth century – had an Irish cousin in the very popular melodramas of Dion Boucicault, whose works were enormously successful in Victorian Ireland ('buffoonery and easy sentiment' might refer both to the stage Irishman of English condescension and the figures of Boucicault's melodramas). The announcement is also redolent of the cultural nationalism which the founders brought to their theatrical venture. They hoped that their vision of an 'ancient idealism' would put them beyond politics as culture performed its benignly unifying mission in a politically divided country. It was to prove a very fond hope.

The theatre movement which Yeats and his confederates inaugurated in 1899 was to endure many vicissitudes and rancorous disagreements before it could claim to be a national theatre in anything other than ambition. From the start it was dogged by controversy. Yet it must be noted that in this movement Yeats found a career of a kind as a man of the theatre (he was to be involved with theatre business for much of his remaining life). None of the other ventures to which he had set his hand earlier in his career had quite offered as much. It is noteworthy, too, that it was a vocation which gave him the chance to focus his attention on an institution and community of fellow workers when a fundamental crisis was beginning to threaten the organic personality of the Magical Order which had been so central to his life in the 1890s. There was in Yeats, one senses, an extraordinary capacity to anticipate changes in his social circumstances almost before they had occurred, so that as one phase in his career comes to a climacteric, the elements of the next phase have already begun to combine. And they do so in a manner which permits the poet to continue to express his primary interests despite the new circumstances.

By 1902 Yeats's fears for the Order of the Golden Dawn had been sordidly vindicated. Further bickering had marred the harmony of the living talisman Yeats believed the Order could be. There were splits and secessions. Sexual scandal forced the Order to change its name. Yeats remained a member of a faction that in 1903 declared itself the Amoun Temple of the Stella Matutina and while he maintained his deep commitment to occult study and a 'strong interest in the Stella Matutina for most of the remainder of his life' (Harper 1974: 125) he does not seem again to have played a leading role of the kind he undertook between 1899 and 1901. Theatre business absorbed his administrative and executive powers and energies.

Yet the kind of theatre Yeats hoped to found in Ireland was not so very different from a magical order and he expected it to perform some of the same spiritual functions as an Order of Celtic Mysteries might have done, or a thriving temple of the Golden Dawn in London. It was to be a theatre in which poetic drama could be reborn. The key to this would be a simple set, with little scenery, in which words would be restored to theatrical priority. As Yeats explained to William Sharp/'Fiona Macleod' in 1897, while the idea of his theatre took shape in his mind: 'One should design a scene, which would be an accompaniment not a ref[l]ection of the text. This method would have the further advantage of being fairly cheap, & altogether novel. It would give one's work the remoteness of a legend. The acting should have an equivalent distance from common reality. The plays might be almost, in some cases, modern mystery plays' (*CL2*: 73–4). That the new theatre movement should have the word at its heart was not merely a poet's aspiration. Magic played a part in forming Yeats's vision for a living theatre. He told AE in November 1899, as he worried at *The Shadowy Waters* (it was published in two early versions in 1900 after fifteen years of brooding on the material): 'I want to do a little play which can be acted & half chanted & so help the return of bigger poetical plays to the stage. This is really a magical revolution, for the magical word is the chanted word' (ibid.: 463–4). Art and religion can be one, since, as he affirmed in 1900: 'The theatre began in ritual, and it cannot come to its greatness again without recalling words to their ancient sovereignty' (*Beltaine*, 1899–1900: 23).

Yeats expected that the audiences for such a drama would at first be small (he was pleased that *The Shadowy Waters* could be played in a drawing-room). As in a magical order, the few would lead the few. Yet the influence of a theatre exercising a magical power could be great. So he informed the readers of the *United Irishman* in April 1902: 'It is certain that nothing but a victory on the battlefield could so uplift and enlarge the imagination of Ireland, could so strengthen the National spirit, or make Ireland so famous throughout the world, as the creation of a Theatre where beautiful emotion and profound thought, now fading from the Theatres of the world, might have their three hours' traffic once again' (*CL3*: 172).

The Irish dramatic movement, in which Yeats was to play a leading role for the next two decades, began in a precise sense, when on 8 May, 1899 Farr's niece Dorothy Paget (her aunt was a member of the cast) spoke a prologue which Lionel Johnson had written for the occasion and the curtain rose on a production of Yeats's *The Countess Cathleen* in the Antient Concert Rooms, Brunswick Street, Dublin. The following night Edward Martyn's *The Heather Field* would play at the same hour. Yeats's play would have four performances and Martyn's three over the following few days under the auspices of the Irish Literary Theatre before the brief season ended on 13 May. Johnson's prologue made explicit reference to the contrast between the two plays. Yeats's offering was 'Sweet as the old remembering winds that wail / From hill to hill of gracious Inisfail'. Of Martyn's contribution to the mini-festival, Johnson advised: 'Stern is the story: welcome it no less,/ Aching and lofty in its loveliness'. Johnson had identified, though the task was not difficult, a fault-line that ran through the movement from its inception. For the contrast between Martyn's Ibsenite realism and Yeats's poetic idealism in that first season of Irish drama was only the first tremor of what would prove over the years to be a seismically significant conflict about the nature of theatre itself, which dogged the movement for years, even when Martyn had severed all his connections with it. For the compromise between two views of theatre which had been implicit in the movement's mission statement could not be resolved so easily in practice.

The list of financial backers (their guarantee was not in fact required because of Martyn's largesse) of that first season did, however, give grounds for hope that the founding triumvirate's wish to unite the differing strands of social and political life had not been otiose. The names included those of John O'Leary, Fenian, and John Pentland Mahaffy, redoubtable Unionist and Fellow of Trinity College, notorious for his low view of the Gaelic revival. Prominent members of the Irish Party in Westminster lent their support, as did pillars of the ruling establishment, including Lord Ardilaun and the Marquis of Dufferin and Ava.

The play itself was as spiritual an allegory as might have been expected to arouse only elevated responses. Performed in a revised version (five acts of the 1892 text had become four), the play was a dreamy expression of some of the writer's fundamental beliefs, as a committed member of the Golden Dawn, about the need for spiritually superior individuals to sacrifice themselves to the greater good of a humanity in thrall to materialism. Set amid famine in a generalized Irish period of antiquity when Christianity and paganism intermingled (Yeats himself stated the 'play is not historic, but symbolic'; *Beltaine*, 1899–1900: 8), *The Countess Cathleen* concerns an aristocratic lady who enters a pact with the devil's agents to save the starving peasants. She barters her soul for gold. At a more personal level, the play allegorizes in its tapestry-like series of representative figures (generic peasants, wily merchants who are demons in disguise, a self-sacrificing martyr to a social cause, the poet) not only Yeats's sense of the spiritual battle he faced as a leader of the people in an Ireland where materialism was making disturbing inroads on an essentially imaginative race; it expresses his own sense of uncertainty in his relationship with Gonne. For in the person of Aleel in the play (Farr took the part) is embodied a poet who admires the Countess's commitment, but who is distracted by the claims of art and transcendent vision. The personal implications of the plot could not have been lost on Yeats, since he had urged Gonne to play the title role. She had resisted his entreaties, despite the dedication of the play to her. She was, she remembered, 'severely tempted, for the play fascinated me and I loved acting, but just because I loved the stage so much I had made the stern resolve never to act. I was afraid it would absorb me too much to the detriment of my work' (MacBride 1994: 176). She, like the Countess, had nobly sacrificed herself for the people.

The play certainly gave Yeats the chance to test his theories about the sovereignty of the word in a revived dramaturgy. It is an elaborately verbal work, in which a rather self-consciously naive peasant speech is set against the grave, stately melancholy of the Countess's richly sonorous verse paragraphs and Aleel's more lyrical intensity and rhetorical elevation of tone. The play in its 1899 production in fact offered two of Yeats's most famous lyrics, 'Impetuous heart, be still, be still' and 'Who Goes with Fergus' (they are printed as 'chants from the work in *Beltaine*). The effect is to suggest how the life of the spirit cannot be subdued even by the terrible circumstances of famine. Indeed it thrives amid the horror. The Countess achieves her paradoxical salvation (God judges the motive, not the deed) in a time of crisis, Aleel summons the spirits of heroic rejuvenation, even when death seems triumphant. The message the poetry seeks to impart in its magical way, in chant and musical incantation, is that Ireland should not be distressed by her limited material assets, nor bemoan her poverty, but trust to her own immense spiritual resources:

> For Fergus rules the brazen cars,
> And rules the shadows of the wood
> And the white breast of the dim sea
> And all dishevelled wandering stars.

At the play's climax the Countess is received into the ranks of the blessed amid the sound of horns that emerges from the heart of light, with the peasants kneeling in wonder and gratitude. It is an apotheosis, or at least Yeats hoped it would be one, 'wherein', as James W. Flannery states it 'the war of the immortal upon the mortal worlds, the struggle of opposites is resolved. In the final tableau, Ireland – symbolised by the kneeling peasants with Aleel among them – is mystically transformed into the perfect nation of Yeats's dreams: a community of people sharing the one religious, cultural, and aesthetic ideal' (Flannery 1976: 149).

Regrettably the actual production failed to fulfil Yeats's hopes for it. The English professionals whom Moore had probably helped recruit to save the project from rank amateurism (he saw himself as a fully accomplished literary man among theatrical neophytes), could not speak verse as Yeats wanted it to be spoken. Only Farr knew how to chant her lines. The small hall and stage could not accommodate Yeats's almost Wagnerian wish for a theatrical climax in which his poetry would be accompanied by haunting visual and aural effects. One sympathetic member of the audience, the Dubliner Joseph Holloway, complained of indistinctness in the actors' efforts and found much of the last act spoiled 'by a creaky door, and the too liberal use of palpable tin-tray-created thunder claps' (Holloway 1967: 7). The critic Max Beerbohm, who reported on this first season of the Irish Literary Theatre for the *Saturday Review* in London (13 May, 1899) found the scenery 'as tawdry as it should have been dim' (cited in Flannery 1976: 149). Yet he was aware of certain strengths in what he had seen. He told his English readership: 'Yeats is so far a dramatist that he can tell things simply and clearly in dramatic form.' However, he discerned that Yeats was 'pre-eminently a poet' (*CH*: 10) for whom the ordering of words is 'chief care and delight'.

Beerbohm perhaps did not reckon sufficiently in this report with the inner turmoil, the self-division that had made the drama a likely vehicle for Yeats. He had nevertheless astutely identified what fascinated Yeats about the theatre at this time. For over the next few years his passion for poetry chanted amid minimal scenery on stage (the production of *The Countess Cathleen* had confirmed his views on the folly of elaborate scenery) and in public performance was to become almost an obsession. Curiously, it might be thought, Yeats announced in 1900 that the Irish Literary Theatre's policy was to produce published plays as far as possible and that no play would be produced 'which could not hope to succeed as a book' (*Beltaine*, 1899–1900: 7). This did not imply, however, that Yeats was keen to privilege the written text over the spoken. Rather, he had become acutely sensitive to the complex relationships that existed between speech and text in literary production, as he himself began to highlight speech after a decade in which he had been profoundly attracted by the idea of a sacred book. Literature, however, was unquestionably a matter of published volumes, and the commercial exigencies of an experimental theatre movement made that inevitable; but it had its true life when realized by the human voice. 'Let us', he wrote in 1902, when with Farr he had begun to experiment with the public performance of his own poetry to the accompaniment of a musical instrument, 'get back in everything to the spoken word, even though we have to speak our lyrics to the Psaltery or the Harp, for, as A.E. says, we have begun to forget that literature is but recorded speech, and even when we write with care we have begun "to write with elaboration what could never be spoken"' (*Samhain*, October, 1902: 9).

For just as Yeats was convinced that magical power was present in the living, organic body of a hierarchical order, so he had come to believe that the magic of poetry was at its most potent when quick on the tongue and vibrant in a human voice, when given body and immediate presence. 'Passion', he observed in a lecture first delivered in 1902, 'is the master of all beauty and a passionate theatre will be always a theatre of beauty, but that beauty will not be in pasteboard or in anything else that is far outside the vital principle but will be in the vital principle itself in the movements of men's bodies and in the sweetness of their voices' (Londraville 1991: 96).

In a real way this was transposing the beliefs of the Golden Dawn to a wider arena; for as Ellic Howe has commented, the ritual ceremonies of the Order 'were like complicated theatrical performances' in which 'correct diction and dignified movement and posture were of great importance (Howe 1972: 67). Farr certainly believed that the sound of words can enter into the innermost being, so that through their powers a glimpse can be caught 'of the great truth that heaven and hell and God can be with us here and now (Farr, 'The Music of Speech', cited in Johnson 1975: 122). And Yeats's performance of his own poetry in the early years of the century, as Stefan Zweig remembered, partook of the ritualistic. Zweig recalled how he declaimed his verses in black monkish garb, standing by a black-covered reading desk in a darkened room, between two slightly scented altar candles, adding atmosphere to 'a melodious, sombre voice' (Zweig 1943: 127).

Yeats's aesthetic scruples and dramatic theories about a ritualistic poetic theatre, challenging as they were, meant nothing to a substantial body of opinion in Ireland. For there were those among his compatriots who were seriously affronted by the very idea of a play such as *The Countess Cathleen* and they had not been slow to voice their outrage. In the years of conflict ahead, which had their most obvious inception in the row over *The Countess Cathleen*, Yeats could rest assured, however, that he had in Lady Gregory a staunch, motherly ally and in Coole a sanctuary from abuse and contumely. He was going to need them both.

6

An Irish Ireland

The trouble began in late March 1899 with Edward Martyn's conscience. Always a delicate organ, as the first night approached it became anxiously inflamed. He was concerned that *The Countess Cathleen* was blasphemous. Martyn took theological advice. His fears were vindicated. Yeats and Lady Gregory both sought second opinions and were pleased to report a clean bill of theological health. Moore was scandalized that art was subjected to such absurd tests in Ireland. It confirmed his opinion that the country, to which he was self-indulgently willing to devote his talents, was a benighted, priest-ridden outpost of Rome Rule. Moore's attitude confirmed Martyn in his view that Moore, who was in fact his cousin, was a sacrilegious reprobate. All might have been lost had not Yeats smoothed Martyn's ruffled feathers and calmed his fears. He withdrew his threatened resignation at Yeats's behest; but the crisis deepened when a public row blew up that threatened to do Yeats and his confederates real and lasting damage. Before Martyn had time to regain his not very secure composure, an enemy, whom Yeats had encountered during the quarrel about Gonne's entitlement to speak on behalf of the Irish cause in the United States, issued a vicious broadside, which made *The Countess Cathleen* a national issue.

Souls for Gold!: A Pseudo-Celtic Drama in Dublin was the coat-trailing title Frank Hugh O'Donnell gave his virulent piece of anti-Yeats polemic. It was an intervention in Irish cultural debate that was to set a particularly noxious agenda for years to come. When the play was finally produced in May 1899 a faction in the audience was expected to protest, so a poet's idealistic vision of an Ireland in harmony as a result of spiritual sacrifice, had the presence of the constabulary to ensure that its performance and the partisan responses of pro- and anti-factions would be guaranted a lively reception. Next day some of the anti-faction, students at University College, Dublin, sent a letter of protest about the play to the papers. One student, on being asked to sign this missive, refused. James Joyce was then seventeen years old. Unfortunately the then more influential Cardinal Michael Logue – stern scourge of Parnell in his hour of trial and enthusiastic supporter of language revival, also took against the play. He denounced it sight unseen.

Although the week was an overall success, Yeats swiftly recognized that more was at stake than simply his own play or even the plans to establish a living theatre in Dublin. He sensed that *Souls for Gold!* was a declaration of war – and that the enemy was altogether more dangerous than anything represented by the likes of the gentlemanly Dowden, or even the self-important Duffy, with whom he had previously tangled. So although his first response to O'Donnell was to assure Lady Gregory 'I hardly think it will do us much harm' (*CL2*: 403), he was quick, after the first production, to defend his play in a letter to the public press which set down the lines of battle. He attacked the Cardinal trenchantly for damning his play without having read it.

Yeats's real target, however, was not Logue, who would have been expected by Yeats to have behaved in the way he had (the Church had always condemned the Fenians, so a literary Fenian could expect no better from that quarter), but the kind of manipulators of public opinion among whom he sensed were ranked his most deadly foes. He rode straight into battle:

'The Countess Cathleen' is a spiritual drama, and the blind bigots of journalism, who have made no protest against the musical burlesques full of immoral suggestion which have of late possessed the Dublin theatres, have called it a blasphemy and a slander. These attacks are welcome, for there is no discussion so fruitful as the discussion of intellectual things, and no discussion so needed in Ireland. The applause in the theatre has shown what party has the victory. (*CL2*: 410)

It was perhaps unwise to declare a victory during a first skirmish, with a long war of attrition ahead. For O'Donnell was speaking for an Ireland that had been genuinely affronted by *The Countess Cathleen*, and on less than the strictly theological grounds that had troubled Martyn's tender conscience. In his elevated magical vision of spiritual leadership Yeats had unwittingly strayed on to very vexed territory indeed.

The poet may have liked to believe that his play was set in an unspecified Irish past made merely poetic by the passage of time. Many in his likely audience would have reckoned its setting to be a direct enough reference to the tragic famine which had occurred in all-too-recent history. Furthermore, the Great Famine of the 1840s was increasingly being employed at the century's end by nationalist propagandists as a definitive example of the malign effects of British rule in Ireland which had, as it continued to have, the support of the Anglo-Irish Protestant caste with which Yeats and Lady Gregory were easily identified. That, in Yeats's imagining of famine conditions, it is an aristocrat who is noble and self-sacrificing, while the peasantry are venal and ripe for subornation by the devil's agents, would have seemed intolerable. To add injury to insult, it seemed that Yeats was perversely rewriting known history in a mischievous way. In the 1840s it had been Protestants who had offered soup to starving Catholics prepared to embrace the reformed faith. 'Souperism', as Conor Cruise O'Brien points out had meant souls for soup. It was understandable that Yeats's play 'embarrassed as well as shocked' (O'Brien 1972: 61). Some anti-clerical nationalists were prepared to cheer the play when it seemed to attack the Catholic church, but that scarcely helped Yeats's idealistic case.

The qualms which Yeats aroused even in thoughtful Irishmen and women with *The Countess Cathleen* allowed less scrupulous individuals to wage war on all Yeats stood for. He could be damned as dubiously Irish, his Celticism a pagan absurdity that only a deracinated product of a corrupt garrison culture could produce. It was worthless to the Irish nation. O'Donnell's rebarbative animus was in fact just the first clumsily directed barrage in what would soon become a more precisely aimed and polemically effective campaign. What one of the participants in that campaign grandiosely dubbed a 'battle of two civilisations', had been joined.

The phrase was D. P. Moran's. Moran was a Waterford-born journalist who had cut his teeth in the London press. He was well armed with a talent for coarse-grained, journalistic raillery (he famously lampooned poor AE as 'the hairy fairy'). He was also an aggressive ideologue who had returned to Ireland with a mission, which he pursued from 1898 onwards in the *New Ireland Review* and then in the vigorously engaged columns of his own newspaper, the *Leader*, which he founded in 1900 (Lyons 1973: 230).

Moran's mission can be summed up in one word: 'de-Anglicization'. Douglas Hyde had introduced this term to Irish cultural debate in a lecture delivered in Dublin in 1892 when he had identified a national imperative as the necessity of de-Anglicizing Ireland. The Gaelic League, established in 1893 to encourage language revival, looked to Hyde's lecture as its founding testament. It had had immediate impact and had gained wide currency in the 1890s. Its central argument was that Ireland had lost her identity when she had lost her language. Unprotected by the veil of her own language, she had been easy prey for the English language that had made of her population a people without true nationality, merely imitative of the population of the neighbouring island. The Irish had lost their native Celtic characteristics and were languishing in a condition of unworthy west-Britonism, neither genuinely English nor authentically Irish. For all the rodomontade of his address, Hyde's analysis of what could be done and his practical proposals were in fact quite modest. He wanted Irish to be respected when Home Rule was achieved and accordingly given academic status in the education system 'on a par with – or even above – Greek, Latin, and modern languages, in all examinations held under the Irish Government'. Indeed, despite the apparent divisiveness of his terminology, Hyde, as his biographers wisely observe, offered 'something for everyone within a national context' (J. Egleson Dunleavy and G. W. Dunleavy 1991: 185). His was an essentially mild, eirenic vision of cultural and linguistic possibility.

The problem was that once the concept of de-Anglicization had been admitted to public life, there were those all too ready to make it a matter of urgent alternatives and not just for themselves. Moran was one such. He too excoriated the west-Britonism of Irish life. He attributed to it the economic and social degradation of the country. For him de-Anglicization could not happen too quickly, since national survival depended on it. Those who in Hyde's gentle view of things were doing their bit by singing Irish songs, or even writing Irish poems and plays in English, were not friends of his cause but at best ridiculous nuisances like AE and at worst enemies like Yeats, to be socially extirpated along with the language they spoke as an Irish *lingua franca*. The future for English in Ireland was not as the basis, along with a revived Irish, of a national renewal, as Yeats believed it could be, but absorption, as Ireland became universally Irish-speaking. 'The foundation of Ireland is the Gael', he pronounced, with the severity of the ideologue and zealot he was beneath his tub-thumping, knockabout journalistic antics, 'and the Gael must be the element that absorbs. On no other basis can an Irish nation be reared that would not topple over by the force of the very ridicule that it would beget' (Moran 1905: 37). Moran believed in an Irish Ireland and had no compunction about attacking in blunt terms all those he believed were inimical to its interests. He kept Yeats in his sights at the turn of the century (though for all his verbal violence he was an opponent of physical force as a political weapon; Toomey 1996: 47).

Yeats's position in Irish life was now an intensified, more publically exposed version of what it had been in the mid-nineties, when, on the one hand he had had to contend with the cultivated literary internationalism of a Dowden, and on the other the nativist, sentimental patriotism of Thomas Davis's literary patrimony, to which Duffy had been so tiresomely loyal. In 1898 the Irish critic John Eglinton had put the case for cosmopolitan individualism in a newspaper debate with Yeats in the columns of the Dublin *Daily Express* with altogether greater subtlety than Dowden had ever done. Their exchanges, along with contributions by AE and another writer, William Larminie, aroused so much interest that they were issued as a book, *Literary Ideals in Ireland* in 1899. It was by no means clear that Yeats had got the better of Eglinton in the argument. On the other flank Yeats had to endure the attacks of Moran, whose nationalism was so advanced that Davis himself had attracted his critical anathema, since the Young Irelander's cultural nationalism had, in his extreme view, never gone far enough.

In articles in the *New Ireland Review*, which were to be published in collected form under the pretentious title *The Philosophy of Irish Ireland* (1905) Yeats had had to accustom himself to being told brutally that 'practically no one in Ireland understands Yeats and his school' (Moran 1905: 103) and to the movement he had led for literary revival being characterized as the last of a series of nineteenth-century 'make-believe[s]' (ibid.). What was worse about Moran's crusade against Yeats was that his Gaelic triumphalism was mixed with self-conscious Catholic piety. In Moran indeed can be seen the formation of a version of Irish identity, which was increasingly to appeal to the Irish middle classes in general, in which a commitment to Irish revival and to Catholicism were joined in a newly vibrant nationalism. For whatever degree of opportunity the post-Parnellite period had in fact offered to *déraciné* Irish Protestants like Yeats, to assume a leading role in national life, was now swiftly diminishing. The pro- and anti-Parnellite factions of the Irish Parliamentary Party, as F. S. L. Lyons notes, had reunited in 1900, and 'middle-class nationalism was again in the ascendant' (Lyons 1973: 243).

Furthermore a new generation of nationally minded activists (the commemoration of 1798, in which Yeats had participated, had renewed national feeling) had committed itself to language revival in the Gaelic League. This generation, especially its priests, teachers, minor civil servants, its educated young in unsatisfactory employment, was closer in spirit to the likes of Moran than they ever could have been to Yeats, however they might individually have regretted the confessional analysis of the Irish social order the *Leader* so vociferously sponsored (for Moran the authentic national identity was Gaelic *and* Catholic; there could be no two ways about that).

Roy Foster has sensibly cautioned us against reading the cultural wars of the first years of the twentieth century exclusively through the eyes of the combatants. What they experienced as a conflict between two starkly opposed camps creates an impression that Ireland as a whole was attentively following every shot fired, every blow received. This was not the case. Most Irishmen and women went their ways oblivious to the action and counter-action of disputing factions in the cultural wars. Their culture was the culture of English-language newspapers, of an Irish-accented version of English-language middle-brow fiction, of the Dublin music halls and of the touring grand opera company. Yeats and Moran shared common ground, ironically, only in their scorn for the complacent and, as they saw it, corrupted life of Ireland's ordinary petit-bourgeois citizens, who, however they could be stirred by commemoration of the patriot dead, or by sentimental literary accounts of a national tradition, were reasonably at ease with their cultural lot at the turn of the century: 'in the early 1900s the majority Irish culture was not that of the cultural ginger-groups, Irish-Irelander or Anglo-Irish' (Foster 1988: 455). It was the culture so intently explored by Joyce in *Dubliners* (1914) and comically in *Ulysses* (1922). Yet it has been estimated that membership of the Gaelic League peaked at around 75,000 in 1906. Between 1900 and 1906 'the number of branches increased from 120 to 985, mainly based in the cities and towns but distributed throughout Ireland' (Hutchinson 1989: 178). So linguistic revivalism was a significantly popular movement (James Joyce was characteristically sceptical about the motivation of its enthusiasts) which made language acquisition an Irish national imperative. From this period onwards, Irish could claim the moral high-ground and those, like Yeats, who knew little or none of it, could be wrong-footed in debate and controversy.

That the struggle between Irish Ireland and the Anglo-Irish literary revival was not quite the titanic thing both sides imagined with their obsessed sense that a civilization was at stake, did not make Yeats's discomfiture in Dublin any the less. It was there he sensed the warfare was centred (although in retrospect in the 1930s Yeats would recall to the poet Thomas MacGreevy how all this controversy had been conducted in an almost comic spirit; MacGreevy n.d.: 11). Among his potential readership in the Irish capital he was experiencing real opposition. It amounted almost to a boycott of his works. By May 1901, as Moran's crusade took firm hold (Yeats had earlier damned him in a letter as an uncultivated autodidact and like all such 'as lively as a Dancing Dervish'; *CL3*: 19), he was forced to report to Lady Gregory that his publisher, on a visit to

Dublin, had found an amazing hostility among the city's booksellers to the poet's books. Yeats's account of this indicates that he knew all too well how perilous the ground had become on which he was trying to stand in Ireland. He was trapped between the rising tide of Catholic national feeling and the obdurate cliff-face of his own caste's disapproval of his Fenian associations:

> Russell [AE] told me before I saw Bullen that clerical influence was he beleived working against me because of my mysticism... Memory of 'The Countess Cathleen' dispute accounts for a good deal. Bullen found the protestant booksellers little better & asked me if TCD disliked me. Magee, the College publisher said 'what is he doing here. Why doesnt he go away & leave us in peace.' He seems to have suspected me of some deep revolutionary design. ...
>
> I imagine that as I withdraw from politics my friends among the nationalists will grow less, at first at any rate, & my foes more numerous. What I hear from Bullen only confirms the idea that I had at the time of 'the Countess Cathleen' row that it would make a very serious difference in my position out side the small cultivated class. (*CL3*: 71)

In such an unfriendly climate it is not surprising that a note of resolute, angry protest entered Yeats's public pronouncements on Irish matters at this time, especially as they related to artistic freedom. 'I believe', he wrote with Protestant directness in one Irish newspaper, 'that literature is the principal voice of the conscience' (ibid.: 119). Nor is it surprising that Yeats tried to keep his London theatrical options open. A visit to Stratford-upon-Avon in the spring to see the Benson Company play the history plays had impressed him greatly. It suggested what a theatre dedicated to dramatic art could do.

It was in London that he began his vocal experiments with Farr, although he admitted in a letter to a newspaper in March 1902 that he knew nothing of music, could not tell one note from another and even disliked music. He had, fortunately, recruited a truly helpful adviser, the musician Arnold Dolmetsch, who fashioned the psaltery (a twelve-stringed lyre-shaped instrument which in Dolmetsch's version 'had 26 alternating strings of fine string and twisted brass arranged an octave apart so that the octave could be played with one finger'; ibid.: footnote 91). Farr, along with her niece Dorothy Paget, gave her first performance of speaking verse (Yeats had advised in an article which had appeared in May that her method was not to be confused with the chanting to be heard in church) to this odd instrument as an illustration to a lecture by Yeats, on 10 June 1902. Yeats well knew, one senses from his article, that this form of art would probably appeal only to a coterie (though Farr and he gave more than twenty such lecture/performances in London in 1903 and together made a tour of provincial British cities in 1906), but the experiment played its part in a period of his life when he was stimulated in a variety of ways by theatrical possibilities which might be exploited in Dublin *or* in London.

Music was involved in another of these. In March 1901 he had attended a Purcell Operatic Society performance of Purcell's *Dido and Aeneas* where he was much taken by the scenery designed by Gordon Craig, illegitimate son of the famous Victorian and Edwardian actress Ellen Terry. He quickly arranged to meet Terry and in 1902 after seeing more of Craig's conception of total theatre (scenery, music, action and words in co-operative concert) with performances of works by Purcell and Handel, he began a collaboration with Craig that was to effect his own developing idea of theatre. At Craig's suggestion, he had a model stage constructed on which he could experiment with stage design and direction.

Yeats also involved himself in the metropolitan effort to renew English theatrical life, then very much in the doldrums because of the myopic censorship exercised by the Lord Chancellor's office. Since 1895 the Examiner of Plays, a G. A. Redford, had ensured that the theatre was closed to the discussion of sex, religion and politics (although the bawdy vulgarity of commercially successful farces did not disturb him). Only in what were essentially private clubs could London audiences have the opportunity of seeing serious contemporary European theatre (where these topics were frankly and controversially broached) or could serious English-language dramatists present their plays. In 1900 Yeats became associated with the embryonic Literary Theatre Club with whose members, such as T. Sturge Moore (who became one of Yeats's close friends), Charles Ricketts and Florence Farr, Yeats hoped to cooperate in a romantic and poetic theatre that served his own dramatic purposes. In the early years of the century the poet worked with others to build on their rather amateur foundations what he hoped would be called the 'Theatre of Beauty' which was eventually constituted as the all too short-lived Masquers Society (*CL3*: 723–4). It was clear in all this that Yeats was still unsure whether or not Dublin would allow the seeds he and his confederates had planted there to grow. Yet as he busied himself in London, he was entering on a period of close collaboration with Lady Gregory which kept Ireland and Irish subject-matter securely in his mind.

For Lady Gregory was offering Yeats more than a home and some discreet patronage. Their relationship seemed to allow Yeats, even in the middle of crises like that affecting his theatrical plans in Dublin or the Golden Dawn in London, to work with a greater sense of stable purpose. Lady Gregory's collaboration in folklore studies gave him more than the material for his own folkloric articles; it encouraged him to accept that such material could be the basis of dramatic experiments like *The Pot of Broth* (first performed in the Antient Concert Rooms in October 1902). This slight comedy which dramatizes a tramp tricking two mean but credulous peasants into supplying him with sustenance, a firm favourite with Irish audiences, which Yeats admitted was largely Lady Gregory's work, brought into his dramatic writing not only a note of humour but a convincing rural demotic. Indeed much of the rural speech in Yeats's drama as a whole was supplied by his friend at Coole.

The Hour-Glass (which had its première in Dublin on 14 March 1903) was also based on folk material which Oscar Wilde's mother, 'Speranza', had included in her *Ancient Legends of Ireland* (1887). In this morality play Yeats introduced a figure which was to fascinate him in much of his future work: the fool who is wiser than the ostensibly wise. Even more importantly, in encouraging Lady Gregory to tell a heroic Irish tale in her *Cuchulain of Muirthemne* (1902), Yeats was also giving himself licence, in defiance of the those who had denounced *The Countess Cathleen* for its heresy and mysticism, to explore an Irish heroic age, pagan and primitive in its implications, savage and brutal in a way which his work had not hitherto been. From July to early October 1901 Yeats worked on a poem of the Irish mythic age, 'Baile and Aillinn' (on 12 July he informed his father that he was at work on 'narrative poems of the Irish heroic age' for the first time since he had written 'The Wanderings of Oisin'; *CL3*: 87). This tale of deathly annunciations is based on a story Lady Gregory was to include in her volume, indicating how closely they were sharing their ideas and work at this time. When at Coole he set the poem aside that summer, it was to work on the first of his plays to take Cuchulain (the central figure in Lady Gregory's narrative), as his own hero, the starkly noble, tragically ironic *On Baile's Strand* (first performed on 27 December 1904). The visit to Stratford-upon-Avon in the spring, to see the history plays, had also encouraged him to attempt a play of Shakespearean scale.

Yeats's growing confidence as a man of letters, who knew he had the support and patronage of Lady Gregory to sustain him through difficulties, was manifested in his keenness in late 1901 to gather together a collection of his essays in volume form. This was probably intensified by his failure satisfactorily to fulfil the contract for *The Speckled Bird*. Although he had not abandoned his attempts to complete the novel, his publisher was impatient and accepted the collection of essays as a means of recouping his investment in a work which did not so far promise well. Yet for Yeats to make more permanent the occasional writings of periodical literature was to risk his reputation in the critical as well as the poetical field (articles in journals were rarely reviewed, books by well-known writers almost always were). When they appeared in 1903 under the title *Ideas of Good and Evil*, Yeats had come to believe, as he told AE, that the book represented his current views only partially ('the book is only one half of the orange'; *CL3*: 369). Yet the volume served as an illuminating commentary on his own career to date, highlighting how much the poet since boyhood had engaged with the transcendental in his imaginings, but never at the complete expense of a passionate involvement with his native land. Yeats's own characterization of Ireland – in a key essay in the volume ('Ireland and the Arts'), as a land where 'love of the Unseen Life and love of country' (*E&I*: 204) combine creatively – might be taken to reflect his own governing concerns as man and artist, as revealed by this collection. Yet, as AE observed in a letter, the book made very public indeed Yeats's commitment to occultism and to the revelatory powers of poetry, for he thought it would do more than anything else Yeats had written, 'to bring the mystical interpretation of life into literature . . . because it shows the long meditation out of which your verse springs' (Denson 1961: 46). The *Athenaeum* accordingly noted, for all the work's technical faults, that Yeats 'never treats a work of art in the distinctively literary way, but as the speech and embodiment of forces that are and have been spiritually at work in the world' (*CH*: 137).

Yeats sensed that he was coming into his maturity as man and writer in the first years of the century. In a letter written when he was in his thirty-ninth year, in January 1904, about the play which he had begun in the summer of 1901,

On Baile's Strand, the poet indicated how much of his own development as a man had gone into the figure of Cuchulain in that work:

> He lives among young men but has himself outlived the illusions of youth. He is probably about 40, not less than 35 or 36 & not more than 45 or 46, certainly not an old man, & one understands from his talk about women that he does not love like a young man. Probably his very strength of character made him put off illusions & dreams (that make young men a womans servant) & made him become quite early in life a deliberate lover, a man of pleasure who can never surrender himself. He is a little hard, & leaves the people about him a little repelled. (*CL3*: 527)

There are elements of a knowing self-portraiture about this (as Jeffares reminds us, in the cycle of plays Yeats wrote about Cuchulain, the hero ages with the dramatist himself; Jeffares 1988: 149), as there are later in the letter when Yeats fleshes out his character: 'The touch of something hard, repellent yet alluring, self assertive yet self immolating is not all but it must be there. He is the fool – wandering passive, houseless & all but loveless' (*CL3*: 527).

For all the poet's increased self-confidence, as Lady Gregory gave him a point of reference in his life and collaborated creatively with him, the poet retained an awareness of the contradictions at war in his own nature, as he made his hero a tragic victim of the central paradox contained in a phrase in his letter: 'self assertive yet self immolating'. The boastful Cuchulain in the play is tricked into unwittingly slaying his own son in a trial of strength and is driven mad with grief. And even as Yeats self-assertively began to come into his own as a man of the theatre, busy in a markedly managerial way in his letters to all and sundry, with plans for theatrical experiments in Dublin and London, his imaginative preoccupation with self-immolation, with sacrifice, still haunted him. For in the Shakespearean pastiche of *On Baile's Strand* Yeats was offering an Irish version of the struggle in Shakespeare's history play between the poet Richard II and the practical man Bolingbroke. In Yeats's sense of things Cuchulain's fate, like that of a poetic English king, is to be preferred to the brutally materialistic exercise of political power.

Self-sacrifice is one of the thematic threads that bind together his own varied attempts at play-writing between 1901 and 1904. The poet's fascination with the act of self-sacrifice is at its most obvious in the play which opened on 2 April 1902 in Dublin with Gonne in the main part. The origin of this work, *Cathleen ni Houlihan* (spelt Hoolihan at first publication) had been in a dream, in which Yeats had seen a 'cottage where there was well-being and firelight and talk of marriage, and into the midst of that cottage there came an old woman in a long cloak' (Pethica 1988: 8). With Lady Gregory's help (and the evidence is clear that she had a major part in the composition of this essentially collaborative work), he cast his dream as a play of peasant life interrupted by a figure who raises realism to the level of potent political allegory.

The year is 1798, the scene is set in County Mayo where the French had landed in Ireland to aid the revolutionary cause. The peasant family is preparing for the wedding of their son, their minds set on the material benefits which will derive from a wise match. An old woman arrives seeking shelter in their home. She speaks enigmatically (but with obvious nationalist significance for an Irish audience) of strangers in her house and of four beautiful green fields (the English were widely regarded as strangers in Ireland, as alien conquerors of the four historic provinces). The impact of the play is less dependent on this overt allegory – the old woman is obviously Ireland herself in familiar guises as the poor old woman or as Cathleen the daughter of Houlihan – but on the way in which a realistic setting is transformed by mesmeric, chant-like rhythms into a site for apocalyptic feeling and an eschatological summons to participate in a transcendental mode of being. The young men of the neighbourhood are invited to enter by way of self-sacrifice the eternal present of national commemoration. The old woman leaves but is heard singing:

> They shall be remembered for ever,
> They shall be alive for ever,
> They shall be speaking for ever,
> The people shall hear them for ever.

As the play ends, the child of the house reports, when asked had he seen an old woman going down the path, 'I did not, but I saw a young girl, and she had the walk of a queen.' It was a curtain line guaranteed to rouse any patriotic Irish audience. Yet the emotional force of the play was rooted in more complex feelings than simple anglophobia or chauvinist enthusiam for a rebel spirit. Yeats and Lady Gregory had mixed a dangerous cocktail indeed. For combining as it did Lady Gregory's fascination as a nationalist for tales of martyrdom in the cause, with Yeats's longing for and belief in magical transformations of reality, *Cathleen ni Houlihan* made of the idea of sacrifice a religious imperative. To give one's life for Ireland was a redemptive act, Christ-like in its transformative potentiality, an act far superior to anything the merely mundane could offer. Toomey has astutely noted its 'uncanny' element and its exploitation of an Irish folkloric *topos*. Cathleen is 'The Lianhan Shee', of whom the poet had read in William Carleton's 'tale of that name' (Toomey 1996: 67).

The image of a young queen, touched by an otherworldly allure, was a stirring one too, given added immediacy by Gonne's playing of the part. Yeats himself wrote to Lady Gregory of how she 'played it magnificently, & with wierd power' (*CL3*: 167). She had agreed to play the part as Yeats hoped she would, since he had acceded to her request that it should be performed by members of a nationalist ginger group she had helped to found in 1900 as Inghinidhe na hÉireann (Daughters of Ireland). Gonne was their president and, as well as offering Irish-language classes to children, they were in association with a broader political and cultural grouping, Cumann na nGaedheal, which included appropriately national dramatic presentations among the activities it encouraged and sponsored. In *Cathleen ni Houlihan* Yeats had at last produced a work of which she could enthusiastically approve. For as an Englishwoman Gonne would have understood how provocative was the image of Ireland in the guise of a young and vibrant queen, in the period when her own country was barely able to adjust to the death of the old queen who had for so long ruled over the British Empire. Within a month of the death of Queen Victoria some 3,000 elegies had been published in Britain and the colonies on that melancholy event. In many of these, as Samuel Hynes reports, 'Her maternal role is so repeatedly mentioned as to suggest that it was a commonplace of her reign' (Hynes 1968: 15).

The young queen, by contrast, whom Yeats and Lady Gregory conjured into existence in the autumn of the year in which Victoria died, was no beneficent aged mother reigning over a settled empire, but a threatening figure, a portent of catastrophes to come for the empire. Together they had created a powerfully subversive image of an alternative sovereignty. That they had done so when England was uncertainly coming to terms with the death of its long-lived ruler, so soon after unexpected defeats in the Boer War had disturbed national self-confidence, made the work even more provocative. So too did its references to aid for Ireland from a foreign power (the French expeditionary force of 1798), in a period in which fears of invasion had intensified in England, following the Fashoda incident of 1898, almost to a state of national panic (the invasion novel remained a staple of popular fiction until the outbreak of the Great War). Gonne must have been especially gratified to play the part since her old enemy Queen Victoria was now dead. In 1900, when the Queen had paid a visit to Ireland, Gonne had been too ill in France to travel to defy her adversary in Dublin. She took her revenge.

Dublin audiences quickly comprehended the extra-theatrical impact of this coat-trailing work. One Anglo-Irishman famously recalled wondering if such plays should be put on unless the people responsible were prepared to shoot and be shot at. Perhaps a more telling summary of the play's effect on national feeling is supplied by the moderate nationalist commentator J. J. Horgan. He wrote in 1948 of the play's visionary conclusion:

> No more potent lines were ever spoken on an Irish stage. All our hopes were in that answer, it had an echo in every heart. It symbolised and rekindled that flame of romantic revolutionary nationalism which was to consume so many of its devotees and which has not even yet been quenched by the healing waters of freedom and experience. Poets have much to answer for. (Horgan 1948: 94)

No one in 1902 really could have anticipated how all-consuming might be the fiery emotions which such a play provoked. That lesson would be learnt when in 1916 and 1919 the flames of revolution took firm hold in Ireland. Yet even in 1902 it was for some a disturbing portent and for others a work of prophetic Irish feeling, which, for the only time in his life, made Yeats a genuinely national figure. He had asserted himself in a play commending self-immolation in the cause of Irish freedom and was accorded the respect that so frequently was withheld by unsympathetic nationalist public opinion.

Other dramatic experiments of this period which engaged with the theme of self-sacrifice were not of a kind that could easily endear Yeats to the audiences which responded enthusiastically to *Cathleen ni Houlihan*. Aristocratic elitism, so offensive in *The Countess Cathleen*, was acceptable in a Fenian version (Fenianism had always espoused an ideology of revolutionary vanguardism in its own elitist cabals) which summoned a chosen few to a sacred, self-immolating destiny. When it recurred as an ideal of artistic and religious commitment, taken to the point of heroic individual self-sacrifice which the common herd could not comprehend, then Yeats's vision of human potential had no ready purchase on the imaginations of his compatriots. *Where There Is Nothing*, composed swiftly by Yeats in September and October 1902 and published in a first version in the same year as a supplement to the *United Irishman*, (30 October, dated 1 November), might have been designed deliberately to forfeit the credit which his success earlier in the year had won him. For if *The Countess Cathleen* had fluttered the religious dovecotes in Dublin, the frank, anarchic heterodoxy of the new play's hero would have provoked pious outrage. Yeats seems to have been aware of this, for the following year he entertained the idea of a London rather than an Irish production, although the work had its inception in his impression that the Irish Literary Theatre required some plays in prose. It eventually opened in a production by the Stage Society (one of the independent theatre clubs which could mount such works beyond the Lord Chamberlain's censorious purview), in a rewritten version of the hurriedly composed script, in June 1904. The play had been published in 1903 in its revised form (which is addressed below) as the first in a projected series of Irish dramatic texts. In a later form it became *The Unicorn from the Stars*, much of which was from Lady Gregory's hand (1908).

Where There Is Nothing dramatizes in five stylistically distinct acts the spiritual quest of a propertied Irish gentleman who is alienated from his own class by the visionary experiences which make of him an isolated malcontent amid the banalities of merely social existence. His odyssey takes him first to a life among the tinker-folk, with whom he celebrates the spirit of licence, holy drunkenness and Tolstoyan Christian anarchism, to the horror of his former acquaintances, then to a monastery where he achieves prophetic powers of utterance in trance states that undermine orthodox Christian authority. He is expelled, and with a few faithful disciples, takes up the life of an itinerant religious teacher until he is slain by the mob, a martyr to his own terrifying dedication. In a compellingly ritualistic scene in the monastery in Act IV, Yeats has his hero, Paul Ruttledge, in potent symbolism, extinguish candles representing the Law, towns, the Church, the very world itself, in the name of a 'religion so wholly supernatural, that is so opposed to the order of nature that the world can never capture it' (Worth 1987: 98). For the play is a dramatic working out of the precept enunciated in *The Secret Rose* that where there is nothing, there is God. But where the tale of that name ended without violence, the play involves the hero's death, the enigmatic metaphysical doctrine on his dying lips. Paul Ruttledge's assertion of his mystical, commanding nature results in self-immolation as he accepts his martyrdom: 'for at death the soul comes into possession of itself, and returns to the joy that made it' (ibid.: 115).

It is not difficult to see this play as a defiant response by Yeats to Irish censure of his own magical ambitions and mystical purposes. He was certainly conscious that there was a good deal of himself in his main character. And there is much in Ruttledge's teaching with which Yeats would have concurred: his Blakean celebration of passionate, disruptive energy, his commitment to ritual as the handmaiden of vision, his questing dedication to the point of self-sacrifice. He sensed too that something of his own less than attractive imperiousness of manner had been at work in the first version of Paul Ruttledge, which he sought to soften in revision. As he himself commented: 'In the old version he did rather ram his ideas down people's throats' (*CL3*: 312). In the new version he hoped to 'make him more emotional, more merely passionate' as he 'tried to show Paul's magnetic quality, his power of making people love him and of carrying them away. I dont think he himself would have been in the ordinary sense sympathetic. . . . People love Paul because they find in him a certain strength, a certain abundance' (*CL3*: 312). One suspects some rueful self-knowledge mingles here with wish-fulfilment.

What the play incontrovertibly dramatizes is how spiritual adventurism risks social obloquy and can demand the sacrifice of life itself. A conviction explored by the poet in the 1890s on the level of an otherworldly, even decadent, religiosity, now finds confident dramatic expression in a loosely structured epic play, which makes the assaults of the conventional mind and of the mob on the free spirit of liberation, real and rebarbatively repressive forces. There is a tone of exuberant contempt in Ruttledge's anarchic rejection of the world which gives the play a relish for conflict that had been absent when battle had been joined principally on the plane of spiritual aspiration. Ruttledge takes disconcerting pleasure in identifying the perambulator and adult preoccupation with its contents as the chief enemy of human promise when he informs his procreative brother 'You have begotten fools' (Worth 1987: 90). Responsibility for neither Shakespear's nor Gonne's progeny had, one imagines, much attracted Yeats in his relations with the two women. He has his hero in this play make a scornful virtue of such inhibition. Paul Ruttledge aspires to higher forms of sacrifice altogether.

As does the hero of a third play of heroic sacrifice, *The King's Threshold*, which Yeats drafted in the spring of 1903. This asserts the right of the poet to be heard in affairs of state. Seanhcan, chief poet of ancient Ireland, stages a hunger strike when he is banished by the King from the Council of State. He refuses to abandon his self-sacrificing campaign as representatives of all the powers in the land who, for corrupt reasons, seek to dissuade him from his course. He holds firm and at the last it is the king who submits, when he is forced to receive his crown from the poet's hand, as if to acknowledge that his sovereignty depends on a higher power than kingship, the power of art. In the version of the play which opened in the Molesworth Hall in Dublin on 8 October 1903, along with Synge's *In the Shadow of the Glen*, Yeats has the play end thus triumphantly. In offering such an upbeat conclusion to his Irish audience, the poet may have been influenced by Lady Gregory, who perhaps suggested that he might provide a 'few happy moments in the theatre' (Flannery 1976: 307–8). In fact the trajectory of the play seems tragedy-bound, which Yeats accepted in his ultimate revision of it in 1922, when the experience of modern hunger striking in Ireland for a political cause had given a note of awful, tragic authenticity to what had existed hitherto only in the annals of folklore. In the version of 1922, the poet dies, another in the list of Yeatsian heroes who pays an absolute price for his ideals.

Yeats's early plays serve notice that he fully understood that the artist and seer would meet forceful opposition to his crusade to spiritualize the world. In *On Baile's Strand* Cuchulain is victim not only of his own nature but of a king's concern for political and dynastic order. In *The King's Threshold*, too, the state seeks to subject the poet to its will. Ruttledge in *Where There Is Nothing* is repelled by his own landlord caste's fatuity of life, but meets his fate at the hands of a zealous mob. In *Cathleen ni Houlihan* it is not the money-grubbing peasantry who are privileged to witness the transformation which makes the old woman a young woman with the walk of a queen, but a young child, whom we must assume has not yet been corrupted by the prevailing acquisitiveness.

Despite an intense preoccupation in these works with the enemies of heroism, with his religious and artistic vocation, and despite his awareness of the even greater sacrifices he might still be called upon to make if he remained true to his calling, Yeats did not foresee the most serious blow to his hopes for Ireland. That blow came in February 1903. He felt it was a devastating act of betrayal of all he had sought to achieve.

Since their work together in the 1798 commemoration and her confession to Yeats of the complications of her past, Yeats and Gonne had maintained a spiritual communion in dreams, visions and 'astral' journeyings. They had met occasionally and corresponded as their differing pursuits allowed. Gonne had supported Yeats in the controversy over *The Countess Cathleen* and encouraged him as one who had 'done wonderful work in waking people up to the Irish ideals' (*GLY*: 107). Yet however close they were on the astral plane, Gonne knew, as the pace of her political engagement quickened, that they could never live as man and wife in the world of political intrigue and revolutionary activism in which she was caught up. She knew he did not care for the political battle to which she was so committed, but tried to assure him in July 1899 that, although their respective commitments at first sight seemed 'very far apart' (*GLY*: 109), they were 'curiously the same only on different planes' (ibid.). A year later she felt it was time to help Yeats to see both her and his own situation more clearly:

> I do not want you to make up your mind to sacrifice yourself for me. I know that just now, perhaps, it is useless my saying to you 'love some other woman'. All I want of you is not to make up your mind *not* to, to put it before you as a duty, that would be wrong the gods do want that, & it makes me very sad. As for me you are right in saying that I will be always to you as a sister. I have chosen a life which to some might be hard, but which to me is the only one possible.... All I want of you is not to build up an imaginary wall of duty or effort between you and life – for the rest the gods will arrange, for you are one of those they have chosen to do their work. (*GLY*: 130)

Life for Gonne had indeed been hard in the years since her 'mystical marriage' to the poet and by 1900 it had become markedly dangerous too, a thing of espionage, betrayals, police surveillance and murderous plots. The Boer War, which broke out in the autumn of 1899, had offered militant Irish nationalists an opportunity to prove that England's difficulty could be Ireland's opportunity. It was time to seize the day. In January 1900 Gonne went to the United States to lecture on the Boer cause. She had revived her association with Millevoye, whose Anglophobic patriotism and high-level official contacts made him an apparently useful ally; but in 1900 as their emotional entanglement came to an undignified and sordid terminus, with Millevoye seeking sexual satisfaction elsewhere, she found herself in a looking-glass world of conspiracy, informers, diverted funds and probable embezzlement. Her plan to plant bombs on British troop ships, with South African and French support, to discourage military recruitment, resulted in her embroilment in the convoluted quarrels of the Irish Republican Brotherhood, with Yeats's old enemy Frank Hugh O'Donnell as the seedy Minotaur of a Conradian labyrinth. As her plans disintegrated, the funds she had raised from the Transvaal's representative in Belgium were intercepted by O'Donnell for his own purposes. Yeats and she had to discourage one faction of the IRB from executing the egregious fellow. They both distanced themselves from the Brotherhood as a result of this murky business.

Gonne remained excitedly committed to the Boer cause, and however much Yeats may have hoped she would be true to their 'spiritual marriage', she was all too likely in these action-packed years, when she was rousing the Irish people to resist recruitment and energetically at work with the Daughters of Erin in raising Irish consciousness, to be susceptible to the claims of another man for whom action was second nature.

John MacBride, a Mayo man and of an age with Yeats, had joined the IRB in his youth. He had emigrated to South Africa, where, on the outbreak of the Boer War, he joined an Irish Brigade, in which he served as a major and as second-in-command. He had seen action and was celebrated as a war hero not only by the Boers but by his fellow countrymen. He had stood up to the British. Gonne met him in Paris in November 1900. They quickly made common cause and Gonne arranged for MacBride to undertake a lecture tour in the United States. She joined him there, since he found lecturing more unnerving than facing enemy fire. He proposed marriage to the Irish Joan of Arc, who would not accept in a time of war. By the early summer of 1902 she was ready for matrimony, though before her marriage to MacBride, she once again had to refuse a new proposal from Yeats that they should make their 'marriage' a more bodily one.

Yeats had been overwhelmingly surprised in December 1898 when Gonne had revealed the secrets of her hidden life with Millevoye. For Yeats, her behaviour had challenged his own vision of her as the transcendent beauty for whom he had sacrificed his youth. He had explained to Lady Gregory in 1899 that she had been caught up in a war of 'blinded idealism against phantasy & eternal law' (*CL2*: 357). It was as though she had been swept along in a battle she could not win. In their 'spiritual marriage' it had in consequence become vital for him that she remain aloof from the forces arrayed against idealism. He could stoop, as one who saw himself as a teacher of a kind, to what he identified in another letter to Lady Gregory, in April 1900, in a fastidiously offensive phrase, as 'the baptism of the gutter' (*CL2*: 512). She could not. She must inhabit an elevated sphere of her own, where she could be available for spiritual union with her poetic lover.

By summer 1902, with the furore over *The Countess Cathleen* still a bitter memory, with D. P. Moran 'intermittently' (Toomey 1996: 60) waging a specifically Catholic nationalist campaign against him, Yeats must have been unsettled enough to be told by Gonne that she had spent a week in a Carmelite Convent in France, where her daughter Iseult had been baptized a Catholic. Gonne's aside – 'I felt a little inclined to be also but felt it would mean limitations of thought so didn't' (*GYL*: 155–6) – cannot have been wholly reassuring to Yeats. He sought to dissuade her from such a momentous step, though in a dream he became convinced that she would take it. Yeats's response in 1903, when he learnt that Gonne did indeed intend conversion to Catholicism and that she was about to marry MacBride, was a measure of how deeply she figured in his own vision of a shared national destiny and how betrayed he felt by what he saw as a capitulation to the enemy.

He learnt of her decision one night in early February 1903, as he was about to give a lecture on the future of Irish drama. By about 10 February he had sent at least four letters trying in vain to save her from herself. He thought she was about to demean their shared cause in a degraded misalliance. The fourth letter – extant in a draft which bears the marks of great agitation – is a painful document indeed. Yeats's caste snobbery, never very far from the surface in his personality, boils up as a noxious anti-Catholic elitism, as if the nightmare of Gonne's apostasy has released a bile he did not customarily allow to influence his feelings. He does not appear wholly in control of himself in this bitter, admonitory letter.

At the outset he reminds Gonne of their 'mystical marriage' which he believed gave him the right to write her such a missive; he reminds her of their work together and warns her of imminent danger and of the terrible risks he considers she is taking: 'For all who undertake such tasks there comes a moment of extreme peril. I know now that you have come to your moment of peril. If you carry out your purpose you will fall into a lower order & do great injury to the religeon of ⟨pure⟩ free souls that is growing up in Ireland, it may be to enlighten the whole world' (*CL3*: 316; the angled brackets indicate decipherable cancelled matter). He tells her too that it is being said in Ireland that her conversion will mean a triumph for the priests. Her action will thrust the people further down into a vitiating dependency on their clergy. By contrast, Yeats had seen her as a force for spiritual liberation because of her freedom of spirit and her independence of mind as an upper-class woman who had embraced the cause of the Irish people:

> You represent a superior class, a class where people are more independent, have a more beautiful life, a more refined life. Every man almost of the people who has spoken to me of you has shown that you influence him very largely because of this ... You are going to marry one of the people .... This weakness which ⟨has⟩ thrust down your soul to a lower order of faith is thrusting you down socially, is thrusting you down to the people. (*CL3*: 316–17)

Accordingly, by her conversion and marriage, Gonne will forfeit her capacity to lead. 'Do not', the poet pleads in mingled admiration, flattery and some impertinence, 'you ⟨whom⟩ seemed the most strong the most inspired be the first to betray us, to betray the truth' (*CL3*: 317). He turns the dagger in the wound when he reminds her of how she had always excoriated the Irish priest-hood as anti-national, for a moment in his anguish acceding to her sanguinary view of the Irish political past. Will it be the priests, he asks her, who will lead the people in their hour of need; for they have always betrayed Ireland and denounced the spilling of blood in the National cause. They have weakened (he casts her own argument back in her face) Irish manhood, broken its pride.

Gonne, who married MacBride in Paris on 21 February 1903, responded with magnanimity to this onslaught. She truly cared for Yeats and the way in which she immediately sought in letters to calm his mind, even though his letter to her had been a presumptuous thing, is touching. She assured him that she had not been vexed and that their friendship would survive. By May of the year she was reaffirming conscientiously to him, what she had already told him in February, that she thought all religions a way to God, as Yeats himself had taught her. She assured him that she had become a Catholic to help her own work: 'it was necessary. . . to become more completely united to the soul' (*GYL*: 170) of the people, more completely to understand their thoughts and the better to help them.

Yet the differences between them were very great. Before the year was out, Yeats had further reason to feel that Gonne and he were antithetical spirits, and that she had indeed gone over to the enemy when she had married MacBride. The occasion of their dispute was the production of John Millington Synge's play *In the Shadow of the Glen*, which opened in Dublin on 8 October 1903, to a chorus of nationalist denunciation in which Gonne joined.

Synge was the Dublin-born son of a Protestant solicitor and a devout, evangel-ically Christian mother. The Synges were a solidly prosperous family with links of kin and loyalty to landed gentry in County Wicklow. In the nice social gradations of Protestant Ireland, the Synges were a cut above the Yeatses. The future dramatist's mother was snobbish and zealous. Left by the death of her husband with a family to raise alone (John was an infant when he was orphaned), she had experienced great distress when her son, like many a Victorian youth, discovered Darwin and lost the strict faith in which she had earnestly instructed him. He had become a drifter, undecided between music or poetry as a way of life. He spent the years between 1895 and 1902 in Paris, where as a student at the Sorbonne he read widely in contemporary literature. Trinity College, Dublin, where the Irish language was taught, largely as a tool useful in proselytism, had given him some knowledge of his country's native language, which he augmented by visits to the western, Irish-speaking Aran Islands. He had made his first visit to the islands in the summer of 1898 and spent part of the next three summers there.

Yeats and he, as we saw, had met in Paris in December 1896. Synge had become involved there with Gonne's branch of the Young Ireland Societies, but, never anything more than a mild cultural nationalist, he had disassociated himself when he learnt of the violently revolutionary ambitions which she and her co-conspirators nurtured. Yeats liked to believe that he advised Synge to give up trying to be a decadent poet and literary critic and to go to Aran to live there as one of the people 'to express a life that has never found expression' (Yeats in Synge 1968: 63), thereby affecting the course of literary history. As Nicholas Grene (Grene 1989: 48–9) has argued, however, it is likely that Yeats in his recollection of the early stages of their relationship conflated the meeting of 1896 with a later Parisian encounter of 1899 after, not before, Synge's first visit to the islands. Given Yeats's ruthlessly cavalier way with chronology in the interests of a personal myth, he was right aesthetically in highlighting that it was Aran and the West of Ireland which gave Synge to know what his subject should be. For it was Aran, as well as an ancestral Wicklow which made of him a dramatist imaginatively engaged by the vitality, pagan energy and exuberance of language and spirit of a social world altogether remote from the reserved decorums of his own invincibly pious Dublin bourgeois background.

In the summer of 1902 Synge's apprenticeship to dramatic art came to an end when he wrote two of his most remarkable works: the one-act plays *Riders to The Sea* and *In the Shadow of the Glen* (subsequently titled *The Shadow of the Glen*). He also embarked on a two-act comic work, *The Tinkers' Wedding*. By winter, in an *annus mirabilis*, he had begun *The Well of the Saints* and his masterpiece, *The Playboy of the Western World*.

In The Shadow of the Glen is not in fact set on the Aran Islands, nor even in the West, but in the County Wicklow of the dramatist's own ancestry. It is not the Wicklow of Anglo-Irish landlordism which preoccupies him in this play but the county of small peasant farms in difficult terrain. The shadowed glen, in which a young married woman ekes out a life of sexual and emotional deprivation in a barren marriage to an old farmer, is a symbol of social isolation and female oppression. The woman of the house is lured away from her spiritual and sexual impoverishment by a tramp who offers her at least, in a wandering life, the chance of some delight, pleasure and simple sociability before she dies. A rural, comedic version of *The Doll's House* (she shares a first name with Ibsen's heroine), *In the Shadow of the Glen* gave scandal to those among the nationalists who found any less than flattering betrayal of the Irish people an occasion for taking offence. That Yeats, their *bête noire*, was a supporter of Synge, only intensified their irritation that the scion of an Anglo-Irish Protestant family would cast a dramatic slur on the chastity and respectability of a Catholic wife. Moran's *Leader* was true to its intemperate form. Its drama critic thought the play one the nastiest he had ever seen and brutally condemned it as 'an evil compound of Ibsen and Boucicault'. The *Independent and Nation* waged a less colourfully expressed but no less zealous campaign against Synge's grave insult to Irish Catholic womanhood.

Once again Yeats had to defend artistic freedom from the philistines, who this time included Madame MacBride. She wrote to him in September, before the first production, that she thought Synge's play 'horrid' and in a second letter disassociated herself from Yeats's dramatic movement before the first night. She told him bluntly: 'We are in a life & death struggle with England . . . & have not time & energy for purely literary & artistic movements unless they can be made to serve directly & immediately the National cause' *(GYL*: 178). By contrast, Yeats wrote in the *United Irishman* on 17 October 1903 to defend Synge's play and to insist, 'One can serve one's country alone out of the abundance of one's own heart, and it is labour enough to be certain that one is in the right, without having to be certain that one's thought is expedient also' *(CL3*: 449). He was answering Gonne's private letter in public. The following week in the same periodical she let it be known that she considered the play one which would please those who had put ease and comfort before patriotic duty and accused Yeats of admitting deleterious 'foreign influences' to his work *(United Irishman*, 24 October 1903). They could scarcely have been more at odds. In the same issue Yeats put his cards openly on the table. He identified his enemies precisely, in terms guaranteed to give wide offence. They were to be found among 'the more ignorant sort of Gaelic propagandist, who would have nothing said or thought that is not in country Gaelic' *(CL3*: 452). He found them too among 'the more ignorant sort of priest, who, forgetful of the great traditions of his Church, would deny all ideas that might perplex a parish of farmers or artisans or half-educated shopkeepers' *(CL3*: 452). And then there was 'the obscurantism of the politician and not always of the more ignorant sort, who would reject every idea which is not of immediate service to his cause' *(CL3*: 452). Gonne was consorting with the enemy, whom he implied in his scornful polemic, were the broad mass of the very people she felt called upon to serve.

Five days after Gonne and MacBride married in France, a great storm struck the West of Ireland. It uprooted trees in the woods at Coole where Yeats had been accustomed to wander since the first summer he had stayed there. In August 1903 he published a slim volume of poems to which he gave the title *In the Seven Woods: Beings Poems of the Irish Heroic Age* (the first poem in the collection was also so titled). Yeats recorded in the volume 'I made some of these poems walking about among the Seven Woods, before the big wind of nineteen hundred and three blew down so many trees, & troubled the wild creatures, & changed the look of things' *(ISW*: 25). When the book appeared, Yeats must have been aware that the stormy events of 1903 had changed much in his own life too. One of the finest poems in the collection is 'Adam's Curse', which dramatizes a poignant, meditative conversation between the poet and two beautiful women about the dedication required by both poets and women in the service of beauty. We know from Gonne's autobiography that the poem was based on a late-summer after-dinner conversation, between Yeats, herself and her sister, of 1902 (MacBride 1994: 317–18). It suggests that the conversationalists found agreement on the sexual equality of effort involved in the Edenic fall, which means that everything beautiful requires 'much labouring' if it is to seem the unstudied work of sheer inspiration. Yet the poem inhabits, not the climate of eschatological expectation, which had so invested *The Wind Among the Reeds* with portent and is still invoked in the title poem of the collection, but an atmosphere of acknowledgment that hopes had been disappointed. Instead of a world and an erotic relationship transformed by a spiritual apocalypse, the poet and his loved one are now cast adrift in mere temporal existence, the emptiness of repetitive accumulation of days and years:

> We sat grown quiet at the name of love.
> We saw the last embers of daylight die
> And in the trembling blue-green of the sky
> A moon, worn as if it had been a shell
> Washed by time's waters as they rose and fell
> About the stars and broke in days and years.
>
> I had a thought for no one's but your ears;
> That you were beautiful, and that I strove
> To love you in the old high way of love;
> That it had all seemed happy, and yet we'd grown
> As weary-hearted as that hollow moon.

The winds which blow in this book are still symbolically suggestive of the spiritual forces which Yeats had earlier invoked in such poems as '*The Secret Rose*' ('*thy great wind blows*') but now they are also the more unpredictable winds of circumstance and history (variously a 'wintry wind' and a 'black wind') that buffet a man who realizes he has arrived at a more complicatedly recollective phase of a troubled life. The predominant tone in the lyrics in the book (which also included, in the 1903 first publication, the two long narrative poems 'The Old Age of Queen Maeve' and 'Baile and Aillinn', as well as Yeats's play *On Baile's Strand*) is one of pained, passionate, yet eloquently complimentary retrospection. Maturity has brought memories freighted with a sense of lost possibilities and beauty no longer in its first flower. A note of dramatic intensity has, however, entered Yeats's poetry, as he situates himself as the poet speaking in poems that admit of contemporary experience of a realized social world and the fraught conflicts of mood and emotion human relations involve. These are no longer the verses of an almost disembodied voice, mesmerically bringing a symbolic universe into revelatory existence, but the poems of a man who has been listening to the voices of actors and performers on stage and in recitals to the psaltery. They are the poems too of a man who has found himself confronted by the challenges of life's ineluctable ambiguities when he had expected a transcendent consummation in a spiritual renewal of Ireland and the world with which his own destiny and that of Maud Gonne were united. Sacrifice, which Yeats had made a primary ideal thoughout his youth, in mid-years would mean not some ecstatic transcendence of the self as death and revelation meet for the hero/martyr, but a condition of enduring personal loss. This is perhaps most clear in the poem that Yeats added to this volume's contents in 1906, 'Never Give all the Heart':

> O never give the heart outright,
> For they, for all smooth lips can say,
> Have given their hearts up to the play.
> And who could play it well enough
> If deaf and dumb and blind with love?

> He that made this knows all the cost,
> For he gave all his heart and lost.

Whatever the truth about Yeats's claim here to have given all his heart in love (this is a poem, we must remember, in which he is mythologizing his own past as earlier he idealized the present and the future, and not a confession) the sense of regret is palpable. The repeated 'all' implies the poet's awareness of the absolute, spiritually uncreative, nature of the sacrifices he has made, to no apparent purpose.

7

The Strong Enchanter

In the autumn of 1901 Violet Martin wrote to her friend and literary co-adjutor Edith Somerville (they were both redoubtable Unionists) that she had seen Yeats and Maud Gonne at the theatre in Dublin. She had met the poet earlier in the year during his summer visit to Coole where she had thought he looked just what she had expected. He struck her as a cross 'between a Dominie Sampson and a starved R.C. curate – in seedy black clothes with a large black bow at the root of his long naked throat' (Lewis 1989: 252). Gonne as a physical presence also made an impact. Martin reported of her appearance in the theatre: 'I . . . thought her looks terrific. The features still handsome the nose salient and short but the badness of the expression was startling. A huge mop of curled yellow hair crowned her big fat body' (ibid.: 256). Gonne was arriving at an age when she could expect such prejudiced comments on the effects of time on her beauty. Even one of the poet's constant friends, as 'The Folly of Being Comforted' records, had observed to Yeats 'Your well-belovèd's hair has threads of grey,/ And little shadows come about her eyes'. For the poet such intimations of the bodily decrepitude which would eventually overtake them both, were heart-breaking.

In the Seven Woods is a book of the heart. In its brief, poignant lyrics of lost love, of beauty about to fade, of bitter-sweet recall, the poet speaks as from a full heart, emotion not so much recollected in tranquillity as in the flood of intense present feeling. In the title poem the poet speaks of how he has 'put away/The unavailing outcries and the old bitternes/That empty the heart' in a poem which is itself filled with heartfelt emotion. In the collection as a whole, where the word 'heart' recurs many times, the energies of an intense utterance seem governed by a pulsating structural rhythm of statement and counterstatement, the rise and fall of feeling, the systolic and diastolic movements of the vessels themselves. 'The Folly of Being Comforted', for example, is structured in two verse paragraphs. In the first the poet reports being advised that since his belovèd's beauty is beginning to decline, he now needs only patience until faded beauty will make his state of unrequited love easier to bear. To this the poet responds, as one emotion sweeps out of the poem to allow it to fill with another: 'But heart there is no comfort, not a grain'. The effect is to make the repeated beats in the poem's final couplet seem much more than an exploitation of an all-too familiar trope:

> O heart O heart if she'd but turn her head,
> You'd know the folly of being comforted.

For *In the Seven Woods* is a book of the body. The heart that beats through its pages is certainly the romantic metonymy for sexual and strong feeling, as in the opening lines of 'The Rider from the North' (subsequently collected as 'The Happy Townland') where the poet imagines 'many a strong farmer/Who's heart would break in two'. It is also the bodily organ which beats in the breast and quickens as the mood of the poet alters. In 'The Song of Red Hanrahan' (subsequently collected as 'Red Hanrahan's Song about Ireland') 'Angers that are like noisy clouds have set our hearts abeat'. For the lips, eyes and hair of Yeats's 1890s' imagining in *The Wind Among the Reeds*, where the body was rendered ethereal and impalpable in a dimension of the symbolic, have been replaced by a consciousness of the 'marrow' into which memory of the loved one's beauty pierces like an arrow 'Made out of a wild thought' ('The Arrow'). In 'The Players ask for a Blessing on the Psalteries and on Themselves', the poet who has experimented with poetry as a spoken thing has his players demand 'Hurry to bless the hands that play/The mouths that speak', in their knowledge that the timeless beauty they seek to produce is also dependent on their mutable bodies and the materiality of 'notes and strings'.

Yeats who had already begun to think of a magical order as a living body, who had sought to make poetry vibrant on the tongue in a living theatre, was now also writing lyrics which implied that verse itself has its source and its life in the body as well as in the mind. The physical reality of the volume, and the familial conditions of production in which these poems were first collected in volume form, augmented the sense that Yeats was newly attentive to his art's bodily, material aspect and to its debt to a labour more akin to physical than mental or spiritual work:

> I said 'a line will take us hours maybe,
> Yet if it does not seem a moment's thought
> Our stitching and unstitching has been naught.
> Better go down upon your marrow bones
> And scrub a kitchen pavement, or break stones
> Like an old pauper, in all kinds of weather;
> For to articulate sweet sounds together
> Is to work harder than all these...'.
>   ('Adam's Curse')

The death of Susan Yeats in 1900 had undoubtedly been a release for John Butler Yeats. It was no longer so necessary to keep up a family home in Bedford

Park, with the difficulties that that involved. Scarcely domestic himself, his wife had never relished the burdens of household management and for many years strokes and her depressions had made her incapable of contributing to work in the home. At his wife's death both his sons were launched in their different ways (Jack Yeats was making his way as an artist, his first solo exhibition had been held in 1897) and John Butler had never been concerned for long that his daughters were not yet provided for and remained unmarried.

In October 1901 an exhibition of his own work, along with that of the great landscape painter Nathaniel Hone, was mounted in Dublin, through the good offices of a family friend, Sarah Purser. Its favourable reception caused John Butler Yeats, amid a good deal of uncertainty at this transitional stage of his life, to consider settling in his native country once again. The idealism and earnest application of his daughters to things Irish in the London of the late 1890s was the factor in the familial chemistry which made this practicable.

The Arts and Crafts movement, over which William Morris had presided as an inspiring spirit in late Victorian Britain, had, by the turn of the century attracted Irish interest. The Arts and Crafts Society of Ireland was founded in 1894, after Morris's advice had been sought. However it was an Irish woman living in England who was to give Arts and Crafts in the country a major stimulus when she decided in 1902 to establish a craft centre there. Evelyn Gleeson had studied art in London where she had met disciples of Morris. She had got to know the Yeats family in Bedford Park, since she was a member of the Irish Literary Society. So when she was advised on health grounds to leave the city, she invited 'Lily' and 'Lollie' to join her in her Irish project. Gleeson rented a house in Dundrum, then a village about six miles from Dublin. The house was duly renamed Dun Emer (Emer's fort – Emer in the Celtic saga being the wife of Cuchulain, skilled in needlework and weaving). The Yeats sisters took a house nearby in November 1902, where they established themselves, with John Butler Yeats also in residence, and set to work. The press was to operate from their new home, Gurteen Dhas.

The aim of their co-operative venture (the partnership with the ill-tempered Gleeson was a fraught one and broke up finally in 1908) was 'to find work for Irish hands in the making of beautiful things'. 'Lily', given her earlier experience with Morris and his daughter, was to be in charge of embroidery, making and selecting designs and training young women as workers. 'Lollie' was to be responsible for hand-printing on a small press which had been acquired second-hand. With such a project in mind she gained some knowledge of type-setting in London. Her poet brother was to serve as editor for the imprint, selecting books for publication. The first two works published were a volume of verse by AE and Yeats's *In the Seven Woods*.

Yeats recorded in one copy of this production that it was the first of his books 'that is a pleasure to look at – a pleasure whether open or shut...' (cited in Wade 1968: 67). The rich decor of some *fin de siècle* artwork now a thing of the past, the design is chaste and uncluttered, the print, as the press itself announced, was 'a good eighteenth century fount of type which is not eccentric in form, or difficult to read'. The end matter advertised other Dun Emer craft products, highlighting the physicality of the book's production. The paper used, the reader is told, was 'made of linen rags and without bleaching chemicals', in a print run of 325 copies. The visual impact of the poems is foregrounded since they are printed in a bold black ink, while some of the other printed matter is in blood-red. The polarities which in Yeats's early poems had been things of wavering indeterminacy, shadowy interfusings of opposed realities, are here associated with precision in the stark colour contrast in the print. The book, both in its contents and its production, acknowledges the material aspects of human existence. It is an Irish book made in Ireland.

In a 1906 publication the poet himself commented on the change of style which the writing for the theatre involved for him, which had in fact affected the poems in *In the Seven Woods*:

> Some of my friends . . . do not understand why I have not been content with lyric writing. But one can only do what one wants to do, and to me drama . . . has been a search for more of manful energy, more of cheerful acceptance of whatever rises out of the logic of events, and for clean outline, instead of those outlines of lyric poetry that are blurred with desire and vague regret. All art is in the last analysis an endeavour to condense as out of the flying vapour of the world an image of human perfection and for its own and not for the art's sake, and that is why the labour of the alchemists, who were called artists in their day, is a befitting comparison for all deliberate change of style. (*VP*: 849)

Aestheticism is eschewed here and while the metaphor of alchemy might seem to give an other-worldly exoticism to Yeats's conception of the artist, his emphasis is on labour producing something substantial as water is condensed out of 'flying vapour'. The spiritual, as it were, is deliberately brought down to earth in an image of human perfection which we can take has its distinctly bodily aspect, as style expresses manful energy in clear, dramatic outlines.

Yeats had been encouraged in such a redirection of his poetic not only by his experiments in the drama, in living theatre and in the experiments he had conducted in oral performance of verse, but by his excited reading in the autumn of 1902 of the works of Nietzsche. Indeed his recruitment of Nietzsche to his personal pantheon of powerful and noble spirits who might direct his own life as man and artist, was a crucial moment in the poet's intellectual and emotional development.

Yeats had probably been aware of Friedrich Nietzsche's narcotic, addictive philosophical and literary works since at least 1896, for in that year 'the *Savoy* included the first of Havelock Ellis's "Friedrich Nietzsche"' series alongside Yeats's "Rosa Alchemica"' (Bohlmann 1982: 1, cited in Worth 1987). And Katherine Worth has suggested that the poet in an 1897 essay on Blake 'seems to be in touch with Nietzsche' (Worth 1987: 20) in the conviction that the artist can transcend good and evil (Yeats claimed that he got the title of his volume *Ideas of Good and Evil* from one of Blake's manuscript works, *CL3*: 313). We know too that he purchased a pamphlet published in 1900 which contained brief extracts from the German's writings in English translation, some time between its publication date and October 1902 (*CL3*: 239).

In the summer of 1902 Yeats had met a rich young New York lawyer, whose practical help was to mean a great deal over the years. For John Quinn, who was in Europe for the first time when Yeats and he met, was to earn himself a role in modern literary history not only as a loyal, wonderfully active friend and patron of Yeats and his family, but as an obsessive, extremely astute collector of modern literary manuscripts and paintings. His name threads through the literary history of Modernism as beneficent friend and strong-willed advocate of those he chose to support (among them Joseph Conrad, James Joyce and T. S. Eliot). Quinn's first gifts to Yeats were copies of Nietzsche's writings.

Back in New York in the autumn he sent Yeats copies of Nietzsche's works, probably *Thus Spake Zarathustra*, then *The Case of Wagner* and *The Genealogy of Morals* (*AM*: 584). By the end of the year, Yeats wrote apologetically to Lady Gregory:

> I have written to you little and badly of late I am afraid for the truth is you have had a rival in Nietzsche, that strong enchanter. I have read him so much that I have made my eyes bad again. They were getting well it had seemed. Nietzsche completes Blake & has the same roots – I have not read anything with so much excitement, since I got to love Morris's stories which have the same curious astringent joy. (*CL3*: 284)

By early February Yeats was thanking Quinn for his gift of Alexander Tille's three-volume edition of *The Works of Friedrich Nietzsche*, in terms which echo his observation to Lady Gregory about his association of Nietzsche with Blake, but which also highlight how the new thinker's influence is imaginative, psychological and literary rather than strictly philosophic. For Yeats could certainly have found in Nietzsche reaffirmation of Blake's antinomial, dialectical vision of reality ('Without contraries is no progression', Blake announced definitively in *The Marriage of Heaven and Hell*). And Nietzsche's separation of the impulses at work in culture between Apollonian and Dionysian energies in *The Birth of Tragedy* shares Blakes's profound consciousness of warring forces invigoratingly at work in the world and in his human nature. But he would also have encountered in Nietzsche's robust, often rhapsodic, veneration for the exercise of power by heroic individuals, a kind of completion of Blake's more mystically focused delight in human energy as a manifestation of the divine life. For if Blake found all divinities in the human breast, and deemed energy eternal delight, Nietzsche preached a doctrine whereby the individual, aware of the power realizable in a human being if he rose to his destiny, might heroically transform the world. Blake's spiritualized humanism, in which the body was sacred as the site of the divine in the world, was given astringency and cutting edge in Nietzsche's celebration of the whole man, body, mind and spirit, acting with elevated self-assurance that the will to power in the struggle of life is an ennobling impulse. Accordingly Yeats told Quinn (who had informed Yeats that he detested certain aspects of Nietzsche's philosophy, such as his 'exaltation of brutality' *CL3*: 239):

> He is exaggerated and violent but has helped me very greatly to build up in my mind an imagination of the heroic life. His books have come to me at exactly the right moment, for I have planned out a series of plays which are intended to be an expression of that life which seem[s] to me a kind of proud hard gift giving joyousness.   (*CL3*: 313)

Denis Donoghue in his *Yeats* (1971), a succinct and telling account of Yeats's career, which emphasizes the poet's debt to Nietzsche, accounts for Yeats's enthusiastic response to the philosopher as rooted in Yeats's psychological needs when he first read him intensely. He argues that 'Yeats's "consciousness as conflict" began to define itself in this excited reading of Nietzsche, when he found himself turning from one mood to its opposite and sought some means of retaining both' (Donoghue 1971: 53). He summarizes persuasively:

> His relation to the strong enchanter is based upon the needs of a particular moment, but it became a definitive relation and was never abandoned or even greatly modified. Specifically, the kinship depends on Nietzsche's terminology of power, the endorsement of will and conflict, his feeling for the theatrical principle, his sense of tragedy, contempt for the herd, glorification of the hero.   (ibid.: 56)

Furthermore, Nietzsche offered Yeats a means whereby the inchoate, fissiparous nature of selfhood could be converted into a positive asset. As a man entering on his maturity, conscious of the conflicting forces − in his Anglo-Irish family, in Ireland and England, in his relations with women, in his intellectual and emotional commitments − which had determined his personal and social experience, Yeats could find in Nietzsche a gospel of self-creation that made of extreme psychological tensions, energizing potentialities. For Nietzsche believed, as he had announced in *Beyond Good and Evil* (an English translation appeared in 1907, but extracts from this work which suggested its general tenor were available in 1903 in an English anthology of his work):

> The man of an age of dissolution which mixes the races with one another, who has the inheritance of a diversified descent in his body − that is to say contrary, and often not only contrary, instincts and standards of value, which struggle with one another and are seldom at peace − such a man of late culture and broken lights, will, on average, be a weak man. His fundamental desire is that the war which is *in him* should come to an end. ... Should, however, the contrariety and conflict in such natures operate as an *additional* incentive and stimulus to life − and if, on the other hand, in addition to their powerful and irreconcilable instincts, they have also inherited and indoctrinated into them a proper mastery and subtlety for carrying on the conflict with themselves (that is to say, the faculty of self-control and self-deception), there then arise those marvellously incomprehensible, and inexplicable beings, those enigmatical men, predestined for conquering and circumventing

others, the finest examples of which are Alcibiades and Caesar..., and among artists, perhaps Lionardo da Vinci. (Nietzsche 1907: 122)

The effects of Yeats's enchantment by Nietzsche's writings were swiftly evident. The man whose sense of special destiny had been nurtured by elitist doctrines and rituals of occultism, found in Nietzsche a counsellor who gave instruction in self-mastery and the dominance of others in social contexts where mere hierarchy, as in a magical order, could not be depended upon to enforce submission. In the hysterical letter to Gonne of early February 1903, in which he had sought to dissuade her from marriage to MacBride, written only a few days after his encomium on Nietzsche penned for Quinn, we see how Yeats had incorporated Nietzschean feeling into the image of himself as a chosen magus responsible for the spiritual health of his people. 'There are people', he insisted to Gonne, '(& these are the greater number) who need the priest <&> or some other master but [there] are a few & you are one of those for whom ... surrender to any leadership but that of their own souls is the great betrayal, the denial of God. It was our work to teach a few strong aristocratic... spirits that to believe the soul was immortal & and that one prospered hereafter *if one laid upon oneself* an heroic discipline in living & to send them to uplight the nation' (*CL3*: 316). To the ideal of noble sacrifice is now added the concept of heroically self-disciplined leadership by the Nietzschean free spirit, instructing a chosen cadre of *illuminati*.

It was in his dealings with theatre business and management that Yeats was able to practise what he sensed Nietzsche had preached. He had seen how fractiously human beings could behave in the Order of the Golden Dawn, and although he had kept theatrical options open in London, he was determined that his Irish theatrical venture would not go the same way as the temple in Hammersmith, with its quarrelling magicians. In the years ahead, theatrical Dublin would give him ample opportunity to exercise a Nietzschean capacity for 'conquering and circumventing others' in the interests of the discipline which he believed essential to high co-operative achievement.

In the years since the spring of 1899, when the Irish Literary Theatre had presented its first season of plays, Yeats had worked assiduously, with Lady Gregory's loyal support, to realize his dreams of a poetic theatre in the Dublin capital. The lack of a developed indigenous theatrical tradition made this a very difficult task. Few could have realized that the labours of those years were about to give birth in the Abbey Theatre founded in the autumn of 1904 and launched with four plays in late December of that year, to a long-lasting institution, which for the first time would make Dublin a recognized centre for the production of innovatory drama.

In the absence in Dublin of anything more than a provincial version of the despised London stage, Yeats had had to depend for a pool of available acting talent on dramatic societies, clubs and associations (like Inghinidhe na hÉireann) where nationalism, an interest in the arts and amateurism went somewhat uneasily hand in hand. Furthermore, in George Moore and the financially supportive, if cautiously pious Edward Martyn, Yeats had two collaborators who had proved very difficult indeed, in their comically different ways.

Moore was a professional, cunningly feline man of letters, whose only real commitment was to his own dedicated sense of artistic standards. Martyn, as interested in church art, music and liturgy as he was in the theatre, was very much the kind of amateur writer who lacked the sustained concentration on his craft which allowed for creative development as an artist. Between 1899 and 1903 there had been much disagreement, some real acrimony, and a lack of unity of purpose among the four principals of the Irish Literary Theatre. Yeats, who could collaborate as a dramatist with Lady Gregory, had found it nearly impossible to do so with Moore. Moore's account of their attempt jointly to author one play, the mythologically based *Diarmuid and Grania*, is a comically absurd highpoint of his autobiographical re-creation of their joint endeavour in *Hail and Farewell* (1911–14). The play had premièred disastrously on 21 October 1901, with the professional English actors who had been retained for the production mangling Irish accents. By the following autumn Yeats and Moore were at daggers drawn, since Moore believed Yeats had stolen from him the plot of *Where There Is Nothing*, and Yeats wrote and published it at speed to claim a copyright he felt was his by right. Moore threatened legal action, but nothing came of his petulant gesture.

Martyn too had reason to feel aggrieved about his experience as a participant in the dramatic movement. His play *The Heather Field*, a forceful Ibsenite study in ruinous obsession – an Irish *Master Builder* – had been an undoubted success in the Irish Literary Theatre's first season. A further play of his, *The Tale of the Town*, was reckoned to require substantial revision, if it was to be produced, which Martyn reluctantly permitted Moore and Yeats to attempt. The extent of Moore's surgery nevertheless distressed Martyn, who refused to allow his name to be associated with the work, when it was produced as *The Bending of the Bough* as part of the second season of plays, presented in February 1900. His financial patronage of the movement could scarcely be depended on for the long term.

Through these years of public controversy, of problems and disputes among the founders of the Irish Literary Theatre, as Yeats tested his own dramatic capacities, he also had striven single-mindedly to ensure, despite the movement's hesitant beginnings, that his enterprise would not run into the sands. When at the end of 1901 it was evident that Martyn would no longer bankroll the venture and that the Literary Theatre would be unable to mount another season of plays, at a time when he was seriously tempted to make London rather than Dublin the focus of his theatrical ambitions, Yeats turned to one of the genuinely gifted of the amateur men of the theatre in the Irish capital: Frank Fay, who with his brother Willie, in the Ormond Drama Company, had trained a group of passably competent actors and had themselves attended to developments in contemporary European theatre. The Fays were associated with Inghinidhe na hÉireann in the production of Yeats's *Cathleen ni Houlihan*. Following the acclaim that play attracted they decided to develop their company into a National Theatre Society. In August 1902 the Irish National Dramatic Society (it soon became known as the Irish National

Theatre Society) was founded. Yeats was elected president with AE, Maud Gonne and Douglas Hyde as vice-presidents. John Synge, among others, was elected to membership. At a later meeting Lady Gregory was brought aboard.

The Fays were a godsend to Yeats. Frank in particular had special skills in the teaching of voice production, based on the tradition of French rather than English theatrical practice. And Willie had a good deal of solid practical experience in mounting plays. But the Fays and the actors they had gathered together could not be trusted to share all Yeats's high ideals for a poetic theatre, where the sovereignty of the word would be respected above all else. Yeats could lecture and write (as he repetitively did in the pages of *Samhain*, the successor to *Beltaine* as the occasional journal of the dramatic movement, which survived the terminal season of 1901 as a periodical of theatrical commentary) on the necessity to make 'the poetical play a living dramatic form again' (*Samhain*, no. 2, October 1902: 10). He could draw together, in his authoritatively stated observations, the strands of Irish dramatic experiment (in the Irish-language productions of the Gaelic League, in Cumann na Gaehdheal and its patriotic cultural work in which amateur dramatics played a popular part) and weave from them a tapestry of his own aspirations. It could picture a dramatic movement dedicated to an essentially religious understanding of the artistic life, for 'every argument carries us backwards to some religious conception, and in the end the creative energy of men depends upon their believing that they have, within themselves, something immortal and imperishable, and that all else is but as an image in a looking-glass' (*Samhain*, no. 4, December 1904: 17). On the less exalted level of daily business in Yeats's own circle, the picture was never so finely realized. At that level of policy disagreement and conflicts of personality, as if in deliberate contrast to the elevated generality and ostensibly even-handed, if judgemental, tone of his prose writings on theatre at this time, Yeats was very much the administrative tyro, who treated opposition with Nietzschean disdain and deliberate brutality.

It is significant that the letter which Yeats wrote to Lady Gregory in December 1902 to tell her that Nietzsche had been her rival in recent months, is largely taken up with the poet's summary dismissal from the ranks of the elect of an unfortunate playwright, who had failed to pass muster. James Cousins, a Belfastman of Methodist background, who had converted to Theosophy when he had transferred to Dublin, was one of the hermeticists whom AE kept under his wing. He had published a crude little farce, which Willie Fay had begun to put into production. Yeats calmly informed Lady Gregory that he had told Fay he thought it rubbish and vulgar (*CL3*: 285). He was spoiling for a fight.

He had not long to wait; for the kinds of factionalism, that had been so troublesome in the Order of the Golden Dawn in London, bedevilled the theatre movement in Dublin too. Cousins was impossibly vain, as Willie Fay reported to Yeats, he alone 'of all the writers' refusing 'to listen to any criticism' (*CL3*: 290). But he had his following. His play was suppressed but the Society revolted, since they felt Yeats had exercised a veto to which he was not entitled over both Cousins' play, and over another, which had been proposed as a substitute. The eventual outcome was the adoption of clear rules by the society. These gave Yeats a key role on a reading committee, which would consider plays submitted for production. In all of this Yeats was a victor of sorts, but the strains between those who wished like Yeats to see the movement achieve on the artistic plane and those who wished the movement to serve a more directly national cause, had become glaringly clear. In the ensuing struggle on the issue to Yeats's chagrin, Gonne would, as we saw, make her nationalist position publicly known.

May 1903 saw the Society in London, where it presented five plays for the Irish Literary Society at the Queen's Gate Hall in South Kensington. Rather than giving offence the players and their repertoire (which included as well as Yeats's *The Hour-Glass* and *The Pot of Broth*, his frankly nationalistic *Cathleen ni Houlihan*) won golden English opinions. Yeats must have been especially gratified that *The Times* emphasized the aural achievement of the Society: 'We had never realized the musical possibilities of our language until we had heard these Irish people speak it' (*Samhain*, no. 3, September 1903: 34). Yeats published *The Times*'s praise of their work that autumn in *Samhain*. He realized that the favourable judgement of so august an organ was a coup, a sign that the Irish would have to take his movement seriously. Yet he was all too conscious that English success was a sword that could be turned against him.

For Dublin remained highly suspicious of Yeats. On 5 April 1903 he wrote to remind his publisher A. H. Bullen not to send his *Ideas of Good and Evil* to the Dublin papers for review, quoting a rule they had agreed. 'Reviews in Dublin papers', Yeats reported in some exasperation, 'sell no copies & I don't see why I should give them the oppertunity of attacking me' (*CL3*: 341–2). In his new guise of Nietzschean superiority in the exercise of an energized will, he was becoming a formidable adversary for his enemies. It took its toll, however, and by the autumn of 1903 he was tired and frustrated by a city which had so crudely responded to Synge's *In the Shadow of the Glen*. His public disagreement with Gonne was a painful business, only intensified by his knowledge that her marriage to MacBride was already a failure. And despite Lady Gregory's support, money was always a problem. In November 1904 Yeats would find himself before a Revenue enquiry in London. The tax authorities had assessed him as earning £500 per annum, a 'preposterous sum' (*CL3*: 665), the poet complained when he asked one of his publishers to supply a statement of what he had paid him in the past three years. It seems the taxman could not imagine that someone so much in the public eye could subsist on less than the round sum he thought appropriate to Yeats's station in life. Apparently Yeats persuaded them of his comparative poverty.

The poet's dedication to the theatre was a costly one, for it took time away from the composition of lyric poems which could command good fees in periodicals and journals. Plays usually had to wait for volume publication and Yeats took no royalities from such profits as their performance generated. His work with Farr in speaking to the psaltery had, however, introduced him to public lecturing as a means of augmenting an income from writing. From early in the century Yeats was aware that he could hold an audience as a public speaker and he had begun preparing a set of lectures which could be presented as occasion demanded. He wrote to Lady Gregory in January 1903 to tell her that he would lecture on 'The Irish Fairy Kingdom' in Cardiff for a fee of £10 and hoped to get £5 for a lecture in London: 'It looks as if lecturing was going to become profitable. Dolmetsch recommends it to me strongly' (*CL3*: 295). This experience meant that when Quinn suggested that he would arrange a financially lucrative lecturing tour for the poet in the United States, in association with the Irish Literary Society in New York, Yeats readily accepted. He must have been glad, as he set sail from Liverpool, with a first class ticket, on the *Oceanic* liner, to shake some of the dust of Dublin from his feet, with its wearisome disputes and rancorous factional politics.

Quinn was crucial in making Yeats's first North American tour the critical and financial triumph it was. Yeats was a well-known figure when he arrived in New York on 11 November 1903. Moreover he was further advanced in a literary career than Oscar Wilde, his Irish predecessor on the lecture circuit in that continent, when he had made a reputation for himself in North America as a gifted, commercially attractive public speaker. Yeats, however, was more obviously Irish than Wilde; he was travelling under distinctly Irish-American auspices and was offering lectures on Irish topics. This could have been a disadvantage. Quinn's achievement was to gain him a hearing at solid rates of remuneration in the American universities, in Ivy League institutions such as Yale, Smith, Amherst, Mount Holyoke, Wellesley, Bryn Mawr and Vassar, where Irish-America could not have been assured of a welcome, as well as at the lesser known or distinctively Irish schools such as Trinity College, Hartford, Connecticut and Notre Dame, Indiana. It is striking that Wilde had lectured at only one specifically college audience in upwards of 140 speaking engagements (Ellmann 1987: 178–81). Quinn and his agent had exploited not only Yeats's reputation in gaining the bookings they did but the moment in North American cultural life when English departments in the universities and colleges (women's institutions were notably involved in the process) were welcoming the living creative writer to the academy. So Yeats found himself addressing large numbers of young American students and mixing freely with the professors of some of the most distinguished of American colleges and universities.

The poet, who could not have matriculated in Trinity College, Dublin, found this gratifying and encouraging. Here at least he could feel properly appreciated and rewarded; the inveterate 'begrudgery' of Dublin viewed from the broad perspectives of North American amplitudes of geography and spirit, could be dismissed as a rancid, puny thing. His sense of Nietzschean superiority became more firmly rooted. He noted in the margin of a selection of Nietzsche's writings how he agreed that 'the lower... cannot make obligations to the higher' (Frazier 1990: 61). In New York, Quinn had dealt with him on the presumption of their shared distaste for the common herd, which was a settled conviction with the acerbic, impatient, capitalist Irish-American lawyer.

Quinn was determined that Yeats's tour would be a financial success. He knew his man, so insisted that the poet should not cash any of the cheques he received, but send them all on to him (NL Ms 30,539). Under this no-nonsense regime, Yeats kept conscientiously to schedule, performed with considerable élan, even as travel wearied him. His success meant that the tour was extended, so by March 1904, when he had completed his engagements, he had managed to accrue the sum of $3230.40 (Reid 1968: 19) as reward for his labours. It was the largest amount of money he had amassed to date.

As important as the money was the chance not only for Yeats to meet distinguished Americans (he had lunch with President Theodore Roosevelt) who took him seriously in the way few did in Ireland, but to gain a sense of an Irish-American constitutency which was open to the kind of cultural nationalism he espoused. Where in Dublin he was excoriated by the likes of D. P. Moran and those who agreed with the Irish Ireland 'philosophy', in the heartland of Irish Catholic America Yeats found people ready to listen to his more inclusive message. At the University of Notre Dame in Indiana he sat up late talking with the Fathers about the fairies. He told Lady Gregory that he had been 'entirely delighted by the big merry priests of Notre Dame – all Irish & proud as lucifer of their success in getting Jews & non-conformists to come to their college. . . . I think these big priests would be fair teachers, but I cannot think they would be more than that. They belong to an easy going world that has passed away, – mores the pity perhaps – but certainly I have been astonished at one thing the general lack of religious prejudice I find on all sides here' (*CL3*: 520).

In one of the lectures which Yeats included in his repertoire for the tour, the poet sketched his vision of the Ireland he hoped might come into existence as a result of the literary and cultural renaissance he now was sponsoring. Abandoned in this lecture is the rather aggressive note of nationalist militancy which had him in 1892 addressing his American readers in the Boston *Pilot* as 'Your Celt' from the capital of the enemy.

Speaking now on 'The Intellectual Revival in Ireland' in the Carnegie Hall, New York in early January 1904, Yeats took the opportunity to defend his movement as in the tradition of Irish patriotism in general and of Young Ireland in particular. But he was at pains to emphasize the comprehensive idealism of its inspiration. He recognizes the forces which Moran and the Gaelic League represent ('Gaelic Ireland is beginning to call the tune, and Gaelic Ireland is the most Irish part of Ireland'; Londraville 1991: 112) and that de-Anglicization involves a 'vigorous industrial movement' (ibid.). Yet his hope is for an Ireland which will bear into the modern world a harmonious, ancient spirituality in which all classes might find fulfilment. Yeats's speech for a moment becomes simultaneously a Utopian dream of Irish unity and a threnody for a vanished civilization. Where Moran had made the battle of two civilizations a matter of vulgar, immediate polemics, Yeats makes of it an inspirational call to cultural preservation and development:

> we Irish do not desire, like the English, to build up a nation where there shall be a very rich class and a very poor class. Ireland will always be in the main an agricultural class. Industries we may have, but we will not have, as England has, a very rich class nor whole districts blackened with smoke like what they call in England their 'Black Country' . . . . Ireland will always be a country where men plow

and sow and reap. And then Ireland, too, as we think, will be a country where not only will the wealth be well distributed among the people. We wish to preserve an ancient ideal of life. Wherever its customs prevail, there you will find the folk song, the folk tale, the proverb, and the charming manners that come from an ancient culture. In England you will find a few thousands of perfectly cultivated people, but you will find the mass of the people singing songs of the music hall – an easy-going vulgar people. In Ireland alone among the nations that I know you will find, away on the Western seaboard, under broken roofs, a race of gentlemen, keeping alive the ideals of a great time when men sang the heroic life with drawn swords in their hands. (ibid.: 113–14)

His speech was an essence of imagined Ireland, filtered through a curious solution – part William Morris and William Blake, part Susan Yeats's prejudice against English vulgarity and John Butler Yeats's detestation of Belfast and personal myth of the non-commercial gentlemanly calling; part Samuel Ferguson's Celtic heroics. The note of ardent, spiritualized nationalism is Yeats's, together with his magniloquent, inflated sense of sacred destiny at work in the processes of history: 'The nations of the world are like a great organ. And in that organ there are many pipes. Each pipe is a nation, and each pipe has its own music, that is the life of the nation . . . it is certain that at last the pipe that is Ireland will awake and that its music will be heard through the whole world!!!' (ibid.: 115). Disappointingly, the audience was smaller than expected (*AM*: 309).

Return to Europe meant that Yeats had to direct his attention to more quotidian matters. While still in the United States he had heard from his sister 'Lily' that Dun Emer Industries was facing a financial crisis. She hoped he would invest some of his lecture receipts in the printing side of the business and in her embroidery work. He was not best pleased, as he wrote to Lady Gregory: 'I confess I do not like the thought that the first money I ever earned beyond the need of the moment will be expected to go to Dun Emer for I suppose that is what is expected' (*CL3*: 548).

Money was also urgently required if Yeats was to sustain his leading role in the Irish theatre movement and to continue to consolidate the reputation of the Irish National Theatre Society. Fortunately real support was available, if from an unlikely quarter. Annie Horniman, with whom Yeats had stood firm against the disruptive indiscipline of the 'Groups' in the Order of the Golden Dawn in 1901, had indicated privately to the poet in April 1902 that she might be prepared to offer financial support to the National Theatre Society. Yeats knew that she would have to approve of its policies if her support was to materialize. Indeed Adrian Frazier has argued (1990: 77) that Yeats's article 'The Reform of the Theatre' in *Samhain* in the autumn of 1903, with its defence of artistic freedom, was part of a crusade of that year to persuade Horniman that he was sufficiently internationalist in outlook to allow her to invest in his enterprise – that he would not use the theatre (he was after all the co-author of *Cathleen ni Houlihan*) to foment rebellion. She had been impressed by Yeats's determination, expressed during the row about Synge's *In the Shadow of the Glen*, to see the Society produce international masterpieces, as well as native plays. Without theatrical talent herself, she was clearly fascinated by, was even in love with, Yeats and was open to persuasion. She probably hoped that by buying the poet a theatre, she might win his affections at some significant level (she grew to detest Lady Gregory as a rival for his favours and attention, who cordially returned the compliment, describing her wickedly as 'like a shilling in a tub of electrified water – everybody tries to get the shilling out'; *L:* 490).

So the Abbey Theatre came into existence in the second half of 1904 through the refurbishment of a building in Abbey Street in Dublin at Horniman's expense. The theatre therefore owed its birth to Horniman's wealth. Energetic, feminist, occultist, drama-besotted, Wagnerite, the often cantankerous Horniman had inherited a substantial sum from her tea-trading English grandparents. And Yeats was not averse, despite the risk of antagonistic comment from the advanced nationalists, to taking English money to realize his dreams for Ireland. Nor did he mind in the least using Horniman's feelings for him, which she translated into substantial subventions to the theatre, so that he could develop a properly national, rather than cosmopolitan repertoire, with international drama as a secondary concern. That she did not share his hopes for Ireland concerned him not at all. There was to be no question of a close relationship, although Horniman entertained unrealistic hopes that Yeats and she might be married. Yeats in fact thought her 'a vulgarian' (Frazier 1990: 154). She was canny enough, however, to ask Yeats to republish his 1903 *Samhain* article in the 1904 issue (which Yeats did in an amended form in 'The Play, the Player, and the Scene') along with her letter of April of that year, offering the theatre and the Society's acceptance of her conditions. It was as if she was rather pointedly reminding Yeats of the ground rules of their co-operation and of the basis of her patronage which meant that the company could use the building she had refurbished rent-free. The same issue of *Samhain* also published Synge's *In the Shadow of the Glen* in defiance of his detractors. Horniman could rest assured that the Abbey would not bend before narrow nationalist assault.

When in 1902 the Fay brothers and the troupe of amateur Dublin actors had invited Yeats to serve as President of the Irish National Theatre Society, they had expected that the poet would be little more than an articulate figurehead. He would make elegant, elevated speeches on public occasions while they got on with the business of running the Society. They could not have been more wrong. For Yeats had set his eyes on a goal. The great magician wanted a theatre of his own where he could direct Irish consciousness as he saw fit. He was not to be gainsaid, as he had been a decade earlier when the libraries scheme had gone awry. With the knowledge that Horniman might finance such a venture if he played his cards astutely, he had systematically worked to achieve that goal.

It was only partly realized when the Abbey Theatre mounted its first productions at the end of 1904. For he still lacked full control. The new theatre continued to operate under rules which with AE's help had been drawn up in February and June 1903, after the arguments about its repertoire. Yeats was on a reading committee, but its recommendations still had to go for a decision to the company in general. This could not continue. Such democracy in matters of art and taste was insupportable. Yeats set to work with a manipulative will. By 16 September 1905 he could report to John Quinn with evident satisfaction: 'I think we have seen the end of democracy in the Theatre, which was Russell's doing, for I go to Dublin at the end of the week to preside at a meeting summoned to abolish it. If all goes well, Synge, Lady Gregory and I will have everything in our hands; indeed the only practical limitation to our authority will be caused by the necessity of some sort of permanent business committee in Dublin' (*L*: 461).

With devastating single-mindedness Yeats brooked no opposition to his plans to alter the legal status of the company to make the actors employees. The opposition was considerable. The actors, who understandably thought the company was their own and Yeats a cuckoo-in-the nest, were not happy to envisage a situation in which they would be holders of a minority of the shares in a limited company. Furthermore, while they might have been happy to become professionals rather than amateurs, the salaries proposed distinguished between them in a divisive way and in some instances were derisively minuscule. Some were offered ten shillings a week; Frank Fay was offered a top-rate at twenty-five shillings a week. At this time a cook in service could command a salary of between £30 and £40 per annum, a general servant could make £15 with room and board added (Hearn 1989: 48); so it seems clear enough on what scale the putative directors of the new company (all of them from a class accustomed to solving the servant problem) were assessing wages for their talented employees. Yeats had confessed in *Samhain* in 1902 that he had once asked a dramatic company to let him 'rehearse them in barrels' on castors so that he could 'shove them about with a pole when the action required it' (*Samhain*, October, 1902: 4). Less amusingly, as 1905 came to a bitter end, he would have been content to see all his actors securely trapped in the barrels of water-tight contracts, so that he could shove them about as he saw fit.

Yeats skilfully exploited the differences between the various parties which had to accede to these proposals, playing off one against the other until he had his way. He exhibited a surprisingly keen business and legal intelligence. But his victory was not won without bloodshed. There were resignations among the company's actors – those who refused to sign the contracts offered. Mary Walker, one of the leading players in Yeats's tragedies, could not make up her mind. Yeats berated her violently, 'his whole being shaken by fits of the most uncontrollable rage' (Frazier 1990: 126, citing Nic Shiubhlaigh). As the year ended, AE objected with a long letter in the measured and searching terms that only an old friend could risk. He counselled Yeats that his personality and manner were self-defeating; he would find himself alone in Dublin, without supporters in the public or in the press, for 'Irish people will only be led by their affections' (*LTWBY*: 153).

Yeats would have none of this. His reply in January 1906 was condescending, a Nietzschean unbending to a lesser soul, momentarily admitted for its own good to the heroic heights:

> I desire the love of very few people, my equals or my superiors. The love of the rest
> would be a bond and an intrusion. These others will in time come to know that I am

a fairly strong and capable man and that I have gathered the strong and capable about me, and all who love work better than idle talk will support me. It is a long fight but that is the sport of it. The antagonism, which is sometimes between you and me, comes from the fact that though you are strong and capable yourself you gather the weak and not very capable about you, and that I feel they are a danger to all good work. It is I think because you desire love. Besides you have the religious genius to which all souls are equal. In all work except that of salvation that spirit is a hindrance.　(*L*: 466)

The friendship did not survive this lamentably pompous, if acute, divigation. The two former art students, intimates of the early Dublin days, were estranged for years. Early in 1906 an inveterate theatregoer and friend of the company recorded in his journal that 'The Greenroom looked quite lonely and strange in the absence of so many old familiar faces and the presence of new' (Holloway 1967: 67).

In these conflicts, which extended to rows with his sister 'Lollie' about literary standards at the Dun Emer Press, Yeats was assuredly driven by his own sense that aesthetic values were at a premium in Ireland. Too many wished to recruit art to immediate nationalist purposes. He had written to Quinn in February 1905 of the 'intense hostility' which he sensed in the general atmosphere in which Synge's *The Well of the Saints* had been staged that month. 'Irish national litera-ture', he had asserted, 'has never produced an artistic personality in the modern sense of the word. . . . We will have a hard fight in Ireland before we get the right for every man to see the world in his own way admitted' (*L*: 447). He had been prepared to fight a fairly brutal campaign: he told Synge that their theatre must have 'somebody in it who is distinctly dangerous' (Frazier 1990: 127, citing Saddlemyer 1982: 88). It infuriated him that his own family could not be depended upon to share his estimate of present dangers.

Naturally Yeats's behaviour was experienced by the family not as a round in his fight with the philistines but as another example of how impossible he could be as a person. John Butler Yeats, who had already in June 1904 expressed a pained wish to 'Lily' that Willie could have 'Jack's tender gracious manner', admitting that the poet sometimes treated him as if he were 'a black beetle' (Hone 1946: 78), entered the fray on his daughters' behalf. On 1 June 1906 he wrote to his son explaining that 'To make Dun Emer a pecuniary success is a matter of life and death to Lily and Lolly. . . . I hope you won't mind my suggesting that you are *gentle* with Lolly' (Lewis 1994: 69). Yeats would have none of it, drawing from his father a rare, precisely aimed rebuke, in which he identified the malign influence of Nietzsche on his son's general attitude: 'As you have dropped affection from the circle of your needs, have you also dropped love between man and woman? Is this the theory of the overman, if so, your demi-godship is after all but a doctrinaire demi-godship. . . . the men whom Nietzsche's theory fits are only great men of a sort, a sort of Yahoo great men. The struggle is how to get rid of them, they belong to the clumsy and brutal side of things' (Hone 1946: 97).

In fact Yeats had by no means managed to repress his own affective and sexual nature ('love between man and woman') in a public quest for social dominance as the leader of the Irish theatrical movement. Rather, the truculence and ill-temper of his polemics and public exchanges, the displays of rage and clumsy bullying, all suggest a man for whom the studied nonchalance of real mastery was an impossible ideal. Frustration and emotional turmoil kept breaking through. The self which in youth he had vainly sacrificed to the symbolic order, in the belief that the world would be renewed, he now sought to overcome in feats of self-mastery as a superior being whose occult adeptship must find expression in the social order as it actually existed. But the needs of his nature could not be gainsaid: the emotions and the body issued their own urgent imperatives.

In 1903 or 1904, following Maud Gonne's 'betrayal' of their 'mystic marriage', Yeats had ended his chaste years in a love affair with Florence Farr. Sexually experienced (Holroyd in his biography of George Bernard Shaw reports that she claimed fourteen lovers when she had her affair with the playwright in 1890; Holroyd 1988: 248). Farr did not take the physical side of male/female relations too seriously. She liked to adopt a worldly, no-nonsense attitude to sexual needs. In her mildly scandalous novel of 1896, *The Dancing Faun*, she had airily offered a New Woman's blasé, disenchanted view of the matter: 'A civilised woman has very little taste for what may be termed pure passion; it pleases her instinct perhaps, but it revolts her intellect, her imagination, her delicacy, her pride' (Farr 1894: 49).

Yeats's and Farr's sexual relationship did not last long. It seems she became bored with him as a lover quite quickly. For the poet however, Farr was one of the very few people with whom he felt able to speak freely, as if without any need to pose. His letters to her throughout the period when his public persona was becoming more and more a stagey thing of imperious attitudinizing, bespeak a man generously permitted needful intimacy of feeling as the fruit of a fairly brief sexual encounter. Yeats was as grateful as the costive side of his nature permitted him to be. In June 1905 he told her: 'I was very glad to get your letter – a dip into the river of life changes even an old hand-writing and gives it a new and meaning face' (*L*: 450). In July, since he was deep in Chaucer, with Morris's great edition for stimulus, he suggested a bicycle trip to Canterbury with 'some harmless person to keep appearances up' (*L*: 456). In January 1906, in the wake of his battle for control of his theatre, in direct contrast to the austere frigidity of his letter to AE, he confessed warmly to Farr:

> You cannot think what a pleasure it is to be fond of somebody to whom one can talk
> – as a rule any sort of affection annihilates conversation, strikes one with a silence
> like that of Adam before he had even named the beasts. To be moved and talkative,
> unrestrained, one's own self, and to be this not because one has created some absurd
> delusion that it all is wisdom, as Adam may have in the beast's head, but not in Eve,
> but because one has found an equal, that is the best of life. (*L*: 468)

Throughout this time, too, the trials endured by Gonne as her marriage to MacBride collapsed in scandal and calumny, gave Yeats much pain. On 26 January 1904 Gonne had given birth to a son, Jean Seagan MacBride (later known as Seán). Yeats must have learnt of this event during his lecture tour of the United States since the page in the *San Francisco Examiner*, devoted almost entirely to him the day after his arrival in the city, also carried news of the birth (Strand 1978: 35). The fact that there was a child involved in the MacBride marriage made the business of separation and divorce almost impossibly difficult. When Gonne's position as the mother of two young children, one of them by a former lover, was added to the fact that her estranged husband was an Irish national hero, the problems she faced might have seemed insurmountable to a less courageous woman. MacBride's behaviour had been atrocious. In late 1904 Gonne learnt that during her absence from their Parisian home, MacBride in a drunken fit had sexually assaulted members of her own household and had even molested the eleven-year-old Iseult (*AM*: 331). Throughout 1905 and 1906 Gonne wrote to Yeats keeping him abreast of a struggle in which she felt herself a truly wronged victim. She declared at the outset: 'I am fighting an uneven battle because I am fighting a man without honor or scruples who is sheltering himself & his vices behind the National cause knowing that my loyalty to it in part ties my hands' (*GYL*: 184–5).

MacBride protected his Irish reputation by taking a case for libel against a Dublin newspaper, which meant that the details of Gonne's case against him were kept from the Irish public, among whom rumours were circulated by his supporters, to her great disadvantage. Her English origins were cited against her. The old accusation that she was in fact a British spy resurfaced. By October 1906, when she visited Dublin, a faction had been inflamed against her. One night in the Abbey Theatre which she attended with Yeats, she was greeted with a shout of 'Up, John MacBride' and a small group in the pit who hissed loudly (Colum 1966: 124). As a result of the court settlement (a separation rather than a divorce because of legal technicalities in the inter-jurisdictional case), Gonne was forced to remain in France, for she feared that in Ireland MacBride would seek custody of their son. This was a bitter blow to one who felt her fate bound up with the Irish national cause. For years she would make her home in Paris and in Normandy.

All this turmoil in Gonne's life horrified Yeats and affected him deeply. The same forces against which he was struggling were also arrayed against the woman to whom he had given his primary loyalties, even if he did not love her as uncomplicatedly as sometimes he liked to believe he did. Nor can it have escaped him on that night in the Abbey Theatre (Lady Gregory's *The Gaol Gate* was playing) that the following month his own version of the doomed love of Deirdre and Naoise would open in the same theatre, with its tragic tale of 'the Irish Helen' (Yeats's note to the first production, cited in Miller 1977: 125). Tragedy was a possibility on the level of personal life as well as on the stage of a heroic poetic theatre. In the play, we see, as Flannery has observed, 'a heroine, who, by functioning in response to her deepest feminine instincts, is driven into conflict with a harsh world of objective masculine values that leads her inevitably to a tragic doom' (Flannery 1976: 45).

Conflict was intense in Yeats's personality at this stage of his life and career. On the one hand he was deliberately cultivating a Nietzschean disregard for common feelings in his relish for triumph in artistic warfare. On the other, lack of intimacy of an unrestrained, fulfilling kind, which he enjoyed only on rare enough occasions with Farr, can be seen as undermining his equanimity and health (he remained a frequent victim of minor illnessess, colds and similar infections) like the return of the repressed. Yet Yeats was not simply in the grip of an affective dialectic, but with considerable insight was seeking to comprehend so that he might utilize as an artist and writer, the truths of experience that a complicatedly fractured awareness of human identity enjoined upon him. He sensed a new energy in his work, activities and human relations that was not simply the effect of a crude Nietzschean will to power. It was probably in early 1906 he told Farr how he could now move people by power, and not by charm, in public speaking. He continued:

> I feel this change in all my work and that it has brought a change into the personal relations of life – even things seemingly beyond control answer strangely to what is within – I once cared only for images about whose necks I could cast various 'chains of office' as it were. They were so many aldermen of the ideal, whom I wished to master the city of the soul. Now I do not want images at all, or chains of office, being content with the unruly soul. (*L*: 469; date uncertain)

In the same year Yeats worked on a series of prose reflections (he described them as 'a curious impressionist book... almost a spiritual diary'; *L*: 476). He would finish these in 1907, and collect them in volume form in December of that year as *Discoveries*, the last production of the Dun Emer Press. In them he pondered the relation of the divided self to the unruly soul and began to develop a view of the artist as one in whom fragmentation is transformed into life-enhancing wholeness of being. For there was always in Yeats an instinct for a richly harmonious mode of social life, which restrained the impulses to mere power for its own stimulating sake. An ethical drive which found expression in a desire for graciousness and sweetness in fulfilled human possibility, made his 'equivalent for Nietzsche's brotherhood of supermen' not 'a gang of superb Irish roughnecks but an intellectual elite' (Ellmann 1964: 96).

Discoveries is primarily concerned with a poet's exploration of what an intensive engagement with the theatre has given him to understand about life and art. Central to his advancement in learning, he acknowledges, is an awareness of how crucial to true art are the living emotions of real men and women. His work, he tells us, has always brought him to the certainty that 'what moves natural men in the arts is what moves them in life, and that is, intensity of personal life, intonations that show them, in a book or play, the strength, the essential moment of a man who would be exciting in the market or at the dispensary door' (*E&I*: 265). The drama of such emotional epiphanies had further instructed Yeats that his own early poetry had been predicated on a false view of the self and what it could achieve. He writes that until he had learnt of the value of 'personality' in literature he had been 'interested in nothing but states of mind, lyrical moments, intellectual essences' (ibid.: 271). In consequence, he had thought of himself 'as something unmoving and silent living in the middle of [his] own mind and body, a grain of sand in Bloomsbury or in Connacht that Satan's watch-fiends cannot find' (ibid.). In other words, he had imagined the self to be some essential, fixed identity, immune in its integrity to the depredations of all that might threaten it.

By contrast he has come to understand, *Discoveries* announces, 'quite suddenly, as the way is, that I was seeking something unchanging and unmixed and always outside myself, a Stone or an Elixir that was always out of reach, and that I was the fleeting thing that held out its hand' (ibid.). He had come indeed to accept the complex, mutable compound which is selfhood, which achieves wholeness of being only when it expresses itself in moments of passion. The essays in *Discoveries* invoke, accordingly, a new cluster of ideals in Yeats's inventory of aspirations: 'energy that comes from the whole man'; 'the normal, passionate, reasoning self, the personality as a whole'. Art should now 'rise out of life as the blade out of the spear-shaft, a song out of the mood, the fountain from its pool, all art out of the body, laughter from a happy company' (ibid.: 295).

It must have struck Yeats as he composed this series of reflections that he and his father were no longer at odds in the stark way they had been when he had first rebelled against John Butler Yeats's Victorian materialism of outlook. For Yeats's father had always been an advocate of personality, sceptical of the value of ideas until they were given voice in a living man's self-expression. In 1905 he had written in a memoir of an old friend: 'Argument is not the test of truth. Meditation, experience of life, hope, charity, and all the emotions – out of these the imaginative reason speaks' (Hone 1946: 87); and in July 1906 he had insisted to his poet son that 'to be a poet it is necessary first of all to be a man. The high vitality and vivid experience, the impulses, doings and sufferings of a Tolstoi, a Shakespeare or a Dante, – all are needed' (ibid.: 93).

Yet however releasing it may have been for Yeats no longer to feel in perpetual warfare with his father, in 1906 Yeats was still uncertain whether or not he could himself write the poetry of 'blood, imagination, intellect running together' (*E&I*: 266). He was still in the poetically barren phase, which had begun in 1898, and which the publication of *In the Seven Woods* had not really broken. Only in his writing for the imagined personalities of the stage could his verse begin to suggest that holistic fusion of aspects of the self that can occur in passionate utterance, which now seemed an aesthetic desideratum for poetry. A Cuchulain or a Deirdre *in extremis* might speak as if made momentarily, magnificently whole in the transport of passionate declamation. For the lyric poet it was more difficult.

For Yeats at this time it was Synge who seemed to have achieved in his own person an exemplary unity of being, in comparison to which he himself remained fearful, as he put it in *Discoveries*, that he would 'be broken to the end' (ibid.: 296). Synge was the integrated measure of his own 'broken' state, the Synge who in his plays had achieved, as he told Quinn in 1907, 'a harsh, independent, heroical, clean, wind-swept view of things' (*L*: 495) in expression of his own wholeness of being. For in Synge, as Yeats recorded after the playwright's death in 1909, he had encountered a man in whom artistic commitment and its expression seemed to have transcended all self-division: 'He had that egotism of the man of genius which Nietzsche compares to the egotism of a woman with child' (*Mem*: 205). To such creative self-possession, compact of identity and alterity, Yeats could only aspire, as the challenges of middle age succeeded those of youth and young manhood.

8

The Mid-life Mask

John Millington Synge's *The Playboy of the Western World* opened in the Abbey Theatre, Dublin on 26 January 1907. Trouble had certainly been expected. When Yeats and Lady Gregory had heard the first two acts of the play read to them in late 1906, they had had misgivings about its possible reception. The cautious Willie Fay had tried to get Synge to alter his script, but the dramatist, apart from a few cosmetic, verbal changes, would have none of it. Rumours spread through the city that Synge, who had already traduced the virtue of Irish womanhood in *In the Shadow of the Glen*, was about to repeat the offence with a vengeance. The first-night audience included a faction ready to make its antagonistic views known.

Even in this overheated atmosphere, when the trouble actually erupted as a near-riot, it was a shock. Yeats was lecturing in Scotland on the evening of the première. Lady Gregory dispatched a telegram to him after the first two acts had passed off in comparative quiet: 'Play great success.' Later in the evening a second telegram followed the first: 'Audience broke up in disorder at the word shift.' Yeats hurried back to Dublin, arriving on 28 January. The theatrical ructions of the week to come would bear little relationship to the kind of magical dramatic movement he had envisaged himself as leading. For instead of hierarchical power flowing from a centre of occult, magisterial poetic drama, all was controversy and ill-tempered conflict. The play had opened on a Saturday evening. The following Monday the police had to be called in to keep order, and although they were a complement of men from the unarmed Dublin Metropolitan Police and not the hated Royal Irish Constabulary, which maintained the peace of the countryside under arms, this understandable action gave a propaganda coup to advanced nationalist opinion, which had set its face against Synge and most of his work. On the Tuesday evening a bunch of Unionists, undergraduates from Trinity College, had also turned up, more to sing, drunkenly, 'God Save the King' in defiance of the nationalists, than to appreciate a night in the theatre.

Yeats announced a debate on artistic freedom in the theatre for the following Monday in terms that poured oil on the flames of controversy which Synge's brilliant, violent and grotesque tragicomedy had ignited. The Dublin newspapers filled up with letters on the Abbey's *succès de scandale*, many of them supportive of Synge. The audience who gathered to hear Yeats's lecture was not. AE, who in what Yeats judged an unforgivable act of base betrayal, by a ruse avoided taking the chair as he had agreed to, and sat amid Yeats's enemies in the gallery. Yeats won himself momentary sympathy from his turbulent audience when he announced himself as the author of *Cathleen ni Houlihan* but overall the occasion went against him. Supporters had stayed away (Synge could not attend) and those enemies who came were not to be denied their polemical triumph. Yeats's father spoke, with an exact appreciation of how to deal with a hostile Dublin audience. In old age, Yeats remembered John Butler Yeats's speech that night as a beautiful lofty moment, for all its broad comedic brio:

> My father upon the Abbey stage, before him a raging crowd.
> 'This Land of Saints,' and then as the applause died out,
> 'Of plaster Saints'; his beautiful mischievous head thrown back.
> ('Beautiful Lofty Things')

For Yeats that week in January 1907 was a defining moment. Henceforth it would be impossible for him to nurture quite the same hopes for his theatre that had sustained him through the long, difficult early years when he had worked to establish the movement. For the forces arrayed against a theatre of poetic beauty, rooted in his own magical view of the universe, were such that even a Yeats, armed with the conviction of his own high calling as adept and artist, could not have been other than daunted. Although he felt, when the dust settled somewhat in early February, that he and his confederates had 'won in the fight' (O'Driscoll n.d.: 34) since educated opinion had rallied to their support, it was perhaps time to redirect his energies. And although the Abbey would be an abiding preoccupation, one senses the tidal energies of Yeats's life beginning to shift once again in 1907 and 1908, as they had done when the Golden Dawn had proved so fractious a body, when he had directed his attention to the theatre as his prime sphere of influence.

Things were undoubtedly changing in Yeats's own circumstances. The end of 1907 would see his father, whose finances were always a problem, set out for a visit to the United States. There he would remain for the rest of his life, under the protective wing of John Quinn, never completely settled but never so unsettled as to wish to return to Europe. Yeats's sisters in 1908 would end their association with the Dun Emer Industries and set themselves up as Cuala Industries, leaving Gleeson to her carpet-making, weaving and design work, while they concentrated (their father's departure to New York undoubtedly gave them the freedom to do so) on printing and publishing. On 16 March Yeats's old mentor John O'Leary died. The poet did not attend the funeral, yet he judged the occasion to be a national watershed, in which the values of one generation were superseded by those of one much less noble. In an essay dated August 1907 entitled 'Poetry and Tradition' (it was published in December 1908), Yeats explained why he could not bring himself to attend O'Leary's obsequies. He admitted that he 'shrank from seeing about his grave so many whose Nationalism was different from anything he had taught or that I could share' (*E&I*: 246). It is very clear from this pained reflection that Yeats believed that those who had attacked Synge and his drama were just the people who would publicly mourn O'Leary, while contravening in their lives and actions all the nobility of spirit and action he had espoused. The death of O'Leary and the reaction to Synge combine in Yeats's mind as he develops a new Irish sociology. It is a sociology which takes full account, for the first time in his writings, of the modern Irish society that had been in the making since the Famine, which he had sought to ignore in his own imaginative celebration of his native country and of the west of Ireland in particular, as a repository of ancient, uncontaminated, Celtic spirituality.

Yeats identifies in this essay 'Three types of men who have made all beautiful things', who 'look backward to a long tradition': aristocracies, the countrymen and the artists. 'Being without fear', Yeats avers, they have all 'held to whatever pleases them' (*E&I*: 251). By contrast, a new class has emerged in Ireland – pragmatic, anxious, modern, informed by the easy suasions of vulgar propaganda (with Sinn Féin – 'Ourselves' – the political movement founded in 1905 by Arthur Griffith, leading the pack) and an unheroic national feeling. Yeats allies himself with an O'Leary who stood for nobility and self-sacrifice but excoriates in a disdainful mood of disappointment 'a new class which had begun to rise into power under the shadow of Parnell' (*E&I*: 259):

> Power passed to small shopkeepers, to clerks, to that very class who had seemed to John O'Leary so ready to bend to the power of others, to men who had risen above the traditions of the countryman, without learning those of cultivated life or even educating themselves, and who because of their poverty, their ignorance, their superstitious piety, are much subject to all kinds of fear. Immediate victory, immediate utility became everything, and the conviction, which is in all who have run great risks for a cause's sake . . . that life is greater than the cause, withered. (*E&I*: 260)

In penning such an article, Yeats indicates that he was thinking of cutting his Irish losses (though the delayed publication may indicate a desire not to burn all his Irish boats at once). For he cannot but have known that he would not lightly be forgiven such patrician disdain for the new Irish order, with which the majority of the country's inhabitants identified. Nor would the Irish democracy all about him struggling to be fully born have been inclined to indulge the aristocratic pretension of this document, its ready assumption that art consorts at its ease with social elevation, as well as with the necessitous spirituality of an impoverished peasantry.

References in the essay to the courts of Renaissance Italy, to 'high rocky places, to little walled towns . . . to all those who understood that life is not lived, if not lived for contemplation or excitement' (*E&I*: 252), would not have met with much sympathy either among those of Yeats's fellow-countrymen whose political and social aims included the transfer of power from the poet's caste to the Catholic nationalist majority. Such elitist imaginings could have cut no ice with the majority of the Irish people who believed their history had been a grim story of religious and political persecution by an elite.

Yeats had been in Italy with Lady Gregory and her son Robert, where they had holidayed together in the spring of 1907, in the aftermath of the storm aroused by *The Playboy* and O'Leary's death. They visited Urbino, Ravenna, Ferrara and Florence. The poet's earlier regard for Castiglione's *The Courtier* (evidenced in his esteem of nonchalance of manner in 'Adam's Curse') was reinforced as Lady Gregory read extracts to him on evenings they shared in Urbino itself. Lady Gregory remembered too how they had arrived in Venice: 'We came ... not to the jangle and uproar of the railway station, but to the heart of the city's beauty, to [the] piazza of St Mark – And as I left him there ... he was as if entranced by the rich colouring, the strange beauty of the joyous Venetian night' (Gregory 1996: 315).

Castiglione's ideal of the courtier humanized for Yeats the more brutal implications of Nietzschean elitism. The Italian's vision of the whole man brought into existence by lifelong dedication to poetry, love and physical prowess, but expressed with *sprezzatura*, effortlessly, became a governing ideal for Yeats as well, defining the poet's sense of true aristocracy. Yeats wrote of it as 'the victory of the soul' which 'was sought in dances, in noble manners, in love songs, and in a laborious training of the body' (*Discoveries: Second Series*, in Skelton and Clark 1965: 89). Castiglione's emphasis on the noble duty of self-fashioning also touched, with humanist delicacy of feeling, a chord in Yeats's own Nietzschean awareness of the role of self-mastery in personal achievement. This helped to refine what was a developing idea of this period of Yeats's life: that the self could make effective use of its powers in the world only in as much as it re-created itself as one mask or another.

An insecure hold on personal identity had always been an aspect of Yeats's experience. The tensions and conflicts of his social formation, the cultural and political crises amid which he had lived as a younger man, the erotic dilemmas he had faced, the complex exchanges of sexual power with which he had engaged in the world of occultism, the rigours of controversy and public debate he had undergone, had never been accompanied by a sense of much growth in self-knowledge, or inner self-assurance. Rather, he was conscious not so much of the actual, sustaining affective and temperamental contents of his own selfhood, as of its ineluctably divided nature. In his autobiography he was to state: 'I know very little about myself and much less of that anti-self: probably the woman who cooks my dinner or the woman who sweeps out my study knows more than I. It is perhaps because Nature made me a gregarious man, going hither and thither looking for conversation and ready to deny from fear or favour his dearest conviction, that I love proud and lonely things' (*Au*: 171). That confession, paradoxically, does bear the imprint of some self-knowledge in its disclaimer of such. For at least it comprehends how the poet's own idea of the mask (fully developed by the time he wrote *The Trembling of the Veil*, where this passage first appeared), his idea of the self and its anti-self, had its source in the kind of self-division which can make a gregarious man a lover of 'proud and lonely things'. But it is a sense of selfhood's potentiality deeply rooted only in an awareness of the conflictual basis of identity.

Yeats in 1907 and particularly in 1908 had ample opportunity to ponder how the self projects itself in the world in so complicatedly variegated a manner that the issue of integrated identity becomes clouded in apparently contradictory performative acts. He had arranged with his publisher, A. H. Bullen, to edit his works for an eight-volume *Collected Works* to appear under the imprint of the Shakespeare Head Press at Stratford-upon-Avon. This would be an appropriate riposte to all his Irish detractors, and Yeats took immense care over it. He wanted to revise much of what he felt had been inadequate about his early work. So for a year, withdrawing from direct engagement with the Abbey, he made this his main business. The edition was to include reproductions of portraits, etchings and drawings of himself. Yeats was especially concerned that these would represent him aright, as he became conscious in a heightened way of the self as a public icon. He wanted the images of Yeats as man and poet to highlight a variegated identity. Augustus John, John Singer Sargent and Charles Shannon were recruited to provide the requisite works of art (though in the end John's 1907 etching was not used; (O'Donnell 87–92). In January 1908 he told John Quinn:

> I am going to put the lot one after another; my father's emaciated portrait . . . beside Mancini's brazen image, and Augustus John's tinker to pluck the nose of Shannon's idealist. Nobody will believe they are the same man. And I shall write an essay upon them and describe them as all the different personages that I have dreamt of being but have never had the time for. (*L*: 502)

It was important to Yeats that this impression of complex, developing variety be created by the images of himself made available in the *Collected Works*. He was worried that such a compendium could seem both definitive and terminal. He had, after all, published almost no new lyric poetry since *In the Seven Woods* and it was as a lyric poet that, primarily, he had made his literary reputation. He explained to Bullen that he had been so insistent on his revisions in the Shakespeare Head edition because he knew he must get his 'general personality and the total weight of [his] work into people's minds, as a preliminary to new work' (*L*: 498). The visual representations of the poet would indicate that the edition was not the memorial of a completed, finally formed, singular man, but a work in progress.

For Yeats *was* beginning to compose lyric verse again. When he published a new collection, *The Green Helmet and Other Poems* in 1910, it would include poems begun in 1908. It would be a volume in which the poet could represent himself in various guises, personal and public, as if portraying himself in a grouped series of portraits and sketches. He appears as a committed man of the theatre, wearied and drained of creative joy by 'plays / That have to be set up in fifty ways' ('The

Fascination of What's Difficult'), eloquent and outraged, by legislation contrary to the landed interest, in a country house 'Where passion and precision have been one / Time out of mind' ('Upon a House Shaken by the Land Agitation'), at the Abbey Theatre paying Douglas Hyde a gracious compliment, at Galway races where 'Delight makes all of the one mind' ('At Galway Races'), in momentary rebuke of a modern world where merchant and clerk have 'Breathed on the world with timid breath'.

In the series of reflections composed in 1908 or 1909, which Yeats thought of as a second set of *Discoveries*, he recorded the observation of a friend, 'very learned in pictures' who explained to him how the portraiture of Castiglione's Renaissance displayed the evidence of generational change. 'Their generation had something present to their minds which they copied. They would imitate Christ or Caesar in their lives, or with [their] bodies some classic statue. They sought at all times the realization of something deliberately chosen, and they played a part always as if upon a stage before an audience, and gave up their lives rather than their play' (Skelton and Clark 1965: 89). *The Green Helmet and Other Poems* suggests a similar stagey deliberation of manner, a poet offering himself as subject for stylized representation with some classical analogue to guide the painter's hand. The theatre, a classical antiquity and mythology, provide opportunities for a poetic portraiture reminiscent of Renaissance iconography. 'The Fascination of What's Difficult', for example, invites us to trope the fatigued man of the theatre as abused offspring of Pegasus, exiled from Mount Olympus. In 'At the Abbey Theatre' Yeats asks the populist Douglas Hyde how to please a whimsically changeable audience: 'Is there a bridle for this Proteus...?'. And throughout the book the beloved's beauty is set in the contexts of Homeric, theatrical and painterly imagining.

Yet for all the managed deliberation of this volume, its aura of achieved public life, in which the poet plays a controlled part, the dramatic timbre of the verse − its driving rhetorical urgency, its moments of histrionic overstatement (all hortatory injunction, anguished interrogation, peremptory utterance) − scarcely bespeak a poet at any kind of peace. For as the first decade of the twentieth century drew to its close, there was much in Yeats's life that was not conducive to emotional tranquillity. Turbulence of feeling breaks through the arranged portraiture of *The Green Helmet and Other Poems* in a new poetry of charged dramatic lyricism. The life of the self again took its revenges, even as Yeats sought to make its discords amenable to the deliberate poses of an iconographically self-aware art.

In 1908 Maud Gonne came back into his life with a renewed and augmented intimacy. The chronology of this mid-life intensification of their relationship is not completely secure; but we know that in 1908 Yeats and she were once again sharing the contents of their dream lives with one another and that Yeats was making evocations with P. I. A. L. (Gonne's name in the Order of the Golden Dawn, which Yeats retained for her). On 26 July 1908 Gonne wrote to Yeats of a dream of the previous night in which he had figured momentously and erotically, in the form of a serpent: 'We melted into one another till we formed only *one being, a being greater than ourselves* who felt all & knew all with double intensity – the clock striking 11 broke the spell & as we separated it felt as if life was being drawn away from me with almost physical pain' (*GYL*: 257).

Yeats had been in Paris in late June in 1908, where he had met Gonne and their spiritual marriage had apparently rekindled. What she probably did not know was that in the spring Yeats had begun a vigorously physical relationship with a woman named Mabel Dickinson, a member of the Dublin United Arts Club, which Yeats had recently joined as an escape from the loneliness of the Nassau Hotel, where he often stayed when in the city. The daughter of a deceased Trinity College Professor of Pastoral Theology (he was the 'much loved vicar of St Anne's, Dawson Street, and dean of the Chapel Royal in Dublin Castle'; Foster, *AM*: 384), Dickinson followed a more earthy profession as a Swedish masseuse and her physique and healthy attitude to things bodily were of a kind likely to seem, to a sexually starved middle-aged man, an exhilarating antithesis to the spirituality of intercourse Gonne seemed to prefer. Yeats wrote to her of the Louvre classic painters, responding to 'clear light, strong bodies having all the measure of manhood' (cited in Kelly 1989: 183). Little doubt it was her body which the statuesque beauties of Ingres and David brought to mind. Yet with an uncanny instinct, Gonne seems to have been able to discern when Yeats was sexually active (even though Yeats kept his affair with the thirty-three-year-old Dickinson a closely guarded secret in Dublin and London), choosing at such moments to engage with him at a level which would give him pause, would keep him in thrall to his idea of her. So just as she had done when he had been sexually entangled with Shakespear in 1897, in 1908 she wrote him letters like that of 26 July. She surely knew that he was vulnerable at the level of occult possibility and such a letter was couched in terms, as William T. Gorski has argued, of an alchemical marriage – just the kind of thing to intrigue and tempt one who had recruited Gonne to the Order of the Golden Dawn: 'Maud must have guessed how irresistible "Willie" would have found her astral adventure, replete as it was with Maud's yearnings, Blakean iconography and the apotheosis of love' (Gorski 1996: 132). Yeats's response was to resort to the woods at Coole, where he was spending the summer, to imagine himself as the great serpent of Gonne's vision, to conjure his own visions of alchemical unions: through the late summer and autumn their spiritual ardour flamed, emotionally singeing them both. In a private notebook the poet kept at this tormented stage of their relationship he wrote of the pathos of his complex feelings for Gonne:

What end will it all have? She has all myself. . . . I was never more deeply in love, but my desire, always strong, must go elsewhere . . . she is my innocence and I her wisdom. Of old she was a phoenix and I fought her, but now she is my child more than sweetheart . . . but in the phoenix nest she is reborn in all her power to torture and delight, to waste and to enoble. She would be cruel if she were not a child, who can always say 'You will not suffer because I will pray'. (Unpublished Ms, cited in Gorski 135).

Gonne visited Dublin in October, where the famous actress Mrs Patrick Campbell took the leading role in Yeats's play *Deirdre*, and she also followed the play to London on her way back to Paris. Yeats journeyed to Paris in late November 1908, to work on a play which was preoccupying him, *The Player Queen*; he hoped Mrs Campbell would once again complement the Abbey troupe. The play was giving trouble (and would not be completed until 1917). He was also taking French lessons, with the usual lack of linguistic success. The major distraction was Gonne, ready to convince Yeats that they were united for ever as spiritual lovers, despite her marriage to MacBride. Now Yeats wanted more.

All the evidence we possess suggests that it was in France in the wintry month of December 1908 that Willie and Maud became bodily lovers, that they gave way to what Gonne herself admitted was 'earthly desire' (*GYL*: 258). As Jeffares observes ('Introduction' *GYL*), her last letter of that year to Yeats, immediately following his departure from France, is couched in the language of shared tenderness and real intimacy. Elizabeth Heine, who has examined the astrological manuscripts of this period, concurs (Heine 1998: 14–15). Yet the letter also implies that Gonne is trying to decide that their relationship will henceforth only be a spiritual one. She addresses her departed lover as 'Dearest' and tells him that once again she has been with him in the astral. She recalls: 'You asked me yesterday if I am not a little sad that things are as they are between us', and gives him a definitive reply:

> I have prayed so hard to have all earthly desire taken from my love for you & dearest, loving you as I do, I have prayed & am praying still that the bodily desire for me may be taken from you too. ... That struggle is over & I have found peace. (*GYL*: 258–9)

Her letter is surely that of a woman ending a physical relationship, about which she feels deeply ambivalent (as a practising Catholic, sexual intercourse with Yeats would have been adulterously sinful for Gonne, since she was still, in her Church's eyes, the wife of John MacBride). For Yeats Gonne's chaste determination must have been seriously unsettling, as he set off for Dublin (he probably received Gonne's letter in Manchester in the middle of his journey) where Mabel Dickinson, healthily unabashed about earthly desire, was complaisantly ready to take the measure of his frustrated manhood.

The poet had left Paris as a great storm settled on the English Channel, making his voyage to England a hazardous one. All the boats got in late. By the first week of January, in dreadfully cold weather, both Yeats and Gonne were ill and commiserating with each other. Yeats blamed their indisposition on some kind of occult attack. Gonne more astutely observed: 'I believe more & more that illness can only take hold of one when one is in some way out of harmony with oneself psychically' (*GYL*: 260).

Yeats had begun to keep a private journal in December 1908. Its first entry was his magisterial poem for Maud Gonne, 'No Second Troy', which would be collected in *The Green Helmet and Other Poems*. The almost immediately following entries for January 1909 and for the early months of the year show little of such ostensible control of mood. Strain expressed itself in morbid, unfruitful self-analysis and fissile emotional health. In late January he admitted to himself how out of psychic harmony he had become: 'I have had a curious breakdown of some sort. I had been working hard, and suddenly I found I could not use my mind on any serious subject' (*Mem*: 140). He had not easily accepted Gonne's attempt to return their relationship exclusively to the astral plane. He had sent her the collected edition of his works and a new poem. She had replied to a letter in which he must have pressed her on the role of fulfilled sexuality in the creative life by insisting 'Michael Angelo denied the power of sex, *for a year* while he was painting the marvel of the Sistine Chapel' (*GYL*: 261). At mid-month, as their difficult correspondence flowed between Paris and Dublin, he had communicated his feelings to his journal: 'Today the thought came to me that PIAL never really understands my plans, or nature, or ideas. Then came the thought, what matter? How much of the best I have done and still do is but the attempt to explain myself to her? If she understood, I should lack a reason for writing' (*Mem*: 141–2).

Then came the news of Lady Gregory's life-threatening illness (probably a cerebral haemorrhage). On 30 January Yeats had visited Synge and found him poorly. He pondered next day, as he acknowledged to himself how serious was the playwright's condition (he was suffering from the terminal stages of Hodgkin's disease, though Yeats did not know of this diagnosis): 'if he dies it will set me wondering whether he could have lived if he had not had his long, bitter misunderstanding with the wreckage of Young Irelandism' (*Mem*: 154). The poet sensed he was about to lose one of his few allies in his own long crusade against the same antipathetic Irish forces, those he had avoided at O'Leary's funeral. As if to conquer self-doubt he tested himself in futile enough controversy about the constitution of the United Arts Club, discovering that he retained, even at such an emotionally perilous period in his life, the ability to manipulate men and women and to gain the upper hand in a public matter.

That disjunction between the private man and his public comportment, seemed to confirm in the sphere of action a theory which had been forming in his mind since he had considered the portraits of himself to be included in his collected edition. In the midst of the intensifying crises of the early months of 1909, which culminated in the death of Synge on 24 March, and of his own emotional collapses, which he feared might be 'the root of madness' (*Mem*: 157), inherited from the Pollexfen line, he refined his theory of the Mask. To the *sprezzatura* Castiglione had encouraged the courtier to express as he emulated some image of noble life, Yeats now added his own conviction that the Mask is a form of self-mastery, a nonchalant, even playful, achievement to be sure, but made necessary by the tragic realities of life and the pain of personal experience.

Yeats in his 1902 and 1903 reading of Nietzsche would certainly have been made aware that the world of continuous struggle which he so compellingly evoked, included the struggle to create a mask. The will to power which Nietzsche had celebrated so fervently could find expression in two related forms of mastery: mastery over the self, and over others, which is made possible by that heroic self-mastery. Castiglione's altogether less brazen, less strident commendation of courtly self-fashioning had offered to Yeats in 1907 and 1908 a version of self-transcendence that dwelt less on the self and its capacity to transcend itself in struggle, than on submission to traditional disciplines and self-refining social customs. The poet himself, absorbing and synthesizing their thought, in 1909 developed his own theory of the Mask, which allowed for the satisfying exercise of power (like that he employed in the Arts Club, as he had done so forcefully and effectively in the Abbey Theatre), but did not depend on any great self-knowledge. In his journal indeed he categorized the culture of the Renaissance as 'founded not on self-knowledge but on knowledge of some other self – Christ or Caesar' (*Mem*: 160). For his theory accepted as a given that the self is by its very nature fissile, and therefore not open to easy self-comprehension. It also is inevitably called upon, given the nature of things, to endure extremes of suffering and emotional conflict. Against these the Mask serves as a defence and a means of self-transcendence in the realm of action and of art, as a form of dramatic performance, an endless play. Yet the adoption of a Mask partakes of tragedy, for it is the exigencies of actual, deeply flawed experience that the Mask permits the poet to transform. So Yeats in a January of deep personal distress arrived at the conviction that:

> There is a relation between discipline and the theatrical sense. If we cannot imagine ourselves as different from what we are and try to assume that second self, we cannot impose a discipline upon ourselves, though we may accept one from others. Active virtue as distinguished from the passive acceptance of a current code is therefore theatrical, consciously dramatic, the wearing of a mask. It is the condition of arduous full life. (*Mem*: 151)

By March he had further concluded:

> I think all happiness depends on having the energy to assume the mask of some other self, that all joyous or creative life is a rebirth as something not oneself, something created in a moment and perpetually renewed in playing a game like that of a child where one loses the infinite pain of self-realization, a grotesque or solemn painted face put on that one might hide from the terrors of judgment, an imaginative Saturnalia that makes one forget reality. (ibid.: 191)

Yet that other self, an escape from the terrors of reality, can, when it dons a tragic mask, involve the soul in new experiences, more profound than the every-day divided, suffering self of the poet could ever have envisaged:

> A poet creates tragedy from his own soul, that soul which is alike in all men, and at moments it has no joy, as we understand that word, for the soul is an exile and without will. It attains to ecstasy, which is from the contemplation of things which are vaster than the individual and imperfectly seen, perhaps, by all those that still live. (ibid.: 152)

Perhaps it attains to the knowledge of the dead (note 'all those that still live'). At this moment in Yeats's journal the reader senses that the poet is daring to enter zones of speculation about which he as yet feels uncertain. He admits: 'I cannot see my way clearly. But I am hunting truth too far into its thicket. It is my business to keep close to the impression of the senses and to daily thought' (ibid.: 153). In the years to come he would penetrate deeply into that thicket, as he sought to explore through the powers of spiritualist mediumship the knowledge possessed by those who more perfectly see in the kingdom of the dead the tragic inevitability of all things, in which knowledge 'the active will perishes' (ibid.: 152). However, from these anguished months on, Yeats's work will be touched with an intensified consciousness that the 'impression of the senses' and 'daily thought' bring pain as well as pleasure (ibid.: 153), tragic suffering as well as the satisfactions of power exercised in the real world about us. And it will be shadowed too by a powerful apprehension that the tragic sense of things may bear on a fundamental condition of being, which we share with all the shades, for whom self as we experience it in its energizing divisiveness is no more. For they traffic with the void, which Yeats at his most bleakly pessimistic, feared as the primary reality at the heart of experience.

As if to step back from that void, at the stage in mid-life when the knowledge of illness and death was hitting home with personal force (Synge was the younger man), Yeats chose to immerse himself in the novels of Balzac. He owned an edition of forty volumes, which he had started to read in February 1908. By the autumn of the following difficult year he had waded through thirty volumes of the French realist, whose worldly understanding of the foibles of human personality, the destinies implicit in social circumstance, he must have experienced as a kind of ballast for an imagination which had been invaded by an intimation of weightlessness, negation and of individual mental and physical fragility. For Balzac's mood is relish for the play on the painted stage, but the substance of his world is a philosophy of a kind which could be accommodated to Yeats's theory of the Mask and even to his esotericism (Gould 1989). The stuff of history and the social could conjoin with impalpable vision. Yeats consumed the novels like a tonic, as in 1909 he struggled to regain a measure of emotional well-being.

In May Yeats and Gonne met once more in London. She quarrelled with him, then apologized handsomely in a letter which was clearly intended to put an end to any hopes he might still have nurtured: 'My loved one I belong to you more in this renunciation than if I came to you in sin' (*GYL*: 272).

A further crisis of this fraught year was, by an odd chance, Balzacian in content, tone and consequence, adding a note of the painfully ludicrous to so much emotional turmoil. Quinn visited Europe in July 1909. He was becoming increasingly interested in British and French art, so could not find the time to visit Ireland for any length of time. He was also tiring of Irish importunity, at its most demanding in the poet's father (he would have been glad to have been able to persuade John Butler Yeats to return to Dublin). Always an irascible man, Quinn was in no mood to be trifled with by Yeats. He heard that the poet had been gossiping around Dublin about Quinn's relationship with his mistress, an American woman named Dorothy Coates, and about his own amatory chances in that quarter. He jumped to the conclusion that Yeats was trying to supplant him in the lady's affections, an impression she was happy to substantiate, to Quinn, for she knew where her interests lay. Quinn confronted the poet and an unseemly quarrel ensued. Quinn was not to be mollified by Yeats's retort, straight from a comic Balzacian contretemps: 'If it had been your wife, yes, but your mistress never' (*GYL*: 276). He found what Yeats called his 'unrestrained sense of comedy' (ibid.: 278) an intolerable insult. They remained seriously at odds for five years. Quinn nevertheless did Yeats the greatest service it was possible for him to do in continuing to support John Butler Yeats in New York. For in so doing he secured the poet freedom from the immediate concern for his father which as a young man he had often found burdensome. With John Butler Yeats safely, and despite his frequent protestations to the contrary, permanently across the Atlantic, Yeats had the cis-Atlantic space to play a mature role as successful man of letters and increasingly renowned poet and theatrical impresario.

By the late summer of 1909 Yeats had been in sufficiently ebullient mood to take on the authorities at Dublin Castle, which did him no harm with such advanced nationalists as were still willing to grant him some national credit. The Abbey put on Shaw's *The Shewing-up of Blanco Posnet*, which had been banned in London by the Lord Chamberlain. His absurd writ did not run in Dublin and Yeats took the kind of delight in cocking a snook at and outmanoeuvring Irish colonial officialdom which suggests that the 'strain' (his own word in a journal entry of August 1909) under which he had been labouring since before the previous Christmas, had not taken any great toll on his fighting spirit. In 1909 he had too contemplated making a more settled commitment to Irish life, for he was mooted unsuccessfully for a post as a lecturer in English at University College, Dublin, in the newly constituted National University of Ireland.

Yeats was at a stage where he was ready for some reconfiguration of the arrangements whereby he lived for much of each year in straitened circumstances in Woburn Buildings in London, in the Nassau Hotel or in rented rooms in Dublin, with summers at Coole. The sumptuously produced Shakespeare Head edition of his works (guaranteed to the tune of £1,500 by Annie Horniman) had not been the commercial success he had hoped it would be. The reviews had been respectful, tending to see Yeats as a representative figure of what Lytton Strachey identified as extreme romanticism. A consensus seemed to be developing that Yeats was to be celebrated as a writer of exquisite lyric poetry in the romantic Irish manner, whose experiments in dramatic art had been a less than convincing distraction from the exploitation of his true gift. There was unquestionably (however Yeats had hoped to suggest otherwise), a fairly general impression abroad, that this series of volumes was a lifetime's body of work, presented to the public for definitive judgement.

In the theatre, too, uncertainty made Yeats conscious that the future would require new arrangements (Frazier 1990: 186–97). From 1906 onwards, particularly after a spring and summer tour by the company in England in that year,

Horniman had complained repeatedly and vociferously about how the theatre was being run. Her *bête noire* was the unfortunate Willie Fay, against whom she directed a tirade of intemperate criticism. She detested the Irish and had invested in a Dublin theatre only because that was where her beloved Yeats chose to work. She found their manners lax, their business methods shoddy and their easy familiarity, particularly between the sexes, intolerable. When she had inherited from her father, she had let it be known that she had £25,000 to invest in the Dublin enterprise, provided it dropped the word 'Irish' from its title and became generally known as the Abbey Theatre Company (this was only partially acceded to) and performed an international repertoire with a strong leaven of English actors to make the loaf rise to her demanding standards (this was not acceded to).

Horniman was willing to move to Manchester where she would fund a repertory company and she tried to induce Yeats to transfer the production of his plays to the planned venue. This attempt by Horniman to manipulate 'her' playwright had brought Yeats in June 1907 to one of those rare moments in his life when he had been forced to declare his position openly, instead of maintaining, as was his wont, complicatedly ambiguous relations with differing individuals in the interests of getting what he wanted. This time he had been forced to chose between Horniman's money and Lady Gregory's friendship, for she and Synge had opposed Horniman's plans with which Yeats had been inclined to compromise. He had hoped the huge injection of funds would give him increased freedom to direct the theatre towards poetic drama, reducing the need to produce more popular peasant plays as money-spinners. His resolve stiffened by Lady Gregory, who appealed to his honour in the matter, he had written what he must have known was a letter which could put an end to his capacity to exploit Horniman's patronage. He decisively informed the Hiberniphobe Horniman, 'I am not young enough to change my nationality – it would really amount to that' (*L*: 500: misdated here, see *AM*: 599). She determined bitterly that she would not waste any more time on a lost cause, since she could not compete with the lure of Kathleen ni Houlihan (*AM*: 599).

Yeats's letter had not provoked an immediate revocation of her support. It meant, however, that Horniman was intent on finding an English alternative for her highly conditional largesse. She had become even more paranoid about the nefarious plottings of the Irish as she sensed Yeats slipping from her, under the constant influence as he was of Lady Gregory's gravitational pull. The Fays became the chief victims of the maelstrom of theatre politics at this time. The brothers resigned from the company in January, 1908.

In September, 1909, with her mind now set on the establishment of a theatre in Manchester, Horniman offered to sell the theatre to the Irish company. By December the terms were agreed, though Yeats cannily ensured that her promised payment for 1910 would be forthcoming as he unabashedly tried to milk the last drop from his rich Englishwoman. She took final insult that the theatre, inadvertently, had failed to shut to mark the death of Edward VII in May 1910.

More was changing for Yeats than the financial support of his theatre. His own relationship with the English and Irish establishments was in transition. So much so that in the autumn 1910 when Dowden became ill and considered retiring from his professorship of English Literature in Trinity College, Dublin, Yeats immediately expressed an interest in succeeding him. One of the Fellows, a congenial and sociable classicist, intimated to the poet that he could be in the running, so Yeats wrote (in a letter in which he misspelt the word 'Professorship'; Edwards 1965: 6) to Trinity's John Pentland Mahaffy to enquire about his chances. Yeats by 1910 would have been glad enough to command a salary of £600 per annum (his father was delighted by the idea) which Dowden's post then entailed. In the event Dowden recovered and resumed his duties. Mahaffy would have preferred it if Yeats could have taken the post, for he recognized the poet's substantial English reputation and the way he had made himself at home with the English upper classes, with whom Mahaffy, an ineffable snob, liked to consort when he could.

For Yeats, who in the 1890s had inhabited the socially anomalous world of London's *déclassé* literary coteries, by 1910 had in fact become something of a society lion. The poet who had dined on his North American tour with professors and local notables, and with the president of the United States, was at the decade's end an invitee at metropolitan literary dinner parties and at the week-ends in the country that were a feature of upper-class English Edwardian social life. As a colourful guest his Irish nationalism could seem, in a period when Home Rule of some kind was awaited from a Liberal government, a pleasing added value to a hostess desirous of graciously argued conversation at her table. In Dublin Yeats could expect obloquy and suspicion among the more militant of his fellow countrymen that his nationalism was an affectation or seriously inadequate. Among Unionists his English success might make a Trinity Chair possible but his earlier Fenian excesses were remembered. So London and the Home Counties, where his poetry and Irishness could open doors on agreeable dining rooms and country houses, took on an attractiveness they never had before. In November 1909 he told his father that he was dining out a great deal and described how at a men's dinner party, given by the critic Edmund Gosse, he had sat next to Prime Minister Asquith. He found him 'an exceedingly well read man, especially, curiously enough, in poetry. Not a man of really fine culture, I think, but exceedingly charming and well read' (*L*: 540). He had also been meeting, he told his father, General Ian Hamilton, a relative of Lady Gregory, whom he assessed as 'a man of the really finest culture, as fine as that of anybody I've ever met' (ibid.: 541). Earlier that year Wilfrid Scawen Blunt had recorded in his diary: 'Yeats is beginning to get fat and sleek; he has cut his hair... he is well dressed...' (Blunt 1922, vol. 2: 252).

Yeats's acceptability in English society meant that when Horniman withdrew her subsidy for the Abbey Theatre, he and Lady Gregory, as Pierce points out, could turn 'immediately to fashionable London society' (Pierce 1995: 164) in an appeal for funds. At a drawing-room meeting held in June 1910 by Lady Gregory at the house of her nephew, Sir Hugh Lane, in Cheyne Walk, Chelsea, the guest list reads surprisingly, if we remember Yeats as a poor young Londoner setting out in the world, sharing sparse apartments in Fountain Court with Arthur

Symons. Yeats addressed an audience of titled ladies and knights of the realm to seek their support for his Dublin theatre. He was something of a celebrity in the English capital, like his even more socially successful fellow countryman George Bernard Shaw, who spoke on the same occasion. Whatever his personal views on political matters, he was a poet of unquestioned distinction who could be depended upon to grace a public occasion with dignity and eloquence. In April 1910 Edmund Gosse wrote inviting him to become a founding member of a proposed English Academy of Letters. Yeats's was the only Irish name among a distinguished list of twenty-seven writers, prominent academics and men of letters who constituted the original membership. Also in 1910, through Gosse's good offices, Yeats accepted Asquith's offer of a Civil List Pension of £150 per annum (Dublin wit swiftly dubbed him 'Pensioner Yeats'). His scrupulous proviso, that in accepting such a benefice he still felt free to participate in a future Irish rebellion, would have seemed just Mr Yeats's endearing way. He was, after all, a romantic poet, but a middle-aged one now, and the times were peaceful.

No doubt Yeats had his eye on his Irish reputation when he entered that caveat, though it must be accepted that his own sense of principle was well developed on key issues (he never remotely countenanced the idea of a knighthood, for example, even when it was seriously mooted by Lady Cunard at the end of 1915). He would too surely have been influenced by his awareness that posterity would make its comment and he would have wished the record to contain such clarifications of motive and deed. For Yeats in 1910 was assembling the poems that would appear in December of that year in *The Green Helmet and Other Poems*. It is a volume that for the first time in a sustained and obvious way presents his own life experience as the stuff of poetry, as he represents himself as a public figure who in private has known sacrifice, struggle and the pangs of unrequited love.

As a collection, *The Green Helmet and Other Poems* (1910) evinces an impression of a poet concerned to stage-manage how he will be seen both by his public and by posterity; even his sufferings in love must be cast in terms of distancing analogy, trope, allegory and addressed from a position of measured retrospection. The volume assuredly occupies a temporal reality of past, present and implied future and not the timeless world of transcendence or apocalyptic consummation which the early volumes sought to enter. However the poet does not submit to mere temporality. A complicated syntax, which generates long verse sentences which weave through skilfully modulated tenses and shift from the active to the passive voice, seeks to control the passage of time to the degree that the poet acquires wisdom from it ('The Coming of Wisdom with Time'). He seeks, moreover, to anticipate the future. So conditional moods simultaneously allow for a note of preoccupying self-assessment, and permit poems to conclude with declarative force: 'Now I may wither into the truth' ('The Coming of Wisdom with Time'); 'we find hearteners among men/That ride upon horses' ('At Galway Races'); 'I'll find the stable and pull out the bolt' ('The Fascination of What's Difficult').

One critic has argued that Yeats's poetry of this period lacks 'the enactment of trauma' (Pierce 1995: 161) and that there is 'little pressure behind the writing' (ibid.: 160). He notes though that the language of *The Green Helmet and Other Poems* is a language of struggle. Pierce concludes, however, that it is 'not a private voice struggling to get heard but a public voice seeking its customary declamatory mode' (ibid.: 162). This underestimates how much that struggle is an attempt to don a mask in the knowledge of time's cruel exactions and of a threatening present. As Edward Larrissy comments, this is a book where 'there is a gradual change of emphasis' from poetry as a kind of music which evokes 'a realm, of images we pursue, to the mask that arrests, by main force of personality, the drift of images, and gives it a unity that is not the unity of reason' (Larrissy 1994: 94).

Bloom complains of this volume that too many of the poems tend to run into one another (Bloom 1970: 169) for the reader, with only the fiercely impressive 'No Second Troy' sufficiently commanding attention. Yet it can be argued, to develop Larrissy's point, that it is this context of reiteration which gives the poem its special force in the collection. The implied poet of the volume is evidently wrestling with repeated moods of loss, bitterness and strain in a spiritual marriage (the first eight poems are headed '*Raymond Lully and his Wife Pernella*' in the Cuala Press edition of December 1910, in mis-allusion to a chaste alchemical marriage; in an erratum slip Raymond Lully became Nicholas Flamel) and in an unsympathetic social environment. Accordingly, the mask of patrician arrogance and social disdain worn in 'No Second Troy' with such 'an audacious drum-roll of overstatement' (ibid.) is done so in irrational defiance of personal suffering and in terror of a tragic gulf between the lover's elevated beauty and the destructive forces of mass democracy. The poem, moreover, is a force field of unresolved feelings and of deep ambivalence about woman, for all its almost Byronic swagger of self-assurance. The appearance of control this poem manages is deceptive. A unity of unreason achieved by the wearing of an arresting mask is no unity at all. ' "It was the mask engaged your mind,/And after set your heart to beat,/Not what's behind" ' counselled 'A Lyric from an Unpublished Play' in the same collection, as it responded to a lover's curiosity: ' "I would but find what's there to find,/Love or deceit" '.

Yeats probably took as stimulus for 'No Second Troy' William Cowper's lines composed in horror of the Gordon riots of 1780: 'When the rude rabble's watchword was "destroy"/And blazing London seem'd a second Troy'. As a student of the Blake who had witnessed the rampant disorders of those few days of eighteenth-century urban riot, Yeats would have been well aware of the sectarian fears and class hatred at work in the violence of that Protestant assault upon Catholicism. Now in Dublin, where his lover has fomented rebellion and class antagonism, it is, in an obvious rewriting of Cowper's lines (Dublin, no more than the London of the Gordon riots, is no second Troy, even if London for a few days 'seem'd' so) a predominantly Catholic mob which may turn on its Protestant masters. It may do so at the behest of an agitator who has caused the poet pain on both the personal and public levels. For in a sense she has gone over to the enemy (in 'King and No King' in the same volume, the poet speaks of himself as one who does not share his lover's 'faith'):

> Why should I blame her that she filled my days
> With misery, or that she would of late
> Have taught to ignorant men most violent ways,
> Or hurled the little streets upon the great,
> Had they but courage equal to desire?

The poet's reply to himself in the poem, in a volume of much questioning self-address, is to make his lover a figure who combines in her person Helen's beauty with Amazonian singleness of purpose and a chaste strength that evokes the goddess Diana:

> What could have made her peaceful with a mind
> That nobleness made simple as a fire,
> With beauty like a tightened bow, a kind
> That is not natural in an age like this,
> Being high and solitary and most stern?

The allusiveness of this verse sentence is fairly precise, as well as operating on the level of high rhetorical generality. It is compact of ambivalent feeling. Toxophily, the primary metaphor upon which it depends for its impact, had been in fact a very popular hobby for well-bred Victorian women and it remained a sport for the wives and daughters of the elite well into the twentieth century. Society papers often included photographs of young, aristocratic females engaged in the sport. Yet it was not natural in a democratic age, when poverty might turn on wealth, Catholic on Protestant, for it suggested aristocracy and upper-middle class graciousness. Yet the antique activity bore its own charge of ambiguous sexual frisson. In her elegant fashion, upper middle-class Edwardian womanhood was sustaining, as she took bow in hand, an image of chivalric warfare in an era when the defeats of the British forces by the Boers in South Africa had shown such traditions and their accompanying weaponry to be irrelevant. That it was 'woman' who achieved this anachronistic iconographic apotheosis lent to her an aura of mythological martial prowess more usually associated with male heroes, when such heroism was becoming increasingly impossible for men. As Cullingford comments of 'No Second Troy': 'the poem's heroine transgresses all the stereotypes of feminity: she is violent, courageous, noble, fiery, solitary, and stern; her beauty is a weapon – a "tightened bow" – rather than a lure' (Cullingford 1993: 81).

Disturbing emancipatory forces therefore are released by the image in this poem of woman/Gonne as chivalric warrior, about which the poet is ambivalent: he seeks to control those energies in what Bloom has identified as a series of closed questions; yet the interrogative structure of the poem resists such an authoritarian impulse, even as it strains syntactically against the possibility of unpredictable responses. The poet both admires and fears what Gonne represents, for she is an active force in the poem in a way in which the Homeric analogue, Helen, was not (she was passive victim of the events, not their agent). The exceptional woman, the poem implies, can achieve heroism, but seeks to restrict that heroism to the past in which it seems itself most naturally to exist and to control it where it might have deleterious effects on the present. For out of place in the present, it becomes complicit with socially destructive agitation and unheroic riot ('little streets upon the great').

The ambivalence of the poem in its response to such imagery of female empowerment is compounded by its evocation of the goddess Diana. Indeed the name 'Diana' had peculiar implications for Yeats, as well as significant, more general, socio/cultural ramifications. For the poet as well as for Victorian and Edwardian culture, it was bound up with uncertain feelings about the role and place in society of exceptional women.

When Yeats began the first draft of his autobiography in 1915, although he knew his words would not be published in their first form in his lifetime, he nevertheless chose to protect Shakespear's name in a pseudonym, 'Diana Vernon'. That of course is the name of the lively, independent-minded, beautiful heroine of Scott's novel *Rob Roy*. 'Diana Vernon sounds pleasantly in my ears and will suit her as well as any other' (*Mem*: 74), the poet, rather disingenuously, remarked in the draft, for in choosing such a pseudonym for his first sexual partner he was attributing real distinction to her. Yeats's apparently casual act of naming in 1915 was an acknowledgement of what he owed to a remarkable woman, to one who at great risk to herself had so generously, as he records in 'Friends', relieved him in 1896 of 'Youth's dreamy load' ('Friends', composed in January 1911). He can scarcely have been unaware in December 1910, as 'No Second Troy' apotheosized Gonne, of Shakespear as a Diana in her own right. She had her own nobility. For she had ignored the shackles of a conventional marriage to defy the constraints of Victorian mores, and had offered him the kind of peace Gonne could not. Shadowing the poem is an ideal of peace in a woman, which is as extraordinary in its way as the violent distinction Gonne represents.

Yeats and Shakespear had in fact renewed their intimacy some time during or shortly after June 1910; and although the evidence does not allow us to assert for certain that they renewed physical relations then or thereafter, it seems possible that in 1910 they did. So although 'No Second Troy' was in existence by the end of 1908, when Yeats selected it for inclusion in *The Green Helmet and Other Poems*, he was surely aware how the recent past bore on the poem's contrast between a 'peaceful' mind and a mind 'made simple as a fire' that had 'filled' his days with 'misery'. When he was preparing the book for a second edition, which Macmillan published in London and New York in 1912, with six added poems, he placed 'Friends' immediately before it, with its gratitude (in one reading of a notable crux) for Shakespear's sexual generosity in his youth. For as Toomey has remarked: 'the recent emotional rapprochement of June 1910 and possibly afterwards must have reminded Yeats of how much he owed in terms of sexual development – "what none can have and thrive" – to Olivia Shakespear' (Toomey 1988: 225). 'No Second Troy', I am arguing, gains something of its undoubted dramatic impact from its ambivalence of feeling about differing forms of exceptional womanhood. Its placement in the second edition of the collection intensifies that contrast, as it appears there following the poem in which

Shakespear (along with Lady Gregory) is praised. Yeats's imaginative renewal through the power of the feminine lay in the future. 'No Second Troy' is a troubled honouring of its diverse expressions.

The stagey direction of *The Green Helmet and Other Poems* as a whole is made to seem a kind of premature maturity of manner and address by the taut energy of the volume's most striking poem, where language is deployed with rhetorical force, despite the conditional grammar. A new awareness of death as a reality, rather than as a metaphor of spiritual transformation when self-sacrifice has run its course, also gives the book a chill air of emotional austerity, despite its slightly plush theatricality ('kings,/Helmets, and swords, and half-forgotten things', 'Reconciliation'). Time has begun to wither even Gonne's beauty, but a friend's illness enforces bleaker truths still:

> Sickness brought me this
> Thought, in that scale of his:
> Why should I be dismayed
> Though flame had burned the whole
> World, as it were a coal,
> Now I have seen it weighed
> Against a soul?
> > 'A Friend's Illness'

In 1909 Synge had 'gone upward out of his ailing body into the heroical fountains' (*Mem*: 205). Lady Gregory had 'very nearly slipped away' (ibid.: 161). In the autumn Yeats's uncle and fellow member of the Order of the Golden Dawn, George Pollexfen, with whom he practised astrology over the years, died after 'Lily' Yeats had heard the banshee. At his Sligo funeral, which Yeats attended, Pollexfen's fellow master masons threw the Acacia spray into the grave, 'Upon a melancholy man/Who had ended where his breath began' ('In Memory of Alfred Pollexfen'). In a haunted poem which Yeats added to the 1912 edition of *The Green Helmet and Other Poems*, the fate of the spirit after death is imagined with a new urgency. 'Ah! when the ghost begins to quicken' the poem asks,

> Confusion of the death-bed over, is it sent
> Out naked on the roads, as the books say, and stricken
> By the injustice of the skies for punishment?
> > ('The Cold Heaven')

It was a question that was to absorb the poet for the rest of his life. He would consult many of 'the books' in quest of spiritualist illumination on the matter; but also seek answers 'out of a medium's mouth'.

9

Darkened Rooms

In the months following the first production of *The Playboy of the Western World,*
Yeats had written a prose drama entitled *The Golden Helmet.* First performed at
the Abbey Theatre in March 1908, it was published in Volume IV of the
Shakespeare Head collected edition of that year. In December 1909, dissatisfied
with the text and its production, Yeats rewrote the play in a ballad metre, in
which form it appears as the title work of *The Green Helmet and Other Poems.* It
was produced as a verse drama at the Abbey on 10 February 1910. In the
volume which bears its amended name, the play adds a note of unrestrained,
rollicking vitality to the prevailing retrospection of the poems. Subtitled 'An
Heroic Farce', the play glorifies Cuchulain, unapologetically contrasting his
capacity to dare all in the cause of fame with the quarrelsome pettiness of
his Irish contemporaries ('Town land may rail at town land till all have gone to
wrack'). Cuchulain is a chosen one, selected by the magical shape-changing
divinity who rules the land:

> And I chose the laughing lip
> That shall not turn from laughing whatever rise or fall,
> The heart that grows no bitterer although betrayed by all,
> The hand that loves to scatter, the life like a gambler's throw;
> And these things I make prosper.

The play has a truculent air, an insouciance of farcical high spirits which
suggests that it is Yeats's contemptuous answer to his own Irish detractors in a
'blind bitter land' ('The Consolation') where Synge had been harried to an early
death. It is the play of a man who refuses to give his enemies the benefit of any
doubt. They are poltroons and mediocrities, good only for quarrelling. As if to
defy those who had found the eroticism of Synge's play unsettling, Yeats makes
Cuchulain the object of dangerous female desire. Emer, his wife, sings an intense
lyric:

> women kind
> When their eyes have met mine,
> Grow cold and grow hot,
> Troubled as with wine
> By a secret thought,
> Preyed upon, fed upon
> By jealously and desire.
> I am moon to that sun,
> I am steel to that fire.

It is while Emer sings this song for the second time in the play, as she fends off with her dagger the furious wives of lesser men, that her erotic energy summons spirit forms, in what is a highly stylized version of the theatricality of a seance. The stage direction runs: 'Suddenly three black hands come through the windows and put out the torches. It is now pitch dark, but for a faint light outside the house which merely shows that there are moving forms, but not who or what they are, and in the darkness one can hear low terrified voices.' Emer is the medium who conjures the Red Man of the play who awards Cuchulain the Green Helmet of honour.

It was apt that this work which expresses Yeats's impatience with his enemies (the devil-may-care fantastical, grotesque quality of the action defies as stagecraft any conventional audience expectations) should have contained this uncanny dramatic moment. For it anticipates what was to become from 1911 onwards a Yeatsian obsession with spiritualism and mediumship, an obsession which demanded the kind of concentrated attention that theatre business and the management of men had required in the first decade of the century.

One consequence of this reorientation of Yeats's interests was once again to make London and England the primary location of his variegated endeavours. For almost a decade (although he had continued to publish his books and essays in England as well as Ireland), Dublin and the Abbey Theatre had been the centre of his artistic activism. From 1911 onwards as he became more and more absorbed by psychic investigation his role in the Abbey diminished (the popular playwright Lennox Robinson who was appointed manager in 1910 would release Yeats from some day-to-day responsibilities). After 1912 his social presence in Ireland was significantly less marked. By 1913 he would spend the summer in England conducting psychic experiments, for the first time since 1897 forgoing the delights of Coole, where Lady Gregory could not, that year, receive him until the autumn. He holidayed in August with the family of Olivia Shakespear's brother Harry, to whom Shakespear had introduced him. In 1911 Harry had married a widow named Edith Ellen ('Nelly') Hyde-Lees, whose daughter, the Hampshire-born Bertha Georgina, Yeats had first met probably in December of the same year (*AM*: 437–8). They had become friendly, since Yeats spent time with her family at various agreeable houses and hotels in the English countryside or by the south coast. In August 1913 Yeats talked intently with her about the experiments he had been conducting that summer. The young Georgie, then twenty years old to Yeats's forty-eight, would remember how fascinated the poet had been by his psychic investigations and how he had recruited her to help him in that work.

Some Irish obligations were sacrosanct. The memory of Synge was to be protected, his reputation cast in appropriate bronze. In May, 1910 during a visit with Maud Gonne at the home she had established for herself and her children in Normandy, he had been working on a long essay on Synge which was intended to serve as preface to an edition of his dead friend's works. It was completed by September of that year. Because Yeats disapproved of some of the editorial decisons of the managing editor of the press, he withdrew his essay, issuing it in July 1911, through his sisters' Cuala Press, as *Synge and the Ireland of his Time*. Yeats used the occasion to restate in more magisterial terms the sociological account of modern Ireland which he had earlier outlined for himself in 'Poetry and Tradition'. He castigated a modern middle-class, Irish nationalism so deficient in imaginative capacity that it had substituted 'a traditional casuistry for a country' (*E&I* 314). It was obvious that Sinn Féin was still his target, with its narrow, separatist ideology that demanded everything should serve the cause. The dead Synge is celebrated as one whose constitutionally apolitical sensibility (a Yeatsian simplification, adopted for the purposes of his myth-making) made him an artist incapable of doing other than expressing his unique vision. The hard battle which Yeats had prophesied in 1905 (in his letter to Quinn) to create in Ireland an artistic personality in the modern sense of the term, was one Synge had fought and won almost without knowing it. For in Yeats's version of him as exemplar his artistic vocation was paramount:

> in Ireland he loved only what was wild in its people, and in 'the grey and wintry sides of many glens.' All the rest, all that one reasoned over, fought for, read of in leading articles, all that came from education, all that came down from Young Ireland – though for this he had not lacked a little sympathy – first wakened in him perhaps that irony which runs through all he wrote; but once awakened, he made it turn its face upon the whole of life. (*E&I*: 320)

For Yeats, the whole of life to which Synge bade his audiences attend, to their vocal discomfiture, encompassed tragedy as well as the full colour of vibrant peasant speech transmuted into poetry. Synge's integrity as an artist was such that he did not flinch from the presence of death in life. That was why he was so attracted to the inhabitants of Aran and the Blasket Islands, averred Yeats, for there were men and women, who 'under the weight of their necessity lived, as the artist lives, in the presence of death and childhood' (ibid.: 325).

Synge in this essay exists in a half-world between the living and the dead. The tenses shift between past and present to allow the dramatist to haunt the text as Yeats's ghostly instructor, death investing his reported remarks with the force of an augury. The sense of tragedy which Yeats associates with his person and *oeuvre* makes Synge a revenant from an advanced state of being, who rebukes the world of compromises and self-betrayal:

To speak of one's emotions without fear or moral ambition, to come out from under the shadow of other men's minds, to forget their needs, to be utterly oneself, that is all the Muses care for. . . . All art is a disengaging of a soul from place and history, its suspension in a beautiful or terrible light to await the Judgement, though it must be, seeing that all its days were a Last Day, judged already. (ibid.: 339)

In 1910 and 1911 Synge played a role in Yeats's intensifying preoccupation with a concept of tragedy as religious revelation, in which the theatre attends as if upon spirits. In 1910, in an essay entitled 'The Tragic Theatre', Yeats wrote 'that in the supreme moment of tragic art there comes upon one that strange sensation as though the hair of one's head stood up' (ibid.: 243). No longer is it the symbol which induces the revelatory trance in Yeats's aesthetic/magical theory, but 'Tragic art, passionate art, the drowner of dykes, the confounder of understand-ing, [which] moves us by setting us to reverie, by alluring us to reverie, by alluring us almost to the intensity of trance' (ibid.: 245). Synge's art was an art which served a similar purpose in 'the substantiation of the soul' (ibid.: 341) which Yeats as spiritualist increasingly sought.

To secure the future of the Abbey in the post-Horniman dispensation also remained a sacred duty. In early 1910, as he anticipated lean times to come, Yeats prepared three lectures which could help to raise money for the company. These were first delivered at the Adelphi club in London before a paying audience in the same year. They were also the lectures which Yeats in part drew on in the United States, during a second tour of that country which he undertook in September 1911, on behalf of the theatre.

Synge's reputation, so much in Yeats's mind since the playwright's death in 1909, arose as a crucial issue during that visit. A faction of Irish America did not wish to be outdone in its morality and national zeal by its Irish and English cousins and chose the Abbey tour which Yeats was accompanying to make its own vociferous protest. Yeats treated the play's antagonists with total contempt, giving many interviews in which he berated Irish America for failing to recognize what even Dublin, Belfast and Cork had eventually granted was work of genius.

The poet's second tour of the United States allowed him to spend some time in New York with his father, though the breach with Quinn remained as wide as ever. There is also evidence that he attended a seance in Boston conducted by a Mrs Chenoweth, the pseudonym of a Mrs Minnie Meserve Soule, whose powers as a medium were at that time under investigation by the American Society for Psychical Research. He returned to London towards the end of October with his spiritual interests fully awake.

Yeats's fascination with spiritualist mediumship probably developed in a dedic-ated form from 1909 onwards. By 1911 and 1912 it had become a fascination which, in various ways, would absorb him for the next fifteen or so years. Some time before 1900, according to Jeffares (1988: 194) Yeats attended a seance with Constance Gore-Booth. In January 1903 he reminded a correspondent that he had promised him an introduction to a spiritualist, since he sensed he would have time that winter and he wished 'to begin really serious investigation' (*CL3*: 294).

He seems then to have begun 'going a good deal to séances for the first time' (*Ex*: 30) and to have got over the terror, revulsion and physical reaction he had experienced in 1888, when he had accompanied Katherine Tynan to such an event. In mid-life the darkened room of psychic experiment and occult communication became almost a humdrum feature of his daily life. For he made it his business to seek out and painstakingly record and assess the powers of well-known and obscure practitioners of the medium's art.

At stake was the fate of the human soul after death and the significance for an understanding of individual selfhood of a communicative spirit world breaking in upon personal consciousness. With the death of Synge and that of his uncle George Pollexfen enforcing a sense of mortality, Yeats was entering on a phase of intense religious speculation. For a period in 1909 he even joined a group which met for the study of the Bible, which a pious member of the United Arts Club in Dublin had organized. He reflected 'Was the *Bhagavad Gita* the "scenario" from which the Gospels were made?' (*Mem*: 150).

Yeats as spiritualist and psychic investigator strikes many people as a preposterous figure. And it must be admitted that the ludicrous was never far absent when in suburban Edwardian drawing-rooms and in seedy flats in Soho, dependent on such paraphernalia of the medium's often consciously fraudulent trade as tin-box trumpets and planchettes, earnest, credulous folk sought to question spirits summoned from the vasty deeps in an atmosphere of occult gullibility. Seances in Paris conducted by Mme Juliette Bisson (specialist in ectoplasm and spirit photography), in May 1914, with Yeats in attendance, suggest even more troublingly how the fad for psychic experiment and spiritualist mediumship constantly threatened absurdity and fatuity. A manifestation of phosphorescent light raised the question whether, in some gross subterfuge, the medium's saliva could have been involved in the uncanny spectacle. The record solemnly advises: 'it would be difficult to make life sized phantoms, one of them resembling Mme B's Mother by spitting' (NL Ms 30,358).

Yeats, among the spirit mediums in the second decade of the twentieth century, for all the triviality of some of the documentary record he has left of his experiences, was by no means an isolated, anomalous figure. In the United States, the experimental work and lectures of the psychologist William James had given a good deal of respectability to psychic investigation, while in England the Society for Psychical Research numbered among its membership two of Britain's most distinguished physicists, Lord Rayleigh and Joseph John Johnson. Rayleigh was a Nobel laureate and in 1908 he became chancellor of the University of Cambridge. He retained his membership of the Society as a vice-president until his death in 1919. Johnson also received the Nobel Prize for physics in 1906. In 1918 he became master of Trinity College, Cambridge after a glittering scientific career which had never meant him repudiating an interest in the paranormal. With such paragons of intellectual respectability ready to risk their reputations among more hard-headed colleagues in pursuit of evidence of the paranormal, it surprises less that a poet of Yeats's anti-materialist, romantic sympathies should have indulged the *outré* excesses of the spiritualist and psychic world.

Furthermore, new media – the telephone, the phonograph, the photograph, the cinematograph – were dispersing human identity in new ways and allowing the dead a kind of presence among the living quite new to human experience (it was no accident that photography of spirits and individuals' auras played a crucial role in investigations of psychic phenomena). Psychology was also developing as a branch of knowledge which took account of self-division and of the possibility that secondary and tertiary personalities of the mediums and sitters, in unconscious co-operation, were at work in mediumship, which became a proper object of scientific attention. Some well-known mediums acceded to this possibility and submitted themselves to psychological investigation. One famous Irish practitioner (to whom in her girlhood Yeats had once explained that he had devised a spool-like gadget with threads and corks, which, attached to a windowsill, would induce the fairies to play a weird music) worked with an experimentalist at Duke University, North Carolina, and eventually concluded that the 'controls' of mediumship are 'principals of the sub-conscious' (Garrett 1968: 92) and the spirits themselves 'entities... formed from spiritual and emotional needs of the persons involved' (ibid.: 94).

Two main approaches were to be found among the many individuals in Britain and Ireland who interested themselves in psychic phenomena in this period (paralleling a similar duality of approach in North America). E. R. Dodds, (who, as a young man, knew Yeats in the second decade of the century in Dublin), subsequently Regius Professor of Greek in the University of Oxford, and an inveterately sceptical member of the British Society for Psychical Research, lucidly distinguished between the two approaches, though they are often mixed in individual minds. The one was that of the occultist who sought experience rather than explanation, the other that of the psychic researcher who wishes to 'abolish' the occult in the clear light of day (Dodds 1977: 97–8).

Dodds thought Yeats an occultist, while he numbered himself among the psychic researchers. Yet for all his dedication to the occult there was a good deal of the investigator in Yeats too. It was probably through a friendship with Everard Feilding, an honorary secretary of the Society for Psychical Research, that Yeats became an associate member of the Society in 1913 and maintained this status until 1928. He had begun attending seances in earnest in 1909 at Cambridge House, the Wimbledon home of William T. Stead, who had published the letters of a dead American woman to himself in book form in 1898 as *Letters from Julia* (subsequently *After Death*, 1914). It was there that Yeats may have made first contact with what seemed to be a spirit anxious to affect how he understood both his own mind and the relationship of the dead with the living. The same spirit, who came at the call of an American medium, Mrs Etta Wriedt, spoke with a strong Irish accent at a seance in May 1912 in Cambridge House through the tin trumpet she employed for such communications. The voice 'claimed to come for "Mr Gates"' (cited in Adams and Harper 1982: 4), that he had been with him since childhood and that the spirits wished to use his hand and brain. In May and June Yeats attended many seances, at some of which Leo Africanus, the familiar who had announced himself to Yeats, came through in an insistent manner. He was intent on instructing the sceptical poet, who despite his doubts, kept detailed accounts of these unlikely proceedings, which continued for several years.

At the same time as Leo Africanus was making himself known to Yeats, the poet was also engaged in an experiment in automatic writing with a young woman named Elizabeth Radcliffe, an acquaintance of Olivia Shakespear, whom he had met in the spring of 1912. He had consulted her during a crisis in his relationship with Mabel Dickinson. Dickinson had communicated to him in May 1913 that she was pregnant by him. Their relationship may have been complicated by the fact that Yeats had 'like several others of the artistic avant-garde, notably Augustus John − . . . enjoyed a casual affair with the beautiful but insipid Alick Schepeler' (*AM*: 474). In the summer of 1912 he had been 'sending Schepeler letters of roguish sexual innuendo from Coole' (ibid.: 474–5). Or perhaps she simply wanted to know how she stood with her poet, as the biological clock ticked. Radcliffe, it seems, proved her clairvoyant credentials in this troubling matter, since her automatic scripts seemed to have prophesied a distressing event and there may have been a point in her writings which encouraged the poet to believe that Dickinson's claim was false, as indeed it was. Yeats, in high emotion, suspected that his mistress had attempted to trap him into an unwanted marriage. He ended their sporadic liaison in an acrimonious scene, which was followed by a truce negotiated between them at the Victoria and Albert Museum in London.

This *démarche* left Yeats considerably shaken and in a state of intense nervous excitement. Some time that summer he wrote to Gonne from a London where the relieved aftermath of crisis had made him highly suggestible:

> My period of trouble is over − I was given a piece of false information that had an overwhelming effect on me & this trouble has gone side by side with the most irrefutable evidence of the survival of the soul & the power of the soul. Various spirits have come to a friend of mine and written their names & dates etc through her hand. I have verified fact after fact . . . No thought reading theory can cover the facts − proof is overwhelming. (*GYL*: 322)

Through the summer Yeats worked with Radcliffe, who had probably helped him to avoid precipitate action when he had first heard Dickinson's alarming news (he thought he would have to marry her).

Radcliffe brought messages in various ancient and modern languages. Three spirits in particular seemed to dominate the transactions: a Thomas Emerson, who passed on details about his suicide, a Sister Ellis and a German woman poet who spoke a language neither Yeats nor Radcliffe knew. Yeats was fascinated and strenuously sought to confirm by more conventional means what he had learned through automatic writing. He even recruited Scotland Yard to help him confirm what Emerson had reported. The mixed emotions of the enthusiastic occultist and the psychic researcher led Yeats through this strange maze of half-comprehended messages and obscure fact until, for a time, he became convinced that something more than the contents of his own and Radcliffe's individual and combined minds were at work in their exchanges. He composed a lengthy document, which he chose not to publish, entitled 'Preliminary Examination of the Script of Elizabeth Radcliffe', in which he pondered his findings, arriving at a rum enough conclusion. As George Mills Harper and John S. Kelly summarize it:

> he postulated that the long dead, having forgotten how to use language, are obliged to communicate by means of the residual memories of the more recently dead, the latter either remaining passive the while, or having already abandoned the shell of such memories. In one of the more striking images in the essay he likens this process to robbers stealing the clothes of bathers. (Harper and Kelly 1975: 135)

The essay is marked by the blend of credulity and the exacting instinct for evidence that could satisfy reason, which would characterize Yeats's traffic with spirit messengers for much of the rest of his life. A few months later, at the end of this work, when he had convinced himself that much more is involved in automatic writing than unconscious memory, he would append a troubled note: 'another hypothesis is possible. Secondary & tertiary personalities once formed may act independently of the medium, have ideoplastic power & pick the minds of distant people & so speak in tongues unknown to all present. If we imagine these artificial beings surviving the medium we can account for haunted houses & most of the facts of spiritism' (ibid.: 171). This suggests that he found it difficult to shake off the fear that all he had discovered had a merely human source in the mind of the medium. However, for Yeats, the concept of secondary and tertiary personalities involved more than psychological import. They could be artificial entities which unknown spirits fabricated from the minds of a medium. So even this apparently sceptical entry carried its weight of occult credulity.

The primary impression of the essay is of a man cautiously hoping, despite his doubts, to discover a structure, an order of things, which could dignify self-division, authenticate such secondary and tertiary personalities on the supernatural, rather than the merely psychological, plane. He hopes ardently that fragmentary human consciousness plays a significant role in some comprehensible, ultimately creative, reality. Somewhat plaintively he observes, as he reckons how strange an institution in the nature of things is the fact of death: 'Death would never have been invented if we were to have the same minds and the same faculties after it as before' (ibid.: 159) According to this essentially forensic document of mingled evidential fact and elaborate speculation, the living and the dead share a reality governed by spiritual laws, as natural laws govern the natural order (early in the essay Yeats admits, only to dismiss in the body of his document, that nature may require in almost evolutionary terms 'a false appearance of spiritual intercourse, a seeming proof of the soul's survival after death'; ibid.: 144).

This essay's tentative quality suggests a mind at the beginning of a new phase of a fundamental quest. In the spring of 1913 Yeats had written to Gonne of having been through a period of '*mental stocktaking*' (*GYL*: 319). In the new phase of his thought which that inaugurated, he would seek an underpinning of his life and work, one which could take account of self-division, death and the afterlife, in the way the Golden Dawn had formerly provided a disciplined, institutional framework in which a will to power, a desire for self-mastery and dominance of others, and a taste for imaginative symbolism, had found controlled expression. Spiritualism was therefore for Yeats a means of access to a kind of institution of the living and the dead, an order of reality in which he might, despite initial distaste at the appeal to egotism which communion with the dead involved, play a significant part as he had played a commanding role among the magicians of Hammersmith and in the effort to establish a mystical theatre in Dublin. On 7 June 1914 (the day he appended the ambivalent note to 'Preliminary Examination') he felt sufficiently confident of the substance of his discoveries to tabulate his convictions in the way he had earlier listed his beliefs in magic in the essay of that name. Now six conclusions can safely be recorded in a private note. The gist of these was that the 'minds of some kind' which write or speak though mediums have powers independent of both mediums and sitters. They even have 'strange power over matter' (Adams and Harper 1982: 12).

It was well that the encounter with Elizabeth Radcliffe so crucially helped to convince Yeats of the likely reality of the spirit world. Although he never could quite get enough evidence to satisfy fully the sceptical side of his mind, and although he was sometimes distressed that so little that was profound came through in the seance room, without such an aid to faith in the supernatural, it might have been difficult for him to account in other than unsatisfying psychological terms, for the strange relationship he concurrently developed with the spirit of Leo Africanus.

Leo was an ubiquitous presence at the many seances Yeats attended between 1912 and 1915. Some were crowded affairs, others were more intimate occasions when Leo seemed to speak directly to him. All this culminated in the seances of 20 and 22 July 1915. At the first Leo predicted that Yeats was to receive 'much recognition'. The second, as Yeats recalled it three weeks later, took their relationship to a new plane of symbiotic intensity:

> He was no secondary personality, with a symbolic biography as I thought possible but the person he claimed to be. He was drawn to me because in life he had been all undoubting impulse, all that his name and Africa might suggest symbolically for his biography was both symbolical and actual. I was doubting, conscientious and timid. His contrary and by association with me would be made not one but two perfected natures. He asked me to write him a letter addressed to him as if to Africa giving all my doubts about spiritual things and then to write a reply as from him to me. He would control me in that reply so that it would be really from him. (cited in Adams and Harper 1982: 13)

For Yeats it must have been gratifying that the spirit which promised him enhanced fame and which wished to associate with him in this close way was that of an aristocratic Moor and sixteenth-century explorer, an authority on

Mohammedan Africa, a scholar of great renown and a 'distinguished poet among the Moors' (ibid.: 23). Foster adduces evidence that Yeats had been subliminally prepared for this manifestation, for his 'work had come back into circulation' (*AM*: 465) in the recent past and was known by at least one of his acquaintances in the Order of the Golden Dawn.

It would be easy enough to read Yeats's encounter with the spirit of Leo Africanus (as Yeats himself did at first) as merely the symbolic expression of a bifurcated nature where scepticism and a highly developed imaginative credulity, nurtured by much colourful speculation and an extravagant dream-life, were in conflict. To do so would be to underestimate how profoundly Yeats needed not to resolve the tensions in his nature but to believe that they had their origins in something more spiritually significant than mere personal and social experience. For such confirmation as Leo supplied that the concept of the Mask was more than a psychological expedient of an uncertain sensibility, but a true account of the nature of human personality, was enormously important to him. It meant that the works of art which spoke as if from the mask of a sensibility that was the polar opposite of his daily self, was no mere human voice. It was the voice of his daimon. In a compelling sense the authors of his poems, like those of William Blake, were in eternity. As Ellmann justly has it: 'he would have supernatural sanction for the pose he had built up since childhood; the mask would be filled with cosmic drama. He would have, too, an explanation of the strange power and purity which he could experience only when writing verse' (Ellmann 1987: 199–200). So Yeats wrote to Leo (probably in the autumn of 1915): 'You were my opposite. By association with one another we should each become more complete; you had been unscrupulous & believing. I was over-cautious and conscientious' (Adams and Harper 1982: 21).

As if to challenge the poet's caution and intellectual scruple, Leo's letter offers an elaborate account of the soul's experience of the afterlife. He acknowledges Yeats's difficulty with such matter. As a man with a residually Christian cosmology, who also inhabits a world where scientific dogma – 'the best opinion of your time' (ibid.: 28) – makes everyone to some degree a sceptic, he is likely to be incredulous when confronted with the supernatural. 'Let science', Leo pontificates, 'build upon obscurities, she has her necessary labour. Wisdom, like all the greater forms of art[,] is founded upon experience' (ibid.: 29). He advises Yeats that, though he is now a complex spirit who uses the minds of the living to sustain a ghostly existence,

> I was also Leo Africanus the traveller, for though I have found it necessary, so stupifying [*sic*] is the honey pot to reread of my knowledge of self through your eyes & through the eyes of others, picking out biographical detail through the eyes of those, who are not conscious of ever having heard my name[,] I can still remember the sand, & many Arab cities.   (ibid.: 38).

For all Leo's eloquence, and for all the poet's tentative hope that through spiritualism he had found himself part of a cosmic order that could give supernatural significance and dramatic energy to his own life and work, Yeats was inveterately doubtful. He reserved to himself the last word in correspondence: 'I am not convinced that in this letter there is one sentence that has come from beyond my own imagination' (ibid.: 38–9). Despite a sense that his hand had been guided as he composed, he admitted: 'I think there is no thought that has not occurred to me in some form or other for many years passed . . . nothing has surprised me' (ibid.: 39).

Even in these intense months of dialogue with his own familiar spirit, which culminated in their haunted correspondence (Leo lives again in it like a figure in historical romance), the habits of mind, which would always give him pause in the face of the most persuasive experience, displayed themselves in characteristic fashion. In May 1914, with his friend Everard Feilding and with Maud Gonne, Yeats had investigated an apparent miracle at Mirebeau in France, where, it was claimed, oleographs of the Sacred Heart had been bleeding copiously. The sceptical poet did the next best thing to putting his hand in the wound; he and Feilding took a sample on a handkerchief. Yeats reported: 'The whole thing puzzled Feilding and myself greatly for of course the orthodox explanation is impossible, and a sceptical explanation difficult' (cited in Harper 1975: 173). Gonne, as Yeats acerbically informed Lady Gregory, fell on her knees early in the day and remained in that position when she could. Yeats was altogether more circumspect. Although keen to have the miracle confirmed, for he sensed it was the kind of event which linked Christianity with the world of pagan antiquity ('The image of Adonis in Alexandria may have dripped with blood'; ibid.: 189) he accepted that when Feilding had the sample analysed at the Lister Institute in London, the result was definitive. On the record he had kept of their occult field trip, he noted: 'Analysis says not human blood' (ibid.: 175). Case closed.

Psychic experimentation in these years did bring Yeats one message which, as it transpired, had vital import for him. He was interested in the phenomenon of 'cross correspondence', in which individual minds received similar illumination. In July 1914 a pious friend advised him in surprising terms against trafficking with spirits. He wanted him to concentrate not on such dark matter but on his own creativity: 'Conquer and subordinate the dark horse to the white one or cut the dark horse away, from your chariot, & send it adrift' (cited in *VPs1*: 7). This echoed symbolically what another correspondent told him had come through in an Automatic Script which dealt with himself. He wrote, noting the similar Platonic imagery: 'It is as you will see very nearly what your controls say. Notice their allusion to the horses of Phaeton and to the sign, the sun (Leo). I do not understand it in the least except that both you and he speak of a dual influence and bad' (ibid.: 7–8).

Yeats's absorption in spiritualism and his social experience in the years leading up to the outbreak of the Great War meant that he was less frequently in Ireland than he had been when his plans for mystical theatre in Dublin were a major responsibility. His psychic investigations too were opening up a mental terrain in which Ireland was only a province of a cosmic imperium from which the spirits came as instructive emissaries. An indication of how Yeats's mind had turned again, as it had in his youth, to much broader imaginative vistas than those of his native land, is perhaps the way in which he responded so enthusiastically in 1912 to the visit to the West of the Bengali poet and sage Rabindranath Tagore. The young man who in Dublin had found Mohini Chatterjee an inspiration, in maturity now wrote an introduction to translations from the Indian poet's work, which made of Tagore a messenger from an orient of the mind, in which 'poetry and religion are the same thing' (*E&I*: 390).

Yeats the poet and successful man of letters must have been aware that not all his readership would have been comfortable with his new obsession with spiritualism and psychic investigation. Such a disinclination to alienate his audience may in part account for the fact that he chose not to publish any of the elaborate documents he had so painstakingly composed on his own experiments and experiences, though he did speak of his belief in the supernatural from public platforms. In only one published work of this early intensive period of involvement with spiritualism (and it did not appear until it served as an epilogue to Lady Gregory's book *Visions and Beliefs in the West of Ireland* in 1920) does the subject arise directly. When it does, it has, a little surprisingly, considerable bearing on the country of the poet's birth that social experience was rendering somewhat subsidiary to his current wide-ranging interests. But the Ireland invoked in this work is an Ireland situated in the kind of universalist context we might expect of a man who had been consorting with a cosmopolitan troop of spirits, who had been pondering the spiritual virtues of an imaginary orient.

Swedenborg, Mediums and the Desolate Places – begun in early 1912 but composed for the most part in the winter of 1913/14 – seeks to link what Yeats had encountered in the seance room with Swedenborg's cosmology (he had reread Swedenborg in 1913) and with the legends and lore of the west of Ireland which he had explored with Lady Gregory fifteen years earlier. The desolate places of his primal, Celtic Ireland offer the same truths about the afterlife that are to be discovered in the seance room from the 'wisdom of some fat old medium' (Gregory 1970: 311), to be examined in the peculiar supernatural architecture of eternity supplied by Swedenborg and experienced in the Noh plays of ancient Japanese tradition, to which Yeats had recently been introduced. All these, in the essay, seem like ante-chambers to a reality where the soul 'lives while in its true condition an unimaginable life and is sometimes described as "of round or oval figure" and as always circling among gods and among the stars, and sometimes as having more dimensions than our penury can comprehend' (ibid.: 333).

The Ireland of 1912 and 1913, however much Yeats may have wished to emphasize the universal implications of its folkloric traditions, was not, in reality marked by much cosmopolitanism, spiritual or otherwise. It was, rather, taken up with its own political affairs which were moving inexorably towards crisis. The promulgation of the third Home Rule Bill in Westminster in May 1912 threatened in Ireland the Edwardian peace that would continue undisturbed in the rest of the United Kingdom for another two years. Through the summer of 1912 the Unionists of the island mustered opposition to the Bill. In July a great meeting of public protest was held at Blenheim Palace, at which Unionist Ireland in general, together with its British supporters, served notice that they would not be bound by the Bill if it was enacted as law.

It was the north of Ireland, where demography allowed the real revolutionary muscle to be exercised, which reacted most dangerously. In September 1912 many thousands of loyalists signed, some of them in their own blood, a Solemn League and Covenant to oppose Home Rule, by force of arms if necessary. By January 1913 the Ulster Unionist Council, acting like a provisional government, decided to organize the local militias, which had already been drilling under the authority of justices of the peace, into a 90,000-man Ulster Volunteer Force. In March 1914 British army officers stationed in the Curragh in the south of Ireland let it be known they would not be used to coerce the Ulstermen. In April the same Ulstermen imported guns from Germany. By the end of 1913 in the south the Irish Volunteers had declared themselves a new, countervailing force, ready to defend what the north would oppose. As the storm clouds of general war broke in Europe, the Irish Volunteers landed smuggled weapons in Ireland. As they did so, British Army guns were turned on an unarmed Dublin crowd. Three people died and thirty-eight were injured. It was the war however which allowed a deceptive truce to be called in the Irish *imbroglio*. The Home Rule Bill was passed in May 1914 (a temporary opt-out clause by county was made permanent in the House of Lords to satisfy the Ulster Unionists). The Act could be placed on the statute book. It became law on 18 September, 1914 but was suspended for twelve months or for the duration of the war, with ambiguities about the Ulster question still intact, but with partition effectively granted.

Dublin in 1913 had had its own more immediate troubles to distract it from the national drama in the making. Revolutionary hopes in the Irish capital, about which Yeats had expressed a patrician contempt in 1908 in 'No Second Troy', under the influence of two labour leader, James Connolly and James Larkin, had begun to find not only courage equal to desire but the organizational capacity and will to take on the major employers and landlords in a city notorious for its grinding poverty. Industrial unrest, which had disturbed Britain since 1911, in Dublin in 1913 found a stage which made a conflict between workers and their employers an epic conflict that seemed to symbolize a titanic struggle between labour and capital in modern society.

The drama began when Larkin tried to unionize the Dublin United Tramway Company, whose owner was a local magnate, William Martin Murphy, newspaper proprietor and landlord. Murphy sacked a number of his workers who dared to join Larkin's union and demanded declarations from his employees that they would not join a strike. A strike ensued on 26 August. Then the authorities proscribed a public meeting called for 31 August. It was wondered whether Larkin, who had been bailed on charges of seditious libel and seditious conspiracy, would be present. The day before there was disorder in the streets. The police ran amok. Two people lost their lives and many were injured. The next day Larkin, a prodigious orator, appeared on a hotel balcony before a large crowd in the city's main thoroughfare. Again the police overreacted and there was further violence. At this juncture, Murphy joined with his fellow Dublin employers in a crusade against organized labour. They 'locked-out' members of Larkin's union. By late September about 25,000 men and their dependants were enduring severe privation. There was sporadic violence as the police tried to keep order. Conservative Dublin reacted with horror and with a determination that labour would not have its way. The Catholic Church, with its lay shock troops in the Ancient Order of Hibernians, advanced nationalists, like Sinn Féin's Arthur Griffith (with the notable exception of a young schoolmaster and writer, Patrick Pearse), the business interest and the ruling class found themselves unlikely allies as fierce reaction raised dykes against what for a moment seemed a revolutionary tide in full flood. Crowds tried to blockade the railway stations and ports when a scheme was attempted to send workers' children for care in England. The police seemed complicit with such outrageous mob-rule. Eventually the tide turned when Larkin failed to get the general support of British trade unionism that he hoped would give him victory. Support for resistance waned as winter settled in. By the end of January 1914 the workers were defeated. And the broad cause of Irish labour was to find itself swamped by the more general Home Rule crisis of 1914 and the Great War which followed so swiftly and catastrophically upon it.

In October 1913 Yeats sent a letter to James Connolly's newspaper the *Irish Worker*, nailing his colours to the mast of liberty. In this letter, appearing on 1 November under the heading 'Dublin Fanaticism', he objected strongly to how the police had failed to defend the rights of citizens when inflamed zealots had prevented men and women and children from leaving the country. It was brave intervention in an extremely dangerous situation. 'I want to know', Yeats challengingly asked

> who has ordered the abrogation of the most elementary rights of the citizens, and why authorities who are bound to protect every man in doing what he has a legal right to do – even though they have to call upon the forces of the crown – have permitted the Ancient Order of Hibernians to besiege Dublin like a foreign army? (*UP2*: 407)

Even though Yeats had long studied the controlled art of self-fashioning, and often operated with a precise appreciation of tactics and strategic interests, the poet in his mid-forties remained a passionate man who could be overcome with intense feelings of anger, perhaps the most eruptive emotion in his psychological make-up. Not all was mask and studied performance. The actions of the mob during the Lockout stirred his fury as little had done since the attack on *The Playboy of the Western World* and, roused by anger, he could act with courageous impulsiveness and noble generosity of spirit. As Cruise O'Brien remarks of Yeats's response to these events, 'he was not only capable of generous indignation – he positively revelled in it' (O'Brien 1972: 231).

Cullingford has insisted that 'a study of Yeats's previous attitudes suggests that Larkin's side' in this conflict 'was the natural one for him'. She adduces in support of this benign view of Yeats's politics how he had been affected by

'O'Leary's praise of artisans, Morris's championship of the workers, Maud Gonne's devotion to the poor' (Cullingford 1981: 82) and invokes 'Yeats's own populism' as further grounds to explain his commitment to the workers' cause in 1913. This latter congeries of feeling, which found most ample expression in the poet's idealistic, anti-industrial, anglophobic, nationalist speeches before Irish American audiences during his first lecture tour in the United States, was, it is true, a perennial source of emotional energy. He undoubtedly hoped, when he thought about it, that a national revival would ameliorate the condition of the Irish urban poor. He could be moved, moreover, by noble action on the poor's behalf. The force of his anger in this letter came, however, much more directly from the fact that William Martin Murphy was both a representative figure and a dangerous opponent in a controversy much closer to Yeats's central concerns than the immediate fate of Dublin's transport workers and of Irish trade unionism.

For through much of 1913 Yeats was engaged in a cultural war on behalf of Lady Gregory's nephew, Sir Hugh Lane, an art collector, connoisseur and dealer in paintings. Since 1903 Lane had been concerned that Dublin should have a gallery in which modern painting would find a place. He had generously offered to the city a collection of paintings (including work by French Impressionists, then less universally regarded than they subsequently became), provided the municipal authorities would earmark funds for a suitable gallery. By 1912, despite some movement in that direction by the municipal authorities, Lane was losing all patience. A subscription fund was established to augment what the public purse would provide. A sense began to get abroad that the whole scheme was an act of Ascendancy condescension to Dublin's citizenry. Lane's aesthetic ambitions did not help to counter that impression. He wanted a bridge gallery across the river Liffey to a design by the English architect Sir Edwin Lutyens. The city fathers squabbled and procrastinated. The employment of an English architect emerged as a contentious issue. By the autumn of 1913 Lane had withdrawn his offer and the bequest seemed lost to the city for ever.

In 1914 Yeats wrote that in 'the thirty years or so during which he had been reading Irish newspapers three public controversies had stirred his imagination: the Parnell controversy, the *Playboy* dispute and the Lane débâcle' (notes to *Res*; no page given). Murphy, who locked out the workers, had been an anti-Parnellite in 1890 and 1891. In the Lane affair he used his newspaper to oppose Yeats. The same people who cited the expense to the city of Lane's proposed gallery were engaged, Yeats reckoned, in a war to the death with trade unionism. Larkin, employing any weapon to harry his enemy, supported Lane's plan. In retrospect Yeats's estimate of the journalistic campaign against Lane and himself, was acerbic: 'As the first avowed reason for opposition, the necessities of the poor got but a few lines, not so many certainly as the objection of various persons to supply Sir Hugh Lane with "a monument at the city's expense," and as the gallery was supported by Mr James Larkin, the chief labour leader, and important slum workers, I assume that the purpose of their opposition was not exclusively charitable'.

In the heat of the quarrel in 1913 Yeats's satiric irony had not been so nicely honed. For the Lane controversy had brought to a head all his angry revulsion for what he identified as the materialistic Ireland that had destroyed Parnell and Synge and which had now disgraced itself again in spurning the magnanimity of Sir Hugh. In 1913 Yeats published two political poems in the Unionist *Irish Times* in Dublin and then in October issued a Cuala Press pamphlet which included a further three contentious poems written that year. The pamphlet was titled *Poems Written in Discouragement*, and in it the poet denounced moneyed Catholic Ireland in vituperative terms. The insult to Lane by those who had ruined Parnell and shortened Synge's life, in 1913 so incensed the poet that he threw all caution to the wind in a satiric assault on his enemies and a demand that enlightened aristocracy and wealth should act with proper regard for its responsibilities to leadership. In these poems, wealth is summoned to a Renaissance Italianate role in giving the people what it needs, while plutocracy in Ireland is pilloried in the figure of Paudeen (a diminutive of Patrick) as an acquisitive, venal, pious force preying upon life itself and betraying all Ireland has stood for in the past. And Parnell, who had only in ruin and death really stirred the youthful poet's admiration, is now a noble, solitary figure – one whose entire life was a patrician gift of service to lesser souls. 'September 1913' (titled 'Romance in Ireland' in its September 1913 printing in the *Irish Times*, it probably hardened opposition to Lane's demands) is the most lethal of these broadsides, couched as it is in the rhythms of traditional balladry (in which national heroes had been apotheosized since the eighteenth century) and employing a heady refrain and a mesmeric imagery of heroic sacrifice set against the grotesquerie of a lampoon. The Ireland of O'Leary is no more, Parnell and Synge are dead, 'All that delirium of the brave' which took Irish heroes to the scaffold or into exile, casually denigrated by those who have lost their childhood capacity for wonder at the walk of a queen, who through the centuries (1913 is definitely not a date like 1798, alas, the title implies) calls young men to her cause:

> What need you, being come to sense,
> But fumble in a greasy till
> And add the halfpence to the pence
> And prayer to shivering prayer, until
> You have dried the marrow from the bone;
> For men were born to pray and save:
> Romantic Ireland's dead and gone,
> It's with O'Leary in the grave.
>
> Yet they were of a different kind
> The names that stilled your childish play
> They have gone about the world like wind,
> But little time had they to pray
> For whom the hangman's rope was spun,
> And what, God help us, could they save:
> Romantic Ireland's dead and gone,
> It's with O'Leary in the grave.

Yeats's disillusionment with Ireland ran deep at this time. In 'To a Shade' he advised the ghost of Parnell, if it has revisited Dublin, to fly hence since 'they are at their old tricks yet' and Hugh Lane has been treated just as he had been: 'An old foul mouth that once cried out on you/Herding the pack'. In a poem written for Lady Gregory (which she wrongly assumed was addressed to Hugh Lane), under the title 'To a Friend Whose Work Has Come To Nothing' he displaced on to his patron his own sense of defeat on the Irish battleground and a consequent determination to retreat from bruising exchanges in public, to personal superiority in private. He counsels:

> Amid a place of stone,
> Be secret and exult,
> Because of all things known
> That is most difficult.

How difficult and lonely such a personal place of stone might be Yeats confessed to Gonne in July 1913. He wrote to her telling her about the Dickinson fiasco. Gonne, it seems, had suggested to him that he only wanted physical love in a woman:

> My gloom this week was from lonliness. . . . There was not a soul I could go to after nightfall & in the winter it is dark at four & after that I cannot use my sight except a very little. I should neither read nor go to the theatre which makes my eyes smart next day (here where stages are very brightly lit). The alternative is to dine out and last week I was ill – could not & even when I am well dining out leaves me worn out with nerves upset. A mistress cannot give one a home & a home I shall never have; but now that it is summer and I can work late I do not mind. (*GYL*: 323)

Earlier in 1913 the possibility had arisen that Yeats might at least have a more secure role in Dublin life than as director of a financially exiguous theatre, working from hotel or rented room. Dowden had finally died on 3 April and once again Yeats had hopes of academic preferment. He would have expected, upon appointment, to have inherited the professor's gracious rooms in the university, where he could have established himself in donnish style in a collegiate home, in default of anything more agreeably domestic. The Board of Trinity College dashed such hopes when it appointed an academic mediocrity to the post, no doubt for Yeats adding to the Dublin discouragements of a discouraging year.

A retreat into mandarin privacy to cultivate his muse was necessarily postponed when the poet discovered in mid-1913 that over the years he had become indebted to Lady Gregory to the tune of £500. He decided to redeem his debt, so on 31 January 1914 he set sail on the *Mauretania* for New York and a third remunerative lecture tour. He also welcomed the chance, as he put it in a lecture in London in December, 1913 to get 'at his own countrymen' (cited in Strand 1978: 130). In the event Yeats's lectures on 'The Theatre of Beauty', 'John Synge and the Ireland of his Time' and 'Contemporary Lyric Poets' (on the poets of the

1890s) did not arouse either the journalistic attention given to the lectures delivered in 1904 or contribute to controversy of the kind which raged around *The Playboy* in 1911. Yeats was asked about Ireland, but it was the general political situation as the problems of Ireland intensified which interested America more than Yeats's quarrels with philistine Dublin. About the Irish constitutional future he remained hopeful, as if he could not bring himself to admit that Sir Edward Carson, the Anglo-Irish barrister who had vocally and energetically adopted the Ulster Unionist cause in his zeal for the Union itself, could actually break the unity of the country. Yeats told the *Detroit Times*: 'I have no idea of what sort of compromise can be arranged, but I believe that one will be worked out' (cited in ibid.: 137).

Such misplaced equanimity indicates that Yeats had failed fully to grasp how the forces that had been unleashed in the north of Ireland, about which he, like his paternal family, had always expressed patrician hauteur were creating an uncompromisingly polarized Ireland. He certainly understood in these years of political crisis the Northern Protestant concern that a Home Rule Ireland might be unduly influenced by the Roman Catholic Church, but knew too how such fear could be exploited by imperialists (*AM*: 458–62). He thought Carson, the Dublin Protestant, member of parliament for Dublin University (T. C. D.) could be depended upon to do the right thing to keep Ireland one, even if his tactics had involved some risky alliances. Carson would tame the northern tiger (Carson, with tragic consequences, was trying to ride the beast in the hopes of keeping Ireland one within the Union). He would not prove the traitor (Foster, *AM*: 513). He was 'too good a patriot for that' (cited in Strand 1978: 137). And the Home Rule settlement which Britain had offered Ireland could release the country from confessional politics in a new tolerant polity (Foster 1998: 101).

Yeats's third tour of the United States, which ended on 2 April 1914 achieved one of its main purposes. He left with £500 to repay his patron. The Civil List pension had made a real difference to his financial standing, for it gave him a basic income upon which to build each year by variegated literary work. A financial statement of 1917 tells us how he was placed at this point in his career. With a £150 pension per annum assured, in 1913 he brought in £522, in 1914 £582. In 1915 he made all of £602, sparing him difficulty in the comparatively lean year, 1916, when his income fell to £323. The year 1917 saw a revival in his fortunes for he earned £590 then (NL Ms 30,358). Such sums were not of course lavish, but they did represent, at last, the sort of income upon which many a salaried middle-class man with a family modestly depended. Yeats, as a single man who could usually summer in Coole, was no longer the impecunious neophyte, starving for his art.

His latest visit to the United States had made him acutely aware of his father's perilous pecuniary position. As John Butler Yeats's biographer discreetly puts it, 'his financial condition had gone beyond its usual precariousness' (Murphy 1979: 415). Fortunately, John Quinn chose to exploit Yeats's return to America by breaking the ice of their five-year quarrel over his mistress. Yeats responded with relief to Quinn's warmly conciliatory overture. The first joint task the reunited friends undertook was to arrive at a scheme whereby Yeats *père* could be made financially secure. Quinn devised a scheme whereby he purchased Yeats's manuscripts and deposited the sums due to the poet in a jointly named trust account, which was periodically used to discharge the debts which John Butler Yeats accrued at his agreeably rackety New York lodging house. There, with its pleasant restaurant, where, most nights, he held court, he would live out his days. The arrangement suited everybody. Though initially Yeats and Quinn may have hoped to tempt John Butler Yeats back to Dublin, where he could be looked after by his unmarried daughters, he stayed on in New York until his death in 1922.

Another personal matter was preying uneasily on Yeats's mind during his United States tour, displacing in an insistent way any concerns he might have felt about the developing political crisis in Ireland, about which he seemed curiously undisturbed in his public utterances. His old collaborator in the theatre, George Moore, had abandoned Ireland in disgust in 1911, convinced that a priest-ridden people was unworthy of his dedication to its aesthetic improvement. His Irish period had borne fruit in two pioneering works of fiction, the collection of realistic short stories of country life *The Untilled Field* (1903), and a subtle psychological novel, *The Lake* (1905). What troubled Yeats was neither of these, but a work by Moore which purported to be an autobiographical account of Moore's role in the Irish Literary Revival in which Yeats and Lady Gregory appeared to considerable disadvantage.

Hail and Farewell poured salt in many tender wounds. The first volume, *Ave*, had appeared in 1911. In that work Yeats had not been best pleased to find their collaboration in the Irish Literary Theatre treated as matter for droll comedy. The second volume, *Salve*, appeared in 1912, but it was the third, *Vale* (1914), which gave particular offence to Yeats. He had read extracts from the forthcoming book in the *English Review* in January and it was their portrait of himself (the first appeared after a long poem by Yeats's old enemy, Aleister Crowley) and a slur on Lady Gregory, which rankled throughout his American tour. At Yale, conversing with a member of the faculty, he 'expressed hatred of George Moore, and said a great many of the events that Moore described in his book, conversations with Yeats, etc., never happened' (Strand 1978: 147)

Moore's crime had been to libel Lady Gregory as an 'ardent soul-gatherer', implying that before her marriage she had engaged in the proselytism which the evangelical traditions of her family deemed a proper activity for a devoutly Protestant young woman. He had also wickedly satirized Yeats's pretensions to aristocracy in a passage of sustained comic deflation: Yeats is seen inveighing against the middle class despite himself being a member of that class, as the scion of 'millers and shipowners on one side, and on the other a portrait-painter of distinction' (George Moore 1976: 540). Moore recounts how Yeats had told AE that he should have been Duke of Ormonde if he had had his rights and recalls AE's sardonic reply, 'I am afraid, Willie, you are overlooking your father.' The satiric note rises to a crescendo as the poet is evoked in full flight on the wings of his pompous rhetoric:

We have sacrificed our lives for Art; but you, what have you done? What sacrifices have you made? he asked, and everybody began to search his memory for the sacrifices that Yeats had made, asking himself in what prison Yeats had languished, what rags he had worn, what broken victuals he had eaten. As far as anybody could remember, he had always lived very comfortably, sitting down invariably to regular meals, and the old green cloak that was in keeping with his profession of romantic poet he had exchanged for the magnificent fur coat which distracted our attention from what he was saying, so opulently did it cover the back of the chair out of which he had risen. But, quite forgetful of the coat behind him, he continued to denounce the middle classes, throwing his arms into the air, shouting at us.   (ibid.: 540–1)

Lady Gregory threatened legal action, but thought better of it. Yeats noted in his journal that Moore's statements about himself were 'too indefinite for any action, though equally untrue' (*Mem*: 269). He observed in his journal entry that Moore had misunderstood his use of the term 'bourgeois', which for him did not so much refer to a class like the middle class, but to a frame of mind and way of life antithetical to artistic endeavour and to aesthetic values: 'The word bourgeois which I had used is not an aristocratic term of reproach, but, like the older "cit" which one finds in Ben Jonson, a word of artistic usage' (ibid.: 270). Yet Moore's satire on the poet's pride of family and comically wistful claims to gentle birth had hit home. Yeats damned Moore as a vulgarian who could imagine himself rich but not 'with fine manners' (ibid.). In contrast to his own lineage, with its merchants, state servants and scholarly clergy, Moore's was a flawed pedigree, all too typical of an Ireland which could produce a William Martin Murphy, an Edward Martyn with his tender conscience, a Moore with his demagoguery and love of the rich:

I have been told that the crudity common to all the Moores came from the mother's family, Mayo squireens, probably half-peasants in education and occupation, for his father was a man of education and power and old descent. His mother's blood seems to have affected him and his brother as the peasant strain has affected Edward Martyn. . . . Both men are examples of the way Irish civilization is held back by lack of education of Irish Catholic women. An Irish Catholic will not marry a Protestant, and hitherto the women have checked again and again the rise, into some world of refinement, of Catholic households. The whole system of Irish Catholicism pulls down the able and well-born if it pulls up the peasant, as I think it does. A long continuity of culture like that at Coole could not have arisen, and never has arisen, in a single Catholic family since the Middle Ages. (*Mem*: 270–1)

The spleen of the occasion probably accounts for some of the venom of this entry in a private journal, with its crass sociology of Irish marriage and its cultural consequences. Nevertheless, its assumption that cultivated continuity depends on a long patriarchal dynasty, in which uneducated Irish Catholic peasant women cannot pull down able, well-born men to their own level, supplies a disturbing context of specifically sectarian feeling for the poem of ancestral pride Yeats chose to stand at the head of his next published collection. *Responsibilities: Poems and a*

Play (1914) prints '*Pardon, old fathers*' as its preface, a poem which expresses gratitude to Yeats's male ancestors alone for bequeathing to him uncontaminated blood (they had avoided the kind of miscegenation so fatal in the case of Moore's lineage:

> *Traders or soldiers who have left me blood*
> *That has not passed through any huckster's loins.*

The poem emphasizes the radical freedom of the Yeats line (the maternal Pollexfen connection is admitted in terms of its masculine, seafaring spirit) from constraint of any kind. From William Pollexfen the poet has learnt that '*Only the wasteful virtues earn the sun*' and, in consequence, in middle age, he admits that he has not been true to an inheritance:

> *Although I have come close on forty-nine*
> *I have no child, I have nothing but a book,*
> *Nothing but that to prove your blood and mine.*

Three things raise this poem above the level of rebarbative and rather ridiculous family pride. The poet is chastened by his own barren parsimony (he had of course published many books, but here he sets the empty singularity of 'nothing but a book' against all the generative potentiality of a 'child') in contrast to a vision of life lived in generous independence of spirit. There is, too, an embattled isolated tone in what T. S. Eliot characterized as a 'violent and terrible epistle' (T. S. Eliot 1957: 262), with its urgent claim on the past, which suggests how profoundly the poet feels alienated from the present. And the poem as a whole sets ancestor worship in the context of spiritualist possibility, which casts across the page the dim light of the seance room, with its atmosphere of uncanny presences. The old fathers may '*still remain/ Somewhere in ear-shot for the story's end*' (in fact the spirit of George Pollexfen was a seance revenant). We feel ourselves, as readers, in company with a poet who reckons as much with the dead as with the living. The effect is simultaneously chilling and bracing.

10

The Lonely Height

For all Yeats's avowed sense of personal inadequacy in '*Pardon, old fathers*' his new book (published by the family firm, the Cuala Press, in May 1914 as *Responsibilities: Poems and a Play*) which he could proffer to his male ancestors in lieu of progeny, was his most substantial collection of verse since *The Wind Among the Reeds* (1899). It included some poems which had earlier found a place in *The Green Helmet and Other Poems* (1910, with a second printing including new work in 1912) and the poems printed in the autumn of 1913 as *Poems Written In Discouragement*. The volume also collected poems which had hitherto appeared only in periodicals, two unpublished poems and a play, *The Hour-Glass*, first performed in a prose version in 1903, extensively revised in 1912 (the 1912 version is in prose and verse).

It was not only the prefatory poem in *Responsibilities* which made the volume a book of the eavesdropping and communicative dead. It is a book of spirits, ghosts and intimations of the afterlife. In 'The Grey Rock' the poet addresses the friends of his youth '*Companions of the Cheshire Cheese*,' whom he imagines as a troop of spirits who '*Kept the Muses' sterner laws*'. Milton's heavenly vision of Lycidas is here transposed to an aesthetic and spiritualist apprehension of the afterlife. In that spirit world the dead may linger, attentive to our call. 'To a Shade' imagines Parnell as revenant who may have revisited the city which had betrayed him. 'September 1913', written in the heat of a polemical contempt for a sordidly pecuniary view of life after death (prayer as insurance policy), invokes the 'delirium of the brave', the heroes of romantic nationalism, and admits they are 'dead and gone' with 'O'Leary in the grave'. But Yeats despatches them as if for their own good, as Parnell is advised to 'Draw the Glasnevin coverlet' about his head, since 'could we turn the years again,/And call those exiles as they were,/In all their loneliness and pain' they would meet calumny and denigration. They have become figures in a national drama, perhaps even 'characters in the drama we ourselves have invented' and are all 'shadows [which] have drunk from the pool of blood and become delirious' (Gregory 1970: 327). The poet wistfully

1 W. B. Yeats by John Sargent, 1908 (National Portrait Gallery)

2 John Butler Yeats, the poet's father (Rex Roberts)

3 Susan Yeats, the poet's mother (Rex Roberts)

4 John O'Leary, the old Fenian, 1894 (Rex Roberts)

5 Yeats by Charles Beresford (National Portrait Gallery)

6 Maud Gonne (National Library of Ireland)

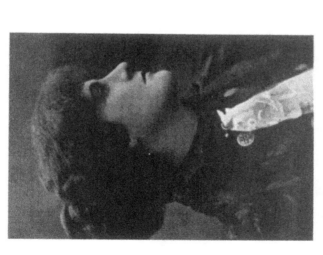

7 Olivia Shakespear (Bodleian Library/*Literary Yearbook*, 1897)

8 Florence Farr (Department of English, University of Reading)

10 John Millington Synge (Hugh Lane Municipal Gallery of Modern Art, Dublin)

9 Lady Augusta Gregory, patron and friend (National Gallery of Ireland)

11 Iseult Gonne from a pastel by Maud Gonne (National Library of Ireland)

(a)

(b)

12a and b W. B. and 'George' Yeats (née Georgina Hyde-Lees) (Rex Roberts)

13 W. B. and 'George' with their children, Anne and Michael, 1929 (Rex Roberts)

14 W. B. Yeats, *c.* 1935 (National Library of Ireland)

counsels: 'let them be' they are 'dead and gone'. Yet the grave can be a centre of visionary potential, even if it remains unawakened. In 'The Mountain Tomb', 'All wisdom shut into his onyx eyes/Our Father Rosicross sleeps in his tomb'. Hell itself in its condition of absolute being ('when midnight smote the air') can be a *mise en scène* of Blakean contraries and the eternal delight of exuberant sexual energy, as in 'The Attack on "The Playboy of the Western World", 1907' where 'Eunuchs ran through Hell and met/Round about Hell's Gate to stare/At great Juan riding by'. For the individual soul, however (and this is a book of the soul as *In the Seven Woods* was a book of the living, beating heart), death and the afterlife are compact of chilling terror and a challenging sense of metamorphosis.

The volume as a whole is marked by an excited elevation of tone, with poem after poem springing from some moment of sudden awareness: of a transitional state of being or feeling or of a defining stage in a process. 'Now all the truth is out' begins one poem, 'Now must I these three praise' begins another. 'Running to Paradise' opens 'As I came over Windy Gap'; 'The Cold Heaven' begins 'Suddenly I saw the cold and rook-delighting Heaven'. A windy dawn, a wild landscape of primitive, cold desolation, morning light in which solitary curlews call, constitute a climate and geography of the soul engaging with last things, the trauma of death and the life to come. Landscape and weather are the portents of a spiritualist eschatology in a Yeatsian book of the soul's personal apocalypse. 'The Cold Heaven', moved to this book from the second printing of *The Green Helmet* in 1912, enacts an intense drama of feelings induced by a cold and detached wintry sky.

At once shockingly immediate in an apperceptive and bodily sense and expansively open to the symbolic order, the poem in two charged sentences engages with the passion of a lifetime and the terror of the soul as it passes from that life to judgement. The authority of the poem's rhetorical trajectory, its energized syntax, is tellingly in conflict with powerful intimations of loss, defeat and self-dispersal. For the poet who can so magisterially dramatize a condition of remorse for deeds done and undone, can imagine too a state of extreme vulnerability, when the authoritative energy of the ego is no more and the poet will be bereft of such commanding powers of speech. Then the ghost will be required to travel in desolate places without known destination.

As part of Yeats's riposte to George Moore's irreverence about his claims on worthy lineage, and as a sustained attack on Catholic Ireland, which Moore and William Martyn Murphy in their different ways represented for the poet, *Responsibilities* certainly has its risible, even its crass, notes. The several poems in which Yeats celebrates Irish beggary as a metaphor of the spiritual freedom the Irish materially minded moneyed class so signally lacks, are without purchase on much beyond the literary salon's version of mendicancy. The hermits, beggars and poor folk of this book are figures of a picturesque poverty, remote from actual immiseration against which Yeats had protested during the Dublin Lockout. In this volume, it is the assault on aesthetic values when Lane's magnanimity was spurned (the larger crises in Dublin and in the United Kingdom of 1912–14 are barely among its concerns and responsibilities), which draws from the poet tones of disdain and personal superiority that escape literary mannerism. 'Paudeen', for example, has the accent of prejudiced revulsion in its estimate of 'the fumbling wits, the obscure spite/Of our old Paudeen in his shop', that makes the volume as a whole open to ugly humours, less the choler of a Swiftian savage satiric indignation, than the bile of social snobbery, class and even sectarian prejudice. In a snide aside in 'To a Shade', the poet observes of the Parnell monument 'I wonder if the builder has been paid.' The Catholic-dominated Corporation of the city which erected the monument could not be depended upon even to pay its bills.

The spiritualist dimension that shadows *Responsibilities: Poems and a Play* moderates the presumptuousness of the book's social attitudes, which would otherwise, as Bloom claims it does, ring 'false, for lack of a sustaining context' (Bloom 1970: 171). For the implied presence of that shadowland enforces an awareness of death as the ultimate democracy. The wind that blows through these poems is no longer the transcendent power it was in *The Wind Among the Reeds*, but a levelling wind which carries away 'the best labourer.../And all the sheaves to bind' ('To a Child Dancing in the Wind'). Even 'Paudeen' admits, in an expansive vision of spiritual egalitarianism, at odds with the social pride of the book as a whole,

> That on the lonely height where all are in God's eye,
> There cannot be, confusion of our sound forgot,
> A single soul that lacks a sweet crystaline cry.

The play included with the poems augments such religious universalism. *The Hour-Glass* (originally written in collaboration with Lady Gregory, now in a new version) pits a sceptical wise man who has taught his pupils that there is no afterlife against a fool who knows that angels walk the hills. A modern version of the medieval Christian morality play *Everyman* (and also an echo of Marlowe's *Doctor Faustus*), the work is a *momento mori* which instils a sense that before death and judgement all are equal. The play ends with the angel of death summoning humankind to his presence:

> I hear the wind a blow
> I hear the grass a grow,
> And all that I know, I know.

The knowledge that death and the soul's fate cast an admonitory light (like the cold heaven of the poem of that title) on the human stage, makes *Responsibilities: Poems and a Play* a book in which commanding accents vie with a consciousness of the fragility of life in time surrounded by the mysterious beyond of eternity. Hell, the angel avers, in *The Hour-Glass*, for those who have denied its existence will prove 'A Lake of Spaces, and a Wood of Nothing'. In face of such possible stripping away of individuality and identity, the facts of ageing, incipient bodily decrepitude and decline of passion that the poems addressed to Gonne and her daughter Iseult record, seem intimations of ultimate tests in store for the soul, for all the dynastic prestige and rhetorical authority the poet has mustered. Then it must go out naked on the road, as the books say. The spiritualist context, I am arguing, renders the elitist purport of the volume more a strained reaction to the levelling fact of death and its unexplored aftermath, than a jaundiced assault on Irish vulgarity. For the decision announced in 'A Coat' that the poet would henceforth abandon a poetic of 'embroideries / Out of old mythologies' for the enterprise of 'walking naked' anticipates not only a stylistic and thematic disrobing, but the soul's imagined spiritual triumph in face of life's sufferings. 'What's dearth and death and sickness to the soul' asks the angel in *The Hour-Glass*,

> That knows no virtue but itself, nor could it,
> So trembling with delight and mother-naked,
> Live unabashed if the arguing world stood by.

The book dismisses that arguing world, the better to prepare for a test which must come to everyman.

The sense that the book registers not just a set of personal responses to local conditions and to particular affronts to *amour propre*, is further generated by the manner in which Yeats exploits mythology in *Responsibilities: Poems and a Play*. For it was in this work that the poet began to employ mythology in a sustained way, not simply as a source for metaphors, symbols and themes, but as an interpretative tool to account for contemporary events and experiences. In the narrative poems 'The Grey Rock' and 'The Hour before Dawn', Yeats sought to make explicit relations between the mythic past and the modern moment in the way he had done implicitly in 'No Second Troy'. Past and present are juxtaposed to indicate that an order of things which found expression in a previous era is repeating itself in the modern world under another guise. What T. S. Eliot identified in a famous review of James Joyce's *Ulysses* in *The Dial* in 1923, as the 'mythical method', where past and present are juxtaposed as if they occupied a shared ontological zone, can be observed at work in such poems as these. For in them mythology is deemed to possess explanatory force for the modern mind. In such writing the incoherencies of the self, dispersed in time, memory and in self-division, the disorder of the social world and of history, are momentarily made amenable to a transcendent pattern inscribed in the old tale. That temporary achievement permeates the present with meanings not otherwise readily available to contemporary consciousness.

'The Magi' announces in its dramatic opening lines the immediate and perennial significance of the mythic journey of the Magi from eastern lands, who sought out the newborn Christ in the gospel account of the incarnation:

> Now as at all times I can see in the mind's eye,
> In their stiff, painted clothes, the pale unsatisfied ones
> Appear and disappear in the blue depth of the sky. . .

In the poem these figures are avatars from a transitional phase in the human past where history fades into mythology. They fill the mind's eye, insistently coming in and out of focus as they undertake their endless quest, determined to make their occult presence known as a rebuke to a failing Christian culture which has made a dead god the basis of an unsatisfactory religious account of reality:

> With all their ancient faces like rain-beaten stones,
> And all their helms of silver hovering side by side,
> And all their eyes still fixed, hoping to find once more,
> Being by Calvary's turbulence unsatisfied,
> The uncontrollable mystery on the bestial floor.

The poem accordingly employs a powerful myth (of the Magi who journey through time in quest of a full incarnation of the divine life) to invest the present moment with intimations of its inadequacy and implicitly to account for that state. The theatrical, stylized formality, ('stiff, painted clothes'), the austere dedication ('pale', 'eyes still fixed') the grandeur, antiquity and stoic permanence that they represent in the poem, cannot find expression in a religion and a culture based upon it, which takes as its founding moment the death of a physically incarnate god. For Calvary is 'turbulence' in the poem, the unsatisfactory outcome of a mystery that cannot be controlled (images of authority, order and collectively intent purposes, by contrast, constitute Yeats's vision of the Magi, who begin to suggest a disciplined army on the march in search of a kingdom to rule, rather than the mystic trio of Christian tradition), the birth of a god on 'the bestial floor'.

The young American poet Ezra Pound, in a very positive review of *Responsibilities: Poems and a Play*, in the Chicago-based journal *Poetry* (where some of the poems in the volume had first appeared), singled out for particular praise the opening lines of 'The Magi'. He approved them as a point in Yeats's development as a poet where the 'pseudo-glamours and glamourets and mists and fogs' which had wafted through much English-language poetry since Yeats had raised them so magically in the 1890s, were finally dissipated in 'hard light'. The poems in Yeats's new book, Pound informed his readers, were 'no longer romantically Celtic' (*CH*: 189). A note which had sounded initially in 'No Second Troy' was now indicative of an exciting new phase in Yeats's career. Pound identified a 'gaunter' style, that sought 'greater hardness of outline' (ibid.: 188).

Pound's endorsement of Yeats's 'change of manner, real or intended' (ibid.) in *Poetry* was not without a certain self-satisfaction. For he believed he had had a guiding hand in it. From November 1913 until the end of January 1914 (when Yeats had set out on his American tour) Pound had in fact been sharing quarters with Yeats in a house in the Sussex countryside, where he had acted as amanuensis and reader to the elder poet, whose weak eyesight had become an increasing problem in the heavy schedules of literary work he set himself. That winter together had been the culmination of a relationship which had gone so far by November 1912 as to allow Pound to amend some of the poems which he had arranged for the Irish poet to submit to *Poetry* (Chicago) for publication. Yeats had baulked at some of Pound's editorial decisions but accepted others in a remarkable deferral to the younger, and as yet, much less accomplished man. At Stone Cottage, the Sussex house they shared in 1913/14, as Yeats revised poems for inclusion in the forthcoming *Responsibilities: Poems and a Play*, Pound had felt sufficiently involved in the process to write to Harriet Monroe, the editor of *Poetry* (Chicago), that 'they look more like the versions I sent first, at least it suits me to believe so' (cited in Litz 1985: 138).

Literary collaboration between Yeats and Pound would have seemed an unlikely outcome when the Idaho-born man in his early twenties arrived in London in 1908. Yeats's first impressions were, that although quite an authority on the troubadours, he was 'a queer creature' (*L*: 543). Pound's initial view of Yeats was compact of unbounded youthful admiration for the poet he knew was the poet of the age, and youthful defensiveness about how Yeats would respond to his characteristically brash overtures. The young American's channel to Yeats was through their shared friendship with Olivia Shakespear and her daughter Dorothy. He turned up at Woburn Buildings in May 1909 and soon became a Monday evening fixture. By 1910 Pound was writing to his mother that Yeats was 'the only living man whose work has more than temporary interest' (cited in ibid.: 130). But he was not overawed. One observer remarked that 'One of his greatest triumphs was the way he stormed 18 Woburn Buildings' and succeeded in reducing Yeats 'from master to disciple' (Goldring 1943: 48). There Pound 'dominated the room, distributed Yeats's cigarettes and Chianti, and laid down the law about poetry' (ibid.: 49).

The relationship between the two poets, the one a mature, celebrated literary figure, the other an ambitious, critically impatient neophyte, developed over several years into a creative symbiosis. Pound was determined to be a literary force in England and he was keen that Yeats, indisputably a poet of major talent (when he met him in 1909 he judged him 'the greatest living poet'; cited in Ellmann 1970: 61), should be identified with the kind of verse he wished to sponsor as poet, critic and editor. Yet he feared that Yeats might be reckoned a monument of the nineties and not as a vital presence. He was aware, as he told Harriet Monroe, in August 1913, that Yeats was 'already a sort of great dim figure with its associations set in the past' (Paige 1971: 21). He had detected, however, the new energized clarity of 'No Second Troy' (though he might have found anticipations of Yeats's later style at an earlier point in his career – in 'Adam's Curse', for example). He set about encouraging Yeats to direct his poetic towards greater verbal precision and concrete statement.

Yeats was not averse to such instruction. The years 1912 and 1913 when Pound was at his most direct as poetic adviser, were a period of artistic uncertainty for the older poet, despite his increasing renown and fashionable prominence in English society. The poems in *In the Seven Woods* and in *The Green Helmet* had been a less than ample harvest for a decade's labour, and there was no assurance that the poetic fertility he had known as a young man could be restored. Since 1910 his only full new book had been a collection of essays, published in the United States in November 1912 as *The Cutting of an Agate*. These, as Yeats observed in 1918 in the preface to the English edition (published 1919), which added new material, were mostly the product of the decade after 1902, when he 'wrote little verse and no prose that did not arise out of some need of the Irish players, or from some thought suggested by their work, or in the defence of some friend connected with that work, or with the movement of events that made it possible' (*E&I*: 219). The 1912 edition is dominated by essays on the theatre and the cultural condition of the Ireland in which Yeats had sought to lead a dramatic movement. So while the volume does contain general reflections on the nature of drama, especially in 'The Tragic Theatre' and in the series titled 'Discoveries', which would affect Yeats's poetry as it became more essentially dramatic, the book does little to suggest a poet convinced of his way forward as an artist. It is retrospective in stance, rather than anticipatory. Its centre of gravity is Ireland and not the England in which Yeats was increasingly spending his time.

Indeed, in the very month that *The Cutting of an Agate* appeared in the United States, the poet was experiencing a bout of very troublesome nervous indigestion, that seemed the somatic expression of deep personal anxiety about his life and work. At such a stage in his career he was undoubtedly flattered and gratified by Pound's attentions. For the energetic, self-confident and ambitious young man combined a high sense of his own artistic calling with a real respect for Yeats's achievement. In early January 1913, his digestion still 'rather queer', Yeats could inform Lady Gregory that he had been allowing Pound to help him with his verses in a collaboration that he wisely compares to their own in the theatre: 'He is full of the middle ages and helps me to get back to the definite and concrete away from modern abstractions. To talk over a poem with him is like getting you to put a sentence into dialect. All becomes clear and natural' (cited in Litz 1985: 139).

Yeats was pleased to set up house with Pound the following winter. Pound was less enthusiastic about the prospect, or at least affected a dutiful gloom. In November 1913 he informed his mother, just before he made the move to Sussex: 'My stay in Stone Cottage will not be in the least profitable. I detest the country. Yeats will amuse me part of the time and bore me to death with psychical research the rest. I regard the visit as a duty to posterity' (Paige 1971: 25). In fact this time together and the subsequent occasions over the following two years, when Yeats shared Stone Cottage with Pound and his young bride Dorothy Shakespear (Olivia's daughter, whom Pound married on 20 April 1914) would affect their work for years to come.

Stone Cottage was a six-roomed, well-set, two-storied stone-built edifice, situated in the depths of the Sussex countryside near the village of Coleman's Hatch. It fronted on a bare heath and at the back gave on a heavily forested hill – the Five Hundred Acre Wood. Yeats for once felt at ease in an English landscape. Undoubtedly both Yeats and Pound, despite the younger man's protestations, valued the intense privacy which Stone Cottage afforded them that first winter together (when Dorothy joined them, things became more sociable). The isolation meant they could each indulge a version of themselves and their sojourn in

Sussex as a retreat from a vulgar and philistine world to refine an aristocratic and traditional art remote from the common herd. They were looked after by a local woman, the appropriately named Alice Welfare (Longenbach 1988: 8). As they settled down to a regimen of reading, writing, conversation and exercise (Pound taught Yeats to fence), Pound soon realized that Yeats was 'much finer *intime* than seen spasmodically in the midst of the whirl' (Paige 1971: 27). Yeats especially, his Irish wounds still aching, found these months of intense reading and discussion with the younger poet whom he found a learned, pleasant companion and a dedicated worker, a truly restorative experience. For they enabled him to deepen his faith in poetry as a magical art, with traditional authority. He could reassure himself that his life had not been wasted, however recalcitrant he had found his fellow countrymen in the difficult years since *The Playboy* riot and the death of Synge.

Just before Pound settled with Yeats in Sussex, he had acquired the papers of the American scholar of Chinese and Japanese, Ernest Fenollosa. At Stone Cottage he began work on them, exploring the Japanese Noh play that first winter of their Sussex period. He shared his discoveries with a much-interested Yeats. Edward Larrissy has written perceptively of this seminal moment in Yeats's career, arguing that Yeats's introduction to the Noh 'was by no means merely an instigation to technical experiment' (Larrissy 1994: 115). For 'Pound's work on the Fenollosa papers allowed Yeats to link themes of tradition, family, the spirit world, desire and the possible void at the heart of human existence in what seemed to him a coherent way' (ibid.). In Larrissy's astute assessment of the appeal of the Noh for Yeats, he highlights how imbued the tradition was with Zen Buddhism. It was a religious and mystical theatre, expressive of ideals of non-attachment to material things. He notes too how aristocratic elitism, the Noh's association with a noble warrior caste, would have made it irresistible to the poet. Furthermore, it combined an obsession with the spirit world with profound veneration for ancestry. It also employed, to Yeats's great fascination, an elaborate symbology of highly stylized dramatic masks.

In Yeats's discovery of the Noh, it is perhaps the fact that the plays were composed by a tradional elite for a fit audience, though few, which most enthused and liberated him. In the essay entitled 'Certain Noble Plays of Japan', published in 1916 as an introduction to a small volume of that name (it was added to *The Cutting of an Agate* in the edition of 1919), when he had himself written drama under the influence of the Noh, he highlighted the kind of audience the Noh theatre drew to its esoteric plays in contemporary Japan and the familial inheritance of the actors themselves:

'Accomplishment' the word Noh means, and it is their accomplishment and that of few cultivated people who understand the literary and mythological allusions and the ancient lyrics quoted in speech of chorus, their discipline, a part of their breeding. The players themselves, unlike the despised players of the popular theatre, have passed on proudly from father to son an elaborate art, and even now a player will publish his family tree to prove his skill. (*E&I*: 229–30)

As in a sense he had done, himself in the prefatory poem to *Responsibilities: Poems and a Play*.

Pound, though he could be sardonic about Yeats's aristocratic pretensions, shared the elder poet's aesthetic elitism, allowing as Yeats did, that a noble lineage and artistic accomplishment could be bulwarks against the philistinism of the age. As James Longenbach has argued indeed, it is possible to view their collaboration at Stone Cottage as a personal attempt to constitute a private hierarchy of elect artists, whose distinctiveness amid the banality of contemporary English culture was akin to that of the true aristocrat's social elevation in an increasingly democratic world. When Pound helped to organize a ceremonial award lunch, held one cold January day in 1914, to mark the seventy-fourth birthday of the elderly poet/landlord and revolutionary Wilfrid Scawen Blunt, which Yeats gladly attended, social and artistic values came together in magnificent, if anachronistic symbolism. The event took place at Blunt's country home in Sussex. The company included Yeats's friend Sturge Moore and an old Rhymers Club acquaintance, Victor Plarr. Richard Aldington and F. S. Flint were invited to represent those of the younger generation of whom Pound approved. Hilaire Belloc arrived after dinner. He had missed something rather special, for peacock was served, which Pound noted 'went very well with iron-studded barricades on the stairway and other mediaeval relics and Burne-Jones tapestry' (cited in Longenbach 1988: 67).

The occasion was not without poignancy. Like Yeats, Blunt, who had inherited the family estate with its 4,000 acres in 1872, had nothing but a book to offer his old fathers to prove his blood. Married to Byron's grand-daughter, whom he treated in his obsessive amorous liaisons with Byronic disregard for her feelings, he lacked a male heir and the estate itself was in considerable financial disarray. Houses, horses and mistresses had taken a heavy toll. In David Cannadine's comprehensive study of the inexorable decline of the British aristocracy between 1870 and the mid-twentieth century, he is presented as a classic case, in which revolutionary commitments in Ireland and Egypt disguised an essential conservatism on land ownership and a reactionary loathing for the middle classes and capitalism as a social force: 'Like many landowners, his real enemy was "the infamous" capitalist system: but in Blunt's case, his exceptionally ardent and passionate nature, combined with his increasingly insecure position on the lower margin of the landed establishment, drove him to express his outraged sense of patrician decency by moving to the left rather than to the right' (Cannadine 1992: 538). Blunt's world, the world of the formidable British landed interest in the United Kingdom and the aristocracy which sustained it (he himself was related to such notables as the Mayos and the Wyndhams), was a world in the process of disintegration as the power of new money and of the plutocratic rich was fundamentally changing a society which now found its centre of gravity in the city of London and its satellites – the centres of maufacturing industry and the colonies of a swollen empire.

Pound and Yeats, in choosing to honour Blunt in defiance of middle-class literary taste (*AM*: 510), were nailing their colours to the mast of a sinking ship, the ship of traditionally based society, with its stable hierarchies of class and achievement, which would founder fatally on the shoals of the great European war which broke out the following autumn. We may take the Blunt dinner (for all Blunt's own anti-imperialism) as one of those many moments in the fateful year of 1914 when the *ancien régime* seemed poised in fateful innocence of the cataclysm to come, taking its pleasures in ignorance of how the years of bloody conflict ahead would speed the process of disintegration that had been undermining their world since the 1870s. We glimpse Yeats again in this Edwardian twilight on the brink of European dark, in the spring of 1914 at dinner in Sir Edmund Gosse's fine house in Regent's Park, 'a pattern of talk...dancing to and fro across the table...easy and effortless' (Stark 1983: 130). It is a striking vignette: 'Beyond Yeats's dark hair and heavy chin like that of some prelate not too ascetic, and Sickert's aquiline profile, the open windows showed heavy garden laburnums pale in candlelight against the sombre leafage of the park' (ibid.).

Douglas Goldring, towards the end of World War II, remembered London on the eve of the Great War. The English capital 'presented the tremendous public spectacle of the wealthiest city in the world working itself up to a crescendo of pleasure and dissipation, to the music of languorous waltzes, punctuated by the popping of champagne corks. If we had no Offenbach to set everyone whirling frantically to tunes in which mad gaiety blended with the tom-toms of death, there was nevertheless a close resemblance between the Paris of the last days of the third Empire and the London which woke with a hangover to face the deluge of blood in August, 1914' (Goldring 1943: 73–4). Yeats spent this last summer of peace, with its brilliant weather and hectic air of hedonism, deep in the spiritualist researches that had taken him in May with Gonne and Feilding to Mirebeau in France. By autumn he had begun further to discharge his obligations to his own familiar dead, as he worked on the memoirs which would become *Reveries Over Childhood and Youth* (published in March 1916). He was also working on 'Swedenborg, Mediums, and the Desolate Places', begun in 1912 and worked on the previous winter, for there he speaks of himself climbing to the top of 'that old house in Soho where a medium is sitting among servant girls' while 'the great battle in Northern France is still undecided' (Gregory 1970: 325; when eventually published, the essay was dated 1914). He imagines the medium being asked for news of some Gordon Highlander or Munster Fusilier, not yet aware of his own death, stumbling on 'amid visionary smoke and noise' (ibid.).

Yeats did not himself need a medium's help to receive disturbing news from France or for a first-hand account of the sufferings of real warfare as it swiftly gathered pace in August and September. In France Gonne, who noted how Yeats had seemed to escape the obsession of the war, heard strange sounds of beating drums in the Pyrenees, the ringing and hammering of a phantom bell that drove Europe to 'an inconceivable madness' (*GLY*: 348) which had taken hold of Europe. For her the war with Germany, in which a hated England was in alliance with a beloved France, was a terrible ordeal. How could she reconcile love for a France under attack with love for an Ireland she hoped could benefit politically from the conflict? She quickly concluded that Ireland had nothing to gain in the war 'except perhaps extra tillage & employment for her people' (ibid.: 351). Gonne had immediately met her personal crisis with characteristic dispatch. She and Iseult presented themselves at a hospital in the Pyrenees to which the French wounded were being transported. They both accepted the rank of lieutenant in the French military and served as nurses to those of the wounded who survived their journey from the battlefields in the north of the country. It was lengthy, harrowing labour. On 7 November 1914 she wrote to Yeats of her 'wild hatred of the war machine' (ibid.)

By December 1914, Gonne was back in Paris with Iseult. She wrote to Yeats describing what modern warfare, with incompetent officers and generals, was exacting on the youth of France and Germany: 'Only 40 or 50 kilometres from Paris in the North and East the fields are vast cemeteries of hastily buried dead' (ibid.: 353). Before too long, Yeats's own circle was to be touched in direct ways by the angel of death that war had so universally summoned in the European theatre.

The twenty-five-year-old T. S. Eliot, hastening back to England from a university summer school in Germany, in the autumn of 1914 found London in the grip of a new mood. In early September he wrote to a friend to say how deeply he had been affected by seeing how the people in two countries had 'taken the affair'. He noted 'the great moral earnestness on both sides' (Valerie Eliot 1988: 57). Yeats, who along with Pound had found the vulgarity and materialist ostentation of the bourgeois insufferable in peacetime, could not have been expected to take the same class's moral earnestness in warfare too seriously. Pound was insouciant. He was delighted when the artist and designer Charles Ricketts (survivor of the 1890s), pronounced: 'What depresses me most is the horrible fact that they can't *all* of them be beaten' (Paige 46). Yet he knew that artists and writers were risking their lives in the slaughter in France. The sculptor Henri Gaudier-Brzeska, whose work he admired, was already in French uniform and had lost seven of ten men in a scouting squad. It was the dullness of trench life the sculptor was forced to endure that struck Pound. At the outset Yeats sought to take the long view. He thought London was reacting neurotically to the war with its rumour and fearful gossip, and counselled that 'unless a sufficient number of people read the history of China steadily they will not know what to do if there is a real disaster' (cited in Pierce 1995: 176). Yet he was not unaffected by news from Europe, especially that in Gonne's anguished letters. In Dublin in November 1914 he confessed where his interests lay in the conflict: 'I have friends fighting in Flanders, I had one in the trenches at Antwerp, and I have a very dear friend nursing the wounded in a French hospital. How can I help but feeling as they feel and desiring a German defeat?' (cited in ibid.: 177). The war however was a distraction from his work.

Yeats could not have known in 1914 that his limited partisanship in the conflict threatened to marginalize him further in the Ireland he had begun to neglect since the death of Synge. For there were those in Dublin in 1914 already contemplating a military rising against British rule. There had been a time when Yeats might have been privy to some such plan or at least in contact with those who were. Now his London domicile and his broad, if scarcely vocal or enthusiastic support of the Allied cause, set him apart from the revolutionary energies that were awakening once again in his native country. As if to highlight the ambiguity of his position – that of a supportive if emotionally disengaged non-combatant in London and an ageing, unaware representative of a superseded national movement in Ireland – in November 1914 Yeats composed a detached poem, 'A Meditation in Time of War'. In this almost indifferent evocation of transcendental perspectives, the poet sees the war *sub specie aeternitatis*. Images of permanence and of flux compose a polarity, which is comprehended by a more fundamental dialectic, that between animate, universal spirit and a materialism that has mankind in thrall to destructive imagining:

> For one throb of the artery,
> While on that old grey stone I sat
> Under the old wind-broken tree,
> I knew that One is animate,
> Mankind inanimate fantasy.

Yeats's remote response to the general crisis and ignorance of Irish developments in the early months of the war allowed him, as others worried about the present and the future, to cast his mind back into his personal past. Moore's caustic satire on his dynastic pride in *Hail and Farewell* would be answered in a recollective account of his own childhood and youth among mighty men, the descendants of a heroically active line of '*old fathers*'. He wrote to his own father on 26 December 1914 that he had completed on Christmas day (spent with Lady Gregory at Coole) the autobiographical work begun that summer. He counselled, in a cautious letter to his father – who was not likely to warm to his son's less than generous treatment of an old family friend, Edward Dowden, set in striking contrast to the nobility of John O'Leary – that his book was 'less an objective history than a reverie' (*L*: 589). Yeats further admitted in this interesting letter that the book was a product of detachment, for by making 1886 or 1887 the terminal date of his memoir, he could exclude many of the living and could 'stand apart and judge' (ibid.).

That judgemental pose certainly helps to account for the book's strange lack of emotional zest, as if the isolation and uninvolvement of the mature Yeats in the general crisis of the autumn of 1914 extends its influence to the recollection of his own childhood and youth (the pain of that past may also account for a certain distance of tone). He chose to ignore the grim horror of the present but could not find in his past a source of imaginative renewal. The dominant mood, as Foster has astutely noted, is 'elegiac passion' (Foster 1998: 102). In his letter to his parent, he states: 'You need not fear that I am not amiable' (*L*: 589) but immediately adds, conscious that is the work's deficiency, 'I shall illustrate it with a photograph of Jack's *Memory Harbour* at any rate' (ibid.). In fact that vibrant, Chagall-like celebration of a primal, village world, serves only to highlight in the 1916 Cuala Press edition, the general atmosphere of joylessness which the poet's reveries evoke. He was determined however to continue the work, even if the sequel could be only for his own satisfaction and not for publication.

January and February of 1915 Yeats spent with Pound and his new bride at Stone Cottage. Pound was reading Wordsworth, Browning and Morris to him in the evenings and Doughty's *Travels in Arabia Deserta*. They sought to ignore the military struggle across the English Channel. Yeats was attracted by Doughty's accounts of Arab djinn, their magic taking him into a world that his precursor, Leo Africanus, had travelled. The war encroached however. Yeats wrote to Lady Gregory with a real sense of foreboding:

> I wonder if history will ever know at what man's door to lay the crime of this inexplicable war. I suppose, like most wars it is at root a bagman's war, a sacrifice of the best for the worst. I feel strangely enough most for the young Germans who are now being killed. These spectacled, dreamy faces, or so I picture them, remind me more of men that I have known than the strong-bodied young English football players who pass my door at Woburn Buildings daily, marching in their khaki or the positive-minded young Frenchmen. (Yeats, cited in Longenbach 1988: 117)

The poet sensed he was a bystander observing a new tragic generation of young men. Those dreamy young Germans reminded him of the poets of his own doomed generation, of the poets of the Cheshire Cheese, who had sacrificed their lives for their art. Soon events gave him to understand that the war would bring tragedy very close to home, that his own immediate circle would not escape the sacrifice of young manhood upon which the western world had so unthinkingly embarked.

At the end of January British troops were on manoeuvres in the countryside around Stone Cottage and on the great moor nearby. Yeats, asked for a war poem for an anthology to aid Belgian refugees, wrote in 'A Reason for Keeping Silent':

> I think it better that at times like these
> We poets keep our mouths shut, for in truth
> We have no gift to set a statesman right.
> (cited in Longenbach, 188, the later version reads 'A poet's mouth be silent' in the newly titled 'On being asked for a War Poem').

Yeats remained preoccupied with his own past as his mind turned to the years which followed the point where he had concluded *Reveries Over Childhood and Youth*. It had been then that he had met Gonne, who had so recently been heroically at work among the injured French soldiery. Such noble activities must have reminded him of her similar work among the poor of Ireland and he composed three poems, 'Her Praise', 'The People' and 'His Phoenix', which celebrate her as she had once been in her original beauty, but primarily esteem her for self-sacrificial devotion to the people, a virtue still governing her actions in France: 'Among the poor both young and old gave her praise' ('Her Praise').

In May 1915 a German submarine torpedoed the passenger liner *Lusitania* off the southern Irish coast. Among the many civilians drowned in that atrocity was Lady Gregory's nephew, Sir Hugh Lane. On the night when the ship was lost, Professor Dowden's daughter Hester, a notable medium, was conducting a seance in Dublin with Lennox Robinson, manager of the Abbey Theatre. According to her biographer, Lane 'came through' before they knew he had perished or was even on board the sunken ship. In subsequent sittings Lane expressed extreme anxiety that a gallery should not be erected in Dublin to his memory but was anxious that a codicil to his will be honoured (Bentley 1951: 38–9). Yeats too was to be haunted by the dead Sir Hugh for many years as the matter of his will became a *cause célèbre*, to the resolution of which Lady Gregory dedicated herself with unflagging determination. She made sure, in her firm way, that Yeats did not slacken in his support of their just cause. For Lane, irritated by Dublin Corporation's unenthusiastic response to his generous offer to donate his collection of pictures to the city, had changed his will, conferring them in the event of his death to the National Gallery in London. Before setting off to America in 1915 (he met his death on the return journey), he had added a codicil to his will rescinding this angry decision and reassigning them to the Municipal Gallery in the Irish capital. The codicil had not been witnessed. So began a dispute between the two cities that absorbed Lady Gregory for the rest of her life and increasingly became burdensome to the loyal, but much less single-mindedly dedicated Yeats.

In March Gonne had written to tell Yeats that her sister's twenty-one-year-old son had been killed in France leading his platoon. In June Pound's friend Gaudier-Brzeska was also killed in action. In October Gonne wrote again to report that her former lover and Iseult's father had lost his son to the 'horror of this war'. She told him of how she had become 'strangely sensitive and clairvoyant' and how she felt 'the great battle & the thousands of souls going out' (*GYL*: 359) before she read of it in the newspapers. By September even the deliberately detached Yeats had noted that 'the anxiety of the war and the many deaths' (*L*: 601) had reduced audiences for the Abbey Theatre both in Dublin and in England.

In London especially, the war had encroached in direct ways. The citizenry had the chance to observe the methods of modern warfare when the Germans launched Zeppelin attacks against the city. In September, following a raid which Robert Gregory had witnessed, Yeats wrote from Coole to his father to report in dispirited and gloomily detached terms on the progress of the war. He expected a fatigued draw. Robert Gregory had heard a London mob cheering the spectacle of a Zeppelin raid: 'High up a Zeppelin shone white under a cloud' (*L*: 588, this letter is misdated by Wade). In October Yeats himself witnessed a spectacular attack while he was working close to the British Museum (Pierce 1995: 179).

In the summer of 1915 Yeats and Pound had tried to help James Joyce, who had moved from Trieste, where he had lived since 1907, to Zurich in neutral Switzerland, to avoid internment as a British citizen for the duration of the hostilities. Yeats hoped he could arrange for a pension to be paid to his fellow Dubliner from the Royal Literary Fund. Through Sir Edmund Gosse's good offices, the deed was done, though not without Gosse's expressed surprise that neither Yeats nor Joyce had been forthcoming in support of the Allied war effort.

The truth was that Yeats, however much tragedy it involved for many, experienced the war as an irritating interference with the work he wished to do. He simply got on with it as best he could. In his letters of the period, he exhibits a mixture of *sang froid*, impatience and determination not to allow the general crisis to distract him from his own more fundamental artistic and spiritual concerns. In fact the years 1914 to 1917 were poetically quite fruitful. He composed over twenty poems (some of them complex metaphysical speculations), which would form the basis of the fairly substantial volume which he would publish in 1917 as *The Wild Swans at Coole*. He mostly divided his time between London and Stone Cottage, where in 1916 he spent the first three months of the year with the Pounds. There were excursions as well to Gonne's Normandy home and to Coole. He continued to visit Mabel Beardsley, sister of the artist, until her death from cancer in 1916. The poem 'Upon a Dying Lady' which he had composed about her between January 1912 and 1914 was included in the 1917 volume. *The Player Queen* continued to give difficulty and in late 1915 he began to rewrite it. He was beginning to feel his years. He wrote of Gonne in the autumn of 1915: 'There is grey in your hair./Young men no longer suddenly catch their breath/ When you are passing' ('Broken Dreams'). He had looked 'death in the face' ('A Deep-sworn Vow') and was increasingly conscious of the aridity encroaching age might bring: 'The holy centaurs of the hills are vanished;/I have nothing but the embittered sun;' ('Lines Written in Dejection').

Yet he remained obsessed by the erotic magnetism of women, their lives entangled with his own. Gonne's daughter Iseult, now twenty-one, had begun to seem more than the 'child' he called her in the sexually charged poem of November 1915, 'Presences', where he set a young girl amid a trio of women, one 'a harlot' (possibly Dickinson, or Dorothy Coates who had broken his friendship with Quinn, the biographers suggest) and one 'it may be, a queen' (Gonne herself). A fourth woman was joining the circle too. There is some evidence that Yeats may have proposed marriage to Georgina Hyde-Lees in November 1915, for she seems to have believed that he had done so (Harwood 1989: 158–9). Jeffares speculates that the exigencies of her war-work (as a student at Cheltenham Ladies College, she was working as a nursing assistant and hospital cook) 'may have caused the matter to be put aside' (*GYL*: 39). It is true that Yeats had kept in contact with the young woman with whom he had discussed his psychic experiments in August 1913. She had entered the Stella Matutina section of the Golden Dawn, probably with Yeats as a sponsor (Jeffares 1988: 217) in 1914 where she took the motto and name N. E. M. O. Georgie and her family remained in friendly contact with the poet, allowing a young woman's feelings of admiration for the distinguished older man to develop into something more personal. She had her eye on him as a possible husband and she possessed a strength of personality and will beyond her years.

Winter in Stone Cottage in 1916 intensified Yeats's fascination with the Noh. Among the Fenollosa papers, Pound had found a Noh text in translation which Yeats seized upon as the basis for a play of his own. Pound introduced him to a Japanese dancer, Michio Ito, who was in London to learn classical and modern dance. In February Yeats quickly dictated *At the Hawk's Well* to Pound. Ito, although not himself an adept of the Noh, would, he envisaged, play a leading role in this new work. Edmund Dulac, artist and designer, would be responsible for masks and costumes. The play was mounted in London privately, at first in Lady Cunard's drawing-room at her house in Cavendish Square, and two days later in Lady Islington's house in Chesterfield Gardens, in aid of the Social Institute's Union for Women and Girls. The première on 2 April 1916 included among its small invited audience T. S. Eliot and the orientalist and poet Arthur Waley, but no drama critics or newspaper photographers. Two days later, the audience at Lady Islington's numbered 300, among them no less a personage than Queen Alexandra (quite deaf, so capable only of appreciating the work's visual impact) gracing what was a considerable social occasion for one of the city's most influential hostesses.

In June 1914 Yeats had completed a poem entitled 'The Fisherman'. It was first published in *Poetry* (Chicago) in February 1916, while he was at work on *At the Hawk's Well*. In the poem he had imagined, in scorn of the kinds of philistine attacks the Abbey Theatre and Synge and Lane in particular had encountered in Dublin ('beating down of the wise/And great Art beaten down'), an ideal Irishman, country-bred, 'wise and simple'. Perforce he had admitted that such a man 'does not exist' for he is 'A man who is but a dream'. Yet the poet records how he cried

> 'Before I am old
> I shall have written him one
> Poem maybe as cold
> And passionate as the dawn.'

The contrast between Yeats's ideal imaginary national audience evoked in this resonant yet wistful poem and the English society audience before which *At the Hawk's Well* was performed in the spring of 1916 could not have been more stark. Without an Irish constituency for his vision of a theatre of accomplishment venerated by the cognoscenti, Yeats fondly hoped that English society hostesses and dilettantes could assemble an audience akin to the Shogun elite that had brought knowledgeable attention to the Noh in Tokugawa Japan. Perhaps a calling in of dues for favours rendered was also involved. For Lady Asquith records in her diary for 11 April 1916 (Asquith 1968: 152) that Yeats was one of ten poets who read from their works at Baroness D'Erlanger's house, in aid of the Star and Garter Fund. The poet, who had made his scruples known when he accepted a pension from the British state, and who had indicated in December 1915 that he would refuse a knighthood, was not incapable of a discreet accommodation with the English establishment when courtesy and obligation required it.

At the Hawk's Well in fact addresses the theme of heroic destiny in a dramatization of Cuchulain at a definitive moment in his life. It can also be read as an
expression of the poet's deep desire for personal renewal as the years began to
advance on him. We see a figure who is strikingly younger than the poet himself
at the time he composed the play. Cuchulain in *At The Hawk's Well* is a young
man whose fate is determined by the events which the play presents. The
destructive effects of old age are represented nevertheless in the figure of the
Old Man, who also plays a crucial part in the drama.

The plot of the piece is simple enough, although it is veiled in an elaborate,
ritualistic stylization (Yeats's adaptation of the Noh form) and the elevated,
liturgical measures of its choric verse (some of which is accompanied by music)
which contrast strikingly with the tense vivid diction of the dialogue. A wandering
man in quest of his destiny (a figure from the Noh), Cuchulain is in search of the
waters of youth and immortality. An Old Man, who has waited by a well where
immortality can be quaffed on the rare occasions when its dry bed fills with water,
and Cuchulain himself, are both tricked of their chance to gain immortality by
the wiles of the *Shidhe* (the fairy folk). The Guardian of the Well performs a
hawklike dance at the moment the waters rise. During this, the Old Man sleeps,
so missing his chance of eternal life once again, but Cuchulain holds her gaze in a
display of courage, which distracts him from his opportunity to put on immortality.

Had the audiences at the London performances in 1916 known their Celtic
mythology they would have realized that this moment of courage seals Cuchulain's fate. Instead of immortality or even a long life which would bring him old
age with 'An old dog's head on his knees,/Among his children and friends', he
would face a tragic destiny. As the play ends, we are reminded that Cuchulain
will meet his fate in a confrontation with the warrior queen Aoife – the hawk-
girl's dance has 'roused up the fierce woman of the hills,/Aoife, and all her troops,
to take your life'. From their doomed sexual and military entanglement will come
the son Cuchulain will slay in ignorance (the event enacted in *On Baile's Strand*).
Cuchulain's fated erotic obsessions with Aoife will involve too the powerful
jealousy of his wife Emer. And he will die at the height of his powers, dispatched
by a blind and cowardly man. Yet his memory will be noble, his instinctual
commitment to living life with full intensity, an image of heroic courage.

At the Hawk's Well is a drama of initiation. Cuchulain passes a kind of test as he
holds the eye of the hawk-girl, which sets him on a path that leads to violence,
passion and death. The Old Man of the play, by contrast, is an idealist who has
given his life in a futile hope of immortality. He knows that he has missed life in
his desire for something more permanent. The dry well filling with water as a
symbol of renewal in the play for him is an ironic one. Only remorse for a wasted
life awaits this old man (as Yeats himself in middle life seems to have feared a
similar fate might be his also). Cuchulain entering on his unique, passionate
destiny seems to have chosen the better part. Or have been chosen for it.

Yeats knew the audience for the first public performance of his play was
unreceptive. He wrote to Lady Gregory that the event was a success, 'though a

charity audience is a bad one' (cited in Miller 1977: 225). When he posted that letter (the postmark is 10 April 1916), he did not of course know that two weeks later a much greater drama would unfold in his native city that would affect the Irish people in a way nothing had done since the ruin and death of Parnell. For the Rising of 24 April 1916, on Easter Monday, would prove a defining moment for the nation, a moment of renewal of a kind Yeats had deemed impossible in the city that had denied the legacy of O'Leary. It was set in motion by the courage of a small group of insurgents and by a mysterious process of transformation which recruited them to a destiny of heroic proportions. It was as if the magical, occult dance of the hawk-girl in *At the Hawk's Well* which determined Cuchulain's destiny, had an equivalent in the lure of Cathleen ni Houlihan as she sent men to the deaths that would alter everything for ever. For the Easter Rising was a fateful event that would profoundly affect in extraordinary ways not only the history of Ireland, but Yeats's own story.

It was not that some form of demonstration was unexpected that Easter Monday. The Irish Volunteers had been openly drilling with fake guns for several years. But few realized that the 'exercises' scheduled for Easter Sunday were a cover for a general uprising, with real guns from Germany promised to support the insurrection. In the event, Sir Roger Casement's plot to land weaponry fell through. It was discovered by the British authorities and he himself was arrested. An order cancelling the exercises was published in the Sunday newspapers by the commander of the Volunteers, but a secret army within that force, the Irish Republican Brotherhood led by a teacher, writer and orator, Patrick Pearse, and a group of armed labour militants known as the Citizen Army, under the trade unionist and agitator James Connolly, were determined to strike a blow for an Irish republic, come what may. On Easter Monday Pearse, with a small force, entered the General Post Office in central Dublin and, having secured the building and raised the Republican flag, read 'The Proclamation of the Irish Republic' before a small crowd of surprised Dubliners. The insurgents also took other strategically placed buildings. After a few days of skirmishing with British troops, the authorities in the city ordered that the occupied buildings be shelled by a gunboat offshore and by the artillery that had been brought hurriedly into the city centre. Much of Sackville Street around the Post Office was destroyed in the fighting and bombardment. After a few days' brave resistance the rebels surrendered to the vastly greater strength arrayed against them. It was all over by Sunday, 30 April.

In proportion to the immense human catastrophe that was the war in mainland Europe (the battle of the Somme began nine weeks later), the Rising was a limited affair. The insurgents numbered at most some 1,600 men. Casualties were relatively light in comparison with a war where thousands perished daily; there were 450 dead and 2,614 wounded (Foster 1988: 483). Many Dubliners were aghast at the folly of the rebels and in the early days of the Rising were distressed by the damage to their city. Rural Ireland was largely indifferent to the fate of Dublin. It was the British response – swift, surgical and uncomprehending of the ghosts they were reawakening – which helped to make of a botched rebellion the sacrificial act of national renewal some of the doomed participants had hoped it might be.

In the first two weeks of May, fourteen of the revolutionary leaders were executed by firing squad in Dublin (a fifteenth execution took place in Cork). These executions, perfectly justifiable to the legal and military mind, which saw them as a proper response to men who had traitorously conspired with the German enemy in time of war, inflamed national feeling, which began to turn inexorably in favour of the men who had died for Ireland, as so many martyrs famed in ballad and poem had done in the past. Among them was Major John MacBride, Maud Gonne's estranged husband. He died bravely on 5 May 1916. Everything had indeed changed.

11

All Changed

Yeats heard the news of the Dublin Rising in England. He was staying in the home of a friend, Sir William Rothenstein, in Gloucestershire. Gonne heard of the Dublin events in France where she was starved for precise information. She immediately wrote to Yeats asking him to send on newspapers with details. At the beginning of May, with a newspaper to hand which Yeats had sent her, she wrote to tell him that she was 'overwhelmed by the tragedy & the greatness' of the sacrifice the revolutionaries had made: 'They have raised the Irish cause again to a position of tragic dignity. They will have made it impossible to ignore Ireland or to say she is satisfied at the conference where at the end of the war, much will be heard about the Right of small nationalities' (*GYL*: 372). This letter indicates that Yeats had expressed the political view in a letter to her, which had accompanied the newspaper, that the deferral of Home Rule at the outbreak of the war had resulted in the tragedy of the Rising. By 11 May, with knowledge of the executions, all such political considerations had been consumed in the fire of Gonne's fervent nationalist faith: 'Major MacBride by his Death has left a name for Seagan [her son by MacBride] to be proud of. Those who die for Ireland are sacred' (ibid.: 375). Later in May, as she brooded on all that had happened and read Patrick Pearse's prison poem, composed while awaiting his execution, she cited in a letter to Yeats lines from *Cathleen ni Houlihan*, in which she had played in 1902: 'The deaths of those leaders are full of beauty & romance & "They will be speaking forever, the people shall hear them forever"' (ibid.: 377).

Yeats's response lacked the ardour and clarity of Gonne's elevated, sorrowful yet exhilarated conviction that the Rising was a redemptive act, a moment of national renewal. Rothenstein reported that he thought his friend was troubled to find himself in England at such a time, when acquaintances had risked their lives in Ireland. Yet he could not unambiguously support what they had done. On 11 May he wrote from London to Lady Gregory confessing that 'The Dublin tragedy' had been 'a great sorrow and anxiety' (*L*: 612). 'I am trying', he told her, to write a poem on the men executed – 'terrible beauty has been born again.' If the English Conservative Party had made a declaration that they did not intend to rescind the Home Rule Bill there would have been no Rebellion. I had no idea that any public event could so deeply move me – and I am very despondent about the future. At the moment I feel that all the work of years has been overturned, all the bringing together of the classes, all the freeing of Irish literature and criticism from politics.   (ibid.: 613)

Yeats also realized that what had happened in Ireland would certainly affect his own life. He was in the process of transferring his copyrights to the successful Macmillan publishing house which would henceforth be his English and North American publishers. That decision, although it did not by any means preclude residence in Ireland, in its definitive quality certainly suggested, along with his increasingly comfortable position in social life in the Home Counties, that Yeats foresaw for himself a predominantly English, metropolitan future. Now with so many deaths in Ireland (and the recent death in England of his friend Mabel Beardsley must have deepened a depressed mood of uncertainty about his own future as the years ran on), he felt a renewed sense of obligation to his native country. On 23 May he wrote to Quinn of his grief and sense of personal responsibility for all that had been lost in so many deaths: 'At the moment I feel as if I shall return to Dublin to live, to begin building again. I look sadly about my rooms for I have just taken in and furnished the floor below my old rooms and so have practically the whole house. I am pleased with the look of things and shall be sad to shift (ibid.: 614). Furthermore Yeats must have realized immediately that the execution of MacBride had direct personal consequences for himself, since that death had released Gonne from the bonds of marriage. That knowledge could not but have stirred up confused feelings, disturbing memories and questions about their future relationship.

In the first instance Yeats attempted to discharge his obligation to the dead heroes. He sought to complete the poem begun in May, in which the phrase 'terrible beauty' would serve as a refrain and resonant culmination, as a proper memorial to them. It is not certain when this poem was composed. It is dated September 25 in the typescript which was used in 1917 to print 25 copies. However we know that he read a version of it to Gonne on a beach in Normandy during the autumn of 1916 (Gwynn 1940: 32). So we can assume it was much on his mind through the summer and early autumn of 1916, as the public mood in Ireland swung irresistibly behind those who had given their lives in the Rising and its bloody aftermath. The poet spent July and August with Gonne and Iseult in Normandy. On 1 July he proposed to Gonne once more, offering her a life away from politics in a world of writers and artists, and was again rejected. Yet her person, presence and imaginative experience found their way, as so often before, into the poem which preoccupied him through the summer of 1916.

From Yeats's earliest writings onwards the concept of ideal beauty and Gonne's earthly form (almost anticipated in 'The Wanderings of Oisin') had been woven together to suggest an intermingling of erotic feeling with expectation of imminent apocalypse and death. From early in Yeats's *oeuvre*, feminized beauty, an abstract idea made languorously available in verses of erotic longing and swooning death wishes, was also associated with something more authoritative: with height and nobility, with instinctive, solitary aristocracy of presence. In 'The Arrow' in *In The Seven Woods* a woman's beauty had been recalled at its inception as 'Tall and noble but with face and bosom / Delicate in colour as apple blossom'. 'No Second Troy' had added martial prowess to the complex of associations which the term 'beauty' involved for the poet. Gonne as female ideal – erotic, death-haunted, noble in dangerous hauteur – constitutes in Yeats's poetic a reiterated idea of the beautiful, so that the term 'beauty' is vested in his work with a powerfully female, sexual aura. As it is in this poem.

'Easter 1916', the poem in which Yeats attempted to resolve his feelings about the event which had so moved him and to memorialize the men whose names had been made sacred by death, is a poem of occult imagining. It seeks to penetrate beneath the appearances of history to comprehend the mysteries of destiny. It seeks too to fathom the depths of a process that has wrought an extraordinary transformation, in which a society apparently engaged in a casual comedy has found itself enacting a drama of tragic significance. Written in the protracted emotional aftermath of the Rising, with Maud Gonne once again free to be courted as muse and marital partner, 'Easter 1916' confronts not only how ordinary men have been cast as heroes, but inscribes the poet's own troubled responses to female beauty and its attendant power. And the repeated phrase 'terrible beauty', in the context of Yeatsian imagining is compact of a strange energizing force and sexual allure. For Yeats, the Rising was a manifestation of occult forces in which the female daimon was at work. Though she is not mentioned directly in the poem, in several complex, even confusing ways, Gonne is a presiding spirit in 'Easter 1916'.

As Yeats worked on his poem the political skies grew even darker. Despite a concerted international campaign in which George Bernard Shaw participated, Sir Roger Casement was hanged in Pentonville prison on 3 August; he had been found guilty of high treason. Yeats had communicated privately with Herbert Asquith, the British prime minister, advising clemency. In this tense atmosphere, Yeats knew any poem by him on the Rising would be a public statement and would be read in the future as his contribution to what increasingly seemed likely to prove a defining moment in his country's history. For the Yeats who had written so dismissively in prose of the generation of Irishmen who had now proved their mettle in battle, to be accepted as the poet of the Rising required some adroit rhetorical manoeuvres. The poet met this challenge by casting 'Easter 1916' as a palinode, which answers his own 'September 1913' in terms that imply that its harsh judgements have been overtaken by events. The opening movement of 'Easter 1916' magnanimously acknowledges how wrong he had been in thinking that the martyrs and he himself had inhabited a world of drab inconsequentiality, which could not change. For now all has changed, 'changed utterly'.

Concessive recantation does however allow the poet his own reservations. The poem does not accept fully that Yeats's earlier assessment of a generation and a society had been in error. Rather, the second rhetorical move of the poem is to suggest how the martyrs' characters and behaviour had enforced an estimate of them and their world in which the heroic played no part, and to accept with a touch of astonishment, as well as humbled recognition, that they have been changed. It is striking that the heroes of a revolution which had brought back tragic dignity to Ireland are represented here as passive figures, altered, in some instances beyond recognition, by a historical change over which they seem to have no control. So powerful has been this transformative energy that even the disreputable MacBride has been affected by it and made fit matter for a noble elegy:

> This other man I had dreamed
> A drunken, vain-glorious lout.
> He had done most bitter wrong
> To some who are near my heart,
> Yet I number him in the song;
> He, too, has resigned his part
> In the casual comedy;
> He, too, has been changed in his turn,
> Transformed utterly:
> A terrible beauty is born.

The phrase 'in his turn' here implies that the actual agent of transformation (and we note the passive voice in which acts of rebellion are recounted) is death by execution itself, for the prisoners in Kilmainham Gaol in Dublin were dispatched singly and in batches over a grim period of days. Yet the poet is not satisfied by that simple response to what had happened, which he could not share with Gonne who accepted that her husband, whatever their unhappy personal history, had been apotheosized by dying for Ireland. The poet wanted to understand what had made the martyrs risk and even, in some cases, court death. He wanted to comprehend how they had been changed as individuals and as figures in a national drama that had taken so tragic yet heroic a turn. And he wanted to participate as poet and mage in the wonder of the event itself.

In the brief portraits of the rebels in the poem's second stanza, feminine attributes are emphasized in two cases and suggested in another. Countess Markievicz, who as Constance Gore-Booth of Lissadell had won Yeats's admiration in her girlhood in the 1890s, is remembered 'young and beautiful' riding to harriers. Her career as a suffragist and socialist agitator, and worker among the poor of Dublin, had made of her a 'shrill' voice in argument, when once no voice had been 'more sweet than hers'. 'Sweet' is a key word here, for Yeats found true femininity to lie in the sweetness of the female voice (in a late poem he asserted 'The women that I picked spoke sweet and low', 'Hound Voice'). The critic and lecturer Thomas MacDonagh, another of the 1916 martyrs, is evoked in ambiguous terms:

> [he] Was coming into his force;
> He might have won fame in the end,
> So sensitive his nature seemed,
> So daring and sweet his thought.

'Force' reminds us here that MacDonagh, the intellectual and university-educated man of letters, had fatefully cast in his lot with men of the 'physical force' tradition in Irish politics. Yet his nature is a feminized one, combining as it does sensitivity and sweetness of thought with daring. Even the sanguinary Pearse (his oratory had made much in the years immediately before the Rising of a necessary shedding of blood), whose 'helper and friend' MacDonagh had been, is gathered into this nimbus of beauty and sensitivity – of the gentler, cultivated, even womanly virtues – for 'This man had kept a school' as well as riding 'our wingèd horse' (the 1916 version of the poem here reads 'wingèd mettlesome horse').

In a detailed analysis of the gender politics of this poem, Cullingford boldly asserts that 'Markievicz stands in for Gonne in "Easter 1916". The Countess, condemned to death for her part in the Rising but reprieved because of her sex, offered a mirror image of Gonne's devotion to her country and what might have been her fate had she stayed in Dublin' (Cullingford 1993: 121). Yeats had often expressed a fear that Gonne would lose her femininity in a political fanaticism bred of abstract patriotism (or ideological commitment) which he did not think proper for women. Such abstraction had made the beautiful girl Constance Gore-Booth had once been, a strident, ignorant woman, wasteful of time and her own beauty. By extension such fanaticism (and the image of the revolutionaries' 'vivid faces', contrasted with the measured sobriety of 'grey Eighteenth-century houses', with which the poem opens, highlights a freakish fanaticism) can destroy the feminine in a man also. And so Cullingford has it that 'Easter 1916...asks whether the sacrifice of change occasioned by obsessive love of country may not give political men as well as political women hearts of stone' (ibid.: 125).

Cullingford is referring in this summary to the central metaphor of the poem, the implications of which are explored in its third and fourth movements. Set in apposition are the flux of natural life and the stone of the fanatic heart which troubles the living stream. Stone as metaphor here, in the context of Yeatsian imagining, intensifies the sense of Maud Gonne as presiding presence in the poem, for it had played a crucial part in Yeats's estimate of her and the dangers which she faced as a person.

A few days before the death of Synge in 1909, Yeats had communicated to his journal his fears for Gonne the political agitator:

> Maud Gonne writes that she is learning Gaelic. I would sooner see her work at Gaelic propaganda than any other Irish movement I can think of, except some movement of decorative art. I fear for her any renewed devotion to an opinion. Women, because the main event of their lives has been a giving of themselves, give themselves to an opinion as if [it] were some terrible stone doll. We {men} take up an opinion lightly and are easily false to it, and when faithful keep the habit of many interests. . . . They grow cruel, as if [in] defence of lover or child, and all this is done for something other than human life. At last the opinion becomes so much a part of them that it is as though a part of their flesh becomes, as it were, stone, and much of their being passes out of life. It was part of her power in the past that, though she

made this surrender with her mind, she kept the sweetness of her voice and much humour, yet I cannot but fear for her.   (*Mem*: 191–2)

Yeats had dreaded what Ireland could do to Gonne and was probably relieved that her estrangement from MacBride had largely kept her out of the country in the years when the sweet voice of a beautiful Gore-Booth had been made strident in the turmoil of agitational politics. He knew too that an entire generation could be affected by the same petrifaction. For those who had destroyed Synge, he had sensed, had been like 'an hysterical woman who will make unmeasured accusations and believe impossible things, because of some logical deduction from a solitary thought which has turned a portion of her mind to stone' (*E&I*: 314).

In the meditative heart of 'Easter 1916', Yeats represents the dangers of fervent, even fanatical, commitment to an ideal, as a dialectic between stone and a living stream, between the immutable and flux. The dialectic brings the 'terrible beauty', longed for by the obsessive and fanatical (the 'enchanted' of the poem), to birth, in an occult dynamic which the poet seeks to comprehend in his intense verses – a dynamic which might indeed have claimed Gonne as another of its human victims, even though her beauty manifests an alluring ideal.

Gonne, finally, is present in the poem, not only because for the poet she was beauty itself and because he had feared her 'flesh' might have been petrified had she stayed in Ireland to become a martyr for the cause, but in the special sense that the imagery of the poem in part derived from her imagination. In September 1911 Gonne had written to Yeats, in sensitive awareness of the complex gender exchanges that constituted their long relationship, that 'Our children were your poems of which I was the Father sowing the unrest and storm which made them possible & you the mother who brought them forth in suffering & in the highest beauty & our children had wings' (*GYL*: 302). 'Easter 1916' is a compelling example of an even more intimate, immediate kind of literary erotics.

In September 1901, when their spiritual marriage was still compulsively intact, Gonne had written to Yeats of one of her vivid waking visions. In a haunted glen she was led by a god and goddess to a stream: 'I went a long way up the stream till I stood by stones marked with 7 & with 9. There standing in the middle of the stream dressed in lily green was a beautiful girl. She stood still & presently sat down by a rock & and a laughing baby child came also dressed in green & leant up against her' (ibid.: 144). Gonne associated this vision with the music of the fairy folk, which she told Yeats she had heard once 'quite distinctly', with 'physical ears'. In 1915 she heard it again. On 7 November she wrote to Yeats that she had been haunted for three days 'by an air with the Rhythm of a dance reel' (ibid: 362). She then recalled where she had heard the air before, when it had seemed to come out of the heart of a mountain, from Slieve Gullion. It had seemed in the past to be connected with the number 16. The air from the mountain, she recollected, had shared the rhythm of '8 hand reels', which she had heard at a Gaelic League music festival. As she thought of this rhythm, which obsessed her in the early days of November 1915, she sensed its colour was green.

The imagery and curious numerology (stream, rock, green-clad fairy folk, the numbers 7 and 9) of Gonne's earlier vision had been bathed in a blissful, almost pastoral, light, as in a Samuel Palmer canvas. The haunting fairy music of 1915, which she had heard before on Slieve Gullion in association with the number 16, provokes in 1915 a prophetic, Wagnerian vision of Irish destiny in the war raging in Europe. She thought of all Europe as dancing to the rhythms of the fairy reel and of the many Irish soldiers who had already given their lives on the battlefield. They were being brought back 'to the spiritual Ireland' from which they had wandered. Some had died without hate and so they could be part of the dance, but others among them had

> died with a definite idea of sacrifice to an ideal, they were held by the stronger & deeper Rhythms of the chants, leading in wonderful patterns to a deeper peace, the peace of the Crucified, which is above the currents of nationalities & storms, but for all that they will not be separated from Ireland for as an entity she has followed the path of Sacrifice & tasted of the Grail & the strength they will bring her is greater. (ibid.: 363)

In the summer of 1916, when Gonne's vision of nationally efficacious Irish sacrifice had been vindicated (the poet was reading, with Iseult's help, the writings of the French Catholic school with, in Jammes and Péguy, its intense version of sacred sacrificial patriotism), Yeats's poem on the Rising entered the territory of his hostess's strange envisioning and numerological arcana. As Helen Vendler has pointed out (with acknowledgment to her students; 1991: 20), the poem itself is a numerological artifact, probably based on the date when the Rising began, 24 April 1916. It is constructed as four movements: the first of 16 lines, the second 24, the third 16 and the final movement 24 once more. This structure gives magical force to the act of poetry itself, for it participates in the mystery of the occasion it honours. 'I write it out in a verse' announces the poet/ mage, 'I number him in the song.'

One of the most moving aspects of this powerful, troubled poem – its taut trimeters disallowing any too easily earned elevation of tone – is its consciousness of two orders of time. In one, day follows day, winter follows summer, minute by minute things change, 'close of day' brings 'nightfall', time is wasted in lingering in the street, in 'nights in argument', sacrifice can be sustained 'too long'. In another order of time, the martyrs of 1916 are entered in eschatological reality, in a permanent present tense that suffuses futurity with national meaning:

> MacDonagh and MacBride
> And Connolly and Pearse
> Now and in time to be,
> Wherever green is worn,
> Are changed, changed utterly:
> A terrible beauty is born.

The numerological structure of the poem enforces a sense that quotidian time has been mastered by a deep structure in history which occasions recurrence. For the basic pattern of the poem, based on the date of the Rising, is rendered twice (16, 24, 16, 24). Yeats's poem embodies recurrence in the sacral dimension of an eternal present. Yet the cost to individuals caught up by the process, which the poem makes palpable, is also sorrowfully, even agonizingly, acknowledged. For 'death' in 'Easter 1916' is not some counter in a saga of patriotic grandeur, as it seems to have been for Gonne. It is a cruel, ineluctable and consequently radical interruption of the minute by minute vitality of daily existence and of the uncertainties of future political possibilities: 'Was it needless death after all?/ For England may keep faith/For all that is done and said.' Yet for all that, patriots and poet have dwelt together at an apocalyptic moment, in a trans- formed order of time and being, which recalls the younger Yeats's conviction at the end of the 1890s that Ireland would be a site of magical renewal, when occult powers would elevate her to a transcendent spirituality: 'A terrible beauty is born.'

Yeats allowed twenty-five copies of the poem to be printed in 1917 for private circulation, though a letter of 5 December 1917 disclaims responsibility for the printing. The date appended to this version (the first published version made some changes to stanza two) was retained in subsequent publications. The effect is uncanny, for the precision of the date (25 September 1916) highlights how time has run on in the days and months since that fateful 24 April, to which the poem is a kind of monument, composed for future reading. It collapses back into the daily order of time from a period of five months when time has been experienced on another dimension. The twenty-fifth of September seems the day after 24 April, which has been brooded upon in arrested, sacral time.

In that everyday world there was much to confuse the poet who had so magisterially risen to the challenge of writing out in a verse his reactions to the Easter Rising as sacred, dramatic event. He sent the poem to Gonne for her comments, which were less than flattering. She was in no mood for a poem that could imagine England keeping faith. She bluntly informed him in November 1916: 'No I don't like your poem, it isn't worthy of you & above all it isn't worthy of the subject'. She resented the idea that sacrifice could turn any heart to stone and twisted the knife of her displeasure by letting him know that Iseult had had difficulty comprehending his work until mother had explained to daughter his 'theory of constant change & becoming in the flux of things' (*GYL*: 384) A month later Gonne plaintively enquired why the poet had not replied.

The truth was that their relationship, always a complex, sometimes a fraught affair, had taken a curious turn. For in the summer of 1916 Yeats had begun to pay court to Gonne's daughter Iseult, then twenty-two years old to the poet's fifty- one. Iseult had visited London in May, hoping to arrange for a passport which might allow her mother to travel to Ireland. Yeats had relished introducing her to his society friends. He sensed he might have had such a daughter had he lived the normal life of other men. In July in Normandy, when Gonne refused what was in all probability a *pro forma* rather than passionately intended proposal, Yeats began to feel Iseult might make a bride for him. He asked Gonne's permission to propose. The presumably bemused Gonne thought it unlikely that the young woman would take Yeats seriously, though Iseult, in her teens, had in fact made a precocious if naive proposal of marriage to the poet (Jeffares 1988: 217). In the autumn Yeats left Normandy, still nursing this possibility in his increasingly troubled mind, for Iseult had flattered him in a flirtatious dalliance. Yet some kind of understanding with Georgina Hyde-Lees had been arrived at in 1915, so with whom did his future lie, if with anyone?

The Easter Rising had, as Yeats told Robert Bridges in June 1916, upset all his 'habits of thought and work' (*L*: 614). It had also set in motion an emotional upheaval in his personal life that had him vacillating in his attraction to three women. Moreover he was uncertain as to where he would live in the years to come. He felt the call of Irish obligation to return to help sustain the cultural resources the Rising had imperilled in Dublin (he had seen the physical destruction on a visit to the city in June 1916). But he was no longer the youthfully vital man with high ambitions for his country who had established the Abbey Theatre in the face of many obstacles. The agreeable life of the English capital held real allure. In May 1916 he allowed his name to go forward for membership of the Savile Club. We can imagine that when he dined with the Ulster writer St John Ervine in Dublin in June in the company of Lady Gregory, the subject came up, for Ervine was a member of the Club, which enrolled the poet in late January 1917. As a London clubman, he cannot have been best pleased that his attempts to explain to English dinner-tables why Irish men and women had thought it necessary to rise in rebellion against Mother England, led to a suspicion that he was sympathetic to Germany in the Great War. There was even talk that his civil list pension might be withdrawn.

A state of depressed uncertainty in his personal life and genuine doubt about where his future might lie may account for the fact that Yeats did not choose to publish his poem on the Easter Rising at this time. This has troubled critics and biographers. Cruise O'Brien adjudges it a telling example of how Yeats mingled cunning with passion (Cruise O'Brien 1965: 240) in his public interventions as a writer. It is indisputable that Yeats would have been nailing his colours to the mast of a vessel, bound he knew not where, by publishing 'Easter 1916' in 1916 or early 1917. So he may well have been keeping his options open in a calculated enough fashion, in declining immediately to enter it in the public domain in the United States, which was still at peace in 1916. Yet Gonne's response to the poem may also have been part of the emotional chemistry at work, for he assuredly needed her good will if his suit with Iseult was to go anywhere. Furthermore, depressed and uncertain as he was, his social success in recent years in England had inclined him to believe that he could influence affairs of state in private conversation. In December 1916, in the company of Lady Gregory he lunched with Asquith at 10 Downing Street, just before the prime minister's resignation. The subject was the Lane bequest (Gregory 1978, vol. 1: 17). In October 1918, during the crisis about conscription being extended to Ireland, he would write to Lord Haldane, at the time chairman of a committee on the machinery of government, that were conscription to be 'imposed upon Ireland', it would 'be neither imposed nor met in cold blood' (O'Driscoll n.d.: 32). By withholding what would have been read in England as a highly partisan poem, Yeats had kept such channels open. Another consideration (which Tom Paulin and Pierce evaluate) was Lady Gregory's anxiety not to prejudice the case they jointly wished to press on the matter of the Lane bequest. Yeats and she planned their campaign in October 1916 and were in the thick of it by January 1917. And finally, one senses that the currents of Anglo-Irish feeling were so uncertain at this time that Yeats would have been chary of releasing his poem into such unpredictable waters.

So Yeats waited to publish his poem until 1920 and the War of Independence between Britain and Ireland, when the die had been well and truly cast and the publication of 'Easter 1916' could have its most decisive impact. From the turbulent year of 1916 the major poem he chose to publish in 1917 was not the rhetorically compelling public poem the Rising of that year had drawn from him, but the more private, nostalgic and poignantly lonely 'The Wild Swans at Coole'. Tellingly this poem echoes 'Easter 1916', completed earlier in the year. The poet in autumnal mood as befits the season, observing nine-and-fifty wild swans on the lake at Coole, in the fourth stanza (in subsequent printings this 'final' stanza became the third) confesses:

> I have looked upon those brilliant creatures,
> And now my heart is sore.
> All's changed since I, hearing at twilight,
> The first time on this shore,
> The bell-beat of their wings above my head,
> Trod with a lighter tread.

The swans exist 'Unwearied still, lover by lover', in a condition of undying 'Passion or conquest'. In what became the final stanza, the poet imagines them in their freedom, flown away, leaving him, as the poem's negotiation of past and present implies, in some future when the changes experienced in a personal autumn will be superseded by those of winter. Change in this limpid, drifting poem (the fact that the stanza order could be altered without breaking a sequence of logic, alerts us to its liquid, brooding introspection) involves no birth, terrible or otherwise, but a heavier tread, an older heart.

In 'The Wild Swans at Coole' Yeats recalls how he had first stayed at Coole nineteen autumns earlier. He must have known all too painfully as he did so, that his heart had been sore then too, since his mistress had left him and Gonne was unattainable. In 1915 and 1916 he had forced himself to relive the anxiety and strain of that time, for he had been at work on a draft of his autobiography, which he knew could be for his eyes alone, in which he frankly explored the emotional and sexual conflicts of a very difficult stage of his life. That raw, confessional text ends on the memory of how Lady Gregory in 1898 had offered him money to travel and had told him 'not to leave Maud Gonne till [he] had her promise of marriage' (*Mem*: 134). Yeats had replied 'No, I am too exhausted; I can do no more' (ibid.). Donoghue reports that pencilled in on the last leaf of the manuscript is 'a working draft . . . of the opening lines of 'Lines Written in Dejection' (ibid.). He also advises that Yeats completed this autobiographical work in late 1916 or early 1917. The poem, which may have been written in October, 1915, was obviously on his mind as, in his account of his early life, he reached that terrible impasse. Now in middle age he fears 'the moon/Can send me no longer the green eyed leopards and the wavering bodies/The green eyed leopards of the moon' (ibid.).

In his confusion and uncertainty (he may well have feared that his seriously muddled emotional life would once again, as it had in 1898, leave him to face the future quite alone), Yeats turned to philosophy to seek to understand himself and the difficulties that confronted him. He also hoped that the book which emerged from these studies and reflections could serve as a token of his sustained regard for Iseult. He still hoped she might entertain a proposal of marriage. Rarely can wooing have been conducted in so strange a guise.

By December 1915, when Yeats had been brooding on the significance of his encounter with Leo Africanus, he had completed a poem of abstract speculation to which he gave the obscure title 'Ego Dominus Tuus' (I Am Thy Master). This explored in a dialogue between two characters, Hic ('this' or 'the former') and Ille ('that' or 'the latter') the theme of self-division that contemporaneously found expression in the elaborately colourful psychic fiction of the letters to and from Leo.

When Yeats in January 1918 published *Per Amica Silentia Lunae*, the work of philosophic reflection upon which he had worked in the winter of 1916–17, he chose to print 'Ego Dominus Tuus' as a poetic introduction to the volume's prose content. The poem in its dramatization of a self-consciously divided nature, highlights the central preoccupations of the text as a whole: how can such a nature be made effectively one? what role does the Mask have in such a process? and does the impetus for unity of being derive from beyond the self in a power which can be depended upon to renew the creative energies of the ageing poet? The poem itself considers how the poets Dante and Keats, the former a sexual profligate by reputation, the latter 'poor, ailing and ignorant', both celebrated in their art images of reality the antithesis of their natures. While the poem is marred somewhat by its rather schematic duologue (Hic seeks to find himself, Ille desires an image the opposite of himself) and a crass stereotyping of the imagined poets to enter them in the dialectic, it does serve as a moving introduction to what follows in its acknowledgement that the poet's speculative concerns have their roots in personal crisis. There is too a note of longing for revelation, renewal, the rebirth of creative power. The poet knows that a superficial kind of writing is possible for those who have lived a life of action and fulfilment, but fears that the few who have sacrificed their lives to achieve a higher art have run terrible risks:

> The rhetorician would deceive his neighbours,
> The sentimentalist himself; while art
> Is but a vision of reality.
> What portion in the world can the artist have,
> Who has awakened from the common dream,
> But dissipation and despair?

The main body of *Per Amica Silentia Lunae* consists of two essays: the first ('Anima Hominis') on the individual self's relationship with its other, its mask; the second ('Anima Mundi') on what can be termed the collective unconscious, which reveals itself in images as if from a supernatural order of reality. Both share a preoccupation with the possibility of poetic sterility, which is associated with the figure of the romantic poet William Wordsworth 'withering into eighty years, honoured and empty-witted' (*PASL*: 43) or some simple piety such as might satisfy 'an old woman' (ibid.: 89). As counterweight to this anxiety, the poet invokes, in a richly associative and beautiful set of images, the hope that he will 'find the dark grow luminous, the void fruitful when I understand I have nothing, that the ringers in the tower have appointed for the hymen of the soul a passing bell' (ibid.: 24). The imagery here implies that revelation may involve a faithfulness unto death, but the metaphor of a mystical marriage and fruitfulness also invests the sexual longing that the text frequently intimates, with sacred, ritualistic dignity.

Through both essays a dialectic between dissatisfaction with the present and doubting hope for the future is explored in a sinuous, subtle poetic prose. This dialectic, and the richly metaphoric writing in which it is cast, makes *Per Amica Silentia Lunae* a deeply human document, for all the obscurities of its doctrinal postulates. We do not have to follow Yeats into his readings and rereadings of the seventeenth-century Cambridge neo-Platonist Henry More, with his metaphysical technicalities on the body as 'vehicle' of the soul, to comprehend the emotional import of this strangely beautiful, haunted text. For the poet's instinct to read the past and daily life as if they were redolent of portent and imminent revelation is rendered in this work as poetic apprehension rather than axiom. Idealist philosophy, occultism and psychic investigation become in *Per Amica Silentia Lunae* the stuff of metaphor. The mumbo-jumbo of the seance room, its tawdry psychic detritus, the abstract arcana of astrology, are reimagined in ample metaphor and given pathos by immediate personal ambiguities of feeling:

> I am persuaded that the Daimon delivers and deceives us, and that he wove the netting from the stars and threw the net from his shoulder. Then my imagination runs from Daimon to sweetheart, and I divine an analogy that evades the intellect. I remember the Greek antiquary has bid us look for the principal stars, that govern enemy and sweetheart alike, among those that are about to set, in the Seventh House as the astrologers say; and that it may be 'sexual love', which is 'founded upon spiritual hate', is an image of the warfare of man and Daimon; and I even wonder if there may not be some secret communion, some whispering in the dark between Daimon and sweetheart. I remember how often women when in love grow superstitious, and I believe that they can bring their lovers good luck; and I remember an old Irish story of three young men who went seeking for help in battle into the house of the gods at Slieve-na-mon. 'You must first be married' some god told them, 'because a man's good or evil luck comes to him through a woman' (ibid.: 31).

As his personal life became intensely problematic and old age began surreptitiously to encroach with its fears of creative and sexual impotence, Yeats produced perhaps his finest single prose work.

The fundamental dissatisfaction expressed in *Per Amica Silentiae Lunae* is with the heterogeneity and aridity of the self. The poet, who sensed his carefully constructed social existence as an Irish man of letters in the English capital had been set in question by the tragic events of 1916 in Dublin, who found himself caught not only between two countries but amid his feelings for three women, began *Per Amica Silentia Lunae* in a troubled, confessional mood. He makes public the kinds of morbid self-doubt he had communicated to his private journal in 1909. The intervening years, despite social prominence and increasing fame, had not significantly reduced a chronic sense of disabling self-division and failure. 'Anima Hominis' opens:

> When I come home after meeting men who are strange to me, and sometimes even after talking to women, I go over all I have said in gloom and disappointment. Perhaps I have overstated everything from a desire to vex or startle, from hostility that is but fear; or all my natural thoughts have been drowned by an undisciplined sympathy. My fellow-diners have hardly seemed of mixed humanity, and how should I keep my head among images of good and evil, crude allegories. (ibid.: 9)

This blends envy with a certain condescension as it contrasts the poet's own sense of his 'mixed humanity' with the unified confidence of others ('crude allegories' in the boldly etched outlines of their characters). He continues: 'But when I shut my door and light the candle, I invite a Marmorean muse.' Such an invocation in solitude of marble certitudes, when the poet states that all his 'thoughts have ease and joy' and he becomes 'all virtue and confidence' (ibid.: 10) inclines him to believe 'for a moment . . . I have found myself and not my anti-self' (ibid.). The main body of the essay refutes this assumption. Self-division is inescapable; indeed is necessary for a truly dramatic poetry. The poet echoes 'Ego Dominus Tuus' and its strictures on much contemporary verse-making: 'We make out of the quarrel with others, rhetoric, but of the quarrel with ourselves, poetry. Unlike the rhetoricians, who get a confident voice from remembering the crowd they have won or may win, we sing amid our uncertainty' (ibid.: 21). To find oneself, even were it possible, is not an option if one is to remain a poet.

This consciousness stimulates the poet to ponder how he had in the recent past sought to transcend the heterogeneity of the self in the adoption of the mask, in accordance with the doctrine he had formulated most explicitly in his private journal in 1909 ('Anima Hominis' quotes from it). Then he had imagined how Renaissance figures had 'made themselves over-mastering, creative persons by turning from the mirror to meditation upon a mask' (ibid.: 41). When he had had this thought, he confesses that he 'could see nothing else in life' (ibid.). Yet he judges now that, in seeking to act on his doctrine, his 'imagination [had become] sterile for nearly five years' (ibid.: 27). He admits: 'I only escaped at last when I had mocked in a comedy my own thought' (ibid.). The problem had been that such self-fashioning was not really an escape from self at all, for all his hope that a mask might allow him to experience how 'another's breath came and went within his breath upon the carven lips' (ibid.: 29). *The Player Queen*, by mocking what was after all still his own thought, opened, he now reckons, his imagination to a more wondrous possibility pondered with mingled excitement and doubt, frankness and caution in *Per Amica Silentia Lunae.*

Yeats had been at work on *The Player Queen* since 1908, when he had hoped the renowned English actress Mrs Patrick Campbell might play the main role. It had given him enormous trouble. 'Anima Hominis' speaks of Yeats tearing up hundreds of pages in his efforts to make something of it. It began first as a prose play of tragic import. In the autumn of 1915, however, he had reported how he conceived the idea of making it 'a wild comedy, almost a farce, with a tragic background' (*L*: 588, misdated). In the summer of 1916 he went back to it (incidentally the generic transition from tragedy to comedy offered a mirror image to the historical process imagined in 'Easter 1916', which tropes a miraculous change from social comedy to mythic tragedy). He had finished this new version by May 1917, making its completion roughly concurrent with the composition of the meditative prose work which refers to it.

The play is set in an indeterminate kingdom at a time of revolution. An actress in a travelling group of players finds herself at the right place at the right time. For Decima, the main character, is disinclined to play her planned role in a play about Noah and the Flood. She wants to play a queenly role and on the abdication of the true queen she assumes the part and wins over the rebellious subjects by the power of her performance. By acting the part she becomes the part. Yet for all the broad farce of the play, its air of gleeful self-parody, *The Player Queen* is no mere amused celebration of opportunistic self-fashioning. There are allusions throughout to an occult process determining the history in which Decima can seize her chance to play the queen. An age is being superseded by an age in a turmoil of events. The cycles of history are obeying a hidden agenda, symbolized – in the almost camp overstatement of the play's manner – by a great white unicorn which is rumoured to inhabit the royal palace. Decima recreates herself and is recreated as she meets a fate over which she can exercise only limited control. A power beyond the self is at work which the play acknowledges in its exuberant, highly self-conscious theatricality. The play's the thing, but the script is written by a hidden hand to a theme of fantastic, inevitable renewal.

Per Amica Silentia Lunae, in its awestruck, almost weightless prose (Ellmann speaks rather too disparagingly of its 'beautiful bottomless style'), attends equally on the chance of renewal and is earnest with the hope that a power beyond the self will make the wearing of a mask something much more than a stratagem to transcend mere heterogeneity. For in the seance room (experience of which is admitted with self-protective urbanity) a man may encounter a presence that seeks him out: 'The Daimon comes not as like to like but seeking its own opposite, for man and Daimon feed the hunger in one another's hearts. Because the ghost is simple, the man heterogeneous and confused, they are but knit together when the man has found a mask whose lineaments permit the expression of all the man most lacks, and it may be dreads, and of that only' (*PASL*: 29–30). So he can affirm, 'We meet always in the deep of the mind, whatever our work, wherever our reverie carries us, that other will' (ibid.: 32).

The second essay in this almost incantatory summoning of regenerative powers beyond the self, 'Anima Mundi', wonders if the seance room and its communicative dead offers assured entry to a storehouse of authoritative images which can so take over an imagination that a man thereby possessed will not know when he is 'the finger, when the clay' (ibid.: 88). For then he will speak as from the mouth of a god in the condition of stone to which the heroes of 1916 had attained by their act of self-sacrifice (in 'Anima Hominis' he asserts: 'I think the Christian saint and hero, instead of being merely dissatisfied, make deliberate sacrifice'; ibid.: 25). The poet's route to that goal is by way of continued, dissatisfied uncertainty. But the rewards may be supernatural: 'Once, twenty years ago, I seemed to awake from sleep to find my body rigid, and to hear a strange voice speaking these words through my lips as though through lips of stone: "We make an image of him who sleeps, and it is not he who sleeps, and we call it Emmanuel"' (ibid.). As Lawrence Lipking states of *Per Amica Silentia Lunae*: 'Yeats clearly wants a poetic renewal that does not depend . . . uncompromisingly on his own personal initiative' (Lipking 1981: 56).

In 1917 the stone in the midst of all – the brutal fact of Easter 1916 and the executions – hardened in Yeats's mind. In 'The Rose Tree' (dated 7 April 1917 in manuscript) he set aside his reservations and wrote a poem which drew on a long tradition of Irish revolutionary and patriotic balladry. Although Yeats here speaks in the voices of Pearse and Connolly, the act of composition and the poem's final stanza, which decisively concludes a debate between Connolly and Pearse on how Ireland might be revived to live again, indicate that Yeats knew the die had been cast:

> 'But where can we draw water,'
> Said Pearse to Connolly,
> 'When all the wells are parched away?
> O plain as plain can be
> There's nothing but our own red blood
> Can make a right Rose Tree.'

Like 'Easter 1916', this poem was withheld from publication at this time.

That Yeats believed the Rising, and in particular the response of the British authorities, had irrevocably altered the shape of things is evidenced in his play *The Dreaming of the Bones*. He worked on this in May and June 1917 and it was substantially complete by that August (though he was still polishing it as late as October 1918). An Irish version of a Japanese Noh play which climaxes with a spirit dance, its message was stark and uncompromising. In a place of mountain and sky, a young man meets a stranger and a young girl. The young man is a rebel who has fled from Dublin and the Rising in which he participated and hopes to make good his escape from Ireland by way of the western coast. He is led by the stranger to a mountain summit, where we realize he is in the company of the spirits of Diarmuid and Dervorgilla, who in Irish nationalist historiography were the pair of lovers who traitorously invited the Normans into Ireland to serve their partisan cause. They are the primal sinners in an Irish Fall which brought conquest and English rule. In Yeats's play, they are condemned to spend eternity in erotic longing for one another. Their lips can never meet and they cannot be released from their torment of desire unless one of their own race forgives them. The young man is tempted to do so, so affecting is their condition, until recognition dawns and he declares he cannot. Forgiveness, in any moral equation he understands, is impossible.

In *The Dreaming of the Bones* Yeats, through the Irish rebel, gave a voice to a congeries of feeling and ideology which had been in the making since the rebellion of 1798 (the date at which he and Lady Gregory had set *Cathleen ni Houlihan*). The young man indicates that he killed in the 'late Rising' not as a violent revolutionary, but as chivalric soldier who took no pleasure in killing British soldiers. His contempt is reserved only for Irish traitors. He is inspired too by a vision of English wrong, Irish potential and the efficacy of blood sacrifice.

Yeats thought *The Dreaming of the Bones* one of the best things he had done, but was consious that it was politically explosive. In June 1917 he told Lady Gregory that he thought it 'the best play' he had written for years but worried that it was 'only too powerful politically' (*L*: 626). He nevertheless contemplated magazine publication in October 1918, but advised that his editor might wish to accompany it with a mitigating note, to discharge some of its subversive energies: 'My own thought is that it might be published with an editorial note either repudiating its apparent point of view or stressing the point of view. England once, the point of view is, treated Ireland as Germany treated Belgium' (ibid.: 654). The problem was of course that England had treated Ireland as Germany had Belgium, not in the distant past, as this letter implies, but in 1916. Feelings were still running extremely high in Ireland and these had been intensified by the conscription crisis of April 1918 which had provoked a sustained campaign of Irish opposition and passive resistance to the prospect of military conscription being imposed on Ireland. A general strike had been observed throughout the country (apart from Ulster) on 23 April.

In truth the imaginative vision of Yeats's play *was* so powerful that its implications could not be rendered anodyne by suggesting that it was simply a dramatic expression of a point of view (as in a Shavian charade). For *The Dreaming of the Bones* is one of Yeats's most remarkable achievements. Its sense of life and politics, history and individual responsibility, implacable memory and forgiveness, peace and war, is seriously unsettling yet, simultaneously, exhilarating. And it plays well on stage, as many of his dramas do not.

In the play the world of Diarmuid and Dervorgilla is associated with an imagery of aristocratic beauty but also with decay and death (these dry bones may dream but will never live again). When Yeats spoke of it, in his letter to Lady Gregory in which he feared its political power, he referred to it as his 'Dervorgilla play' (*L*: 626), which perhaps indicates that he associated that world with a feminine sweetness in the past that a harsher present would cast aside (though he is referring to Gregory's own play of that name, first performed in 1907). The play's Chorus carries most of the work's metaphoric freight. For it is three musicians who invoke in their chants and songs a world in which 'wine ... fills to the top/A grey-green cup of jade/Or maybe an agate cup'. They echo a 'Music of a lost kingdom' and dreamily brood on images of sterility and loss:

> Those crazy fingers play
> A wandering airy music;
> Our luck is withered away,
> And wheat in the wheat-ear withered,
> And the wind blows it away.

In shocking contrast they also sound a brutal savage note, with images of raw bestiality summoning new energies:

> My heart ran wild when it heard
> The curlew cry before dawn
> And the eddying cat-headed bird;
> By now the night is gone.
> I have heard from far below
> The strong March birds a-crow.
> Stretch neck and clap the wing,
> Red cocks, and crow!

Dawn is breaking, forgiveness is a dream of the fading darkness and of a superseded world of compromised graciousness. The savage god is at hand.

The effect of this metaphoric antithesis is a chill sense of ambiguity of feeling and of tragic inevitability. The past is both beautiful and fatally corrupted. It weighs on the present as if seeking an absolution that cannot be granted. For the present is an outcome of that past, and its consequences cannot be set aside. Dawn, when invigorating energies break through this moral impasse, must be greeted with exhilaration, but such a redefinition of the context in which the play poses the issue of forgiveness, also terrifies. The play wavers poignantly between a mood of acquiescence before the implacable nature of the moral dilemma it dramatizes and mingled excitement and horror at the prospect that a new state of things now obtains. What is starkly certain however is that Easter 1916 is another event of definitive significance in Irish history, like the guilty lovers' crime. It stands as a stone in the midst of all. It no longer matters whether England keeps faith or not. Quotidian time is now after the resurrection time, as before it was post-lapsarian time. All changed, changed utterly.

Yeats first published this work in its early form in January 1919, the month, by strange chance, in which the first shots were fired in what became the Irish War of Independence.

As if to instruct himself that things had indeed changed irrevocably, in late March 1917 Yeats had purchased from the Congested Districts Board a Norman keep at Ballylee in County Galway for £35, which he intended to renovate as a home for himself and for a woman who might be prepared to share it with him as a wife. He had had his eye on this property since 1916 when Robert Gregory, his patron's son, had suggested to him that he should purchase it. There was a cottage adjacent, which could also be made habitable to allow residence, whilst more extensive work was carried out on the tower itself (the structure was sound, but the interior and roof required considerable work).

The poet had never before owned any property and this toe in the waters of proprietorship gave rich symbolic satisfaction. He was a Yeats acquiring title on a building in the Irish west, close to Coole. His father was especially gratified. He congratulated his son: 'It is all a symbol of the poetical life, a thirst for the soil, and you have it to the centre of the earth. It is in Ireland, another thirst instinctive, and therefore of the poet. And it is old, therefore again a poet's desire' (cited in Jeffares 1988: 219).

Yeats himself found the prospect of spending extended periods of time in the country very restorative. In a letter to Shakespear written the day before taking possession, when he confessed to not being 'in the best of spirits', he also remarked 'I shall never be in good health but in the country. I have been better since I came here than I have been for months' (*L*: 625–6). He observed the woods full of crabtrees in flower, the cherry trees. There were fruit trees in the cottage garden and a mass of flowers. He had taken enthusiastically to house planning with a Dublin architect who had visited the site, so that the cottage could be extended with kitchen, bathroom, sitting room and three bedrooms. A thatched roof would complete a rural retreat. In the tower proper would be two noble rooms. He was envisaging an architectural expression of his ideal social order: 'My idea is to keep the contrast between the medieval castle and the peasant's cottage' (ibid.: 625).

The experience of ownership and domestic responsibility seems to have settled Yeats somewhat at a perplexing period of his life. In June 1917, writing to his father of how he had recently been setting in order his system of belief (*Per Amica Silentia Lunae*, we must take it, was the work he had in mind) he tropes on homely labour: 'One goes on year after year gradually getting the disorder of one's mind in order and this is the real impulse to create. Till one has expressed a thing it is like an untidy, unswept, undusted corner of a room' (ibid.: 627).

Yet who was it all for? He told his father that his painter brother Jack could use the cottage when he wanted to paint Connacht scenery. He envisaged how he would store possessions there, so allowing him to reduce his rent on Woburn Buildings, since he would need less space in London. Yet in such plans and speculations one may detect a note of wistfulness.

In 'Ego Dominus Tuus' the poet had invoked his daimon:

> I call to the mysterious one who yet
> Shall walk the wet sands by the water's edge,
> And look most like me, being indeed my double,
> And prove of all imaginable things
> The most unlike, being my anti-self.

Lipking remarks of this passage that 'a shrewd reader of men, viewing these lines in 1917, might well have guessed that Yeats was looking for a wife. Indeed, *Per Amica* (dedicated to a lost love) proved his last fling at bachelorhood' (Lipking 1981: 54). And Foster (*AM*: 518–19) has indeed movingly revealed how this passage of the poem had its source in a moment in 1914 when Yeats had been reminded of his mystic marriage to Gonne, as he longed to meet face to face with the divine image of himself.

Soon a young bride would be walking by the stream that ran past the foot of his tower. She would bring more than he could have imagined when he hoped in 'Ego Dominus Tuus' for an encounter with his anti-self, who, as he had it there, would 'disclose/All that I seek'.

12

Occult Marriage

The circumstances of Yeats's marriage were less than auspicious, though he himself believed that the month of October 1917 was astrologically a most propitious time for him to enter on the hazardous experiment of matrimony. That his marriage to Georgie Hyde-Lees turned out as well as it did might indeed suggest that some higher power had Yeats's interests at heart; for the union was in fact contracted amid so much emotional turmoil and confusion of motive that spectacular disaster should have been the most probable outcome.

In August 1917 Yeats had visited Maud and Iseult Gonne in Normandy where he renewed his suit for Iseult's hand. She was moody, sickly from over-indulgence in cigarettes, flirtatiously affectionate but no more inclined to marry Yeats than she had been the previous summer. Her mother he found surrounded by the usual menagerie which included a laughing parrot whose forte was peals of hysterical laughter. By September Gonne herself was 'in a joyous and self forgetting condition of political hate' (*L*: 631) he had not hitherto encountered. In April, Florence Farr, the woman to whom Yeats once had felt he could tell everything, had died of cancer in Ceylon, where she had spent her final years as headmistress of a school. Yeats in Normandy, as he tried to prepare lectures which he hoped would help to pay for the renovation of his west of Ireland tower, must certainly have felt that the future would be a solitary one. For the gulf between his mind and Gonne's was strikingly evident. She was intensely anxious to return to Ireland to renew the kind of political activities about which Yeats had so often felt queasy. They quarrelled about whether London was a better place for Iseult to establish some sort of independent life for herself than Dublin. Yeats became finally convinced, though not without distress, that Iseult was fixed in her determination to reject his suit. In September they all travelled together to Southampton, in hopes that an onward journey to Ireland might be arranged for Gonne and her daughter. At the port the two women were subjected to a police search as suspected spies. Allowed entry to Britain they were refused leave, under the Defence of the Realm Act, to set foot in Ireland. Yeats wrote to Lady Gregory 'as you can imagine life is a good deal at white heat' (*L:* 632).

Over the next weeks the heat remained at the same febrile temperature. Yeats, whose feeling for Iseult combined besotted erotic fascination and avuncular concern, was gratified when a librarianship was found for her in London, for that significantly relieved him of the responsibility he felt for her and allowed him, in what must inevitably seem a rather cold-blooded reorientation of his marital intentions, to proceed with marriage to Georgie Hyde-Lees. Hyde-Lees had remained in the wings of his affections, as it were, during the episode with Iseult. He had proposed by the end of September.

The details and emotional significance of this very confused period in Yeats's life remain ultimately obscure. Harwood, who has examined such facts as can be established in detail, highlights the 'fear and indecision' Yeats felt as his amatory affairs gathered to a head. He felt he must marry, as his astrological chart advised, but he found it more than difficult to bring himself to the point of actual commitment. Harwood argues persuasively that a letter from his prospective bride's mother to Lady Gregory indicates ambivalence on Yeats's part about what he hoped would be the outcome of this new proposal of marriage. For on learning that Mrs Tucker (Georgie Hyde-Lees's mother) was adamantly not in favour of her young daughter (with the possibility, or so she believed, of important work in the Foreign Office awaiting her) marrying a man as old and as successful as Yeats, the poet apparently told her of his feelings for Iseult. And Mrs Tucker in turn commented darkly to Lady Gregory that fortunately her daughter had 'no knowledge of all this unpleasant background' (Harwood 1989: 157). Harwood adduces from this and from the way Lady Gregory forcefully tried to set her mind at rest on this score, that Yeats was 'perhaps unconsciously, trying to sabotage' (ibid.: 159) his chances of marriage with Hyde-Lees, as a result of emotional confusion and almost insurmoutable indecision. He comments: 'the parallel with his strong reluctance to consummate his relationship with Olivia in 1895–6 is obvious' (ibid.). Even if there was no such deep pattern in Yeats's confused behaviour at this time, the fact that he may have let slip in a letter to Mrs Tucker 'more than he meant to' about his recent courting of Iseult Gonne, in an effort to be 'honest – but not too frank, and sincere – but not too revealing' (Saddlemyer 1989: 197), does indicate a very uncertain state of feeling.

The higher power that brought this near fiasco to a happy resolution was not in the heavens, but at Coole. It was Lady Gregory who managed to bring the reluctant but lonely prospective husband to the sticking point, having first been persuaded that Yeats's intentions were in fact honourable, if ill-expressed. Some home truths must have been spoken. The mistress of Coole was particularly scathing about Yeats intending to marry Hyde-Lees in the clothes he had purchased to woo Iseult. It was also the redoubtable Lady Gregory who managed to persuade Hyde-Lees's mother that Yeats could be a suitable husband for her daughter, even though Mrs Tucker had sensed 'If Georgie had an inkling of the real state of affairs she would never consent to see him again, if she realised it after her marriage she would leave him at once' (ibid.). Yet it may be, as

Saddlemyer has suggested, that in all this toing and froing the mother did not know her daughter as well as she thought. Saddlemyer insists that Hyde-Lees was by no means 'the simple naive rebound'. It was she who went up to London, as Saddlemyer points out *without* her mother' (ibid.) for the publishing of the bans, which is certainly evidence of her determination to play a part in resolving an undignified muddle that had gone on long enough (since 1915 indeed, she may well have thought). Perhaps it also bespeaks a decisive calculation.

Yeats and Hyde-Lees were married on 20 October 1917 at Harrow Road Registry Office in London, with Pound as best man. As Georgie Yeats's cousin Grace M. Jaffe recalls, the bride's extended family learnt of the marriage only gradually, for the ceremony 'was conducted in almost complete secrecy' (Jaffe 1987: 144). It was well that the occasion was not public, though Jaffe in recollection may have exaggerated its clandestine quality, for strains in the couple's relationship surfaced immediately, bringing the union in its early days almost to the point of rupture.

Matrimony plunged Yeats into a slough of deep despond, in which he could only find relief in composition of two poems (initially named 'The Lover Speaks' and 'The Heart Replies'; subsequently published as the two part 'Owen Ahern and his Dancers'), which admitted the 'madness' to which his heart had brought him. The poet has his heart question of a young woman, in self-mocking despair:

'How could she mate with fifty years that was so wildly bred?
Let the cage bird and the cage bird mate and the wild bird mate in the wild.'

It is unimaginable that Yeats showed these two poems to his young bride as they honeymooned at the Ashdown Forest Hotel. It seems he sent them to Lady Gregory to hide away in safe keeping, referring to them, in the letter in which he promised them to her, as poems of 'the misery' he had endured immediately after his marriage (though he believed too that from that misery had come poems which were 'among the best' he had done). It is not difficult to imagine, although she almost certainly had not at that disturbing juncture read these poems of eruptive emotion and anxious fears of entrapment, that it was Yeats's young wife who most frighteningly felt the bars of a cage close about her. For she discovered, as her mother feared she might, that she had married a man who still hankered after another. Before her marriage she would have known of the poet's long-term love for Gonne, but she may not have realized how deeply absorbed and guilty he felt about what had recently transpired between himself and Iseult. Yeats still felt he might have waited for Iseult to change her mind. As her mother had foreseen, Georgie Yeats, aware of the insult to herself this implied and the nearly impossible situation it created, was inclined to leave her new husband without ado (Ellmann 1987: xiv). The fact that Iseult wrote to Yeats and that he replied to her must have deepened her alarm (*GYL*: 392). That she did not leave is evidence of a remarkable strength of will wedded to a commitment to the older man who had so confusedly, even irresponsibly, entered on marriage with her. It was she who would save their union and who would over the next five years build for her complicatedly shy, difficult, demanding, wonderfully gifted, psychologically vulnerable and sexually unfulfilled spouse, a domestic, emotional and spiritual life that was fundamentally to renew him as man and artist.

The volume of poems that Yeats published in November 1917, at the Cuala Press, shortly after their honeymoon ended, was a warning, if she needed such, of the immensity of the challenge she had accepted in choosing to remain with Yeats. For that book, which his sister and publisher noted 'Finished' on 10 October, ten days before the poet's precipitate marriage, was burdened with complicated feelings for the several women, other than George (as Yeats called her) herself, who had made his life so difficult for so many years. It was marked too by a gloomy sense that the visionary gleam of lunar inspiration, so full a presence in his early poetry, had deserted him for ever.

The title poem, 'The Wild Swans at Coole', set a mood of autumnal restropection for the volume as a whole, in which ageing and the diminution of visionary power are bitterly regretted. In 'Men Improve with the Years' the sexual implications of encroaching old age are acknowledged with wry despair, when the poet addresses a young beauty (the poem was composed in Normandy in July 1916):

> O would that we had met
> When I had my burning youth!
> But I grow old among dreams,
> A weather-worn, marble triton
> Among the streams.

The poet is now a stone monument in the living streams, foolishly dreaming that age has so improved him that he can yet win the desire of his heart. 'The Collarbone of a Hare' expresses, in an insouciant flourish, a desire to solve the problem of sexuality in a debonair promiscuity ('change my loves while dancing/And pay but a kiss for a kiss'), but the manner is more wistful than convincing.

The troubled water of sexual and emotional life is the central matter of the book. For *The Wild Swans at Coole* includes a suite of poems (a majority of them written in the autumn of 1915 and winter of early 1916) in which Gonne is the dominant presence. The effect of reading these as a group in the context of a volume in which old age and declining masculine prowess are bitterly resented by the poet, is to create a portrait of a man in deep personal crisis.

Yet to say that Gonne is a presence in the volume and in these poems is to simplify. The title of one of them 'Presences' should alert us to the fact that woman appears in these poems in various guises, more as the multiple figure of womanhood than as a particular person, though the biographers labour to establish specific identities. The poem imagines, in a haunted night of strange dreams, a revision, as it were, of Wyatt's courtly poem of sexual licence and decline, 'They flee from me',

> That women laughing, or timid, or wild,
> In rustle of lace or silken stuff,
> Climbed up [the poet's] creaking stair.

> One is a harlot, and one a child
> That never looked upon man with desire,
> And one, it may be, a queen.

The imagery of wildness and of queenliness predominates in the representation of woman in the volume. For the feminine presences invoked are summoned to a world of wild creatures: the swans of the title poem, a hawk who will not be caged, the mountain hare, dark leopards and holy centaurs, one of which is 'Drunk with the unmixed wine'. Robert Gregory's woodcut of a unicorn, printed here as a frontispiece (it was first used in the Dun Emer Press edition of *Discoveries*, 1907) introduces us to a dream territory of fabulous wild creatures in which woman figures as a shape-changing object of ubiquitous desire, at once familiar of 'heroic mother moon' and queen or nobly self-sacrificing lady in whose presence the poet sinks his 'head abashed' ('The People'). She is also the focus of mingled praise ('She is the foremost of those I would hear praised'), tender retrospection ('There is grey in your hair/Young men no longer suddenly catch their breath/When you are passing'; 'Broken Dreams') and bitter recall of a life frustrated ('And all because of some one/Perverse creature of chance'; 'On Woman').

Among the best of the poems in the volume, such full-hearted poems as 'Her Praise' and 'Broken Dreams' achieve a tone of richly expansive, conversational control. It is as if the poet has truly learned his trade, has mastered a medium. Yet it can only be employed to recall past fires ('I knew a phoenix in my youth'; 'His Phoenix') or to anticipate future acts of recollective praise. The present is uncertain. In 'The Fisherman' even an audience for the poet's work is in doubt. Death is a presiding spirit, as if to give deeper poignancy to the fading erotic charge which the book also registers in its evocation of female presences. The poem 'Upon a Dying Lady' was highlighted as a sequence on the contents page. That makes death's unkind attendance on a most gracious, stylish woman (the poem was that written about the lingering death of Mabel Beardsley, the tragic artist's sister) a central movement of the volume's variegated but significantly elegiac music. In knowledge of death memories are insubstantial as breath, a poem a mere 'mouthful of air' (the trope derives from *At the Hawk's Well*, the haunted play that was included in the volume). 'An image of air' ('Broken Dreams') is all that remains when death must be confronted, or when the unconscious overwhelms the conscious mind:

> always when I look death in the face,
> When I clamber to the heights of sleep,
> Or when I grow excited with wine,
> Suddenly I meet your face.
> ('A Deep-sworn Vow')

The second edition of *The Wild Swans at Coole*, which Yeats published in 1919 (removing *At the Hawk's Well*) added among seventeen new poems a number which gave notice that the experience of marriage to a living woman, as distinct from consort with an idealized image of an unrequited love, had had its very real effects. 'Soloman to Sheba' introduces a note of fulfilled, collaborative human feeling to a book that had on its first appearance been predominantly a record of emotion recollected in solitude:

> Sang Solomon to Sheba,
> And kissed her Arab eyes,
> 'There's not a man or woman
> Born under the skies
> Dare match in learning with us two,
> And all day long we have found
> There's not a thing but love can make
> The world a narrow pound'.

More cryptically, 'Under the Round Tower' is an epithalamium that exploits an imagery of erotic and occult implication. It imagines a 'golden king' and 'silver lady', partners in an alchemical marriage, in their round tower

> Bellowing up and bellowing round,
> Till toes mastered a sweet measure,
> Mouth mastered a sweet sound,
> Prancing round and prancing up
> Until they pranced upon the top.

Domesticity too had its pleasures. So 'In Memory of Major Robert Gregory' (the poem Yeats wrote for Lady Gregory's air-pilot son, killed in action on the Italian Front on 23 January, 1918 and collected in 1919 in the expanded edition of *The Wild Swans at Coole*) has the poet 'almost settled', pondering those who 'cannot sup . . . /Beside a fire of turf in th'ancient tower' with the new occupants of the house. Yet the air of domestic satisfaction that pervades this poem disguises how unconventional, indeed extraordinary, a thing Yeats's marriage had turned out to be in the early months of the couple's life together. 'The Phases of the Moon' (a complex poem of doctrinal speculation) and 'The Double Vision of Michael Robartes' (a poem of visionary contemplation) in the second edition of *The Wild Swans at Coole* lay new claim on the lunar powers that Yeats recently had feared had waned forever. The latter poem has the poet's persona Michael Robartes profess his gratitude, despite the ambiguity of the visions he has been vouchsafed, that he 'ignorant for so long,/Had been rewarded thus'. One senses the tone is expressive of Yeats's own profound gratification that the leopards of the moon had not departed forever, as some of the critics of the book had asserted. The English critic Middleton Murry had argued indeed, despite these evidences of rekindling poetic fires in the enlarged version, that Yeats's 'creative vigour' had failed him and that the title poem was in fact a swan-song: 'It is eloquent of final defeat; the following of a lonely path has ended in the poet's sinking exhausted in a wilderness of grey. Not even the regret is passionate; it is pitiful' (*CH*: 218). Murry had thought him lost among 'the phantoms of the individual brain' which 'left to their own waywardness, lose all solidity.... To anchor them he needs intelligent myth' (ibid.: 217).

The leopards of the moon had returned in the person of Yeats's young wife. Disturbed by her husband's mood on their honeymoon and anxious to distract him from his brooding on Maud and Iseult Gonne, she had attempted a session of automatic writing, only to discover a ready facility for that spiritualist practice which Yeats had found so fascinating in Elizabeth Radcliffe. It was a gift she was to exploit to remarkable effect in the early years of a marriage which might otherwise have foundered. For it quickly made her a daily focus of the poet's almost insatiable curiosity about the paranormal, about the possibility of spirit communication, and gave her the means by which she might direct, without obviously appearing to do so, a conjoint exploration of their relationship, especially as it bore on Yeats's past life as a single man.

To suggest that George Yeats exploited her gift in the interests of marital security is of course to risk a crudely reductive account of one of the strangest acts of imaginative collaboration in all literary history. The fact that the 'Communicators' (the overall term they settled on for the spirits who 'came through') insisted that the experiments take place without observers present, or 'unbelievers in the house' does encourage scepticism. But one can imagine that the worldly-wise young George fully recognized how risible what they were about together could be made to seem by unsympathetic critics, and accordingly made sure that their activities would remain private by communicating a spiritual interdiction on publicity. For what they in fact were about was something very remarkable indeed. From tentative beginnings in a honeymoon hotel in the Ashdown Forest in October 1917 the poet and his wife set themselves to a regime of punishing self-discipline, record, study and eventual publication in book form in Yeats's *A Vision* (1925) of their joint findings in elaborate and protracted Spiritualist experiment. What probably began as a wifely stratagem, at once sexually alluring and suggestive of hidden feminine powers (to which Yeats had always been susceptible) became a way of life – arduous, demanding, psychologically risky as well as fruitful. George Yeats herself later confessed to Olivia Shakespear that her first intention had indeed been to ' "make an attempt to fake automatic writing" ', but that she had found herself ' "seized by a superior power" ' (letter 9 July, 1928, cited in V. Moore 1964: 253).

From the start that higher power seemed to transmit significant matter. The first message, as Yeats informed Lady Gregory on 29 October 1917, counselled 'with the bird ... all is well at heart' (*L*: 633), which the poet took as an exonerating message about Iseult Gonne. Even more amazingly for Yeats, what George Harper identifies as the first preserved Script, that for 5 November 1917, focused 'on man's dual nature in the psychological polarities of sun and moon, objective and subjective' (*VPs* 1: 8). An image that expressed this polarity was particularly exciting, for the medium's control, who gave his name as Thomas of Dorlowicz, spoke of what Yeats in time took to be two horses 'one white one black both winged both necessary to you' (*VPs* 1: 56). Yeats recalled, as the communications continued, his friends' 'cross correspondence' of 1914. As Harper summarizes this strange moment of creative renewal in Yeats's life: 'Although the mystery of the amalgamation in Yeats's mind may never be resolved, we may be sure that as a result of the cross-correspondence ... Yeats associated the white and the black horses with the sun and the moon, which form the basic psychological polarities of *A Vision* ... 5 November was one of the most important days of his life' (Harper 1987, vol. 1: 11–12). So, from November 1917 until early 1920 when the predominant communicative method of choice became 'sleeps' in which a rich, mutual dream-life was recorded and explored, the couple worked through numerous sittings of 'automatic writing'.

Psychic experiment would sustain Yeats's interest from the ending of the Great War, through a war of independence and civil war in his native country, and survive the birth of a daughter and a son to the couple, who incorporated their small family into a vision of an occult marriage which at last gave the poet the kind of institutional authority as mage and poet he had always so sedulously sought. For the dynamic released between the poet and his spouse as they worked together to tap the energies with which their minds seemed to be in touch, partook of the kind of imaginative and personal empowerment he had sought in an occult order, in a poetic national theatre and among the serried ranks of the spirit dead that thronged the seance rooms of London, Dublin and Paris.

Since their marriage they had spent much time alone. Neither partner was really close to a circle of immediate family and they had not settled sufficiently to establish a social life. So on 31 December 1919 Yeats informed Quinn that he and his wife had been 'practically alone' together since 1917, with George every evening in his study helping him with his work (*VPs* 1: 47). In this isolation they had been taken up by the unfolding drama. That Yeats granted the serious possibility of genuine spirit communication from the dead at this time is evidenced, nevertheless, in his continuing attempts to contact the spirit of Lady Gregory's nephew, Sir Hugh Lane, with the practical purpose of learning the whereabouts of a signed codicil to his will. About this testamentary task Yeats wrote: 'I think that one should deal with a control on the working hypothesis that it is genuine. This does not mean that I feel any certainty on the point, but even if it is a secondary personality that should be the right treatment' (cited in Harper 1987: 175).

On the basis of such a hypothesis the Yeatses conducted a fascinating, wholly absorbing two-hander. The poet scrupulously, insistently, sometimes bullyingly, formulated questions of the spirits (he was sceptical of individual communications but was absorbed overall by the activity itself) and George Yeats, through her guides and controls, offered written replies of varying appositeness and revelatory significance. Sometimes the medium baulked, refusing to accommodate Yeats's demanding personality. She could also be brusque and dismissive in the replies she recorded for her avidly curious and obsessional husband. In such an emotionally perilous process George Yeats may not have been fully or consistently aware herself how much of what she was doing was consciously directed by her, or how much was the product of a highly developed capacity to allow her own unconscious mind expression in relationship with the mind of the powerful, masterful man she had married. As a person she possessed a keen sense of the histrionic, and was sensitively appreciative of all that was theatrical in life despite a powerful instinct for personal privacy. Margaret Mills Harper has reported ('"This Other Aquinas"', 13) that she was an avid collector of play-scripts and that she donated many to the experimental theatre group, the Dublin Drama League, of which she was a member in the 1920s. She was also a gifted linguist, capable of quoting freely from German, Italian and French (Saddlemyer 1989: 194), which indicates a capacity to imagine herself in various cultural settings. In the production of the Automatic Script her zest for the drama and the play of personality in different societies and eras could find expression. For the various lodgings she shared with her husband in the early years of marriage welcomed in their frequent sessions together, a cast of 'Guides' and 'Controls' who were implicated in the developing plot of their own relationship. The Guides had the oddly touching names of natural objects – Apple, Rose or Leaf – as if giving voice to the familiars of an intimately domestic exchange; the Controls bore the more portentous names, as if of mythical personages: Dionertes, Thomas of Dorlowicz, Ameritus, Aymor.

A drama of multiple personalities allowed George Yeats to attribute, and encouraged Yeats to attribute, what was transpiring between them to powers over which she could be deemed to have only partial if any control. So she shaped for herself emotional and discursive spaces in which to conduct both a daily life and a complex affective transaction with an older man whose powerful personality might otherwise have overwhelmed her essential privacy (Marcus 1988: 241). That much of what preoccupied them in their erotically charged exchanges involved sexuality, their own sexual life and Yeats's obsession with Gonne, George Yeats's desire for a child, probably gave an imperative and addictive quality to the elaborate drama they were enacting together (though at times, particularly during her pregnancies, two of which came to term and one which did not, George Yeats wearied of the whole enterprise).

At moments in the Script (published in 1992) and in their reaction to it, it becomes clear that they understood how they were engaged in a complex, collaborative activity. A Guide and a Control put it this way: 'This system is *not* preexistent – it is developed & created by us & by you two or you three now [the Yeatses' first child, a daughter Anne had recently been born] from a preexisting psychology – all the bones are *in* the world – we only select & our selection is subordinate to *you both* – therefore *we* are dependent on you & you influence our ability to develop & create by every small detail of your joint life' (*VPs* 2: 240). Margaret Mills Harper reports that Yeats considered this 'important enough to copy it verbatim into the large Card File he used to organise ideas from the Script in preparation for writing *A Vision*' (Margaret Mills Harper 1988: 53–4).

In December 1917, at the end of a traumatic year in his life, Yeats wrote to Lady Gregory from London to tell her of his happiness with George. He could report that George and Iseult had become friendly. George was to give Iseult a dress as a Christmas present. Yeats confessed, conscious that his new status as married man had changed his relationship with Lady Gregory: 'My wife is a perfect wife, kind, wise, and unselfish. I think you were such another young girl once' (*L*: 634). There is a hint here that he knows his patron and friend's feelings for him had perhaps been more than merely motherly. And he cannot have forgotten as he told her how his new wife had made his life 'serene and full of order' (ibid.) and had domesticated his rooms in Woburn Buildings, that Lady Gregory many years before had helped him similarly, when he had almost gone under emotionally, following his break with Shakespear.

It was fortunate that George Yeats numbered domestic organization among her talents, for marriage to Yeats was to test severely her gift for home-making. The property which Yeats had purchased and was renovating in Ballylee was not yet ready (any woman would demur at the idea of starting her marriage amid bricks and mortar). So their first year together was a peripatetic introduction to the kind of life Yeats had lived for many years and which he did not really seem inclined to abandon completely as a husband. After their honeymoon the couple spent a while in Stone Cottage. In December they removed to London, only to retire once more to the country, since the city was at risk of serious bombardment from German Zeppelin raids. From January to early March 1918 they were in Oxford at 45 Broad Street, in 'charming old rooms near the Bodleian' (*L*: 643). The poet had determined to live in Ireland but imagined he could make Oxford his English outpost, where he could establish a centre for his Noh plays. A letter from the poet Frank Pearce Sturm advised him that 'a machination of the stars' had taken Yeats to Oxford: the university city was 'about to become a great centre of spiritual learning' (*LTWBY* 2: 345). The spring then took the Yeatses to Ireland where they stayed in the depths of the Wicklow countryside at Glenamalure and at the ancient ecclesiastic site at Glendalough in the same county. In April they paid a visit to the recently bereaved Lady Gregory at Coole, still in mourning for her son. Ever bountiful, she lent them a house which she owned near their tower, where they spent the summer supervising the builders and carpenters.

Before his marriage Yeats had been in correspondence with a local builder about the renovation of Thoor Ballylee, showing a surprising capacity (which had served him well in theatre business as well) to attend to practical matters when that was necessary. His wife immediately shared this task with him and swiftly became expert on the wearisome minutiae of construction. Yeats, still a disciple of sorts of William Morris, wrote of his 'dream of making a house that may encourage people to avoid ugly manufactured things' (*GYL*: 393–4). By late September their home was approaching a habitable condition and they moved in together for two or three days. Gonne had generously suggested that they use, at nominal rent, a house on which she had a lease in Dublin. This was an elegant Georgian residence at 73 St Stephen's Green, the fashionable city centre square, where at the end of the same month they settled to await the birth of their first child, who was due the following February. Gonne's offer was all the more gracious since her own address at that time was Holloway Gaol in London. She had been incarcerated there since the early summer. For Gonne had been arrested in Ireland, to which she had travelled in disguise in early 1918, on suspicion of being involved in a plot with the German enemy. Her son Seán had spent part of the summer with the Yeatses.

In November 1918, during the great influenza epidemic of that year, the heavily pregnant George became seriously ill with pneumonia. The strain of this on Yeats probably helped to precipitate the serious quarrel which broke out between the poet and his former muse in that month. Gonne too had been ill in prison and after representations to various authorities, in which Yeats had joined, tuberculosis was diagnosed. She was released and promptly gave the slip to the unfortunate detectives charged with watching her. Once more she made her way in disguise to Ireland, to turn up on the Yeatses' doorstep, though she had grounds to consider it more her own than theirs. The poet (who had that summer written to her that they would move out if Gonne could manage to get to Dublin), anxious about the stress the discovery by the police of a fugitive on the premises would occasion his sick and pregnant spouse, refused her entrance. The quarrel was bitter but blessedly short. By the end of January 1919, following a brief stay in the Wicklow village of Enniskerry and at a spa hotel west of Dublin, the Yeatses had moved along the square to number 96 St Stephen's Green. In June 1919 Yeats finally gave up his rooms in Woburn Buildings in London, which for so long had been a focus point for his metropolitan life. That summer the Yeatses spent some time in their increasingly habitable residence at Thoor Ballylee. October saw them move to 4 Broad Street, Oxford, a house they had arranged to rent earlier in the year, on a six-month renewable lease.

It had been a happy thing indeed, given the perilous condition of his relationship with his young bride that George Yeats's first communication with the spirit world had brought Yeats conscience-salving news about Iseult. For the message that all was well with 'the bird' had effected an extraordinary transformation in his mood. As he informed Lady Gregory: 'The strange thing was that within half an hour after writing of this message my rheumatic pains and my neuralgia and my fatigue had gone and I was very happy. From being more miserable than I ever remember being since Maud Gonne's marriage I became extremely happy. That sense of happiness has lasted ever since' (*L*: 633). The evidence of the Automatic Script indicates, however, that he was by no means so comprehensively released by his marriage and George's message from the burden of past experience as this letter.

Essentially the Automatic Script involves two things. It develops the system of historical and psychological schematization, which was revealed, to a scarcely excited world in 1926, with the first publication of what would prove to be Yeats's most curious, idiosyncratic work *A Vision* (dated 1925 but issued in January 1926). It also explores in detail the poet's relationships with Olivia Shakespear, Maud and Iseult Gonne and with George herself in a protracted series of what amount to sessions of depth analysis that bespeak a profoundly troubled relationship with the past. There is of course a good deal of overlap between these two preoccupations. The effort to assess psychologically a wide variety of personages, both historical and contemporary, significant to Yeats in various ways and to varying degrees, involved both much debate not only about how George and Yeats judged the past, but about how they related to their own circle. It involved Yeats also in self-assessment and raised the fraught matter of why he had led so unsatisfactory an emotional and sexual life until his marriage with George. They spent a great deal of time pondering what they learnt were 'Moments of Crisis', which appear in the script as abbreviations: IM is Initiatory Moment, CM is Critical Moment, OM is tantalizingly left without gloss, and BV is Beatific Vision. They sought to understand their own and others' lives in relation to this developmental psychological model, with what they recognized as 'knots', analogous to the Freudian concept of complexes. Yeats certainly knew about the theories of current psychology and associated them with spiritualism. For H. W. Nevinson remembered him discoursing in October 1916 at Woburn Buildings on his earlier spiritualist experiments, and then on 'Freud and Jung, and the Subconscious Self, applying the doctrine to art' (Nevinson 1935: 340).

Among the early communications had been the following lengthy reflection upon the nature of the truly creative individual:

> The antithetical self is necessarily always the temptation because it offers a contrast to the primary. If the primary had no contrast to look upon there would be consequent absorption in a morality outside itself which would be accepted as a thing against which there could be no conflict – in the case where either the primary or *antithetic* self is almost predominant it produces the idiot or the fool as distinct from lunacy.
>
> Genius is implied in the conflict for domination – where the antithetical is *much stronger* but not predominant it has the practical force of the primary self to control it – it is when the primary self becomes submerged that lunacy ensues – And learn this
>
> The fool is born so – the predominant self submerges him from birth – nothing changes that
>
> The lunatic is gradually predominated by *one or the other* & therefore may *be cured*
>
> The fool is predominated by the *antithetical* or dream self from birth – the lunatic may be predominated *by either*   (*VPs*: 170)

The script was confirming what Yeats had sensed since the first decade of the century when he had developed his theories of the self and anti-self and of the Mask. The self was constitutionally divided but the conflicts within it could be a source of creative energy if antithetical force was channelled aright. The communications were expansively emphasizing the role of the antithetical self in true genius but reminding that the dangers of folly or lunacy could only be avoided in the exercise of the 'practical force of the primary self', which serves as a control.

The process of self-analysis with which Yeats was engaged with his wife was undoubtedly a risky business. That it was conducted without emotional disaster is a testament to the remarkable self-control and maturity of the young woman Yeats had so uncertainly wed. Before her marriage George had been accustomed to a fairly sociable life, despite the essential privacy of her nature. Her intimate friend Dorothy Shakespear had given her access to the advanced thought of intellectual and artistic London in the years before the Great War. At Olivia Shakespear's salon she could have met such luminaries of that world as

'Wyndham Lewis, the sculptor Henri Gaudier-Brzeska, the pianist Walter Morse Rummel, Richard Aldington, Hilda Doolittle ('HD'), William Carlos Williams, T. E. Hulme' (Harwood 1989: 130). She had too as a girl travelled widely in Europe with her mother, so we must assume that she was by no means unsophisticated or unworldly. She may well have gathered before her marriage that Yeats had been sexually initiated by the person who was now her aunt by marriage, the mother of her best friend. But she must have been surprised to discover that the pair had been close as recently as 1910 (about sexual intimacy between Yeats and Shakespear at this time, even the 'communicators' were reticent). It is a measure of the effectiveness of the 'Automatic Script' as a distancing device, which permitted the couple to address sensitive emotional issues on a non-attributable basis, that they were able to negotiate together a way of dealing with Yeats's complicated sexual history that brought them together rather than driving them apart.

For Yeats a great deal was at stake in his occult marriage. He was informed on 30 June 1919 that 'script depends on the love of the medium for you' (*VPs* 2: 323). The issue was whether or not in the therapeutic exchanges on which he had embarked with a loving, sexually vital, self-dramatizing young woman, he could release a new wave of creativity which would carry him as an artist over the shoals of middle life and the sterile rocks of encroaching old age. Could the antithetical in his nature flourish again without lunacy or vitiating folly? What now of the leopards of the moon? What of all those years of lack when he had sacrificed life and love to an image?

The nature and quality of the Yeatses' life together is a recurrent topic in the Automatic Script. George Harper has estimated that about three-quarters of the Script were devoted to 'highly personal matters' (Marcus 1988: 234). Sexual intercourse and family planning are introduced in ways that suggest George was anxious to instruct her less than fully experienced husband in the facts of married life, without undermining his male confidence. Significantly, Gonne is an object of sustained critique in the Script. In the complicated past lives summoned into imaginative existence in the text (in one Yeats was an itinerant preacher of Sodomite tendency), in which Yeats and his several women all seem to have shared in a repetitive, continuing psycho-drama, Gonne is accused of having hated George Yeats and with trying to destroy her.

Through the Automatic Script the impression gathers force that George Yeats was engaged, in years of isolated labour, in a complicated, perhaps only half-conscious, emotional education and restoration of her middle-aged husband, in the interests both of their marriage and of his continued artistic capacities. He was a man who had for many years buried a private world of feeling beneath the mask of a public pose, allowing it expression only in the dramatic utterance of the poetry that might dry up as the years wore on and mannerism froze the blood of what remained of a creative sensibility. George Yeats seems to have sensed from quite early in her marriage that sexual fulfilment and her husband's creativity were intimately linked in their relationship. She was not averse too to instructing him on the nature and necessity of female orgasm in a happy marriage and on the need to maintain his own sexual potency by repeated intercourse (Cullingford 1993: 111). But his imaginative survival profoundly absorbed her. In Oxford on 20 November 1919 this thematic of the Script reaches a revelatory and personal climax.

Earlier in the month Yeats had been exploring, with the help of Ameritus, how thought may be transferred not only from living persons to others but also from the dead. Harper sums up what was involved in this series of exchanges:

> It is, indeed, clear that any theory of automatic writing must necessarily be founded upon the assumption that thought can be transferred from spirits to humans through a living medium. . . . Having explored various extensions of this basic assumption, Yeats was now prepared to take the final leap: was it not possible for ideally endowed humans, say prophets and seers, to receive complexes of related ideas, including works of art, from the Anima Mundi without the agency of a medium or control? (Harper 1987 vol. 2: 346–7).

Yeats was anxious to know how such communication could occur and was exhilarated to learn that in dreams and at moments of life-crisis images are made available, not thought. The image comes with its attendant emotion. It is accompanied by thought, but it is the image that possesses the true power for it has a 'special character' bound up with 'spiritual thought or pity or desire'. Seeking clarification of all this Yeats asked his guide about Keats's poem 'Ode to a Nightingale'. He queried of its author 'Do you mean that his thoughts at time of composition still remain & can be transferred to us.' In reply came the tantalizing information: 'They remain because transmitted & *received* at time' (*VPs* 2: 474). With this encouragement the poet moved inexorably through a question and answer session of Socratic rigour to learn, in Harper's words, 'The work of art is a part of the racial unconscious; it exists for all time as an archetypical image in the world's memory, the Anima Mundi' (Harper 1987 vol. 2.: 354). What Yeats had claimed as truth in his essay on 'Magic' had now been sanctioned, as it seemed, by direct revelation. Though now the concept of the symbol was reconfigured in that of the image, which conjoined emotion and thought in its own characteristic mode of spiritual power. For Yeats such knowledge must have felt like a renewal of his poetic vocation in a call from beyond to once more credit dream as the source of envisioning creativity.

For several days Yeats concentrated on this revelation until Ameritus on 20 November expressed fatigue and stated that he felt 'Absolutely dried up'. What followed was one of the most intriguing exchanges in the whole series of transactions between Yeats and his curiously gifted spouse. The aridity of the control stimulates a session on the role of sexual mutuality in mediumship, which by extension seems to bear on the same force in poetic inspiration.

Yeats responds to Ameritus's 'dried up' condition by asking how there had in fact been script in the final three months of his wife's pregnancy with his daughter Anne, when, as he delicately puts it, sun in moon had been impossible. The control replied:

Depends on subject − in the present complex script it would be impossible because the sex element is part of the matter − There was no sex element in last Nov Dec Jan Feb Script

The daimonic relation is essential *after* both have undergone both CM's

The exchange continues compellingly (Yeats is addressing Ameritus):

3. Why especially after
3. to avoid a negative

4. To the intensity or the harmonisation of the force that is necessary to you
4. intensity now

5. It is wholly mechanical force that you lack
5. No − there is also lack in medium

6. Do you mean by that that you lack creative force
6. That is so but mediumship in this case is dependent on certain emotions & as well as that I lack creative force

7. What is that other element which sun in moon gives which is not defined as emotion or instinct? That element whose absence causes a lack in medium. [For 'sun in moon', that is, sexual intercourse, Yeats here uses the astrological signs]
7. Mediumship in this case arises because of certain sexual emotions − When those lack there is no mediumship

8. Is a long excited preliminary important in the present case
8. What is important is
turn over
[MW x 3] that both the desire of the medium and her desire for your desire should be satisfied − that is to say her desire & you as the image of her desire must be kept identical

9. Does a force or a truth come though the Image
9. In *this* case there cannot be intellectual *desire* (not intellectual interests) without *sexual & emotional* satisfaction − therefore without intellectual desire there is no force *or* truth especially *truth* because truth is intensity

10. Is the essential thing in emotion & sexual satisfaction the fixing of the image
10. *Yes*

11. Is that which intellectual desire seeks in correspondential relation to the image
11. *No*

12. Is it in some other indissoluble relation with that image
12. No its *essential* is the *self-moving* (*VPs* 2: 486–7)

It is striking that, even at this late stage in their transactions in Automatic Script, when George Yeats had largely settled for writing in her own hand, that she has recourse, in matters so intimate, to mirror writing (indicated by the abbreviation MW above).

Yeats must have fully understood the implications of what he was being told. For the concept of the Image employed in this intricate conversation was already that which had been employed to explain how great art comes into human consciousness from the Anima Mundi. Now he was being told that mediumship which bears its truth in the Image is dependent on a fulfilled sexual relationship in which both partners find satisfaction. It can scarcely have been lost on him that what was true for mediumship was true for poetic creation, for they both involve the Image. Indeed experience since his marriage would have instructed him, had Ameritus not, that mediumship, the Image and his own poetry were intimately related, giving added force to Ameritus's advice about the significance of a harmonious sex-life enjoyed by two mutually aroused partners as being necessary to creativity. For since that day in Ashdown Forest in 1917 Yeats's own creative work had been increasingly dependent on a collaborative engagement with his wife's mediumistic powers.

There were three ways in which husband and wife became collaborators in a joint artistic enterprise in the early years of the Yeatses' marriage. There were works, the principal of which was Yeats's play *The Only Jealousy of Emer*, which he sought to relate as he wrote them, to the material generated by their joint labours. There were, even more interestingly, poems which had their imagistic source not in Yeats's imagination but in that of his wife and in the communications of her guides and controls. And there were, in a way which would prove sustainedly inspirational for the poet, the poems written by Yeats which took for granted as the context of their intellectual and emotional engagement with reality, the psychological, historical and metaphysical system of thought he and his wife were so patiently establishing together, the system which would be given to the world in *A Vision*, under Yeats's name alone.

On 3 November 1917 Yeats wrote to Lady Gregory that he had begun a new Cuchulain play indicating that it was changing shape under the influence of what he had lately been feeling (unpublished letter, cited in Harper 1987 vol. 1: 6). January the 14th of the new year has him announce to the same correspondent 'Today I finished my new Cuchulain play' (*L*: 645). The intervening weeks had seen the poet and his wife earnestly engaged on the psychic experiment in which the play itself, *The Only Jealousy of Emer* had figured as a significant preoccupation.

The Only Jealousy of Emer, like *The Dreaming of the Bones*, is based on the Noh form. Music, dance, ritual action and masks are combined to explore elemental aspects of human existence in a reality that encompasses metaphysical realities and the presence of a spirit world. Where *The Dreaming of the Bones* had followed 'most closely the form of the Noh dream play' (Born 1984: 43), Yeats's new play for dancers and masked actors also had a Japanese source, but was also influenced by the kinds of stories Lady Gregory had collected in *Visions and Beliefs*, 'in which supernatural spirits seek power through possession of living bodies' (ibid.: 45). In the play a figure of Yeats's heroic alter-ego, Cuchulain, has been possessed by Bricriu, the mischief-making Celtic spirit of disorder and discord among gods and men. On stage there also crouches the ghost of Cuchulain, on the point of beginning his journey into the next world.

Cuchulain has apparently perished in his fight with the waves with which *On Baile's Strand* concluded. Queen Emer, his wife, is by his side. She in her wisdom has sent for Cuchulain's young mistress, Eithne Inguba, for she knows that the hero is not dead, merely 'bewitched', and that Eithne may help to save his life:

> I am but his wife, but if you cry aloud
> With the sweet voice that is so dear to him
> He cannot help but listen.

On Emer's instruction Eithne kisses the figure of Cuchulain, only to provoke Bricriu into speech from the mouth of the figure he has entered. A malign spirit of the Sidhe, Bricriu knows that the fairy Fand loves Cuchulain. Perversely determined to keep him from Fand, he offers Emer a terrible bargain. If she renounces any hope of future domestic, matrimonial happiness with her husband, then he can be restored to life. At the play's climax Emer is allowed to see Fand tempt Cuchulain in an alluring dance, offering him eternal beauty and an ecstasy of forgetfulness:

> at my kiss
> Memory on the moment vanishes:
> Nothing but beauty can remain.

Cuchulain hesitates, remembering not his many casual liaisons, nor indeed his young mistress, but the wife whom he senses he has lost. In the moment of hesitation Emer makes her act of renunciation. Cuchulain wakes as himself, wearing his heroic mask, but it is Eithne who claims him and it is in her arms that he seeks refuge from the terrifying experience through which he has passed in the region between life and death.

As a drama the play is certainly affecting. Its setting on a sea-shore allows the action to inhabit a liminal zone that can admit both human and spectral characters in a convincing imaginative space. Images of sea and storm, of frail sea-birds compared to a woman's beauty, make it an atmospherically charged theatrical artifact in which eroticism and magic seem to mingle in a world of shape-changing and spirit possession. And at its heart is a complex but very human relationship between a wife and a mistress and a genuinely dramatic dilemma. Indeed Emer's self-sacrificing act of renunciation raises questions for audience and reader alike. How does wifely love compare with that of the woman as *amor fati* (Fand), and with that of the woman who brings revivifying sexual dalliance (Eithne)? On his awakening, it is Eithne who claims that she has won Cuchulain back from the sea, though the audience knows that it was Emer who gained his release. Is a wife's love, accordingly, something that can sustain a man, though he doesn't know it, which involves the self-immolation of his spouse, her preparedness to give him up when he faces personal catastrophe in love of another? Is her only true enemy, the only focus of a necessary jealousy, the ghostly but intense desire for an *amor fati* and not for the passing fancy like those women who 'the violent hour passed over/Are flung into some corner like old nut-shells'? In view of Yeats's past life, and his future behaviour as a person willing to entertain emotional and erotic affairs with attractive younger women, while remaining a conventional family man (albeit of a somewhat semi-detached variety), such questions have obvious enough biographical point.

Yeats himself, however, saw in his play a great deal more than the dramatization of such fairly commonplace, though undoubtedly interesting, personal issues. For Yeats, deep in psychic experiment with his medium wife, *The Only Jealousy of Emer* bore in very exciting ways on the kinds of psychological, spiritual and metaphysical truths that were unfolding in their collective mind as they worked together on the Automatic Script. The play gave him a set of apparently archetypical figures in terms of which he could interrogate the Communicators, thereby investigating, at a remove, as it were, his own troubled experience of selfhood. The characters of his play became symbolic counters in the elaborate experiment he was conducting concurrently with its composition.

Between November 1917 and January 1918 the broad outline of what was to become the system of thought adumbrated in *A Vision* was also taking shape in the Automatic Script. For the possible range of human personality type was being categorized according to a system based on twenty-eight phases of the moon. Differences in personality were being attributed in part to varying degrees of subjectivity and objectivity at work in the individual. This involved the Yeatses in placing figures such as Shakespeare, Socrates, Milton and an idiosyncratic list of lesser literary and artistic figures, together with notable historical personages, in a phase of the moon that accorded with a personality type on the scale of subjectivity and objectivity. Friends and aquaintances were similarly categorized, as were those with whom Yeats had had his most intimate relationships: Maud and Iseult Gonne, Lady Gregory, George herself. Yeats was allowed to share phase 17 with the great poet Dante, as well as with the lesser English lyric poet Landor. Characters from *The Only Jealousy of Emer* (and some of the imagery of the play derives from the Script) were also accorded their respective phases of the moon, Cuchulain at 12, Eithne at 14, Fand at 16 (and at 15, the full of the moon, when subjectivity is at its greatest, where only soul as perfect beauty can exist), Emer at 18 (Harper 1987 vol. 1: 126). It is furthermore clear that these characters share their categories with Yeats, Iseult, Maud and George respectively, so that Yeats's play must be read, if we are to follow its author's intentions, as a ramifying study of archetypical representations of himself and the three women he has loved in elaborate interrelationship. As such the play becomes a detailed attempt at self-analysis based on permutations of category (among which are included the four elements, points of the compass, planets, astrological signs, parts of the body) employed by a man who understands how complicatedly divided personality in fact is. To begin to comprehend personality will require, it seems, a system of categorization which is capable of identifying various patterns among a large number of variables and intriguing permutations.

There is in all this a curious impression of two minds absorbed in a high degree of systematic abstraction, which suggests that Yeats may have become absorbed by the elaboration of the system itself, whatever its implications. Margaret Mills Harper, who has studied the Yeatses' collaboration intensively, has observed that 'the quality of the System that shows George's contribution most clearly is its diagrammatic character. As we know from numerous occult notebooks and papers, W. B. could cast a horoscope, trace Hebrew letters or astrological symbols, or copy a kabalistic drawing with the best of his fellow adepts in the Order of the Golden Dawn. In his schooldays, he had been keen on mathematics. Nevertheless, charts and numbers seem to have been George's passion. She concludes: 'In general, my sense is that W. B. provided images and literary allusions while George was interested in pinning information down by means of historical dates, lists, charts, or other organizational methods' (Margaret Mills Harper, 1997: 16–17).

What Yeats also supplied was an intense degree of personal fascination, as if he recognized almost from the first that his wife's powers offered him a last chance to come to terms with the meaning of his experience in a way he had never done before. So while one is struck in the Vision Papers by the ramifying detail of the System which is coming into existence in its pages, one is also conscious how much emotion on the poet's part energizes the enterprise. There is a fierce intentness, for example in Yeats's interrogations as he seeks to relate the characters of *The Only Jealousy of Emer* both to the emotional entanglements amid which the Automatic Script came to birth and to the System that the script was making available to him.

The Automatic Script was also supplying images and themes for the poems upon which the poet was at work in these exciting and renewing years. The spirits had informed Yeats that they had come to give him 'metaphors for poetry' (*PFEP.* 12) and it seemed they were keeping their promise. A session in Dublin of the Automatic Script for 7 January 1919 suggests how great was their largesse. George sketched a diagram of the ruined church and castle at Cashel in Co. Tipperary, surrounding it with symbolic objects. Yeats used such symbols in two poems ('Another Song of a Fool' and 'The Double Vision of Michael Robartes') which he was to include among the final poems of the second edition of *The Wild Swans at Coole*, and in a third poem ('Towards Break of Day'), which was to be collected in his next volume *Michael Robartes and the Dancer* (1921). The poems so generated reflect the imagistic relationships, like those in George's diagram between an eye, a book, a hand holding a rod and a butterfly, a Maltese cross carried by a bird (Albright 1992: 600). In a further example of such creative interchange 'Another Song of a Fool' employs some of these images to state:

This great purple butterfly,
In the prison of my hands
Has a learning in his eye
Not a poor fool understands.

Once he lived a schoolmaster
With a stark denying look,
A string of scholars went in fear
Of his great birch and his great book.

The session of 7 January had begun with a question in George's hand 'Why have you made this drawing?' Thomas's reply seemed intended for Yeats:

You are empty – drained dry – the true moment for vision – a new influx – must come this time from the past – you are drained dry from looking into the future & exhausted by the present – passivity is dangerous in the present & *future so go to the past* – a historical & spiritual past – the church the *Castle on the hill*   (*VPs* 2: 162)

There then follows the mysterious communication

Dreams
I gave you dream each – now I give you two more in one – at
Castle
Hand & eye
waterfall & stag
Hand – eye
waterfall
touch – desire to grasp
eye – desire to see
possessive hand – desiring eye   (*VPs* 2: 162)

There is doubt about the exact date of composition of Yeats's poem 'Towards Break of Day', but what is clear is that the poem itself, originally titled 'The Double Dream', is the result of discussion between husband and wife of their complementary dream life and that it employs imagery which the Automatic Script was suppying to the poet. The poem begins

Was it the double of my dream
The woman that by me lay
Dreamed, or did we halve a dream
Under the first cold gleam of day?

One implication of this is that the completed poem itself, with its images of waterfall and stag, touching and seeing (possessive hand that touches and desiring sight that seeks its ideal), drawn from the Automatic Script and from the couple's individual dreams, is itself a dream made whole (the poem suggests in its apposition of touch and sight that the couple had somehow each dreamed half of the same dream) in an act of collaborative creativity.

The main aesthetic consequence of Yeats's obsessive psychic experimentation in the early years of his marriage was a marked reorientation of his poetry towards present vital, challenging experience instead of towards the past and its disappointments and failures in love, which had been so much in his mind since 1914, when he had begun to compose his autobiography. It is present apprehended, however in the kind of visionary, phantasmagoric terms which had only rarely (in 'The Cold Heaven' for example) seemed possible to him since the publication of *The Wind Among the Reeds* in 1899. This can render it as troublingly obscure as it is hauntingly mysterious. Poems like 'The Double Vision of Michael Robartes' and 'The Phases of the Moon', in their direct exploitation of material and concepts derived from the Automatic Script and accompanying dreams and meditations, risk on the one hand theological tedium and on the other absence of communicable meaning. Yet the two decades since 1899 in which Yeats's poetry had laboured to give his diction a tougher edge and his rhythms a more urgent, supple movement, had equipped him to begin writing in his fifties a visionary and metaphysical verse that could conjoin abstract concepts and occult learning with a sense of bodily reality and immediately experienced historical processes. In his final two decades of life Yeats was to write the body (both male and female) in history, in a way he had never done before. And it was a history which, for all its grim contingencies in a period of Anglo-Irish warfare and postwar European crisis, could be comprehended in terms both exhilarating and terrifying, derived from a system whose authors were in eternity. It is almost certainly the case that Yeats could not have coped as an artist with the demands both of old age and the period of crisis in which he was living, in the extraordinary way he did, had not his wife's Communicators brought him their metaphors for poetry and supplied him with the basis of a system of thought and feeling which offered an interpretative myth whereby he could seek imaginative meaning amid the cumulative indignities of bodily decrepitude. To the institution of an occult marriage Yeats as poet owed a great debt, as do we his readers, who discover in his later writings a body of work which confronts in its heroic and radically disturbing fashion, the crisis faced by the religious imagination in the modern world.

13

The Weasel's Tooth

In the years in which Yeats and his wife were so assiduously at work to schematize both history and human psychology Europe and Ireland were in the midst of a revolutionary series of political reconfigurations. The imperial age had begun to disintegrate following the immense blood-letting of the Great War and the uneasy armistice of 1918 which had ended it. Revolution in Germany hastened the armistice which concluded the war in November. In the east, Austro-Hungary was in disarray in the wake of the collapse of the Hapsburg monarchy. In Russia a spectacular revolution that had broken out in November 1917, which was to change the map of Europe for the rest of the century, quickly gave way in the summer of 1918 to a civil war in which the victorious Allied powers in the Great War intervened unsuccessfully to defend ancient authority. In Ireland an anti--imperial struggle, which was to serve as a model for many subsequent anti-colonial movements around the world, was conducted by a small guerrilla army with an intensity and ferocity that was an immediate effect of the intimate and local scale of the military operations engaged in by the belligerents. In the United Kingdom the Reform Act of 1918 greatly expanded the parliamentary electorate (women over thirty would vote for the first time that year in the December General Election).

In Ireland the memory of 1916 still burned bright in the popular mind. The recent anti-conscription movement also gave a keen edge to political life. In the General Election the country returned a majority of Sinn Féin candidates who had stood on an abstentionist, separatist and republican ticket. They quickly established a seccessionist assembly (Dáil Éireann) in Dublin in January 1919, under whose putative authority (although it was suppressed in the autumn of 1919 and could only meet clandestinely and infrequently) an Irish Republican Army (the offspring of the IRB and the Irish Volunteers who had planned 1916) waged a campaign of violence and intimidation with the intent of undermining the British capacity and will to govern the island. Force was met with force, atrocity with atrocity. The British recruited a notorious auxiliary force of English recruits to reinforce an over-stretched Royal Irish Constabulary, which was responsible for law and order outside Dublin. The repressive viciousness of the force (dubbed the Black and Tans on account of a uniform which combined constabulary dark bottle-green with military khaki) in the districts in which they operated well beyond any rules of war, radicalized even conservative elements of the Irish population who might not have felt unambiguously in favour of the revolutionary implications of Sinn Féin's constitutional programme. By 1920 local elections had given Sinn Féin considerable political control over Ireland outside the nine northern counties of the province of Ulster. The moderate Home Rule policy of the Irish Parliamentary Party was swept from the local stage it had occupied in Ireland since 1900. In the military field terror and counter-terror achieved an ongoing stalemate between the British and Irish combatants. In February 1920 the British government began to set in place legislation which would begin to permit two devolved parliaments to be established, one in Dublin the other in Belfast. The government thereby signalled, in a way which would prove fatally contentious in the south of the country, that the foreseeable future would effectively be a partitioned one. Fighting continued in the south until July 1921 when a truce was arranged to allow for a period of negotiations.

Against such a dramatic backdrop, the Yeatses' private preoccupations with the occult patterns of history and the fate of the soul in the phases of the moon can seem at once a heightened, nervously excited reaction to a turbulent and dangerous period and an episode of almost quixotic emotional self-inflation. As history made and remade itself about them in 1919 and 1920 their days were filled with their occult work and an obsessive attention to portents, astrological charts, signs of imminent revelation. By 1920 and in the years immediately following, as George Harper and R. A. Martinach have remarked, Yeats's 'house must have been redolent with the smell of roses, violets, incense, roast apples and burnt feathers (all of which had become part of a code), and clamorous with the sound of owls, cats, whistles and spirit voices which are frequently mentioned' (*VPs* 3: 3). A typical entry in one of Yeats's *Sleep and Dream Notebooks* describes a late summer night in Oxford in 1920:

> After Dionertes had been speaking for some time there was a bird's cry which he said was an Owl, & he made me keep silent that he might listen but it did not come again. A little after the clocks began to strike 12; and he asked me what sound that was. I told him & again he asked me to keep silent. When the last strike was finished he said 'Sounds like that are sometimes a great pleasure to us'. (*VPs* 3: 41)

The ambiance of the Yeatses' home life, where magic, obsessively courted as a daily, lived experience, was colourfully caught by the youthful C. S. Lewis when he wrote to a friend of visiting the poet and his wife at Broad Street, Oxford in March 1921:

> It was a very funny room: the light was supplied by candles, two of them in those 6-ft. candle-sticks that you see before the altar in some English churches. There

were flame-coloured curtains, a great many pictures, and some strange foreign-looking ornaments that I can't describe. The company sat on very hard, straight, antique chairs: except Mrs Yeats who lay on a kind of very broad divan, with bright cushions, in the window. (Hooper 1979: 286)

In this stageily arranged interior the poet's talk 'was all of magic and apparitions'. Lewis commented that the effect of Yeats's presence was to impress on him that a great deal of the sort of thing he had glimpsed *chez* Yeats, was going on all round him. He would have been even more surprised by the Yeatses' *ménage* had he known that Mrs Yeats was then pregnant with a son whom they would name Michael. He came into the world on 22 August 1921, with the parental expectation that, as an incarnation of an ancestor, he would complete the ideal tetradic family of occult tradition. The Yeatses had been convincing themselves for some time that AE's 1896 prophecy of an Irish avatar, was about to be fulfilled.

The Yeatses had in fact been disappointed in 1919 when the birth of their first child, Anne, on 26 February, had revealed that she could not be the long-awaited avatar. Thomas as spirit communicator admitted about three weeks later that '*we cannot influence sex*' – a moment in the overheated, sexually charged, self-immersed emotional transactions (similar in kind to those recorded in the annals of Freudian and Jungian analysis) of these years that suggests to what degree Yeats and his partner were risking, in protracted psychic experiment, a credulous *folie à deux*.

Yet their working relationship, with its ambition, dedication and occasional foolishness, was not only renewing the imaginative energies of the poet in middle age, while giving him a system of thought and related images to explore experimentally in verse and drama. It was also the direct source of poems which, intimately implicated with the detail of the couple's mutual psychic studies as they were, nevertheless bore portentously and disturbingly on the many crises unfolding simultaneously in Europe and Ireland.

In Galway in April 1918, during their first visit with Lady Gregory, the Yeatses were engaged together (though George Yeats seems to have been hesitant about such psychic work being done at Coole, which was certainly not her territory) in an attempt to discover whether the image of a funnel, which they had established earlier in analysing the conflicts in human personality, could also apply to history. They were told it could and through a series of complicated questions and answers with illustrative diagrams, began to develop a cyclical theory of change, with history as an ascending and descending spiral of energies that recoil from a centre. An ascending period is marked by democratic collectivism, a descending period emphasizes the individual. Periods so affected can equivalently be identified according to the lunar symbolism of the phases of the moon. The birth of Christ was read off in this complex act of historicism as a key date. It was at phase 2 and 27 simultaneously. The year 1918 becomes a phase 12, which Aymor, one of the instructors then at work with the Yeatses, characterized as a period of 'violent reaction against central power – throwing over of kingship & centralised rule – going towards individual subjectivity' (*VPs*: 1: 422). It emerges that the probable unit of history is a thousand years, which allows Thomas, putting Aymor right about some of the confusions of the system, to assess 1918 as a time when 'the world's civilization is apart from the centres that is why aymore mistook / Christ at same place as before' (*VPs*: 1: 428).

Metaphors and ideas that would form the basis of a famous poem were coming directly from the instructors. For 'The Second Coming', composed in January 1919 and published in November 1920, would begin, the funnel having being replaced as term by 'gyre',

> Turning and turning in the widening gyre
> The falcon cannot hear the falconer;
> Things fall apart; the centre cannot hold.

And in the rest of the session of 16 April 1918 and on the following evening at Coole, Yeats's consciousness that he was living through a period of fundamental change was encouraged by the responses Thomas gave to his insistent interrogator. Is a new incarnation imminent? Must not the two hundred years ahead resemble those before the birth of Christ? Will the period of disturbance last until 1950? Will war be followed by civil war? And perhaps most troublingly, for a poet who increasingly found a democratic age rebarbative: 'Is not world as spiral ascends getting farther from reality that being central line' (*VPs* 1: 433). All the answers implied that a time of terrible chaos was at hand before a new incarnation would inaugurate a new era.

The manuscripts of Yeats's poem of international disorder and prophetic summoning of a new incarnation to succeed the 'mere anarchy' of the present, refer to events of the previous year. They make implicit reference to the Treaty of Brest-Litovsk of 3 March 1918, which envisaged control of semi-autonomous Baltic states and the Ukraine by postwar Germany. The specificity and reaction of the poem's early drafts is suggested in fact in cancelled lines such as 'The germans to Russia to the place' and 'And there's no Burke to cry aloud no Pitt' (Stallworthy 1963: 16–25). January 1919, when Yeats finished the poem, was the month in which the Spartakist Uprising was put down with much blood in Germany; civil war raged in Russia with the Franco-British Expeditionary Force enforcing a coastal blockade. In Paris a general Peace Conference opened on the twentieth of the month. Next day Dáil Éireann met for the first time in the Mansion House in Dublin. That day two members of the Royal Irish Constabulary were murdered in County Tipperary by a group of Volunteers. This action, though unsanctioned by any higher Irish authority, in retrospect came to be seen as the first blow struck in the guerrilla War of Independence. Yeats spent much of this monumental month questioning his instructors about the gyres, cycles of history, the birth of Christ and the coming avatar soon to be revealed in the person of an expected son (George Yeats was eight months pregnant with Anne). On 24 January Yeats asked 'Is the Sphynx . . . a form of love?' (*VPs* 2: 190) Subsequent questions reveal the poet pondering the reversals of history as a Nietzschean transvaluation of values of the kind addressed with awesome phantasmagoric power in the 'The Second Coming'. The Sphinx is the central image in a vision of epochal parturition.

Yeats withheld this poem, with its blank verse urgencies and authoritative rhetorical tone, from publication for twenty-two months, perhaps because the birth of Anne Yeats in February 1919 did not bring forth the avatar of expectation. A future child might be the new Messiah. So Yeats between February and June 1919 composed for his first child the tender, anxious poem 'A Prayer for My Daughter' which prayed, in fear of a future 'Dancing to a frenzied drum', that her life would be one in which a bridegroom would 'bring her to a house/Where all's accustomed, ceremonious' ('The Second Coming' had recoiled in horror from the spectacle of 'the ceremony of innocence' being drowned in a blood-dimmed tide). 'A Prayer for My Daughter' was first published in November of the year of Anne Yeats's birth.

Whatever the reason for Yeats's delay in publishing the poem written in the last weeks *before* Anne's birth, the postponement meant that when it was eventually published, 'The Second Coming' seemed to bear more on Irish affairs than on the general European crisis which had been its primary inspiration (Malcolm Brown 1972: 170–1). Its association with the birth of his own child was occluded, though this was to be restored when the poems were published sequentially in Yeats's volume of 1921 *Michael Robartes and the Dancer*, the poem of general apocalypse being followed therein by the more personal work. Had, however, 'The Second Coming' been published in the spring of 1919 it would have seemed a poem of nearly unambiguous revulsion from current revolutionary violence and the overwhelming of ancient aristocratic courtesies that only a new order might restore after a terrible period of transition. When the poem did in fact appear the atrocities of the Black and Tans, committed in the name of established authority, which had taken place in the intervening twenty-two months, meant that the poem could be read as an Irish cultural nationalist's horrified reaction to the months of terror in Ireland, in which the poet sought to maintain a prophetic voice in the face of an outbreak of atavistic political savagery in his own land. The interpretative emphasis could now fall not on the reprehensible acts of European revolutionaries as viewed by an alarmed social conservative, but on the Irish *imbroglio* as the tide of a new flood, of politicized anarchy amid which the best lacked 'all conviction' while the worst (on both sides) were filled with 'passionate intensity'.

Though the publication context of 'The Second Coming' initially made it seem a response to local horrors, its mythic generality has made it perhaps the single best known of Yeats's later poems ('increasingly this is seen as Yeats's central poem'; Bloom 1970: 317). It has been celebrated by most critics and many readers as a prophetic anticipation of the monstrous unfolding of twentieth-century world history. Its images have gone into popular consciousness, its resonant phrases into the language. On the level of its myth-making, however, Bloom has entered a stern caveat (ibid.: 127–325). He judges the poem flawed since it illegitimately exploits the Christian expectation of the Second Coming of Christ to express the poet's hopes and fears about a second birth of 'the antithetical divinity or spirit'. From this imaginative sleight-of-hand knotty interpretative problems derive, which Bloom addresses with considerable command. Though it is not clear he intended it, Seamus Deane has recently supplied a compelling rereading of 'The Second Coming' which answers Bloom. For in Deane's account it is accepted that of course the poem refers not to a second coming in the Christian sense but to a second birth of the avatar and he accepts with Bloom that Yeats relished the prospect considerably: 'Yeats spent so much of his life in the pursuit of those deep energies of the occult, almost cancelled in the modern world, that he could scarce forbear to cheer their sudden arrival' (Deane 1997: 175). Where Deane's reading surpasses Bloom's is in his awareness of how Yeats's contradictory emotions of horror and welcome for the 'rough beast' of the poem, are ultimately visible in its 'inner dialogue between a highly present male voice and an almost wholly concealed female one' (ibid.: 179). And he understands too how this mythologically expressed conflict bears on the local context. For he sees 'The Second Coming' as an exploration of the possibility that what had been unleashed by the Easter Rising may be a struggle between revivifying and destructive energies, between the demonic and the bestial. Deane sums up, arguing that Yeats is asking a troubling question in this poem of History's repetitious revelations (its second comings): 'Can the Bestial find a Bethlehem in which it can be born again as the demonic? Can the mob be born again as a people, as a nation? That would truly be a second coming. It became known as Fascism' (ibid.: 180).

Since the Easter Rising Yeats had indeed pondered the consequences of the bloodletting. In May 1918, at the height of the conscription crisis, he had written in a letter of the dangerous condition of feeling among 'the wild bloods' in the country: 'the old historical passion is at its greatest intensity' (*L*: 649). Between 1919 and 1921 that intensity was in full spate, drowning 'the ceremony of innocence' in a 'blood-dimmed tide'. As the war with England quickened its pace with acts of assassination and British military oppression, Yeats wrote of his very real fears that Ireland would follow the road of Russian revolution: 'What I want is that Ireland be kept from giving itself (under the influence of its lunatic faculty of going against everything which it believes England to affirm) to Marxian revolution or Marxian definitions of value in any form. I consider the Marxian criterion of values as in this age the spear-head of materialism and leading to inevitable murder. From that criterion follows the well-known phrase "can the bourgeois be innocent?"' (*L*: 656, date uncertain).

The temptation to leave the country to its folly was a real one. An invitation to take up a two-year lecturing post in Japan, which arrived in July 1919, was a chance, as he wrote to Quinn, 'to go away until the tumult of war had died down, and perhaps Home Rule established' (*L*: 659). The publication (in slightly amended form) of his 1912 North American collection of essays, *The Cutting of an Agate*, had been greeted in London by the *Times Literary Supplement* in terms that suggested it seemed like a voice from a past overtaken by history. A war had intervened. 'In 1914' the reviewer opined (in fact it was the poet Walter de la Mare) 'we could have quietly woven these essays into our literary life'

(*CH*: 226). In 1919 a harsher judgement is demanded: 'Mr Yeats's edification, his aphorisms, chiselled, recondite, and profound . . . will convert only the converted. He engraves his fine prose for a little clan' (ibid.: 230). And T. S. Eliot, the American ex-patriot, staking his own claims to a European patrimony, read in the essays a sensibility so different from his own as to allow him to assert 'the difference is not only personal, but national' (ibid.: 231). Eliot's review appeared in *The Athenaeum* in July under the heading 'A Foreign Mind'. A sense that he might never return and a concern for what would happen to his abandoned tower in his absence kept Yeats, who might well have had enough of England as well as Ireland, from accepting the tempting Japanese offer.

It was his ambition to complete the renovation at Thoor Ballylee, so that it might be 'a fitting monument and symbol' as well as a soundly roofed dwelling-place which meant that Yeats was to spend almost five months of 1920 in North America. His lecture tour there, to raise funds for the building work he planned, took place as violence intensified in Ireland. Dublin was under nightly curfew. Policemen were shot in various parts of the country. In March, in Cork city the police ran amok following the death of one of their number. The mayor protested and demanded the withdrawal of the force. He was murdered in his bed for his pains in an act that a coroner's jury identified as state terrorism. Republican prisoners went on hunger strike in London and in Belfast. By April about 400 of the auxiliaries (the Black and Tans) had been recruited in England. (There would be 9,500 of them by the end of the war). A terrible cycle of brutality and revenge was in motion. In Galway Lady Gregory was having trouble with tenants in a land dispute. She feared for the future of Coole and the estate. In her journal she recorded how there was news in Gort of a man who had 'been shot dead, in his house over a matter of dividing land' (Gregory 1987 vol. 1: 153). On 5 May, even more alarmingly, her brother Frank wrote from Roxborough to tell her how he and his family had been forced out of their home by an armed gang, who in the name of the Republic ordered them to quit on suspicion that he was a government spy.

Yeats and his wife had set sail for the United States on 13 January 1920. George Yeats had been keen to travel and to meet people after the isolated early years of their marriage. Yeats had wanted to introduce his father to his young wife and had hoped that they could persuade him to return to Ireland. In the event, John Butler Yeats was delighted with his daughter-in-law but was as cunningly obdurate as ever about doing anything other than what suited him, which did not include repatriation in his eighties (Yeats accepted financial responsibility for his continued residence in New York). Unsuccessful in that object of their journey, the Yeatses certainly got to see much of the country in eighteen weeks. The poet's lectures were quite amply rewarded, despite an anxious time when it transpired that the agency which had arranged his lecturing venues was on the point of bankruptcy. Once again he was a success at the lectern, though one member of an audience, who had heard him lecture in 1903 and 1911, commented 'Young Shelley has become middle-aged Coleridge, – quite another man' (Strand 1978: 191).

Given the situation in Ireland it was unsurprising that Yeats was frequently asked about political matters. However, the subjects of the lectures he had prepared for his tour were almost ostentatiously apolitical. It was as if in a period of brutal political struggle the poet wished to defend the role of art as a force in human affairs. But Yeats's audiences and the press wanted to hear what the author of *Cathleen ni Houlihan* and the Irish poet of the age had to say about Sinn Féin's campaign of violence and about British repression. When pressed he confessed that he hated the violence and even tried to suggest that Sinn Féin could not be held accountable for what the militarists in the movement were doing. He suspected, however, to his great distaste, that violence would prove more efficacious than all the work of constitutional and cultural nationalists in forwarding the Irish case for self-government. In Toronto he admitted: 'One of the Irish leaders once said: "If you want anything from the English Parliament you must go to the Commons with the tail of a cow in one hand and the head of a landlord in the other"' (cited in Strand 1978: 179).

The Yeatses' North American tour, finally a financial success, was not so crucial an event in the poet's life as the two earlier visits had been. Two encounters, however, offered symbolic recognition of the public man Yeats had indisputably become. In March a young Japanese man spontaneously presented the poet with a 550-year-old samurai sword, as a mark of respect for his achievement. The gift of Sato's sword, which initially embarrassed Yeats by its munificence, was to enter his imagination as a potent icon. And in May Yeats met Eamon de Valera for the first time in his native city of New York. The maker spoke with the maker of history.

The American tour was significant in a private sense for the Yeatses in one respect, other than the financial. This bore on the occult aspect of their relationship. In Pasadena, California, on 29 March the spirit Dionertes, then in communication with the couple, indicated that he 'preferred to use other methods – sleeps' (*VPs* 3:1) in his trafficking with them. They accordingly began a process of enquiry which involved the frequent record and study of the contents of their dreams, as well as questionings of a half-asleep partner, along with meditations over matter revealed by speech delivered while asleep. It also made for intent reflections on the portents daily life constantly offered (even on North American journeys by 'sleeper' train, no less). Much of this material was recorded in sleep and dream notebooks. The activity was continued from March 1920 until March 1924.

The Yeatses returned to Europe in early summer. During Yeats's absence Iseult Gonne had been married. In 1919 she had conceived an infatuation for a young fellow almost eight years her junior, Harry Francis Stuart (an Ulsterman, poet and the novelist-to-be, who had only recently left Rugby school in England). In June Gonne wrote to Yeats that 'the marriage is a 'tragedy'. She then asked him to intervene if he could to save Iseult from the violence, sloth and sadistic miserliness of Stuart's behaviour towards her. Gonne reported in July: 'He behaves like a lunatic – or perhaps only like a vicious English public school boy would behave to a fag' (*GYL*: 404). All was not well with the bird. Once again a woman to whom he had proposed and by whom he had been rejected had contracted a foolish and destructive marriage to an unsuitable husband (and this time a northerner to boot, confirming family prejudice). Yeats set off for the lonely valley of Glenmalure in County Wicklow where the young couple were living in rancorous enmity in a house which Gonne herself had purchased. It was set high up in the glen Synge had imagined as the setting for his play of marital misalliance, *The Shadow of the Glen*. Yeats found Iseult ill and run down. So he efficiently arranged for her to spend time in a Dublin nursing home. For the moment that was all that could be managed in a nearly impossible situation.

In August George Yeats suffered a miscarriage and in the autumn Yeats himself had to have his tonsils removed in an operation performed 'with his usual exuberant gaiety' by the Dublin surgeon, wit and poet, Oliver St John Gogarty (shortly to be immortalized as Buck Mulligan by James Joyce in the opening chapter of *Ulysses*, 1922). A haemorrhage seemed momentarily life-threatening, investing with a *frisson* of mortality the poem Yeats had composed in Gonne's house in Glenmalure, while waiting for surgery. For just before he wrote 'On a Picture of a Black Centaur by Edmund Dulac' (first published in 1922) Yeats had pondered how 'eternity is not a long time but a *short* time' (*Hone*: 327). He might in the autumn of 1920 have had his chance to stretch out his limbs in a longer sleep than the drunken brief eternity that that poem invokes with its allusion to the seven sleepers of Ephesus.

Autumn also brought the war of independence home to Yeats with shocking immediacy. Gort in County Galway, so long the focus of Yeats's idyllic vision of the Irish west, was traumatized by the murderous activities of the Black and Tans. Lady Gregory's response, her republican convictions deepening with every grim month that passed, was to publish anonymously in the *Nation* in London, from October 1920 until January 1921, a series of articles that chronicled the barbaric brutality of the British auxiliary forces in her own district, where a policy of reprisals was evidently in unchecked operation. In early November a young pregnant mother of three was shot in nearby Kiltartan. On 14 November Lady Gregory recorded in her journal 'Yesterday morning I awoke with the words in my ears; "And the Leaves of the Tree are for the Healing of the Nations"; ah, if we could but find that tree!' (Gregory, 1987 1: 200).

The poet's response to this new phase of Irish history, when temporizing of any kind became impossible for most nationally inclined Irishmen and women, was to invoke another altogether less pacific arboreal image. On 23 October 1920 he had finally made his poem 'Easter 1916' in a slightly revised version, fully available in the pages of the London-published *New Statesman*. In November he nailed his colours even more firmly to the mast (though by 1920 the words 'England may keep faith/For all that is done or said' in the poem of the 1916 Rising rang with corrosive irony) when he published in *The Dial* (in the United States) a series of poems (including 'Easter 1916') some written, as we noted, in 1916 and 1917, but then withheld. 'Sixteen Dead Men', 'On a Political Prisoner' and 'The Rose Tree' were Yeats's most frankly republican works since the first performance of *Cathleen ni Houlihan* in 1902. In the circumstances of November

1920 there could be little doubt where Yeats now stood on the Irish question. It was in imaginative understanding of the Pearse who had followed the summons of the young woman with the walk of a queen. 'The Rose Tree' echoes, as do the final lines of 'Easter 1916', the tradition of Irish republican ballad-making and calls to mind the Liberty-Tree of the revolutionary period of the 1790s which was the inspiration of the 1798 rebellion during which Yeats had set his propagandist play.

In 1965 Conor Cruise O'Brien iconoclastically marked the centenary of Yeats's birth by portraying him in an influential essay as a man who combined passion and a strategic self-serving political cunning through most of his life. Yet even O'Brien was forced to admit the political courage which Yeats displayed in publishing such poetry at such a time: 'To publish these poems in this context was a political act, and a bold one: probably the boldest of Yeats's career' (O'Brien 1965: 239). O'Brien however tempers this recognition by arguing that Yeats remained cautious even in outrage in publishing the poem 'Sixteen Dead Men', with 'the most explicit bearing on contemporary politics', in America. Yeats must also have reckoned by late 1920, O'Brien assumes, that the future would hold some kind of independence for an Ireland in which he would have hoped to play a role. So he was establishing his credentials, but at a safe distance. Yet he also wrote an incendiary poem entitled 'Reprisals', which he intended to publish in England and only desisted at Lady Gregory's request, since she felt its contents were insincere, dragged her son from the grave and would offend his widow. It may well have done for she shared Robert Gregory's pro-British sentiments and she had always resented Yeats. She could not have been happy with how Yeats, in his 'An Irish Airman Forsees his Death' (first published in the second edition of *The Wild Swans at Coole*; (1919)) had represented her imperially minded husband as a kind of neutral who had given his life in 'a lonely impulse of delight'. Now Yeats addressed Gregory's ghost to tell him that a British military rabble were murdering at will his father's tenants, beyond the purview of law or parliament.

O'Brien's assessment of Yeats's stance in the autumn of 1920 and the winter of 1921 lacks generosity. More and more evidence came in (and Lady Gregory's articles were an important contribution to a lengthening charge sheet) that English public opinion was being sickened by what was being done in the name of England, and was turning towards the possibility of a settlement. Yeats was comfortably established in Oxford where he had spent the spring and early months of the summer pleasantly with his wife, holding evenings to which he invited selected undergraduates, welcoming friends, visiting his friend Lady Ottoline Morrell on occasional weekends at Garsington, near Oxford. She gathered together at her social events the literary and intellectual lions of Blooms-bury, not all of whom would have been in concessive mood about Sinn Féin politics and republican violence (though their hostess, a recent convert to radical Irish politics, was). Yeats's energy levels must also have been diminished in the autumn by post-operative weakness (in a notebook entry of 19 November he spoke of a 'slow recovery' *VPs* 3: 53) and his wife was coping with the sorrow of a miscarriage. He could have kept silent, letting things take their course, without undue personal disturbance of his English way of life. None of these things prevented him delivering an incandescent denunciation of Britain's policy and action in Ireland at a debate in the Oxford Union in February 1921. Mr De Valera must have been gratified to have such a voice ('Pensioner Yeats' no more) added to the chorus of those who spoke in support of the Oxford motion in the chamber itself and who welcomed its sentiments in the country at large. The motion stated that the Union would 'welcome complete self-government in Ireland and condemns reprisals'. It was carried by a substantial majority.

O'Brien's charge that Yeats published 'Sixteen Dead Men', with its incendiary image of the dead of 1916 loitering 'to stir the boiling pot', in America rather than London because of a constitutional incapacity to shake off a calculating political prudence, can be further set in question. For Yeats collected it, along with the other 'republican poems', including 'Easter 1916', in the slim volume of verse he published in February 1921: *Michael Robartes and the Dancer*. Issued in Dublin by the Cuala Press, it would, we can be fairly sure, have come to the attention of the military authorities in the city, in the way a poem published in a small American literary magazine would not have. Though Yeats was 'certain Dublin Castle knew that he and Lady Gregory were not essentially interested in politics' (Pierce 1995: 212), he was making his loyalties clear at a defining moment, in a way that bespeaks a more resolute national commitment than O'Brien allows.

History enters Yeats's poetry with a vengeance in *Michael Robartes and the Dancer*. As well as the poems directly addressing the matter of 1916, the volume includes 'The Second Coming' and 'The Leaders of the Crowd', with its disdainful admonishment of demagoguery – a poem that suggests Yeats's fear that a poet's privacy is at risk in the current turmoil:

> How can they know
> Truth flourishes where the student's lamp has shone,
> And there alone, that have no solitude?
> So the crowd come they care not what may come.
> They have loud music, hope every day renewed
> And heartier loves; that lamp is from the tomb.

The final image here implies that the Yeatsian poetic truth has its source in the afterlife. That truth, learned from the spirits and in much study, can make some kind of order of the painful history to which the collection so openly bears witness in the directly Irish poems and in 'The Second Coming'. 'A Meditation in Time of War', composed, as we noted, in November 1914 (first published in *The Dial* and *The Nation* in November 1920) proposes that even such immense historical events as a war partake of unreality as compared with the living unity of all things.

It was in *Michael Robartes and the Dancer* that Yeats began to reveal to the world the kinds of things he had been recently learning by the light of an occult lamp. In the second version of *The Wild Swans at Coole*, in 'The Phases of the Moon' and 'The Double Vision of Michael Robartes', Yeats had already begun to ponder the significance of his personal life and of human experience in the light of his emergent 'system'. In a number of elaborate notes to the new volume, two of which amounted almost to essays in themselves (the most extensive annotations to a volume of his verse since *The Wind Among the Reeds*), Yeats introduced concepts (their source disguised in a fiction that involved both a correspondence between Michael Robartes and Owen Aherne, revived from the poet's early prose, and an imaginary Arab mystical Christian sect, among whom Robartes had sojourned, the Judwalis), that originated in the automatic writings. He even provided a geometric figure of two interpenetrating cones or gyres as a representation of the soul in the body, with the technical observation: 'It had its origin from a straight line which represents, now time, now emotion, now subjective life, and a plane at right angles to this line which represents, now space, now intellect, now objective life; while it is marked out by two gyres which represent the conflict, as it were, of plane and line . . . ', and so on and on, in a manner which verges on a parody of abstraction.

Yet in the volume as a whole this hyper-abstraction contrasts not only with the rhetorical urgencies of the poems on Irish politics and the general historical crisis of 'The Second Coming', to which the note on the gyres is a commentary, but with the sensual pulse of its love poetry. Those who heed the leaders of the crowd may wake each day in hope of 'heartier loves'. The poet of these poems, it is fictively implied, is one who manifestly enjoys a more exotic, more elaborately erotic, yet no less bodily, love. The volume as a whole sets in apposition history, metaphysics, eternity with the body – male and female – in an amused, even self-mocking awareness that the erotic is a force that can vie powerfully with abstraction. And that apposition is the stuff of a drama of a complex experience in which male and female voices are caught up in the 'fundamental contestation in the book between the lyric poet and metaphysical philosopher' (Sidnell 1996: 113).

It is not, it should be emphasized, that the male voice in the dialogue poems in the volume (the title poem, 'Solomon and the Witch' and 'An Image from Past Life') speaks for philosophy and the mind, the female for the lyric impulse of the body. What these poems suggest rather is that the work of the poet and his wife together has begun to produce poetry with collaboration as well as conflict as a controlling theme. In these the issue of gender, highlighted in the title poem, begins to dissolve in the dramatic tensions and releases of the erotic moment, a male *and* female occult epithalamium in which the he and she are not quite forgotten (as in Donne's version of sexual ecstasy) but interrelate even as they are presented in debate or in post-coital or matrimonial disputation.

The title poem of the collection has been tellingly situated by Cullingford in the context of the suffragist movement which was redefining the relations between the sexes in the postwar period. She suggests how the persona of Michael Robartes, the Yeatsian *alter ego*, imagined as recently returned, in the fiction of the book, from his travels, allows the poet to address a modern young woman in terms of 'an increasingly embattled chauvinism'. Robartes would allow the Dancer as female only beauty, bodily pleasure and the 'physical coherence' (Cullingford 1993: 92) of her art. Cullingford argues that Yeats uses the character of Robartes 'to test both his own prejudices and the inherited generic norms of love poetry against feminist objections and demands' to conclude: 'In 'Michael Robartes and the Dancer' Yeats uses the lyric form to stage a social quarrel about the effect of changing sexual roles; but it is also that quarrel with himself, out of which, he insisted, poetry is made' (ibid.). In the poem the dancer is allowed (and it is the poet who still is the permissive agent of her empowerment) her answers back, inserting herself in direct speech into the discursive space of the poem in a way in which the female voice had not hitherto been represented in Yeats's poetry (if we except a mild conversation in 'Adam's Curse').

This infringement of Robartes's patriarchal attempt to restrict women's role, sets a note for the book. However the book includes 'A Prayer for My Daughter'. Composed in the year when the Sex Disqualification (Removal) Act, protecting female employment rights, was passed in Westminster, this poem envisaged a future of leisured ease for the poet's first child. It includes too 'Easter 1916', with its vision of men in thrall to a terrible beauty that turns the heart to stone. That is to say the book registers a troubled ambivalence of feeling about woman's social role and her place in the poet's own imagination. In 'Solomon and the Witch' nevertheless, a female voice offers its own estimation of the bodily pleasure to be derived from the marriage bed. Sheba in the poem is an occult bride whose lunar powers make her the sexual partner, under 'the wild moon', of a Solomon who expatiates wordily after intercourse upon the risks and failures of sexual love. She reminds her man in a comic, human exchange, that love does not involve an apocalyptic, conclusive consummation. It demands a constant renewal of their mutual passion:

> 'The night has fallen; not a sound
> In the forbidden sacred grove
> Unless a petal hit the ground,
> Nor any human sight within it
> But the crushed grass where we have lain;
> And the moon wilder every minute.
> O! Solomon! Let us try again.'

'Solomon and the Witch' is Yeats's poem of compliment to a young bride, a modern woman, who responded to the emancipatory spirit of her time in demanding and, for a time, achieving sexual equality with her husband. She was also the person who took a good deal of the lead in what was to be the decisive step taken by the couple over the next year or so which was to see them abandon England as a place of part-residence each year and to make Ireland their primary home.

In April 1921 Yeats was at work on a poem which bore unnervingly on any such decision. Then entitled 'Thoughts upon the Present State of the World' (subsequently renamed 'Nineteen Hundred and Nineteen'), the poem recalled incidents that had occurred in Kiltartan in 1920:

Now days are dragon-ridden, the nightmare
Rides upon sleep: a drunken soldiery
Can leave the mother, murdered at her door,
To crawl in her own blood, and go scot-free.

The Yeatses, for financial reasons, had sub-let their Oxford house, and were staying in a country cottage in Berkshire, where George Yeats longed for Ballylee, despite the unsettled state of the country as a whole. Ireland might be safe for a visit, but a determination to settle there permanently with a young daughter and another child on the way, could well have given a young English mother pause. The truce in the Anglo-Irish war of the summer of 1921 and a treaty negotiated in the following months between representatives of Dáil Éireann and the British government which essentially granted the twenty-six counties of southern Ireland Dominion status, might have allowed a more sanguine view of Ireland's future to encourage removal from England to an Irish home. The birth of their son, in August 1921, in the first month of peace following the truce, might also have seemed to the couple, their tetradic family now complete, to augur well. But by the end of the year Yeats was grimly depressed about his native land. He wrote to Shakespear: 'I am in a deep gloom about Ireland for though I expect ratification of the treaty from a plebiscite I see no hope of escape from bitterness, and the extreme party may carry the country. When men are very bitter, death and ruin draw on as a rabbit is supposed to be drawn on by the dancing of the fox' (*L*: 675). In 'Thoughts upon the Present State of the World' Yeats had written of 'the weasel's tooth' as metonymy of the violence of feeling that fed a climate of atrocity. That feeling now involved fratricidal, feral impulses. Although, as Yeats states in the same letter, he and his wife were planning to live in Dublin, with 'George very urgent about this' the poet's anxieties were obvious. He imagined going to live in some far land for the sake of the children, for in the turmoil that might ensue neither England nor Ireland could be a fruitful home for them. And Japan, which had beckoned two years earlier, had never fully left his mind, even though his wife had ruled it out for them as a place to live.

Since 1918 Yeats had been at work on a fourth play for dancers, based on the Noh theatre. This play along with *At the Hawk's Well*, *The Dreaming of the Bones* and *The Only Jealousy of Emer* had been published in London that October as one of *Four Plays for Dancers*. Entitled *Calvary*, the play was an early exploration of ideas on the subjective and objective personality, derived from the automatic writings, which Yeats would present much more fully in future years. As a study in the strange dedication of the self-sacrificing victim, the Christ whose single-mindedness is incomprehensible to the very people he dies to save, the play had its immediate relevance in an Ireland which had embraced in hunger-strikes like that of the mayor of Cork, Terence MacSwiney, in October 1920, the martyrology of sacrificial heroes. In the play Christ dreams back (or relives) his passion only to discover that Lazarus and Judas reject him once again, and that the Roman soldiers cannot grasp how his death might have any significance whatsoever. It was a warning that the condition of such heroism is essentially that of solitude, its outcome uncertain. *Calvary* was not produced in Ireland in Yeats's lifetime. It was, however, published in Japan in a Japanese translation in 1922.

February 1922 saw the Yeatses, who in June 1921 had taken rented accommodation in the Oxfordshire market town of Thame, decide upon permanent residency in Ireland. The pleasant house they had rented in Thame, where their son had been born, had set Yeats thinking of dynastic responsibilities and familial property. Before the Yeatses left Oxford he had finished a new autobiographical prose work *Four Years* which appeared from the Cuala Press in December 1921. This work undoubtedly reminded him of the problems he had experienced as a young man with an impecunious father who had signally failed to support his household.

He was at work too, in this summer and autumn of insecure peace in the Anglo-Irish struggle, completing a further set of autobiographical recollections of his young manhood which recounted his laborious efforts in the cause of Irish cultural nationalism after the fall of Parnell and during the heady years of political struggle at the end of the old century (these new autobiographical works were to appear in collected form in October 1922 as *The Trembling of the Veil*). The Ireland that was and the Ireland that might now be were both in his mind, mingled with his own hopes and fears for his family. Premonitions of the future found expression in September 1921 when *The Dial* printed 'Thoughts upon the Present State of the World', with its recognition that an era of near universal peace in nineteenth-century Europe had given way in the new century to a period when visceral hatreds gave birth to black imaginings and blood-lust. Vicious acts of violence that had been raised to the level of mythic generality in 'The Second Coming' in this poem are given a local habitation and a name. The 'rough beast' is now the incubus of a fourteenth-century County Kilkenny woman, Dame Alice Kyteler, who had, in the legend about the witchcraft for which she was tried and executed, sacrificed cocks and peacocks to her demon lover:

> But now wind drops, dust settles; thereupon
> There lurches past, his great eyes without thought
> Under the shadow of stupid-pale locks,
> That insolent fiend Robert Artisson
> To whom the love-lorn Lady Kyteler brought
> Bronzed peacock feathers, red combs of her cocks.

In the summer of 1921 Yeats had also begun a poem, in part inspired by the elegance of Lady Ottoline Morrell's country house, which pondered the ambiguous origins of the Georgian houses of the Irish countryside in the land to which he was contemplating a return. It took account of the expropriatory violence which had shadowed their cultural achievement and the risks they now faced in a period when dynastic deterioration was only one of the dangers which faced them. This poem, 'Ancestral Houses', was the first of what was to become a remarkable sequence to be entitled, on its first publication in *The Dial* in January 1923, 'Meditations in Time of Civil War'.

In February 1922 George Yeats, with financial acumen and dispatch, purchased for the family a large house on Merrion Square in south central Dublin. Centrally placed in one of the most elegant of the Georgian terraces that gave Dublin some of the grandeur which, for all the dereliction and decay over 100 years of economic decline since the Act of Union of 1800 had effected, still made it a national capital of some style and pretension. This act of familial determination was given significance of a poignant kind for Yeats, not only because it meant a return to his natal city of the definitive kind he had hitherto avoided, but because only a few days before the transaction was complete, which gave the poet a substantial Dublin home, John Butler Yeats died in New York.

George Yeats had fortuitously been able to strike a really good bargain in Dublin and she envisaged letting out parts of the ample accommodation to tenants. So Yeats could feel that the return to Dublin was a kind of triumph, in which he overcame the disagreeably straitened conditions of his youth in the city. He sorrowed that his father, who had delighted the previous summer in the birth of an heir to his son, had not lived to see how family fortunes had turned dramatically for the better: 'I wish he could have lived to see us in Dublin' (*L*: 678).

For Yeats, in 1922, to envisage himself settled in Dublin involved a good deal more than living as though to the manner born in a splendid Dublin town-house on the southern side of a Georgian square whose western side boasted the National Gallery and Leinster House, the home of the Royal Dublin Society which became the seat of the national parliament. For one thing Dublin residence of a permanent kind made Yeats available in an immediate way to the two sisters with whom his relations as an editor of the Cuala Press had often proved tricky and sometimes downright exasperating. They had, moreover, learnt in 1921 that they would lose their lease on Cuala in May 1922, where they had conducted their business since 1908 (though the blow did not in fact fall until the summer of 1923; Murphy 1995: 214). This made their future uncertain. Then 'Lily' Yeats took her father's death very hard, falling ill with what was to prove the first serious symptoms of the total breakdown of her always precarious wellbeing which climaxed in 1923. Even more challengingly, the hopes of the summer and autumn of 1921 that Ireland would enjoy a peaceful future were dashed in the most terrible way in the spring and summer of 1922.

In January 1922 Dáil Éireann ratified the Treaty which the Irish emissaries had negotiated in the last months of 1921. A sizeable rump led by Eamon de Valera rejected both the terms of the treaty and the decision to ratify it. The seeds were set of a civil war which broke out in April 1922 when forces loyal to the de Valera faction in the independence movement occupied the strategically and administratively important Four Courts building on the northern bank of the River Liffey in central Dublin. Violence which had been simmering throughout the country began to boil over, as the Provisional Government led by Michael Collins, one of the most daring and able of the former freedom fighters, tried to establish its authority in the face of opposition led by erstwhile colleagues in the struggle against the British.

The Yeatses had not planned to occupy their new Dublin home immediately. In February 1922, in a letter expressing his belief that the political situation in Ireland would settle in a few months, Yeats had told Shakespear of their intent to spend the spring and summer at Ballylee. They would return to Oxford in the autumn to make the final move to Dublin. Such optimism meant that Yeats, his wife and young family found themselves in some real danger during the early months of what proved to be a bitter, dirty war.

On 8 March 1922, just before he set off for Ireland Yeats wrote to Shakespear that he had been reading 'the new Joyce'. Joyce had published *Ulysses*, his extraordinary experimental fiction of Dublin life, a month before in Paris on 2 February. So Yeats must have been among its earliest readers in Britain or Ireland. He confessed only to have got through thirty pages (in June 1923 he admitted that he had not yet been able to finish the book) but noted that it has 'our Irish cruelty' (*L*: 679). In the following month Yeats would have to live amid Irish cruelty himself. He kept on trying with *Ulysses* but found a more congenial companion for the stresses of civil war in the Trollope of the Barchester novels. He worked on his autobiography and was pleased to listen to sections of Lady Gregory's memoirs, upon which she was also at work. The composition of *A Vision*, with its lunar vistas, kept his mind from immediate events (the first book of that volume concludes with 'Finished at Thoor, Ballylee, 1922, in a time of Civil War' (*AVA*: 117).

The spring and summer of 1922 was the first occasion on which the tower itself proved fairly habitable. George Yeats was busy transforming the place. Her husband told Quinn that she made 'at every moment a fourteenth century picture'. The hawthorn was gloriously in bloom. For most of the time all seemed peacefully undisturbed. The wider surrounding area was in the hands of the government forces who held Galway city. They patrolled by day. By night the Irregulars began to move about the countryside, issuing threats to landlords, seizing land, seeking to exert a rule of terror. Still, in the idyllic peace of Gort and Ballylee it was difficult to believe that anything was happening at all. In May, however, news came of the murder of Protestants in Cork, apparently as reprisals for pogroms against Catholics in Belfast. Yeats felt some alarm and wondered whether out of 'murder and rapine will come not a demagogic but an authoritative government' (*L*: 682).

By early June Yeats had finished *The Trembling of the Veil* (the preface is dated May 1922) and fell ill with post-creative exhaustion. For the rest of the month the poet and his wife recorded the contents of 'sleeps', taking up an activity they had interrupted in September of the previous year. On 16 June Dionertes gave him advice on his health, but the other communications of this month, the only ones recorded for this period, turn once again to the old question of the poet's love for Gonne and his divided selfhood which had caused so much trouble in affairs of the heart. On 20 June George Yeats wrote: 'the action into which the mind is completed is one which satisfies the intellectual & moral nature' (*VPs* 3: 118). The spirits were confirming her husband's recent preoccupations, for *Hodos Chame-liontos* (the third of five sections in *The Trembling of the Veil*) had concluded that in great artistic masters

> The two halves of their nature are so completely joined that they seem to labour for their objects, and yet to desire whatever happens, being at the same instant predestinate and free, creation's very self. . . .
>
> And these things are true also of nations, but the Gate-keepers who drive the nation to war or anarchy that it may find its Image are different from those who drive individual men, though I think at times they work together.   (*TOV*: 153–4)

Possibly in April Yeats had queried in a letter to Shakespear whether 'litera-ture' would 'be much changed by that most momentous of events, the return of evil' (*L*: 680 date uncertain). In *Hodos Chameliontos* he offered a vision of what that change might now entail: an artistic unity of being in a man which might prove exemplary for a nation in the process of tearing itself apart. For the Unity of Culture which Yeats now confesses he had once dreamed of in Ireland, which might have raised a divided self and a nation out of heterogeneity ('that multi-plicity of interest and opinion, of arts and sciences'; *TOV*: 149, which *The Trembling of the Veil* explores as the ground of the young poet's fragmented experience), could only come now, in the ultimately divisive horror of civil war, from some absolutely transformative act of the poetic imagination.

The horror intensified over the next few months, in the country at large and at Gort and Ballylee. The government forces in six weeks of summer fighting drove most of the 'Republicans' (so-called because they rejected the treaty with Britain in the name of the Republic declared by Pearse in 1916) south and west so that their final stand would take place in the southern province of Munster. With the new state's army occupying towns and cities, their enemies retreated to the hills and safe houses in the countryside to engage in the guerrilla tactics that had served them well in the War of Independence. From August onwards Collins's army was confronted with the problem of 'ambushes, sniping, destruction of roads, blowing up of bridges and breaking of railway lines. The task which the army thus faced from mid-August on was to prevent the guerilla tactics from destroying the economic life and social fabric of the country' (Valiulis 1992: 167). It took until late in the following spring for the Republicans to abandon their increasingly lost cause.

The Yeats family in their western fastness experienced at first hand the effects of the Republicans' military strategy. For a week all communication with the outside world was broken off. In mid-August the poet wrote to his friend Sturge Moore of how among the large houses for miles around, only Lady Gregory's and Martyn's had escaped a Republican raid (the Republicans were looking for arms, cheerfully enough firing many houses of the hated Ascendancy as they left, so that government forces could not billet in them). He told of how a motor had just passed 'with a National soldier and a coffin up on end and what I suppose were the relatives of the dead man' (Bridge 1953: 46). He reported too on blocked roads and a fear that his own bridge might be dynamited. It almost immediately was. Yeats and his wife were allowed to place their children in an upper room of the tower before the mine was exploded by the midnight raiders (Hone 1946: 349). As Yeats later recalled of this anxious, unsettling time 'One felt an overmastering desire not to grow unhappy or embittered, not to lose all sense of the beauty of nature.... Presently a strange thing happened. I began to smell honey in places where honey could not be, at the end of a stone passage or at some windy turn of the road, and it came always with certain thoughts. When I got back to Dublin I was with angry people who argued over everything or were eager to know the exact facts' (*Au*: 580).

The poem which Yeats composed about this experience, the sixth in the sequence 'Meditations in Time of Civil War' is a reverent prayer, in the midst of violence, that the benign forces of nature, the honey-bees, should build in the empty nests of the starlings in the crumbling masonry of the poet's tower. Yet Yeats did not choose to conclude his meditation with prayer (the customary terminus of a religious meditation) but with vision. In the final poem of the sequence the poet unfolds a vision of apocalyptic terror in which mindless evil overwhelms civilization. The tone of this is remote both from the piety of the sixth poem of the sequence and from the anger about the civil war that Yeats would find in Dublin when he returned there. It dramatically releases in its rhetorical urgencies, as from the heartless depths of a haunted unconscious, as graphic and imaginatively expansive a set of images as anything in Yeats's *oeuvre*. Simultaneously fascinating and repellent, an almost cinematic sequence of strange yet curiously apt iconographic moments, it induces in the reader not anger but awe, a chilling sense of the romantic sublime in a vision of evil. In its final stanza the poet is represented as enduring a solitary despair and as coming to a recognition of what must now be his principal preoccupation:

> I turn away and shut the door, and on the stair
> Wonder how many times I could have proved my worth
> In something that all others understand or share;
> But O! ambitious heart, had such a proof drawn forth
> A company of friends, a conscience set at ease,
> It had but made us pine the more. The abstract joy,
> The half-read wisdom of daemonic images,
> Suffice the aging man as once the growing boy.

14

Senator and Seer

The Dublin to which Yeats and his family returned on 20 September 1922 was a city in the grip of profound uncertainty about the future as well as anger and sorrow at recent events. Arthur Griffith, one of the principal architects of Irish independence and a crucial figure among the pro-Treaty elected representatives who had won a definitive general election in the early summer, had died suddenly on 12 August from a cerebral haemorrhage, apparently brought on by overwork. Ten days later Michael Collins had met his death at the hands of a sniper, when the convoy in which he was travelling was ambushed in County Cork. Most of the nation had mourned a heroic young warrior killed in action. General Mulcahy, at the head of the army in Collins's place, issued an address to his troops: 'Let no cruel act of reprisal blemish your bright honour'. Yeats's sisters at the Cuala Press, who had lived anxiously enough through the violence of the recent past in Dublin and who supported the new state that was seeking to establish itself, published a text of his noble, but sadly ineffectual address, in Celtic lettering.

The new Parliament met on 9 September and formed a government which in October voted draconian powers to the army to arrest, try and execute its enemies. It also passed the Irish Free State Constitution Bill which brought the new state into legal existence on 6 December. Executions were summarily carried out both immediately before and after that date in reprisal for deaths inflicted by Republicans. The new dispensation had been forged in the blood of former comrades. And before hostilities ceased seventy-seven men were to die in this fashion. The new government governed from heavily fortified buildings on Merrion Square, with ministers spending nights in their offices for fear of assassination. The young minister for home affairs, Kevin O'Higgins, who authorized executions, understood forebodingly that in defending the state's authority in such brutal fashion, he had signed his own death warrant. The seeds of terrible future bitterness were being laid as Irishmen and women took over the duties and challenges of self-government. Writing to a friend of the bitterness of that terrible year the young Irish poet Austin Clarke caught a general mood: 'everything here has become darker and Dublin is as ugly and violent as Belfast now.... It seems to me that a self-destructive period is beyond the expression of verse.... If one were purely a dramatist and sufficiently aloof one might be able to study the amazing maelstrom of revengeful passions, cupidity and...falsehood that has swept the people of every shade of opinion and transformed quiet citizens into bloody-minded disciples of force. But silence seems best' (cited in Thompson 1997: 292).

In thinking of his return to Dublin Yeats reckoned that there might be some public role for himself amid the turmoil. He had been nominated by Sinn Féin as a delegate to an Irish Race conference which he had attended with Maud Gonne in Paris the previous January. In July Queen's College in Belfast conferred an honorary degree on him, as did his father's *alma mater*, Trinity College, Dublin, in December. His distinction was being afforded formal Irish recognition. When he took part at the end of the year (which had begun so sadly with the death of John Butler Yeats) in the colourful ceremony in the eighteenth-century Public Theatre of the college where two generations of Yeatses had been educated, the poet was also a newly created senator of the Irish Free State – a very public man indeed, 'a personage' as he reported in gratification to Shakespear. The horoscope he had cast for the moment when he took his oath of office had signalled trouble ahead for the Irish Free State but 'announced personal safety for himself' (Pearce 1961: 11).

The senate of the bicameral legislature established under the terms of the Treaty was a curious body. It was an assembly of sixty persons with powers of veto on legislation, to which the new government had agreed to nominate half of its membership 'with a view to the providing of representation for groups of all parties not adequately represented' in the Dáil, or lower house. The head of government, President Cosgrave, was in fact keen to prove that the former Anglo-Irish Protestant caste had nothing to fear in the new order, so the national minority of which Yeats as a nationalist with a Fenian past was an unusual part, was heavily represented. In a remarkable demonstration of his bona fides Cosgrave ensured, as one historian has sardonically pointed out, that in this first senate 'in a land of Catholic commoners sat twenty-four non-Catholics and fifteen titled persons' (Fitzpatrick 1975: 160). It was in fact an assembly in which bankers, lawyers and merchants would determine the tone and content of much of the debate, but Yeats nevertheless saw his appointment as a way of getting a few of his pet projects on the public agenda. He had been appointed as one of three senators qualified to advise on education, literature and the arts. The post also carried an emolument which by the end of Yeats's tenure of office in 1928 amounted to the not insubstantial sum of £360 per annum. There were a few others among the membership who shared his concern for the cultural life of the country.

In October 1922 Yeats had written to Shakespear of the disturbed Dublin he had found when he had returned to the city from County Galway: 'One meets a minister at dinner, passing his armed guard on the doorstep, and one feels no certainty that one will meet him again' (*L*: 690). By December, when Yeats accepted appointment to the senate, the executions had made assassinations of public representatives even more likely than they had been in October. In a December letter the poet made light of the danger, suggesting that the senator's income would be compensation of a kind for the chance of being shot at or his house being burned or bombed. On 4 January 1923 he informed the English poet Robert Bridges that life was 'interesting, but restless and unsafe – I have two bullets in my windows' (ibid.: 696). An armed guard was provided for his door-step in Merrion Square. Gonne, as a diehard Republican, was arrested in January, but not before she wrote to Yeats threatening permanent estrangement because of his betrayal in siding with the Free State which was executing patriots. Her response to the increasingly draconion powers of a regime which had interned her son Seán in June 1922 and her son-in-law Stuart in August, had been to organize a Women Prisoners' Defence League. In a military raid on her St Stephen's Green house in November government soldiers had burnt a large cache of her papers, including many of the poet's letters to her. Yeats thought only of using his influence to see that she had warm blankets in gaol. Passion, it seems, had cooled. She was swiftly released, but when on her rearrest in April 1923 she went on hunger strike in solidarity with other women engaged in that baleful form of protest, Yeats reminded the leader of the government, President Cosgrave, that his important prisoner was in frail health (*GLY*: 44). When Iseult Gonne was also briefly imprisoned, he made similar representations.

In London in January 1923, where he was once again raising the perennial issue of Dublin's right to the Lane bequest, Yeats did try to renew his contacts in the English governing class to see if a peace in Ireland could be brokered, but to no avail. In the same month Oliver St John Gogarty, the surgeon who had removed Yeats's tonsils, now also a senator, was kidnapped by Republicans as he took a bath in his own home. He escaped almost certain death in a desperate Liffey swim, having outwitted his captors.

Pierce speculates on the basis of epistolary evidence that in January or early February of 1923 Yeats was so unnerved by the dangers of Dublin that he entertained the possibility of leaving Ireland for good. Certainly January had been a terrible month for supporters of the government, and for some of Yeats's acquaintances. The execution of thirty-four Republican prisoners in that single month was met with a concerted outbreak of fire-setting in the houses of prominent citizens in various parts of the country. Republican headquarters had in fact issued an order that the houses of senators should be attacked. On 29 January the comfortable Dublin home of Senator Horace Plunkett, was mined. It was then burned the following night. The fire took with it thirty paintings by AE, some paintings by Jack Yeats and destroyed a house which had been at the centre of progressive unionist social thinking about Ireland since 1906. Plunkett, whom Yeats had known for many years, had given his life to the social improvement of the Irish countryside. He took the attack very personally, resigned from the senate and stayed away from the country for two years (West 1986: 202–7).

In such circumstances, forgetting the good auguries of the horoscope, Yeats may have felt immediate, acute fears for his life and for the safety and future of his family. With hostilities terminated by Republican defeat by May 1923, Yeats wrote to Shakespear of how his health had recently improved. He partly attributed the amelioration to 'the passing away of the strain of civil war' (*L*: 699). So the *sang froid* of some of his letters in this period may disguise a time when panic momentarily set in question his capacity to cope with Dublin at war. Pierce has suggested indeed that it was George Yeats, determined that her husband should not imperil his reputation before the bar of history, by quitting his post, as it were, who reminded him of responsibilities greater than the personal or the familial.

For Yeats Ireland in 1923 offered him an opportunity, like none he had enjoyed since the heady days of 1897 and 1898 of actually influencing in a direct way the development of his country. In the same letter in which he reported on his improved health to Shakespear he wrote of 'the slow exciting work of creating the institutions' (*L*: 698) of the new nation. Compared with the troubled, passionate young man who had worked alongside Gonne in the politically inspired commemoration of the 1798 Rebellion, the man who set his hand to this complex task had many advantages which the years had brought. He was unquestionably a figure of public account, honoured in Britain and in Ireland and signally respected in the United States. The award of the Nobel Prize for Literature, which was announced in November 1923, added full international lustre to an already very substantial reputation. Perhaps Yeats's modest assertion, in a letter to Edmund Gosse, that he took this as an honour given to him not as an individual but as a representative of 'a literary movement and of a nation' (ibid.: 701), had its source in a semi-conscious sense of the awful possibility that he might have forsaken Ireland earlier in the year. Be that as it may, he was pleased that the honour meant he had a greater chance of being 'listened to' in Dublin 'than ever before' (ibid.). The award presentation in Sweden impressed him enormously, the Swedish court winning over the Irish Republican Brother of old with its gracious honouring of accomplishment. He felt himself 'moved as if by some religious ceremony' (*Au*: 544).

In addition his finances were on a sounder footing than they ever had been. To his royalties, civil list pension and senator's salary could now be added not only the income from his wife's investments but from his own. For he invested £6,000 of the Nobel Prize of £7,500, (Jeffares 1988: 272) much of it in Irish railway shares. This Nordic windfall was a very timely one, for though his father's death had relieved the poet of one financial responsibility, he had in recent years been helping to support his two sisters. And 'Lily' Yeats's health was giving grounds for serious concern. Consumption was diagnosed, though incorrectly.

More fundamentally, the poet found strength to engage with the task of moulding the new institutions of state, since he himself inhabited the institution of a marriage that generated the kind of collaborative centre of occult power that he had sought as a basis for authoritative action for much of his life. The Irish Free State may have consolidated its position in a democratic election in which a majority triumphed over a minority that remained committed to revolutionary violence. Yeats's intervention as senator and public man in 1920s Ireland, how-ever did not come from a mind acquiescent to the tenets of mass democracy. Rather he welcomed the chance that an embryonic polity afforded as an oppor-tunity to effect a return 'to conservative politics as elsewhere in Europe' (*L*: 693).

The poet who began in 1923 to play a public part on the Irish stage once again was therefore invigorated by a marital relationship that had brought him sexual fulfilment, occult knowledge, a sense of destiny and the written materials in which he might cast his thoughts into an empowering unity. For the early years of the Irish Free State were the years in which Yeats worked intensely to complete his labours on the revelations of the Automatic Script, on what had also come from the spirit world in 'sleeps' and in dreams (employing the elaborate system of cards which he developed for filing and cataloguing data). In the mornings of his new Dublin life he wrestled with the problem of how to produce from all the revela-tions a work which could be a sacred book for an age that, even in Ireland, had at best a deficient sense of the sacred. In the afternoons when the senate was in session (he spent 'on average three hours in the chamber every fortnight', Fitzpatrick 1975: 163), he engaged with a pedestrian world of order papers, motions and legislative detail.

A 'sleep', which reported the instruction of a spirit named Carmichael, of 14 December 1920, recorded by George Yeats, gives a sense of the kind of thing the poet as acknowledged legislator in the democratic parliament might have been pondering of a morning in his study before he took his seat in the senate chamber. George Yeats had queried what had caused the rapid changes of the recent past in Europe, to be told:

> Nations begin by being pure & because pure conquered. They then absorbed into themselves the conquered and became impure.... Foreign financial interests in a nation is a form of impurity. When people have unity of culture the transference of thought & image goes through the whole people. In the past pure races have been made by blood, but bloods are now so mixed that in the future they will have to be made by culture. (*VPs* 3: 63)

He might also have been assessing and filing information from 'sleeps' in which it was intimated that among certain groups of people, for whom the term 'covens' was used for a time, such thoughts and images already circulated telepathically. On 6 April 1921 Yeats, in response to a series of dreams, had speculated revealingly: 'Does not the classical age adore the emblems of the Roman power. This time will it not be the adoration of the power of the mass on the one hand, & that of "the groups" which are to re-create unity of culture on the other' (ibid.: 87). Unity of culture could re-create a pure race, the instructors made clear, but it required an initiated elite to achieve that necessary renewal of the nation.

Yeats in the early years of the Irish Free State worked and lobbied to create an Irish Academy and to transform the Abbey into a state theatre. The latter was a pressing concern. For since Synge's controversial triumphs the company had become notable not for a poetic theatre of passionate, poetic implication but for a steady diet of realistic drama of a local life. Yeats's own poetic plays had seemed idiosyncratic abberrations in his own theatre. The audiences preferred the known to the Noh and commercial exigencies would always determine repertoire unless the state could be persuaded to patronize a theatre that could risk real experiment. The kind of theatre which might promote 'unity of culture' directed by an illuminated elite would be impossible in a strictly commercial context. In an open letter to Lady Gregory, published in 1923 in the *Irish Statesman*, the Dublin periodical AE had begun to edit earlier that year, Yeats had confessed that the success of the Abbey as a purveyor of realism had been for him 'a discouragement and a defeat' (cited in Hunt 1979: 134). By 1923 Yeats and Gregory were ready to hand over the theatre to the government, an offer which was repeated to the same lack of effect in 1924. Strenuous lobbying did mean however that the company was granted a subsidy in the year 1925–6. The subsidy was raised and made annual the following year but it came with a government representative on the Board, risking the complete artistic independence it had hitherto jealously protected. Yeats must have reckoned the risk worth taking in the divided and contentious world of theatrical Dublin in the 1920s, with his eye set on the dream of unity of culture in the new order of things.

For the condition of theatrical life in the Dublin to which Yeats had returned reflected the more general, divided state of the country at large. There were those content that the Irish theatre should supply a drama in which the life of ordinary people, so long denied political independence and cultural respect, should find representation in the recognizable world of farm-kitchen and small-town parlour. In Dublin the Dublin Drama League, founded with Yeats's blessing in 1918 by Lennox Robinson, to present contempory European drama, thought otherwise. This small avant garde circle of enthusiasts, among whom George Yeats was happy to circulate and work, found the conventions of the typical, successful Abbey play of the period stultifyingly provincial. They were allowed to take over the Abbey stage for their productions on nights when it was free. So it is possible to read this division in the cultural life of the period as indications of a more general division in society as a whole, between those who found Ireland sufficient unto itself and those who were anxious that national life be leavened by influences from beyond Irish shores. A conflict between an increasingly aggressive nativism and a sometimes superficial internationalism of outlook, espoused by a beleaguered minority, most of whom were writers, was, indeed, to mark cultural debate in Ireland for the rest of Yeats's life, intensifying markedly in the 1930s. It was not a discursive arena in which Yeats by any means felt at ease, since its polemics involved oversimplifications at variance with his own complex synthesis of eclectic spiritual elitism with national feeling.

Such divisions in Irish society which Yeats, as the years went by, found more and more alienating, in the early 1920s, it is true, lacked the immediate viciousness of the politics that the civil war had left in its bloody wake. The theatre, artistic production and cultural debate could not however escape completely that bitter legacy. In April 1923 the Abbey Theatre presented a first play by a new playwright, the work of a Dublin working-man, a Protestant with a history of labour and national agitation behind him. Sean O'Casey's *The Shadow of a Gunman* was a daring production to mount in the last month of the civil war. Its characterization of a patriot of the War of Independence as a *miles gloriosus* and cowardly prating poet, was likely to offend Free Stater and Republican alike. It was followed in March 1924 by O'Casey's even more dangerously relevant *Juno and the Paycock*, which dramatized not only the horrors of executions carried out on former companions-in-arms in the civil war but suggested how years of revolution and violence had benefited nobody, least of all the poor. It invoked in its final scene a 'state of chassis' as a prevailing condition of Irish being.

In writing such plays O'Casey was intervening in an over-heated, dangerously volatile, even explosive crucible of feeling. And Yeats as director of the Abbey was aiding and abetting him. It was a crucible in which was increasingly added not only the bitter elements of violently divided politics but a direct, vigorous, unabashed sectarianism.

Yeats had encountered Catholic opposition to his work before. D. P. Moran in the *Leader* at the turn of the century had never been disinclined to imply that Yeats as a Protestant from the English garrison, should not be dabbling in Irish affairs. Yet there had been something almost amusingly rhetorical about Moran's crudely boisterous bluster. And Ireland in the early 1900s was a place with a great deal yet to be played for. Moran's voice among many competing voices was not something to be unduly worried about, even when it was offensive. By the 1920s, with the memories of violence and civil war polluting the atmosphere, cultural polemic took on a sharper edge. With what was viewed as a native government in place for the first time, albeit one that many considered seriously compromised in its acceptance of the Treaty, ideology became less a matter of debate and exchange of views about a possible Irish future, than a contest about actual political and social power. Culture was seized on as a weapon ready to hand in a nasty fight. For there were ideologues ready to argue that Ireland was a Catholic country and that the new state should seek to ensure that its distinctively Catholic culture should be protected from contamination by alien elements. A measure of the aggressively anti-Protestant and xenophobic attitudes that prevailed in some comparatively influential circles is provided by the response of the Dublin-published *Catholic Bulletin* to Yeats's Nobel prize. It was greeted with a ill-tempered outburst, entirely of-a-piece, with the venomous crusade it had been waging against Anglo-Ireland and writers like Yeats, Gogarty and AE who presumed to speak for it and for Ireland:

> Paganism in prose or in poetry has, it seems its solid cash value: and if a poet does not write tawdry verse to make the purse heavier, he can be brought by his admirers to where the money is, whether in the form of an English pension, or in extracts from the Irish taxpayer's pocket, or in the Stockholm dole.   (cited in T. Brown 1985: 57)

The *Catholic Bulletin* was an extremist organ, with only a small circulation, but it was edited by a man who was a respected figure in the Sinn Féin movement. The attitudes which found noxious expression in its pages were by no means restricted to cranks and vocal extremists but represented a point on a spectrum of Catholic and nationalist public opinion that would prove unreceptive to Yeatsian ideals of the social order.

The fact that in the senate Yeats swiftly identified himself with a group of independent senators who made it their business to protect the interests of the former Unionist inhabitants of the new Free State (he joined the Kildare Street Club, a bastion of privilege at the epicentre of Ascendancy society) did not allow his voice to sound very effectively in the broader Irish community. It has been argued (Hone) that Yeats took these steps because he believed he could influence his effective, worldly colleagues in the direction of his developing concept of an Anglo-Irish tradition of magnanimous service to the nation with totemic eighteenth-century figures such as Swift, Grattan and Burke, with Parnell their inheritor, as inspiration. If this was the case it was a rather fond hope, for his new coadjutors (such as Andrew Jameson the whiskey distiller) were practical men, defending the immediate economic interests of their caste and class. And Yeats's identification with this group, though he did not always vote with them on specific issues, certainly made his position ambiguous to say the least, in the broad church of nationalist Ireland, now giving some credence to sectarianism.

In 1923 and 1924 Yeats became a public man in a way that he had never been before. In the senate he spoke on such matters as the location of parliament, censorship of films, damage to property ('This Country will not always be an uncomfortable place for a country gentleman to live in, and it is most important that we should keep in this country a certain leisured class'; Pearce 1961: 38), national health insurance, inspection of prisons and Northern Ireland. He also spoke on the cultural matters that interested him more deeply: Irish manuscripts, the National Gallery and the School of Art, the National Musem, the role of the Irish language in national life ('I wish to make a very emphatic protest against the histrionics which have crept into the whole Gaelic movement'; Pearce 1961: 57). Yet all was not a measured, occasionally rather portentous contribution to a well-ordered assembly of worthies. Yeats's occult life was bearing its own strange artistic fruit, even as he attended to the tediums of an order paper and the protocols of parliamentary exchange. And the artist in him could not resist more dramatic, risky engagements with his experience, the kind that had always energized his imaginative being.

By July of 1923 he was writing to Sturge Moore for a big design for his philosophy book of which he had then written 120 pages. September of that year saw him complete a version of a daring poem to be entitled 'Leda and the Swan'. In January 1924 he published in *English Life and the Illustrated Review* a lengthy, richly complex poem entitled 'The Gift of Harun El Rashid', (the spelling of the proper name went through several permutations), which exploited an elaborate fancy to dramatize how his personal life had been affected by marriage. It had brought him a gift of 'Desert Geometry' (when the poem was included in his philosophy book *A Vision*, 1925, it was titled 'Desert Geometry or the Gift of Harun Al-Raschid').

The poem in fluent, buoyant iambics (an uncommon register in Yeats's *oeuvre*) transposes the reader into a world of multiple fictions. We are back with the imaginary Arab world with its invented Judwalis, which supplied the context for the extended notes in *Michael Robartes and the Dancer*). Kusta Ben Luka, whose memory the Judwalis sect had kept green in the religious tradition that included the image of interpenetrating gyres, is now the grateful recipient, as an ageing philosopher, of a young bride with mediumistic powers. The hazy stories of this act of enlivening generosity, written about by Ben Luka in an intimate letter to a friend, are fancifully deemed by Yeats to have been recollections of what was contained in a little book discovered 'by some Judwali scholar or saint between the pages of a Greek book' (Yeats supplied an extensive, pseudo-historical note to the poem when it was republished later in 1924).

This highly complicatedly fictional context in which the poem was entered in 1924 was of course no real disguise for any reader who wanted to consider it as a version of the poet's own life. The famous man who had married a young bride in 1917 could not really have hoped to publish such a poem without at least stimulating some prurient speculation. Many of its lines gave grounds for wondering what exactly the distinguished senator's home life was actually like, if his poem was other than a older man's Browningesque fantasy:

> Upon a moonless night
> I sat where I could watch her sleeping form,
> And wrote by candle-light; but her form moved,
> And fearing that my light disturbed her sleep
> I rose that I might screen it with a cloth.
> I heard her voice, 'Turn that I may expound
> What's bowed your shoulder and made pale your cheek';
> And saw her sitting upright on the bed;
> Or was it she that spoke or some great Djinn?
> I say that a Djinn spoke. A live-long hour
> She seemed the learned man and I the child.

The oddly transparent disguise of this poem serves, I would argue, a purpose other than concealment. Though Yeats's contemporary readers, without access to knowledge about the Automatic Script and the spirit instructors, might only have interpreted the poem as a narrative of imaginative renewal in marriage with a young woman, the fact that the poem had an autobiographical content was obvious enough. What the poem offers is in fact a pseudo-disguise cast as pseudo-history and scholarship, presented in fictions within fictions, in a context of inferred, multiple textuality. This bears on its meaning.

Through much of the poem it is inferred that the truth which marriage has brought are truths of the body and truths made known by the body. Yet the poem is also about writing and about the attempt to explicate in the words of a letter or in a philosophy what are the significances of the diagrams Ben Luka's bride draws in the sand while sleep-walking.

The signs and shapes;
All those abstractions that you fancied were
From the great Treatise of Parmenides;
All, all those gyres and cubes and midnight things
Are but a new expression of her body
Drunk with the bitter sweetness of her youth.
And now my utmost mystery is out.

What Yeats was about as he constructed his system from the material George Yeats had supplied, this poem implies, is the impossible task of representing what may be unrepresentable in words. Wisdom of and derived from a living body that had been the vehicle of revelation and renewal could perhaps find a strange geometric expression in diagrammatic form, but not easily in 'poor words'. Words would be only inadequate substitutes for embodied truth at its most vital in the passionate body and at its most starkly austere in 'desert geometry'. Verbal acts of representation accordingly partake of necessary, but arbitrary, stylistic arrangements of experience. They are forms of fiction which must seem fancifully textual, lacking originating author, when confronted with the 'utmost mystery'.

A passage that Yeats wrote as he worked on the composition of *A Vision* links this poem with the labours he had set himself in 1924 and 1925, as he sought to complete his strange new book. It reveals that he did indeed see his task as a most difficult search for the words to represent what only geometry can model precisely. It is a passage of mingled uncertainty and confidence that he was not wasting his time in the strange, burdensome avocation he had accepted for himself:

> As I write I find myself looking for words that do not exist to express what can be expressed accurately in geometric lines – three times this morning I had given up in despair [?did] I not remember that this task has been laid upon me by those who cannot speak being dead & who if I fail may never find another interpreter. Kusta ben Luka himself once so learned & so eloquent could now, lacking me but twitter like a swallow. (cited in Harper 1987 vol. 2: 408)

If the publication of such a poem invited speculative prurience in Yeats's readership, several of his forays into politcs in 1924 risked greater damage to a reputation as sage senator responsibly engaged with matters of the democratic state that the poet's demeanour and delivery in the Senate suggested he had in mind. In February he gave an interview for the *Irish Times* which appeared under the headline 'From Democracy to Authority: Paul Claudel and Mussolini – A New School of Thought'. The occasion was a Dublin Drama League production of a play by Paul Claudel. Yeats comes over as a pontificator of magisterial indiscretion: 'Authoritative government is certainly coming, if for no other reason than that the modern State is so complex that it must find some kind of expert government, a government firm enough, tyrannical enough, if you will, to spend years in carrying out its plans' (*UP2*: 433). The success of Mussolini in Italy, who

had marched on Rome to seize power in October 1922, is set against such long
historical perspectives, as part of a univeral turn away from vulgar individualism
to mass movements led by exceptional persons. Democracy as fruit of the
Enlightenment is now, Yeats avers, withering on the vine: 'I see the same
tendency here in Ireland towards authoritative government. What else can
chaos produce even though our chaos has been a very small thing compared
with the chaos in Central Europe?' (ibid.: 435). He hoped for a steady movement
towards 'the creation of a nation controlled by highly trained intellects' (ibid.).

February 1924 was a less than tactful time for an Irish senator to voice such
subversive opinion (though the fact that Yeats included among recommendations
in this interview his opinion that the state should encourage 'proper teaching in
the designing of lace' must have dampened somewhat its apocalyptic impact).
Since January trouble had been brewing in the Free State army. Efforts to
professionalize and demobilize that force after the civil war had led to great
internal tensions. Officers who found their powers diminished in March 1924
were on the point of mutiny. The democratic institutions of state survived only by
dint of some extremely adroit political manoeuvres, verbal fudgings and decisive
action in which Yeats's acquaintance Kevin O'Higgins played a skilful part. For a
period of ten days or so in March a *coup d'état* was an all too real possibility.
Kidnappings and assassinations had been planned. A march on Dublin might
have put paid to the country's infant democracy. Yeats could have seen rule by
the few sooner than he expected. There is evidence, however, that Yeats, who
had the ear of a certain younger army officer, did the state some service in
alerting the independent senators about what was afoot. There may have been a
conduit to Cosgrave and O'Higgins: 'His authorities were unnamed, but they
were usually young men, and always dark in complexion, who called upon him
late at night' (*Hone*: 382).

Yeats was happy to see established order maintained. Approaching sixty, he
nevertheless still relished a good public row and welcomed the invigoration of
conflict. The summer of 1924 offered both.

When Yeats had completed the first version of 'Leda and the Swan' he had
explained to Lady Gregory that the poem had its inspiration in 'his long belief
that the reign of democracy is over for the present, and in reaction there will be
violent government from above, as now in Russia, and is beginning here'
(Gregory 1978 vol. 1: 477). As he later outlined, its immediate political relevance
to the Irish and international situation became less obvious as he wrote the poem.
Yet it retained, in its graphic, deliberate, dramatic representation of a sexual
assault and rape, a highly shocking voltage. It was first published in Ireland safely
enough in a Cuala Press volume, *The Cat and the Moon and Certain Poems* in a limited
edition in July 1924 and at a distance in *The Dial* in June. The poem had been
originally commissioned by the *Irish Statesman* (of which Yeats was a director). But
AE, the editor, who knew his periodical's readership and its sponsor Horace
Plunkett, had understandably demurred (George Yeats shared her husband's
view that AE was prudent to the point of pusillanimity; she thought he had the
moral courage of a flea) when he saw what he had been offered. He most

certainly did not want to face suppression (Yeats wanted to title his poem 'Annunciation', adding to the risk) with so much needing to be said about the state of Ireland in a periodical to which he contributed very largely himself. With the nonchalant irresponsibility, that signalled the personality differences between himself and AE that always made their friendship an unlikely, intermittent affair, Yeats delightedly seized a chance to see the poem locally in print in a way that would make it a point of public contention.

Francis and Iseult Stuart, with the young painter Cecil Salkeld and the writers Liam O'Flaherty and F. R. Higgins, had decided to produce a provocative monthly to be entitled *To-morrow*. They approached Yeats for support. The ageing poet, who welcomed contacts with a rising generation of radical spirits who were agitated by questions of national culture, drafted an editorial for the first edition, which was attributed in the magazine to Stuart and Salkeld. Expecting 'an admirable row' Yeats loftily opined in an act of patrician ventriloquism, 'we are Catholics, but of the school of Pope Julius the Second and of the Medician Popes' who had patronized great artists. By contrast 'What devout man can read the Pastorals of our Hierarchy without horror at a style rancid, coarse and vague, like that of the daily papers?' A summons for artists everywhere to 'call back the soul to its ancient sovereignty' (*To-morrow*, vol. 1, no. 1: 4) was not likely in such a context to meet with much Irish approval.

It was not the editorial which provoked most comment. Rather, a short story by Lennox Robinson about an Irish peasant girl who when raped by a tramp imagines herself pregnant by the Holy Spirit gave most instant offence. Yeats's Leda poem, which also appeared in same issue of *To-morrow* in August 1924 swiftly became associated with a story which affronted piety chose to regard as a blasphemy. From 1924 on the *Catholic Bulletin* would inveigh against the 'putrid "Swan Poem"' or the '"Stinking Sonnet"' as a target that stood for everything they detested about the poet (Cullingford 1993: 148). It damned Yeats as a leading spirit in a cabal of Ascendancy pagans who wished to corrupt the pure Catholic and Gaelic soul of Ireland.

Yeats had got his 'admirable row' and, as he had hoped, the periodical was threatened with suppression. Even the conventionally pious President Cosgrave had got to hear of it. *To-morrow* ceased publication after the second issue.

August saw Yeats in fighting mood, welcoming contention. At the Tailteann Games which the government had inaugurated to enliven in an appropriately Celtic fashion the rather dull social climate of postwar Dublin, there was announced the result of a literary competition, judged by Yeats and Robinson. They chose the poems of one Francis Stuart as worthy of the prize. At the Tailteann Banquet on 2 August Yeats once more, as he had done to the members of the Golden Dawn more than two decades before counselled discipline as against freedom. In her analysis of this speech and the draft that preceded it, Cullingford has argued (Cullingford 1981: 149–50) that by 'discipline' Yeats meant 'self-discipline' not the kind of enforced discipline that Russia was experiencing under the Bolsheviks. It was not therefore inconsistent for the partisan of Irish freedom to admire Mussolini. Italy was not being subdued in the name of an abstract Utopia but accepting the self-imposed necessity of discipline. This is a nice distinction and probably a fair one given, at this time, Yeats's merely basic knowledge of Fascism. Yet it is the kind of distinction that gets easily lost in the heat of political exchange and in circumstances other than the rather ineffective if colourful pageantry of the Tailteann, such speeches could have proved more dangerous than they were in the Dublin of 1924.

The essentially pacific and innocently aesthetic nature of the poet's engagement with Irish public life is indicated not by this speech and the *Irish Times* interview but by the enthusiasm with which Yeats set off for London that month on a government sanctioned mission. He had not been dreaming of black-clad armies to assert the Irish nation's will. Rather he hoped to get Charles Ricketts to design robes for judges in the Free State courts (Gregory 1978 vol. 1: 575), which could replace the all-too English wig and gown. This engaging fashion fancy, like the poet's scarcely brutal hopes for native lacemaking, came to nothing.

In the late summer and early autumn of 1924 Yeats was the complete man. He possessed wife, children, elegant home, position, reputation, honours and some public power on issues that interested him. He had, too, been revising his writings for a Macmillan Uniform Edition of his works, which would, it was probably hoped, make the Nobel Laureate's achievement readily available to a wide international readership. He was furthermore deeply absorbed by his 'philosophy', which he hoped to finish quickly for Werner Laurie, publisher of *The Trembling of the Veil*. Laurie had agreed to publish *A Vision*, to appear as the autobiographical volume had done, as a limited, signed and numbered edition. Yeats's life seemed set fair for a vigorous yet settled old age, with Dublin as the centre of his activities. Even news of the death in New York in July of John Quinn, who had been ill with stomach cancer for some time, was not the blow it would have been earlier in Yeats's life. Fate willed, as so often before, a future the poet could not perhaps have expected, for all his scrying and reading of astrological charts.

As winter drew on physical problems began for the first time to interfere seriously with Yeats's always busy daily life. His sight in one eye was almost gone, and slight deafness was a sign of advancing years. He was also overweight and periods of over-indulgence in tobacco were taking a toll on heart and lungs. Exercise became difficult because of shortness of breath. Though Lady Gregory recorded in her journal for 11 November that Yeats, who was visiting her at Coole looked 'a picture of health and in high spirits' (Gregory 1978 vol. 1: 603), he was in fact suffering from worryingly raised blood pressure and was advised by his doctor to rest. George Yeats decided forthwith that he should have an Italian break and at the end of November the couple set off for Capri and Sicily. So began a period of fifteen years, in which Yeats would endure much ill-health and would frequently seek to restore his constitution through periods abroad, until his death in the south of France in January 1939. He would spend his old age in the same peripatetic fashion as he had his youth and young manhood.

This first of his late journeyings was a pleasant and enriching holiday for a man whose career, for all its public glamour, had been marked by extraordinary and unremitting years of literary toil (the correspondence the Nobel Prize had generated had added to an already extremely onerous daily burden of letter-writing, discharged throughout a long life with great faithfulness).

In Italy the Yeatses spent time in Sicily, Capri and Rome. Even on what was intended by spouse and doctor as a complete break Yeats was working. The conclusion of the fourth book of the 1925 edition of *A Vision* is followed by the note 'Finished at Syracuse, 1925' (*AVA*: 252) while the dedication is dated February at Capri. He met Pound again, who had left London in 1920 convinced that there was 'no longer any intellectual *life* in England' (Paige 1971: 158). Italy in the full tide of Fascist experiment appealed to Pound greatly. After four years of Paris he had recently moved to Palermo before making a permanent home in Rapallo. The Irish poet took the chance, when the couple eventually made their way to Rome after about two months' recuperation in the south, to explore with the help of George Yeats's Italian, 'the spiritual antecedents of the Fascist revolution, an event which Yeats considered . . . as at least equal in importance to the proletarian conquest of Russia' (Hone 1946: 368). As his first biographer, who met the Yeatses in Rome at this time, recalls, the poet who had read Croce on Vico in 1924, further whetted an appetite for the modern Italian philosophers who seemed to underpin the new Fascist state. The writings of Gentile, particularly as they pertained to educational theory and practice, especially interested him as he learned of them in summaries of Italian texts supplied by his wife.

Yeats returned to Ireland in the spring, his own 'philosophy' ready for the publisher, his mind and imagination refreshed by new reading and new sights. The rich imagery of Michelangelo's Sistine Chapel, which he had visited frequently and photographed, had told him that Irish Catholicism, with its distrust of the body, its puritanical fear of sexual irregularity of any kind, was an aberration in the church universal. Yet when such tolerance of the flesh was combined with a rigid legal code in respect of matrimony and divorce, as in Italy, the effects he believed were socially deleterious. This was an insight he was to exploit almost immediately upon his return to Ireland.

In February a procedural process began to make it impossible for the Irish parliament to introduce any bill allowing for divorce in the state. Yeats in anticipation of speaking against the resolution prepared a speech. When the chairman of the senate ruled this resolution out of order on constitutional grounds, Yeats promptly published an article in the *Irish Statesman* (14 March), based on what he would have said, guaranteed to offend many Catholics and also to disturb mightily members of the Church into which Yeats himself had been baptised, the Protestant Church of Ireland. For many in that community thought it best to keep a low profile in a country where a significant number of their fellow citizens regarded them as suspect remnants of the *ancien régime*. Yeats had no truck with such caution, roundly condemning a legislative attitude which bespoke a desire on the part of the majority 'to impose . . . Catholic convictions upon members of the Church of Ireland and upon men of no church' (*UP2*: 450). He warned that such a policy would further divide the Protestant North from the rest of the country. Yet the heart of his argument, adducing Italy, Spain and pre-revolutionary France in support of his thesis, was that 'the price that you pay for indissoluble marriage is a public opinion that will tolerate illegal relations between the sexes' (ibid.). And in a passionate affirmation of the classical Protestant view of divorce, he urged resistance to fanaticism in the name of liberty. Upon a small minority would depend the free future of a country that had fought for its freedom from Britain.

In June Yeats got his chance to speak in the senate on the issue of divorce. For in that month the senate debated and passed a resolution that effectively made divorce and remarriage a legislative impossibility. Yeats spoke from a written text with magisterial, incandescent intensity to a house that was less than receptive to his disdainful admonition on the necessary separation of the powers of church and state; on the unreliability of biblical texts: on the laxity of morals in Catholic countries; on the sexually notorious reputation of the piously Catholic patriot Daniel O'Connell. Yeats reached a rhetorical crescendo in defence of his own Protestant caste:

> We against whom you have done this thing are no petty people. We are one of the great stocks of Europe. We are the people of Burke; we are the people of Grattan; we are the people of Swift, the people of Emmet, the people of Parnell. We have created the most of the modern literature of this country. We have created the best of its political intelligence. (Pearce 1961: 99)

Yeats certainly knew that his speech, which cost him dearly in emotional and physical energy, was an act of defiance. He was deliberately fomenting conflict in identifying his own stock, the Protestant people of Ireland, with an elitist libertarianism that the country could ill afford to lose. For the people from whom Yeats's pantheon of great men had sprung were not associated in the popular Irish mind with love of liberty, but with centuries of oppression of the native Irish at the behest of an alien garrison. Yet beneath the inflammatory rodomontade of Yeats's speech there runs a strain of genuine concern, that had surfaced in his article in the *Irish Statesman*, for the spiritual destiny of the nation. Conflict, he believed, the cut and thrust of dialectic, was necessary to its genuinely religious health and conflict was what he was prepared to give it, at whatever cost to his health and social ease. For he had been awaiting the proofs of a book which he earnestly hoped would offer a vision of the future to the young country in whose senate he served. Central to that work was a principal of conflict, a war at the heart of things which raised life when it was comprehended aright, from materialist banality to spiritual miracle made manifest at shocking moments of annunciation. That book was aptly entitled *A Vision*.

It appeared to almost universal disinterest in a print run of 600 expensive copies for subscribers in January 1926. It received a review from AE in the *Irish Statesman*. AE was respectful, but reckoned: 'It is not a book which will affect many in our time' (*CH*: 272). One can readily see why he arrived at that conclusion.

The text of *A Vision* gives ample evidence that Yeats was all too aware that many would regard his book as a folly. When he had first started to talk about his findings in Dublin in 1919, as the novelist Douglas Goldring reports, his audience, mostly elderly women, had 'stared at him goggle-eyed' (Goldring *The Nineteen-Twenties*: 118, cited in Pierce 1995: 304). His dedication to the volume recognized that he might 'disappoint those that come' to his book through some interest in his poetry alone. He advised them to dip into a book that he could have made richer had he worked on it for another year. And he admitted that it was incomplete: 'I have not even dealt with the whole of my subject, perhaps not even with what is most important, writing nothing about the Beatific Vision, little of sexual love' (*AVA*: xii). In the body of his work he counsels that 'only long familiarity with the system' (ibid., 21) can make part of it intelligible and recognizes that one section must have been found by the reader 'very troublesome' (ibid.: 149). Almost immediately after its publication Yeats began to think he had failed his Communicators in giving to the world a flawed document. In the second version, published in 1937, he confessed that the first version filled him with shame; 'I had misinterpretated the geometry and in my ignorance of philosophy failed to understand distinctions upon which the coherence of the whole depended' (*AVB*: 19).

Yet it is not only the inconsistencies and impenetrabilities of the work that can repel the reader of this work. Its bizarre juxtaposition of fanciful romance with complex psychological categories explored through a dizzying set of permutations tracked in a private, often obscure terminology, its geometric concepts and diagrams, historical charts, cultural histories and Spiritualist speculations are indigestible as a whole.

Yeats as man and artist had obviously invested a great deal in this book, for all that he wrote self-deprecatingly of its early reception: '*A Vision* reminds me of the stones I used to drop as a child into a certain very deep well. The splash is very far off and very faint...A few men here [he was writing from Dublin in March 1926] are reading me, so I may found an Irish heresy' (*L*: 712). It was the fruit of seven years painstaking psychic work with his medium wife and of arduous attempts to cast what he had learned through that collaboration into coherent form. The revision of the text would become also a central preoccupation for years to come. So the critic and biographer is faced not only with an obscure and difficult text to explicate but with the problem of how such a strange work bears on a major writer's creativity and on the works which he produced in the final thirteen years of his life. Yeats himself thought of his book as 'a last act of defence against the chaos of the world' and he hoped 'for ten years to write out' of a 'renewed security' (unpublished letter, cited in Harper 1987 vol. 2. 407–8).

The primary critical problem is a problem of kind. Much of the book is couched in the curiously technical, abstract jargon that Yeats had derived or developed from the private language of the automatic writings (tinctures, Will, Mask, Creative Mind, Body of Fate, Husk, Passionate Body, Celestial Body, Spirit) and suggests the systematic organization of a treatise that purports to instruct a reader in a body of knowledge painstakingly accountable to observable data. The charts and geometric diagrams – in which the interpenetrating gyres which had already accompanied the first volume publication of 'The

Second Coming' ramify to the point of tedium – also suggest a study of axiomatic truth. If only the reader were more attentive, more assiduous in study all would be revealed, the text somewhat pedagogically implies. However its complicated contents come, as does the poem 'Desert Geometry Or The Gift of Harun Al-Raschid' (employed as a preface to Book II), wrapped in ostentatious fictionality.

The introduction is supplied by Owen Aherne, who recounts how he met Michael Robartes in 1917, recently returned from his Near Eastern sojourn. Robartes is anxious to know the whereabouts of Mr Yeats (as social comedy, as Archibald has argued, the whole thing is impossibly arch) who he believes misused him as a merely fictional character in 'Rosa Alchemica'. He tells Aherne of his journeys, which first took him to the Polish city of Cracow where he accidently came on a book 'Speculum Angelorum et Hominorum' by a scholar named Giraldus (whose scholarship did not extend as far as the genitive plural of *Homo*). The book had been left behind in the lodgings of Robartes's Polish mistress by an unfrocked priest. From Cracow thence to Arabia, where Robartes found among the Judwalis and in their drawings on the sand the same structure of thought as contained in the book of Giraldus. Robartes is anxious to enlist the help of either Yeats or Aherne in publishing his discoveries. At last he gets to meet Mr Yeats who consents to write an exposition based on the diagrams Robartes has taken from Giraldus's text. Aherne concludes his introduction by stating that 'Mr Yeats's completed manuscript now lies before' him. He gives the date and place of composition of his own text as 'LONDON, *May*, 1925'. Immediately before the title page to the volume as a whole is a woodcut, attributed to Giraldus's book, of the author of the 'Speculum'. It is captioned 'Portrait of Giraldus', but executed by Edmund Dulac, exhibits (as the poet instructed it should) a striking likeness to Yeats himself. He may even be winking. Fiction unfolds further within these enfolded fictions in another contribution by Owen Aherne, 'The Dance Of The Four Royal Persons'. This links Robartes' account of a diagram in Giraldus called 'The Great Wheel' with the desert geometry of the Judwali sect, from which, Aherne sceptically explains, Mr Yeats took his 'poem of Harun al-Raschid'. Fiction and reality implode in these increasingly absurd narratives with their obviously 'fake' apparatus. The effect is to encourage the reader to interrogate the status of what follows. The sense of vertiginous fictionality that this layered text deliberately, if somewhat tiresomely, induces, sets in question the literal truth of anything it contains.

What it essentially does contain is a vision of life as most profoundly itself when in conflict – 'all things dying each other's life, living each other's death' (*AVA*: 183). It is a work which accepts conflict as the condition of the spiritual. As such it is Yeats's manifesto for the new Ireland in which he himself had enthusiastically embraced controversy and conflict. It was a summons to the new state to relish such conflict as a spiritual resource which would enable it to transcend the bitter divisions of the civil war. Conflict, comprehended as the source of creative energy rather than disabling divisiveness, would vitalize the country and save it from the materialism of an age which would deny the immortality of the soul and destroy the living body of the nation. *A Vision* was a poet's prophetic book which did not so much forecast the future as challenge the present. As so often before, Yeats's ambitions for his work and his country were to meet with crushing disappointment.

15

Visionary Modernist

A Vision comprises four books. The first, 'What The Caliph Partly Learned', is divided into two parts in which the system is painstakingly, though often confusingly, explained and explored. Book Two, 'What The Caliph Refused To Learn', translates the system into an impenetrable solid geometry. Book Three, 'Dove or Swan', assesses human history in the light of the system, while Book Four 'The Gates of Pluto' offers a guide to the soul's after-death experience. Though the work is often baffling and as a whole repels by its very oddity its basis is not complex.

The work explores a primary duality. Human personality can be measured on a scale of objectivity and subjectivity (what Yeats also terms 'primary' and 'antithetical'). The former is a solar, the latter a lunar state. In Yeats's system complete subjectivity (which he associates with Unity of Being, a desirable condition too absolute for any living person) is at the full of the moon, complete objectivity is at the dark of the moon. Between these two poles are twenty-six phases of the moon, on what Yeats terms 'The Great Wheel': 'all possible human types can be classified under one or other of these twenty-eight phases' (*AVA*: 12) according to the proportion of subjective or objective 'tinctures' at work on the personality. 'Human life', Yeats insists, 'is impossible without the strife between the Tinctures' (ibid.: 14). The human person, furthermore, has four faculties which constitute the tinctures, and here the problems start. For not only are the faculties given the less than helpful names which Yeats had derived or developed from the Automatic Script but they are defined in ways that deepen the obscurity. The four categories are *Will*, the *Creative Mind*, the *Body of Fate* and the *Mask*. By *Will* Yeats means 'feeling that has not become desire because there is no object to desire; a bias by which the soul is classified and its phase fixed but which as yet is without result in action' (ibid.: 14–15). By *Mask* Yeats means 'the image of that we wish to become, or of that to which we give our reverence'. *Creative Mind* is 'all the mind that is consciously constructive' (ibid.: 15). *Body of Fate* is the actual physical body and the environment and social circumstances with which the person must contend. In Yeats's elaboration of this set of categories *Will* and *Mask* are predominantly Lunar and *Creative Mind* and *Body of Fate* are predominantly Solar. In *A Vision* the lunar or antithetical faculties seem to be preferred since they are subjective and creative, but all four are necessary in a dynamics of the human person. *Will* and *Mask* are always paired in opposition as are *Creative Mind* and *Body of Fate*. At its clearest Yeats is imagining a drama of the faculties which can be compared 'to the *Commedia del Arte* or improvised drama of Italy'. In this

> The stage manager having chosen his actor, the *Will*, chooses for this actor, that he may display him the better, a scenario, *Body of Fate*, which offers to his *Creative Mind* the greatest possible difficulty that it can face without despair, and in which he must play a rôle and wear a *Mask* as unlike as possible to his natural character (or *Will*) and leaves him to improvise, through *Creative Mind*, the dialogue and the details of the plot. (ibid.: 17–18)

At this point the system of classification, which might have been accepted as a complex symbol of forces in conflict in the human psyche, starts to become (as Graham Hough has argued) not only obsessively complicated but increasingly arbitrary in relation to anything we might sense to be lived experience. For what might have seemed a way of thinking about the human personality as a compound of subjective and objective impulses with character dependent on a tendency towards one or other of these polarities, is refined to the point of near-total obscurity. Not only are there true and false forms of *Mask* and *Creative Mind* (which seem to offer the possibility of choice in a closed system) but the symbol of the Great Wheel is employed to establish the ratio of the faculties in the person, according to a set of rules which is never clearly established in the text. It has to be inferred from their use, as Hough demonstrates. When this system is eventually grasped it is obvious enough that Yeats has used it (the 'Communicators' helped in this labour) to assemble a set of biographical, psychological and critical analyses which exemplify how living and dead persons represent varying permutations of the faculties.

This second part of Book One (though confusingly Yeats has no heading for Part Two), makes for much more interesting reading than the definitions of Part One or the geometric conundrums of Book Two. For the human interest of learning at what phase Yeats places friends, contemporaries, historical personages, writers living and dead, gives to a system that would otherwise seem arbitrary and mechanical to the point of whimsy, a novelistic psychologism. The personalities at the early phases, it is true, do seem as factitious as most astrological typologies, lacking felt life. Human interest intensifies however as we move around the Wheel to Phases Fourteen to Twenty-four, which include Keats, many beautiful women (Phase Fourteen), William Blake, some beautiful women (Phase Sixteen, where we know from the Automatic Script, Gonne was placed by the Communicators), Dante, Shelley (Phase Seventeen, where the poet himself was placed), Shakespeare, Balzac, Napoleon (Phase Twenty), Queen Victoria, Galsworthy and Lady Gregory (Phase Twenty-four). What the deepening human feeling of Part Two of Book One (entitled, 'The Twenty-eight Embodiments') suggests, is that the abstraction of Book One, Part One, and the 'desert geometry' of Book Two, enabled Yeats to assess in his own writing the warring constituents of his personality with a greater precision and self-knowledge than he had ever done before, even in his autobiographical works. And he was enabled too to see his obsession with Gonne more steadily than hitherto. Of 'some beautiful women' at Phase Sixteen Yeats writes:

> They walk like queens, and seem to carry upon their backs a quiver of arrows, but they are gentle only to those whom they have chosen or subdued, or to the dogs that follow at their heels. Boundless in generosity, and in illusion, they will give themselves to a beggar because he resembles a religious picture and be faithful all their lives, or if they take another turn and choose a dozen lovers, die convinced that none but the first or last has ever touched their lips, for they are of those whose 'virginity renews itself like the moon'. (*AVA*: 74)

Images from Yeats's own plays and poetry combine here in a passage which bathes Gonne as the representative beautiful woman, in the dispassionate light of understanding both granted and accepted. At Phase Seventeen Yeats has a psyche whose primary experience is that of the Will 'falling asunder'. The intellect must 'synthesise in vain' and 'The being has for its supreme aim . . . to hide from itself and others this separation and disorder' (ibid.: 75). A portrait emerges of man wracked by a knowledge of self-division but driven by a desire for synthesis, of man in whom conflict is an energizing principle, in whom the antinomies of life are creatively incarnate. There is a tone of proud self-acceptance in this entry, a refusal either to sentimentalize the past or to imagine that the future will allow any armistice in the war within:

> The being, through the intellect, selects some object of desire for a representation of the *Mask* as *Image*, some woman perhaps, and the *Body of Fate* snatches away the object. Then the intellect (*Creative Mind*), which in the most *antithetical* phases [of which Phase Seventeen is one] were better described as imagination, must substitute some new image of desire; and in the degree of its power and of its attainment of unity, relate that which is lost, that which has snatched it away, to the new image of desire, that which threatens the new image to the being's unity. (ibid.: 76)

Book Three of *A Vision* 'Dove or Swan' ('Leda and the Swan', here titled 'Leda', is printed as an introductory poem) which extends the principle of conflict in human personality to history, takes the gyres of Book Two as an explanatory image of the processes at work in historical change. Where conflict is essential in the dynamics of personality, history in both its creative and destructive guises in this book is explicable in terms of endless antitheses. The main body of the text here, for all the efforts to map the past according to geometric patterns, is a boldly synoptic cultural history of Europe which emphasizes the fine plastic arts as manifestations of the *Zeitgeist*. A resolute historicist, Yeats comprehends the past as a series of distinct periods and seeks to understand development and degeneration as they are determined by cyclical movement. As the human soul in many incarnations moves through the phases of the moon, history moves according to the spirals of primary and antithetical gyres in complicated cycles of 2,000, 1,000 and 500 years. In some wonderfully assured passages Yeats writes of the apogees of human culture, at the end of the fifth century AD in Byzantium, for example. Yet the real purpose of the book is neither art criticism nor historical illumination but warning and annunciatory excitement. The period from the Renaissance to the frightening present moment is Yeats's main burden and in his account of this period he offers an interpretation of the contemporary crisis which enters *A Vision* in the literature of Modernist anxiety.

Yeats shares with the T. S. Eliot of *The Waste Land* (1922) a conviction that modernity has involved a terrible desacralization of the world. Since the scientific revolution, religion, in its Christian form, has been in retreat and materialism has almost universally overwhelmed the sacred. The unified culture of Christendom, Yeats argues, gave way to individualistic personal expression. This in the end was no match for the power of a materialistic world view. The contemporary world is marked by a reductive objectivity and concomitant political and artistic degeneration:

> Personality is everywhere spreading out its fingers in vain, or grasping with an always more convulsive grasp a world where the predominance of physical science, of finance and economics in all their forms, of democratic politics, of vast populations, of architecture where styles jostle one another, of newspapers where all is heterogenous, show that mechanical force will in a moment become supreme. (*AVA*: 206–7)

Yet at such a moment of 'ever more abundant *primary* information' its opposite, '*antithetical* wisdom' (ibid.: 209) waits in the wings as it were for the next gyre. It will come like the violent annunciation of 'Leda and the Swan', of the birth of Christ which 'vexed to nightmare' twenty centuries of 'stony sleep'. Yeats is exhilarated by the prospect: 'when the new gyre begins to stir, I am filled with excitement' (ibid.: 210).

That excitement is confirmed by the avant garde art of the 1920s, in which Yeats discerns two impulses that encourage him to believe 'some revelation is at hand'. In the works of Pound, Eliot, Joyce and Pirandello, which he addresses towards the end of 'Dove and Swan', the poet reckons that objectivity has reached an extreme point, at which it seems to summon its opposite into proleptic existence: 'It is as though myth and fact, united until the exhaustion of the Renaissance, have now fallen so far apart that man understands for the first time the rigidity of fact, and calls up, by that recognition, myth – the *Mask* – which now but gropes its way out of the mind's dark but will shortly pursue and terrify' (ibid.: 212). The experiments of the Englishman Wyndham Lewis and the Romanian Brancusi, of the Scandinavian Milles, are adduced as works by 'masters of a geometrical pattern or rhythm which seems to impose itself wholly from beyond the mind, the artist "standing outside himself"' (ibid.: 211).

These comments on literary and artistic Modernism – on the Cubist experimentation of the period, the fragmentation of logical processes in literary hyperrealism – which attribute the shocking originality of new art forms to the 'mind's dark' and to things which come 'from beyond the mind', are intriguing in their own right. Yet they bear most forcibly on Yeats's own text, as if to instruct us on its complicated status. For *A Vision* is a work which comes from the dark of the mind and from beyond the mind, if we are to give any credit to the introductory narratives and to 'Desert Geometry or the Gift of Harun Al-Raschid' (included in the contents under that title). It is, too, a work of extraordinary factual rigidity in which the variations of human type are arranged according to an apparently 'scientific' taxonomy. It offers furthermore a geometry that claims analytic relevance to both the human person and to history. For Yeats has in fact contributed his own highly experimental text to the experimentalism of its period. *A Vision* breaks down human experience and history into what can be read as a 'given' series of abstract and mechanical patterns that bear the same kind of relation to reality as Cubist portraiture does to the persons it ostensibly portrays. They involve perspective and a deliberately objective eye. However Yeats's objective perspectivism coexists in his text with an awareness of its opposite – the subjective reality of bodily and spiritual life to which myth bears witness in its compelling way. The final book of *A Vision* translates us unapologetically to the dimension of myth as if to summon into existence the antithetical art whose imminence Modernist experiment anticipates in its negative way.

All of which is to say that *A Vision*, even in the form he quickly came to think of as seriously flawed, played a crucial part in Yeats's life as a poet in the 1920s and 1930s. For by attempting to organize human experience and history into a unified system he seems to have satisfied some deep need of his nature for pattern and structure in reality. This satisfaction of a need, or the sense that it could be satisfied, which had been central to his being from youth onwards, was a profoundly releasing thing for Yeats. For it freed him to confront his life and times in the faith that they were meaningful in and of themselves and not because they reflected an as yet uncomprehended reality which lay beyond them. That existence could be made amenable to an intricately complex pattern of oppositions, however arbitrary or even bizarre in absolute terms, allowed the poet to engage with the drama of self and world with an imaginative certitude both that he could trust his powers and trust that life would offer its own symbolic and mythic annunciations of the antithetical. Intricate structure elaborated gave him the energy to accept that conflict in the world as he experienced it was the true poet's only destiny. He could even accept a new era which would come 'bringing its stream of irrational force' (*AVA*: 213) secure in the conviction that 'organic groups, *covens* of physical or intellectual kin melted out of the frozen mass' (ibid.: 214), were harbingers of an antithetical age struggling to be born.

'The Gates of Pluto' is Yeats's *Book of the Dead*. In it the poet offers a Spiritualist's guide-book to 'death's dream kingdom' and explores the stages of recall or dreaming-back, purgation and renewal, through which the soul is imagined as passing before reincarnation. It is less than fully committed, however, to the idea of a dimension beyond existence in which final rest is attained. Escape from the cycles of reality may be desired but is so long deferred as to be almost meaningless as an object of the spiritual exercises death inaugurates. 'We may say' Yeats avers 'that the dead remain a portion of the living' (ibid.: 227), so great is their involvement, in the various stages of their purgation, with what they have left behind. The impression mounts that the afterlife is merely a new realization of the antinomial reality that experience in this life has afforded. It is a further dance of dynamic permutations (of 'Principles' not 'Faculties' in the world of the spirit) which allows for moments of ecstasy, but no escape from mere experience. Yeats puts this in terms of a dark conceit, but his message is that experience is all we will ever really know. There are some souls, it is true, who have completed their cycles ('Those who wait' Yeats dubs them) but the spirit 'will almost certainly pass' from what seems an otherworldly extension of life's conflicts, 'to human rebirth because of its terror of what seems to be the loss of its own being' (ibid.: 236). In the difficult concept of the Thirteenth Cone (adverted to in the 1925 version of the book and developed in the 1937 version), it is true, Yeats does ponder the possibility of deliverance from all cycles, but without real zest or much theological clarity. The concept seems incorporated into the system as a means of subverting at the last its overall determinism, rather than as the desirable goal of all human striving. Unity of Being in this life is the key aspiration of *A Vision* and its God is no mysterious Thirteenth Cone but the process in which Unity of Being can endlessly be sought. In the midst of the process failure and loss are the customary companions of spiritual ambition.

On 30 June 1921, when he was himself close to death John Butler Yeats had written to his son to make some telling observations about his work as a poet and dramatist:

> When is your poetry at its best? I challenge all the critics if it is not when the wild spirit of your imagination is wedded to concrete fact. Had you stayed with me and not left me for Lady Gregory, and her friends and associations, you would have loved and adored concrete life for which as I know you have a real affection. What would have resulted? Realistic and poetical plays – poetry in closest and most intimate union with the positive realities and complexities of life. And that is the world that waits, so far in vain, its poet. I have always hoped and do still hope that your wife may do for you what I would have done. (Hone 1946: 280–1)

'The Gates of Pluto', in its own very curious way, suggests that George Yeats had indeed performed for Yeats a service of the kind which John Butler Yeats had hoped she would. For the text her mediumship had brought him did not allow him to transcend experience, but, even as he contemplated the afterlife, brought him back to what he would celebrate, in a poem still to be written, as 'complexities of mire and blood' ('Byzantium'). As he testified in a letter to his future biographer, possibly in 1927: 'We are in the midst of life and there is nothing but life' (*L*: 728). When she read the published volume, Shakespear immediately recognized this about the 'Dove or Swan' section. She found it an oppressive read: 'I think it is rather terrible – all so unending & no rest or peace till one attains an unattainable goal' (*LTWBY* 2: 467–8).

Through much of the 1925 version of *A Vision*, for all its over-elaborate adumbration of abstract concepts, there hovers too the presence of a hauntingly undefined, complex entity – what Yeats calls the Daimon. Variously conceived of as the unconscious, the true self, the 'image' of 'Ego Dominus Tuus', an attendant spirit distinct from the self, the Daimon is a female 'other' whose influence on the self adds to the impression that the text as a whole has a sexual inspiration. For Yeats in *A Vision* was writing the body of a bride who had brought him erotic self-understanding and poetic renewal. As one commentator has argued, the poet 'was using the system both to acquire a muse and as a balm for the knot of his own unhappy love' (Croft 1987: 83). To this one might add that the work of seven and more years with his wife had enriched his sense of sexuality to the degree that the feminine in his own nature, his female Daimon, became a living presence in his conscious mind, available as a creative resource for art. For as Thomas Parkinson has suggested, a lifelong 'dependence on various women' (Parkinson 1982: 201) had prepared the poet to feminize the Daimon as something akin to the Anima in Jung's thought. Certainly the poet's unconscious allowed for such androgyny. In fact in one of Yeats's recorded 'sleeps', a strange gender exchange had taken place, which dramatizes how marital collaboration in Spiritualist experiment with George had stimulated transferrals of male and female identity, akin to those Gonne had once suggested were involved in his poetic achievement:

> I saw in a dream a hercules – I had no memory of George using that word – lying naked alseap or resting. I wonder how a woman could desire such a great coarse strength & and then it seemed to me I became a womans mind & I felt the desire of the strength & I touched his genital organs, but this did not seem to awake. (*VPs* 3: 87).

So *A Vision* which seemed in 1926 to have sunk without trace, is a key Modernist text – in its self-referential fictionality, in its Cubist abstraction and in its considerable investment in the potential powers of myth to apprehend and restore spiritual reality in a desacralized, materialistic age. It is Modernist too in its sense of historical crisis and in its awareness of the conflictual forces at work in the human psyche, an awareness that even challenges the basis of sexual self-identity. Its tiresome obscurities, the portentousness of some of its more hiero-phantic imaginings, its implied status as sacred book, also allow us to identify it as an example of Modernism in one of its most extreme forms. If the book did not admit the inexorable claims of the body and complex lived experience, it would seem merely a folly, a fascinating futility in an avant garde movement which, at an early stage of its development, found its *reductio ad absurdum*. As Daniel Albright has cogently stated it: 'Yeats was a Cubist only with the proviso that the reader must decubify the *image*, must try to recover the uninflected beauty that lies beyond it. What is important is not the stylistic arrangement of experience, but experience itself, immediate, carnal, unspeakable' (Albright 1997: 100). In as much as it allows recovery of such 'uninflected beauty', it makes an aesthetic claim on our attention as we discover amid its often tedius arcana, passages of singular, starkly strange intensity:

> I IMAGINE the annunciation that founded Greece as made to Leda, remembering that they showed in a Spartan Temple, strung up to the roof as a holy relic, an unhatched egg of hers; and that from one of her eggs came Love and from the other War. But all things are from antithesis, and when in my ignorance I try to imagine what older civilisation she refuted I can but see bird and woman blotting out some corner of the mathematical starlight. (*AVA*: 181)

A Vision was Yeats's summons as well to the new Irish state to find its spiritual destiny as an antithetical nation that would prefigure a general reversal of a materialist world order, now in its death throes. The gyres were inexorably turning, but individuals and nations were free to decide how they responded to the challenges of the age. Yeats hoped that conflict, the dominant subject of his prophetic book, would be the catalyst of spiritually invigorating change. He himself was more than ready to stir the pot. A chance to do so arrived almost immediately, in February, 1926.

Sean O'Casey's daringly iconoclastic play *The Plough and the Stars* opened at the Abbey Theatre on the eighth of the month. Yeats sensed he had not only a masterpiece on his hands but the makings of a first class row. For not only did O'Casey's play represent the Easter Rising in a less than heroic light but the second act, set in a public house, had a prostitute in symbolic apposition to the figure of a patriot orator, recognizably Patrick Pearse. Outrageously, the flags of the Citizen Army and of the Republic were brought on stage in Rosie Redmond's dubious company.

The first night passed off without incident but by the fourth the forces of protest had organized. They were led by Republican women, widows of patriots, and by diehards, inflamed by what they took to be an unforgivable slur on the martyred dead. During Act Three they invaded the stage and brought the performance to a halt amid general mayhem. Yeats delivered himself of a prepared speech in which the audience was berated: 'you have disgraced your-selves again'. The protesters were escorted from the theatre by the police, to allow the performance to conclude.

One member of the audience recalled that some of the protesters were armed. When she heard Yeats's contemptuous speech she 'fled the theatre, convinced that the poet's words would lead to murder' (Devitt 1988: 20). Yeats had made sure that they would be recorded in next morning's *Irish Times*. The following Saturday armed men tied to kidnap some of the players. Yeats sought police protection for his company. On 21 February he wrote to H. J. C. Grierson, whose edition of Donne he had been rereading, of the invigorating effects of conflict: 'One never tires of life and at the last must die of thirst with the cup at one's lip' (*L*: 711).

Yeats, relishing conflict, was nevertheless set on higher matters. Even before the publication of *A Vision*, conscious of its difficiencies, he had for the first time set himself to a serious study of philosophy. He was helped in this by an extended correspondence with his friend the painter Sturge Moore, brother of the English analytic philosopher G. E. Moore. It was a curious enough exchange in which the anti-materialist, spiritualist Yeats engaged, by proxy as it were, with the anti-idealism of Bertrand Russell and Moore. Yeats would have none of their limited view of Mind: 'Russell and his school cannot escape from the belief that each man is a sealed bottle. Every man who has studied psychical science by watching his own life knows that we share emotion, thought and image' (Bridge 1953: 68), wrote Yeats impatiently on 5 February 1926. Yeats read G. E. Moore's famous essay of 1925 *A Defence of Common Sense* and Sturge passed on his observations to the less than impressed philosopher. Sturge transmitted his brother's refutations to Yeats. Yeats responded by immersing himself in Whitehead's *Science and the Modern World*. He found much that appealed. Whitehead's was an aristocratic mind to set against Russell's 'plebeian loquacity', (*L:* 714). He could see how Whitehead could be synthesized with the immaterialism of the Irish eighteenth-century thinker, Berkeley. He turned to Spengler's *Decline of the West*, which he found gratifyingly consistent with 'Dove and Swan' in *A Vision*. George Yeats read to him when poor eyesight and fatigue took their toll, as Yeats sought to build a philosophic as well as mythological bulwark against a world-view in which objective knowledge and sense data were a final court of appeal.

There was Plotinus' *The Enneads* to wrestle with in the English translation by the Irish journalist, scholar and Republican Stephan MacKenna (the fourth of five volumes appeared in 1926). And senate business took time away from poetry as well as philosophy. His wife wanted the poet to give up the senate to concentrate on his writing, but Yeats was determined to stay on, if only to keep a worse man out. For all her commitment to the Irish cause George Yeats sometimes thought her excitable husband was becoming too nationalistic, crudely anti-English. There was a surfeit of Yeats relations to be indulged. In the summer she wrote to her friend the Irish poet and art historian Thomas MacGreevy of her hatred for her adopted country. She was patently bored. In March she had had to accompany Yeats on senate business to inspect a progressive school run by the Sisters of Mercy in Waterford. Yeats's interest in education had burgeoned, influenced by the writings of Gentile, and his friendship with the Irish minister for education. George Yeats did not share her husband's new-found enthusiasm. Despite the admirable piety of the nuns, she found the decor of the Waterford convent tastelessly provincial, the food disagreeable, and the measures of brandy and milk in the Mother Superior's parlour excessive. The poet, in a rare burst of domestic curiosity, enquired how often the floors were washed (T. C. D. Ms. 8104/37).

There were important contacts to be maintained and significant affairs of state to attend to. On 23 April the Yeatses dined with Kevin O'Higgins and his family, despite the slight rupture and dose of measles which Yeats had suffered earlier in the month. In May he was appointed chairman of the Coinage Committee to oversee the design of an Irish coinage. He took great pains over this (the task was accomplished by 1928). Summer and autumn meant visits to Thoor Ballylee, work on his *Autobiographies* which would appear towards the year's end, and on an English-language version of Sophocles' *Oedipus the King*, which had interested him as a project since about 1904. He was thinking too about composing a version of the same playwright's *Oedipus at Colonus*, which would occupy him during the coming winter months. He was also busy with scenarios of a new play of his own about Christ and the followers of Dionysus (*The Resurrection*, 1931). He was surprised when a drawing of two lesbian lovers, 'in the full stream of their Saphoistic enthusiasm' (*L*: 715), got into his dreams. And he was writing poetry – love poetry and a poem based on his visit to the Waterford school, to be entitled 'Among School Children'. His reflections on Byzantium in *A Vision* bore autumn fruit in a poem, 'Sailing to Byzantium'. Lady Gregory kept his nose to her grindstone too, ensuring that he did not neglect his duties on behalf of the Lane bequest. They took him to London to lobby politicians about the issue. In December his version of Sophocles' masterpiece played at the Abbey to general acclaim. As one Irish critic noted of a later Abbey production of the work 'we watch Doom stalk, almost tangible on the . . . stage' (Alec Reid, cited in Bradley 1979: 129).

Doom would stalk again all too tangibly upon the stage of Irish public life. Yet by the end of 1926 Yeats appeared to have recovered much of his strength and was, even in his early sixties, capable of enormous expenditures of energy. He was thinking of getting to grips, in a further autobiographical work, with the years 1900 to 1926, as a final great effort and 'test' for his 'intellect' (*L*: 711). He had also felt able in 1926 to publish as a short book entitled *Estrangement*, sections of the private journal he had kept in 1909. In this he made fully public his doctrine of the Mask and contemptuously threw down the gauntlet against the forces of vulgar extremism in Ireland: 'All empty souls tend to extreme opinion' (*Aut*: 469). Such extremists had destroyed Synge and they were still rampant in the attack on O'Casey's play. Yeats was self-confidently preparing for action on behalf of a new coadjutor. The new year was to bring not the stimulation of renewed battle for the soul of Ireland but sickness, national tragedy and weeks in which Yeats's own life seemed at real risk as his health became perilously uncertain.

Acutely painful arthritis was followed by influenza in January and February 1927. Work for the Coinage Committee took time. A threat to Irish copyright for authors in a bill before the senate involved the poet from March to May in lengthy, vigorously argued contributions to the controversy that resulted in the bill's eventual defeat (Yeats's final senatorial achievement; he resigned in September 1928). Summer at Thoor Ballylee, where as always the poetry had been flowing, brought the Yeatses the terrible news of the assassination on 10 July of their friend and efficient minister in the Free State government, Kevin O'Higgins. O'Higgins had been shot while walking from home to Mass and died in his own house after several hours of great suffering. Among those arrested on suspicion of his murder was Seán MacBride, the dedicated IRA man whom Gonne's son Seagan had become. The gyres were grinding finely indeed.

Yeats composed two poems (during several months of charged creativity in which a series of major poems were written) in direct response to this seismic event in the Irish body politic, 'Blood and the Moon' and 'Death'. Both are poems of cold anger. The former, a phantasmagoric celebration of Anglo-Irish racial pride and eighteenth-century individual intellect with Swift, Goldsmith, Berkeley and Burke as exemplary figures, challenges 'Odour of blood on the ancestral stair' with a contemptuous question: 'Is every modern nation like the tower/Half dead at the top?' Yet the poem as a whole is full of dismay at modern incoherence and failure of will. By contrast, 'Death' defiantly proclaimed

> A great man in his pride
> Confronting murderous men
> Casts derision upon Supersession of breath;
> He knows death to the bone –
> Man has created death.

In August, Constance Markievicz died, following her sister Eva who had passed away the year before. Although Yeats had hated the Countess's socialist politics he could not but recall with emotion the beauty of the two sisters at Lissadell, where he had first known them many years before. In early winter he wrote 'In Memory of Eva Gore-Booth and Con Markiewicz', with its limpid nostalgia, historical assessment and visionary acceptance of life's variety: 'The innocent and the beautiful/Have no enemy but time. . . .'

Not everything however could be absorbed into the vision of unifying apocalypse with which this poem so strikingly concludes. Gonne had broken her epistolary silence with Yeats in January 1926. Civil war disagreements had been circumspectly set aside. Seán's arrest revived the note of contention between them. A series of increasingly acrimonious letters was exchanged, rehearsing old quarrels and political disagreements. Yeats let it be known that he had been saved from Republicanism by his reading of Balzac. He said the novelist had made authoritative government interesting to him. Gonne could not stomach his support of the Irish Free State. Their difference seemed absolute. Yeats, still profoundly shaken by the murder of O'Higgins, was all for law and order. She could not comprehend how he could choose to ally himself 'to the deadly quiet exterminators of love' (*GYL*: 440). Their correspondence would be desultory in the years to come.

In August 1927 Yeats issued a Cuala Press selection of his poems of the 1920s, under the title *October Blast*. It contained some of the poems he had decided to include in his next major collection, *The Tower* (named for the poem of that title and because it and several other of the poems in the book are set at Thoor Ballylee). He was anxious that the book, upon which he set great store, would be an impressive iconic artifact. He had recruited Sturge Moore the previous May to execute an appropriate design for the cover. In September he gave instructions: 'the Tower should not be too unlike the real object or rather . . . it should suggest the real object. I like to think of that building as a permanent symbol of my work plainly visible to the passer-by. As you know, all my art theories depend upon just this – rooting of mythology in the earth' (Bridge 1953: 114).

In the event Yeats's poetic testament to certain forms of permanence in a mutable world might have appeared posthumously. For between the writing of that letter to Moore, telling him that Macmillan had all the manuscript of his book in hand, and the publication of *The Tower* on 14 February 1928, Yeats fell seriously ill. In October a bad cold went to his chest and congestion of the lungs set in with high fever and delirium. With some strength restored, his wife took him south – to Algeciras, then to the warmth of Seville (where, alarmingly, he bled from the lungs) and to Cannes in the south of France (where he was recuperating under strict doctor's orders when *The Tower* appeared in London).

It was grimly appropriate that Yeats should have been recovering from serious illness when *The Tower* first appeared, for the title poem engages with the decrepitude and testy delirium of old age before fading, in an exquisite diminuendo, into a gathering darkness that figures encroaching death. The first poem of the collection 'Sailing to Byzantium' imagines too how 'once out of Nature' the poet who among the sexually active young sees himself as as 'a tattered coat upon a stick', will be gathered into 'the artifice of eternity'. It signals that this is a book that can adopt after-death perspectives from which to sing of 'what is past, or passing, or to come'. It was appropriate too that it should have been published in the aftermath of Yeats's great distress at the death of O'Higgins ('the finest intellect in Irish public life, and I think, I may add, to some extent my friend', Yeats recorded in 1933; *WS*: iv), for much of the book deals in the turbulent history that had unfolded so savagely in Ireland since 1912.

Moore's design for the book's cover and its dust-jacket offers a bold image of a four-square tower embossed in dark green against a gold background. Power and permanence are its symbolic import. Yet the tower is reflected in the eddying waters of a stream as if to suggest both Heraclitean change and the interrelationship of image and reality that mirroring evokes. The cover accordingly serves as a visual introduction to the book's contents (it was published without the poet's preface that Yeats usually included in his collections).

The Tower is unabashed at the idea of power. In many of its most sonorous lines Yeats permits himself the exercise of a rhetoric of command, a tone of summary authority. Power and knowledge, yoked as they are in the penultimate line of 'Leda and the Swan' (included in the collection), seem the entitlements of the poet as master of occult wisdom and deep culture:

> I have prepared my peace
> With learned Italian things
> And the proud stones of Greece,
> Poet's imaginings
> And memories of love,
> Memories of the words of women,
> All those things whereof
> Man makes a superhuman,
> Mirror-resembling dream.
>
> ('The Tower')

In 'Meditations in Time of Civil War' the power of a violent and bitter man is honoured as the foundation upon which the civilization of a great house is reared in stone and the poet in his tower has a samurai sword beside pen and paper on his table. The amplitude of the poems in the volume itself, the range of poetic form employed with assured, at times almost nonchalant, accomplishment, suggest indeed a poet writing at the height of *his* powers. Yet power celebrated and exercised in this self-consciously masterful book is in no way immune to an ironic vision. Rather the emotional force of the collection is dependent on a drama in which power is humiliated by decline, decay, disintegration and catastrophe. The decline of physical powers to which the volume bears frustrated witness is inevitable in an order of things fashioned by the 'Primum Mobile' in which 'the very owls in circles move' ('Meditations in Time of Civil War'). For this is a book of time's revenges. It opens in 'Sailing to Byzantium' with the poet as aged man, a 'paltry thing' among 'the young in one another's arm', and ends with 'All Souls' Night' in which the poet after midnight communes with the spirits of dead friends and companions. Youth, age, memory and death are the volume's thematic constants (developed with a new terse, direct energy in 'A Man Young and Old'), finding complex expression in 'Among School Children' (the poem Yeats composed about his visit to the Sisters of Mercy school in Waterford). A 'sixty-year-old smiling public man' among the children, who stare at him for a moment in wonder, enters on an extended reverie in which he imagines the childhood of a former lover and ruefully broods on his and her present condition, in lines that mix regret and self-mockery:

> Her present image floats in to the mind –
> Did quattocento finger fashion it
> Hollow of cheek as though it drank the wind
> And took a mass ['mess' in later printings] of shadows for its meat?
> And I though never of Ledaean kind
> Had pretty plumage once – enough of that,
> Better to smile on all that smile, and show
> There is a comfortable kind of old scarecrow.

Permanence, like power, in the book is shown as subject to time's inexorable depredations. In 'Meditations in Time of Civil War' the poet's wall 'is loosening' and he can imagine a future of dynastic decadence in which it would be prefer- able for the tower to become a roofless ruin in which

> the owl
> May build in the cracked masonry and cry
> Her desolation to the desolate sky.

'Nineteen Hundred and Nineteen' states starkly 'Man is in love and loves what vanishes,/What more is there to say?' In poem one of 'Two Songs from a Play' even a great city will vanish to be succeeded by a new one: 'Another Troy must rise and set,/Another lineage feed the crow.'

Transience provokes a longing for permanence in the volume's primary anti-nomy. Art might offer a kind of permanence for the poet set upon a golden bough in a holy city of the imagination, but the achievement of the book as human drama depends on the unflinching way in which it engages with the brute facts of time and of history. The first four poems of the collection test the powers of art to the limit against a backdrop of historical crisis and find them insufficient bulwarks to meet the flood-tide. Annunciation seems its only real capacity and what this sequence announces is in no way consolatory. Art can only afford a vision of turbulent change, sublime in its awesomeness perhaps, but terrible nonetheless.

'Sailing to Byzantium', 'The Tower', 'Meditations in Time of Civil War' and the retitled 'Nineteen Hundred and Nineteen' are collected in that order. This means that the poem that adverts to events that took place during the war of independence follows the poem set during the civil war. By thus reversing the chronological order of these events, Yeats highlights how the first four poems, all of which are dated by the poet (with what must be deliberate inaccuracy), are a sequence which from 1927 dreams back as it were a passage of years which took Europe, Ireland and the poet from before the Great War, through revolution and civil war to the present moment of horrified uncertainty about the future. For the last of these poems dated in its title and the text as 1919 (supposedly the date of composition which in fact took place in 1920–1), refers to talking 'seven years ago' of 'honour and truth', which casts the sequence back to 1912, the year in the Ulster crisis when the threat of violence and armed power became key terms in the modern Irish equation. And throughout the sequence it is violence and its destructive energies that so alarm a poet who longs for some permanence in a world where 'All men are dancers and their tread/Goes to the barbarous clangour of [a] gong' ('Nineteen Hundred and Nineteen'). For the year 1919 is made to bear a mythical import in the poem as a date symbolic of the epochal transition that had been inaugurated by the Home Rule crisis in 1912 and the Great War which followed it (from 1921, the date of completion to the outbreak of general European hostilities in 1914 is also covered by the phrase 'seven years ago'). It is a moment in which a dream of unending stability (the Victorian peace, 'Public opinion ripening so long') had given way to 'Violence upon the roads'.

The implication of this dreaming back through an historical period is that the aesthetic and philosophic aspirations of 'Sailing to Byzantium' and 'The Tower' are recollected by the reader as responses to the horrors that follow them in the text. Powerful as these two poems are, and though they are dated and placed as if to suggest a culmination in the poet's wisdom and poetic power, their momentary visions of stasis and the calm of a hard-achieved, philosophic mind seem, in a sequential reading, no match for what follows them. For the final two poems conclude with visions of apocalypse and bestial annunciation which anticipate the epochal image of historical change which is 'Leda and the Swan', printed as the eleventh poem in the book and dated 1923. Their force is such as to cast in radical doubt the ways in which the poet has sought through the sequence to allow art and wisdom redemptive valency in a disordered world. So intense is the humiliation of a humanist ideal of the poet as transformative agent in the sequence that in 'Nineteen Hundred and Nineteen' Yeats himself joins, in an act of savage, bitterly satiric self-laceration, those whose medium is mockery. Even they must bear the brunt of his exactions:

> Mock mockers after that
> That would not lift a hand maybe
> To help good, wise or great
> To bar that foul storm out, for we
> Traffic in mockery.

Extremity is a theme in much of Yeats's late poetry. These lines from a poem of high ambition in *The Tower*, a response to the present state of the world as its earlier title indicates, are a hint of the bitterness to come. Yet they do not strike a discordant note in a volume in which the poet often manages a register of ostentatious authority. For an undercurrent of feeling in the work as a whole is failure, as romantic ideals long held sacrosanct meet recalcitrant realities. The site of romantic utterance in Yeats's poetry had often involved certain figurative withdrawals from the modern world, suggested indeed by some of the titles of his volumes. *In the Seven Woods* and *The Wild Swans at Coole*, had made an Ascendancy demesne the site of imaginative commitment to 'high laughter loveliness and ease' ('Upon a House Shaken by the Land Agitation'). Even a volume like *Responsibilities* had measured the pusillanimity of current Irish national feeling against a romantically conceived version of a wild Irish countryside, remote from the settled world of town and grocer's shop, where liberating beggary coexists with pride in the Big House tradition ('Running to Paradise'). *The Tower* is a further act of withdrawal; it registers a Norman keep in the Irish west as the place where the poet can write his will and make his soul. In 'Meditations in Time of Civil War' the poet focuses on 'My House', 'My Table', 'My Descendents', 'The Road at my Door' (in the titles of poems two, three, four and five of the sequence) in a deliberate series of acts of self-isolation, which can still permit a rhetoric of command but in a context that implies its increasing impotence. For who can be the implied audience of such a sequence uttered *in extremis* from the tower of the volume's title poem? Hence the bitterness, the sense of failure for a poet who iteratively employs the first person pronoun as egotistical sublime through the title poem as a last ditch stand in face of all that threatens the authority of the poet's vision. Hence the ghostly presence of Wordsworth in the text – at the conclusion of 'Meditations in Time of Civil War' for example – for he had represented for the writer of *Per Amica Silentia Lunae* the desolation of vanished powers and conventional decline into conservative old age. Hence too the rejection of romantic escapism in 'Nineteen Hundred and Nineteen' where 'the half-deceit of some intoxicant' is eschewed.

Yet *The Tower* is by no means simply to be registered as a late entry in the tradition of Romantic disillusionment, with tragic irony at its tonal epicentre. Its drama is too complex for that, its poetic too charged by an awareness of imaginative renewal. For the drama of the book, all noble commitment to literary and cultural tradition in full consciousness of declension, defeat and loss, is conducted in a theatre of competing discourses which opens itself to the feminine as a source of creative power. And it does so in a poetry that confidently moves among its symbols all the while recognizing the difference between stabilizing symbol and the world experienced as process.

The creative presence of the feminine is most fully celebrated in 'The Gift of Harun Al-Rashid' where its narrative account of an enriching occult erotics is a humane antithesis to some of the darker apprehensions of sexuality in the book. Historical change may be a product of such inhuman forces as can only be figured in tropes of divine rape ('Leda and The Swan') or of impregnation by an evil spirit ('Nineteen Hundred and Nineteen'). Yet even in the midst of horrors that demand metaphors of lust and possession to give them poetic body, the poet can admit moments of feminine nurture as a natural force (images of mother birds offer hints of natural beneficence in both 'The Tower' and 'Meditations in Time of Civil War', where in the loosening masonry 'The mother bird brings grubs and flies'; which make the murder of a mother by a drunken soldiery in 'Nineteen Hundred and Nineteen' an atrocious infringement of taboo and an assault on nature). That man and woman together can create a protective, loving community in a family is celebrated with gentle concern in 'A Prayer for my Son', an evocation of Herodian perils.

Love in its sexual guise is the theme of 'A Man Young and Old', a testament in this volume of historic occasions, to the ahistorical power of obsessional erotic entanglements. An amatory male biography of youth and age (in its pamphlet printing the sequence was represented as the songs of a young and old 'Countryman') it is set in the timeless world of traditional balladry. The sequence takes a young man through a stony world of feminine, lunar indifference to his fate as unrequited lover, to besotted, death-threatening desire, to sympathy with a young woman's fear of entrapment in love. The second section of the sequence, old age's regret for lost sexual opportunity, expresses erotic pride at past sexual dominance of 'the first of all the tribe'. It recognizes that mature desire is its own wild season, in which the language of courtly romance can be superseded by something altogether more earthy. What had begun as a work in which the young man is in thrall to woman, ends with the old man learning from women of female desire satisfied and unsatisfied. From those he had desired and loved in youth he hears in cheerfully illicit sexual gossip,

> How such a man pleased women most
> Of all that are gone,
> How such a pair loved many years
> And such a pair but one,
> Stories of the bed and straw
> Or the bed of down.
>   ('The Secrets of the Old')

Such intimate instruction provokes the man to wildness in the final poem ('His Wildness'), a state which in Yeats's poetic vocabulary, as Cullingford has observed, 'is frequently attributed to women' (1993: 182). In fact the sequence ends with a gender exchange which has the old man 'all alone' living in memory, ready to 'nurse a stone/And sing it lullaby'. His sexual destiny is complete as he takes on the role of a mother to the heart of stone which he had discovered in his first love, when he had hoped for a 'A heart of flesh and blood'. For the old, sexuality involves a mutuality of earthy bawdry which enables the man to feminize his being. That can release him from a youthful idealization of 'beauty's murderous brood' to the degree that he can simultaneously perform a female task and accept his masculine pride: 'I'd have a peacock cry/For that is natural to a man/That lives in memory.'

There is a certain truculence of tone in this sequence, as if to say that the poet, for all that the work assumes an ahistorical world of perennial feeling, knows he is dealing in his own history and in a way which would affront his Irish contemporaries. The metaphors of heart, stone, moon and tree had been for too long properties of his high romantic art for their use in such a poem of carnal candour (a 'shriek' in this sequence can be both the anguish of sexual frustration and a sadomasochistic moment in anticipation of orgasm) to seem anything other than provocative. As terrible annunciations served notice in the great historical poems of this volume, that the future would bring an antithetical age, Yeats began to produce poems that bore witness to female power and to the drama not only of permanence and change but of male and female, body and body. In the final few years of Yeats's life this desire to write the body, including the female body, accounts for some of the more excessive, extravagant attitudes in his verse, wilful crudities of feeling and expression, factitious barbarisms. In *The Tower* however it results in the laconic zest of 'A Man Young and Old' and the ecstatic final stanza of 'Among School Children', both of which establish the volume as a more complex achievement than the extended 'Ode to Dejection' in the nineteenth-century Romantic/apocalyptic mode, it might otherwise have been.

'Among School Children' is quintessentially a poem of the body: the body in age weighed down by sixty winters, in childhood, and in sexual maturity. It is a poem of eyes, cheek, hair, plumage, head, thighs, fingers, even irreverently 'the bottom of a king of kings'. The body is pleasure and pain, in 'Honey of generation' and the 'pang' of birth. It is 'struggle' and 'labour'. Bodily as the poem is, an air of impalpability nevertheless pervades its musings. Memory casts back and forth across a fluid temporal space, an image 'floats' into the mind, the intensity of the non-existent past dims present awareness: 'She stands before me as a living child.' And an eternity of permanent forms shadows the text, in antithesis to the mutable conditions of bodily existence. For 'Plato thought nature but a spume that plays/Upon a ghostly paradigm of things.' Tantalizingly, between the two orders of being, symbolic images attain a permanence of bodily form. What they symbolize – 'all heavenly glory' – being unattainable, they 'break hearts'. At this emotional crisis of the poem, where body and image are poised in juxtaposition, the poet rises to a celebration of bodily existence that becomes an image of life's unitary fullness. In rejecting spiritual pleasure as the fruit of asceticism and beauty and wisdom bred of 'despair' and 'midnight oil' respectively (female beauty and male poetic wisdom are equated as desiderata) the poet can rejoice in 'Labour' as 'blossoming or dancing':

> O chestnut tree, great-rooted blossomer,
> Are you the leaf, the blossom or the bole?
> O body swayed to music, O brightening glance,
> How can we know the dancer from the dance?

An image of earthly rootedness, of a permanence of a sort, is imaginatively associated with the momentary glory of a human body in ecstatic motion, in which dance and dancer seem joined in unity of being.

The way in which 'Among School Children' moves fluently between bodily and symbolic orders of being is undoubtedly a register of how *The Tower* as a whole is not overwhelmed by the romantic irony it also painfully admits. The living presence of the feminine in the book and the sense of bodily wisdom it contains find expression in a poetics notably free from constraint and inhibition. The conflicted self as dilemma has been superseded by a dramatic speech in which self-division is rendered as vital, energized drama. Nor is *The Tower* burdened by a religiose, solemn need to find every occasion redolent of the symbolic, as the early poetry so often was. It inhabits a palpable world of historical event and bodily experience that can be set, the revelations of *A Vision* assumed, in a context of mythological meaning. So symbolism can be exploited with ease and self-assurance in a consciousness that no symbol can be complete ('I am satisfied with that' says the poet in 'Nineteen Hundred and Nineteen' as he recalls how the 'solitary soul' has been compared to a swan); but symbols make possible a poetry that engages a drama of body and soul.

> O sages standing in God's holy fire
> As in the gold mosaic of a wall,
> Come from the holy fire, perne in a gyre,
> And be the singing masters of my soul.
> Consume my heart away; sick with desire
> And fastened to a dying animal
> It knows not what it is; and gather me
> Into the artifice of eternity.
> ('Sailing to Byzantium')

The final stanza of 'Among School Children' and this dramatically intense stanza from the volume's opening poem are moments of transcendent authority in *The Tower*. As such they bear witness to the power of the image to embody meaning momentarily arrested in the flux of history and of time, in defiance of failed romantic envisioning. They manage to be at the same time wonderfully exhilarating and strangely unsettling in the context of the book as a whole. For so centripetal are their energies, so separable as achieved monological utterance are they from the poems in which they appear, that they can alert the reader to features of the text of *The Tower* which subvert the high drama of its competing personal discourses and its assured, practised deployment of symbol. For *The Tower* can be read not only as a book in which a poet, renewed by marriage and all it brought, managed to supersede the romantic irony of failing powers in charged dramatic and symbolic writing, but as a text invaded by Modernist problematics.

Like *A Vision*, to which it owes its sense of an underlying cosmic scheme that allows for seemingly unstudied, apparently spontaneous symbolic expression of the truths of human experience and history, *The Tower* is a markedly self-referential text. Key poems advert to the fact that what a poem does is generate text. 'It is time that I wrote my will' announces the poet in the title poem and follows his declaration with lines that are both a description of what such a document might contain and the legal instrument itself: 'I leave both faith and pride/To young upstanding men.' And this section of the work concludes a poem that has stepped in and out of the fiction that a character whom Yeats created as a young man, Red Hanrahan of the *The Secret Rose*, shares his ontological status with the poet himself (an elaborate footnote compounds the transparent literary sleight-of-hand; the ghosts of the card-players in Hanrahan's story have been seen, we are told, in 'what is now' the poet's bedroom). For it is he whom the poet must question on the ambiguities of his own past. Self and the self's creation weave a fictive uncertainty about the stability of authorial presence in a text that highlights the creative, equivocal role of narrative in memory and art. In 'Meditations in Time of Civil War' and in 'Nineteen Hundred and Nineteen' we are reminded in imagery of pen and paper – 'The half-imagined, the half-written page' – that a poem finds its life not as utterance from a living person but as literary artifact, as an 'ingenious lovely' thing. 'The Gift of Harun Al-Rashid' once again comes with a fictional framing footnote.

The footnotes that Yeats supplied to the poems in his book emphasized not only the reading that had inspired individual works but the act of literary appropriation. In a lengthy note to 'The Tower' he acknowledges an unconscious debt to a poem by Sturge Moore and a misremembering of Plato and Plotinus. Of 'Among School Children' he erroneously confesses 'I have taken "the honey of generation' from Porphyry's essay "The Cave of the Nymphs".' These oddly unhelpful admissions do serve a function in alerting us to how complicatedly intertextual the book in fact is. Shelley Wordsworth, Coleridge and Keats, the Irish folk poet Anthony Raftery are unnamed presences in allusion and echo. The Shakespeare of the history plays, which the poet had seen in sequence at Stratford-on-Avon in 1901, appears by virtue of the term 'Falstaffian' in poem five of 'Meditations in Time of Civil War', Milton by virtue of an allusion to *Il Penseroso* in poem two. Homer and Chaucer are directly named in the book. The cumulative effect of this textual instability in which a body of contemporary writing is open to the powerful presence of others' work, is to undermine the univocal authority of Yeats as poet. He engages a violent present in texts that would seek to sustain a tradition of masterful, even epic, art that has its origin in

Homer. Yet the presence of his precursors highlights how radically fragmentary is his achievement in *The Tower*, where moments of epical personal authority and of unified consciousness emerge from a poetic in which the verse sequence seems the nearest approximation to a protractedly discursive art the modern age can allow. *The Tower* with its assumed mythology, its self-conscious textuality, its cast of historical and literary characters, its echo chamber sonorities in which a literary tradition lives on as the ghost of itself, its moments of charged intensity, its elaborately composed individual works arranged to form a group of sequence poems, in 1928 can be read, I am arguing, as a companion work of T. S. Eliot's poem of 1922, *The Waste Land*. It is not a comparison Yeats would have found congenial, since his book is richer in tones of grandeur, its textures more ornamental, and its several parts are structurally more coherent than those of Eliot's work, but it does set *The Tower*, like *A Vision* before it, firmly in the context of the Modernism of the 1920s. Sensitivity to the *Zeitgeist* had always been a Yeatsian strength. It had not deserted him with old age. Yet old age had also brought him intimate appreciation of female power, celebrated in this volume with the worldly zest that sets it apart from Eliot's mandarin, misogynistic lament for a lost classical order.

16

Home and Abroad

On 23 February 1928 Yeats confessed to Lady Gregory (from Rapallo) that *The Tower* astonished him 'by its bitterness' (*L*: 738). He was nonetheless gratified that it sold 2,000 copies in the first month of publication. It was his most immediately successful book. His renown as a Nobel laureate had made Yeats a fashionable name for the book-buying public, but the commercial success of the collection was helped by the critical reception which acknowledged the power and originality of the work itself. As the poet recorded 'Even the Catholic press is enthusiastic' (ibid.: 740). T. S. Eliot in the *Criterion* published the poet John Gould Fletcher's review which allowed that Yeats 'corresponds, or will correspond, when the true literary history of our epoch is written, to what we moderns mean by a great poet' (*CH*: 287). He judged that *The Tower* was not merely 'a collection of anthology specimens . . . but what is essentially a *Weltanschauung*' (ibid.: 286).

As for Yeats himself, he was tired of bitterness, associating it with the Ireland to which he had returned in April 1928, where he was plunged into a painful controversy with Sean O'Casey about the playwright's new play *The Silver Tassie*. Yeats was responsible for its rejection by the Abbey and wrote a letter of essentially accurate but severe critique to O'Casey, who took the reverse to his burgeoning career very badly. Yeats's Olympian tone rankled: 'The mere greatness of the world war has thwarted you; it has refused to become mere background, and obtrudes itself upon the stage as so much dead wood that will not burn with the dramatic fire' (*L*: 741). The poet longed, he told Shakespear, to live abroad that he might 'find some new vintage' (ibid.: 742).

The Yeatses had seemed so settled in Dublin at the end of 1923 with Merrion Square house, Nobel laureateship and senatorial business making the poet very much the public man. Five years on, advancing years and ill-health a constant consideration, fundamental domestic change was on the agenda. George Yeats had told her friend Thomas MacGreevy in March that she feared her husband had been undergoing an intermittent nervous breakdown for more than a year. She wondered how wise she had been to have children, given the poet's condition

(T.C.D. Ms 8104/57). In July the Yeatses sold their Dublin house and moved to a rented flat in Fitzwilliam Square, which they intended to use when in Dublin, though spending the winter months in Rapallo. They had an option on an apartment there in the small town Yeats had found 'indescribably lovely', where in February he had felt he could escape Irish bitterness and 'find some measure of sweetness and of light, as befits old age' (*L*: 737).

In Rapallo he had sensed a new poetic forming – 'bird songs of an old man, joy in the passing moment, emotion without the bitterness of memory' (ibid.) – and was now keen to get back to Italy's revivifying light and climate. There too he had begun to write a new prose work which he would call *A Packet for Ezra Pound*. The Yeatses spent the autumn of 1928 in their Dublin quarters (Thoor Ballylee was judged too damp) and set off for Rapallo in November. They had taken a lease on the flat for six months. The poet, who had not allowed his name to go forward for re-election to the senate in September, relished the freedom from responsibilities his new life allowed. He felt as if he were on board 'a ship at sea before they discovered wireless' (Gregory 1987 vol. 2: 337). He could forget for a while the exhausting battle he had relished fighting in a mood of high spirits that autumn in pugnacious journalism, against the impending Irish Censorship of Publications Act (he judged it 'ridiculous to the man of letters' and a real threat to intellectual liberty). George Yeats who had managed the break-up of their Merrion Square house (though not without some complaint about her husband who rested in Howth during the disturbance of moving) now set to painting the Rapallo flat. She chose Chinese red. Yeats said he shed a personality as it replaced a ninetyish green (T.C.D. Ms. 8104/67).

By February 1929 George Yeats reported to MacGreevy that the poet, who had visited Rome in January and experienced there a few days of constant fatigue, was once more full of themes. He was at work on a series of twelve lyrics that could possibly be set to music. In March he had completed three of them to his satisfaction. He thought them the opposite of his recent work, 'all praise of joyous life, though in the best of them it is a dry bone on the shore that sings the praise' (*L*: 758). A week later he had another two poems for music on paper. By the end of the month, in a sustained burst of creativity, he had nine poems for the sequence. He confessed to Shakespear some consternation at this unaccustomed facility: 'I am writing more easily than I ever wrote and I am happy, whereas I have always been unhappy when I wrote and worked with great difficulty' (ibid.: 761). By the end of April he had written nineteen new lyrics as the number kept mounting.

Rapallo also meant renewed conversation with Pound (Yeats was completing his prose work addressed to his old friend and sparring partner) and new acquaintances among a small circle of literary and artistic people who had settled in the Italian town (it reminded Yeats of the little town in Keats's 'Ode on a Grecian Urn'). Among these were his fellow Nobel laureate, the German dramatist Gerhart Hauptmann (whose alcoholic prowess impressed the comparatively abstemious poet) and the young avant garde composer, George Antheil. Yeats interested Antheil in writing music for three of his plays and he did in fact produce the score for *Fighting the Waves* (a prose version of *The Only Jealousy of Emer* first produced in August, 1929 in the Abbey Theatre with the choreographer and dancer Ninette de Valois in the part of Fand). The circle met frequently at the Hotel Rapallo where they shared a taste for detective stories. To Antheil's consternation the great poet, who often talked of the visitations of spirits from as far afield as Dublin, would tip his soft felt sombrero to the ghost of his indigestion, whom he had christened William. The occult mage grew whimsically humorous as he relaxed.

A Packet for Ezra Pound was published in Dublin by the Cuala Press in the summer of 1929. It was a fragmentary little volume that made extraordinary revelations in a lapidary prose. For Yeats in this text, which, with revisions, would serve as an introduction to a new version of *A Vision*, made public how that work had its origin in his wife's automatic writing and 'sleeps'. Yeats's sister 'Lollie' at the Press wondered about her brother's sanity (*Hone*: 406). She consulted AE, who advised publication on the grounds that it would interest future biographers: 'it is intimate & personal more than anything he has yet written' (NL Ms 9969/478). He was referring to the second of the three prose pieces that made up most of the book. The first and the third in mingled conversational, abstract and mythological mode offer an account of Yeats's relationship with Pound and his work. A quizzical affection for the younger poet does not disguise Yeats's incapacity to warm to Pound's *Cantos*, the sequence of long poems upon which Pound had been engaged for more than a decade. Yeats could discern no principle of organization in this work, despite the 'mathematical structure' Pound implied he was employing. Yet time might allow fuller comprehension.

That possibility stimulates Yeats in the second prose piece to reveal how his own book of 'classification by a series of geometric symbols' (*PFEP*: 12), which he had taken up into his own imagination in *The Tower*, came into existence – and the eerie story unfolds with its record of mysterious sounds and smells, its automatism, scholarly deliberation and moments of superstitious fear: 'the mediaeval helpless horror at witchcraft' (ibid.: 22). As recently as the end of 1927 or early 1928 the Communicators had in fact returned, for Yeats tells in this essay of how one afternoon during his convalescence in Cannes, George Yeats had walked in her sleep and had spoken with the voice of a spirit who wished to object to all the philosophic reading the poet had been doing since the earlier revelations.

In the third prose piece, a letter to his fellow poet, Yeats counsels Pound against political engagement ('do not be elected to the Senate of your country' he pompously advises). Rather he hopes that Pound will accept 'the introduction of a book which will, when finished, proclaim a new divinity' (ibid.: 35). For he senses, as he cites his fellow poet's famous poem 'The Return' (with its delicate evocation, as Yeats reads it, of classical deities tentatively returning to the world), that Pound and he share a faith in cyclical annunciations and in the sacredness of art. Pound, already deeply committed to Fascism, Yeats implies, should stick to the high vocation of poetry and steer clear of direct engagements with politics.

This odd publication, which included two poems, subsequently titled 'At Algeciras: a Meditation on Death' and a poem in which the poet recollected his religious instruction in youth, 'Mohinee Chatterjee', tells us two things about Yeats at this point in his life. As always he hankered after artistic collaboration and a community to sustain his creativity. Pound and Rapallo were fulfilling that constant need. And he was continuing to speculate about the significance of the revelations which had come to him so strangely. Even more explicitly than in the 1925 publication of his findings, he linked his work to avant garde Modernist art, to the kinds of thing he probably talked about with Ezra Pound, just as they had shared ideas a decade-and-a-half before at Stone Cottage: 'Some will ask if I believe all that this book contains, and I will not know how to answer. Does the word belief, used as they will use it, belong to our age' (ibid.: 32). When Yeats published *A Packet for Ezra Pound* as the introduction to the second version of *A Vision* (1937) he had rewritten this passage to highlight how his conception of belief bore on the kind of relationship to truth that he discerned in Modernist aesthetics – in the work of Wyndham Lewis and Brancusi. His system, like their cubes and ovoids, was a stylistic arrangement of experience which had helped him 'to hold in a single thought reality and justice' (*AVB*: 25).

The collection of poems Yeats published in the United States later in 1929, *The Winding Stair* (also distributed in Britain), revealed how experimental an artist he truly was. For in the sequence entitled 'A Woman Young and Old', which comprised the greater part of the volume, he supplied a provocatively iconoclastic companion work to 'A Man Young and Old' (which had been included in *The Tower*).

This sequence had largely been composed in 1926 (it was left out of *The Tower*, where it might have appeared with its companion poem, for a reason the poet could not subsequently recall) though the final poem 'From the *Antigone*' dates from the late months of 1927, when Yeats had been so horrified by O'Higgins' death. In October of that fateful year he had communicated to Shakespear that he was still of the view 'that only two topics can be of the least interest to a serious and studious mind – sex and the dead' (*L*: 730). 'A Woman Young and Old' is a daring study of female sexuality and desire, given erotic intensity by the knowledge of old age and death.

The sequence is daring not only in his frank subject matter, an insouciant riposte to the threat of censorship in Free State Ireland and to its prudish Catholicism, but in its dramatic exploitation of poetic forms. Albright has described it as a kind of 'experimental theatre' in which part of the drama is derived from 'the clash of genres' (Albright 1992: 744). The dominant notes struck are the rhythms and direct unenchanted realism of traditional balladry with its tales of love won and lost, of seduction and betrayal, birth and death, its dramas of male and female suffering. These notes are made to sound subversively in a sequence which simultaneously evokes the formal and thematic traditions of high art: the religious and love poetry of the Renaissance, Shakespearean drama, mythopoeic Modernist symbolism. The effect is a drama of answering-back in which a female voice is reckoned most authentically itself in a mocking,

knowing wisdom of the body, expressed in zestful scorn of male spiritual
presumption:

> What lively lad most pleasured me
> Of all that with me lay?
> I answer that I gave my soul
> And loved in misery,
> But had great pleasure with a lad
> That I loved bodily.
>
> Flinging from his arms I laughed
> To think his passion such
> He fancied that I gave a soul
> Did but our bodies touch,
> And laughed upon his breast to think
> Beast gave beast as much.
>   ('A Last Confession')

Yet such iconoclastic, gratified utterance is only one moment in the complex
drama of the sequence which represents female sexual identity from childhood to
old age in difficult relationship with masculinity. That relationship is inevitably
figured not only in the ribald poetics of the ballad but in the male imaginings of
high art, especially love poetry, through which the woman of the sequence must
also seek to express herself against the grain of her true being. A power play is
assumed in the dramatized exchanges of the sequence. Its drama is accordingly as
much the drama of conscious, manipulative role-playing (the 'dissembling' and
'coquetry' of 'A First Confession') as it is that of a frankly uttered female desire in
conflict with the male's wish to determine the discourse of love.

In the tautly stylized, theatrical sexual politics of 'A Woman Young and Old'
moments of mutuality are certainly achieved. The ironically titled 'Her Triumph'
has casual female sexuality 'mastered' by the shock of an overwhelming sexual
encounter, with its shared orgasmic surprise:

> And now we stare astonished at the sea,
> And a miraculous strange bird shrieks at us.

'Chosen' makes such mutuality a gift of 'subterranean' and 'maternal' rest from a
woman to a journeying man (the poem is a pained but celebratory female reply to
Donne's wintry love lyric of depressive negativity 'A Nocturnal upon St Lucie's
Day, being the shortest'). 'Her Vision in the Wood' however is a dark, sadomasochistic, mythic study in the slavery and tyranny of sex, its intimacy with pain
and death. The dessicated old woman of the poem, in a wine-dark sacred wood
at midnight (Fraser and *The Golden Bough* supply the setting and the archetypical
atmosphere) tears her body in sexual frustration. She summons with her blood-
stained finger a vision of the body of a man wounded by a boar (Adonis from
classical mythology, Diarmuid, the doomed lover of Grania in Celtic mythology).

The horror of what she sees challenges the stately *ottava rima* of the verse scheme (the form used to such affirmatory effect in 'Among School Children', which this poem cruelly echoes). The elevated painterly achievement of the woman's vision is radically disturbed by a realization of what it actually portends. Artistic representation of the sexual *imbroglio*, the poem implies, cannot hide the agonizing pain that lies at its heart: 'they had brought no fabulous symbol there/But my heart's victim and its torturer'. For if female wisdom of the body can give man a maternal breast to rest upon and can instruct him in the truth that tragedy (the 'stone' in the midst of all with which 'A Man Young and Old' had concluded) can make sexual comfort a deeply passionate experience ('Consolation'), death awaits woman as it does man. Both know the torture of love and descend to 'the loveless dust' ('From the *Antigone*') with which this sequence, as bleak at the last as its companion work, concludes.

'A Woman Young and Old' was Yeats's first extended attempt to give voice to female sexuality in his poetry (in drama *The Only Jealousy of Emer* had sought to explore the sacrificial love of a wife for an errant husband). In so explicitly associating feminine erotic experience and power with the ballad as against the formal traditions of high art, Yeats was of course making a statement about that sexuality. He was implying that female desire was transgressive, wild, elemental, rather than civilized and containable in a poetics of noble romance, courteous decorum and painterly mythic symbolism. For even childish desire is figured in the sequence as beyond male control ('his hair is beautiful/Cold as the march wind his eyes' replies a child to her censorious father in the Blakean exchange of 'Father and Child').

The formal tensions, between a folk-art and the literary tradition, of 'A Woman Young and Old' are an indication that Yeats understood how the expression of mature female sexuality called for a radical poetic, one less imbricated with a tradition of high art in which the female had been recurrently entered in Western literature as a trope of male transcendental imagining or as a site of erotic fascination or misogynist revulsion. In the extraordinary weeks of creativity that Yeats enjoyed in Rapallo in the spring of 1929, he was discovering such a poetic, a poetic that would form the basis of a remarkable third sequence of poems about sexual experience, 'Words for Music Perhaps'. The composition of that vital, exalted, gross text would prove a recurrent distraction from other work over the next few years until 1933, when it was first published entire. It would add to the explicit carnality of 'A Woman Young and Old' a strand of sensual mysticism that came as if reported from dangerous zones of feeling where the religious and obscene meet, where sensuality, Godhead and death are encountered in the blinding light of eternity.

In the winter of 1929 and 1930 Yeats came perilously close to death himself. There had been something valedictory about the autumn of the year. A stay at Thoor Ballylee had proved how uncomfortable and damp it could be for an elderly man with arthritis and inconvenient for a wife who had to cycle some miles for provisions. The poet would never live there again. In August he had been tempted by another offer of a teaching post in the east, a professorship on the Japanese island of Formosa (£1,000 for a year with a residence and travelling expenses), until his wife ruled it out as unsuitable for the health of their son Michael. In September 1928 he had completed a poem in praise of a now ailing Lady Gregory and of Coole Park (the house, woods and garden had been sold to the Ministry of Lands and Agriculture in April 1927 and rented back by the redoubtable chatelaine, who had been battling breast cancer since 1923). The poem, with its autumnal evocation of swallows coming and going was, when he first collected it in 1932 as 'Coole Park, 1929', redolent of an era at an end. It was a premature funerary encomium to a 'laurelled head'.

In London on his way back to Rapallo the poet once more haemorrhaged from the lung. In December 1929 in Italy he was stricken with Malta fever and became so seriously ill that on Christmas Eve he made a hurried will, which was witnessed by his fellow poets, Pound and Basil Bunting. Recovery, which took the most of four or five months, was taxing, with frequent relapses. Bunting remembered him at this time strolling along the promenade in 'a long overcoat and a broad brimmed hat' (Bunting 1974: 40) apparently lost in reverie, but ready for any gossip with his cronies, as his spirits revived.

Sex and death preoccupied the convalescent poet, who moved with his wife up the moutains to Portofina Vetta at the end of March 1930. In April he began a new poem on Byzantium (Stallworthy 1963: 115), which opens in an eerie, hallucinatory evocation of the city as a post-death state of consciousness. And he was reading and brooding on Jonathan Swift's *Diary to Stella* with its evidences of the great Dean's ambiguous and highly charged sexual dilemmas. Yeats believed Swift 'almost certainly hated sex' (*Ex*: 334). The Dean's sexual anguish is the crux of the play Yeats wrote in 1930, *The Words upon the Window-Pane*, which was produced by the Abbey Theatre in Dublin in November of that year.

The play is unique in Yeats's body of dramatic works since it is set in the room of a contemporary Dublin lodging-house and concerns everyday folk. Its manner is the prosaic realism that the Abbey had made popular in many of its commercially successful productions. Its matter is far from realistic. For the cast of vulgar and trivial people in the play have gathered for a seance, and their Spiritualist credulity is rewarded by something they did not expect – an encounter with what seems to be the spirit of Jonathan Swift himself and his two women friends Hester Vanhomrigh ('Vanessa') and Esther Johnson ('Stella'). The stuff of an imaginary dance-play, akin to that of *The Dreaming of the Bones*, this play, which unfolds within a frame of apparent realism, radically challenges the limits of its ostensible technique. In the imagined play-within-the-play, which is brought to verbal life in the voices that take over a medium's body, Swift is trapped in the purgatory of a tortured conscience. He contends with 'Vanessa' whom he refuses to marry, so fearful is he that their progeny will carry his incipient madness to another generation. He has instructed her in the rigours of a Roman stoicism; but she cannot hold to that cold creed and to his horror places his hand upon her breast. She challenges him to accept both his passionate nature and the demands of the body. By contrast with the aroused 'Vanessa', 'Stella' is submissive and gentle; yet Swift abuses her in a different way by his obsessive concern that she live to care for him in the old age which he dreads with all his soul. He demands that she outlive him to close his eyes at death.

The Swift of this play is a disturbing, dramatically arresting study of a man who, loathing the democracy of an age he sees in the making, is destroyed by a pathological need to control both himself and the future. A bitter misanthropy is directed towards male and female and ultimately his own person. 'Perish the day on which I was born!' (the text is from the Book of Job), he cries through the voice of the medium, as the curtain falls. In biographical terms the main impact of this theatrically very powerful play is not just that Swift as a ghostly stage presence expresses (in slightly exaggerated form as Yeats himself advised) some very Yeatsian sentiments about the horrors of a solitary and decrepit old age. Nor is it enough to note that the sceptical student of the play, who is working on a Cambridge doctorate on Swift, evokes his subject as an eighteenth-century anti-democratic mind in a way that accords with Yeats's own sense of his Protestant Irish precursor. Rather, the biographical force of the work is to be found in its conviction that the tragedy of Swift, expiring a driveller and a show, was a sexual tragedy. To deny the body, as Yeats had done for so many years in his young manhood, was to tempt a Swiftian fate, as he now understood.

In the final moments of *The Words upon the Window-Pane* the medium reports her vision of Swift *in extremis*: 'I saw him very clearly just as I woke up. His clothes were dirty, his face covered with boils. Some disease had made one of his eyes swell up, it stood out from his face like a hen's egg' (*W&B*: 62). It is a portrait of a ruined old man with his brain gone, deserted by his friends, both 'Vanessa' and 'Stella' long dead, beaten by a servant to keep him quiet. In the months when Yeats was writing this play with its final image of physical and mental disintegration the poet had good reason to concern himself with his own physical appearance and condition. Grave illness had left him looking truly old for the first time (as a photograph taken in convalescence painfully reveals). And when he returned to Dublin by way of London, after a slow boat journey, in July 1930, it was in part because he had agreed to have his portrait painted by Augustus John. Swift was much in his mind as he contemplated this 'great honour'. In the diary he kept in 1930 he noted how he stood before a mirror wondering whether John might not 'obliterate what good looks' (*Ex*: 307) he had. He remembered how much he had disliked John's earlier etching of him, but recognized that he had identified a truth of his social nature:

> Always particular about my clothes, never dissipated, never unshaven except during illness, I saw myself there an unshaven, drunken bar-tender, and then I began to feel John had found something that he liked in me, something closer than character, and by that very transformation made it visible. He had found Anglo-Irish solitude, a solitude that I have made for myself, an outlawed solitude' (*Ex*: 308).

Anglo-Irish solitude was what Yeats admired most in Swift and in the other figures of the Protestant Irish eighteenth century ('that one Irish century which escaped from darkness and confusion'; *W & B*: 7) which now represented for him a tradition of anti-materialist passion, of hatred for scientific abstraction, which could serve as an intellectual bulwark against a vulgarizing, democratic modernity. For Swift haunted Yeats in 1930 and 1931; he was 'always just round the next corner' (*Ex*: 345). He felt for him an intensity akin to family feeling: 'Thought seems more true, emotion more deep, spoken by someone who touches my pride, who seems to claim me of his kindred, who seems to make me a part of some national mythology...' (ibid.). Swift in Dublin in his solitude and pride was a mind that could temper his own, as it struggled against the new democratic state that had sold the pass on its finest traditions of heroically individual conservatism. For Yeats's Swift was not the rational Christian moralist of an Augustan English classicism, but a belated Irish inheritor of a Renaissance ideal of a passionate unity of being he could never achieve. His solitude and extremity of vision were the consequence of his sufferings in an antithetical age in which first England, and then Ireland after the battle of the Boyne in 1690, surrendered to the empiricism of Bacon, Newton and Locke. As Archibald has succinctly stated: 'eighteenth-century Ireland contained "a Renaissance echo," fragile and combative, still struggling to keep the seal' (Archibald 1975: 189). Archibald's summary of Yeats's recruitment of Swift and the Irish eighteenth century to his own national mythology is crucial:

> With genuine, if wayward, historical accuracy and with great imaginative conviction, he celebrates the Anglo-Irish Augustans as outsiders, rebels against the orthodoxies and inadequacies of their time, who 'found in England the opposite that stung their own thought into expression and made it lucid' (ibid.)

The saliency of this summary of the poet's encounter with Swift and his century is not only that it throws light on Yeats's celebration in old age of an Anglo-Ireland which in youth he had largely repudiated, but that it supplies a context for us to read the significance of the many representatives of a rebellious, wild, uncivilized estrangement that populate Yeats's late work. They share a Swiftian hatred for what the triumph of a mechanistic, materialistic world-view has everywhere brought into being. Even Ireland, for all Yeats's long-held hopes for it, has been a victim of the malign, reductive force of modernity. It was as if the Belfast of familial legend had become the measure of the contemporary world order. Only beggary and the heroic role of the estranged outsider remained, if pride of family, of traditional kindred and of nation were to be vindicated.

Swift, in the years in which Yeats was obsessed by him, had to share space in the poet's imagination with the figure of a woman who had insinuated herself into the poet's mind with candid persistence. 'Crazy Jane', as he came to call her, was a female version of the Swiftian estrangement and hatred to which Yeats had committed himself as a vital creative force.

Yeats based this unexpected *alter ego*, in whose voice he could speak of things closed to a poetic persona of high romantic seriousness and occult hermeticism, on an old woman nicknamed Cracked Mary, who lived close to Gort in County Galway. She was a 'local satirist', with 'an amazing power of audacious speech'.

He recalled that one of her 'great performances' was 'a description of how the meanness of a Gort shopkeeper's wife over the price of a glass of porter made her so despair of the human race' that she got gloriously drunk: 'The incidents of that drunkenness [were] of an epic magnificence' (*L:* 785–6). It was this figure who in February and March of 1929, 'when life had returned' to him 'as an impression of uncontrollable energy and daring of the great creators' (*WS:* 5) he found himself admitting to his imagination as he wrote a series of poems in which she began to speak as if he were a medium voicing her spirit. These poems became part of the sequence 'Words for Music Perhaps' (published in Dublin by the Cuala Press in 1932, in *Words for Music Perhaps and Other Poems*) and included, in a slighter different and expanded form, in Yeats's volume of 1933 *The Winding Stair and Other Poems* (1933). In the sequence the Gort satirist is crossed with the figure of Crazy Jane, a mad, forsaken girl in English folklore.

Crazy Jane in this sequence is an explicit advocate of the body, who in an unrepentant old age transgressively affirms the power of her own sexual desire in youth and age. She is an unabashed celebrant of the pleasure principle in bold defiance of the bishop of the sequence who would do all he can to bring her under the control of his life-denying ordinances. She does not so much answer back as refuse to take his admonishments as anything but impertinent absurdities. Kin of Macbeth's witches, she is an alternative centre of spiritual authority in the sphere of sexual politics, who conducts by night her own counter-rituals:

> Bring me to the blasted oak
> That I, midnight upon the stroke,
> (*All find safety in the tomb*)
> May call down curses on his head
> Because of my dear Jack that's dead.
> Coxcomb was the least he said:
> (*The solid man and the coxcomb*).
> ('Crazy Jane and the Bishop')

The Crazy Jane sequence is formally cast, in its rhythms and nonsense refrains, to suggest a blend of the traditional ballad with the folk lyric, which, as Cullingford rightly judges, allows the poet to emphasize 'the messy, libidinous and subversive powers of folk culture' (Cullingford 1993: 233) It inhabits a pre-modern world, with Jane, her journeyman lover Jack and the Bishop posed in comic opposition like figures in a perennial, oral folk-tale or medieval fabliau. The obscene punning and *doubles entendres* of Jane's speech ('whole', 'hole'; 'a birch-tree stood my Jack') certainly add a cheerfully cynical, Chaucerian air to the sequence ('Jack had my virginity and bids me to the oak'). Yet for all the pre-modern atmospherics and timelessness of the wild setting – tree, road, grass, sky, tomb – it is not difficult to read the sequence, as Cullingford does, as another of Yeats's wilfully audacious critiques of modern Ireland, where church and state were in alliance to ensure that the Irish body politic would control male and female sexuality through an interdiction on divorce and a draconian censorship.

It would be quite wrong however to restrict the implications of this buoyant, exhilarated set of poems to an Irish context, or to allow wider significance only as a brave Yeatsian attempt to give voice to the feminine in his own identity ('so masculine a figure; yet how feminine is the expression of the face' was A. L. Rowse's impression of the poet in 1931; Rowse 1979: 125). For the sequence addresses metaphysical and religious issues of the kind that were to trouble Yeats increasingly in the final years of his life.

In a diary entry for 15 September Yeats observed 'Descartes, Locke, and Newton took away the world and gave us its excrement instead. Berkeley restored the world' (*Ex*: 325). The polarity is between reductive mechanism and the philosophic idealism which Yeats hoped would supply a metaphysical foundation for his own system. He was reading Berkeley intensively with the help of a young Italian student. The student was at work with J. M. Hone (the poet's first biographer) on a book on the Irish immaterialist ('idealist and realist alike' Yeats called him; *E&I*: 405). In the summer of 1931 Yeats was writing an introduction for this volume. Swift, in contrast with Berkeley, as the poet judged it, had gone mad partly in his horror at the world the mechanists had revealed. He was a victim of a historical as well as personal crisis. The excremental in his work (the fourth book of *Gulliver's Travels*, his poems 'Cassinus and Peter' and 'Celia'), was attributable to that crisis, in which the world was stripped of its transcendence. Yeats in old age hoped desperately that the phase of human thought inaugurated by the scientific revolution of the seventeenth century was coming to an end and that for his contemporaries its reductive explanatory force would diminish (he tried to dismiss science from serious attention as the 'opium of the suburbs'; Finneran 1991: 568). Yet as he began to face the reality of his own death a corrosive nihilism became a recurrent mood. A Swiftian horror of a desacralized world could not be easily historicized and rendered nugatory, as Yeats himself was afflicted by intimations of absolute negation at the heart of things.

'Words for Music Perhaps', of which the Cazy Jane sequence is a substantial part, is an attempt to admit the full force of the Swiftian sense of reality, yet to remain a celebrant of life and its ambiguities. Swift and Blake are presiding spirits, as if the English mystic's ebullient assertiveness can raise an Irish satirist's despair to the level of a redemptive metaphysic:

> 'A woman can be proud and stiff
> When on love intent;
> But love has pitched his mansion in
> The place of excrement;
> For nothing can be sole or whole
> That has not been rent.'
> ('Crazy Jane Talks with the Bishop')

As Archibad has argued, 'Words for Music Perhaps' is where Yeats confronted the hatred and passion he recognized with fellow-feeling in his Anglo-Irish precursor, and where he tried to put 'the poetry back into sex without ignoring the privy walls' (Archibald 1975: 205). He was answering a basic question: 'how to affirm life without dismissing Swift?' (ibid.: 201)

Poetry is immanence in this text where the divine and bodily excess are yoked together in tones of mingled abjection, defiance and exaltation. God is in the gross facts of sensuality, as he is in states of innocence (and the sequence reverses the Blakean progression from innocence to experience; the girl of the second lengthier part of the work is an amatory *ingénue* in comparison with the flagrant Crazy Jane). Sexual desolation, violence, erotic extremity are the context which the Crazy Jane poems supply for the calmer, youthful sexual hopes of the young girl and her suitor in the second part, where both long for permanence in love but know death is a stimulant of profound desire. In the final poems of the sequence the adult complexity and range of love is explored in poems of sexual nostalgia, mother-love, adultery, satiation, elemental rage, celebration, vitalism:

> 'Whatever stands in field or flood
> Bird, beast, fish or man,
> Mare or stallion, cock or hen,
> Stands in God's unchanging eye
> In all the vigour of its blood;
> In that faith I live or die.'
>
> ('Tom the Lunatic')

The overall effect of the sequence is such as to register sexuality in its diverse strangeness as the presence of the sacred in the world. Its tenderness and its violence, its lyrical intensities and its foul physicality together insist that life is pregnant with transcendence, even as love is poignantly subject to time and to death. At moments some of the stridency, the willed aggression, that too often mar Yeats's final poems of celebration, threaten with portentousness the predominant tone of free-flowing spontaneity that makes 'Word for Music Perhaps' overall an alluringly libidinous performance. Its textual erotics, in which epigrammatic, sexual frankness is contained in a verse of limber, lightfooted rhythmic effects, in which refrains are adroitly employed to suggest musical accompaniment, are such as to make it one of Yeats's most unpretentiously accomplished works. It has in the main an unforced self-assurance, a liberated immediacy of tone and texture that is unique in modern poetry (though some of Auden's songs seek a similar music of sinew and nerve, where Yeats sings of body and blood). It answers the Swiftian degradation of life with a vision of sex that does not deny squalor but sees it as one of the guises in which transcendence is known in the flesh:

> I broke my heart in two
> So hard I struck.
> What matter? for I know
> That out of rock,
> Out of a desolate source,

Love leaps upon its course.
('His Confidence')

It was just such a miraculous stream of poetic life as this sequence releases that the novelist Virginia Woolf noted in the man himself when she met him in Ottoline Morrell's house in November 1930. Even after his near fatal bout of Malta fever in December 1929 and his lengthy convalescence, Woolf found Yeats 'vital, supple, high charged & altogether seasoned & generous' (Woolf 329). From his talk and theorizing she got, as she recorded in her diary, 'a tremendous sense of the intricacy of the art; also of its meanings, its seriousness, its importance, which wholly engrosses this large active minded immensely vitalised man. Wherever one cut him, with a little question, he poured, spurted fountains of ideas'. She was impressed too 'by his directness, his terseness' (Woolf 1980: 330).

The years 1931 and 1932 were to test both Yeats's generosity and his energy. At the end of 1931 the Cuala Press was in financial crisis. Since Easter 1931 'Lily' Yeats's health had once more been deteriorating rapidly (in 1929 family suspicion that her ailments were psychosomatic had finally been disproved when she was diagnosed with a seriously malformed thyroid gland). She could no longer play any real part in the business. Yeats paid off the bank overdraft of £1,800, dipping into his Nobel Prize money to do so. (Murphy 1995: 244). The winter of 1931 and 1932 saw him spend a great deal of time at Coole where Lady Gregory was slowly and painfully dying. She, who had so often been a source of strength for the poet, now needed him, and Yeats answered the unspoken call, though it can only have been a sorrowful and distressing thing to watch a proud woman succumb at last to a wasting disease. He read Balzac again in the months he spent at Coole, which inspired the essay 'Louis Lambert'. In February 1931 he composed 'Coole and Ballylee, 1931' a poem which moved beyond encomium of an individual, as its earlier companion work had been, to extol a confederacy of ambition as it goes into the shadows:

> We were the last romantics – chose for theme
> Traditional sanctity and loveliness;
> Whatever's written in what poet's name
> The book of the people; whatever most can bless
> The mind of man or elevate a rhyme;
> But all is changed, that high horse riderless,
> Though mounted in that saddle Homer rode
> Where the swan drifts upon a darkening flood.

Lady Gregory died during the night of 22 May 1932. Yeats, who in her last weeks had brought her pain-killing drugs from Dublin, was in the capital when he heard the news that the end was near. He hurried to Coole to honour and mourn the dead woman who he believed had been for almost forty years his strength and conscience. He knew that a tradition was dying with her. Big Houses like Coole would no longer be centres of cultural power in a country that was now dominated by the democratic forces of rejuvenated republican nationalism, led by Eamon de Valera, who had taken power following the general election of February that year. Within a decade the house at Coole would be sold and razed to the ground. Only the grounds and woods would remain as testament to all the intense life they had known – and the tree on which Lady Gregory had encouraged her pride of literary lions to carve their names.

Yeats was turning sixty-seven when Lady Gregory died. Coole would never again be the place where he could go in the assurance that he would be made welcome. He had lost a home as well as a friend and fellow-worker. Yet as so often before at defining moments in Yeats's life, when Lady Gregory died he had already begun the process of assessing his past and recasting the moulds in which his experience would be shaped in the future. Almost a year before her death he had delivered most of the material for a proposed 'Edition de Luxe' to Macmillan in London, with all the sense of accomplishment and of an *oeuvre* in the making that that involved. Six days later at Sturge Moore's house in London he met an Indian monk Shri Puohit Swami, with whose work he became fascinated in early 1932, and with whom he would establish a collaborative relationship of five years duration, reviving his youthful interest in Hindu thought.

In May 1932 the Yeatses had taken a thirteen-year lease on Riversdale, a comfortable, suburban house below the Dublin mountains in Rathfarnham, County Dublin to the south-west of the city. In July the family moved into what would be Yeats's last Irish home. The poet at first regretted the great rooms of Coole as he settled in the gracious but not grand, leafy suburbs; but George Yeats brought her skilled hand to bear on the décor and soon the poet was domestically at ease. There were ample gardens, fruit trees, a bowling green, tennis lawns and croquet on the grass (Yeats became quite the adept at croquet). By the end of July the poet wrote to Shakespear to share his pleasure: 'This little creeper-covered farm-house might be in a Calvert woodcut, and what could be more suitable for one's last decade? George's fine taste has made the inside almost as beautiful as the garden which has some fame among gardeners' (*L*: 799).

So in the period before and after Lady Gregory's death Yeats was engaged on the editing of his own past work, was bringing old projects towards completion and was embarking on new enterprises. The final section of his autobiography 'Dramatis Personae', begun in 1927, with its lampoons of Martyn and Moore had to await Moore's death in 1933, before the work could be completed for publication (it appeared in 1935; Martyn had died in 1923). This account of the years 1896–1902 achieved a tone of comic zest, as if the poet was exhilarated, with Moore and Martyn both dead, that he is still able to live a life of multifaceted creativity and action in the way he had done since early manhood. In 1931, as well as preparing the 'Edition de Luxe', he had been finishing his play *The Resurrection* (first imagined in the summer of 1926) and had been at work on a series of reflections (*Wheels and Butterflies*, 1934, which collected his recent drama together with prose commentaries), as well as working on Berkeley and on Swift. Major poems that would be collected in the Cuala-published *Words for Music Perhaps and Other Poems* in November 1932 had been included in the material he sent to Macmillan for the 'Edition de Luxe' and these would form a substantial part of the contents of the volume published in London in September, 1933 as *The Winding Stair and Other Poems*. And that collection would supply an impressive chronological conclusion indeed to Yeats's *Collected Poems* (November, 1933). Yeats's *Collected Plays* was published in November, 1934.

Furthermore, in the Irish public sphere he was determined that an Academy of Letters should be established to encourage solidarity among living Irish writers and to fight the censorship. And his good offices as an intermediary between Ireland and England were still sought. In the spring and early summer of 1932 he was an unofficial go-between in an attempt to resolve the issue of the oath of allegiance parliamentary representatives in the Irish Free State were required to make to the English monarch. Yeats's own position on the question over which the civil war had in part been fought, was outlined in an interview, published in the *Daily Express* in London in July 1932. He thought the oath should go since he believed that it was a rag to the red bull of Communism and extremism in Ireland, though 'he certainly d[id] not wish to see Ireland a republic outside the British Commonwealth' (Harwood 1988: 87). By the autumn of 1932 Yeats's plans for the Irish Academy of Letters were well afoot. Nineteen founder members were recruited and a smaller number of associates for the body which came into formal existence on 14 September. Money was needed to support the new institution (and to help too with refurbishment at Riversdale). So once more Yeats set out for the remunerative United States of America and a lecture tour.

The poet travelled by ship to New York, arriving on 26 October 1932 from which city he re-embarked for Europe on 22 January 1933. As before, his North American sojourn was a financial success, netting about £700 for himself and his family and about the same sum for his Academy (more than enough for its purposes, he felt). He had found time too to attend an impressive seance in Boston. He also met T. S. Eliot once more at a dinner at Wellesley College. Their meeting was remarkable only because they had little to say to one another. Another younger American poet was more impressed. Marianne Moore thought he entranced a Boston audience in December: 'he is hearty, smiling, benevolent, and elegant with a springiness and vigor that no invalid could very well counter-feit' (Costello 1998: 286).

In America Yeats most frequently gave a lecture entitled 'The New Ireland'. It involved a good deal of comment on contemporary Irish letters, setting them in a broad historical context that involved four great tragic eras of Irish experience since the war at the end of the sixteenth century which led to the Flight of the Earls. Then a great bell had tolled and similar bells had rung at the end of each succeeding century, as era followed era. The import of this lecture was that the new Ireland was living in the wake of a tragic history which had reached a terrible climax at the fourth bell which sounded to mark the defeat and death of Parnell. As Yeats had it later (in a prose reflection based on this lecture): 'the accumulated hatred' for England 'was suddenly transferred . . . to Ireland' (*VP*: 835), bringing a passion for reality and a satiric genius to Irish writing, as evidenced by Joyce's *Ulysses* and by the work of such younger novelists as Liam O'Flaherty (whose anti-censorship novel *The Puritan*, 1931, Yeats admired). The literature of modern Ireland then was not to be seen as some perverse misrepresentation of Irish reality from which the people had to be defended by an absurd censorship, but an expression of that reality in all its tragic self-destructiveness: 'We had passed through an initiation like that of the Tibetan ascetic, who staggers half dead from a trance, where he has seen himself eaten alive and has not yet learned that the eater was himself' (ibid.).

The Olympian historicism of Yeat's reflections on Irish history at this time, their magisterial economy of judgement, tonally served to distance the poet from the tale of suppression and tragedy they unfolded. Yet Yeats could not have been unaware, as he pondered how Ireland had changed over the course of four centuries, that change was once again working its way through the Irish body politic (his lecture implied that a fifth bell would sound at the end of the twentieth century). His concentrated broodings on Irish history and politics during and subsequent to his American tour, and in an article published in England in January 1932, entitled 'Ireland, 1921–1931', reflect how much his experience of living in the Irish Free State and participating in its governance had affected him. It had roused real political passion (as his adventures with Gonne in the 1890s had never quite done) and made him attentive to the political process as it effected change. It had also made him very vulnerable to political excitement.

The accession to power in February 1932 of de Valera was not entirely unwelcome to Yeats although he was a supporter of his opponent Cosgrave, who had held power since 1922. In 1932, in his article on the politics of the Irish Free State, he had been quite sanguine about a de Valera victory in the then forthcoming election. And when de Valera won he recognized and appreciated the new prime minister's robust antagonism to England and his determination to remove the oath of allegiance. He could see in him the makings of a strong leader like those who in the last decade had arisen in continental Europe. In Ireland in February 1933 he told Shakespear that she was right in comparing the Irish leader to Mussolini or Hitler 'All three have exactly the same aim so far as I can judge' (*L*: 806). Presumably Yeats meant that each of the three strongmen wished to govern through acts of will and conviction. That very month de Valera displayed both, when he chose summarily to dismiss from office his colourful and popular chief of police, General Eoin O'Duffy. That act was to bring O'Duffy to Yeats's Rathfarnham home in mid-summer, in hopes of a liaison than might have made Yeats a party to a *coup d'état*.

A week before the 1932 election, elements in the Irish army who feared that de Valera, having abandoned the gun, would come to power by the ballot box, formed an organization which they called the Army Comrades Association (the ACA). They were concerned that de Valera might settle old civil war scores and thought their association could be some kind of defence against political revenge. In the event, while de Valera did not try to purge the army which under Collins had defeated the Republicans in the civil war, he did seem willing to turn an indulgently blind eye on the activities of the IRA, which was still armed and acting under military discipline. He released Republican prisoners from gaol and was apparently unconcerned when Republicans tried to break up opposition at

election meetings, under the slogan 'no free speech for traitors'. In these circumstances, in which a fear of Republican violence was mixed with paranoia about a
Communist threat, the ACA swiftly developed as a paramilitary force which by
the autumn of 1932 could claim 30,000 members. In July 1933, six months after
his dismissal as chief of police, O'Duffy became leader of this force, renamed the
National Guard. With its zest for marches and public displays of mass support, its
uniform of Blueshirts (its members were popularly known as 'the Blueshirts'), its
raised arm salute, it was inevitable that it should seem an Irish version of
continental Fascism, though its impact on Irish society had more to do with
residual civil war animosities than with any profound ambition radically to
reconstruct Irish society according to corporatist Fascist principles.

In the spring of 1933 de Valera began to turn against the IRA. There were
fears in the very disturbed political atmosphere of these months that the IRA
might respond to de Valera's apparent *volte face* by seizing power and imposing
Communism on the country. By August the National Guard was ready to
contemplate a pre-emptive coup of its own. Yeats, in semi-retirement among
the fruit trees and on the croquet lawn at Rathfarnham, was stimulated enormously by the political commotion. In April he wrote of how he was trying with
eminent colleagues 'to work out a social theory which can be used against
Communism in Ireland – what looks like emerging is Fascism modified by
religion' (*L*: 808). In July 1933, just before O'Duffy took over as leader of the
National Guard, Yeats wrote to Shakespear:

> Politics are growing heroic... I find myself constantly urging the despotic rule of the
> educated classes as the only end to our troubles... I know half a dozen men any one
> of whom may be Caesar – or Cataline. It is amusing to live in a country where men
> will always act. Where nobody is satisfied with thought... Our chosen colour is
> blue, and blue shirts are marching about all over the country. (*L*: 811–12)

The poet evidently hankered to play the role of philosopher to the new
movement (Gentile to Mussolini) and his army friend, a Captain Dermot Mac-
Manus who had been his conduit to O'Higgins a decade before, who did not
think the idea impossible, brought O'Duffy out to see Yeats that summer in late
July. The poet convinced himself (or allowed MacManus to persuade him to
reserve judgement), that his visitor had potential, though O'Duffy was not likely
to prove a Caesar or a Cataline. It was difficult to imagine him heading a
government of all the talents, for he was an ill-educated if practical man. Yeats,
who had been revising *A Vision*, talked philosophy to an uncomprehending
O'Duffy. But the poet was ready to do his bit for the cause ('Doubtless I shall
hate it' he assured Shakespear, 'though not so much as I hate Irish democracy'; *L*:
813). He composed some marching songs for the Blueshirts, though whether they
found them serviceable is not known.

By September Yeats had come to his senses. A monster meeting of Blueshirts
in Dublin had been proscribed by the government and a force which had
threatened a march on the capital was shown to be a toothless tiger. O'Duffy

quickly became not the leader of an extra-parliamentary mass of marching militants, roused to fervour by Yeatsian doggerel with autocratic rule by an educated elite as their goal, but the head of a new opposition political party that succeeded the old Free State party which Cosgrave had led for nearly a decade.

In 1934, with the Blueshirts absorbed back into democratic politics, Yeats attributed his folly of the previous year to a temporary fit of fanaticism. He explained that he had in politics 'one passion and one thought, rancour against all who, except under the most dire necessity, disturb public order, a conviction that public order cannot long persist without the rule of educated and able men' (*VP*: 543). So he had foolishly entertained preposterous notions about the Blueshirts and his own possible contribution to their movement. He had realized soon enough that he was supporting thuggish but ineffectual 'rioters in the cause of peace' (*L*: 820), and rewrote his marching songs for publication in the English *Spectator* magazine in ways which would render them immune to party conscription. There they appeared on 23 February 1934 ('Three Songs to the Same Tune') as an aggressively jaunty, exaggerated and obscure defence of defiant Irish militarism, ironized by the mocking refrains and irregular rhythms to which no marching feet could keep time.

Cullingford in her conscientiously detailed study of this episode essentially accepts Yeats's own account of his behaviour in the summer of 1933. She rightly insists that Yeats's involvement with the Blueshirts was 'never formal and existed largely in his own overheated imagination' (Cullingford 1981: 207) and makes much of the fact that Yeats saw the Blueshirts as a last resort if the IRA and economic troubles combined to bring chaos. He was responding to Irish disorder by envisaging a 'despotic rule of the educated classes' (ibid.: 204), rather than rule by a Fascist gang. There is good sense in this, although Cullingford ignores the degree to which Yeats in old age did not really want to be sensible. To a personality that had always admired the authoritarian imposition of order on human affairs (of the kind he had preached in the Order of the Golden Dawn at the turn of the century) there was something inherently attractive about hierarchy and command. It was absurd to expect O'Duffy to embody such ideals, but Yeats's flirtation with his movement bespeaks more than a midsummer madness. It suggests his boredom with bourgeois democratic politics and the ordinary, daily life they serve, for all that he dreaded disorder; as it suggests too his relish for drama, vitality, the heroic, the irrational, passion. Such attitudes might have made him a temporary fellow-traveller of an Irish Fascism had O'Duffy been the man to lead it; though the instinctive libertarianism that warred in his nature with his rage for order would soon, one suspects, have made him an outlaw of such a regime.

Despite his disillusionment with O'Duffy and his whimsically rueful admission that the summer of 1933 had been a season of general fanaticism in Ireland by which he had been affected, Yeats's political fastidiousness was not such at this time that he rejected the Goethe Plakette, which he was offered by a Nazi-dominated Frankfurt in February 1934. There is clear evidence that he had a good idea what kind of regime had recently been installed there, for on Christmas Day 1933 in a rare late letter to Gonne he had written of Polish Jews he had met at a PEN Club meeting in London: 'Much as they hate Germany for baiting Jews they hate it more for putting down the Polish language' (*GYL*: 449). In Frankfurt *The Countess Cathleen* was performed in his honour, its Wagnerian ambition no doubt making it a suitable piece for such a place at such a time. Hone, in an evasive footnote to his biography of the poet (he was writing in neutral Ireland during the Second World War), reports that Yeats was awarded the prize 'as author of *The Countess Cathleen*' (*Hone*: 403). Perhaps the Nazi Oberbürgermeister of the city, who awarded the prize, appreciated its celebration of higher spiritual values as they contrast with the worldliness of two venal devils in the play, who appear disguised as Eastern merchants.

As well as being the author of *The Countess Cathleen*, Yeats at the beginning of 1934 was the author of the new book of powerful poems which were, as we noted, published in London in the autumn of 1933. Some of the poems in *The Winding Stairs and Other Poems* offer a definition and defence of reactionary political extremism. 'The Seven Sages', for example sites radical conservatism in the Irish eighteenth century and find its inspiration in a hatred of Whiggery:

> but what is Whiggery?
> A levelling, rancorous, rational sort of mind
> That never looked out of the eye of a saint
> Or out of drunkard's eye.

Hatred, which the poet identifies not with marching feet in this poem, but with men 'who walked the roads' and who 'understood that wisdom comes of beggary' is preferable to a reductive, democratic rationality. And given the maimed condition of an Ireland in which four bells had tolled, hatred and fanaticism were inevitable, a matter for remorse certainly, but somehow exhilarating as a perversely heroic destiny, akin to sainthood or dipsomania:

> Out of Ireland have we come.
> Great hatred, little room,
> Maimed us at the start.
> I carry from my mother's womb
> A fanatic heart.
> ('Remorse for Intemperate Speech')

Yeats's footnote to this poem, which informs that he pronounces 'fanatic' in the 'older and more Irish way' (in which, he states, there is emphasis on none of its syllables), 'so that the last line of each stanza contains but two beats' makes the stresses fall here on 'A' and 'heart', like the beat of the natural organ itself. Fanaticism is a physical condition in Ireland, nurtured in the womb of the nation. Can it really be judged, since extremism is a condition of birth and fate?

Political extremism in this volume has a psychic correlative in excesses of mood and attitude: in 'derision' in the face of death ('Death'), in ostentatious self-forgiving and the blessedness which ensues ('A Dialogue of Self and Soul'), in prayerful mysticism in which 'men dance on deathless feet' ('Mohini Chatterjee') and in the sexual daring of the two sequences, 'Words for Music Perhaps' and 'A Woman Young and Old' which comprise more than half of its individual contents. A book of honoured individuals – writers, philosophers – it is predominantly a book of women. *The Winding Stair and Other Poems* opens with 'Two girls in silk kimonos' ('In Memory of Eva Gore-Booth and Con Markiewicz'), closes with 'From the "Antigone"', contains the two elegiac poems for Lady Gregory and a tenderly amusing poem for her grand-daughter ('For Ann Gregory'), as well as a vision of a child-bearing moon '(The Crazed Moon') and of the Virgin Mary as mother of an avatar ('The Mother of God'). Woman appears in the book variously as a stabilizing counterweight to the wilfully histrionic states of feeling the poet indulges, sometimes tiresomely it must be said, or as the embodiment of an innocent eroticism, a transgressive wildness and religious power all of which can reinvigorate an old man given to regrets and remorse, as well as to outrageous fits of hatred and fanaticism. In 'Stream and Sun at Glendalough' a moment of blessed renewal is rendered in terms of female sexual experience, as though such bliss depends on the poet achieving a feminine nature with, as Yeats saw it, an indifference to repentance: 'What motion of the sun or stream/Or eyelid shot the gleam/That pierced my body through?' And in 'Byzantium', as if to remind a poet who makes hatred an inspiration, that the body is the true site of spiritual wisdom, the dance of the spirits in the holy city of eternity is for all the stasis evoked in the poem, rhythmically orgasmic, climactic, a transcendent variation on the mire and blood of human sexuality. The poem may salute 'glory of changeless metal', yet, as Crazy Jane would have poet and reader instructed, '"Love is all/Unsatisfied/That cannot take the whole/Body and soul"':

> At midnight on the Emperor's pavement flit
> Flames that no faggot feeds, nor steel has lit,
> Nor storm disturbs, flames begotten of flame,
> Where blood-begotten spirits come
> And all complexities of fury leave,
> Dying into a dance,
> An agony of trance,
> An agony of flame that cannot singe a sleeve.
>   ('Byzantium')

That even so transcendental a poem as 'Byzantium' should remind, in a final pulsation, of the rhythms of the body, is not surprising, given a major preoccupation of the volume. For in *The Winding Stair* the poet dramatically represents himself as wrestling with the ineluctable 'extremities' between which 'Man runs his course' ('Vacillation'). The vision of an antinomial reality which had been the burden of *A Vision* is now tested to the limit to see whether it offers anything but unending process: 'All those antinomies/Of day and night' ('Vacillation'). Only the knowledge of the dead and the momentary blessedness of unity of being, are allowed by the poet to release humanity from choices that involve, given the nature of choice, partial experience, loss and terror. In 'Blood and the Moon', for example, the imaginative ideal of a rightly ordered polity, where governing authority is grounded in soundly idealist philosophic principles, is challenged by the terrible reality of power divested of any values other than a 'mathematical equality', established and maintained through the shedding of innocent blood. For Sato's sword is 'Still razor-keen' ('A Dialogue of Self and Soul') and a key symbol of the volume is an 'All-destroying sword-blade still/Carried by the wandering fool' ('Symbols'); so if history is chosen as the arena of a self-dramatizing poetics it will require a gothic imagery of blood and moon to tell it true. Under the clay in 'Oil and Blood' are 'vampires full of blood': 'Their shrouds are bloody and their lips are wet.' And, if at the last, self is chosen instead of soul, Man instead of God, in the fundamental antinomies dramatized in the book (Donoghue 1986: 79), then that will involve not only the noble and beautiful things Coole offered to the poet but the reductive and demeaning ignominy of

> the frog-spawn of a blind man's ditch,
> A blind man battering blind men;
> Or that most fecund ditch of all,
> The folly that man does
> Or must suffer, if he woos
> A proud woman not kindred of his soul.
> ('A Dialogue of Self and Soul')

Yet it will also involve, the book is able to intimate, the wisdom of the body in which Crazy Jane is learned. For in her sense of things the poet seeks what might be left of soul as he reckons with the consequences of the choice announced at the conclusion of 'Vacillation': 'Homer is my example and his unchristened heart.' It is as if Crazy Jane is given in *The Winding Stair and Other Poems* the responsibility of saving Yeats's system, so sedulously constructed in *A Vision*, from the nihilism that haunts its apprehension of eternal, antinomial process. Not even she could quite manage that.

17

An Old Man's Frenzy

On 11 November 1933 Yeats wrote to Shakespear about an apparition which had recently visited him seven times. A child's hand, arm and head had appeared to him as he lay in bed, showing him a five of diamonds or of hearts. The poet was anxious to know what Shakespear made of this portent. She replied: 'Perhaps you'll have a fortune or a new love-affair... I believe at about 70–5 men often fall in love...' (Harwood 1988: 92). In offering this prescient interpretation Shakespear was not to know that the now agèd poet was suffering from a serious impediment to future affairs of the heart. As well as bringing recurrent serious illnesses, the decades had taken their toll in failing sexual powers (though arteriosclerosis compounded by sporadic bouts of heavy smoking was probably the main cause of sexual difficulties; mild diabetes may also have played its part).

In April, the cruellest month, Yeats submitted himself to a London sexologist and surgeon, the ostentatiously homosexual Harley Street consultant Norman Haire, who performed for the poet the Steinach rejuvenation operation. Yeats had excitedly read of this procedure in Haire's book *Rejuvenation* (1924) and hoped that what was in fact a partial vasectomy, would vitalize both mind and body. In the event, the evidence suggests that the poet did not regain bodily competence as the result of Haire's ministrations but he certainly felt that the imaginative vigour which he had always associated with sexual prowess, returned full-fold. The operation gave him a huge psychological boost. Ellmann cites an unpublished letter of 1935 in which the poet speaks of 'the strange second puberty' that the operation had given him, 'the ferment' that had 'come upon [his] imagination' (Ellmann 1987: 28).

Yeats quickly found women prepared to indulge him in a second puberty as adventurous as his first had been constrained. In October 1934 he met a twenty-seven-year-old actress Margot Collis (née Ruddock), divorced and recently remarried, with whom he soon became intimate. In December of the same year another attractive woman, the left-wing novelist Ethel Mannin, entered his life and began an improbable affair with the elderly, mystic poet, in which politics were off-limits. Both these affairs were conducted in England. Mannin, in her mid-thirties when she met Yeats, had a comfortable London house near Wimbledon Common at which her occasional lover spent weekends. Later in the decade, Yeats also took a small flat in the city where he could entertain a friend in privacy. Mannin and Collis were both beautiful but where Mannin was worldly, sociable and progressive, with a wide circle of friends and acquaintances – writers, publishers, journalists, socialist activists – Collis was highly-strung, something of an ingénue, socially not fully formed. Yeats fell for her eyes and melodious contralto voice, her cut-glass fragility, her youthful potential. Later he reflected of her that 'there was something hard, tight, screwed-up in her, but were that dissolved by success she might be a great actress...' (Margot Ruddock n. d.: ix). She wanted to be a poet. By the end of November 1934 Yeats was composing for her:

> The Age of Miracles renew,
> Let me be loved as though still young
> Or let me fancy that it's true
> When my brief final years are gone
> You shall have time to turn away
> And cram those open eyes with day.
> (McHugh 1970: 34)

The affair with Mannin was altogether less intense, more amusingly companionable. Warmed by good Burgundy Yeats was treading 'the antic hay with abundant zest'; but 'once off the materialistic plane of wit and wine, gossip and anecdote' (Mannin 1937: 81) they did less well. Early on in their relationship they hit an impasse that might have ended it. Together with the dramatist Ernst Toller, Mannin urged Yeats to support a propaganda campaign to propose that the German writer Carl von Ossietsky, who had been gaoled by the Nazis, be awarded the Nobel Prize. Yeats refused, though considerably distressed by the request. He gave as his reason that as an Irish poet he had no interest in European affairs and that he had only ever supported such a campaign when, at the urging of Gonne, he had signed a petition on behalf of Casement. Months later the political rift between them still rankled and the poet wrote to his mistress in self-exoneration, hoping that she would not cast him out of her affections: 'Do not try to make a politician of me... Communist, Fascist, nationalist, clerical, anti-clerical, are all responsible according to the number of their victims. I have not been silent; I have used the only vehicle I possess – verse' (*L*: 850–1).

A pattern quickly established itself in this the penultimate phase of Yeats's long unsettled life: the distinguished poet lived as a *paterfamilias* in Rathfarnham (the Yeatses had given up their Rapallo flat in the summer of 1934), meanwhile venturing forth to England recurrently, where he conducted a complicated life of sexual dalliance and erotically charged relationship with the several women who in their various ways shared his last years. George Yeats was *complaisant* it seems; her role often was that more of a mother than a wife, who came to the rescue when her ailing husband's health was unequal to the hectic amatory pace he set himself.

This is delicate territory. All marriages have their own inherent dynamics and it can be a presumption for the biographer to attribute feelings to partners where there is no evidence to substantiate conjecture. All we have to tell us in the public record in this case of a spouse's feelings about her husband's considerably less than clandestine adulteries of the mind and heart, if not fully of the body, are that George Yeats said to her wandering poet: 'When you are dead people will talk about your love affairs, but I shall say nothing, for I will remember how proud you were' (Ellmann 1987: 29). And perhaps we should leave it at that, allowing a loyal and patient wife the dignity of her silence. Yet the matter of Yeats's late philandering is a troubling one, not, it must be said, because the spectacle of an old man in pursuit of sexual gratification and intimacy is itself particularly unsettling, but because of what the Yeatses' marriage had been.

In George Yeats, who had brought her poet the overwhelming miracle of the automatic writings, Yeats had found a life-partner with whom he had lived in intimate, fruitful collaborative labour within the institution of an occult marriage. For their marriage, as well as being the usual blend of domesticity, private satisfactions and familial obligation, had been in truth the kind of dynamic relationship which Yeats had sought throughout his life in his quest for esoteric knowledge and power. It had attained in fact the ideal of a tetradic completion with the birth of their two children. That Yeats in the last five years of his life, when his wife was in her sexual prime, felt impelled to seek elsewhere for things he perhaps could not find in such a marriage, raises questions that have not been addressed by his biographers. None have mentioned indeed that the pressures of looking after two young children, one of whom was sickly, with little or no help, told on George Yeats and may well have affected her feelings for her often tiresome spouse. Undoubtedly delicacy and fine feeling for George Yeats have encouraged reticence, as well as a certain man-of-the-world tolerance of a great man's peccadilloes. Michael Yeats has told us that as a boy he scarcely knew his father (Michael Yeats n. d.: 28–37).

Ellmann comes closest to offering a convincing explanation of the poet's errancy. For Ellmann Yeats was determined in old age to make up for all the lost time of a youth and young manhood when he had 'starved upon the bosom of his fairy bride': 'He was determined to make his last years count.' He seemed as well to be 'determined to cultivate extravagance, as if at their utmost bound things took on at last their true shapes and colors' (ibid.: 29). For Ellmann, this involved a new phase of the poet's career when he wrote of old subjects with 'greater explicitness and freedom and greater awareness of ultimate implications' (ibid.: 29). There is force in this, but what it does not do is fully take account of how such 'extravagance' of action and art bespeaks a failure of Yeatsian faith in the powers of strongly disciplined institutions, which had driven him through most of his adult life. For the 'failure' of an occult marriage with its profound intimacies of body and imagination, was, so to speak, conclusively indicative of the failure of all the institutions – a magical order, a nation, a theatre, the communicative dead, in which Yeats had placed his faith at various times. Each of them had been unable to inaugurate a sacred renaissance in the modern world. So in his last increasingly desperate years, Yeats deliberately sought the sacred not in institutions of any kind but in the extra-territorial (all the lovers in his later life were Englishwomen though his final love, Edith Shackleton Heald, had Irish ancestry and as a journalist had covered the war of independence), in the flagrant, the barbaric, in the overwhelming miracle of the unclothed body, beyond inscription. Adultery was a necessity as it were; sexual identity was dissolved in the polymorphously perverse (of Yeats's four final lovers, two were lesbian by sexual orientation).

A measure of the urgency with which Yeats in his final years demanded that experience give him in immediate ways what institutions had ultimately denied him was his intensifying interest in a ritualized primitivism in which raw sexuality and religion found mingled embodiment. In *The Resurrection* for example, which he had been writing and revising since 1926 until it was first performed at the Abbey Theatre on 30 July 1934, Christ appears in his resurrected body as the consummation of a festival of Dionysian worship, of a frenzied dance of sexual ambiguity. In Dionysius there is neither male nor female, Greek nor Jew, only 'something that lies outside knowledge, outside order'. The theatrical effect of this play, in which discussion of a Shavian kind about religious doctrine between a Greek, a Hebrew and a Syrian gives way to a hair-raising encounter with the beating heart of the risen god, is to enforce an awareness of all religion as ritual which gives direct, sensuous experience of an eroticized divinity. The Christ of Christian faith in this play is summoned from the tomb by the orgiastic ritual of the pagan festival. And the sense of the spiritual, as Yeats in his introduction to the play said it must, comes with a shocking, violent sensationalism.

The Resurrection was one of two Yeats plays that were produced for the first time on 30 July 1934. Along with it the Abbey presented the phallically titled *King of the Great Clock Tower*. The actual play delivered on the suggestiveness of its title, in a dramatic action that further reflected the poet's deepening interest in sexuality, religion and primitive ritual. In the play's brief course we meet a king who has taken a mysterious, coldly beautiful woman as his queen (played in the first production by Ninette de Valois). A strolling player declares passion nurtured for the beauty of the Queen about which he has only heard. When he does see her in the flesh, he finds her less beautiful in fact than in imagination, but declares that he will continue to praise her in song, for he has been told in a vision that on the stroke of midnight he will kiss the mouth of the Queen. For this impertinence the King has him summarily beheaded. When his head is brought to the affronted sovereign his Queen dances at his orders with the severed head, which mysteriously begins to sing. As the clock strikes the last stroke of midnight she presses her lips to the lips of the head.

Figured in this terrible and ecstatic scene, the text asserts, is 'desecration and the lover's night' (*KOGCT*: 12). In his commentary on this curious crossing of the decadent symbolism of Wilde's *Salomé* with folk-tale directness, Yeats adverted to the religious meanings he intended: 'The dance with the severed head ... is part of the old ritual of the year; the mother goddess and the slain god' (ibid.: 19). How precisely the erotic dance enacted on stage before the Abbey audience was to be understood in this anthropological, ritualistic sense is not fully clear, though an aura of religious import, of judgement nigh, is clear in the tolling of the clock at the midnight hour. Yet the play itself functions more effectively as a study in the psychology of desire, attainment and the destructive power of sexual obsession than as anything more chthonic.

The Resurrection was more obviously the religious play of the first-night double-bill. Yet the context in which Yeats first collected the text of *The King of the Great Clock Tower* (in a form with which he quickly became dissatisfied, for it was soon transposed from prose to verse and then completely rewritten as another play, *A Full Moon in March*) accentuates the religio-erotic/ritualistic implications he wished the play to embody. For it is followed in *The King Of The Great Clock Tower, Commentaries And Poems* (Cuala Press, December 1934) by a compellingly strange poem on the death of Parnell, which makes his funeral a pagan, ritual sacrifice. In that poem the interment of an Irish leader is rendered as a religio-erotic ritual, in which human sacrifice might have renewed the land, as in a primitive fertility cult. Instead the Irish have lived through an era of bitterness and hatred, of political extremism, of mob rule masquerading as state and ecclesiastical power, an era of lies 'bred out of the contagion of the throng'. A sacral renewal of the social order is no longer likely; no modern leader has 'eaten Parnell's heart'. Only the memory of Swiftian solitude remains as an inspirational image for modern Ireland. For Parnell had shared Swift's invigorating pessimism, the wisdom bred of passion and terrible self-control: 'Through Jonathan Swift's dark grove he passed, and there/Plucked bitter wisdom that enriched his blood.' Yet, if modern Ireland has definitively failed both Swift and Parnell in the public sphere, in sexual experience the true religious *frisson* may still be recovered on a personal level. For such is the heterodox message of 'Supernatural Songs', the obscure poetic theology of sex with which the volume concluded.

In the last years of his life Yeats deliberately sought variegated sexual experience and wrote of sexuality with direct abandon, sometimes with a wilful virility of tone, a coarse-grained violence that can easily repel:

> Whence had they come,
> The hand and lash that beat down frigid Rome?
> What sacred drama through her body heaved
> When world-transforming Charlemagne was conceived?
> ('Whence Had They Come?')

As Albright has suggested, it may be that 'Yeats used fantasies of erotic vehemence as artificial stimulants to his flagging imaginative energies – the artistic equivalent of the Steinach rejuvenation operation' (Albright 1992: 750). More was involved, however, than the continued vitality and creativity of an ageing poet. For in sexuality Yeats was seeking, as death drew closer, the transcendental illumination of consciousness that ritual magic had once seemed to promise. In his late poems of sexual daring, danger, suffering and exalted ecstasy, in poems such as 'Supernatural Songs', Yeats was developing a personal sexual mysticism, in which the body was the way of wisdom:

> God guard me from those thoughts men think
> In the mind alone
> He that sings a lasting song
> Thinks in the marrow bone.

This sexual mysticism of the marrow bone involved too a heterodox theology which in 'Supernatural Songs' introduced the feminine into the concept of godhead and made the transcendent explicitly erotic in a way which even the sexually charged vision of 'Byzantium' had not been. In the person of an old hermit of early Christian Ireland named Ribh, Yeats imagined a version of the island's ancient faith which 'had come from Egypt, and retained characteristics of... older faiths that have become so important to our invention' (*KOGCT*: 45). In 'Supernatural Songs' in the poem entitled 'Ribh Prefers An Older Theology' (subsequently titled 'Ribh denounces Patrick') the poet has his heterodox mouth-piece damn the national saint for the abstract masculinity of his Trinity (tradition has the saint teaching his doctrine of a triune deity with the humble Irish shamrock as symbol of the one-in-three). Ribh offers in contrast 'A father, mother, child, (a daughter or a son)/That's how all natural or supernatural stories run' and a divinity of eternal generation ('Godhead begets Godhead'). For Ribh the Christian doctrine of a masculine Trinity is associated with the incompleteness that makes human lovers strive in sexual intercourse to increase their kind. Lacking such completeness they produce mere 'multiplicity', whereas a fuller theology that admitted the feminine to its holy family would bring freedom from 'the mirror scalèd serpent' of multiplicity and allow participation in the perpetual self-regeneration of true godhead. As Yeats told Shakespear, 'The point of the poem is that we beget and bear because of the incompleteness of our love' (*L*: 824). The first of the 'Supernatural Songs' ('Ribh At The Tomb Of Baile And Aillinn') had envisioned in tones of ecstatic conviction what such celestial intercourse might be like:

> The miracle that gave them such a death
> Transfigured to pure substance what had once
> Been bone and sinew; when such bodies join
> There is no touching here, nor touching there,
> Nor straining joy, but whole is joined to whole;
> For the intercourse of angels is a light
> Where for its moment both seem lost, consumed.

The beauty of this moment of sexual apotheosis should however not be allowed to disguise the fact that late Yeatsian sexual mysticism, as represented in the heresies of Ribh, has radically shocking implications. It expresses a revulsion from human fertility. The second of the 'Supernatural Songs', 'Ribh Prefers An Older Theology', written in late July 1934, strikes a note that sounds more and more clearly in Yeats's last works. Natural reproduction of the species is denigrated in the name of a transcendent renewal of the bodily self, in which the futile copying of human beings is replaced by the regeneration of divinities. Sexual supernaturalism is only for the daring few. The herd cannot be expected to join the poet in his transcendence of reproductive sex; it must, in the end, be subject to eugenic control, for 'the common breeds the common,/A lout begets a lout' (Three Songs to the One Burden' written in 1939) as a late poem has it, in lines that are scarcely redeemed by the fact that they are attributed to a 'Roaring Tinker' and are framed by the mysterious refrain '*From mountain to mountain ride the fierce horsemen.*'

Yeats published a new version of 'Supernatural Songs' in 1935, with additional poems, to accompany his plays *The King of the Great Clock Tower* (now in verse) and *A Full Moon in March* (the completely revised version of *The King of the Great Clock Tower*, which Yeats preferred, though he never saw it performed). The new version made more explicit the elitism of the sequence. It added as a new third poem 'Ribh in Ecstasy', in which the heretical theologian is granted a momentary experience of supernatural sex. After such unity of being, such ecstasy, daily life can only seem a 'common round' to be resumed in sorrow:

> My soul had found
> All happiness in its own cause or ground.
> Godhead on Godhead in sexual spasm begot
> Godhead.

Only the few, though, are granted the privilege of conscious beatitude. The rest, like the representative 'girl or boy' of 'Whence Had They Come?' (another new poem in the sequence) must

> Cry at the onset of their sexual joy
> 'For ever and for ever'; then awake
> Ignorant what Dramatis Personae spake.

By contrast with this mystical elitism, the play which gave the title to the volume of two plays and a selection of poems, published in November 1935 as *A Full Moon in March*, might be read as a work of such ravishing carnality that it redeems the flesh without recourse to the aggressively Olympian supernaturalism that sounds its superior note in some of the 'Supernatural Songs'. In this play an imaginative concentration on dung, blood, virginity, the body, on procreative desire that must bring 'desecration' with its satisfaction, does not preclude the play ending with a dance of erotic veneration for the act of love. In the action the King of the first version has been dropped and we are left with a folk-tale queen who will give herself to the one who sings most beautifully of his love for her but who orders the decapitation of those who displease her. The Swineherd of the play, with his talk of dung and blood, revolts the Queen and he is beheaded forthwith. Then she dances with the severed head in an explicitly orgasmic drumbeat of climax and diminuendo. A virgin queen, as the singing head announces, has been brought down to the level of any Jill who murdered her Jack. Her ecstasy has been bought by her surrender to the gross, bloody physicality of sex. For sexual fulfilment in the earthly body can be achieved only at the sacrificial cost of psychological virginity in a taboo-breaking, transgressive satisfaction of desire. Yet the act of love is also a dance of death. 'What do they seek for? Why must they descend?' asks one member of the play's chorus, to receive the reply that echoes from the first version of the drama: 'For desecration and the lover's night'.

Sexuality in this book is compulsively explored as ritual, as a supernatural means of illumination for the heterodox few and as a degrading, ecstatic descent into the common experience of any pair when they couple like beasts in the mire and dust. For the Swineherd in *A Full Moon in March* senses that human pro-creation is appalling in contemplation. 'When I look into a stream', he confesses, 'the face/That trembles upon the surface makes me think/My origin more foul than rag or flesh'. These conflicting ways of representing sexual experience in the book are not however made the stuff of dramatic opposition, in the way a dialectics of mood and fact, dream and reality, were so heroically dramatized in *The Tower*. Rather, the reader senses that the writer is flagrantly engaging in extreme emotional experiments as he pushes a mood or idea to the point of greatest intensity and accompanying exhilaration or revulsion. An impression is generated that this work is the product of a mind that is no longer fully expecting reality to be comprehended in any system, however compact of inescapable antinomies. Rather it indulges extremism of perspective and attitude, since various radical ways of apprehending the world stimulate excitement, intensity – jolt consciousness out of the dread of nullity. The voltage level of the book is high. Individual poems are wonderfully concentrated. Abstract concepts are given the force of a heterodox catechism but the repeated shocks of its highly charged, consistently assertive rhetoric soon begin to leave the reader fatigued by an artificially generated current of feeling. The refrain of the first of 'Three Songs to the Same Tune', re-collected here from *The King of the Great Clock Tower*, has a crude mechanical energy that the poems in the book as a whole do not quite escape: 'Down, down, hammer them down,/Down to the tune of O'Donnell Abu.'

During his final years of life as he sought the stimulation of new and varied sexual experience with its compensatory influence on what he feared was a flagging inspiration, Yeats was simultaneously attracted by an oriental vision of the spiritual life. That involved its own kinds of extremism too and it can seem but one more aspect of the Yeatsian investment, as the poet's life drew towards its end, in the intensity and strangeness of radically disorientating, extra-territorial perspectives on reality.

Yeats's collaboration with Shri Porohit Swami was the stimulus for his late investigation of Hindu mysticism which bore fruit in the introductions he supplied to the Indian Swami's publications. Yeats found there narratives of religious feeling quite unlike the religion of his boyhood, the 'Irish Protestant point of view that suggested by its blank abstraction chloride of lime' (*E&I*: 428). In the Swami's autobiography and in the writings of his spiritual master, Yeats could luxuriate, orthodox for a moment, in a mode of spirituality that had its own version of theologically sanctioned supernatural sex. For he had learnt that 'An Indian devotee may recognise that he approaches the Self through a transfiguration of sexual desire' (*E&I*: 484). He learnt too of a sexual/spiritual technique that perhaps bore on his own diminished physical condition:

> There are married people who, though they do not forbid the passage of the seed, practise, not necessarily at the moment of union, a meditation, wherein the man seeks the divine Self as present in his wife, the wife the divine Self as present in the man. There may be trance, and the presence of one with another though a great distance separates. (*E&I*: 484)

The poet could ponder too, as he immersed himself in Hindu thought, complex sexual exchanges between East and West that reflected on a world-historical scale the fluid ambiguity of sexual identity: 'The West impregnated an East full of spiritual turbulence, and that turbulence brought forth a child Western in complexion and in feature . . . perhaps the converse impregnation has begun, the East as male . . . We have borrowed directly from the East and selected for admiration or repetition everything in our own past that is least European, as though groping backward towards our common mother' (*E&I*: 432–3).

Yeats's association with his Swami and the reading and study it provoked account for the deliberate orientalizing of his late poetry. As they had been at the outset of his career, Ireland and India are venerated by the poet in his final years as very ancient cultures in which the oldest wisdom of the world took deep root in traditions of pilgrimage, of sacred rivers and lakes, of holy mountains. The life of pilgrimage invoked in Yeats's introduction to Shri Porohit Swami's translation of his master's book *The Holy Pilgrim* has its Irish equivalent in pilgrimage to Lough Derg, with its fastings and penitential extremes ('The Pilgrim'). Since 'every civilisation began, no matter what its geographical origin with Asia' (*VP*: 837; Yeats citing 'a famous philosopher') Yeats's late poetry inhabits a kind of world geography in which ancient Ireland – with its mystic sites, Celtic crosses, burial mounds – is made to seem the spiritual kin of India, Japan, China, Alexandrine Egypt. This easily comparativist perspective gives to Yeats's last collections of verse an imaginative spaciousness and universalism that is the antithesis of the truculent Anglophobic nationalism that some of his late ballads also indulge, and to the crude elitism of his social attitudes in some of his poems. Where Yeats's early poetry, in an act of imaginative appropriation, had made the English language take account of the mysterious otherness of Irish place-names, locales and mythologies, this late poetry anticipates English as the language of a liberated, post-colonial world in which ancient, shared identities could be rediscovered in the language of the dispossession. In this emancipatory freeing of

English from its tribal and geographic roots, and from colonial oppressiveness, politics and nation become subsumed in a mood of all-encompassing spirituality which knows that *sub species aeternitatis* and in the light of universal human destinies, a narrow nationalistic self-interest fades into insignificance. In such a mood Yeats could write in 1937:

> I am no Nationalist, except in Ireland for passing reasons; State and Nation are the work of intellect, and when you consider what comes before and after them they are, as Victor Hugo said of something or other, not worth the blade of grass God gives for the nest of the linnet. (*E&I*: 526)

Yet late Yeatsian orientalism is not just a matter of sexual theology and technique, gender exchanges and enhancing, comparativist perspectives. Oriental supernaturalism in late Yeats has its ascetic aspect, its extremism of self-denial that the poet admits is a 'self-abandonment unknown to our poetry' (ibid.: 470). For he knew that Hindu mysticism in its ascetic form seeks to 'pass out of . . . three pentitential circles, that of common men, that of gifted men, that of the Gods' to find a cavern on a holy mountain, 'and so pass out of life' (ibid.: 469). To western ways of thought such ascetic intensity is distinctly unappealing and can be difficult to distinguish from nihilistic life-denial. And in Yeats's late poetry the way of the east can indeed seem the way of terrifying negation that leads to the knowledge that reality has its basis in non-being. 'Supernatural Songs' concludes with 'Meru' and the chilling lines:

> Hermits upon Mount Meru or Everest,
> Caverned in night under the drifted snow,
> Or where that snow and winter's dreadful blast
> Beat down upon their naked bodies, know
> That day brings round the night, that before dawn
> His glory and his monument are gone.

In this mood the East for Yeats in his last years is the Buddha, whose 'empty eye-balls knew/That knowledge increases unreality, that/Mirror on mirror mirrored is all the show' ('The Statues'). Eastern thought intensified his growing fear, as death approached, that there was nothing behind the 'superhuman/Mirror resembling dream' ('The Tower') that man had made to disguise from himself the truth of nihilism, from 'the desolation of reality' ('Meru').

The social circumstances of Yeats's last years could scarcely have been more different from the extremes of asceticism that he was reading about in Hindu writings. Not only did he have a comfortable home in Rathfarnham and in Mannin's London house a pleasant retreat from that city, in which he was a welcome guest, but in the early summer of 1935 he paid his first visit to Penns in the Rocks, the Sussex country seat of Lady Gerald (Dorothy) Wellesley, estranged wife of the future Duke of Wellington. Yeats had been recurrently ill with congestion of the lung for most of 1935 and he quickly came to look upon his new friend's house as a replacement for the Coole which had so often in the past allowed him to recover from the stresses of metropolitan life. That Wellesley offered sexual intimacy of an emotional if perhaps not a physical kind, as well as her gracious house and her elevated social standing, as gifts to the elderly poet, made Penns in the Rocks a very agreeable substitute for Lady Gregory's Coole. Like Gregory, Wellesley had literary ambitions. It was her poem 'Horses', which Yeats admired, that first brought them together through the good offices of their mutual acquaintance Lady Ottoline Morrell. Wellesley was delighted that Yeats took her poetry seriously, to the extent that he collaborated on a set of poems with her, wrote extensively to her on poetic matters and included swathes of her boringly mannered verse in the *Oxford Book of Modern Verse*, the anthology which under his editorship appeared at the end of 1936.

Wellesley was an androgynous figure and Yeats welcomed the chance their relationship afforded to experiment flirtatiously with his own sexual identity. In October 1936 he wrote to tell her: 'O my dear, I thank you for that spectacle of personified sunlight. I can never while I live forget your movement across the room just before I left, the movement made to draw attention to yourself' (*L*: 864). A month later, as intimacy deepened, he wrote 'My dear, my dear – when you crossed the room with that boyish movement, it was no man who looked at you, it was the woman in me. It seems that I can make a woman express herself as never before. I have looked out of her eyes. I have shared her desire' (*L*: 868).

Yeats's old age of sexual and religious experiment did not escape the folly it so obviously risked and at moments disaster threatened. The years were closing in. In June 1935 the poet's seventieth birthday had been celebrated with public honours and a special PEN Club dinner in Dublin. In July AE, the poet's oldest friend, died in Bournemouth and was buried, with Yeats in attendance, in the Irish capital. In October a lump was removed from the poet's tongue, but was found to be benign. He found the thought of another northern winter intolerable; Dublin was once again loud with anticlerial attacks on the Abbey Theatre. The fatigue of all the reading he had done as editor of the anthology of modern verse that he was preparing for the Oxford University Press was taking its toll as well. He decided to head for the south and more agreeable climes.

Unfortunately his storm-tossed voyage with the Swami to Majorca in the late autumn of 1935, to spend the winter away from the damp cold of London and Dublin, in theological study and translation of sacred texts, was undertaken in the improbable company of the bizarre Mrs Gwyneth Foden. This colourfully vulgar lady of a certain age had attached herself to the English circle that had surrounded the Swami with effusive, feeble-minded admiration. Ostentatiously theatrical (on the voyage she got herself up on one occasion in the garb of an Indian temple dancer), an exploitative hypochondriac, devoutly attached to the Swami, she was for a brief time the object of the poet's unaccountable infatuation. Yet his regard for her did not extend to respect for her very limited literary powers (a book entitled *My Little Russian Journey* was published in 1935). At a party given by the British Consul in Majorca Yeats, his tongue loosened by drink, let his opinion of her work be known. Mrs Foden was inconsolable.

In no time she quarrelled too with her guru. The lady forsook both Swami and poet (who had once more succumbed to ill-health), and hurried back to London where she waged a war of righteous disillusionment against the Swami's reputation and against that of the poet who was caught in her line of fire (Harwood 1988: 105–7).

High farce gave way to something more alarming. In February and March Yeats was nursed through serious illness by George Yeats who had arrived at the beginning of February to take the situation in hand. She found her husband breathless and with his heart missing a beat. Then the poet's slow convalescence was interrupted by the astonishing appearance of Margot Ruddock in May, her wits astray. Having acted in the London production of *The Player Queen* in October 1935, she had been sending Yeats packets of her poetic compositions which the poet had not bothered to read. He had in fact angrily advised her to stop writing. Now in a phase of the severe mental illness which was eventually to overtake her completely, Ruddock's distress focused obsessively on the issue of her talent. In the crisis of a Majorca May Yeats suddenly discovered 'in broken sentences, in ejaculations, in fragments of all kinds . . . a power of expression of spiritual suffering unique in her generation' (Ruddock n.d. xi). Yeats's response to her verse, fulsome after apparent neglect, precipitated what may have been a suicide attempt. She tried to jump into the sea, but instead danced crazedly on the shore (drawing from Yeats in January 1937, the gentle, sorrowing poem 'Sweet Dancer').

The next day the demented woman left for Barcelona, where her eccentric, self-threatening behaviour landed her in hospital with a broken knee. The British Consul there summoned the Yeatses by telegram and the poet had to make himself responsible for the financial cost of her repatriation to London. Yeats reported on this set of circumstances, in a letter to Shakespear, in a tone which probably disguised his shock. He regretted that the expenditure would cut into his wardrobe allowance for the coming year. But Yeats had wanted immediate, intense, erotic experience which brought with it when it came, greater dangers than enforced sartorial economies. The Barcelona incidents got into the London papers and the poet reckoned he would have to keep a low profile when he got back to England. The Swami had wisely set sail for India to escape the Foden problem, from where he would never return.

The Ruddock fiasco had in fact interrupted the completion of one of the most grotesque and wild of all Yeats's works, the play *The Herne's Egg*, which he had begun to write when he arrived in Majorca and before ill-health made work impossible for a time. He completed it when he got to back to Ireland in late June. A black-comedic farce it offers as extremist a vision of sexual excess and religious heterodoxy as anything in the Yeatsian canon. Risk in the poet's personal affairs had its correlative in daringly outrageous dramatic experiment.

The play (published in 1938, but unperformed in Yeats's lifetime) is set in Celtic antiquity and in six brief scenes dramatizes the conflict between freedom and destiny in the person of a saga hero. The hubris of heroism that would seek to deny fate in the play is represented by Congal (the doomed hero of the nine-teenth-century Irish poet Samuel Ferguson's epic poem of that name) and the implacable role of fate in human affairs, is symbolized by a huge heron or 'herne', which exercises absolute power over individual destiny. *The Herne's Egg* engages therefore with the conflicts of Greek tragedy in which a hero struggles to escape an ineluctable curse. Its helter-skelter action, rendered in spare urgent verse, its wilfully stylized symbolism (a donkey appears as a mechanical toy) and its outrageously gross narrative (the play turns on the rape of a priestess of the heron god by seven drunken soldiers) anticipate a theatre of the absurd in which human suffering is the stuff of dark comedy. In combination the tragic plot and the grotesquerie of manner produce an exuberantly savage drama in which a terrible human destiny is staged as metaphysical farce.

For the biographical critic the play (which would place exceptional demands on a producer) is of special interest, for it self-consciously restates in radically new terms some of the poet's key imaginative concerns and interrogates the nature of theatre itself. At its heart is the vision of life in the control of supernatural agencies and of destinies shaped by acts of divine impregnation. For the plot, such as it is, presents a conflict between Congal and Attracta, the priestess of the Great Herne. Congal does not believe in the existence of the Great Herne, the divinity who is shaping his end at the hand of a fool. He thinks him the fantastic product of a virgin's wish-fulfilment. He supposes Attracta can be cured of her delusions by a night of repeated sexual congress with his soldiery. In fact Attracta, in a divinely inspired trance knows herself possessed of the god in a night of mysterious passion. As we see in her authoritative exchanges with Congal the following day, she is a Leda who has put on Zeus's knowledge with his power. For a moment she is no longer merely the priestess but the bride of a god. The male chauvinism of Congal and his men is shown to be ridiculous in face of woman as priestess and goddess.

Where these familiar themes of incarnation and female empowerment in a sexualized supernaturalism were formerly expressed in Yeats's *oeuvre* in tones of elevated portentousness, ecstatic revelation, sublimity, and more recently in blasphemous, profane zest, in this subversive play they are explored in a dramatic context which admits a scarifying vision of cruel absurdity at the heart of things. Richard Cave (to whose interpretation I am indebted) has rightly associated *The Herne's Egg* with Jarry's *Ubu Roi*, which Yeats had greeted with such horror as a young man, when he saw its first performance in Paris. *The Herne's Egg* is Yeats's glimpse of a savage god who is brutally indifferent to the humanity which Congal and Attracta begin to share as the play ends. For her final tenderness for the dead hero, who has perished at his own hand – a fool trying to avoid the prophecy that he would die at the hand of a fool – is made merely poignant in face of an absurdist set of stage effects: a donkey braying, a moon with a round smiling face, a laughing man, and the hero and heroine in the classic theatrical poses of death and grief. It is a scene from Ionesco or the Beckett of *Waiting for Godot* (the most self-consciously histrionic of the latter's dramas) which must leave an audience bewildered as to the responses intended. The institution of theatre to which Yeats had given so much of his life seems to be cast in radical question by a play which mocks the protocols of the medium itself. 'Being confronted relentlessly by such an absurdist vision' Cave argues, 'we have by now lost all sense of decorum that would help us to decide the appropriate response. We are learning what it it is like to live under the sway of a savage god' (Cave 1997: 374).

In the summer of 1936, following these months of dramatic experiment, of illness and of emotional and domestic crises, the poet satisfied himself with an essentially epistolary and literary eroticism. He and Wellesley worked together on one of her ballads, exchanging suggestions by letter, until Yeats could confess towards the end of July 'Ah my dear how it added to my excitement when I re-made that poem of yours to know it was your poem. I re-made you and myself into a single being. We triumphed over each other and I thought of *The Turtle and the Phoenix*' (Wellesley 1964: 82). And from this collaboration came Yeats's own complex ballad on bodily and spiritual love 'The Three Bushes'. This further stimulated a series of quietly erotic lyrics, perhaps the most intensely sensual of all Yeats's poems, physically frank in their acknowledgement of the body – its bestiality, its decrepitude and sexual failure – yet limpidly reverential in tone. How grateful Yeats felt to his aristocratic lover for this late gift of unforced inspiration (in the context of much willed extremity of mood and attitude in the late works, the sequence seems artlessly inevitable) is evidenced in the poem he composed for her that August, 'To Dorothy Wellesley'. In this an English landscape for once enters fully into a Yeatsian imagining. It can do so since the countryside around a lover's home ('Rammed full/Of that most sensuous silence of the night') is expressive of her own sensuality, of the daring, passionate sexuality she represents:

> What climbs the stair?
> Nothing that common women ponder on
> If you are worth my hope! Neither Content
> Nor satisfied Conscience, but that great family
> Some ancient famous authors misrepresent,
> The Proud Furies each with her torch on high.

In the final two years of his life Yeats, however much the climacteric of his affair with Ruddock may have alarmed him, continued to court various kinds of extremism with a kind of hectic abandon. Where so often in the past his personal, political and artistic life had been governed by a highly strategic, manipulative but ultimately astute eye for the way power permeated the order of things, in his old age he was prepared to indulge feelings for their own invigorating sake, whether in his relations with women, in subversive dramatic experiment, or, perhaps most surprisingly, in Anglophobia. So the poet who received in February 1937 that quintessentially English institutional accolade, an invitation to join the British intellectual and social upper circle, in election to the Athenaeum (under rule two which meant that he paid no entry fee), was also the poet who had recently waxed violently indignant against John Bull in frankly inflammatory verse broadsides. A ballad in praise of Parnell who had 'fought the might of England/And saved the Irish poor', composed in September 1936, was followed in succeeding weeks by two incendiary poems on Casement. Composing them strained his health. He had a 'black fortnight'.

Even in old age the climate of renown, notoriety and controversy in which he had lived for so much of his life remained Yeats's proper element. If anything his devil-may-care outspokenness and indifference to critical opinion, as he became less inhibited by considerations of *realpolitik*, made him a more controversial figure than he had ever been before. He was delighted when the *Irish Press* (the daily paper de Valera had founded to support his Republican Fianna Fáil party) printed 'Roger Casement' in February 1937, together with a photograph of the poet and an editorial which said that for generations to come his poem would 'pour scorn on the forgers & their backers' (Wellesley 126). Wellesley had to confess her sadness as an English woman who feared his Irish venom would spread 'yet more hatred for many centuries' (Wellesley 1964: 127).

At a less populist level Yeats's introduction to and selection of poets in *The Oxford Book of Modern Verse*, which appeared in November 1936, was almost wilfully calculated to annoy a new generation of poets and critics who had identified T. S. Eliot as the poet of modernity. They could scarcely have been expected to welcome the poems of Edith Sitwell, never mind those of Dorothy Wellesley, under such a rubric. The latter poet was afforded generous space for forgettable poems, while Eliot was admitted to the volume as a 'satirist rather than a poet' (Yeats 1936: xxii) who appealed to a degenerate readership: 'Eliot has produced his great effect upon his generation because he has described men and women that get out of bed or into it from mere habit' (ibid.: xxi). Thomas Hardy was represented by only four poems, while the young Irish poet Austin Clarke, to his chagrin, was excluded entirely from a volume with a distinctly Irish note sounding in the poems of Synge, James Stephens, Oliver St John Gogarty, F. R. Higgins and in the Gaelic translations of Frank O'Connor (Yeats enjoyed the friendship of the younger men Higgins and O'Connor, in his last Dublin years).

It was especially offensive to many in England that there was no room for work by the 'war poet' Wilfred Owen. In his introduction to the volume Yeats gave as the grounds of exclusion the highly debatable judgement that 'passive suffering is not a theme for poetry' (ibid.: xxxiv). He responded to the furore in a letter to Wellesley in which he opined that Owen 'was unworthy of the poets' corner of a country newspaper' for he was 'all blood, dirt and sucked sugar-stick'. He was unrepentant that he had excluded 'a revered sandwich-board man of the revolution' (*L*: 874).

At a deeper level Yeats's antipathy to the poets of the Great War was less that their poetry took passive suffering for a theme, but that it did not take tragic joy. For in the last years of his life the poet was developing a new aesthetic which demanded that joy, not sorrow or pity for suffering (Owen had written that the poetry was in the pity of his verses), be the fruit of a tragic vision. The experiment of living as if experience could be encountered in direct unmediated fashion, without the sustaining, organizing and empowering structures of institutions and related systems of thought, belief and traditional symbolism to give it meaning, results in an emphasis on 'tragic joy' in Yeats's late aesthetic statements. It introduces too a chill, exhilarating atmosphere to some of his late poems in which the horrors of a violent century are contemplated without despair. Nietzsche is once again a presiding spirit in the Yeatsian universe (though Yeats emphasizes the powers of the imagination, rather than those of the will). For death is no mere theme in this poetry but a kind of weightlessness inducing the heady awareness that, as Yeats had told Sturge Moore in 1929, 'The last kiss is given to the void' (Bridge 1953: 154).

Yeats explained his ideal of tragic joy most fully in an essay penned in 1937, 'A General Introduction for My Work' (it was commissioned for a projected complete edition). He pondered there among other things how throughout his long career he had depended as a poet on traditional poetic form. Indeed the institution of verse itself was something in which he never lost faith. He reckoned that what he called 'ancient salt' was the 'best packing' for the poetry of self-division, that as a writer of dramatic lyrics he had for so long struggled to compose. In these the mask had served his turn. He had committed his 'emotion to sheperds, herdsmen, camel-drivers, learned men, Milton's or Shelley's Platonist, that tower Palmer drew' (*E&I*: 522). Now he senses that those who don the masks of a tragic art attain a transcendent mode of conscious-ness, in which the creative divisions of the self are not merely dramatically expressed in traditional verse, but subsumed in an intimacy with the super-natural, experienced directly. The god descends (though traditional verse form retains its invocatory power). For in Shakespearian tragedy

> The heroes of Shakespeare convey to us through their looks, or through the metaphorical patterns of their speech, the sudden enlargement of their vision, their ecstasy at the approach of death. The supernatural is present, cold winds blow across our hands, upon our faces, the thermometer falls, and because of that cold we are hated by journalists and groundlings. There may be in this or that detail painful tragedy, but in the whole work none. I have heard Lady Gregory say, rejecting some play in the modern manner sent to the Abbey Theatre, 'Tragedy must be a joy to the man who dies'   (ibid.: 522–3)

'Nor', avers the poet, 'is it any different with lyrics, songs, narrative poems' in which 'the rhythm is old and familiar, imagination must dance, must be carried beyond feeling into the aboriginal ice' (ibid.: 523).

At a key moment in *New Poems*, the last collection of verse by the poet to appear in his lifetime (it was published by the Cuala Press in May 1938), that altered condition of consciousness, that elevated state, seems present as rhythm, image and poetic occasion conjoin to offer a hint of what such self-transcending sublimity might feel like. The volume opened aggressively with 'The Gyres' (this poem was probably written in the second half of 1936). A hortatory, rhetorical performance, 'The Gyres' tries to summon the god by violently proclaiming his doctrine. A Nietzschean belief in eternal recurrence can here be the basis of a species of tragic nihilism. The processes of historical change, the turnings of the gyres, repulsively barbaric as they are in effect, must be reckoned of no account by those who look on to 'but laugh in tragic joy'. The tone is Olympian and crudely dismissive of human suffering: 'What matter though numb nightmare ride on top/And blood and mire the sensitive body stain?.' We who know that the cycles of time will bring back all that is being destroyed as 'Irrational streams of blood' stain the earth, will take joy in what we see, assured as we are by a privileged long view on things. 'What matter' the poem forcefully repeats, as if to convince not only reader but poet, in a wilful pouring forth of injunctions, defiant assertions and exclamation marks. The effect is rebarbative; the poem is rescued as poetry from mere rhetorical rant only by nostalgia for 'a more gracious time' implicit in high-flown phrase-making ('In ancient tombs I sighed'; 'Lovers of horses and of women').

By contrast the second poem in the volume, 'Lapis Lazuli' (written in July 1936), concludes in a mesmeric oriental calm. Image, rhythm and a tone of elevated resignation induce a sweet sense that the terrible, tragic vistas of historical disaster, which in others provoke hysteria and antagonism to art itself, can be comprehended by an aestheticized spirituality that takes full account of a tragic reality to which, in the occident, Shakespearean drama (memorably invoked earlier in the poem) responded in its own apocalyptic, yet ultimately joyful way. A piece of lapis lazuli carving (which had been donated to Yeats by a young poet to mark his seventieth birthday), offers the poet a scenery of the mind in which an elevated calm modulates into a music of achieved gaiety. The carving on the stone is of two Chinamen and their servant. A long-legged bird, symbol of longevity flies over them. The servant carries a musical instrument. Yeats recounts all this with lapidary precision as he imagines the trio ascend a mountain amid snowfalls, until they come upon a little halfway house. Then consciousness is slowly raised by its own imagining to the condition of shared vision:

> and I
> Delight to imagine them seated there;
> There, on the mountains and the sky,
> On all the tragic scene they stare.
> One asks for mournful melodies;
> Accomplished fingers begin to play.
> Their eyes mid many wrinkles, their eyes,
> Their ancient, glittering eyes are gay.

These final lines of 'Lapis Lazuli' constitute a kind of still point in what was in fact a disturbingly variegated collection, in which the poet's last experiment in living finds expression in poems of raw brutality ('The Spur'), erotic frankness ('The Lady's Third Song'), social alienation from a democratic age ('The Curse of Cromwell'), nihilistic doubt of the worth of living in face of death ('What Then?'), bitter vehemence on English and Irish politics, with 'The Great Day' (one of a series of fragments which Yeats told Wellesley contained the essence of his politics), representing the poet as political nihilist:

> Hurrah for revolution and more cannon shot;
> A beggar upon horseback lashes a beggar upon foot;
> Hurrah for revolution and cannon come again,
> The beggars have changed places but the lash goes on.

This nasty poem does however highlight in cartoon form a controlling imaginative preoccupation in what would have otherwise been a book remarkable in Yeats's *oeuvre* for its lack of structural cohesion. Its vision of high and low is one that recurs through the volume. The world in which these poems come to their varied life is one of elevation and abasement, lofty heights and abjection, erect energy and deathly impotence. The heroism involved in individual commitment to a lofty display of personality is wonderfully praised in 'Beautiful Lofty Things', as if sheer force of life energy could raise humanity beyond the body as 'straight back and arrogant head' achieve apotheosis: 'All the Olympians; a thing never known again'. But at moments the undignified bodily implications of these polarities is quite explicit, as in 'The Wild Old Wicked Man', with its bitter, sexual refrain:

> 'All men live in suffering
> I know as few can know,
> Whether they take the upper road
> Or stay content on the low,
> Rower bent in his row-boat
> Or weaver bent at his loom,
> Horseman erect upon horseback
> Or child hid in the womb'
> *Day-break and a candle end.*

Elsewhere the volume, less obviously troubled by sexual fate, evokes a terminal condition of life in which proud men, drinkers, dancers, keep their feet ('Stand upright while you can' advises 'Come Gather Round Me Parnellites') in knowledge of a universal doom that awaits them all:

> The lovers and the dancers are beaten into the clay,
> And the tall men and the swordsmen and the horsemen
>   where are they?

Perhaps the poet can share something of the elevated wisdom evoked in 'Lapis Lazuli', through 'frenzy' achieving 'An old man's eagle mind' ('An Acre of Grass'); but he can only do so in the grim awareness that 'under every dancer' there is 'A dead man in his grave' ('A Drunken Man's Praise of Sobriety') and that 'fame and virtue rot' ('The Ghost of Roger Casement'). 'Lust and rage' may still 'dance attendance' upon a poet who is still spurred into song by these partners ('The Spur') but impotence, death, the grave are intimate with the bed of love:

From pleasure of the bed,
Dull as a worm,
His rod and its butting head
Limp as a worm,
His spirit that has fled
Blind as a worm.
('The Chambermaid's Second Song')

The penultimate poem in the collection, the measured and elegiac 'The Municipal Gallery Re-visited', managed to transpose the volume's recurrent polarity between elevation and abasement into a new register, into a key of gravely ceremonial recollection of the past. This tonal shift carefully seeks to suggest that the extremities of experience the rest of the volume expresses can still somehow be brought under poetic control by the last institution left to a troubled poet – the institution of verse-making itself in a traditional, elegantly formal stanza. Contemplating, in the Dublin gallery to which the title refers, the images of the immortals, who with Yeats had together imagined modern Ireland into vibrant existence, the poet sinks down as if in prayer. From the depth of emotion the poem elevates itself in its elaborate octaves (in a poem about absence and unmentioned death, stanza five mysteriously lacks an eighth line) to an encomium for a generation and a self-composed epitaph:

You that would judge me do not judge alone
This book or that, come to this hallowed place
Where my friends' portraits hang and look thereon;
Ireland's history in their lineaments trace;
Think where man's glory most begins and ends
And say my glory was I had such friends.

Vendler remarks of this poem: 'by giving us an epitaph to speak over him, [Yeats] effectively makes himself a corpse by the end of the poem, but a corpse apotheosised by the glorious company he keeps. Yeats's greatest group elegy is finally an elegy for himself' (Vendler 1980: 230–1). In the brief time left to him following the composition of this poem in the autumn of 1937, Yeats was to strike the elegiac note again, but not with such controlled reticence of feeling. The contemplation of his own imminent death became, however, the last challenge of his artistic career and he met it with the extraordinary imaginative energy that had been the resource of a lifetime. The pressure of immediate experience, high and low, various and turbulent, to which Yeats responded in *New Poems*, was to remain as a poetic resource to the end; but it was to be accompanied in the last year of his life by the intimate certitude of his own death and by a terrible need to warn.

18

Stroke of Midnight

In early January 1938 Yeats left Ireland to winter once more by the Mediterranean. On arrival in the south of France he was ill for a few days but recovered to correct the proofs of *New Poems*, which would appear in the early summer. The poet wrote to Wellesley of his pleasure in the new book, telling her that these poems of the last few years pleased him better than anything he had done. He had got 'the town' out of his verse and achieved a 'nonchalance' that encouraged him to believe he was opening a new vein of creativity. He hoped that he would 'watch with amusement the emergence of the philosophy' of his poetry, 'the unconscious becoming conscious', which seemed to increase the force of his work (*L*: 904).

As so often before in a long life of artistic renewal, Yeats was in the process of remaking himself and gathering his energies to meet creatively what lay ahead. His last year of life would be a preparation for the death he knew was imminent, and a confrontation with the ultimate mystery of that divided selfhood which for so long had been the dynamic of his writings. Encroaching death allowed a final freedom of expression. As he permitted some of his deepest feelings, prejudices and fears to come to the surface, he produced in the course of less than twelve months a body of astonishing, powerfully troubling work. It is characterized at its best not only by the sense of frank immediacy which makes *New Poems* a volume of extreme occasions, directly experienced, but by an urgent attempt to warn of a politically threatening future, and a determination to comprehend the past, while struggling to cope with the shocking certainty of personal dissolution.

That the poet knew he had entered on a new and final phase of his career is clear enough. In May 1937 he had announced his retirement from public life, a significant step for a man who had ostentatiously lived in the public eye for almost fifty years. The month before that announcement he had allowed his poem 'What Then?' (probably composed in 1936) to appear in the magazine of the Dublin school he had attended in the 1880s. That poem had sounded a note of pride in a task complete, as well as expressing anxiety about what might lie ahead.

'The work is done,' grown old he thought,
'According to my boyish plan;
Let the fools rage, I swerved in nought,
Something to perfection brought';
But louder sang that ghost 'What then?'

In April he had seen his work on Eastern religious thought come to fruition with the publication of *The Ten Principal Upanishads*. In October the revised edition of *A Vision*, which had preoccupied him since the publication in 1926 of the first version, was published in London by Macmillan. One critic has highlighted how this text, the version most familiar to readers, since it was published commercially, is a work of exuberant fictionality. The comic spirit that permeates it (Hazard Adams 1995: 164) is that of a sensibility relishing its antithetical status at the last and beyond the grave.

Yeats had worked too in 1937 on the general introduction for a proposed complete edition of his work. Posthumously printed (the complete edition was aborted), the introduction's rhetoric is distinctly testamentary, its tone that of a magisterial, if digressive, summing-up. There had also been something a shade valedictory about the dinner held by the Irish Academy of Letters on 17 August in Dublin, at which the fund arranged by a Testimonial Committee in the United States, to allow the poet to enjoy his twilight years without financial stress, was formally announced. Yeats published part of his speech for that occasion as a record of the event, along with 'The Municipal Gallery Revisited' and another poem, to mark the committee's generosity (that genesis accounts in part for the formal quality of the elegy). On 30 August Macmillan in New York published *The Autobiography*, bringing the major body of his autobiographical prose writings together in a single volume. In November and December the poet was rearranging the affairs of the Cuala Press. The year's end also saw the publication of *Essays 1931 to 1936*. The decks were being cleared for a journey.

Yet as so often in Yeats's life, the sense of one phase of his life ending as a new, if necessarily final, one began, was accompanied by the stimulation of novel interests that maintained the poet's vigorous zest for daily living. As always, his life instincts were strong (although at moments death attracted as an escape from the burdens of ill-health) and he retained his genius for creative collaboration. In 1937 an interest in the new medium of radio, that had stirred as early as 1926, became for a few months a kind of obsession. The old interest in verse spoken to a simple musical accompaniment resurfaced. Under expert instruction he quickly became quite a skilled broadcaster. Only ill-health prevented him enjoying work with the BBC again in 1938.

And he had a new woman friend. Edith Shackleton Heald came into Yeats's life at a fortuitous moment. The affairs with Mannin and Ruddock were over, though Yeats tried to encourage Ruddock in her career before her sanity broke down completely, by involving her in his experiments with broadcasting (her volume of poems *The Lemon Tree* had appeared in May 1937 with a handsomely sympathetic introduction from Yeats himself) and he kept up a friendly correspondence with Mannin. Wellesley's mental health at the end of 1937 was uncertain too and Yeats was undoubtedly relieved that in England he had Heald's comfortable home, Chartry House, Steyning, opened to him as another extra-territorial sanctuary.

Heald had moved into Chartry House in 1934 where she lived with her sister. Both women were successful journalists. Journalism had indeed made Edith Heald independent in more than the financial sense, for she was a bold free-thinker with a low view of the economic slavery so many women endured in marriage. She had met Yeats in her youth but now in her fifty-fourth year she began an intimate, if frequently epistolary, relationship with the elderly poet whom she had earlier admired in print for his 'grave manners and melodious conversation' (Souhami 1988: 215), his air of occult mystery combined with an Irish practicality. When they were apart Yeats wrote to her passionately in terms that suggest they were lovers. At Chartry he had a room specially set aside for his use and he was made comfortable and was looked after. She accompanied him to Monte Carlo at the beginning of January, and remained with him until George Yeats arrived in February. He returned to England in March.

A new relationship was accompanied by a new project. To help the finances of the Cuala Press Yeats had decided to issue a series of tract-like publications in which he would write about whatever interested him at the time. In December 1937 he explained to Mannin what he intended for the first issue in the series:' 'I must in the first number discuss social politics in so far as they affect Ireland. I must lay aside the pleasant paths I have built up for years and seek the brutality, the ill breeding, the barbarism of truth' (*L*: 903).

Among the 'truths' that Yeats sought to propagate in his first tract, which he worked on in the early months of 1938, were those of 'alarmist, hereditary eugenics' (Bradshaw 1992: 190). In the gross piece of truculence which *On the Boiler* (1939) is, the aged poet combined his distaste for the mere multiplication of the human species with a conviction that the future of civilization must be assured through eugenic engineering. Yeats had joined the Eugenics Society in London in 1936 and had studiously read eugenic statistical literature and current works on intelligence testing. He corresponded with the secretary of the London society on points at issue in his tract as he composed it. The fact that he chose in *On the Boiler* to represent his own ideas as the ravings of a mad ship's carpenter of his Sligo boyhood tells us that he knew he was espousing a vicious elitism in his polemic, which even some of his correspondents in the eugenics movement would find shocking. But whatever its reception, a text on ill-breeding must itself be ill-bred, barbaric.

It certainly is. Yeats in fact relished the fact that his readers would be 'horrified or incredulous' (ibid.: 210) on first encountering his violently anti-democratic ideals (parliaments along with other extant forms of government for him were 'trash'; *OTB*: 13). The senator who had spoken constructively on educational matters in the Irish parliament, the poet of 'Among School Children', now licenses himself to announce through his unconvincing persona that 'it seems probable that many men in Irish public life should not have been taught to read and write, and would not have been in any country before the middle of the nineteenth century' (ibid.: 11). From the scarcely educable mass of the Irish there now emerges 'some typical elected man, emotional as a youthful chimpanzee, hot and vague, always disturbed, always hating something or other' (ibid.: 12). By contrast able men 'whether six or six thousand, are the core of Ireland, are Ireland itself' (ibid.: 13) and that essential elite is not reproducing itself as the masses proliferate. At moments the writing in *On the Boiler* registers a true *frisson* of Swiftian paranoia – 'the mere multitude is everywhere with its empty photographic eyes' (ibid. 25) – but for the most part it does not transcend a tone of crassly wilful coat-trailing. The poet envisages the Irish future after a coming civil war between the few and the many as a Prussian tyranny (though the small army required to keep invaders from the shore need not necessarily be highly disciplined). He absurdly hopes for 'the victory of the skilful, riding their machines, as did the feudal knights their armoured horses' (ibid.: 19). The new Irish army will keep at bay the 'disciplined uneducated masses of the commercial nations' (ibid.: 30) principal among which, one assumes, will be England, where 'the English mind, excited by its newspaper proprietors and its schoolmasters, has turned into a bed-hot harlot' (ibid.: 35). In the meantime social hygiene is a public duty of government: 'Sooner or later we must limit the families of the unintelligent classes and if our Government cannot send them doctor and clinic it must, till it gets tired of it, send monk and confession box' (*OTB*: 20).

It can be argued that Yeats in this egregious work was merely expressing in an outspoken, deliberately repellent way the ideas that had preoccupied many thinking people since at least the Edwardian years in England. Florence Farr, indeed, in Yeats's immediate circle, had recommended 'careful breeding' in her book *Modern Woman* in 1910. And Yeats was far from alone in the 1930s in fearing the coarsening of the social fabric which population growth in industrial modernity seemed to involve. His vision of the city as a site of 'discordant architecture, all those electric signs, where modern heterogeneity has taken physical form' (*E&I*: 526) could be matched by many equivalent passages in the literature of the period in which modernity itself is indicted as the source of cultural degeneration.

What disallows such a tolerant historicizing of this last Yeatsian 'enthusiasm' (the term is Cullingford's) is the way his elitist extremism finds powerful, imaginatively compelling expression in some of his final poems and in the last new work for the stage which Yeats lived to see performed. What might be dismissed as mere follies in the prose work (the call to arms in a new war, when the destructive power of modern munitions and weaponry was well-known, for example) in the creative achievements of Yeats's last year take on an altogether more sinister weight of significance. These works suggest that what Yeats sought to characterize in *On the Boiler* as the provocative rantings of an obviously comic/ironic figure (the mad ship's carpenter McCoy) came from sources in his own sensibility which lay beyond such exculpatory masking. Yeats, as Donald Torchiana reminds us in profferring a benign, almost humanistic assessment of *On the Boiler*, had in truth always believed in 'Able men, a unified Ireland, a country based on the soil, the intellectual and literary contributions of famous men' (Torchiana 1966: 343). And he was convinced by the 1930s that the family and its rights – 'Inherited wealth, privilege, precedence' – played a crucial part in sustaining a healthy society. Persuaded that there was 'overwhelming evidence that man stands between two eternities, that of his family and that of his soul' (*L*: 911) he desperately wanted, as his time ran out and as the international crisis of the 1930s deepened, to defend in his writings the well-born dynasty as a site of benevolent social power in face of attacks on its entitlements by Communist, Fascist and parliamentary democrat alike. Yet as he did so his sense that in Ireland the true foe was neither of the two great political movements in conflict in continental Europe, but obscurantist Catholicism, which in the name of democracy suppressed free thought, stirred up in him moods of frenzied prejudice against the common herd that have nothing benign about them. He, his kindred and those he included in his small circle of the elect were under direct, punishing attack in the country for which he had once nursed such hopes and he seized his chance to hit back, caring little whom he offended.

The poems of Yeats's final year of life make much of the invigorating satisfactions of violence. War can be relished, for 'when all words are said/And a man is fighting mad/Something drops from eyes long blind/And he completes his partial mind' ('Under Ben Bulben'). And had not Pearse said 'That in every generation/Must Ireland's blood be shed' ('Three Songs to the One Burden')? The dilemmas of selfhood and of history can be resolved in a cult of war and blood. 'Hound Voice', a fluently nasty celebration of social elitism, of terror transcended in blood-lust and of the predatory instinct, concludes with eloquent urgency:

> Some day we shall get up before the dawn
> And find our ancient hounds before the door,
> And wide awake know that the hunt is on;
> Stumbling upon the blood-dark track once more,
> Then stumbling to the kill beside the shore;
> Then cleaning out and bandaging of wounds,
> And chants of victory amid the encircling hounds.

War in these last poems can be welcomed too because it can be fought in a good cause – the regeneration of civilization. The artist's duty in the deepening crisis of modernity ('the filthy modern tide' of 'The Statues') is constantly to keep before the 'secret working mind:/Profane perfection of mankind' ('Under Ben Bulben'). The forms of the perfected human body, the poet's ultimate inspiration, are the goal of a eugenic war which must be waged if the Irish nation is to return to its ancient omens:

> Poet and sculptor, do the work,
> Nor let the modish painter shirk

What his great forefathers did,
Bring the soul of man to God,
Make him fill the cradles right.
('Under Ben Bulben')

The rant of such a poem, with its obnoxious denunciation of 'Base-born products of base beds' could perhaps be tolerated easily enough along with the foolishness of *On the Boiler*, were it not so mesmeric a performance. For 'Under Ben Bulben', half magical incantation, half grim testament, has a charge of savage energy and a cold, dogmatic power ('ancient Ireland knew it all') that makes it especially appalling as a very dubious aesthetic experience. Skill here is complicit with a repulsive politics and a deficient ethical sense. As it is in the equally unnerving, authoritative strangeness of such poems as 'The Statues' (probably written between April and June 1938) and 'A Bronze Head' (probably written at some time during the same year). These two obscure meditations brood on the mysterious role of sculptural representation in summoning a select few ('We Irish born into that ancient sect', if only they could recognize it) to a proper appreciation of the spiritual destiny which is theirs. Both are poems which endow elitist politics with a terrible sublimity. A rhetoric and imagery of the sublime allow a politics of elitist prejudice to seem a form of heroic spirituality that transcends the degradation of less exalted, more commonplace modes of thought and feeling. 'A Bronze Head' directly associates such elevated exorbitance of emotional stance with eugenics and the blood a eugenic war will necessarily spill, in a performance as unapologetically anti-humanistic as anything in the poet's *oeuvre*.

In composing *On the Boiler* Yeats had imagined, in a note which did not get into the final version, 'centuries of bloodshed' before a government of 'the best born of the best' (Bradshaw 1992: 208) could be set in authority all over Europe. 'A Bronze Head' admits the possibility that the world is so degenerate that even massacre may come too late to save it. The poem poses a museum bronze of a woman in old age against the 'foul world in its decline and fall'. The artifact sets the poet brooding on the various bodily forms through which the woman had expressed her divided nature during a long life. Now all that seems living in the bronze is her eye like a bird's eye, which scans the sky for something 'to make its terror less'. The woman of the poem imagined in youth and age (Gonne we can assume from the many poems which Yeats had addressed to her over the years) is a multiple presence here – tender, awesome, fanatical, magnanimous. Compact of contraries, her very self-divisions made her ultimately the extraordinary creature she had always been. So remarkable was and is her person, perhaps she was possessed of a supernatural power ('I thought her supernatural') which as a 'sterner eye' looked through her eye

On gangling stocks grown great, great stocks run dry
Ancestral pearls all pitched into a sty,
Heroic reverie mocked by clown and knave,
And wondered what was left for massacre to save.

The world, this poem concludes in a kind of savage despair, has degenerated to the point where not even massacre could restore it. What shocks about the poem is that its crudely apocalyptic conclusion is reckoned by the poet an appropriate response to his 'bringing together clairvoyance and a pathos of immense nobility' (Bloom 1970: 453) in an evocation of Gonne in all her personally destructive ambiguity. A true humanity of feeling and an elitist brutalism share the aesthetic space of a deeply felt utterance. The reader is left wondering which generates the other in the poem and in the poet, troubled as much by the question as exalted by the undoubted power of the work as art.

Critics have struggled to cope with the ethical implications of Yeats's late writings. Most have had recourse to contextualization of one kind or another – as if the affront of such works can somehow be rendered bearable by understanding. It has taken a severe reader of Irish literature, the post-colonial critic David Lloyd, to accept fully the mesmeric capacity of Yeats's later poems 'to return and to haunt' (Lloyd 1993: 59) while addressing directly their appalling, bleak authority: 'The terror of these poems [he writes of the later political poems in general] lies in the relentlessness with which they discover death at the heart of culture and at the base of the state. Though their exultation in violent acts of the will points the way towards a fascist politics, it draws that political solution from a desperation by no means capable of offering the consolatory myths of belonging on which fascism relies for its legitimation' (ibid.: 79).

Not that Yeats did not care in a special way about belonging. The eugenic enthusisam of 1937 and 1938 was Yeats's expression of a deeply rooted fear that 'the gradual effacement of the well or highly born' (Wellesley 1964: 178) was taking place throughout Europe. He certainly hoped that the process could be reversed by eugenics, birth control and sound legislation in Ireland. According to his first biographer he had in fact read 'a great number of popular books on Hitler's Germany, taking satisfaction that a Nazi law passed in 1933 allowed 'ancient and impoverished families' to 'recover their hereditary properties' (Hone 1946: 467). So perhaps the filthy modern tide could be turned by firm action and members of his own Protestant caste could recover what Land Acts and revolution had taken from them since the 1880s.

Yet Yeats could not really have been surprised that he was living at a time of overwhelming degenerative crisis in which Protestant Ireland had suffered. For his own system, so painstakingly adumbrated in *A Vision*, and much of his reading of recent years in social philosophy and history (he was especially drawn to Hegel, Vico and that modern prophet of western decline, Arnold Toynbee) all confirmed that reality was cyclical and that no civilization was immune to declension. The gyres would turn irrespective of human will or desire. What Yeats defined as a 'rule of kindred' (*E&I*: 526) would of necessity arise as an age gave way to the reversal of an age. Eugenics could only expedite the inevitable. Given such a determinist conception of history the hysteria of Yeats's last enthusiasm seems oddly otiose, an eruption of social prejudice and ugly autocratic feeling in a mind no longer always able to keep its darkest energies at bay, even though his own system had given him the conceptual means to do so.

In the second version of *A Vision* (1937) Yeats had expanded on the concept of the Thirteenth Cone introduced in passing in the first edition. In the second version it is offered as an addition to the twelve cones or 2,000 or so year cycles of historical time that turn incessantly. As such it seems to involve a reality where 'All things are present as an eternal instant.' It seems to be 'a timeless realm, offering a haven from the endless inexorable revolution of the Yeatsian wheels' (Hough 1984: 116). The Thirteenth Cone can be understood as a point where radical human freedom, as distinct from the experience of a limited kind of freedom which the complex ramifications of the system also allow, is finally possible: 'The particulars are the work of the *thirteenth sphere* or cycle which is in every man his freedom. Doubtless, for it can do all things and knows all things, it knows what it will do with its own freedom but it has kept the secret' (*AVB*: 302).

It is the heavy sense of inevitable process at work in history and of the inexorable in the human condition that dominated Yeats's mind at the last, for all his eugenic obsession. The deterministic aspects of his system seemed to weigh more than did its intimations of a possible freedom from necessity he had sought to figure in the concept of the Thirteenth Cone in *A Vision*. The refrain (and many of the poems of Yeats's last year exploit refrain, a poetic technique appropriate to a vision of eternal recurrence) of 'Three Songs to the One Burden' implies as much: '*From mountain to mountain ride the fierce horsemen*'. Freedom keeps its secret. 'Three Marching Songs', ('Three Songs to the Same Tune', substantially revised by the poet in December, 1938), resounds to the mysterious sound of marching feet as history passes on its own way, unaffected by mankind.

In an exquisite lyric, probably completed in April 1938, 'Long-legged Fly', even three figures associated by the poet with moments of world historical change which they influenced, (Caesar, Helen, Michael Angelo) find their minds, as the poem's refrain has it, '*Like a long-legged fly upon the stream*' moving upon silence. What would seem to be epochal in human agency is in fact generated by a dynamic greater than individual volition. And in Yeats's last poem, 'The Black Tower', completed 21 January 1939, even in the tomb there is no escape from the demands of a history that always threatens to repeat itself, as another refrain insists:

> *There in the tomb the dark grows blacker,*
> *But winds come up from the shore,*
> *They shake when the winds roar,*
> *Old bones upon the mountain shake.*

The inexorable as a given of existence is the grim theme of *Purgatory*, the short play which Yeats wrote in the spring and early summer of 1938. It had its première, with stage design by his daughter Anne, at the Abbey on 10 August during a festival of plays and lectures at the theatre (there were revivals of *Cathleen ni Houlihan* and of *On Baile's Strand*, while F. R. Higgins gave a lecture on 'Yeats and Poetic Drama in Ireland'). Austin Clarke attended the first night of *Purgatory* and gave a jaundiced report in a letter to a friend (the newspaper reviews in Dublin were kinder):

Yeats's play was pathetic. It had the usual interesting idea – this time the eternal recurrence in terms of the bridal night, or as the old man coarsely puts it, the sexual act. The scene is the ruin of a great house looking a bit like the Coliseum. In the foreground the tramp scion of a great family which gave statesmen and generals to the empire. With him his get. Coconut horse hoofs indicated haunted house. Father and mother appear in tableaux vivants at the windows. The tramp had murdered his roistering progenitor and now stabs his son who was grovelling on the ground for some pennies. The author hobbled on the stage and made a speech about his infirmities. The dearer seats were full but the back pit half empty.   (Thompson 1997: 659).

Clarke's scathing summary catches some of the play's savage horror and lets us glimpse Yeats on a final occasion in public in his native city. Yet it is wide of the mark in failing to grasp the tragic import of an excoriating vision of irrevocable action as ineluctable destiny.

Purgatory in less than 250 lines of tautly dramatic verse, mostly the old tramp's monologue, manages to induce a sense of time and eternity in intimate proximity (though its brevity on stage makes this a difficult play to carry off theatrically). Of the play Yeats stated on the first night: 'I have put there my own conviction about this world and the next' (*L*: 913). In both dimensions there can be no escape from the consequences a crime of miscegenation has wrought. The Old Man's mother had married a jockey to satisfy her lust. She died in childbirth giving birth to him, her only child. He murdered his own father but not before that base-born product of a base bed had in his cups burnt down the family seat which had become his by marriage. Now with the son whom he 'got/Upon a tinker's daughter in a ditch' the Old Man revisits the wreck of the great house to see the ghost of his parents beget him and to kill his own offspring with the blade he used on his father. He hopes the pollution of a dynasty can be arrested by this second murder and his mother's ghost released from its purgatorial, repetitive re-enactment of her crime. At curtain-fall the Old Man realizes there can be no such escape and the play ends with his anguish and guilt: 'Appease/The misery of the living and the remorse of the dead.' Only silence answers this haunted cry.

Elitist ideals and eugenic panic certainly find expression in this packed dramatic text. The notion of a polluted genealogy is made the more horrific in a stage image of a blasted tree before a ruin which replaces the rich fertility that had once marked an aristocratic tradition. And the Old Man's murder of his son can be read indeed as a very practical act of eugenic cleansing (*Purgatory* was first published with *On the Boiler*). The fact that the Old Man declared the destruction of what is manifestly an Anglo-Irish, eighteenth-century house 'a capital offence' also gave a distinct social and political significance to the work.

The social references in the text, as W. J. McCormack has tellingly argued (McCormack 1985: 382–4), are not restricted to the eighteenth-century origin of the house but bear more precisely on recent nineteenth-century Irish social history when Protestant Ireland was beginning to take cognizance of its essential insecurity in the country. Accordingly the Old Man's caste prejudice, revolted as he is by his mother's infringement of a class taboo and the sectarian debasement that that implies in the play, makes him more than the celebrant of an idealized Irish eighteenth century. He becomes the voice of urgent, more contemporary Protestant anxieties, expressing in local terms the crisis for social privilege implicit in democratic mass society in the twentieth century. Yet he is also the fruit of a flawed pedigree, and his action in bringing his son to witness the appearance of his progenitor making love to his mother, which in the play he can almost be said to stage himself, is inescapably the action of a corrupted being. For in his own person and actions he is the embodiment of a familial doom, played out in the strange 'white light' of eternity which falls on the stricken tree in the final movements of the drama.

The awful sense of necessity that this irony releases on stage (which makes all the Old Man's actions and utterances partake of an ineluctable pollution), renders elitism and eugenics the ideological machinery of a tragic vision, implicating them with the evil in whose coils the participants in the drama will be trapped for ever. History in this severe study in a dynasty's fall from grace, in a context which reflects a universal crisis for distinction of any kind in a heterogeneous, levelling modernity, can only be experienced as tragedy, entered under the signature of a terminal irony. In *Purgatory*, therefore, the eugenic 'enthusiasm' is subsumed as a dubious attraction to a nasty theory in a profoundly disturbing apprehension of the determinism implicit in consciousness experienced as unappeasable consequence.

It must be said however that the work, even as such a heavily ironized tragedy, is as sinister a performance as some of the poems composed in the poet's last year. For *Purgatory*, far from giving us a hero for whom 'joy' is the achievement of suffering as the audience experiences a cathartic release in a religious expansion of awareness at his death, leaves us only in a state of stunned horror at its shocking conclusion. In effect the play throws down the gauntlet of its own cruel, despairing cynicism that not even a tragic redemption can be imagined in the modern world. The play, I am arguing, is an example of the eschatological nihilism of reaction *in extremis*, in which in the 1930s Fascism often found a not-unsympathetic climate for its own lethally nihilistic vision of social destiny.

On 12 August 1938 Yeats wrote to an Irish paper for the last time to explain that his play was a plea for 'the ancient sanctities' (Torchiana 1966: 357). As the summer drew to its close, Yeats had his own ancient sanctities to ponder. On 22 August he wrote inviting Maud Gonne to visit him in Rathfarnham. As they parted for the last time she was surprised when Yeats told her 'Maud, we should have gone on with our Castle of the Heroes, we might still do it' (*GYL*: 48). She had thought him lost to any cause she might favour, but even in the ill-health that made rising from his seat to greet her very difficult, the old fires burned. Then on 7 October came news of a specially poignant kind to stir an old man's memories. Olivia Shakespear had died suddenly on the third of the month. Yeats wrote to Wellesley that for more than forty years Shakespear had been the centre of his life in London. He grieved for her and their shared past: 'For the moment I cannot bear the thought of London. I will find her memory everywhere' (*L*: 916).

It was indeed a time for memories (in mid-October the last Sligo Pollexfen also passed away) and for Yeats to settle his own accounts with himself. In two poems completed in the autumn of 1938 and published in the last month of the poet's life, the past weighed heavily. One, the last of his dialogue poems, wrestled in a grimly trochaic rhymed verse with the poet's own role in Irish history and with the fear of death. But where earlier dialogue poems had been conducted between conflicting poetic selves, 'Man and the Echo' has 'Man' answered by 'Echo' which repeats only what has been said. Selfhood at the last has to confront itself. The other poem, the magisterially recollective 'The Circus Animals' Desertion' (Yeats had probably begun this poem at the end of 1937), acknowledges that Yeats's artistic achievement, his 'circus animals' that he put on show, has been based on an aesthetic which honoured and exploited the transformative powers of the symbol, the image, the dream, more than the fissured, ignoble self, 'my heart', from which they all derived. Now the heart is troped as a 'foul rag-and-bone shop' presided over by a 'raving slut/Who keeps the till'.

Yet as death approaches for Yeats even the heart, the self, is a less substantial thing than these images of a palpable detritus would suggest. For a trancelike imaginative vertigo marks some of Yeats's last writings – spectral reports from death's ante-chamber – where the self both resists and accept its own dissolution and metamorphosis. So in *On the Boiler* Yeats confesses:

> Now that I am old and live in the past I often think of those ancestors of whom I have some detailed information . . . . Then, as my mood deepens, I discover all these men in my single mind, think that I myself have gone through the same vicissitudes, that I am going through them all at this very moment, and wonder if the balance has come out right; then I go beyond those minds and my single mind and discover that I have been describing everybody's struggle, and the gyres turn in my thoughts. (*OTB*: 22)

In 'The Apparitions', composed in the spring of 1938, an old man even at a moment 'of joy', which fills him with an almost sexual 'strength', records '*Fifteen apparitions have I seen;/The worst a coat upon a coat-hanger*' – an unnerving attack of ontological horror 'of the increasing Night/That opens her mystery and fright'. No longer is the kiss *given* to the void but an *amor fati* takes a man in an annihilating embrace.

Yeats was excited by the chance the Abbey festival in August gave him to see *On Baile's Strand* once again. Cuchulain, he wrote to Wellesley seemed to him 'a heroic figure because he was creative joy separated from fear' (Wellesley 1964: 184). The experience provoked a last brief play in which, as at various stages in his life, he explored his deepest feelings about his own sense of reality through identification with the figure of the ancient Irish hero. Transcendence of the fear of death is a controlling theme in *The Death of Cuchulain*, to which Yeats dictated finishing touches on his own deathbed in January 1939.

In late October 1938 the poet left Ireland for England where, as Louis MacNeice records, the beast of history was prowling 'at every door' and barking 'in every headline' (MacNeice 1966: 129). Wellesley told the poet, in the wake of the Munich crisis of the early autumn, that the future filled her with dread: 'The creative people must go on with their jobs, there is nothing else to do' (ibid.: 189). By early November Yeats in the final phase of his own extraordinary creativity had completed a prose version of his play. On 26 November, with his wife, he left London once more for the south of France, his mind still full of his new work. When Wellesley visited the Yeatses in their Côte d' Azur hotel in December the poet was able to read the almost completed poetic version to her.

The Death of Cuchulain offers three contrasting stage images of Cuchulain meeting his death. The terminal ironies of *Purgatory* are not evaded. For the play has a bitter prose prologue spoken by an old man, who extravagantly denounces the modern world, 'this vile age' which will probably misinterpret the play. And the hero is given the *coup de grâce* not by an enemy hand but by a fumbling Blind Man, who kills for the pathetic reward of twelve pence. The hero is the bound, helpless victim of the economics of the greasy till. However where *Purgatory* was a vision of awful necessity, the figure of fate in this play, the Morrigu, Goddess of War, does not overwhelm Cuchulain's spirit even as it endures its own dissolution. Cuchulain quits himself as Cuchulain. And he does so in the presence of feminine sexual powers which make his spiritually courageous death a strangely co-operative act. Cuchulain may declare triumphantly, in face of the ambiguities of history, 'I make the truth', but his death is accomplished as the women he has known in life together weave his personal destiny. In one telling epiphany his mistress Aoife, whose son Cuchulain had mistakenly slain on Baile's strand, binds him to the death-stone with her veil. The image is ambiguously sexual; love and hate mingle in their last, confessional conversation together. After the hero's death, his wife Emer dances before his symbolically represented severed head, achieving, as Richard Cave has suggested, a dramatic embodiment of 'the process of depersonalizing the self which exactly complements Cuchulain's own inner progress' (Cave 1997: 383). And both of them hear the sound of a few bird-notes, which Cuchulain apprehends as the song of his own 'soul's first shape'. Male and female are at one at the moment of transmogrification. Then a song summons the ghosts of heroes.

The co-operative process of dying is the matter of the entranced, calm measures of 'Cuchulain Comforted', the poem which came as a wonderful imaginative afterthought to the poet's last play. Composed in Dantean *terza rima* and completed in January 1939 this twenty-five line masterpiece follows Cuchulain beyond the portals of the underworld. For all the grave chastity of tone with which the poet accompanies his *alter ego*, Cuchulain's transition to a new order of non-being is an arresting one, for he must make his journey, not in the company of women, but of cowards who come before him as Shrouds. He is invited by one of the cowards who meet him to obey an ancient rule and make a shroud. Yet as Seamus Heaney has movingly sensed, the feminine remains as a spiritual resource even among the shades:

We witness here a strange ritual of surrender, a rite of passage from life into death, but a rite whose meaning is subsumed into song, into the otherness of art. It is a poem deeply at one with the weak and the strong of this earth, full of motherly kindness towards life, but also unflinching in its belief in the propriety and beauty of life transcended into art, song, words. (Heaney 1980: 71–2).

The Shroud who speaks to the dead hero promises him that his life 'can grow much sweeter' if he joins in the collective duty of plying the needle that sews the garment of death. The homely craft here is associated with that sweetness which in Yeats's poetry had always been a glory of the womanly voice:

> They sang, but had nor human tunes nor words,
> Though all was done in common as before;
>
> They had changed their throats and had the throats of birds.

Yeats died on the afternoon of 28 January 1939 in the south of France in a small room above the Mediterranean. Both Dorothy Wellesley and his wife George Yeats shared the death vigil. The poet's letter of 4 January, written to a woman friend, had had the ring of last words about it:

It seems to me that I have found what I wanted. When I try to put it all into a phrase I say, 'Man can embody truth but he cannot know it'. I must embody it in the completion of my life. The abstract is not life and everywhere draws out its contradictions. You can refute Hegel but not the Saint or the Song of Sixpence. (*L*: 922)

Epilogue: Afterlife

The poet's remains were interred in a cemetery at Roquebrune, near where he had died. It was hoped that this would be a temporary measure so that his body could be more appropriately laid to rest in Drumcliffe churchyard, County Sligo, where, 'Under bare Ben Bulben's head', his ancestor had laboured as rector. World war broke out in the September following Yeats's death, making that impossible until 1948 (the year Ireland declared itself a republic), when an Irish naval vessel was dispatched to bring the poet back to his native land. When the cortège arrived in Sligo, it was received by members of the Irish government, including, in another turn of the gyre, Seán MacBride, then minister for external affairs. Dignitaries, poets and immediate family mingled around the grave on a rainy September day, after the Church of Ireland service.

Yeats's literary afterlife suffered no such unsettling interruptions. The obituary notice of his life and career were extensive, but it was the English poet W. H. Auden, in his elegy 'In Memory of W. B. Yeats', composed February 1939 and published in New York in March and in London in April of that year, who responded most challengingly as a poet to Yeats's death. He understood that the death of a poet, as Joseph Brodsky has remarked, is 'about as definite as a poet's own production, i.e., a poem, the main feature of which is its last line' (Brodsky 1987: 123). By his death, Auden announced, Yeats 'became his admirers', his ghostly existence now nothing but 'A way of happening, a mouth'.

Yeats's death of course was not his last line in the simple sense that much of his work was to be posthumously published. Death, however, changed both the conditions of publication and the reception of his work. Throughout his life Yeats's poems and plays had undergone complex processes of revision and contextualization over which the poet had astutely sought to retain strict control. Now the *oeuvre* was the responsibility of his widow and the editors and publishers she chose to collaborate with her in the task she undertook with great dedication and acumen: the execution of Yeats's richly diverse and voluminous literary estate. The woman who had brought Yeats so much in life, in death brought him a great deal as well.

Yet with Yeats's death the new work that she allowed to enter the public domain, and the editions of published work that she sanctioned would inevitably be assessed by critics and biographers as adding to the knowledge of a life that was complete. And it was the life of a poet whom T. S. Eliot in a lecture, delivered at the Abbey Theatre in June 1940, identified as 'one of those few whose history is the history of their own time, who are part of the consciousness of an age, which cannot be understood without them' (Hall and Steinmann 1961: 307).

The first task was to arrange for the Cuala Press to publish *Last Poems and Two Plays* and *On the Boiler*. Just before his death Yeats had drawn up a table of contents which seemed to suggest the shape of a new book in the making (though it is not known whether he suggested the title). *Last Poems* followed those wishes. Almost all its contents were the poems and plays he had written or completed in the final death-haunted year of his life. The volume mingled lyrical insouciance, rant, recollection, with intimations of terror and acceptance of death itself as process ('Cuchulain Comforted'). It opened with the testamentary 'Under Ben Bulben', so that the rest of its contents, when it appeared in July 1939, seemed to echo from beyond the grave (Webb 1991: xlii). *On the Boiler* with its exhortation 'seek some just war', came out, as we saw, that autumn.

There was a record to establish before Yeats's life became too much the property of his admirers and others. Yeats's friend Joseph Hone was given sanction by George Yeats to produce a life, published by Macmillan in 1942. A warmly sympathetic, socially astute account (Hone shared Yeats's Anglo-Irish background), with a telling eye for the novelistic detail, much could not yet be said: about the affair with Olivia Shakespear (her identity was disguised), about Maud Gonne (who would live on until 1953) and her pre-marital amatory history, about Yeats's late career of dalliance and perhaps most of all, about the extent of George Yeats's collaboration with her husband in the composition of *A Vision*. Mrs Yeats died in 1968.

It was the poet Louis MacNeice who after Yeats's death inaugurated the full-scale critical assessment of the poetry that his achievement demanded. This was not without its own significance, for the young Ulster-born poet of Anglo-Irish stock was then experiencing, as international war threatened, a conflict of loyalties between his native Ireland and the England in which he had been educated and where he was making a career. He worked on his book *The Poetry of W. B. Yeats* in the spring and summer of 1939, completing it after the outbreak of hostilities that were to make his own crisis of identity especially keen. For Ireland had chosen neutrality in the world war (a stance Yeats's last poem 'The Black Tower' can be seen to advise). So there is a distinct sense in his book (published in February 1941) that MacNeice was assessing Yeats as a way of sorting out a personal muddle about his native country. Yet as a poet and reader of poetry he was also keen to characterize Yeats's legacy to practitioners, while as poet/critic and man he understood that Yeats presented a test case of a very special kind on the question of belief in poetry and life.

One of Yeats's finest critics, Richard Ellmann, acknowledged in 1967 that MacNeice's book on Yeats was then 'as good an introduction to that poet as we have' (Ellmann 1967: 11). It is also useful as a work whose several preoccupations anticipate the critical response to Yeats's poetry as it has developed in different parts of the world and in different contexts, in the six decades since his death.

In 1950 the editors of a book entitled *The Permanence of Yeats* (published in New York) indicated that the question of belief, earlier explored by MacNeice, had become a key critical issue in respect of their case that Yeats was 'certain to remain a major figure in the poetry of the century' (Hall and Steinmann 1961: 1). They concede: 'the greatest obstacle to his full acceptance has been the persuasion . . . that he is a poet of "magic," and that his poetry partakes of the limitations and rootlessness of magic' (ibid.). That undoubtedly remains a key critical issue in Yeats's reception – despite the voluminous scholarship (much of it conducted in the United States) his work has attracted on issues as diverse as his relationship to Romanticism, Modernism, politics, post-colonialism, feminism – made all the more pressing as detailed information has been made available on the centrality to Yeats's imagination of esotericism and spiritualist experiment. The present volume has sought to contribute to discussion of this critical issue by allowing that centrality to appear in its pages, to suggest that it is no longer possible simply to say that Yeats's beliefs offered him the metaphoric and symbolic means of expression for essentially humanist feelings he would have had without such 'exotic' preoccupations. This has been a study of a writer for whom magic, ritual and 'communication' with the dead and with spirits were profoundly experiential things which affected how he felt and thought about human life, about its passions and its meanings. And the artistic consequences were not always congenial to liberal humanist moral feeling.

In his native country, questions about national identity and his contribution to Irish cultural history have been matters of concern, as they were in MacNeice's study. The poet Thomas Kinsella might be taken indeed as identifying a specifically Irish agenda on Yeats's career, when he concluded in a lecture delivered in New York in 1966, that he was a writer '*in* the Irish tradition . . . but isolated in the tradition' (Kinsella 62). For Kinsella Yeats was possessed of an ambiguous greatness: 'capable, perhaps of integrating a modern Anglo-Irish culture, and which he chose to make impossible by separating out a special Anglo-Irish culture from the main unwashed body' (Kinsella 1970: 64). Subsequent critics have been more severe, identifying an Anglo-Irish strategy of self-preservation in Yeatsian cultural politics and in the Literary Revival project as a whole. That interested movement, so the argument tends to run, bequeathed to the nation disabling myths of national essence and dangerously idealist conceptions of cultural unity. And the deepening Northern Irish crisis of the 1970s and 1980s gave these debates a sharp political edge; as when in 1984 Seamus Deane characterized as 'the pathology of literary unionism' (Deane 1984: 10) a passage in Yeats's late prose, where he had agonized over the fact that even though Irish by nationality, he owed his literary soul to England. Since the 1970s Irish feminism has also subjected the idea of the Irish nation itself, imagined as a feminine entity, to a vigorous critique, in which Yeats has been an object of attack for his patriarchal mythologizing. Roy Foster, attentive to these matters in his own cultural criticism, in the first volume of his life of the poet (published in 1997) has now given Irish criticism of Yeats an opportunity to test such critical positions as have preoccupied it in the last thirty years against a scrupulously detailed realization of the day to day deeds and thoughts of Yeats the man and thinker.

Foster concentrates on Yeats the doer in his biography rather than Yeats the writer (though he does reflect most insightfully on *Reveries Over Childhood and Youth*). Naturally, poets and poet/critics have followed MacNeice in seeking, as fellow makers, to learn what they can from the master. MacNeice himself, in his critical encounter with Yeats, was encouraged to credit his faculty for dream, and in the poetry of his later years he allowed for the imaginative powers of myth in a way he might not have done had Yeats not offered exemplary sanction. By contrast MacNeice's friend W. H. Auden judged Yeats's legacy was chiefly technical. Yeats had elevated the occasional poem to the level of high artistic seriousness and had 'released regular stanzaic poetry, whether reflective or lyrical from iambic monotony' (Hall and Steinmann 1961: 313).

T. S. Eliot in his Abbey lecture implied that Yeats's chief influence on his successors would be as an example of artistic integrity, as he had been for his younger contemporaries. He thought it had been 'good for them to have the spectacle of an unquestionably great living poet, whose style they were not tempted to echo and whose ideas contradicted those in vogue among them (ibid.: 297). Eliot's intuition has, largely, been vindicated. Many poets have admired Yeats without trying to adapt his manner to their own poetic usage. When the grand Yeatsian manner, assured of the poet's calling, has been affected by some of Yeats's English-language successors, windy portentousness has sometimes been the result. Not all such poems, however, have been failures. The American Allen Tate's 'Winter Mask: To the memory of W. B. Yeats' is a skilled, sombre salute to Yeatsian trochaics, while his best-known work, 'Ode to the Confederate Dead' (composed during Yeats's lifetime), owes much to the elder poet's meditative achievements in the later verse. Tate's fellow-American, Theodore Roethke, who was deeply indebted to Yeats, especially in the form and rhythms of his elegant love poems, in one poem admitted how difficult it was as a modern poet to avoid his tones: 'I take this cadence from a man named Yeats; / I take it and I give it back again' ('Four for Sir John Davies').

Paradoxically the need thus expressed to avoid Yeats's influence is proof of his sustained capacity to affect the course of modern poetry. Another American, John Berryman, for example, whose first published collection of poems in 1940 was heavily Yeatsian in manner, confessed of his youthful obsession with the Irish poet: 'Yeats somehow saved me from the then crushing influence of Ezra Pound and T. S. Eliot – luckily as I now feel – but he could not teach me how to sound like myself (whatever that was) or tell me what to write about' (cited in Arpin 1978: 15). He had met his hero in 1937, when Yeats had told him he no longer revised his poetry, except in the interests of a 'passionate syntax'. When Berryman did find his own voice, the Yeats who had so mesmerized him as a young man lived on in ghostly fashion in the intricately emotional stanza form of one of his major works, 'Homage to Mistress Bradstreet' (ibid.: 15). And in England

Philip Larkin's first collection *The North Ship* (1945), published as it was after three years in which the young poet had tried to 'write like Yeats' (Larkin, cited in Timms 1973: 25) was dominated by the poetics of the dead poet. It was only when Larkin discovered the poetry of Hardy as counterweight that he was able to strike a true tone of his own. Yet Larkin's became a poetic voice that never lost the power, absorbed from Yeats, to raise articulate speech to levels of emotional intensity which suggest mysteries as yet uncomprehended by a secular idiom (as in the final stanza of his famous poem 'Church Going').

In a broader fashion Yeats lives on in twentieth-century English-language poetry in the poetic fashion for the sequence. Certainly T. S. Eliot's *The Waste Land* and Ezra Pound's *Cantos* almost made this the normative Modernist form. But Yeats himself had understood how 'detachable ideas had deprived' poets 'of the power to mould vast material into a single image' when, in 1913, he had questioned: 'What long modern poem equals the old poems in architectural unity, in symbolic importance?' (*E&I*: 354).

In Ireland especially, the sequence poem has been a predominant twentieth-century form, in which poets have sought to address a fractured history in a mode for which Yeats's 'Meditations in Time of Civil War' might be read as a foundational text (though Pound and Eliot are also seminal figures for this seam of Irish imagining). Patrick Kavanagh's *The Great Hunger* (1942), Thomas Kinsella's 'Nightwalker' (1968), John Montague's *The Rough Field* (1972) and *The Dead Kingdom* (1984), Brendan Kennelly's *Cromwell* (1983) are representative works, while Seamus Heaney's *North* (1975) offers its series of Bog People poems in a volume that seeks, as he informs us in his essay 'Feeling into Words', in a violent time to discover 'befitting emblems of adversity'. The phrase is from 'Meditations In Time of Civil War'.

Heaney in fact has engaged as critic with the poetic achievement of Yeats more fully than any other Irish poet since MacNeice (though Brendan Kennelly's essay 'W. B. Yeats: An Experiment in Living' bears eloquent witness to forty years experience of reading Yeats 'with deepening joy'; Kennelly 1994: 247). Heaney's 1992 estimate of Yeats's 'essential gift' is striking. He celebrates an 'ability to raise a temple in the ear, to make a vaulted space in language through the firmness, in-placeness and undislodgeableness of stanzaic form. But the force is also present in his persistent drive to "teach the free man how to praise"' (Heaney 1991: 790).

This testimony to the palpable presence of Yeats as poet in the last decade of the twentieth century, it should be stated, has its confirmation not merely in continued academic interest in Yeats's life and work, but in the popularity of his verses with a wide reading public. The love poems ('He wishes for the Cloths of Heaven', pre-eminently) continue to be widely anthologized. 'No Second Troy', 'The Cold Heaven', 'Easter 1916', 'The Irish Airman Foresees his Death', 'The Wild Swans at Coole', 'The Second Coming', 'Sailing to Byzantium', 'Among School Children', 'The Circus Animals' Desertion' are indisputably poems of canonical authority. And many readers of Yeats would understand MacNeice's 1941 conclusion that if he were making an anthology of shorter English poems, there was no other poet in the language from whom he would choose so many.

By contrast, Yeats's plays have found few advocates beyond enthusiasts in the academy (his prose is read as the prose of a poet, though had Yeats remained the exquisite of the 1890s he was deemed to be when he composed *Reveries Over Childhood and Youth*, that work would probably now enjoy the status of a minor classic). Even in Ireland and at the Abbey Theatre his drama is scarcely part of the living repertoire. Revivals are dutiful or marked by opportunistic eccentricities of production.

It may be however that Yeats's greatest contribution to world drama is to be found in the more general impact of his collaborator Gordon Craig's concept of total theatre, which he shared with Yeats. And certain of his plays have enjoyed a very remarkable afterlife indeed, in as much as they influenced the dramaturgy of Samuel Beckett, who remarked that he would give the 'whole unupsettable apple-cart' of George Bernard Shaw's dramatic canon 'for a sup of the Hawk's Well, or the Saints', or a whiff of Juno, to go no further' (cited in Roche 1994: 24). In associating Yeats's *At the Hawk's Well* with the achievements of Synge and O'Casey, Beckett was paying Yeats the dramatist a remarkable compliment. And Beckett's own drama with its intense minimalism of style, shares with Yeats a vision of the stage where the rhythms of language and scrupulously choreographed movement call to the eye of the mind images of mesmeric strangeness, in which theatre seems to achieve the condition of austere ritual. It is fitting therefore that Beckett's ghost play for television, ... *but the clouds* ... (first televised 1977) should salute Yeats, one great twentieth-century writer recognizing another, in employing the final lines of 'The Tower' as a haunting conclusion to a haunted work. In this work a man in old age seeks to recall the image of a lost love (a Yeatsian theme indeed), only to have the words she inaudibly speaks, at the last come fully to his own mind, like a communication from the dead: ' but the clouds of the sky ... when the horizon fades ... or a bird's sleepy cry ... among the deepening shades'.

By such acts of creative appropriation, one senses, the permanence of Yeats is movingly secured.

Works Cited

Adams, Hazard. 1995. *The Book of Yeats's Vision: Romantic Modernism and Antithetical Tradition*, Ann Arbor: University of Michigan Press.

Adams, Steve L. and Harper, George Mills. 1982. 'The Manuscript of "Leo Africanus"', *Yeats Annual*, no. 1, pp. 3–47.

Albright, Daniel (ed.). 1992. *The Poems*, London: Everyman's Library.

——. 1997. *Quantum Poetics: Yeats, Pound and the Science of Modernism*, Cambridge: Cambridge University Press.

Alford, Norman. 1994. *The Rhymers Club: Poets of the Tragic Generation*, New York: St Martin's Press.

Antheil, George. n.d. *Bad Boy of Music*, London: Hunt and Blackett Ltd.

Archibald, Douglas.1975. 'The Words Upon the Window Pane and Yeats's Encounter with Jonathan Swift', in *Yeats and the Theatre*, eds Robert O'Driscoll and Lorna Reynolds, London and Toronto: Macmillan, pp. 176–214.

—— 1986. *Yeats*, Syracuse, NY: Syracuse University Press.

Arnold, Bruce. 1998. *Jack Yeats*, New Haven: Yale University Press.

Arnold, Matthew. 1866. 'The Study of Celtic Literature' parts one and two, *Cornhill Magazine*, XIII, January to June, pp. 282–96, 469–83.

Arpin, Gary. 1978. *The Poetry of John Berryman*, Port Washington, NY and London: Kennikat Press.

Asquith, Lady Cynthia: 1968. *Diaries, 1915–1918*, London: Hutchinson.

Auerbach, Nina. 1982. *Woman and the Demon: The Life of a Victorian Myth*, Cambridge, Mass. and London: Harvard University Press.

Balliett, Conrad A. 1979. 'The Lives – And Lies – of Maud Gonne', *Eire/Ireland*, vol. 14, no. 3, pp. 17–44.

Beckson, Karl. 1992. *London in the 1890s: A Cultural History*, New York and London: W. W. Norton and Company.

'Bedford Park' 1881, *Harpers New Monthly Magazine*, no. CCCLXX, vol. LXII, March, pp. 481–90.

Beltaine, (ed. B. C. Bloomfield). 1970. *English Little Magazines*, no. 15, London: Frank Cass and Co. Ltd.

Bentley, Edward. 1951. *Far Horizon: A Biography of Hester Dowden, Medium and Psychic Investigator*, London: Rider and Company.

Bloom, Harold. 1970. *Yeats*, New York: Oxford University Press.

Blunt, Wilfrid Scawen. 1922. *My Diaries, Being a Personal Narrative of Events 1888–1914, with a Foreword by Lady Gregory (Part One)*, London: Martin Secker.

Bohlmann, Otto. 1982. *Yeats and Nietzsche: An Exploration of Major Nietzschean Echoes in the Writings of W. B. Yeats*, London: Macmillan.

Born, Karen. 1984. *Players and Painted Stage: The Theatre of W. B. Yeats*, Sussex: The Harvester Press; New Jersey: Barnes and Noble.

Bornstein, George (ed.). 1995. *Under the Moon: The Unpublished Poetry by W. B. Yeats*, New York and London: Scribner.

Bradley, Anthony. 1979. *William Butler Yeats*, New York: Frederick Ungar Publishing.

Bradshaw, David. 1992. 'The Eugenics Movement in the 1930s and the Emergence of *On the Boiler*', *Yeats Annual*, no. 9, pp. 189–215.

Bridge, Ursula (ed.). 1953. *W. B. Yeats and Sturge Moore: Their Correspondence, 1901–1937*, London: Routledge and Kegan Paul.

Brodsky, Joseph. 1987. 'The Child of Civilization', in *Less Than One: Selected Essays*, London: Penguin Books.

Brown, Malcolm. 1972. *The Politics of Irish Literature: From Thomas Davis to W. B. Yeats*, London: George Allen and Unwin Ltd.

Brown, T. 1985. *Ireland: A Social and Cultural History, 1922 to the Present*, Ithaca and London: Cornell University Press.

Bunting, Basil. 1974. 'Yeats Recollected', *Agenda*, vol. 12, no. 2 Summer, pp. 36–47.

Cannadine, David. 1992. *The Decline and Fall of the British Aristocracy*, London: Papermac.

Catholic Bulletin. 1924. vol. XIV, no. 1, January, p. 6.

Cave, Richard (ed.). 1997. *W. B. Yeats: Selected Plays*, London: Penguin Books.

Chesterton, G. K. 1992. *Autobiography*, Sevenoaks, Kent: The Fisher Press.

Cohen, Marilyn. 1997. *Linen, Family and Community in Tullyish, County Down, 1690–1914*, Dublin: Four Courts Press.

Collini, Stephen. 1991. *Public Moralists: Political Thought and Intellectual Life in Britain 1850–1930*, Oxford: Clarendon Press.

Colum, Mary. 1966. *Life and the Dream*, rev. edn, Dublin: The Dolmen Press.

Costello, Bonnie (ed.). 1998. *The Selected Letters of Marianne Moore*, London: Faber and Faber.

Croft, Barbara. 1987. '*Stylistic Arrangements*': *A Study of William Butler Yeats's* A Vision, Lewisburg: Bucknell University Press; London and Toronto: Associated University Presses.

Cullingford, Elizabeth Butler. 1981. *Yeats, Ireland and Fascism*, London and Basingstoke: Macmillan.

———. 1993. *Gender and History in Yeats's Love Poetry*, Cambridge: Cambridge University Press.

Deane, Seamus. 1984. *Heroic Styles: The Tradition of an Idea*, Derry: Field Day Pamphlets.

———. 1997. *Strange Country: Modernity and Nationhood in Irish Writing since 1790*, Oxford: Clarendon Press.

Denson, Alan (ed.). 1961. *Letters from AE*, London, New York and Toronto: Abelard-Schuman.

Devitt, John. 1988. 'The Plough's the Thing', *Riverun*, vol. V, pp. 19–21.

Dodds, E. R. 1977. *Missing Persons: An Autobiography*, Oxford: Clarendon Press.

Donoghue Denis. 1971. *William Butler Yeats*, New York: Viking Press.

———. 1986. *We Irish: The Selected Essays of Denis Donoghue*,. Sussex: Harvester Press, vol. 1.

Dowden, Edward. 1895. *New Studies in Literature*, London: Kegan Paul, Trench, Trübner and Co. Ltd.

Dunleavy, Gareth W. and Dunleavy, Janet Egleson. 1991. *Douglas Hyde: A Maker of Modern Ireland*, Berkeley, LA and Oxford, University of California Press.

Edwards, Philip. 1965. 'Yeats and the Trinity Chair', *Hermathena*, no. CI, Autumn, pp. 5–12.

Eglinton, John (ed.). 1914. *Letters of Edward Dowden and his Correspondents*, London: J. M. Dent and Sons; New York: E. P. Dutton and Co.

——. 1937. *A Memoir of AE: George William Russell*, London; Macmillan.

Eliot, T. S. 1957. *On Poetry and Poets*, London: Faber and Faber.

Eliot, Valerie (ed.). 1988. *The Letters of T. S. Eliot* vol. 1, *1898–1922*, London: Faber and Faber.

Ellis, John, and Yeats, W. B. 1893. *The Works of William Blake, Poetic, Symbolic and Critical*, 3 vols. London: Bernard Quaritch.

Ellmann, Richard. 1964. *The Identity of Yeats*, London: Faber and Faber.

——. 1967. 'Foreword' to *The Poetry of W. B. Yeats*, by Louis MacNeice, London: Faber and Faber, pp. 9–11.

——. 1970. *Eminent Domain*, London and New York: Oxford University Press.

——. 1987. *Four Dubliners*, London: Hamish Hamilton.

——. 1987. *Oscar Wilde*, London: Hamish Hamilton.

——. 1987. *Yeats: The Man and the Masks*, London: Penguin Books.

Farr, Florence. 1894. *The Dancing Faun*, London: Elkin Mathews and John Lane; Boston: Roberts Brothers.

——. 1910. *Modern Woman: Her Intentions*, London: Frank Palmer.

Finneran, Richard (ed.). 1991. *W. B. Yeats: The Poems*, London: Macmillan.

Fitzpatrick, David. 1975. 'W. B. Yeats in Seanad Éireann', in *Yeats and the Theatre*, eds Robert O'Driscoll and Lorna Reynolds, London and Toronto: Macmillan, pp. 159–75.

Flannery, James W. 1976. *Yeats and the Idea of a Theatre*, New Haven and London: Yale University Press.

Fletcher, Ian. 1987. *Yeats and his Contemporaries*, Sussex: Harvester Press.

Foster, R. F. 1988. *Modern Ireland, 1600–1972*, London: Allen Lane, the Penguin Press.

——. 1989. 'Protestant Magic: W. B. Yeats and the Spell of Irish History', *Proceedings of the British Academy*, vol. LXXV, pp. 243–66.

——. 1993. *Paddy and Mr Punch in Irish and English History*, London: Allen Lane, the Penguin Press.

——. 1998. 'Yeats at Fifty', in *Ideas Matter: Essays in Honour of Conor Cruise O'Brien*, eds R. English and J. M. Morrison, Dublin: Poolbeg Press.

Frazier, Adrian. 1990. *Behind the Scenes: Yeats, Horniman and the Struggle for the Abbey Theatre*, Berkeley, LA, London: University of California Press.

Garrett, Eileen J. 1968. *Many Voices: The Autobiography of a Medium*, New York: G. P. Putnam's Sons.

Goldring, Douglas. 1943. *South Lodge: Reminiscences of Violet Hunt, Ford Madox Ford and the English Review Circle*, London: Constable and Co. Ltd.

Gorski, William T. 1996. *Yeats and Alchemy*, Albany NY: State University of New York Press.

Gould, Warwick. 1989. 'A Crowded Theatre: Yeats and Balzac' in *Yeats the European*, ed. A. Norman Jeffares, Gerrards Cross: Colin Smythe.

Gourvish, T. R. and O'Day, Alan, (eds). 1988. *Later Victorian Britain, 1867–1900*, London: Macmillan.

Gregory, Lady Augusta. 1914. *Our Irish Theatre: A Chapter of Autobiography*, New York and London: G. P. Putnam's Sons, the Knickerbocker Press.

——. 1970. *Visions and Beliefs in the West of Ireland Collected and Arranged by Lady Gregory: With Two Essays and Notes by W. B. Yeats*, Gerrards Cross: Colin Smythe.

——. 1971. *Coole*, ed. Colin Smythe, with a Foreword by Edward Malins, Dublin: The Dolmen Press.

——. 1978, 1987. *Journals*, vols. 1 and 2, ed. Daniel J. Murphy, Gerrards Cross: Colin Smythe.

——. 1996. *Lady Gregory's Diaries 1892–1902*, ed. James Pethica, Gerrards Cross: Colin Smythe.

Grene, Nicholas. 1989. 'Yeats and the Re-Making of Synge', in *Tradition and Influence in Anglo-Irish Poetry*, eds T. Brown and N. Grene, London: Macmillan, 47–62.

Gwynn, Stephen (ed.). 1940. *Scattering Branches: Tributes to the Memory of W. B. Yeats*, London: Macmillan.

Hall, James and Steinmann, Martin, (eds). 1961. *The Permanance of Yeats*, New York.

Halloran, William I. 1998. 'Yeats and Fiona MacLeod', Part 1, *Yeats Annual*, no. 3, pp. 62–109.

Hardwick, Joan. 1996. *The Yeats Sisters: A Biography of Susan and Elizabeth Yeats*, London: Pandora.

Harper, George Mills. 1974. *Yeats's Golden Dawn*, London: Macmillan.

——. 1975. 'A Subject of Investigation: Miracle at Mirebeau', in *Yeats and the Occult*, ed. George Mills Harper, London and Toronto: Macmillan, pp. 172–89.

——. 1987. *The Making of Yeats's* A Vision, two vols, Basingstoke and London: Macmillan.

——. and John S. Kelly. 1975. 'Preliminary examination of the Script of E[lizabeth] R[adcliffe]', in *Yeats and the Occult*, pp. 130–71.

Harper, Margaret Mills 1988. 'The Medium as Creator: George Yeats's Role in the Automatic Script', *Yeats: An Annual of Critical and Textual Studies*, no. 6, pp. 49–71.

——. 1994. 'Yeats's Collaborative Modernity', in *Irishness and (Post) Modernism*, Lewisburg: Bucknell University Press; London and Toronto: Associated University Press.

—— 1997. Paper delivered, Milwaukee, USA.

Harwood, John. 1988. 'Olivia Shakespear: Letters to W. B. Yeats', *Yeats Annual*, no. 6, pp. 59–107.

——. 1989. *Olivia Shakespear and W. B. Yeats*, London: Macmillan.

——. 1992. ' "Secret Communion": Yeats's Sexual Destiny', *Yeats Annual*, no. 9, pp. 7–30.

Heaney, Seamus. 1980. 'Yeats as an Example?', in *Yeats, Sligo and Ireland* ed. A. Norman Jeffares, Gerrard's Cross: Colin Smythe, pp. 56–72.

——. 1991. 'William Butler Yeats', in *The Field Day Anthology of Irish Writing*, vol. II, ed. S. Deane, Derry: Field Day Publications and Faber & Faber.

Hearn, Mona. 1989. 'Life for Domestic Servants in Dublin, 1880–1920', in *Women Surviving: Studies in Irish Women's History in the 19th and 20th Centuries*, eds. M. Luddy and C. Murphy, Dublin: Poolbeg Press.

Heine, Elizabeth, 1998. 'Yeats and Maud Gonne: Marriage and the Astrological Record, 1908–09', *Yeats Annual*, no. 13, pp. 3–33.

Heyck, T. W. 1982. *The Transformation of Intellectual Life in Victorian England*, London and Canberra: Croom Helm.

Holloway, Joseph. 1967. *Joseph Holloway's Abbey Theatre*, eds R. Hogan and J. O'Neill, Carbondale and Edwardsville: Southern Illinois University Press; London and Amsterdam: Feffer and Simons Inc.

Holroyd, Michael. 1988. *Bernard Shaw*, vol. 1, *1856–1898: The Search for Love*, London: Chatto and Windus.

Hone, Joseph (ed.). 1946. *J. B. Yeats: Letters to his Son W. B. Yeats and Others*, New York: E. P. Dutton and Co. Inc.

Hooper, Walter. 1979. *They Stand Together: The Letters of C. S. Lewis to Arthur Greeves, 1914–63*, London: Collins.

Horgan, J. J. 1948. *Parnell to Pearse: Some Recollections and Reflections*, Dublin: Browne and Nolan.

Hough, Graham. 1984. *The Mystery Religion of W. B. Yeats*, Sussex: Harvester Press; New Jersey: Barnes and Noble.

Howe, Ellic. 1972. *The Magicians of the Golden Dawn: A Documentary History of a Magical Order, 1887–1923*, London: Routledge and Kegan Paul.

Hunt, Hugh. 1979. *The Abbey: Ireland's National Theatre, 1904–1979*, Dublin: Gill and Macmillan.

Hutchinson, John. 1989. *The Dynamics of Cultural Nationalism: The Gaelic Revival and the Creation of the Nation State*, London: Allen and Unwin.

Hynes, Samuel. 1968. *The Edwardian Turn of Mind*, London: Oxford University Press.

Jaffe, Grace M. 1987. 'Vignettes', *Yeats Annual*, no. 5, pp. 139–53.

James, Henry. 1905. *English Hours*, London: William Heinemann.

Jeffares, A. Norman. 1984. *A New Commentary on the Poems of W. B. Yeats*, London and Basingstoke: Macmillan.

——. 1988. *W. B. Yeats: A New Biography*, London, Sydney, Auckland, Johannesburg: Hutchinson.

Johnson, Josephine. 1975. *Florence Farr, Bernard Shaw's New Woman*, Gerrards Cross: Colin Smythe.

Kelly, John. 1987. ' "Friendship is the only House I Have" ', in *Lady Gregory, Fifty Years After*, eds Ann Saddlemyer and Colin Smythe, Gerrards Cross: Colin Smythe, pp. 179–257.

——. 1989. 'Caelum Non Animum, Mutant', in *Yeats the European*, ed. A. Norman Jeffares, Gerrards Cross: Colin Smythe, pp. 160–84.

Kennelly, Brendan. 1994. *Journey Into Joy: Selected Prose*, ed. Åke Persson, Newcastle-upon-Tyne: Bloodaxe Books.

Kinahan, Frank. 1988. *Yeats, Folklore and Occultism: Contexts of the Early Work and Thought*, London and Boston: Unwin and Hyman.

Kinsella, Thomas. 1970. 'The Irish Writer', in *Davis, Mangan, Ferguson? Tradition & The Irish Writer*, Dublin: The Dolmen Press.

Kuch, Peter. 1986. *Yeats and AE: 'The Antagonism That Unites Dear Friends'*, Gerrards Cross: Colin Smythe.

Larrissy, Edward. 1994. *Yeats the Poet: The Measures of Difference*, London and New York: Harvester/Wheatsheaf.

Lewis, Gifford (ed.). 1989. *The Selected Letters of Somerville and Ross*, London and Boston: Faber and Faber.

——. 1994. *The Yeats Sisters and The Cuala*, Dublin: Irish Academic Press.

Lipking, Laurence. 1981. *The Life of the Poet: Beginning and Ending Poetic Careers*, Chicago and London: University of Chicago Press.

Litz, J. Walton. 1985. 'Pound and Yeats: *The Road to Stone Cottage*', in *Ezra Pound Among the Poets*, ed. George Bornstein, Chicago and London: University of Chicago Press, pp. 128–48.

Lloyd, David. 1993. *Anomalous States: Irish Writing and the post-Colonial Moment*, Dublin: Lilliput Press.

Londraville, Richard (ed.). 1991. 'Four Lectures by W. B. Yeats, 1902–4', *Yeats Annual*, no. 8, pp. 78–122.

Longenbach, James. 1988. *Stone Cottage: Pound, Yeats and Modernism*, New York: Oxford University Press.

Lynch, David. 1979. *Yeats: The Poetics of the Self*, Chicago and London: University of Chicago Press.

Lyons, F. S. L. 1973. *Ireland Since the Famine*, London: Collins/Fontana.

MacBride, Maud Gonne. 1994. *A Servant of the Queen*, eds A. Norman Jeffares and Anna MacBride White, Gerrards Cross: Colin Smythe.

MacCarthy, Fiona. 1995. *William Morris: A Life for Our Time*, London: Faber and Faber.

McCormack, W. J. 1985. *Ascendancy and Tradition in Anglo-Irish Literary History from 1789 to 1939*, Oxford: Clarendon Press.

MacGreevy, Thomas. n. d. 'W. B. Yeats – A Generation Later', *University Review*, vol. III, no. 8, pp. 3–14.

McHugh, Roger (ed.). 1970. *Ah, Sweet Dancer: W. B. Yeats: Margot Ruddock: A Correspondence*, Dublin: Gill and Macmillan.

MacNeice, Louis. 1966. *Collected Poems*, London: Faber and Faber.

McTernan, John C. 1992. *Memory Harbour: The Port of Sligo*, Sligo: Arena Publications.

Mannin, Ethel. 1937. *Privileged Spectator*, London: Jarrolds Publishers.

Marcus, Philip. 1988. 'The Authors Were in Eternity – Or Oxford: George Harper, and the Making of *A Vision*', *Yeats Annual*, no. 6, pp. 233–44.

Meir, Colin. 1974. *The Ballads and Songs of W. B. Yeats: The Anglo-Irish Heritage in Subject and Style*, London and Basingstoke: Macmillan.

Mikhail, E. H. 1977. *W. B. Yeats: Interviews and Recollections*, vol. 1, London: Macmillan.

Miller, Liam. 1977. *The Noble Drama of W. B. Yeats*, Dublin: The Dolmen Press.

Mitchell, Anthony. 1914. *Biographical Studies in Scottish Church History*, London and Milwaukee: The Young Churchman.

Moore, George. 1976. *Hail and Farewell* ed. Richard Cave, Gerrards Cross: Colin Smythe Ltd.

Moore, Virginia. 1964. *The Unicorn, William Butler Yeats's Search for Reality*, New York: Macmillan Company.

Moran, D.P. 1905. *The Philosophy of Irish Ireland*, Dublin: James Duffy and M. H. Gill and Son Ltd.

Murphy, William M. P. 1979. *Prodigal Father: The Life of John Butler Yeats, 1839–1923*, Ithaca and London: Cornell University Press.

——. 1995. *Family Secrets: William Butler Yeats and his Relations*, Dublin: Gill and Macmillan.

Nevinson, H. W. 1935. *Fire of Life*, London: J. Nisbet and Co. Ltd., in association with Gollancz.

Nietzsche, Friedrich. 1907. *Beyond Good and Evil: Prelude to a Philosophy of the Future*, (trans. Helen Zimmern), Edinburgh and London: T. N. Foulis.

O'Brien, Conor Cruise. 1965. ' "Passion and Cunning" An Essay on the Politics of W. B. Yeats', in *In Excited Reverie*, eds. A. Norman Jeffares and K. W. G. Cross, London and New York: St Martin's Press.

——. 1972. *States of Ireland*, London: Hutchinson.

O'Donnell, William H. 1985. 'Portraits of W. B. Yeats: This Picture in the Mind's Eye', *Yeats Annual*, no. 6, pp. 81–103.

O'Driscoll, Robert. n. d. 'Letters and Lectures of W. B. Yeats', *Irish University Review*, vol. III, no. 8, pp. 29–55.

O'Rourke, T. 1889. *The History of Sligo, Town and County*, Dublin: James Duffy and Co. Ltd.

Olsen, Donald J. 1976. *The Growth of Victorian London*, London: B. T. Batsford Ltd.

Oppenheim, Janet. 1985. *The Other World: Spiritualism and Psychical Research in England, 1850–1914*, London: Cambridge University Press.

Owen, Alex. 1989. *The Darkened Room: Women, Power and Spiritualism in Late Nineteenth Century England*, London: Virago Press.

Owens, Gary. 1994. 'Nationalist Monuments in Ireland, c. 1870–1914: Symbolism and Ritual', *Ireland: Art into History*, eds Raymond Gillespie and Brian P. Kennedy, Dublin: Town House; Niwot, Colorado, Roberts Rinehart Publishers, pp. 103–17.

Paige, D. D. (ed). 1971. *The Selected Letters of Ezra Pound*, London: Faber and Faber.

Parkinson, Thomas. 1982. 'This extraordinary Book', *Yeats Annual*, no. 1, pp. 195–206.

Pater, Walter. 1986. *The Renaissance: Studies in Art and Poetry*, the World's Classics, Oxford and New York: Oxford University Press.

Paulin, Tom. 1992. *Minotaur: Poetry and the Nation State*, London: Faber and Faber.

Pearce, Donald R. (ed.). 1961. *The Senate Speeches of W. B. Yeats*, London: Faber and Faber.

Perkin, Joan. 1993. *Victorian Women*, London: John Murray.

Pethica, James. 1988. ' "Our Kathleen": Yeats's Collaboration with Lady Gregory in the Writing of *Cathleen ni Houlihan*', *Yeats Annual*, no. 6, pp. 3–31.

———. 1992. 'Patronage and Creative Exchange; Yeats, Lady Gregory and the Economy of Indebtedness', *Yeats Annual*, no. 9, pp. 60–94.

Pierce, David. 1995. *Yeats's Worlds: Ireland, England and the Poetic Imagination*, New Haven and London: Yale University Press.

Pittock, Murray G. 1993. *Spectrum of Decadence: The Literature of the 1890s*, London and New York: Routledge.

Putzel, Stephen. 1986. *Reconstructing Yeats*: The Secret Rose *and* The Wind Among the Reeds, Dublin Gill and Macmillan; Totowa, New Jersey, Barnes and Noble.

Reid. B. L. 1968. *The Man From New York: John Quinn and his friends*, New York: Oxford University Press.

Report of the Committee of Enquiry into the work carried on by the Royal Hibernian Academy, 1906.

Roche, Anthony. 1994. *Contemporary Irish Drama: From Beckett to McGuinness*, Dublin: Gill and Macmillan.

Rowse, A. L. 1979. *A Man of the Thirties*, London: Weidenfeld and Nicolson.

Ruddock, Margot. n. d. *The Lemon Tree*, London: J. M. Dent and Sons.

Ryan, W. J. 1894. *The Irish Literary Renaissance: Its History, Pioneers and Possibilities*, London: published by the author.

Saddlemyer, Ann. (ed.) 1982. *Theatre Business: The Correspondence of the First Abbey Directors: W. B. Yeats, Lady Gregory and J. M. Synge*, Gerrards Cross: Colin Smythe; University Park: Pennsylvania State University Press.

——— and Smythe, Colin, (eds). 1987. *Lady Gregory, Fifty Years After*, Gerrards Cross: Colin Smyth.

———. 1989, 'George Hyde Lees: More than a Poet's Wife' in *Yeats the European*, ed. A. Norman Jeffares, pp. 191–200.

Samhain (ed. B. C. Bloomfield), 1970. *English Little Magazines*, no. 14, London: Frank Cass and Company Ltd.

Shakespear, Olivia. 1896. *The False Laurel*, London: Osgood, McIlvaine and Co.

Shiubhlaigh, Maire Nic. 1955. *The Splendid Years: Recollections of Maire Nic Shiubhlaigh*, Dublin: J. Duffy.

Sidnell, Michael J. 1996. *Yeats's Poetry and Poetics*, Basingstoke and London: Macmillan.

Sigsworth, Eric M. 1988. *In Search of Victorian Values*, Manchester and New York: Manchester University Press.

Sinnett, A. P. 1881. *The Occult World*, London: Trübner & Co.

Skelton, Robert and Clark, David R. 1965. *Irish Renaissance: A Gathering of Essays, Memoirs, Letters and Dramatic Poetry from the* Massachusetts Review, Dublin: The Dolmen Press.

Skultans, Vieda. 1983. 'Mediums, Controls and Eminent Men', in *Women's Religious Experience: Cross Cultural Perspectives*, ed. Pat Holden, London and Canberra: Croom Helm.

Souhami, Diana. 1988. *Gluck, 1895–1978*, London: Pandora.

Sri, P. S. 1994. 'Yeats and Mohini Chatterjee', *Yeats Annual*, no. 11, pp. 61–76.

Stallworthy, Jon. 1963. *Between the Lines: Yeats's Poetry in the Making*, Oxford: Clarendon Press.

Stark, Freya. 1983. *Traveller's Prelude*, London: Century Publishing.

Strand. Karin Margaret. 1978. *W. B. Yeats's American Lecture Tours*, University Microfilms International.

Sturgis, Matthew. 1995. *Passionate Attitudes: The English Decadence of the 1890s*, London: Macmillan.

Sussmann, Herbert. 1995. *Victorian Masculinities: Manhood and Poetics in Early Victorian Literature and Art*, Cambridge: Cambridge University Press.

Symons, Arthur. 1899. *The Symbolist Movement in Literature*, London: William Heinemann.

——. 1918. *Cities, and Sea-Coasts and Islands*, London: Collins.

Synge, John Millington. 1968. *Collected Works*, vol. 3 *Plays, Book 1*, ed. Ann Saddlemyer, London: Oxford University Press.

Taylor, Lawrence. 1995. *Occasions of Faith: An Anthropology of Irish Catholics*, Dublin: Lilliput Press.

Thompson, Mary. 1997. *Austin Clarke: A Literary Life-Chronology*, Ph D, University College, Dublin.

Thuente, Mary Helen, (ed). 1979. *Representative Irish Tales* by W. B. Yeats, Gerrards Cross: Colin Smythe.

Thwaite, Ann. 1985. *Edmund Gosse: A Literary Landscape*, Oxford and New York: Oxford University Press.

Timms, David. 1973. *Philip Larkin*, Edinburgh: Oliver and Boyd.

Toomey, Deirdre. 1988. ' "Worst Part of Life": Yeats's Horoscope for Olivia Shakespear' *Yeats Annual*, no. 6, pp. 222–6.

——. 1992. 'Labyrinths: Yeats and Maud Gonne', *Yeats Annual*, no. 9, pp. 95–131.

——. 1993. 'Away', *Yeats Annual*, no. 10, pp. 3–33.

——. 1996. 'Moran's Collar', *Yeats Annual*, no. 12, pp. 45–83.

Torchiana, Donald. 1966. *W. B. Yeats and Georgian Ireland*, Evanston: Northwestern University Press; London: Oxford University Press.

Valuilis, Maryan Gianella. 1992. *Portrait of a Revolutionary: General Richard Mulcahy and the Foundation of the Irish Free State*, Dublin: Irish Academic Press.

Vendler, Helen. 1980. 'Four Elegies', in *Yeats, Sligo and Ireland*, ed. A. Norman Jeffares, Gerrards Cross: Colin Smythe, pp. 216–31.

——. 1991. 'Technique in the Earlier Poems of Yeats', *Yeats Annual*, no. 8, pp. 3–20.

Wade, Allan. 1968. *A Bibliography of the Writings of W. B. Yeats*, 3rd edn. rev. and ed. by K. Alspach, London: Rupert Hart-Davis.

Waller, P. J. 1983. *Town, City and Nation*, London: Oxford University Press.

Washington, Peter. 1993. *Madame Blavatsky's Baboon: Theosophy and the Emergence of the Western Guru*, London: Secker and Warburg.

Watson, George (ed.). 1991. *W. B. Yeats: Short Fiction*, Harmondsworth: Penguin Books.

Webb, Timothy (ed.). 1991. 'Introduction', *W. B. Yeats: Selected Poetry*, Harmondsworth: Penguin Books.

Welch, Robert, (ed.). 1993. *Writings on Irish Folklore, Legend and Myth by W. B. Yeats*, Harmondsworth: Penguin Books.

Wellesley, Dorothy (ed.). 1964. *Letters on Poetry from W. B. Yeats to Dorothy Wellesley*, London, New York and Toronto: Oxford University Press.

West, Trevor. 1986. *Horace Plunkett: Co-operation and Politics, An Irish Biography*, Gerrards Cross: Colin Smythe; Washington, D. C.: Catholic University Press of America.

Wood-Martin, W. G. 1992. *History of Sligo, County and Town*, Dublin: Hodges and Figgis.

Woolf, Virginia. 1980. *The Diary of Virginia Woolf*, vol. 3, 1925–30, London: The Hogarth Press.

Worth, Katherine. 1987. *Where There is Nothing by W. B. Yeats, The Unicorn from the Stars by W. B. Yeats and Lady Gregory*, Gerrards Cross: Colin Smythe; Washington, D.C.: Catholic University of America Press.

Yeats, Michael. n.d. *Cast a Cold Eye: Memories of a poet's son and politician*, Dublin: Blackwater Press.

Yeats, William Butler. 1892. *The Countess Cathleen and Various Legends and Lyrics*, London: T. Fisher Unwin.

———. 1936. 'Introduction', *The Oxford Book of Modern Verse*, London: Oxford University Press.

Yeats, William Butler and Johnson, Lionel. 1908. *Poetry and Ireland*, Dublin: Cuala Press.

Zweig, Stefan. 1943. *The World of Yesterday: An Autobiography*, London: Cassell (1987 printing).

Select Bibliography and Guide to Further Reading

Yeats's Works

Bibliographic Information

Bibliographical information on publication of Yeats's works and selected secondary literature up to 1968 is given in Allan Wade, *A Bibliography of the Writings of W. B. Yeats*, 3rd edn, rev. and ed. by K. Alspach, London: Rupert Hart-Davis, 1968.

Poetry

Collected Poems of W. B. Yeats, ed. Augustine Martin, London: Vintage, 1992.
The Collected Poems of W. B. Yeats, London: Macmillan, 1950.
Under the Moon: The Unpublished Early Poetry of W. B. Yeats, ed. George Bornstein, New York: Scribner, 1995.
The Variorum Edition of the Poems of W. B. Yeats, ed. Peter Allt and Russell K. Aspach, New York: Macmillan, 1957, repr. 1973.
W. B. Yeats: Selected Poems, ed. with an introduction and notes by Timothy Webb, Harmondsworth: Penguin Books, 1991. This edition usefully gives alternative versions of some of the selected poems.
W. B. Yeats: The Poems, ed. and introduced by Daniel Albright, London: Dent, Everyman's Library, 1992; rev. edn 1994.
W. B. Yeats: The Poems, ed. Richard Finneran, London: Macmillan, 1991.
Yeats's Poems, ed. A. Norman Jeffares, London: Macmillan, 1989.

Drama

Collected Plays of W. B. Yeats, London: Macmillan, 1952.

The Herne's Egg by W. B. Yeats, ed. with an introduction and notes by Andrew Parkin, Washington, D.C.: Catholic University of America Press; Gerrards Cross: Colin Smythe, 1991.

The Variorum Edition of the Plays of W. B. Yeats, ed. Russell K. Alspach, London and New York: Macmillan, 1966; repr. 1979.

Where There Is Nothing by W. B. Yeats and *The Unicorn from the Stars* by *W. B. Yeats and Lady Gregory*, Washington, D.C.: Catholic University of America Press; Gerrards Cross: Colin Smythe, 1987.

W. B. Yeats: Selected Plays, ed. with an introduction and notes by Richard Cave, Harmondsworth: Penguin Books, 1997.

See also the Cornell Yeats (Cornell University Press).

Selected Prose Writings

A Critical Edition of Yeats's A Vision, eds. George Mills Harper and Walter Kelly Hood, London: Macmillan, 1978.

A Vision, London: Macmillan, 1962.

Autobiographies, London: Macmillan, 1955.

Essays and Introductions, London: Macmillan, 1961.

Explorations, London: Macmillan, 1962.

John Sherman and Dhoya, ed. Richard Finneran, Detroit: Wayne State University Press, 1969.

Letters to the New Island, eds George Bornstein and Hugh Witemeyer, New York: Macmillan, 1989.

Memoirs, ed. Denis Donoghue, London and Basingstoke: Macmillan, 1972.

Mythologies, London: and New York: Macmillan, 1959.

The Secret Rose: Stories by W. B. Yeats: A Variorum Edition, eds Philip Marcus, Warwick Gould and Michael Sidnell, Ithaca and London: Cornell University Press, 1981.

The Speckled Bird, ed. and annotated by William H. O'Donnell, Canada: McClelland and Stewart, 1976.

Uncollected Prose by W. B. Yeats, vol.1, ed. John P. Frayne, London: Macmillan; New York: Columbia University Press, 1970.

Uncollected Prose by W. B. Yeats, vol. 2, eds John P. Frayne and Colton Johnson, London: Macmillan, 1975; New York: Columbia University Press, 1976.

W. B. Yeats: Prefaces and Introductions, ed. William H. O'Donnell, London: Macmillan, 1988.

W. B. Yeats: Short Fiction, ed. with an introduction and notes by G. J. Watson, Harmondsworth: Penguin Books, 1995.

W. B. Yeats: Writings on Irish Folklore, Legend and Myth, ed. with an introduction and notes by Robert Welch, Harmondsworth: Penguin Books, 1993.

Occult Writings

Yeats's Vision *Papers*, vols 1, 2 and 3, general ed. George Mills Harper, London and New York: Macmillan, 1992.

W. B. Yeats: *A Vision and Related Writings*, ed. A. Norman Jeffares, London: Arena, 1990.

Selected Editions of Letters

The Collected Letters of W. B. Yeats, vol. 1, 1865–1895, ed. John Kelly, associate ed. Eric Domville, Oxford: Clarendon Press, 1986.
The Collected Letters of W. B. Yeats, vol. 2, 1896–1900, eds Warwick Gould, John Kelly and Deirdre Toomey, Oxford: Clarendon Press, 1997.
The Collected Letters of W. B. Yeats, vol. 3, 1900–1904, eds John Kelly and Ronald Schuchard, Oxford: Clarendon Press, 1994.
The Gonne–Yeats Letters, 1893–1938, eds Anna MacBride White and A. Norman Jeffares, London: Hutchinson, 1992; Pimlico, 1993.
The Letters of W. B. Yeats, ed. Allan Wade, London: Rupert Hart-Davis, 1954.

Electronic Sources

The W. B. Yeats Collection on CD-ROM, Cambridge: Chadwyck-Healy, 1998.

Secondary Literature

The secondary literature on Yeats is intimidatingly vast. The following is a basic guide arranged, as far as possible, by topic. A useful *vade mecum* for students of Yeats is David Pierce, *State of the Art W. B. Yeats: A Guide Through the Critical Maze*, Bristol: Bristol Press, 1989. See also Richard J. Finneran (ed.), *Anglo-Irish Literature: A Review of Research*, New York: The Modern Language Association of America, 1976 and *Recent Research on Anglo-Irish Writers*, New York: Modern Language Association for America, 1983. The standard guide is K. P. S. Jochum, *W. B. Yeats: A Classified Bibliography of Criticism*, 2nd edn revised and enlarged, Urbana and Chicago: University of Illinois Press, 1990.

Commentaries on Yeats's works

Jeffares, A. N. *A New Commentary on the Poems of W. B. Yeats*, London and Basingstoke: Macmillan, 1984.
Jeffares A. N. and Anthony Stephen Knowland. *A Commentary on the Plays of W. B. Yeats*, London: Macmillan, 1975.
Unterecker, John. *A Reader's Guide to W. B. Yeats*, London: Thames and Hudson, 1959.

Contexts and Literary History

Brown, Malcolm. *The Politics of Irish Literature*, London: George Allen and Unwin Ltd, 1972.
Ellis-Fermor, Una. *The Irish Dramatic Movement*, London: Methuen, 1939.

Fletcher, Ian. *W. B. Yeats and his Contemporaries*, Sussex: Harvester Press, 1987.

Harris, D. *Yeats, Coole Park and Ballylee*, Baltimore and London: Johns Hopkins University Press, 1974.

Howes, Marjorie. *Yeats's Nations*, Cambridge: Cambridge University Press, 1996.

Kiberd, Declan. *Inventing Ireland*, London: Jonathan Cape, 1995.

——. *Synge and the Irish Language*, 2nd ed, Dublin: Gill and Macmillan, 1993.

Loftus, Richard J. *Nationalism in Modern Anglo-Irish Poetry*, Madison and Milwaukee: The University of Wisconsin Press, 1964.

Loizeaux, Elizabeth. *Yeats and the Visual Arts*, New Brunswick and London: Rutgers University Press, 1986.

Lyons, F. S. L. *Culture and Anarchy in Ireland, 1890–1939*, Oxford: Clarendon Press, 1979.

Marcus, Phillip L. *Yeats and the Beginning of the Irish Renaissance*, 2nd edn, Syracuse, New York: Syracuse University Press, 1987.

Mc Cormack. W. J. *Ascendancy and Tradition in Anglo-Irish History from 1789–1939*, Oxford: Clarendon Press, 1985.

Miller, J. Hillis. *Poets of Reality: Six Twentieth-Century Writers*, London: Oxford University Press, 1966.

Pierce, David. *Yeats's Worlds: Ireland, England and the Poetic Imagination*, New Haven and London: Yale University Press, 1995.

Power, Patrick. *The Story of Anglo-Irish Poetry*, Cork: Mercier Press, 1967.

Stead, C. K. *The New Poetic: Yeats to Eliot*, London: Hutchinson, 1964.

Torchiana, Donald. *W. B. Yeats and Georgian Ireland*, Evanston: Northwestern University Press: London: Oxford University Press, 1966.

Watson, G. J. *Irish Identity and the Literary Revival: Synge, Yeats, Joyce and O'Casey*, London: Croom Helm; New York: Barnes and Noble, 1979.

Welch, Robert. *Irish Poetry from Moore to Yeats*, Gerrards Cross: Colin Smythe, 1980.

Wilson. Edmund. *Axel's Castle: A Study in the Imaginative Literature of 1870–1930*, New York: Scribner, 1931.

Wilson, F. A. C. *W. B. Yeats and Tradition*, London: Methuen, 1957.

Worth, Katherine. *The Irish Drama of Europe from Yeats to Beckett*, London: Athlone Press, 1978.

Lives

Alldritt, Keith. *W. B. Yeats: The Man and the Milieu*, London: John Murray, 1997.

Coote, Stephen. *W. B. Yeats: A Life*, London: Hodder and Stoughton, 1997.

Ellmann, Richard. *Yeats: The Man and the Masks*, London: Penguin Books, 1987.

Foster, R. F. *W. B. Yeats: A Life*, vol. 1: *The Apprentice Mage, 1865–1914*, Oxford and New York: Oxford University Press, 1997.

Hone, Joseph. *W. B. Yeats, 1865–1939*, London: Macmillan and Co. Ltd, 1942.

Jeffares, A. N. *W. B. Yeats: A New Biography*, London, Sydney, Auckland, Johannesburg: Hutchinson, 1988.

Brief Lives

Macrae, Alasdair D. F. *W. B. Yeats: A Literary Life*, Basingstoke: Macmillan, 1995.

Martin, Augustine. *W. B. Yeats*, 2nd edn, Gerrard's Cross: Colin Smythe, 1990.
Tuohy, Frank. *Yeats*, Dublin: Gill and Macmillan; London Macmillan, 1976.

General Critical/Biographical Studies

Archibald, Douglas. *Yeats*, Syracuse, NY: Syracuse University Press, 1986.
Donoghue, Denis. *William Butler Yeats*, New York: Viking Press; Glasgow: Fontana, 1971.
Drake, Nicholas. *The Poetry of W. B. Yeats*, Harmondsworth: Penguin Books, 1991.
Ellmann, Richard. *The Identity of Yeats*, London: Faber and Faber, 1964.
Henn. T. R. *The Lonely Tower*, London: Methuen, 1950; rev. edn, 1965.
Jeffares, A. N. *W. B. Yeats: Man and Poet*, London: Routledge and Kegan Paul, 1949; 2nd edn, London: Kyle Cathie, 1996.
Larrissey, Edward. *Yeats The Poet: The Measures of Difference*, London and New York: Harvester/Wheatsheaf, 1994.
MacNeice, Louis, *The Poetry of W. B. Yeats*, London: Faber and Faber, 1967.
Peterson, Richard F. *William Butler Yeats*, Boston: Twayne Publishers, 1982.
Rajan, B. *W. B. Yeats: A Critical Introduction*, London: Hutchinson, 1965.
Smith, Stan. *W. B. Yeats: A Critical Introduction*, London: Macmillan Education, 1990.
Stock, A. G. *W. B. Yeats: His Poetry and Thought*, Cambridge: Cambridge University Press, 1961.
Thurley, Geoffrey. *The Turbulent Dream: Passion and Politics in the Poetry of W. B. Yeats*, Queensland University Press, 1983.
Unterecker, John. *A Reader's Guide to W. B. Yeats*, London: Thames and Hudson, 1959, repr., 1975.
Ure, Peter. *W. B. Yeats*, Edinburgh: Oliver and Boyd, 1963.
Whitaker, Thomas. *Swan and Shadow: Yeats' Dialogue with History*, Durham, NC: University of North Carolina Press, 1964.

Yeats and the Romantic/Symbolist Tradition

Adams, Hazard. *Blake and Yeats: The Contrary Vision*, 1st pub. 1955, New York: Russell and Russell, 1968.
Bloom, Harold. *Yeats*, New York: Oxford University Press, 1970.
Bornstein, George. *Yeats and Shelley*, Chicago and London: University of Chicago Press, 1970.
De Man, Paul. *The Rhetoric of Romanticism*, New York: Columbia University Press, 1984.
Hough, Graham. *The Last Romantics*, London: Duckworth, 1949.
Kermode, Frank. *Romantic Image*, London: Routledge and Kegan Paul, 1957.
Rudd. M. *Divided Image: A Study of William Blake and W. B. Yeats*, London: Routledge and Kegan Paul, 1953.

Yeats and Modernism/Post-Modernism

Emig, Rainer. *Modernism in Poetry: Motivations, Structures, and Limits*, London and New York: Longman, 1995.

Levenson, M. *A Genealogy of Modernism: A Study of English Literary Doctrine 1880–1922*, Cambridge: Cambridge University Press, 1984.

Longenbach, James. *Stone Cottage: Pound, Yeats and Modernism*, Oxford: Oxford University Press, 1988.

Materer, Timothy. *Modernist Alchemy: Poetry and the Occult*, Ithaca and London: Cornell University Press, 1995.

Orr, Leonard. *Yeats and Postmodernism*, Syracuse: Syracuse University Press, 1991.

Smith, Stan. *The Origins of Modernism: Eliot, Pound, Yeats and the Rhetoric of Renewal*, New York, London, Toronto, Sydney, Tokyo, Singapore: Harvester Wheatsheaf, 1994.

Stead, C. K. *Pound, Yeats, Eliot and the Modernist Movement*, Basingstoke: Macmillan, 1986.

Yeats and Politics

Craig, Cairns. *Yeats, Eliot, Pound and the Politics of Poetry*, London: Croom Helm, 1981.

Cullingford, Elizabeth. *Yeats, Ireland and Fascism*, London and Basingstoke: Macmillan, 1981.

Freyer, Grattan. *W. B. Yeats and the Anti-Democratic Tradition*, Dublin: Gill and Macmillan, 1981.

McDiarmid, Lucy. *Saving Civilisation: Yeats, Eliot and Auden Between the Wars*, Cambridge: Cambridge University Press, 1984.

North, Michael. *The Political Aesthetic of Yeats, Eliot, and Pound.* Cambridge, New York, Port Chester, Melbourne, Sydney: Cambridge University Press, 1991.

Stanfield, Paul Scott. *Yeats and Politics in the 1930s*, London: Macmillan, 1988.

Tratner, Michael. *Modernism and Mass Politics: Joyce, Woolf, Eliot and Yeats*, Stanford, Cal.: Stanford University Press, 1995.

Yeats and Women

Cullingford, Elizabeth Butler, *Gender and History in Yeats's Love Poetry*, Cambridge: Cambridge University Press, 1993.

Keane, Patrick J. *Terrible Beauty: Yeats, Joyce, Ireland and the Myth of the Devouring Female*, Columbia: University of Missouri Press, 1988.

Kline, Gloria. *The Last Courtly Lover: Yeats and the Idea of Women*, Epping: Bowker Publishing Company; Ann Arbor: UMI Research Press, 1983.

Toomey, Deirdre, ed. *Yeats and Women*, 2nd edn, Basingstoke: Macmillan; New York: St Martin's Press, 1997.

Yeats and Magic/Folklore

Flannery, Mary Catherine, *Yeats and Magic: The Earlier Works*, Gerrards Cross: Colin Smythe, 1977.

Harper, George Mills. *Yeats's Golden Dawn*, London: Macmillan, 1974.

Hough, Graham. *The Mystery Religion of W. B. Yeats*, Sussex: Harvester Press; New Jersey: Barnes and Noble, 1984.

Kinahan, Frank. *Yeats, Folkore and Occultism: Contexts of the Early Work and Thought*, London, Boston, Sydney, Wellington: Unwin and Hyman, 1988.

Moore, Virginia. *The Unicorn: William Butler Yeats's Search for Reality*, New York: Macmillan Company, 1964.

Thuente, Mary Helen, *Yeats and Irish Folklore*, Dulbin; Gill and Macmillan; Totowa, NJ: Barnes and Noble, 1980.

Yeats and Poetics

Adams, Joseph. *Yeats and the Masks of Syntax*, London and Basingstoke: Macmillan, 1984.

Beum, Robert. *The Poetic Art of W. B. Yeats*, New York: Frederick Ungar Publishing Company, 1969.

Dougherty, A. *A Study of Rhythmic Structure in the Verse of William Butler Yeats*, The Hague and Paris: Mouton, 1973.

Perloff, Marjorie. *Rhyme and Meaning in the Poetry of Yeats*, The Hague: Mouton, 1970.

Yeats as Dramatist

Bradley, Anthony. *William Butler Yeats*, World Dramatists, New York: Ungar Publishing Co., 1979.

Dorn, Karen. *Players and Painted Stage: The Theatre of W. B. Yeats*, Sussex: The Harvester Press; New Jersey: Barnes and Noble, 1984.

Flannery, James. *W. B. Yeats and the Idea of a Theatre: The Early Abbey in Theory and Practice*, New Haven and London: Yale University Press, 1976.

Friedman, Barton R. *Adventures in the Deeps of the Mind: The Cuchulain Cycle of W. B. Yeats*, Princeton and Guildford: Princeton University Press, 1977.

Good, Maeve. *W. B. Yeats and the Creation of a Tragic Theatre*, Basingstoke: Macmillan, 1987.

Miller, Liam. *The Noble Drama of W. B. Yeats*, Dublin: Dolmen Press, 1977.

Moore, J. R. *Masks of Love and Death: Yeats as Dramatist*, Ithaca and London: Cornell University Press, 1971.

Qamber, Akhtar. *Yeats and the Noh*, New York and Tokyo: Weatherhill, 1974.

Skene, Reg. *The Cuchulain Plays of W. B. Yeats*, London: Macmillan; New York: Columbia University Press, 1974.

Taylor, R. *The Drama of W. B. Yeats: Irish Myth and the Japanese No*, New Haven and London: Yale University Press, 1976.

Ure, Peter. *Yeats the Playwright: A Commentary on Character and Design in the Major Plays*, London: Routledge and Kegan Paul, 1963.

Vendler, Helen. *Yeats's 'Vision' and the Last Plays*, Cambridge, Mass.: Harvard University Press, 1963.

Index

Note: WBY refers to William Butler Yeats; JBY refers to John Butler Yeats (father).

Abbey Theatre, Dublin: actors' discontent
(1905) 161; T. S. Eliot's lecture
(1940) 378, 380; first opens
(1904) 153, 160; Horniman's rift with
WBY (1907) 180; O'Casey's plays
291–2, 311; *The Playboy* ructions
(1907) 168–9; state subsidy 290–1;
US fund-raising by WBY 190; WBY's
diminished role 188; WBY's takeover
of 161–2
Academy of Letters: English 182; Irish 338
'Adam's Curse' 144, 148
'The Adoration of the Magi' 98
adultery, WBY's final years 345–8
aesthetic movement (1890s) 58, 60
afterlife: in *Responsibilities* (1914) 208–10;
WBY's search for (1909–24) 190–8
aging: in *The Tower* 316; WBY's
consciousness of 147–8, 222, 224;
WBY's regrets (1917) 249
alchemical marriage 246–66
allegory, *Cathleen ni Houlihan* 135
Ameritus (spirit control), exchanges
with 259–61
ancestor worship, WBY's aesthetic
elitism 207, 215–16
Anglican Church in Ireland 3–6, 299–300
Anglo-Irish culture, WBY's legacy 379
Anglo-Irish Protestants 142–3, 287, 293
Anglo-Irish war (1919–21), truce (1921) 280

Anglophobia, WBY's later ballads 353,
358–9
Apocalypsism 112–13
Armstrong, Laura 27
Arnold, Matthew 63–4
art: Victorian England 13–14; WBY's
Modernism critique 307–8
artistic freedom: debate on (1907) 169;
WBY's defence of 159
Arts and Crafts movement 75, 149
astrology: in Yeatses' marriage 246–7
At the Hawk's Well (1916) 223–4, 250, 382
Athenaeum, WBY's election to (1937) 358
Auden, W. H. 377
autobiography: *The Autobiography*
(1937) 365; 'Dramatis Personae'
(1935) 337; *Reveries Over Childhood and
Youth* (1916) 2–3, 7–8, 14–17, 22–3,
29, 217–20, 382; *The Speckled
Bird* 113; *The Trembling of the Veil*
(1922) 281; 'The Wanderings of
Oisin' 44; *The Wind Among the Reeds*
(1899) 111–14
Automatic Script *see* automatic writing
automatic writing 193; George Yeats
252–8; Gonne critique 258; nature
of 258–61, 263–6; *A Vision* (1926,
1937) 300–3, 304–11; WBY's
concerns of state (1920s) 290
avatar, AE's prophecy 269

'Baile and Aillinn' 133
ballads: Anglo-Irish 81; WBY's
    Anglophobic nationalism 353, 358–9
Balzac, Honoré de 178
Beardsley, Aubrey 59
Beardsley, Mabel 250
Beckett, Samuel 382
Bedford Park, London 13, 16, 23–5
Beerbohm, Max 124
Belfast: JBY's dislike of 159; sectarianism
    7–8; WBY's dislike of 5–6
Belloc, Hilaire 216
Berkeley, George 334
Berryman, John 380
Besant, Annie 40
Big House ideal, WBY's 25, 336
bindings: *In the Seven Woods* 149–50;
    Moore's design for *The Tower* 315;
    poetry editions 75
biography, Joseph Hone (1942) 378
Black and Tans 268, 271, 273, 275
Blake, William 67, 150–1
Blavatsky, Helena Petrovna
    (Madame) 33–9
Blenheim Road (no. 3), Bedford Park 47, 60
Blunt, Wilfrid Scawen 216
Boer War 139–40
bohemianism, literary 59–60
A Book of Irish Verse (1895) 89
British establishment, WBY's entry into
    (1910) 181–2
British imperialism 57
British Society for Psychical Research 38,
    192
Broad Street (no. 4), Oxford 255–6,
    268–9, 276, 280
Butler, Mary 4

Campbell, Mrs Patrick 175, 240
Canada, lecture tour (1920) 274
Carson, Sir Edward 204
Casement, Sir Roger 225, 229
casualties, Great War 221
Cathleen ni Houlihan (play) (1902) 134–6,
    139, 156
Catholicism 6–7; conflict with Yeatsian
    ideals 292–3, 297, 299–300, 368;
    Gonne's conversion to 141–2; Irish-
    American 158; nationalism

connection 129–30; social power 45;
    WBY's tirade against its women 206
Celtic Order of Mysteries 92–3
The Celtic Twilight (1893) 19, 40–1
Celticism 62–6
censorship in English theatre 132
change, cyclical theory of 269–71
changelings, Irish folklore 19–21
chant, *Cathleen ni Houlihan* 135
Christianity: and paganism 348–9; in
    retreat 307
Church of Ireland (Anglican) 3–6, 299–300
circulating libraries, Ireland 85
Civil List Pension 182, 204
Collins, Michael 282, 284, 286
Collis (née Ruddock), Margot 345–6, 356,
    365–6
Communicators, spirit 192–7, 237, 252,
    254, 259–61, 269–70
conflict: Abbey Theatre takeover
    (1905) 161–2; artistic warfare
    (1905–6) 164–5; Christian and
    mythic in *The Second Coming* 271–2;
    Hail and Farewell (Moore) 205–6; *The
    Playboy*, Abbey Theatre ructions
    (1907) 168–9; religious (1925) 292–3,
    297, 299–300; WBY with father
    (1887) 32, 162; in WBY's
    consciousness (1903) 152; WBY's
    philosophy of 300, 302–3, 311
consciousness: altered states 102; conflict
    in (1903) 152
Contemporary Club, Dublin 28, 68
Controls, automatic writings 254
controversy: *The Countess Cathleen* 126–7,
    131; Irish cultural divisions 129–31;
    Irish Literary Society 85–6; Irish
    poetry critique 90; Sir Hugh Lane's
    art gallery 201–2, 221; WBY in old
    age 359–60
Coole Park, Co. Galway 106–7, 110, 336–7
Corbet, Robert 11
Cosgrave, President William 287–8
The Countess Cathleen (play) 122–5, 126–8,
    131, 342
*The Countess Kathleen and Various Legends and
    Lyrics* (1892) 74–5
The Courtier (Castiglione) 171
Craig, Gordon 131–2, 382

'Crazy Jane' (WBY's *alter ego*) 332–5
creativity: WBY on 257; WBY's own
   258–9, 261
criticism of WBY 378–82
Crowley, Aleister 115
Cuala Press: financial crises 157, 336, 365;
   inception 149–50; WBY's
   posthumous publications 378; WBY's
   tracts (1938) 366
Cuchulain: *At the Hawk's Well* 224; *The*
   Death of Cuchulain 374–6; *The Golden*
   Helmet 187–8; *On Baile's Strand* 374;
   The Only Jealousy of Emer (1917–18)
   261–3; WBY's self-portraiture in 134
'Cuchulain Comforted' 375–6
cultural nationalism: Irish 85–9, 98, 120,
   271; Irish American 158
cultural politics: Ireland (1890s) 85–90, 98,
   126–31; WBY's legacy 379
Cumann na nGaedheal 135, 155
The Cutting of an Agate (1912) 214
cyclical theory of change 269–71

Dáil Eireann 267, 270, 280
de Valera, Eamon 274, 282, 339–40
de-Anglicization of Irish life 128–9, 158
death: in 'Easter 1916' 234; in 'The Gates
   of Pluto' 308–9; Great War
   carnage 218, 221; in *Responsibilities*
   (1914) 209–11; of WBY (1939) 376;
   WBY's poetic confrontation with
   (1917) 250
The Death of Cuchulain (1939) 374–6
Decadence, *fin de siècle* 58–60
Deirdre 175
depth analysis, Yeatses' automatic writing
   sessions 256–7
Dickinson, Mabel 174, 193
Discoveries (1907) 165–6
divorce, WBY's legislature stance 299–300
Dodds, E. R. 192
Dolmetsch, Arnold 131
domesticity, WBY's adoption of 251
Dowden, Bishop John 10–11
Dowden, Edward 10, 12, 26–7, 29, 89–90,
   181
drama: WBY's absorption with 118–25,
   134, 150; *see also* Abbey Theatre; Noh
   plays

The Dreaming of the Bones (1918) 241–3, 261
dreams: automatic writing 263, 265;
   Gonne's relationship with WBY 102;
   WBY's concerns of state 290; Yeatses'
   psychic research 274
drugs, WBY's experiments with 102
Drumcliffe 3, 4, 377
Dublin: Abbey Theatre 153, 160–1, 188,
   190; bitterness in new Irish State
   (1922–3) 286–8; Easter Rising
   (1916) 225–6, 227; hostility towards
   WBY (1901) 130–1; industrial unrest
   (1913) 199–201; Irish Literary
   Society controversy 85–6; JBY's
   studio 26; plays 134; socio-religious
   divisions 87; WBY returns (1922)
   286; WBY's frustration with (1903)
   156–7
Duffy, Sir Charles Gavan 85–6

'Easter 1916' 229–36, 275
Easter Rising (1916) 225–6, 227–35,
   241–2
Edith Villas (no. 14), London 12
'Edition de Luxe', WBY's work on
   (1931–2) 337–8
Edwardian period, heroic women 184–5
Eliot, T. S. 223, 273, 307, 359; Abbey
   Theatre lecture (1940) 378, 380;
   Great War 218; WBY's
   influence 381
elitism (WBY's): aesthetic 215–16;
   eugenics 366–70, 372–3; on Gonne's
   marriage 141–2; last poems 369–70;
   mystical 351; Nietzsche's influence
   153, 157, 171; social 117, 170–1
enemies, WBY's identification of
   (1903) 144
England: establishment acceptance of
   WBY (1910) 181–2; theatre 131–2;
   WBY's psychic experiments
   (1913) 188
English Academy of Letters 182
English language 82; later poetry 353–4
English Romanticism 79
epitaph, WBY's own 363
Essays 1931 to 1936 (1938) 365
establishment, WBY's entry into 181–2
ethics of WBY's late writings 370

eugenic engineering, WBY's promotion of 366–70, 372–3
Europe: first days of the Great War 217–18; political upheavals (1918–19) 270
executions: Easter Rising (1916) 226, 228, 230; Irish Free State (1922) 286, 288
extremism: WBY's eugenics (1938) 366–70, 372–3; WBY's later works (1930s) 352, 358–9

fairies, Irish belief in 19–21, 63
Fairy and Folk Tales of the Irish Peasantry (1888) 19
faith, WBY's beliefs 116–18
famine: Ireland (1897) 100–1; *see also* Great Famine
Farr, Florence 40, 53, 114–15, 131; WBY's affair with 163; death of (1917) 246
'The Fascination of What's Difficult' 173
Fascism 373; Ezra Pound 326; Germany 341–2; Ireland 340–1; Italy 299; WBY's flirtation with 340–2; WBY's last poems 370
Fay, Frank and Willie 154–5, 161, 180
Feilding, Everard 197, 217
feminism 279, 379
Fenians 29, 51, 64, 137
Ferguson, Sir Samuel 1
finances (WBY's): 1903–4 US tour's success 157–8; Abbey Theatre support 180; improvements in (1914, 1923) 204, 289; lack of (1888, 1890s) 30–1, 108–9; Lady Gregory's support 108–9; National Theatre Society 159
Fitzroy Road, London (no. 23) 12
Foden, Mrs Gwyneth 355–6
folk tradition, Ireland 16–20, 38, 80–1, 197–8
'The Folly of Being Comforted' 147–8
Freud, Sigmund 83
A Full Moon in March (play) 351–2

the Gael 129
Gaelic language 81
Gaelic League 130, 158
Gleeson, Evelyn 149
Goethe Plakette, WBY's acceptance of (1934) 341

Gogarty, Oliver St John 275, 288
Golden Dawn *see* Order of the Golden Dawn
The Golden Helmet (play) 187
Gonne, Iseult 222; marriage to Harry Francis Stuart (1919) 274–5; WBY's interest in 234–5, 237, 246–8, 256
Gonne, Maud 87–8, 92, 112; appearance 47–8, 147; birth of Iseult 102; birth of son 163–4; campaign against Irish Free State 288; *Cathleen ni Houlihan* 135–6; Catholicism conversion 141–2; Celtic Order of Mysteries 93; charisma 101–2; death of (1953) 378; death of first child (1891) 51–2; Diamond Jubilee protest 98–100; Easter Rising response 227; family background 50; first meeting with WBY 47–50; Great War conflicts (1914) 217–18; Holloway imprisonment (1918) 255–6; husband's execution (1916) 226, 227–8; Irish nationalism 47–51, 139–40; last visit to WBY (1938) 373; marriage to MacBride 142, 163–4; military nursing in France (1914) 218; 'No Second Troy' allusions 183–6; Normandy visit with WBY (1917) 246; physical relationship with WBY (1908) 175, 178; poems in praise of 220; refused entry to Ireland (1917) 247; renewed intimacy with WBY (1908) 173–6; rifts with WBY 145–6, 256, 314; 'spiritual marriage' to WBY 102–4, 141; tells WBY of Millevoye and children 102; visions 92, 102, 232–3; WBY's fears for 231–2; as WBY's female ideal 49, 228–9; WBY's first marriage proposal (1891) 51; WBY's letters to (1913) 203; WBY's renewed marriage proposal (1916) 228
Gore-Booth, Eva 88, 314
Great Famine (1840s) 127
Great War (1914–18): armistice 267; on the brink of 217; carnage in France 217–18; Gonne's vision of Irish destiny 233; poets of 359; WBY's emotional detachment 219–20

Great Wheel 304–5
The Green Helmet and Other Poems
(1910) 172–3, 175, 182–3, 185–7
Gregory, Lady Augusta 19–20, 105–10,
126, 130–1; *Cuchulain of
Muirthemne* 132; death of (1932)
336; death of son (1918) 251, 255;
denounces Black and Tan barbarity
(1920–1) 275; *Hail and Farewell*
satire 205–6; illnesses 176, 186,
330; Italian visit with WBY
(1907) 171; Lane bequest 221,
236; *Visions and Beliefs in the West of
Ireland*, 198, 262; role in WBY's
marriage to George 247; WBY's
collaboration with 132–6, 138;
WBY's letters to 220, 227–8,
254–5
Gregory, Major Robert, death of
(1918) 251, 255
Guides, automatic writings 254
gyres 307

Heaney, Seamus 381
Henley, W. E. 57–8, 64
Hermetic Society, Dublin 32–4
The Herne's Egg (play) 356–7
heroic age, Irish 133, 144, 147–8
heroic women, Edwardian age 184–5
heros, Nietzschean 151–3
Hindu mysticism 352–3
history: cyclical theory of change 269–71;
of Ireland explored in US tour
(1932–3) 338–9; in *The Secret Rose* 96;
in *A Vision* 306–7
Home Rule 98–9, 227–8, 268
Home Rule Bill: (1893) 98, (1914) 198–200,
204
Hone, Joseph 378
Horniman, Annie 114–15, 159–60,
179–80
The Hour Glass (1903) 132, 156, 210–11
Howth, near Dublin 12, 16, 26–7
Hyde, Douglas 68, 128–9
Hyde-Lees, Bertha Georgie (later
George Yeats) 188, 222, 235;
marriage to WBY (1917) 246–8; *see
also* Yeats, Bertha Georgie
'George'

Ideas of Good and Evil (1903) 133, 150,
156
identity: Irish 129; WBY's insecure sense
of 171–2
imagery: Gonne's waking visions 232–3;
Irish magical 47, 79–81
*In the Seven Woods: Being Poems of the Irish
Heroic Age* (1903) 144, 147–8
In the Shadow of the Glen (Synge) 142–3
incarnation: Christ's birth 269, 270–2;
second – prophesied by Yeatses'
spirits 269–72
Inghinidhe na hÉireann 135, 153, 154
Inns of Court, London 60
IRA *see* Irish Republican Army
Ireland: ancient compared with the
orient 353; Anglo-Irish war truce
(1921) 280; Arts and Crafts
Society 149; civil war (1922–3)
282–5; cultural divisions 85–90,
291–3; cultural politics 85–90, 127–9;
de-Anglicization 128–9, 158;
Diamond Jubilee protest 98–100;
guerrilla war of independence
(1916–21) 270–5; intellectual
malleability 84; land reform 30;
magical imagery 47, 79–81;
mythology 83; nationalist unrest
(1914) 218, 219; North of 5–6;
polarization (1914) 204; politics
(1912–13) 198–202, 204; Sinn Féin
election victories (1918–20) 267–8;
state terrorism (1920) 273;
theatre 153–5, 159–60, 179–80;
WBY's poetry critiques 333; WBY's
schooling in (1881) 26
Irish Academy of Letters 338
Irish America 158, 190; WBY's lecture
tour (1903–4) 158
Irish feminism 379
Irish folklore 16–21, 38, 80–1, 197–8
Irish Free State: Constitution Bill
(1922) 286; inception (1922) 286–7;
trouble averted (1924) 296; WBY
created Senator (1922) 287
Irish identity 129
Irish language 81–2; revivalism 128–30
Irish Literary Society 63, 85–6, 156
Irish Literary Theatre 120–5, 153–4

Irish National Theatre Society 154–6, 159–60
Irish nationalism 29, 62, 85, 98–101, 162; in *Cathleen ni Houlihan* 135–6; Catholicism connection 129–30; de-Anglicization 128–9, 158; Gonne 47–51, 139–40; Lady Gregory 106; revolutionary 136; *Sinn Féin* 170, 189, 267–8; spiritualized version 158–9; WBY's social elitism 170–1
Irish Parliamentary Party, Home Rule policy 268
Irish rebellion centenary (1898) 99–101
Irish Republican Army (IRA) 267, 339–40
Irish Republican Brotherhood 51, 140, 225
Irish Volunteers 199, 225
Italy: WBY's visit with Lady Gregory (1907) 171; Yeatses' visit (1925) 299
Ivy League, WBY's lectures (1903) 157

James, William 191
Japanese Noh plays 215–16, 223–4, 262, 280
Jarry, Alfred 119, 357
John, Augustus 172, 331
John Sherman (1891) 17–18, 48–9
Johnston, Charles 28
journalism: Edith Heald 366; WBY as slave to (1890) 109
Joyce, James 126, 221–2, 283, 307

Kennelly, Brendan 381
The King of the Great Clock Tower (play) 349, 351–2
The King's Threshold (play) 138–9

'The Lake Isle of Innisfree' 18, 31
The Land of Heart's Desire (play) 19–20
land reform, Ireland 30
Lane bequest 221, 236, 288
Lane, Sir Hugh: art gallery controversy 201–3; death in SS *Lusitania* sinking (1915) 221; posthumous concerns about gallery 221; WBY's attempts at spirit contact 253
language: English 82, 353–4; Irish 81–2, 128–30

Larkin, Philip 381
Last Poems and Two Plays (1935) 378
lectures 156–7; artistic freedom fiasco (1907) 169; WBY's 1903–4 US tour 157–9; WBY's 1911 US tour 190; WBY's 1914 US tour 203–4; WBY's 1920 US tour 273–4; WBY's 1932–3 US tour 338
'Leda and the Swan' 296–7
Leo Africanus (spirit of) 192–3, 195–7, 237
Lewis, C. S. 268–9
liberalism, WBY's (1913) 200–1
library project, Irish 85–6
literary culture: Irish need for 89; London 55–6
Literary Theatre Club 132
Logue, Cardinal Michael 126–7
London: *At the Hawk's Well* society performances (1916) 223–4; Great War eve (1914) 217; Irish Literary Society controversy 85–6; literary culture 55–6; theatre 131–2, 134; Theosophical Society 32–3; urban change 23–4; WBY's childhood in 22–3; Zeppelin attacks (1915) 221
love, sacrifice in 95–8, 110–12, 145–6
love affairs, WBY's second puberty 345–8, 355–6, 358, 365–6
love triangle: *The Only Jealousy of Emer* 262–3; *The Secret Rose* 111; SS *Lusitania*, sinking of (1915) 221
lyric verse, WBY's resumption of (1908) 172–3

MacBride, John 140–1, 163–4, 226, 227–8
MacBride, Seán (Gonne's son) 313–14, 377
MacNeice, Louis 378–9
madness, caused by fairy interference 20–1
'The Magi' 211–12
magic: critical issue of WBY's work 379; Irish imagery 47, 79–81; WBY's beliefs in 116–18; Yeatses' preoccupation with (1919–20) 268–9; *see also* occultism
Majorca, WBY's visit to (1935) 355–6
Mallarmé, Stéphane 72
Mannin, Ethel 345–6, 365–6

Markievicz, Constance 230, 231, 314
marriage: Gonne to MacBride 142, 144;
    'spiritual' with Gonne 102–4, 141;
    WBY to George (1917) 246–8;
    WBY's fulfilment in 251; WBY's
    poetry 293–5
Martyn, Edward 120, 126, 154
Marxism, WBY's fear of 272
Mask, theory of the 176–8
materialism, WBY's rejection of 37, 47,
    58, 79, 307, 332
Mathers, Samuel Liddell (MacGregor
    Mathers) 71, 92–3, 114–15
meditative rhythms 77
mediumship: Madame Blavatsky 35;
    Spiritualism 36–9; WBY's spirit
    messengers 192–4; Yeatses' sexual
    mutuality 259–61; Yeatsian
    obsession 188, 190–8; *see also* seances;
    Spiritualism
Merrion Square (no. 82), Dublin 282,
    325
Michael Robartes and the Dancer (1921) 271,
    277–9
middle classes, Ireland 129–30
Middleton, William 8–9, 14
Millevoye, Lucien 50, 102
Milligan, Alice 89
Modernism: John Quinn 151; *The
    Tower* 323; *A Vision* 310; WBY's
    critique of 307–8
moon phases: history 269, 307; personality
    types 263
Moore, G. E. 312
Moore, George 60, 120, 126, 153–4,
    205–6, 209
Moore, T. Sturge 132, 312, 314–15
Moran, D. P. 128–30, 292
Morrell, Lady Ottoline 355
Morris, William 57, 149
Murphy, William Martin 201
music 131–2
mysticism 32–4; essays 133;
    Hindu 352–3, 354; in WBY's later
    sexuality 350–1
mythology: Cuchulain's fate 224; and
    fact 307; in *Responsibilities* (1914)
    211–12; Victorian preoccupation
    with 83

naming: Hiberno-English 82; Irish place-
    names 81
national culture, Irish divisions 291–3
National Guard (Blueshirts) 340–1
National Literary Society, Dublin 85
nationalism: Scottish/Irish comparison
    1–2; *see also* Irish nationalism
New Poems (1938) 360–4
Nietzsche, Friedrich, influence on
    WBY 150–3, 155–7, 162, 167, 360
nihilism, *Purgatory* 373
'No Second Troy' 183–6
Nobel Prize for Literature (1923) 289
Noh plays 215–16, 223–4, 261, 280
numerology: Gonne's waking visions
    232–3; structure of 'Easter 1916'
    233–4

oath of allegiance, WBY's involvement in
    (1932) 338–9
O'Brien, Conor Cruise 127–8, 276
O'Casey, Sean 292, 311, 324
occult marriage, WBY's to George 246–66
occultism 32–40, 52, 68–9, 192; critical
    issue of WBY's work 379; Easter
    Rising 229; influence on WBY's
    poetry 270, 277–8; symbolist
    movement 71–2; Yeatses'
    preoccupation with (1919–20) 268–9;
    see also automatic writing; magic;
    mediumship; Spiritualism
O'Donnell, Frank Hugh 126–7, 140
Oedipus the King (Sophocles), WBY's English-
    language version 313
O'Higgins, Kevin, assassination of
    (1927) 313, 315
Oldham, C. H. 30
O'Leary, Ellen 47–8
O'Leary, John 28–30, 47–8, 50, 169–70
On Baile's Strand (1904) 133–4, 139, 262, 374
On the Boiler (1939) 366–7, 369, 374, 378
The Only Jealousy of Emer (1917–18) 261–4
Order of the Golden Dawn 52, 54, 69–70,
    71; crisis 114–15; decline 121;
    resignation pamphlet 115–18; WBY's
    resignation from 115
orient, compared with west of Ireland 33–4
orientalism, late Yeatsian 352–4, 361, 365
Owen, Wilfred 359

Oxbridge, women's colleges 53
Oxford Book of Modern Verse, WBY's
    editorship 355, 359
Oxford Union, WBY's republican stance
    (1921) 277

A Packet for Ezra Pound (1929) 325–6
paganism, and Christianity 348–9
painting: brother Jack's talents 24; JBY
    abandons law for 11–14
Pan-Celtic universalism 93
Parnell, Charles Stewart 52, 98–9; death
    of (1891) 84; in WBY's poetry 349,
    359
patronage: Annie Horniman 159–60;
    Lady Gregory 132–6
'Paudeen' 210
Pearse, Patrick 225, 231
peasantry, Irish folk-mind 81
Penns in the Rocks, Sussex 354–5
Per Amica Silentia Lunae (1918) 237–41
personality: WBY's own 14–15; Yeatses'
    classification 263–4, 304–7
philosophy 237–9, 312
photography, psychic phenomena 192
The Playboy of the Western World (Synge) 143,
    168, 187
The Player Queen 239–40
plays, WBY's influence on successors 382
Poems (1895) 74–5, 79–82, 89
Poems and Ballads of Young Ireland (1888) 66
Poems Written in Discouragement (1913) 202
Poet Laureateship 74
poetry: Automatic Script influences
    264–6; change of style (1906) 150;
    'Crazy Jane' 333–5; creative burst at
    Rapallo (1929) 325, 329; creative
    vigour renewed (1917) 251–3;
    dramatic intensity (1903–6) 145–6;
    early 76–8; on Easter Rising 228–34;
    female sexuality (1927, 1933) 327–9,
    333–5; final years 364–5, 368–9;
    iconography 110–11; Irish civil
    war 285; Irish place-names 81–2;
    Irish shortcomings 90; lasting
    popularity 381; lyric verse
    resumption (1908) 172–3; magical
    imagery 47, 79–81; marriage to
    George 248, 293–5; metaphysical

verse 266; occultism influence 270,
    277–8; O'Higgins' murder 313–14;
    orientalizing of later works 353;
    pre-marriage (1917) 249; republican
    works (1920) 275–7; 'The
    Rose' 75–6, 79; sense of loss
    in 145–6; symbolism 71–7; wartime
    output (1914–17) 222; women as
    enchantresses 42–3; *see also* individual
    works
The Poetry of W. B. Yeats (MacNeice) 378
politics: de Valera's accession to power
    (1932) 339–41; *The Dreaming of the
    Bones* 242–3; Ireland 84–5, 198–202,
    204, 267–8; Irish cultural (1890s)
    85–90, 98; WBY's flirtation with
    extremism (1933) 340–3; WBY's
    indiscretions (1924) 295–8; WBY's
    republican courage (1920) 275–7
Pollexfen, George (uncle), death of
    (1909) 186
Pollexfen, Susan (later Yeats) *see* Yeats,
    Susan (mother)
Pollexfen, William (maternal
    grandfather) 8–9, 14, 207
The Pot of Broth (1902) 132, 156
Pound, Ezra 307; best man at WBY's
    wedding (1917) 248; in Italy 299,
    325–7; WBY's collaboration
    with 212–16, 220, 222; WBY's
    influence on 381
power: Nietzschean will to 151–2, 176–7;
    in *The Tower* 315–16
A Prayer for my Daughter (1919) 271, 279
Pre-Raphaelites 13, 42–3, 46
Presbyterianism 5–6
pretensions, WBY mocked by Moore 205–6
professionalization, Victorian society 53–4
professions, women's entry into 53
Protestantism 3–6; Anglo-Irish 142–3,
    287, 293; Church of Ireland 3–6,
    299–300; insecurities in Ireland
    (late 1930s) 370, 372–3
psychic studies 191–8; automatic
    writing 252–66; cyclical theory of
    change 269–70; influence on WBY's
    poetry 270, 277–8; prophecies
    270–1; *see also* British Society for
    Psychical Research, occultism

psychological model, Yeatses' 257
psychology 192
public speaking *see* lectures
Purgatory (1938) 371–3, 375
Purohit Swami, Shri 352–3, 355–6

Quinn, John 151, 157–8, 169; death of
(1924) 298; quarrel over mistress
(1909) 178–9; WBY's reconciliation
with (1914) 204–5

Radcliffe, Elizabeth 193–5
radio, WBYs skills as broadcaster 365
Rapallo, artistic circle 325–7
Rathfarnham 337, 339, 346, 354
Rathgar villa, Dublin 25
'A Reason for Keeping Silent' 220
reductionism, WBY's detestation of 334
Reform Act (1918) 267
relationships: Mabel Dickinson 174, 193;
Florence Farr 163; Maud
Gonne 47–51, 87–8, 92, 102,
139–46, 153, 173–8, 203; Lady
Gregory 105–10, 160; Georgie Hyde-
Lees (later George Yeats) 188–9, 222;
Ezra Pound 212–15; John Quinn
204–5; rift with 'AE' 161–2;
Olivia Shakespear 90–3, 185; John
Millington Synge 142–4; with
women 41–2
religion: *The Countess Cathleen* 126–8;
freedom 117–18; Irish divisions
126–9, 131; oriental 352–3, 365; and
sexuality 348–9; symbolism 73;
WBY's youthful crisis 31–2
republicanism 275–7; *see also* Irish
nationalism
Republicans: civil war (1922–3) 284;
defeat of (1923) 289; executions of
(1922) 286, 288
Responsibilities: Poems and a Play (1914)
206–7, 208–13
The Resurrection (play) 43–5, 348–9
Reveries Over Childhood and Youth (1916) 2–3,
7–8, 14–17, 22–3, 29, 217–20, 382
revivalism, Irish language 128–30
Rhymers Club 61–2
rhymes, magical properties 78
Rhys, Ernest 61

rhythm: meditative 77; purpose of 76–7
Riders to the Sea (Synge) 143
ritual magic, WBY's belief in 116–18
Robinson, Lennox 297
Roethke, Theodore 380
Royal Irish Constabulary 268
Ruddock, Margot (later Collis), Majorca
fiasco (1935) 345–6, 356, 365–6
Russell, Bertrand 312
Russell, George William ('AE') 14, 28, 32,
58, 80, 112; artistic freedom debate
betrayal (1907) 169; death of
(1935) 355; WBY's rift with 161–2
Russian revolution (1917) 267

sacrifice: Irish nationalism 135; mortal
love to the ideal 95–8, 111–12,
145–6; WBY's commitment to his
art 95–8; in *Where There Is
Nothing* 138; *see also* self-sacrifice
St Stephens Green (nos. 73 & 96),
Dublin 255–6
Sandymount Avenue, Georgeville,
Dublin 11
Sandymount Castle, Dublin 11
Sargent, John Singer 172
satire: Lane gallery controversy 202;
Moore against WBY 205–6
Schepeler, Alick 193
school: Dublin (1881–3) 26; Godolphin,
London (1877–80) 22, 24–5
science, WBY's schoolboy interest in 26
seances 192–4; Leo Africanus 195–7; SS
Lusitania sinking (1915) 221; Madame
Blavatsky 35; Spiritualism 36–9;
WBY's terrifying experience
(1888) 37; *see also* automatic writing;
mediumship
'The Second Coming' (1920) 270–2, 277–8
The Secret Rose (1897) 96–8, 111, 113
sectarianism, Belfast 7–8
self-analysis, Yeatses' 257, 264
self-government, Irish calls for (1921) 277
self-portraiture: in fictional characters 134,
137–8; *see also* autobiography
self-sacrifice: drama themes 134, 136–9;
mortal love to the ideal 95–8,
111–12, 145–6; in *Where There Is
Nothing* 138; *see also* sacrifice

selfhood: Nietzsche's influences on
WBY 152; theory of the Mask
177–8, 257; WBY's discovery of
166–7; WBY's divided 171–2,
364; WBY's struggle for self-
definition 84
Senate: WBY's appointment to 287;
WBY's appointment to (1922) 287;
WBY's performance in (1923–4) 293
'September 1913' 202
sexuality: automatic writings 257–8; Dean
Swift in *The Words upon the Window-
Pane* 330–1; explored in
poems 327–9, 333–5, 348–63; Gonne
as female ideal 228–9; Gonne's
'spiritual' union 102–4, 141; late
Victorian age 58–9;
mysticism 350–1; WBY's
'Daimon' 310; WBY's failing powers
rejuvenated (1933) 345–8; WBY's
first affair 90–5; in WBY's
marriage 254, 258–61, 279; WBY's
regrets on ageing 249; WBY's
repression 41, 47, 95; woman's erotic
magnetism 222
Shackleton Heald, Edith 348, 365–6
The Shadowy Waters (play) 119, 122
Shakespear, Dorothy 214, 220
Shakespear, Olivia 90–5, 101, 185, 345,
373
Shakespeare Head collected edition
(1908) 187
Shannon, Charles 172
Sharp, William 93
Sinn Féin 170, 189, 267–8
Sinnett, A. P. 33–4
sleep: WBY's concerns of state 290;
Yeatses' psychic research 274
Sligo 1–3, 6–9, 16–17, 88; WBY's final
burial (1948) 377
Sligo Steam Ship Navigation Company 9
Smithers, Leonard 59
social snobbery (WBY's): on Gonne's
marriage 141–2; Irish
nationalism 170–1; in 'Paudeen' 210
socialism 57
solitude, Anglo-Irish 331–2
'Soloman to Sheba' 251
soul, fate after death 193, 209–11

Souperism 127–8
South of France: final year (1938) 364;
WBY's initial burial in (1939) 377
Southward Irish Literary Club 62–3
The Speckled Bird 133
spiritual union, WBY with Gonne 102–4,
141
Spiritualism 36–40, 178, 186; Gonne 52;
in *Responsibilities: Poems and a Play*
208–11; WBY's spirit messengers
192–4; Yeatsian obsession 188,
190–8; *see also* automatic writings;
mediumship; seances
state terrorism, Ireland (1920) 273
'The Stolen Child' 19
Stone Cottage, Sussex 214–16, 220, 222,
223, 255
story-telling, WBY's mother 16–17
suffragist movement 278–9
surrogate motherhood, Lady
Gregory 107–10
Swedenborg, Emanuel 78
*Swedenborg, Mediums and the Desolate
Places* 198
Swift, Dean Jonathan, WBY haunted
by 330–2, 334–5
Swinburne, Algernon Charles 74
Symbolism, role in poetry 71–3, 75–80
'The Symbolism of Poetry' (essay) 76–7
Symons, Arthur 59–61, 71–3
Synge, John Millington 119, 142–4, 166–7,
188–90; death of (1909) 176, 186
Synge and the Ireland of his Time (1911) 189–90

Tagore, Rabindranath 198
Tate, Allen 380
Taylor, John F. 28–9
Taylor, Lawrence 7
technique, early poems 76–7
The Ten Principal Upanishads (1938) 365
Tennyson, Alfred, Lord 74
theatre 118–25; conflict (1907) 168–9; *The
Countess Cathleen* 126–8; Ireland 134,
153–5, 159–60, 179–80; WBY's
interests in England 131–2, 134; *see
also* Abbey Theatre; Noh plays
Theosophical Society, London 32–8
Thomas of Dorlowicz (spirit control) 252,
254, 269–70

Thoor Ballylee 25, 243–4, 255–6; move to (1922) 283–5; relinquished (1930) 329; renovation tour 273
Todhunter, John 10
Tone monument 101
The Tower (1927) 314–23; compared with *The Waste Land* (Eliot) 323; self-referential nature 322; success 324
trade unions, Dublin (1913) 199–201
tradition, Irish folk 16–20, 38, 80–1, 197–8
tragedy: concept of 190; as religious revelation 190
tragic joy 359–60
Treaty, Anglo-Irish (1921) 280, 282, 284
The Trembling of the Veil (1922) 281, 283–4
Trinity College, Dublin 10
Tuatha de Danaan 93
Tucker, Mrs (Georgina Hyde-Lees' mother) 247
Tynan, Katherine 17, 30–1, 37, 48, 54

Ubu Roi (Jarry) 119, 357
Ulster 5–8, 268
Ulster Unionists 199, 204
Ulster Volunteer Force 199
Ulysses (Joyce) 283
Unionism, Edward Dowden 27
United Irish rebellion centenary tour (1898) 99–101
United States (US): Abbey Theatre fund-raising tour (1911) 190; WBY's 1903–4 tour 157–9; WBY's 1914 tour 203–5; WBY's 1920 tour 273–4; WBY's 1932–3 tour 338
universalism, Pan-Celtic 93

Verlaine, Paul Marie 71–2
Victoria, Queen, death of (1901) 136
Victorian period: England 13–14, 23–4; materialism 37, 58, 79; mythology preoccupations 83; professionalization 53–4; rhythms in poetry 77; Sligo 6–7, 9
violence, WBY's last poems 368–9
A Vision: 1925 edition 252–4, 256; 1926, 1937 editions 300–3, 304–11, 371; 1938 revised edition 365

visions: dream 106–7; Gonne 92, 102, 232–3

'The Wanderings of Oisin' 44, 47
The Wanderings of Oisin and other poems (1889) 39, 43–6, 74
war: Anglo-Irish (1921) 280; Irish civil war (1922–3) 282–5; Irish war of independence (1916–21) 270–5; WBY's last poems 368–9; *see also* Great War
The Waste Land (Eliot), compared with *The Tower* 323
Watt, A. P., appointment as literary agent 109
Weckes, Charles Alexandre 28
Wellesley, Lady Gerald (Dorothy) 354–5, 358–9, 364, 366, 376
Where There Is Nothing (play) 137, 139, 154
Whistler, James 22
'The White Birds' 51
'The Wild Swans at Coole' 236
The Wild Swans at Coole (1917) 222, 249–51, 277–8
Wilde, Oscar 31, 59, 157
The Wind Among the Reeds (1899) 110–14
The Winding Stairs and Other Poems (1933) 342–4
Woburn Buildings (no. 18), Bloomsbury, London 92, 109–10, 256
women: emancipation 39, 267; as enchantresses 42–3; heroic Edwardians 184–5; sexuality explored in poems 327–9, 333–5; social role 278–9; Spiritualism 38–9; in WBY's mid-life poetry 249–50; working independence 53–4
Woolf, Virginia 336
words, WBY's employment of 78
The Words upon the Window-Pane (play) 330–1
work, professionalization of 53

Yeats, Benjamin 4
Yeats, Bertha Georgie 'George' (née Hyde-Lees, wife): automatic writings 252–8; boredom with Ireland (1926) 312; death of (1968) 378; death of WBY (1939) 376; early marriage

days 248–9; emotional education of WBY 258–61; marriage to WBY (1917) 246–8; Merrion Square house purchase (1922) 282; pregnancies 254, 255–6, 259–60, 269, 275; qualities 257–8; WBY's late philandering 346–7; WBY's posthumous publications 377–8; *see also* Hyde-Lees, Bertha Georgie
Yeats, Elizabeth 'Lollie' (sister) 12, 53–4, 149, 169
Yeats, Jack Butler (brother) 12, 24, 55, 149
Yeats, Jervis 4
Yeats, John Butler (father) 3, 8, 10–15, 148–9; Abbey Theatre speech (1907) 169; Comptean positivism 10, 20, 32; death of (1922) 282; Dublin studio 26–7; letter to WBY (1921) 309; reproof to WBY (1906) 162; settlement in New York (1907) 169, 179, 204–5
Yeats, Michael (son) 347
Yeats, Reverend William Butler (paternal grandfather) 3, 4–5
Yeats, Susan Mary 'Lily' (sister) 11, 55, 149, 169; illness 282, 289, 336
Yeats, Susan (née Pollexfen, mother) 8, 10–18, 21; death of 148–9
Yeats, William Butler: art school (1884) 27–8; artistic uncertainty (1912–13) 213–14; birth of (1865) 11; birth of daughter, Anne (1919) 253, 254, 269, 271; birth of son, Michael (1921) 253, 269, 280; British doubts about loyalty (1917) 235; childhood 2–3, 7, 11–17, 22–3; creative burst (1929) 336; death of (1939) 376; Easter Rising (1916) 227–35, 241–2; emotional collapse

(1909) 176–7; Establishment acceptance (1910) 181–2; family history 3–5, 8–15; father's conflict with 32; father's death (1922) 282; final year (1938) 364; first love affair 90–5; Great War detachment (1914–15) 219–22; honorary degrees (1922) 287; ignorance of Irish developments (1914) 218–19; impecuniousness 87–8, 108–9, 156; influence on successors 380–1; Irish controversies 126–31; late philandering (1930s) 346–8; marriage to George (1917) 246–8; maturity 133–46; mental stocktaking (1913–14) 194–5; mid-life tensions 173–4; mother's death (1900) 21; personality 14–15; physical decline (1924) 298, 313; poetically barren phase (1898–1906) 166; poetry's lasting popularity 381; Pound detects style change 212–13; quest for wife 234–5, 237, 244–5; religious crisis 31; reputation established (1895) 74; return to Dublin (1922) 282, 286–7; rifts with Gonne (1926) 145–6, 256, 314; schooldays 24–6; Senator of Irish Free State (1922) 287; serious illnesses 315, 329, 356; spiritual union with Gonne 102–4, 141; surrogate mother in Lady Gregory 107–10; tonsils surgery (1920) 275; uncertainties in personal life (1916–18) 235–9; workers' rights championship (1913) 200–1; young adulthood 30–41
Young Ireland movement 66, 158